MW00413265

GITA PRESS AND THE MAKING OF HINDU INDIA

PRAISE FOR THE BOOK

'We sensed that our childhood world was not innocent, that it was part of an ideological edifice that needed engagement and articulation in all its complexity. What a pleasant surprise to find precisely this done so well in Akshaya Mukul's *Gita Press and the Making of Hindu India* . . . Akshaya Mukul's sensitive and learned account is as topical as it is historical.' —Vasudha Dalmia, thewire.in

'Akshaya Mukul tells a textured story of . . . heady ideological cross currents. The book brilliantly situates the press at the intersection of several far-reaching social and political currents, and uses it as a window to illuminate notable social transformations in north India.' —Pratap Bhanu Mehta, *The Indian Express*

'[T]his is a first-rate piece of scholarship which will be one of the standard works on the subject for a long time . . . This book is about the thinking man's Hindutva. It is about true Indian conservatism.' —Aakar Patel, *India Today*

'Among the several achievements of Akshaya Mukul's new book, *Gita Press and the Making of Hindu India*, the most significant is its below-the-hood scrutiny of Hindutva—the design of its engine, the kind of fuel it runs on, and the levers controlling its movement and acceleration . . . Mukul transforms his historical chronicle of a single religious press into a magisterial account of the socio-cultural, economic and human forces at play in the politics of Hindutva.' —G. Sampath, *The Hindu*

'By focusing on the history and money behind the press, Mukul eschews a boring narration of prejudice in favour of a gripping history of Hindu nationalism and the coming of age of India's Marwari, Aggarwal and Baniya communities complete with politics, holy visitations, and sex scandals.' —Aman Sethi, thewire.in

'Mukul's research is breath-taking in its spread . . . The result of his work is this once-in-a-lifetime book, a must for those who want to understand the Hindu revival movement.' —Bhupesh Bhandari, *Business Standard*

'[Akshaya] does readers a great service in illuminating a piece of history that has largely been forgotten by the purveyors of the myth around new political stars and the 'awakening' of a new Hindu India.' —Ullekh N.P., *Open Magazine*

GITA PRESS AND THE MAKING OF HINDU INDIA

AKSHAYA MUKUL

HarperCollins *Publishers* India

First published in hardback in India in 2015 by
HarperCollins *Publishers* India

Copyright © Akshaya Mukul 2015

P-ISBN: 978-93-5177-230-9
E-ISBN: 978-93-5177-231-6

2 4 6 8 10 9 7 5 3

Akshaya Mukul asserts the moral right to be identified as the author of this work.

The views and opinions expressed in this book are the author's own and the facts are as reported by him, and the publishers are not in any way liable for the same.

All rights reserved. No part of this publication may be reproduced, stored in a retrieval system, or transmitted, in any form or by any means, electronic, mechanical, photocopying, recording or otherwise, without the prior permission of the publishers.

HarperCollins *Publishers*
A-75, Sector 57, Noida, Uttar Pradesh 201301, India
1 London Bridge Street, London SE1 9GF, United Kingdom
Hazelton Lanes, 55 Avenue Road, Suite 2900, Toronto, Ontario M5R 3L2
and 1995 Markham Road, Scarborough, Ontario M1B 5M8, Canada
25 Ryde Road, Pymble, Sydney, NSW 2073, Australia
195 Broadway, New York, NY 10007, USA

Typeset in 11/14 Adobe Jenson Pro at
SÜRYA

Printed and bound at
Thomson Press (India) Ltd

To
My parents
Manorama and Madhusudan

Contents

Introduction

Jaydayal Goyandka was an itinerant Marwari businessman based in Bankura, Bengal. A trader in cotton, kerosene oil, textiles and utensils, his work took him to small towns like Chakradharpur (now in Jharkhand) and Sitamarhi in Bihar, and occasionally to Kharagpur and Calcutta. Goyandka had earned a reputation for honesty, offering 'sahi bhav' (right price) and 'sahi taul' (right weight). After business hours he exchanged his ledgers for the Gita, either reading or discussing the text. Over the long years of travel he had formed groups of friends in these towns, mostly other businessmen, who joined him in satsangs (religious congregations). With time these groups expanded; the biggest was in Calcutta where meetings were held at first in the houses of Goyandka's friends and then in an open space behind the fort near Eden Gardens. Soon, even this became too small, so the group rented a place in Banstalla Street and named it Gobind Bhawan. The year was 1922.[1]

Gobind Bhawan became Goyandka's new home in Calcutta. He was fast losing interest in business, keen instead on developing a network of Gita discussion groups, having transformed himself into some kind of an expert whose expositions were praised in Calcutta. What he and his fellow satsangis missed was an authentic translation of the Gita along with a faithful commentary. Gobind Bhawan bankrolled the publication of two editions of the Gita running into 11,000 copies from Vanik Press of Calcutta, but the outcome was considered unsatisfactory, in terms of scholarship as well as production values.

After much deliberation, the group decided to set up its own publishing house, a kind of religious entrepreneurship born out of the desire to produce a definitive version of Goyandka's favourite religious text. Ghanshyamdas Jalan, a businessman from Gorakhpur, who was a friend and also distantly related to Goyandka, suggested that the proposed press be set up in his town. He offered to run the press along with his business partner Mahavir Prasad Poddar. Jalan rented a small house for the press and hired Sabhapati Mishra as the lone employee whose job would be to distribute free copies of the Gita in nearby villages and among children. The manuscript of the text was being sent in batches from Calcutta. By April 1923 Gita Press was ready to print its first translation of the Gita with commentary, on a hand press bought for Rs 600.

But it was only in 1926 that Gita Press truly came to life as a serious player in the fast-emerging Hindi publishing world of the early twentieth century. The seeds of its development into the most successful religious-genre publishing house were sown, not by Goyandka and his associates' concern for one religious text, but by an acrimonious debate between reformists and conservatives in the larger Hindu world.

The occasion was the eighth annual conference of the All India Marwari Aggarwal Mahasabha, one of the community's most influential organizations, held in the oppressive Delhi heat of March–April 1926. Here, leading industrialist Ghanshyam Das Birla expressed his strong disagreement with Atmaram Khemka's speech extolling the virtues of sanatan Hindu dharma (the eternal form of the Hindu religion believed to have existed from time immemorial) as being central to India's salvation. Birla, a devout follower of Mahatma Gandhi, suggested that such views would be better articulated through a journal devoted to the subject rather than at a meeting of a community organization. Birla's off-the-cuff remark led to the start of a new era in religious publishing that would lend weight to the then nascent conflation of Hinduism and Indian nationalism.

The Marwari Aggarwal Mahasabha was headed by Birla's fellow industrialist Jamnalal Bajaj, with Khemka as secretary of the reception committee. As it turned out, Khemka's speech was itself a rebuttal of Bajaj's highly progressive presidential address in which he had asked the Marwari community to turn its gaze inwards and change with the times.[2] Bajaj, like Birla, a convert to Gandhian principles, raised social issues that most members of the community found unpalatable: inter-caste marriage, expressing concern over the extravagance of marriage celebrations, arguing against the practice of financial speculation, condemning child marriage and asking Marwari women to give up their traditional dress and jewellery. He was scathing in his criticism of the business practices of the Marwaris and their lack of concern for the wider society.

Khemka's response stressed the relevance of traditional Hindu values to the making of an eternal 'Indian' culture. It soon became public that Khemka's speech-writer was Hanuman Prasad Poddar, Birla's friend from the days of their youth and a fellow participant in the Rodda Arms Conspiracy. A rising star of the Marwari world in Bombay, Poddar was equally at ease with Gandhi and with the Hindu Mahasabha, which had been set up in 1915 during Haridwar Kumbh mela (fair) as a body to safeguard Hindu interests. Successive failures in business had not dented his image in a community where commerce took precedence over everything.

Poddar had carved a niche for himself as a man of religion, holding satsangs on the Gita, Ramayana and other religious texts. After meeting Jaydayal Goyandka (also a distant cousin), first in Calcutta and later in Bombay, Poddar began to consider him a mentor, and taking his advice became a full-time kathavachak (preacher of sacred texts) fully immersed in the world of religion and sacred Hindu texts. All the while, Poddar stayed connected to the Hindu Mahasabha, his political alma mater, where he cut his teeth in militant Hindu nationalism.

Poddar's belief system would have a bearing on the character and content of the journal *Kalyan*, conceived by Goyandka and other senior members of the Marwari Aggarwal Mahasabha to turn Birla's challenge into a reality. Thus, two entities were born in the span of three years: Gita Press, the publishing house in 1923, and *Kalyan*, the monthly journal in 1926. Both were under the overall control of Gobind Bhawan Karyalaya in Calcutta, an institution managed by Goyandka.

The birth and eventual success of Gita Press/ *Kalyan* can be better understood through three distinctive but inextricably woven factors. One was the consolidation of Hindi at the end of the nineteenth and beginning of the twentieth century as the language of Hindus, and the rapid growth of its public sphere in which journals, newspapers, publishing houses and public figures played an important role—with the colonial state keeping a sharp watch through its widespread machinery of informants and tough laws.[3] Two, Gita Press/*Kalyan* was a Marwari enterprise with a difference, where profit took the back seat. At the forefront was religious philanthropy in the name of saving sanatan Hindu dharma—an obscurantist version of it. In terms of ambition, it was a grand enterprise, unlike anything the Hindi literary world had witnessed till then or would see in the future.

Three, and most important, the 1920s was a period of competing political communalism between Hindus and Muslims. The entire nationalism debate was getting vitiated by religious schisms, exacerbated by a series of communal riots on the issue of cow protection throughout the Hindi heartland of the United Provinces and Bihar. Congress leaders like Madan Mohan Malaviya (who had founded the Hindu Mahasabha), Purushottam Das Tandon, K.M. Munshi, Seth Govind Das and others who were not enthused with Congress politics lent support to the Gita Press/*Kalyan* enterprise. The coming together of sanatan dharma leaders like Malaviya and the Arya Samaj in 1923 at Banaras and the decision to make common cause on cow protection and reconversion to Hinduism (shuddhi) bolstered the conservative Hindu groups further.[4]

Malaviya and Poddar's association preceded *Kalyan*. Banaras Hindu University had been started by Malaviya in 1916, and as a young Marwari in Calcutta, Poddar had organized many meetings at which Malaviya spoke when he came to the city to raise funds for the university. Over the years Malaviya had a deep impact on Gita Press, providing it ample fodder during the communally rife period between 1940 and 1947. The birth of the Rashtriya Swayamsevak Sangh (RSS) in 1925 in Nagpur, with which Gita Press would later forge a close alliance, completed the overall scenario in which *Kalyan* got a firm footing and became a success story unlike any other journal of the 1920s.

The Rise of Hindi

The first quarter of the twentieth century saw Hindi score over Urdu, Hindustani and Persian after an intense battle waged largely on communal lines from the mid-nineteenth century. Bharatendu Harishchandra, writer-poet-publisher-polemicist and a language fanatic from Banaras, led the movement for Hindi. Touted as the father of modern Hindi literature, Bharatendu had begun his career as an Urdu writer and maintained till 1871 that Urdu was the language of his pachhain (western) branch of the Aggarwal clan.[5] His position changed as the issue of language grew more sharply divided on religious lines. In 1877, Bharatendu's ninety-eight-verse speech '*Hindi Ki Unnati Par Vyakhyan*' (Lecture on the Progress of Hindi) at the inaugural meeting of the Hindi Vardhini Sabha in Allahabad established his standing as leader of the Hindi movement. More diatribes against Urdu would follow from Bharatendu, but he did not live to see the result of his efforts. He died in 1885 at the age of thirty-five. The year 1893 saw the establishment of the Nagari Pracharini Sabha in Banaras, the most influential body for advocating use of the Hindi language and the Devanagari script. And in 1910 came the Hindi Sahitya Sammelan in Allahabad with similar intent.

The Nagari Pracharini Sabha sought to popularize the Nagari script through its magazine *Nagari Pracharini Patrika* and the literary journal *Saraswati* founded in 1900. In 1897, when Madan Mohan Malaviya presented Sir Antony MacDonnell, lieutenant governor of the North-Western Provinces and Oudh, with the Nagari Pracharini Sabha's petition *Court Character and Primary Education in N-W P. and Oudh* accompanied by 60,000 signatures, the response was non-committal.[6] Therefore, MacDonnell's order in 1900 on the use of Nagari as a court script came as a surprise. It was a battle very smoothly won, from which a bruised Urdu would never recover. The division—Hindi for Hindus, Urdu for Muslims[7]—had more or less been completed, exemplifying Bharatendu's famed couplet that one's own language is the source of all progress.[8]

The 'MacDonnell Moment'[9] of 1900 'when two distinct languages—Hindi and Urdu—were being given official endorsement'[10] opened new vistas for Hindi. The decision to allow the use of Nagari script in the courts along with Persian acted as a game changer in the language debate. By the second decade of the twentieth century, Hindi had risen to prominence and found a firm footing in what is commonly known as the Hindi heartland—today's Uttar Pradesh (UP), Uttarakhand, Bihar, Jharkhand, Madhya Pradesh, Chhattisgarh, Rajasthan, Delhi, Haryana and Himachal Pradesh. The centre of action in Hindi literature and journalism moved to the United Provinces (present-day Uttar Pradesh) from Calcutta, especially after the Partition of Bengal in 1905.

For Hindi, which claimed a hoary past, pre-dating Muslim rule in India, the period from the 1870s to 1920s was one of intense churning, be it in terms of grammar, syntax or choice of dialect. Khari Boli emerged as the dominant dialect used by writers, poets or commentators, and in the journals that would mushroom throughout the Hindi heartland but more specifically in Banaras and Allahabad. These were centres of learning, with Banaras Hindu University and Allahabad University producing a whole generation of writers, poets, journalists and politicians.

In 1902 the journal *Saraswati* was taken over by Chintamani Ghosh of the Indian Press, Rabindranath Tagore's publishers in Calcutta. Outgoing editor Babu Shyamsundar Das suggested that Mahavir Prasad Dwivedi succeed him. Dwivedi—a one-time railway clerk, signaller and later clerk in the transport department—was mostly self-taught. His seventeen-year stint as editor of *Saraswati* is called the Dwivedi Yug (Dwivedi era) during which the Hindi language was successfully refined and beautified.[11] A votary of Hindi as the national language, Dwivedi was in favour of letting regional languages flourish locally, and translating literary works in these languages into Hindi.[12]

Saraswati was not alone in providing a 'diversified space for Hindi journalism' ranging from social reform, scientific experiments, history, archaeology, moral issues and the role of women, to literary criticism and translations of classics.[13] There were other journals, like *Madhuri*, brought out by the leading Lucknow publishing house Naval Kishore Press from 1921. Similar to *Saraswati* in its sweep, ambition and design, *Madhuri*, edited by Roopnarayan Pandey and Dularelal Bhargava, achieved the same literary standing.

The 1920s saw a surfeit of journals fill the Hindi public sphere, proclaiming Hindi's independent status, free from the encumbrance of Persian and Urdu. Like a restless child out to prove he has come of age, almost all of them brandished their version of nationalism, often mixed with Hindu nationalism. Hindi became a defining component of national identity, both pre- and post-Independence.[14] It was a period of intense mixing of language, identity and nationalism.

Some of these journals had the backing of major publishing houses and, therefore, strong chances of survival; others were exercises in passion—a love for Hindi and for the power of print. In the coming years, three of them—*Chand* (1922), *Matwala* (1923) and *Hindu Panch* (1925)—would have a direct and indirect bearing on the life of *Kalyan*.

Chand, essentially a woman's journal, under the editorship of Ramrakh Sahgal, embarked on a unique method of boosting its circulation and hence fortune by bringing out six special issues on a wide range of subjects: capital punishment (*Phansi Ank*), prostitutes (*Veshya Ank*), Marwaris (*Marwari Ank*), Kayasthas (*Kayastha Ank*), untouchables (*Achhoot Ank*) and literature (*Sahitya Ank*). While commercially most of them were a huge success, selling as many as 15,000 copies each, the journal's tendency to publish vulgar stories and indulge in no-holds-barred personal attacks drew widespread flak from the likes of Premchand—guest editor of *Chand*'s special number on literature—and Banarsi Das Chaturvedi, editor of *Vishal Bharat* and self-proclaimed conscience-keeper of the Hindi literary world. Even if the idea was to expose social ills, the Hindi intelligentsia did not support making a public spectacle of these. What had particularly irked Premchand was *Chand*'s *Marwari Ank* of 1927 that painted Marwari women as being lustful and promiscuous, not sparing the men either. The strong Marwari community immediately sued Sahgal, but the damage had been done. *Kalyan*'s criticism of the *Marwari Ank* was subdued as the issue had also exposed an infamous sex scandal in Gobind Bhawan, its parent body based in Calcutta.

Hindu Panch's strategy was different. It was provocative in its tone, strident in language and content, courted controversy openly—yet cleverly. What could one say of a weekly that stated its fivefold mission on the cover—Hindu Sangathan (Organization), Shuddhi Sanskar (Culture of Reconversion), Achhootoddhar (Removal of Untouchability), Samaj Sudhar (Social Reform), Hindi Prachar (Spread of Hindi)—and a motto on its cover page that openly spelt out its goal of restoring the dignity of Hindus, saving the Hindu name, bringing

Hindu rule to India and waking Hindus up from their slumber (*Lajja Rakhne Ko Hindu Ki, Hindu Naam Bachane Ko, Aaya Hindu Panch Hind Mein, Hindu Jati Jagane Ko*).

Hindu Panch claimed to be working for the defence of the Hindu religion.[15] But the articulation of this defence was not very sharp despite the occasional article on the merits of sanatan Hindu dharma by the likes of Ganesh Damodar Savarkar, the eldest of the Savarkar brothers.[16] The task was better undertaken by Gita Press and *Kalyan*. *Hindu Panch* would focus on reports of Muslims attacking and abducting Hindu girls and widows, carrying highly objectionable columns like '*Choti Banam Dadhi*' (Brahmin Tuft versus Muslim Beard) where Muslims would be derided and their alleged acts of high-handedness against Hindus in general and Hindu women in particular would be reported. While *Hindu Panch* brought out special issues on Lord Krishna (6 September 1928), Lord Rama (29 March 1928), Vijayadashami (28 October 1926) and the Hindu Mahasabha (12 April 1928), it also had a special issue on the Congress (30 December 1926)—a clever balancing act. Two years later, *Hindu Panch* thanked Jawaharlal Nehru for visiting its editorial office in September 1928 and called him 'adarsh veer' (ideal hero). Nehru was reminded that the 'nation is bigger than a community and even more important than the nation is world humanity' . . . 'You belong to that world humanity.'[17]

Marwari Munificence

Essayist, polemicist, journalist and a first-rate satirist Bal Mukund Gupt finds pride of place in all histories of Marwaris as a leading literary figure—next only to Bharatendu Harishchandra. Like Bharatendu, Gupt also died young, at the age of forty-two. Passionate and acerbic, Gupt would spare no one, not even his own community. On learning that the Calcutta Marwaris had opened a school that would impart education in English, Hindi and Sanskrit to their boys, Gupt, writing under the pseudonym Shiv Sambhu Sharma in *Bharatmitra*, the Calcutta journal he edited, hit out at the community telling them not to 'dare come near knowledge'. Instead, he said, it would be better if they worshipped the camel that had brought them to

Calcutta, and if possible bring a camel to the city zoo since it did not have one. He wrote, 'Your wealth has been acquired through hard work and mental machinations. Whatever you have is yours and not related to knowledge. People who cannot digest your prosperity are whispering "vidya, vidya" (knowledge, knowledge) in your ears. Of what use is vidya? You cannot wear or eat it. If you have money hundreds of knowledgeable persons bow before you even if you are a fool. They praise your sad face . . . without education you have become Raja and Rai Bahadur and the future only knows what more is in store.'[18]

Gupt's dig came at a time when Marwaris across India had consolidated their position as the top mercantile community that worked through a wide, often complicated, network of sub-castes and village affiliations going back to Rajasthan. Now they were aspiring to gain wider social acceptability and standing in tune with their growing clout in business. For this vaishya or trading-class community, the quest for education and social status was a big leap.

With Marwari domination of the growth of Indian capitalism in the late nineteenth and early twentieth century, two crucial but contradictory things happened.[19] One, the community became an object of jealousy and derision, the butt of jokes and condemned as being self-aggrandizing, like the Jews in Europe. Two, the Marwaris themselves were undergoing an identity crisis of a peculiar kind. Here was an economically powerful community that did not have the commensurate social standing. Their simple lifestyle did not help their quest for status either. However, the decline of landed gentry across north India and the overall economic situation of the early twentieth century saw the Marwaris take centre stage, a process Lutgendorf terms 'semi-involuntary upward mobility', in which vaishyas became the new kshatriyas, owning villages and getting kshatriya titles like Raja. For instance, as Timberg points out, Raja Gokuldas of the banking firm of Sevaram Khushalchand of Jabalpur reportedly owned 158 villages: 'Most of these estates were picked up at forced sale for tax defaults.'[20] These upwardly mobile Marwaris often donated generously to religious and social causes.

Marwari munificence greatly contributed to their social standing, but came with its own share of tensions—a simple personal life pitted against a public persona based entirely on liberal charity mostly religious and social in nature. As Lutgendorf says, 'Merchants faced a crisis of identity that reflected the classic tension in Hindu society between upward social aspiration and downwardly imposed order', and in the 'special circumstances of the period, the interaction of these forces in the assertion of new identities helped fuel both nationalism and religious revival'.[21]

Marwaris were not alone in their search for a social identity. Intermediate castes like the Ahir Yadavs and Kurmis, with the influence and active help of the Arya Samaj and Ramanandis respectively, were at the forefront demanding kshatriya status. They had started wearing the sacred thread and formed caste associations like the Ahir Yadav Kshatriya Mahasabha in Haryana (1910) and the Gop Jatiya Mahasabha in Bihar (1912). The Kurmis, helped by the Ramanandis in tracing their lineage to Rama and Krishna, formed several caste associations like the Kurmi Sabha and All India Kurmi Kshatriya Mahasabha (1910).[22]

The Yadavs, traditionally worshippers of cows, played an active role in the cow-protection movement and setting up of gaurakshini sabhas in the late nineteenth and early twentieth century. The cow as a cause of communal strife between Hindus and Muslims had already entered the daily discourse of national politics. Various sanatan Hindu dharma sabhas were advocating a complete ban on cow slaughter. From the 1870s to the early twentieth century, a series of communal riots on the issue of consumption of cow meat by Muslims further polarized the two communities.

The Marwaris with their economic might were at the forefront of bankrolling gaurakshini sabhas (cow protection associations) while the Yadavs took on the mantle of foot soldiers at the time of riots. Cow protection was also one of the pronounced goals of Gita Press, for which *Kalyan* was used as a vehicle with two special issues, *Gau Ank* (Issue on Cows) and *Gau Seva Ank* (Issue on Service to Cows), besides innumerable articles on cows in various issues of the journal. Poddar, along with Prabhudatt Brahmachari and Karpatri Maharaj, was instrumental in getting many slaughterhouses closed post 1947. He was part of one of the largest processions of sadhus and members of right-wing parties like the Jana Sangh and organizations like the RSS, Hindu Mahasabha and various sanatan dharma bodies, on a dharna (protest) outside Parliament on 7 November 1966.

Playing an important role in the cow-protection movement, a key facet of sanatan Hindu dharma, was not the only way in which Marwaris gained social standing. This was also achieved through building temples, shelter houses, schools and hospitals as well as sponsoring recitations of the *Ramcharitmanas*. *Aggarwal Jati Ka Itihas*[23] lists hundreds of works of charity bankrolled by rich Marwari businessmen throughout the country. The writers add a disclaimer that the list that runs into thirteen pages is just a cursory one and to put together an exhaustive list would be impossible. The book does mention the role of Marwari philanthropy in the use of print technology to further the cause of sanatan dharma as well as to highlight the ills afflicting the community. In the view of the writers, Hinduism could only be saved by following the principles of sanatan dharma that had existed in the golden past but was being marred in the present 'dark age'. Gita Press founders Jaydayal Goyandka and Hanuman Prasad Poddar find rich mention in this book, as in many other histories of the Marwaris.[24]

Kalyan and Gita Press might have become the most successful print ventures to salvage and consolidate the spread of sanatan dharma, but the initiative and goal itself were not new. Two brothers in Bombay, Ganga Vishnu Bajaj and Khemraj Krishnadas Bajaj (originally from Churu) were among the earliest Marwaris to take to printing as a business and bring out Hindu religious works. In 1871, the duo started the Shri Venkateshwar Press from a single room in the Moti Bazar area of Bombay. By 1880 they had moved to a bigger place in Khetwadi, formally launching the Sri Venkateshwar Steam Press.[25] *Hanuman Chalisa* and *Vishnu Sahasranam* were the earliest titles to come out, and in the next few years the press printed 2,800 titles, almost the entire pantheon of texts on religion, spiritualism, philosophy, culture and history. In 1896, the brothers launched *Venkateshwar Samachar*, a non-controversial weekly that kept itself aloof from politics during the most intense period of the national movement in the first quarter of the twentieth century.[26] As we shall see later, Venkateshwar Press would print the first thirteen issues of *Kalyan* for Gita Press.

In 1889, the weekly *Rajasthan Samachar* was started from Ajmer, financed by Samarthan Das, a Marwari businessman. Its avowed aim was to be a mouthpiece of the Arya Samaj and spread the teachings of Swami Dayanand Saraswati. By 1912, *Rajasthan Samachar* was a daily and, significantly, had moved away from the ideals of the Arya Samaj to promote sanatan Hindu dharma. Editor of *Bharatmitra* Bal Mukund Gupt severely criticized the paper for this shift, pointing out that even articles by social reformists had stopped appearing in *Rajasthan Samachar*. Gupt blamed the Bharat Dharma Mahamandal, a key proponent of sanatan dharma, for the change.[27]

Then there were publications like the Calcutta-based fortnightly *Marwari Gazette* (1890) that highlighted the problems of Rajasthan in general and Marwaris in particular. Its focus was on education for Marwaris, social and religious solidarity, and societal control to contain the growing streak of individualism among members of the community. Departing from the prevailing Hindu view that abhorred foreign travel, the *Marwari Gazette* celebrated such forays, as when the Raja of Khetri went abroad in 1897: 'The Raja's foreign travel is a daring act that would open the doors of progress.'[28]

The publications so far were mostly philanthropic or business efforts of individual wealthy Marwaris. It would be a while before community bodies would get involved in bringing out journals with the aim of reforming the new generation that had apparently deviated from the simple Marwari way of life, the ideals of sanatan dharma being the prescription for the desired correction. Through such initiatives, Marwaris replaced the 'aristocracy and wealthy landlords' as religious patrons, and changed 'the kshatriya–brahmin interface of Hindu society' to a 'vaishya–brahmin interface' that eventually resulted in the 'Marwari-ization of Hinduism'.[29]

Marwari Sudhar was the first such initiative from Ara in Bihar. Launched in 1921 through the efforts of Navrang Lal Tulsiyan, Haridwar Prasad Jalan and Durga Prasad Poddar, *Marwari Sudhar* had a non-Marwari editor in Shivpujan Sahay, among the tallest Hindi writers of his era. Sahay's efforts saw a journal primarily catering to Marwaris become a serious voice in Hindi journalism. Published from Balkrishna Press in Calcutta, it attracted the best names of the Hindi world, such as Ayodhya Singh Upadhyay 'Harioudh', Ramcharit Upadhyay, Suryakant Tripathi 'Nirala', Ram Naresh Tripathi, Bhagwati Charan Varma and Viyogi Hari. For the little over two years that the journal was in existence, Sahay fiercely protected his editorial freedom. Often, substandard articles came in from Marwaris who assumed they had the right to have their contributions published in the community journal. Sahay would reject such contributions sternly but without malice. His autonomy as editor was evident even in the inaugural issue, where, in his editorial comment, Sahay wrote: 'Marwaris have very little regard for learning. Even if a small fraction of their time spent in business was used for learning, the community would have been leading the nation.'[30]

Sahay's forthrightness would pit him against prominent Marwari writers in Hindi like Baijnath Prasad Deora and Shyamlal Deora. They sought an apology for his critical comments on Marwari writers in the inaugural issue. Sahay, however, made it clear that though he was a true well-wisher of Marwaris, he would not succumb to pressure from a few misguided youth and writers. The promising journal ceased publication in 1923 when the newly founded All India Marwari Aggarwal Mahasabha proposed another journal, *Marwari Aggarwal*, as the community's mouthpiece. The new journal edited by Hemchandra Joshi had a three-pronged goal: to eradicate ill practices among Marwaris, to spread the message of the All India Marwari Aggarwal Mahasabha and to revitalize the Marwari community.

Marwari Sudhar and *Marwari Aggarwal*, with their primary mission of reforming the community, advocated a life that struck a fine balance between commerce, profit and spiritualism but failed in suggesting a specific path to that goal. Within a few years, some prominent members of the Marwari Aggarwal Mahasabha decided to strike out on their own. Thus was born *Kalyan*, the first-of-its-kind religious monthly with a single-minded focus on spreading sanatan dharma as the sole saviour, not only of Marwaris but of Hindus in general.

The Political Context

The later decades of the nineteenth century and the early ones of the twentieth were a time of rising religious antagonism between Hindus and Muslims, marked by frequent riots and competitive communalism. Besides the battle for supremacy between Hindi and Urdu, incidents of cow slaughter and music before mosques were becoming flashpoints between the two communities—from the major riot of 1893 in Azamgarh, Mau and adjoining areas on the issue of cow slaughter during Bakr-Id, to the resurgence of widespread violence in 1917 in Bihar's Shahabad, Gaya and Patna.[31] The idea here is not to repeat the vast body of work done on these and other points of conflagration, but to situate them in the context of the birth of Gita Press and how *Kalyan* became a successful vehicle for articulation of religious and communal issues, a trend that continues till today.

The fuzzy divide between religion and politics in the first two decades of the twentieth century ensured that even the Congress, at the vanguard of the national movement, could not keep itself aloof from the cow protection issue. Way back in 1891, a gaurakshini sabha meeting took place during the Nagpur session of Congress.[32] Interestingly, this religious matter continued to impact politics even after Independence. From the 1920s, Poddar was at the forefront of cow protection, supported by a motley mix of sadhus like Prabhudatt Brahmachari, a host of sanatan dharma organizations, the Hindu Mahasabha, RSS and later the Bharatiya Jana Sangh, and a not-so-insignificant section of the Congress consisting of leaders like Seth Govind Das, former Mahasabhaite Jagat Narayan Lal (who was later a minister in the Congress government in Bihar) and many others.

The Hindu Mahasabha and Arya Samaj came together in Banaras in 1923, and decided to make common cause on cow slaughter and reconversion. A relatively young Congress, despite its claim of maintaining a distance from religion, failed to remain neutral. By then, leaders like Madan Mohan Malaviya, Rajendra Prasad and other conservatives had found a firm foothold within the party, forcing it to engage with religiously volatile issues. Meetings of the Hindu Mahasabha from 1922 onwards would regularly take place along with Congress annual sessions. This continued till 1937 when the relationship between the Mahasabha and Congress formally ended.

As gaurakshini sabhas grew in strength and the opposition to cow slaughter became strident, communal riots became the order of the day to salvage the honour of gau mata, the cow as mother. Ninety-one riots took place in the United Provinces between 1923 and 1927,[33] not limited to cow protection as the communal universe of Hindus and Muslims was simultaneously populated with issues such as music before mosques and prabhat pheris (singing of bhajans, etc., in processions at dawn).

Even as the Hindu Mahasabha and other communal organizations pursued their agenda, internal contradictions in the Congress were becoming apparent, adding to the Hindu–Muslim divide. This was most notably witnessed in Allahabad, in the contest between the inclusive and exclusive politics of Motilal Nehru and Madan Mohan Malaviya respectively, during the local body election of 1927. The Malaviya group, under the banner of the Congress, blocked all attempts to strike an amicable deal in 1925 on the matter of Hindu religious processions with music passing before mosques. Another attempt at reconciliation by Nehru in 1926 also failed. Malaviya along with Bishan Narayan Dar represented a perfect blend of 'nationalist and Hindu causes'.[34] This mixture would become potent in the coming years and sharpen the communal divide. Consistently placated by British high officials, Dar and Malaviya became the dominant voices of the religious right in the United Provinces. In the case of Malaviya, who was Congress president in 1919, what added to his rightist stature was his membership of the Viceroy's Council, founding of Banaras Hindu University, control of the daily *Abhyuday* and active association with many religious organizations in various parts of the country, especially Allahabad and Banaras.

In Kanpur, a similar blurring of lines between nationalism and religious revivalism led to Muslims losing faith in the Congress. Muslim intransigence had already taken firm shape during the 1913 Kanpur Mosque affair, when the decision to relocate a small mosque for building a road, though approved by community leaders, led to widespread protests among local Muslims, forcing the British provincial government to rethink its strategy of working through mediators. By the early 1920s, as the practices of prabhat pheri, shuddhi (reconversion to Hinduism) and sangathan (organization) gained ground in the United Provinces, the industrial town, despite its massive migrant population, could not remain untouched. Already suspicious of the government after the 1913 mosque incident, what added to the Muslims' discomfiture was Congress sponsorship of prabhat pheris and Hindu-only akharas (gymnasiums) in the city, funded by the Municipal Board.[35]

Congress's open patronage of these communal symbols, coupled with party workers resorting to coercion and violence in 1931 to force a bandh against the execution of Bhagat Singh, degenerated into full-fledged rioting in Kanpur. Gone was the bonhomie between the two communities witnessed during the Khilafat agitation and the non-cooperation movement. Forty-two mosques and eighteen temples were destroyed during the 1931 riots, not to speak of the many lives lost. Among these was Congress leader Ganesh Shankar Vidyarthi, who was also editor of the daily *Pratap*. Gandhi wrote in *Young India*: 'The death of Ganesh Shankar Vidyarthi was one to be envied by us all. His blood is the cement that will ultimately bind the two communities. No pact will bind our hearts. But heroism such as Ganesh Shankar Vidyarthi showed is bound in the end to melt the stoniest hearts, melt them into one. The poison has however gone so deep that the blood even of a man so great, so self-sacrificing and so utterly brave as Ganesh Shankar Vidyarthi may today not be enough to wash us of it. Let this noble example stimulate us all to similar effort should the occasion arise again.'[36]

As editor of *Kalyan*, Hanuman Prasad Poddar too felt that Vidyarthi's killing warranted comment. He termed the incident a reflection of how Indian humanity was fast degenerating. 'This demonic excitement's victim has been a man who was out there to douse the fire of mutual hatred.'[37] For the barely five-year-old *Kalyan* this was the beginning of its mixing of religion and politics.

In that era of competitive communalism, the Hindu Mahasabha's shuddhi, sangathan and prabhat pheris, equally patronized by Congress, was matched by the Muslim practices of tabligh (propaganda) and tanzim (organization). Tanzim was a direct response to sangathan and prabhat pheris[38] and tabligh to shuddhi. Further, in 1924, the Muslim League would meet separately, outside the umbrella of Congress, and Muhammad Ali Jinnah would make a demand for autonomy in areas where Muslims outnumbered Hindus. Thus, the religious schism of the 1920s and '30s redefined the politics of nationalism, and became a driving force behind Partition and its bloody aftermath.

Within this triangle of Hindi/Hindu journals, Marwari munificence and the blurring of the demarcation between religion and politics, especially in the United Provinces, exists the story of Gita Press. Religious separatism—termed 'communalism' in the approved secular discourse—was a reactive ideology; so one sees both Hindu and Muslim revivalist movements stuck in a chain of reactions to each other. This study of the phenomenon of Gita Press/*Kalyan* will show how Hindu revivalism constituted a response to various forces—of modernity and Western education, of challenge from other religions (in particular Islam), and of change within Hindu society itself.[39]

The Significance of Gita Press and Kalyan

In 1893, Pratap Narayan Mishra castigated readers of his journal *Brahman* for not being serious in their commitment to the goal of Hindi-Hindu-Hindustan. This taunt was taken seriously by many Hindi journals whose politics in the national context was still in the process of getting defined. In specific terms, despite the communalization of the Hindi–Urdu debate at the turn of the century, it had not yet expanded enough to disturb the peaceful, if tenuous, coexistence of the two communities. Periodicals of different genres surfaced, some related to women (*Chand, Jyoti, Grihalakshmi*), to children (*Balak*) and to education (*Shiksha Amrit, Shiksha Sevak*), besides the magazines of the Arya Samaj. These became vehicles to express the aspirations of the expanding class of literates.

Religious journals became critical to this expression. Religion was gaining ground as a subject of debate in the public domain, and gradually came to be reflected in the pages of journals of various genres. Even irreverent ones like *Matwala* could oppose but not ignore religion. It was no longer about Hindi but Hindu religiosity as well.

What added to the debate was the gradual communalization of politics. It is important to understand how Gita Press with its journal *Kalyan* came to occupy the space relating to public discourse on religion. It is not that there were no exclusive journals dealing with Hinduism in general and sanatan Hindu dharma in particular. The monthly *Sanatan Dharma Pataka* started in 1900 from Moradabad and continued till the late 1920s, but its failure to adopt new printing technology as well as the evolving a reader-friendly style of writing limited its circulation and influence, and it remained a local initiative.[40] In the 1920s, when the irreverent *Matwala* regularly attacked votaries of sanatan dharma, the weekly *Dharma-Rakshak* was launched in retaliation. But it too failed to make any impact.

What contributed to *Kalyan*/Gita Press's distinguishing presence and immediate success was the fact that its promoters and editor did not remain impervious to the larger political changes taking place in the colonial period. The propagation of sanatan dharma, with all its emphasis on texts, rituals, social practice and institutions was mixed with the ideals of nationalism. Vasudha Dalmia prefers to call sanatanis traditionalists, and makes the fine distinction between them and revivalist/reformist movements like the Arya Samaj and Brahmo Samaj, arguing that 'incessant change and exchange' took place between traditionalists and revivalists.[41]

Monika Hortsmann, taking from Paul Hacker's interpretation of neo-Hinduism, argues that the *Kalyan* variety of Hinduism fell in the same category: 'Its roots are nationalistic; it makes a universal claim to universalism, to religious hegemony within the boundaries of India while reaching out beyond these to Hindus overseas, it is missionary in the sense that it strives to rally the Hindus in India and the lukewarm expatriates under the single umbrella of the one universal dharma'[42]

The story of Gita Press and *Kalyan* diverges from, even partially subverts, Benedict Anderson's notion of print capitalism and its role in the creation of 'monoglot masses' that led to a 'national identity'.[43] Anderson's basic premise is that booksellers were interested in profit alone and exploited the 'revolutionary vernacularising thrust of capitalism'. This influenced the manner in which pre-Christian-era literature was taken to the public. Gita Press differed in the sense that profit was not at the core of its enterprise. Its promoters were Marwaris, the prominent mercantile class, who at the beginning of the twentieth century were moving towards industrial capital. They were definitely not averse to profit, but not from a venture like Gita Press, an 'indigenous model of proselytization'[44] whose object was defence of the Hindu religion. Goyandka would later acknowledge that popularization of Gita and other texts in Hindi was important to counter the efforts of Christian missionaries.[45]

At the same time, Gita Press recognized the opportunity that print provided at a juncture when Hindi was coming of age, and used it to take the message of sanatan dharma to the hinterland through *Kalyan* and cheap but high-quality, mass-produced editions of the Ramayana, Gita, Mahabharata, Puranas and other Hindu religious texts. Paul Arney calls Gita Press the 'leading purveyor of print Hinduism in the twentieth century'.[46]

In fact, the printing of religious texts contributed to the consolidation of Gita Press in a big way. These texts were the proverbial best-sellers, led by the *Ramcharitmanas*. The print version of the *Ramcharitmanas* widened the scope for its recitation—this was now no longer the preserve of the priestly class. There was no longer the need to copy texts by hand, which had limited their availability. By 1983, Gita Press had sold nearly 5.7 million copies of *Ramcharitmanas*; in that year alone, there were two print runs of 100,000 copies each.[47]

It needs to be pointed out that, in contrast to the Gita, Ramayana, Mahabharata, Puranas and Upanishads, the Vedas were neglected by Gita Press. Though articles in *Kalyan* referred to these most ancient of texts, Gita Press never published translations or even the original texts. Poddar explained to one of his biographers that he had not been able to take up the task owing to the absence of authoritative voices on the Vedas. 'He believed that the available translations of Vedas did not match up to the dignity and prestige of the originals. Therefore, despite a keen desire, he could not succeed in making this source of Indian culture available to the general public.'[48]

Gita Press's popularization of the *Ramcharitmanas* and other works coincided with a rise in the number of professional kathavachaks of these texts. At least two, Radheshyam Kathavachak (1890–1963) and Narayan Prasad Betab (1872–1945), gave the *Ramcharitmanas*, Puranas and Mahabharata new meaning by composing plays based on stories inspired from these texts. The kathavachaks' singular contribution was rendition of the *Ramcharitmanas* in popular verse, which became the basis of Ramlila performances.[49] Gita Press relied on its own kathavachak Kripashankar Ramayani, who not only wrote for *Kalyan* but also participated in the discourses that the publishing house organized from time to time. Ramayani's rendering of the Ramayana has been kept alive by his followers through a web portal.

Recognizing the power of oral tradition, Gita Press, within a few years of coming into existence, had organized Gita and Ramayana sabhas that would regularly hold recitations throughout the country. It had published a pocket-sized Ramayana 'specifically for an all-India recitation during Chaitra Navratra (the period of Ram Navami) observances in 1939 and had promoted it for months in *Kalyan*'.[50] Lutgendorf argues that Gita Press's 'encouragement of mass reading of the *Manas* during the nine nights of goddess worship again suggests the role of the epic as a synthesizing element in North Indian religion, specifically as a mediator between the traditions of Vaishnava devotionalism and Shaiva/Shakta worship'. *Manas,* he says, became the 'text of choice for filling any vacuum in popular religious practice'.[51] This mixture of print and oral propagation worked as a perfect strategy for Gita Press's mission of re-establishing the superiority of sanatan dharma. The impact was significant in a society—especially in the United Provinces—where literacy levels were low.[52] However, the popularization of the *Ramcharitmanas* among people of all classes through printed versions did little to change the social order in villages or towns.

Right from 1789, when the Chronicle Press of Daniel Stuart and Joseph Cooper prepared Nagari fonts in Calcutta, book publishing in India had been fraught with failures. The introduction of lithography in India in the 1820s made printing easier and cheaper, yet success was either confined to state-sponsored initiatives like the translated texts published by Fort William College, missionary publishers, or much later commercial publishing enterprises like Naval Kishore Press of Lucknow established in 1858. As French-born Calcutta printer Haji Mustapha succinctly put it: 'Printing in this country requires a young man and a rich man, and I am neither.'[53] Gita Press, the initiative of not-so-young but rich Marwari men, never encountered failure though occasionally it did face serious threats of closure.

Before Gita Press, the publication of religious texts was on the agenda of publishing houses like Naval Kishore Press. Ulrike Stark discusses how printing texts like the Ramayana, Mahabharata and Puranas had started from the beginning of the nineteenth century and even Muslim publishers were involved in the task.[54] It could have very well been argued that the dissemination of religious texts by established publishers like Naval Kishore Press would have left no space for other religious publications in north India.

In such a context, the launch of Gita Press and its eventual success may be largely ascribed to its monthly *Kalyan*—the first journal to be devoted exclusively to the Hindu religion. The existing journals, political, literary, women- or child-specific, did devote a few pages to religious issues that reflected the growing concerns about identity among readers. The increasing communalization of Indian politics in the 1920s contributed to this identity crisis in a big way. Gita Press's declaration in *Kalyan* that the all-round decline in society was the result of Hindus having moved away from the path of religion made it clear that here was a journal that meant business insofar as defending the religion was concerned. Gita Press's defence of religion was a 'solution to an existing societal crisis', to the 'dark age' that 'threatened order and well-being in society'.[55]

Significantly, there was also recognition by the promoters of Gita Press that *Kalyan* should specifically address the crisis that the Marwari community faced internally and in the eyes of society. Gita Press founder Jaydayal Goyandka was aware of the widespread anger and distrust that Marwari trade practices evoked. In the second year of *Kalyan* he addressed the problem within the trading community. Refusing to lay the entire blame on the colonial government (a common refrain during the period), Goyandka 'condemned the traders themselves for their moral and emotional decline as their transactions were riddled with lies, fraud and cheating'. He ascribed such practices to 'lobh' or greed that 'had brought on the decline of the community and was manifested in practices of speculation, in the widespread adulteration of food and other illegal or shady business practices'. He also warned them that 'immoral business practices would bar them from spiritual merit and also, as a consequence, from the attainment of god'.[56] Over time, *Kalyan* took to instilling the fear of god in its readers to dissuade them from indulging in acts that were against the tenets of religion and morality. An ingenious 'bania' (trading-class) model of devotion or bhakti was invented, that promised sure-shot salvation if the well-laid-out path of sanatan dharma was followed.

One of the key assets of Gita Press was its ability to resolve the conflict between, in Monika Freier's words, 'reformist organizations like the Brahmo Samaj and Arya Samaj and traditionalist organizations based on sanatan dharma principles for the larger project of Hindu nationalism promoted by organizations like the Hindu Mahasabha and Bharat Dharma Mahamandal'. To achieve this, Freier argues, 'Gita Press founders deliberately styled their writings as religiously and politically impartial. Instead of focusing on the difference with other Hindu sects or sampradayas, they offered a framework for emotion cultivation that could serve as an ideal point of reference and identification for the Hindu community as a whole.' However, Gita Press has only partially translated Freier's argument that the 'new political philosophy demanded effacement of all existing divisions of caste, creed and religious sects'.[57] Though it has kept away from attacking other Hindu sects or reformist organizations like the Arya Samaj, Gita Press has not changed its rigid stance on the validity of the caste system.

Gita Press no longer has to contend with the towering presence of someone like B.R. Ambedkar, who it viciously attacked—'himself of hinvarna (low caste) who has married a Brahmin in old age and introduced Hindu Code Bill'[58]—but that does not mean that the Press can loosen its grip over the idea that 'those who do noble deeds are born as Brahmins or Kshatriyas and those who indulged in bad deeds are born as chandals'.[59] As in the past, for Gita Press the doors of sanatan Hindu dharma are so well locked from inside that neither Gandhi's ambivalence on caste nor Ambedkar's stout criticism of it can waft through. It has place only for the top three varnas and the consequent benefits—a monotonous pattern for centuries now—that accrue to them on the basis of birth. The mission, therefore, of working for all Hindus and be their spokesperson remains a mere promise whose time will never come. Its publications also continue to propagate gender stereotypes that relegate women to the inner world of the household while men dominate in the outer world.

But the aspect of Gita Press and *Kalyan* that has the greatest significance in present times is the platform it has provided for communal organizations like the RSS, Vishwa Hindu Parishad (VHP) and many others. Arney points out that Gita Press was 'able to take advantage of the introduction of mass printing technology and successfully promote a homogeneous, popular, bhakti-oriented brahminical Hinduism to which spiritual aspirants of many theological and sectarian persuasions could relate'.[60] He cites a special issue of *Hindu Chetna*, a VHP publication, which came out in 1992 in honour of Poddar. The issue carried a 1964 interview of Poddar by Shivram Shankar Apte, earlier with the RSS and later loaned to the VHP. Poddar, who was among the founders of the VHP, told Apte that it was Gita Press that 'sowed the tolerant ideals that have now blossomed into the plant of the Vishwa Hindu Parishad'.[61]

Gita Press and its flagship *Kalyan* would grow and prosper as the only indigenous publishing enterprise of colonial India that continues till this day. Other Hindi journals of the period, whether religious, literary or political, survive only in the archives to be read by scholars interested in unravelling the heady days of Hindi and Hindu nationalism.

Today, *Kalyan* has a circulation of over 200,000 copies while the English *Kalyana-Kalpataru* has a circulation of over 100,000. And the key mission of Gita Press—publishing cheap and well-produced editions of the Gita, Ramayana and Mahabharata—is a stupendous success, unheard of in the world of publishing. For instance, in April 1955 when President Rajendra Prasad visited Gita Press, a pamphlet was published which stated that Gita Press, in the thirty-odd years since its inception, had printed and sold 6.157 million copies of the Gita and 2.08 million copies of the Ramayana. Not including *Kalyan* and *Kalyana-Kalpataru*, 27.8 million copies of all Gita Press publications had been sold in the market.[62] As of February 2014, 71.9 million copies of the Gita have been sold; for the *Ramcharitmanas* and other works by Goswami Tulsidas the figure is seventy million copies, while nineteen million copies of the Puranas, Upanishads and ancient scriptures have been sold. Then there are the tracts and monographs on the duties of ideal Hindu women and children, of which 94.8 million copies have been sold so far, while more than sixty-five million copies of stories from India's mythic past, biographies of saints and devotional songs have been bought.[63] Though the bulk of the titles (739 to be precise) are in Hindi and Sanskrit, Gujarati titles number 152, the second highest after the combined figure for Hindi and Sanskrit. Gita Press also publishes in Telugu, Oriya, English, Bangla, Marathi, Tamil, Kannada, Assamese Malayalam, Nepali and Punjabi. Urdu publications were started in the 1990s, but only two titles have come out so far.

Writings on Gita Press

Considering the significance of Gita Press and *Kalyan*, what is surprising is the near-total lack of critical evaluation by its contemporaries. During his lifetime, Poddar dabbled in Hindi politics by encouraging the Hindi Sahitya Sammelan, but the Hindi world largely ignored him and the publications of Gita Press. In fact, it was left to hagiographic accounts by insiders like Bhagwati Prasad Singh and Shyamsundar Dujari to praise Poddar as a Hindi litterateur of great calibre and Gita Press as an agent of literary awakening. Authoritative accounts of Hindi literature bypassed or made cursory mention of Gita Press. It is possible that early chroniclers of the Hindi world were too preoccupied with the considerable turmoil in the world of Hindi language and literary endeavour to pay attention to the output of a religious publisher.

However, the silence on Gita Press continued throughout the twentieth century. This may be ascribed to the fact that the study of the making of the Hindi public sphere is itself of recent origin. In many ways Vasudha Dalmia's brilliant 1997 study could be said to have heralded the process of mapping the Hindi literary and public sphere. This was followed by several scholarly works of high quality that looked at various aspects of the Hindi world. Alok Rai's *Hindi Nationalism* (2001) traced the evolution of Hindi and how upper-caste monopoly of the language, by making Hindi too dependent on Sanskrit, took away its vivacity built through easy give and take with Persian and Urdu. Charu Gupta's *Sexuality, Obscenity, Community: Women, Muslims and the Hindu Public in Colonial India* (2001) was another milestone, followed by Francesca Orsini's *The Hindi Public Sphere: Language and Literature in the Age of Nationalism* (2002). Works on individual publishing houses, journals, pamphlets, etc., were still elusive, Ulrike Stark's *An Empire of Books: The Naval Kishore Press and the Diffusion of the Printed Word in Colonial India* (2007) being the first comprehensive work on the life and times of this leading publishing house from Uttar Pradesh. Recently, Shobna Nijhawan in *Women and Girls in the Hindi Public Sphere: Periodical Literature in Colonial North India* (2012) has evaluated a set of women's journals like *Stri Darpan, Grihalakshmi* and *Arya Mahila* and girls' periodicals like *Kumari Darpan* and *Kanya Manoranjan*, taking the study of the Hindi public sphere into a new realm.

Through all this, Gita Press has been relegated to an odd paragraph, appendix or footnotes. This formidable religious publishing house has not been the subject of any detailed study. The few doctoral dissertations on Gita Press and Mahavir Prasad Poddar from the universities of Gorakhpur, Allahabad and Banaras have been hagiographical in nature, failing to critically evaluate its role in the larger world of religious publishing houses and journals that existed in Uttar Pradesh. One M.Phil. work from Delhi University and monographs and articles by foreign scholars like Monika Hortsmann, Monika Freier and Paul Arney have provided tantalizing glimpses, but fall short of taking a comprehensive view of one of the most successful publishing houses of the twentieth century that continues to flourish today.

Arney attributed the 'neglect of Gita Press' to a host of reasons.[64] First, there was the 'anomalous status of the establishment in relation to the concepts of sampraday (sect), ashram (school for religious learning), publisher and factory'. To add to this, he said, Gita Press's principle of 'shun(ning) publicity on ideological grounds' and its refusal to indulge in worship of individuals (vyaktigat puja) kept scholars away from evaluating the publishing house or its editor. Arney also thinks that 'English-language scholarship' never took sufficient note of Gita Press's overwhelmingly rich body of work because it was in Hindi.

The Poddar Papers

When I began working on the history of Gita Press, all I had were the best wishes of historian Wendy Doniger. During my university years I had spent long months in the National Archives and the Nehru

Memorial Museum and Library (NMML), but very little direct literature could be found there on either the institution or the individuals who ran it. However, various admirers of the institution spoke about its success and its contribution in the making of a Hindu public sphere. Each one had a story on Gita Press or Poddar more gushing, more reverential than the other. Goyandka was rarely mentioned, and facts did not matter.

In Gorakhpur, Gita Press officials continued to maintain collective silence on crucial academic questions. Its mammoth library and bookshop had everything but the story of the press, or information about Poddar or Goyandka. 'Vyaktigat puja' was still anathema for the publishing house; so while the writings of Poddar and Goyandka continued to dominate Gita Press publications even after their death, there were no writings on the two founders. As I moved from hope to despair, an old acquaintance suggested I go to Gita Vatika at the other end of Gorakhpur. Poddar had lived the better part of his life and even breathed his last there. His family and a few close associates still live in separate quarters there. In Gita Vatika, which had the air of a commune, I met Harikrishna Dujari, whose father and elder brother had both served Poddar and Gita Press their entire lives. An affable man in his seventies, Dujari was the sole window to a world now gone. He was warm and reticent in equal measure. The first few hours were spent talking about Poddar, affectionately called Bhaiji, and Goyandka, who was Sethji to the world.

Dujari agreed to give me access to old issues of *Kalyan* but made it plain I would have to get them photocopied, an arduous exercise in a city where load-shedding is the norm. Over the next few days, as he watched me shuttle between Gita Vatika and the photocopier's shop, I guess he realized I was serious about the project. First, he offered me a room in Gita Vatika so that I could save time commuting from my hotel in the centre of Gorakhpur. And then, in a matter-of-fact tone, which I now call Dujariesque, he said he had some letters that Bhaiji had written and received. Knowing full well that *Kalyan* itself was not going to be of much help, I requested him to share whatever he had.

What started as a promise of a few letters turned out to be a veritable flood of information on Poddar and Gita Press. I had not yet shifted to Gita Vatika but did not mind leaving my hotel at the crack of dawn to pore over those papers. Dujari would give me file after file of correspondence, pamphlets, manuscripts of hagiographies written on Poddar, government records and all that constitutes a robust archive. In the sweltering Gorakhpur heat, sometimes Dujari would ask me to look at files in the room where Poddar had died. Reading the private papers of a public man in a room full of his memories can be surreal. But in the dimly lit room, as the prospect of the project brightened, I realized the Gita Press story needed to be told differently, and that there was much more to Hanuman Prasad Poddar than had so far been apparent. Besides, the Poddar Papers not only tell the tale of Gita Press, but fill a crucial gap in the history of Hindu nationalism in both colonial and post-colonial periods, telling of how the success of the RSS, Hindu Mahasabha and Jana Sangh was built by foot soldiers such as the makers of Gita Press. Dujari even agreed to let me photocopy the files and I struck a deal with a new photocopy shop that would open early and close late. My days were spent in this shop getting copies made of documents, most of which had not seen light for decades.

During my many subsequent visits to Gorakhpur, I became a resident of the Gita Vatika guest house, following the rules of austerity, eating satvik (pure) food in their small mess where a maharaj (brahmin cook) worked. I literally burnt the midnight oil going through the files that Dujari would leave with me every day. Each time he said no more files were left, I would prod him, urge him to make sure, and the next morning, more would appear. For Dujari, Poddar was a saint, but he found it difficult to comprehend why someone from the English-speaking world was keen to write on him and Gita Press. Finally, in February 2012, Dujari threw up his hands and took me to the room that housed the Poddar Papers in boxes and on bookshelves. He was right; I had literally seen each and every bit of them. In my overenthusiasm I had got everything photocopied, barring the contents of one box—which when opened drew me to tears. The resident joint family of pests, many generations of whom had fed themselves on history, had deprived us of some of the most crucial papers of Poddar's last years. What is left at Gita Vatika is on the brink of extinction and needs serious attention. Even the extra set of copies I made for Dujari will soon fall prey to heat and humidity.

In Delhi, after each visit to Gorakhpur, I spent days at the NMML going through the papers of Jamnalal Bajaj, G.D. Birla, Seth Govind Das, Madan Mohan Malaviya and others. As I joined the dots, the picture that emerged was of a giant twentieth-century Hindu missionary and a mammoth publishing house whose fascinating, quiet and often troubling story was not limited to its primary task. It was a crucial cog in the wheel of Hindu nationalism that struck up alliances with everyone: mendicants, liberals, politicians, philanthropists, scholars, sectarian organizations like the RSS, Hindu Mahasabha, Jana Sangh and VHP, and conservative elements within the Congress.

In the following pages, the story of Gita Press unfolds as we first look at the lives of two individuals, Hanuman Prasad Poddar and Jaydayal Goyandka, and place them within the larger paradigm of 'ascetic nationalist masculinity'.[65]

The thematic chapters that follow describe the founding of *Kalyan*, its early years and the manner in which Poddar created a web of national and international contributors for the journal and its English-language counterpart, *Kalyana-Kalpataru* started in 1934. Apart from examining the making of Gita Press and important events in its life, the book looks at how the goals of a religious publishing house in a small UP town intersected with the aims of communal Hindu organizations and nationalism at flashpoints in history from 1926 onwards,[66] and provides an account of the as yet unchronicled role of Gita Press during the years leading to Partition. Through the pages of *Kalyan*, it not only accentuated the Hindu–Muslim divide, criticizing Gandhi both privately and publicly, but also fanned communal hatred.

The post-Independence years saw Gita Press again become a vehicle of Hindu organizations during the agitation against the Hindu Code Bill and in the cow-protection movement. Politically too, the press became more active, openly seeking votes for orthodox organizations like the Ram Rajya Parishad, Hindu Mahasabha and others, as well as expressing strong views against the spread of communism. The Poddar Papers provide an insight into the hitherto unknown central role of the Gita Press in Hindu nationalist discourse.

Poddar also meticulously kept records of his correspondence with leading Hindi writers, intellectuals, artists, political leaders and many organizations. This helps in narrating the relationship Gita Press had with the Hindi literary world and the manner in which it created a visual iconography of the Hindu religion, an exercise that saw artists who later earned a name as Progressives also participate. Further, Poddar's papers highlight his tumultuous relationship with Gandhi, something that has escaped the scrutiny of scholars of Hindu nationalism.

Through a detailed analysis of primary and secondary sources—mostly the pamphlets, pedagogic in nature, that were brought out by Gita Press and *Kalyan*—we are able to appreciate the important role Gita Press played in creating a unified face of Hinduism. This was done without diluting its stance on core principles of sanatan Hindu dharma such as caste divisions and the responsibilities of women that included grounding the male child in Hindu morality so that he would not lose his bearings in the outer world. Integral to the narrative was the depiction of Muslim men as the 'other'—'libidinous, sexually dissipated and voluptuously lustful'[67]—from whom Hindu women had to be protected at all costs.

In the overall analysis, the Gita Press project of promoting the supremacy of Hindu identity continues unabated, though without the towering presence of Goyandka and Poddar. The two luminaries continue to dominate the pages of *Kalyan* and other publications. At a time when politics has become more divisive, Gita Press's template is unchanged, and its political agenda remains undiluted, as does its fond hope that India will one day become Hindu.

[illegible] This brings into focus the relationship [illegible] [illegible] [illegible] which [illegible] [illegible] [illegible] [illegible] [illegible] Poddar's [illegible] relationship with [illegible] [illegible] nationalism.

[illegible] analysis of [illegible] and [illegible] [illegible] that were brought out by [illegible] [illegible] [illegible] women [illegible] [illegible] [illegible] women that included [illegible] [illegible] [illegible] [illegible] [illegible] [illegible]

In the overall analysis of the Gita Press [illegible] of Hindu [illegible] community [illegible] [illegible] [illegible] [illegible] and Poddar [illegible] of Kalyan and [illegible] [illegible] Gita Press [illegible] [illegible] [illegible] Hindu.

9: A Twentieth-century Hindu Missionary and His Mentor

Hanuman Prasad Poddar, the founding editor of *Kalyan*, headed this first-of-its-kind religious journal for forty-five years from 1926 till his death in 1971. By any standards it was a unique feat, and Poddar was no ordinary editor. The tale of the man, the myth and the magic, stretches across 6 kilometres of Gorakhpur. At one end of this stretch stands the office of Gita Press with its colossal ornate gate; at the other, in Shahpur, on the road to Banaras, is Gita Vatika, Poddar's home for over four decades. Here one feels the holy presence of the man who claimed to have conversed with gods.

The area surrounding Gita Press has a strong Muslim presence in the mohallas of Ghantaghar, Basantpur, Reti and Mirzapur, criss-crossed by serpentine alleys, crowded and noisy. In contrast, Shahpur is by the side of a straight road, an area that is relatively quiet and poor, with open drains, roadside tea stalls and the heavy humming presence of the famed mosquitoes of Gorakhpur.

Inside the press, or outside in its huge bookshop, hundreds of works by Poddar are prominently displayed. But for the visitors who come in droves, Poddar merely remains writer-editor extraordinaire. The absence of even a single book on him reinforces the larger philosophy of Gita Press—religion in defence of society and not for the promotion of an individual.

Poddar's grandson Rasyendu Fogla, a successful businessman, lives with his family in Gita Vatika and manages a trust that was set up in Poddar's memory. Gita Vatika publishes scores of books on Poddar, and those of his writings that never got published by Gita Press. Another trust set up earlier, the Radha Madhav Seva Sansthan, is also part of Gita Vatika and has published works on Poddar's life. At neither Gita Press nor Gita Vatika is Poddar referred to in the past tense. Instead, the title Nityalilalin (ever-present) is used, an exercise in deification.

The story of Poddar here deliberately precedes that of Jaydayal Goyandka, businessman-turned-spiritualist, the man whose vision was behind Gita Press and also Poddar's spiritual mentor who would not let him stray from his work at *Kalyan* despite temptations to join the nationalist movement or become an aide to Mahatma Gandhi. Since their 'first meeting in 1910 or 1911 an amalgamation and, as it seems, also a mutual intensification of visions and actions' had taken place, and as Poddar acknowledged, it was Goyandka who 'encouraged him in his religious enterprises'.[1]

Goyandka hovered over Gita Press as a divine presence, never involving himself in the mundane task of running its daily affairs. He kept a close watch on its functioning and publications, while giving Poddar all the freedom as editor. Every time Poddar made a request to be relieved of his duties, Goyandka would refuse, saying that both Gita Press and *Kalyan* would be nothing without Poddar and that continuous publication of *Kalyan* was the ultimate dharma for the protection of Hinduism.

Thus Gita Press became synonymous with Poddar, making him a prisoner of the image that Goyandka had created for him. Poddar would sometimes sulk, would leave Gorakhpur and spend long spells in his native Ratangarh, but the work of Gita Press and *Kalyan* and Goyandka's moral pressure as well as blunt persuasion would draw him back. Goyandka, the mysterious[2] man of the Marwari world, was a grihasta-sadhu (householder-mendicant) who, when not giving sermons, was an incessant traveller in search of spiritual solace. Occasionally, he would be the final arbiter for Marwari families in disputes over the division of businesses and assets. While Goyandka remained the force behind Gita Press, Poddar was its public face.

Hanuman Prasad Poddar: Birth and Childhood

The word Poddar is derived from the Persian term potdar—'pot' meaning treasury or storehouse and 'dar' its keeper. It was a title common during the Mughal period, conferred on those manning the resources of rulers, be it food or the treasury. The title was commonplace in the principalities of Awadh till the abolition of zamindari in 1950.[3]

Officials involved in transferring revenue collected from the tehsils to state and Central governments were called Poddars.

Hanuman Prasad belonged to the Bansal gotra (exogamous sect) of Marwaris, and the family traced its roots to Ratangarh in Bikaner. His grandfather Tarachand was a prominent businessman of the town who, unlike many from his community, had not stirred out of Ratangarh in search of better business opportunities. Married with two wives—something of a family tradition—Tarachand had a son by each of them. In later years, Tarachand broke his rule against going to videsh ('foreign land', a common term for any place outside Ratangarh and Bikaner) and allowed his elder son Kaniram to branch out on his own. However, *Desh Ke Itihas Mein Marwari Jati Ka Sthan*, a definitive history of the Marwaris, states that members of the Poddar clan had already moved to Calcutta's Burrabazar as cloth merchants.[4]

Three days' camel ride from Ratangarh brought Kaniram to Kuchaman railway station from where a circuitous route through Calcutta took him to Shillong. Through the large Marwari network Kaniram was aware of the opportunities in this cantonment town. Marwaris like Navrangram Agarwala of Churu (Rajasthan) had already made a name for themselves in Assam from the mid-nineteenth century as traders and suppliers of British military rations.[5]

The business prospered and soon more Poddars from Ratangarh joined Kaniram in Shillong. But there was a vacuum in his life: he and his wife Ramkaur Devi did not have a child. A lady with religious and spiritual bearings, Ramkaur had sought the blessings of shamans and mystics, with no result. The fear of the business scattering without a successor to hold it together led the couple to formally adopt Bhimraj, Kaniram's younger brother. Kaniram and Ramkaur bequeathed the entire business and property to the younger brother who managed the Calcutta end of Kaniram's business that was expanding throughout eastern India. The adoption had the blessings of their father Tarachand Poddar and prominent members of the Marwari community and close relatives.

Ramkaur's childless state was known to her family guru Meher Das, a Vaishnavite, as well as many god-men of the Nathpanth (Ratangarh had been the seat of the Nathpanthis and various Hindu religious sects for 600 years). A series of yagnas (offerings to fire) invoking Lord Vishnu, followed by feeding of the poor and brahmins, saw Meher Das predict to Ramkaur that her sister-in-law-turned-daughter-in-law Rikhibai, the wife of Bhimraj, would be blessed with a son. The prophecy of the godlike character of the yet-to-be-born Poddar came from another god-man, Motinath Maharaj aka Tuntia Maharaj, who had considerable influence on the Bikaner royal family.

Motinath said Rikhibai's son would have three distinguishing marks: the holy mark of Shri on his forehead, hair on his shoulders and a mole on his right thigh. Besides this, the baby would be born with a wire-like object in his mouth and only after this was pulled out would he cry. Various accounts of Poddar's birth—published, written and unwritten—highlight how he was born with exactly these marks, indicating an extraordinary life ahead. His aunt-cum-grandmother Ramkaur, an ardent Hanuman devotee herself, named the boy Hanuman Bux—changed to Hanuman Prasad many years later when he was a young man working in Calcutta. Till her death Ramkaur always reminded Hanuman how he was the gift of God and ordained for big things.

Thus, the deification of Hanuman Prasad Poddar had begun even before his birth on 17 September 1892 to Rikhibai and Bhimraj Poddar. His birth—the first son after a long time—brought collective joy to the Poddar clan. The family business of food supply to the British army's Eastern Command had brought considerable wealth and heft to the Poddars, but the lack of a successor had been a cause of concern. The joy was short-lived as Rikhibai succumbed to illness in 1894, leaving behind two-year-old Hanuman Bux to grandmother Ramkaur's care.

In 1896, an earthquake devastated Assam. Two of Hanuman Prasad's cousins died and he barely managed to survive. Ramkaur naturally ascribed the child's survival and extrication from the rubble to his magical powers. The earthquake impacted the Poddar family business severely. Kaniram, who was contemplating shifting to Calcutta, passed away in 1899. His adopted son Bhimraj moved to Calcutta with his new wife and family. Hanuman Prasad was left alone in Shillong with his grandmother. A series of tragedies followed in the family that saw seven-year-old Hanuman Prasad relocate to Ratangarh with his grandmother.

Jorawarmal's school in Ratangarh, the first he went to, equipped the child with the mahajani system of accounting and its variants practised in different parts of Rajasthan. But formal education would elude him. He resisted Ramkaur's attempt to send him to an Urdu-medium school in her parents' town, Amritsar. Even at the age of seven, he felt Urdu education was against Hindu culture and the samskaras (ritual practices) of his family and community. His Ratangarh stay brought him close to the various god-men his grandmother had sought blessings from before his birth. It is here that he first read the Gita. Memorizing verses from the text fetched eight-year-old Hanuman a gift of fruits from Swami Bakhnath, one of whose followers later took him on as a disciple after a formal ceremony. These were the years of Hanuman's initiation into elaborate brahminical rituals like the sacred thread ceremony that Marwaris (originally of the vaishya class) had adopted in the late nineteenth century as part of their further reorientation in terms of caste from kshatriya to brahmin.[6] This involved vegetarianism and wearing of the sacred thread.

Hanuman was married in 1904, at the age of twelve, to Mahadevi, daughter of Gurumukhraj Dhandaria of Ratangarh. In later years, Poddar would make much of his family's, especially his grandmother's, benevolence in persisting with the marriage despite Mahadevi having been afflicted with smallpox that had scarred her face. After the wedding, Hanuman Prasad moved with his wife and Ramkaur to join his father's cloth business in Calcutta. This would completely change the course of young Poddar's life. Calcutta, the capital of India was the omphalos of the British Empire in all respects—political, social and economic.[7] The next few years would see Hanuman Prasad lead the multiple lives of a businessman, God-seeking bhakt, man with literary aspirations and a revolutionary to boot.

Calcutta: Politics and Sedition

Hanuman Prasad's initiation into religious, cultural and later political life in Calcutta was through the Sanatan Dharam Pustkarini Sabha that his father had set up along with Madangopal Kothari, Shivnarain Vyas and Shivprasad Acharya. Though small in scale and operation, the Pustkarini Sabha was part of the larger trend of revival movements that stressed the articulation of orthodox Hinduism through such bodies.[8] Such sabhas had started appearing from the end of the nineteenth century.

Bhimraj's Pustkarini Sabha invited god-men and preachers for satsangs and lectures, and these interactions strengthened Hanuman Prasad's interest in the ritualistic form of Hindu religion, the Gita as the final arbiter of human life and issues like cow protection. These were to form his lifelong mission at Gita Press. It was in this period too that Hanuman Prasad met Jaydayal Goyandka.

If Goyandka and the Pustkarini Sabha instilled in Hanuman Prasad a belief in the superiority of sanatan dharma, his membership of the Hindu Mahasabha taught him how the objects of reconversion and cow protection could be achieved through communal political mobilization. Also, as a young delegate at the Calcutta Congress session in 1907, Hanuman Poddar had been influenced by the 'extremist' group led by Bipin Chandra Pal. So by the time he had his first interaction with Mahatma Gandhi, Poddar's political world view had already been firmed up. When Gandhi arrived from South Africa in Calcutta through Rangoon in 1915, Poddar as a Mahasabhaite welcomed him at the Alfred Theatre and presented him with a memento. A unique, often tempestuous, lifelong relationship was later forged between the two.

Calcutta also provided opportunities for Hanuman Prasad to associate with journalists and leading lights of the Hindi world at the forefront of the acrimonious debate on Hindi–Hindustani. Many of these relationships are documented in the privately held rich personal archive at Gita Vatika, especially with Laxman Narayan Garde, editor of *Bharatmitra* and a regular contributor to *Kalyan*,[9] and Ambika Prasad Vajpayee, bank-clerk-turned-journalist, editor of *Nrsimh*, and later the political paper *Svatantra* who remained Poddar's friend and a contributor to *Kalyan*.[10] Vajpayee had a role to play in Poddar's attraction towards Tilak's Home Rule League. Then there was Jhavarmal Sharma, editor of the conservative Marwari paper *Calcutta Samachar*; and the tallest of them all—Mahavir Prasad Dwivedi, editor of the prestigious *Saraswati*, who after retirement wrote for *Kalyan* and corresponded at length with Poddar. *Calcutta Samachar* later became *Hindu Sansar*, a daily that was deeply immersed in the ocean of sanatan dharma.[11]

Poddar's biographies—published and unpublished accounts based on extensive interviews with him—mention his closeness with editors of Bengali newspapers. His earliest acquaintance was with Brahmabandhab Upadhyay, editor of *Sandhya*, and a Brahmo and a Catholic at various stages of his life. He was also secretary of the Printers' and Compositors' League set up in 1905 at the height of the Swadeshi movement. *Sandhya*'s 'uninhibited use of the language of the streets and its vitriolic and often vulgar abuse of the feringhee and all who aped his ways' as well as its open invocation to readers to 'remain a Hindu and a Bengali' would be reflected in Poddar's writings in *Kalyan* during the years of Partition and early Independence.[12]

Then there were Aurobindo Ghose, Shyamsundar Chakrabarty, Subodh Chandra Mullick, all associated with *Bande Mataram*, and Bhupendranath Dutt, editor of *Yugantar* who openly professed violence as the way to fight the British decision to partition Bengal.

Of all the Congress politicians, Poddar's most enduring relationship was with Malaviya, both ideologically and personally. He would also build a close relationship with Malaviya's second son Radhakant whose failure as a commission agent resulted in a huge financial loss that he attempted to offset with money that his father had collected from the Birlas for the Congress. As a result, the equation between the father and the son became tense and the two communicated with each other through Poddar.[13] Malaviya and Poddar worked closely on several issues concerning the protection of the rights of Hindus. Even in a minor matter of funding for a gaushala (cow shelter) at Barhaj (in Deoria district, United Provinces), Malaviya would ask Poddar and Baba Raghav Das for help.[14]

Poddar also counted the mercurial Panchkouri Banerjee as one of his friends. After the demise of *Bande Mataram*, *Sandhya* and *Yugantar*, Banerjee kept the strident anti-British tone alive through his daily *Nayak*.[15]

Poddar's personal life, meanwhile, had been unfortunately eventful. Mahadevi had died during childbirth in 1909 followed, within a few days, by her infant. In 1911, Poddar got married again to Subtibai, daughter of Seth Mangturam Saraogi, but she too died in childbirth in 1916. The same year, Poddar was married for the third time, to Ramdei

Bai, daughter of Sitaram Sanganeria, a rich businessman from Assam. Hanuman Prasad, who had joined the Swadeshi movement and already switched to wearing khadi, would try his best to influence his new wife to discard her foreign-made clothes.[16]

The heady world of Bengal's politics, in which violence played a defining role, did not leave the Marwari locality of Burrabazar—engrossed in its business and community matters, profit and philanthropy—untouched. In the wee hours of 21 July 1916, the neighbourhood was rudely awakened when a British sergeant, an Indian inspector and seven or eight policemen raided the house on Zakaria Street where leading Marwari businessman Ghanshyam Das Birla lived. Birla himself could not be found, but in the next few hours, a house in Sutapatti was raided and Omkarmal Saraf was arrested. By afternoon, a raid in Clive Street resulted in the arrest of Hanuman Prasad Poddar and Jwala Prasad Kanodia.

The next day's *Calcutta Samachar* reported the raids, but in a muted tone, expressing ignorance about the cause of the arrests. The highly editorialized news report said, 'This incident has created a big wave among Marwaris of Burrabazar . . . It is not clear for what crime these young men have been taken away by police. Whatever it is this incident is new to Marwari world. We cannot think of anything these young men could have done. The entire Marwari society is surprised. We expect government to take a well-considered decision.' The paper continued in a reverential tone: 'We do not for a moment doubt the justice of government, but at the same time we cannot give up our well-established notions about the innocence of our young men. We hope that the Bengal government will, at an early date, consider the case of the young Marwaris who have been arrested, and do justice to them.'[17]

Two days later, *Calcutta Samachar*, either unaware of the facts about the arrests or withholding these from its readers, was still lamenting: 'Who would not be surprised to find jowar grow in a farm that has never seen that crop? There is not a single case of sedition by Marwaris who are the original inhabitants of the land of Rajputs.'[18]

Calcutta Samachar was not alone. Other newspapers too expressed bewilderment at the arrests and speculated about the reasons. These varied from the murder of a deputy superintendent of police Basanta

Kumar Chatterji (*The Englishman*) to the killing of police officers in Calcutta and constables in Mymensingh (*Sanjivani*). *Hitavadi* said the arrests had caused 'great public surprise', while *Marwari*, like *Calcutta Samachar*, emphasized the apolitical nature of the community, how they had been extremely loyal to the government and had never been found to be implicated in any crimes, let alone political ones.

Burrabazar was rife with rumours.[19] One was that the arrests had been made to extort money from the Marwaris. It was said that the son-in-law of a rich Marwari had been arrested and that the government would release him if Rs 30 lakh were paid, which would be transferred to the war fund.

The raids of 21 July led to the recovery of thirty-one pistols, and soon it was revealed that the arrests related to the Rodda Arms Robbery case of 1914. The Sedition Committee of 1918 headed by Justice Rowlatt described this as an 'event of the greatest importance in the development of revolutionary crime in Bengal'.[20]

Calcutta-based R.B. Rodda & Company was one of the largest firms importing firearms and ammunition. On 26 August 1914, company clerk Sirish Chandra Mitra had collected a consignment of 202 boxes from the customs clearance office. He came to the company's godown with only 192 and left saying he would return with the rest, but never did. The ten missing crates contained fifty Mauser pistols of .300 bore and 46,000 cartridges. Every pistol was numbered and these numbers existed in the records of Rodda & Company. The Sedition Committee report claimed that forty-four of these pistols had been immediately distributed among nine revolutionary groups and had been used in fifty-four cases of dacoity. 'After August 1914, probably there was not a single revolutionary act in Bengal in which pistols of Rodda Company were not used. With great difficulty police managed to recover 31 of these pistols,' the report said.[21]

The Poddar Papers include a large number of documents related to the case, including those of the Bengal government's political department and Poddar's detailed 1955 interview to the Akhil Bharatvarshiya Marwari Sammelan that was involved in contributing to the large book project on the freedom struggle to be brought out by the Government of India. In the interview, Poddar denied that G.D. Birla had anything to do with the Rodda Conspiracy, saying that memory failed him about the whereabouts of G.D. Birla on the day of the police raid. Maybe he had been in Bombay or Ootacamund, Poddar said. Authoritative accounts of Birla's life corroborate the claims of his innocence but state that he had been packed off by the family to Mukundgarh in the Shekhawati region of Rajasthan.[22]

In the interview, as well as in various published accounts, Poddar revealed the inner world of Marwari youth and how a number of their social and literary organizations were actively involved in subversive activities and had close links with revolutionary leaders and groups that were active during the Swadeshi movement. G.D. Birla was integral to these groups, and Poddar, in his interview, while underlining that his memory could be failing him, said he himself had been a member of the Swadesh Bandhab Samiti. This fact is not corroborated elsewhere, and Medha Kudaisya refers to Poddar as a member of the Anushilan Samiti, who regularly funded and attended its meetings.[23] Poddar's own interviews and correspondence contain references to his close relationship with another member Sakharam Ganesh Deuskar, a Marathi scholar proficient in Bengali, who wrote *Desher Katha*, a best-seller on the Indian economy.[24]

The foremost society for Marwari youth was the Marwari Sahayak Samiti, with four subcommittees that worked secretly, dealing separately with national issues, social reform and revolutionary activities. The Marwari Samiti was modelled on the lines of the Anushilan Samiti where members had to take a vow to put the country before self and maintain secrecy at all costs. The meeting venues changed frequently—from Birla Garden in Liluah to the residence of Phoolchand Choudhury or the family garden of Nagarmal Modi. The majority of its members were Marwaris, some of whom would dominate Indian business later in colonial and post-colonial India. Among its members were Hanuman Prasad Poddar, Banarsidas Jhunjhunwala, Jwala Prasad Kanodia, Rameshwar Prasad Morarka, Ghanshyam Das Birla and many others. The entire list of members was not available to any one of them. Poddar himself admitted that there was a 'huge difference between the public work and secret aspect of the society'.[25]

Throughout his life Hanuman Prasad Poddar maintained that his association with the Gita dated back to his revolutionary days. The Sahitya Sambandhini Samiti, another of the secret committees run by Marwari youth under the patronage of Jugal Kishore Birla, elder brother of Ghanshyam Das, had published *Tikawali Gita*, one of the earliest Hindi translations of the Gita by Baburao Vishnu Paradkar. What drew Poddar to it was its cover showing Bharatmata with the Gita in one hand and a sword in the other. The book had become an instant success, selling in the thousands and adding to the growing influence of religious revivalism on revolutionaries. In an article for *Kalyan* in 1938, Paradkar wrote of how *Tikawali Gita* was banned by the British for its influence on revolutionaries and the Sahitya Sambandhini Samiti was put under a close watch.[26]

With such an elaborate arrangement of secret societies and serious resolve to act, all the young Marwaris needed was a chance to showcase their valour. The Rodda Conspiracy proved to be their single moment under the revolutionary sun. In the aftermath of the arrests, the Marwari elders of Calcutta would regret the incident, viewing it as a grave act of digression from the path of business and loyalty to British rule.

There were slight variations in the Marwari accounts of the Rodda Conspiracy. New names cropped up as many of those who carried out the act—notably Hanuman Prasad Poddar and Prabhu Dayal Himmatsingka—were out to prove themselves as reluctant revolutionaries, or at least to minimize their role.

After the disappearance of the ten boxes along with clerk Sirish Chandra Mitra, the problem was finding a safe house for the arms and ammunition. The Poddar Papers state that Hanuman Prasad's domestic help Sukhlal played a major role, as did Baburao Vishnu Paradkar.[27] The boxes were spread across various locations in and around Burrabazar: Harrison Road, Nai Tola, Kannulal Lane, the gaddi (business establishment) of Banarsi Prasad Jhunjhunwala on Chitpur Road, two boxes to Omkarmal Saraf's house at Sutapatti that eventually got transferred to Poddar's gaddi on Clive Street. Some of the stuff were sent to Chandernagore. Himmatsingka, then a student of law and actively involved with revolutionaries, helped transfer two boxes to Poddar's business establishment from Saraf's. A cache of ammunition was kept in G.D. Birla's house as well for some time.

Poddar said in an interview that his shop was searched immediately after the incident but no action was taken due to his father-in-law's contacts in the police. He also disputed the version that a few pistols had been recovered from his shop. 'All the pistols were given away to Bengalis (revolutionaries),' he stated. The residence of Sirish Chandra Mitra, already under surveillance for his alleged involvement in the murder of two British men, was also searched but nothing could be found. In fact, Mitra's role in the Rodda case could never be established. He went underground.

The police laid a trap to identify those behind the Rodda Arms Conspiracy. Phoolchand Choudhury was approached by a CID inspector with the information that a Bengali revolutionary had named him, Birla, Himmatsingka, Poddar, Kanodia and Saraf as ringleaders. He is said to have been asked by the inspector for a bribe of Rs 10,000 to bury the investigation. The group discussed the inspector's proposal and decided to report him to his superiors. Choudhury, a government employee, reported the matter to his boss, an Englishman and the brother-in-law of Calcutta Police Commissioner Charles Tegart. The commissioner acted swiftly and dismissed the corrupt inspector. After due diligence, Tegart was convinced of the involvement of Choudhury and the others, and arrest warrants were issued under Section 120 of the Indian Penal Code. Himmatsingka was the first to be arrested and externed for two years from Bengal in March 1916 under the stringent Defence of India Act. A few months later, all the others, except Birla, were arrested.

Poddar and his friends were kept for a fortnight in Dullanda House, a former mental asylum.[28] They first refused to eat the pitiable jail food. Jhavarmal Sharma, the editor of *Calcutta Samachar*, stepped in to organize home-cooked food for the Marwari revolutionaries. Saraf was the first to be let off on 3 August 1916 for lack of evidence.

Various explanations have been suggested for Birla's absence on the day of the raid and the subsequent deletion of his name from police records—ranging from a prior tip-off to his growing clout in business world of Calcutta that helped the family deploy the best resources. Poddar's private papers claim that Baijnath Kedia, an important member of the Marwari Sahayak Samiti, was sent to meet Birla in Bombay to apprise him of the developments, while Hindu Mahasabha leader Ashutosh Lahiry's version is that the Birla family had to spend Rs 1 lakh to escape the police dragnet.[29] Another version is that the family approached Sir Kailash Chandra Bose, who was close to the British establishment in Calcutta and was a friend to Marwaris. Bose is believed to have stood surety for G.D. Birla with the Lal Bazar police, and Tegart too helped the family in good measure, forging a long-term relationship that led to his heading Birla's London-end of business after retirement.[30]

After a fortnight in Dullanda House, Poddar, Choudhury and Kanodia were sent to Alipur Jail. Poddar said they were not tortured there, but Choudhury was sent to his native Punjab where he suffered at the hands of the local police. Their arrest under the Defence of India Act allowed the British government to keep them in jail without trial. By an order of 21 August 1916, Poddar was interned in Simlapal, a nondescript village 38 kilometres from Bankura town.

The internment order signed by J.G. Cummings, secretary to the Government of Bengal, said: '. . . in the opinion of the government of Bengal, there are reasonable grounds for believing that Hanuman Prasad Poddar . . . has acted, is acting and is about to act in a manner prejudicial to the public safety'. Poddar was then directed to report to the superintendent of police of Bankura, where the SP ordered Poddar to live in the house of Adhar Chandra Rai—letting the police have free access to his room at any time. His movements were limited to a small area around the house, and he was banned from interacting with anyone 'not permanently domiciled within the limits of village'. Significantly, he was not allowed to speak with schoolchildren, students or schoolteachers.[31]

In January 1917, news came that Ramkaur was seriously ill, and on 12 January Poddar was given a week's parole to visit her. She passed away in December 1917, when Poddar was given two weeks' parole 'to put his affairs in order'. The government turned down his request for a third parole in April 1918, and in May 1918 came the order that he was not to 'enter, reside or remain within the confines of the province of Bengal'.[32] After fifteen months of internment, his wife Ramdei was allowed to join him.

Poddar's life had taken a different direction during the confinement in Simlapal; as he later admitted, the experience brought him closer to God. He would also never forget how the Marwari world of Calcutta had shunned his family. His distant cousin Jaydayal Goyandka (whose alter ego he would become in the future), Banarsidas Jhunjhunwala (member of the Marwari Sahayak Samiti and Poddar's co-accomplice in the Rodda Conspiracy but not an accused), and friends Jhavarmal Sharma and Ramkumar Goyanka were the few people who had visited his family and helped them. The rest of the Marwari world of Burrabazar, led by the elders, had been busy shedding its revolutionary skin.

Less than a month after the arrests, the Marwari community had sought the help of Sir Kailash Chandra Bose to restore their standing with the British government. Bose was invited as a special guest to the meeting of the Marwari Association. Outgoing president Rai Bissesar Lall Halwasya Bahadur set the tone when referring to the arrests, saying, 'Marwari community is deeply attached to the government and we therefore hope that the arrested young men will be fully able to vindicate their character.' More important, he exhorted young Marwaris to 'remain free from the contamination of political thoughts and ideas of harmful nature'. In his speech, Bose 'dwelt on the loyalty of the Marwari community, which he said was always regarded as an object of admiration by the other communities'. He 'regretted the recent arrests of some Marwari youth, and hoped that this would prove only a solitary instance'.[33]

Thus, the one revolutionary act of the Marwaris was suppressed by the dominant conservative elements in the community with a zeal that was no less revolutionary. The protagonists of the Rodda Conspiracy were exhorted to keep away from politics for the rest of their life. G.D. Birla was soon back in Calcutta and got active with business and community affairs through the Marwari Relief Society. He became one of Gandhi's closest aides and a proponent of ahimsa. Himmatsingka, then a law student, was to become a prominent lawyer, while Poddar would be the stormy petrel of religious publishing in the country.

Bombay: A New Direction

With the externment order in hand and a young wife and a half-sister to take care of, Hanuman Prasad Poddar now faced the problem of finding work. The Marwaris of Calcutta had already distanced themselves from him, so the family headed for their native Ratangarh, but work did not come.

One day a letter arrived from Jamnalal Bajaj, asking Poddar to come to Bombay. Bajaj promised to get Poddar started in business in this commercial centre. What awaited Poddar when he arrived in Bombay in 1919 was a huge network of intellectuals, political leaders and philanthropists; also a new Marwari world less closed than that in Calcutta, owing to its new-found wealth from industry and interaction with the wider world. This account of Poddar's Bombay years is entirely based on interviews he gave to close aide Gambhirchand Dujari, which also formed the basis for Poddar's biography by Bhagwati Prasad Singh.

Jamnalal Bajaj, the leading light of the Bombay business world and one among the few industrialists who were close to Gandhi, stood by his promise to Poddar, though the latter's experience of business was scant. In fact, most of the accounts on Poddar are silent about his independent business in Calcutta, though he himself mentioned to Gambhirchand Dujari that he had a jute business in Dacca in partnership with Naurangrai Ramchandra, and that during one of his business trips there in 1912 he had met Ma Anandamayi.

In Bombay, Bajaj helped Poddar start various ventures, from a brokerage firm in partnership with Gulabrai Nemani dealing in cotton, to share brokerage with Srinivas Das Balkrishnalal Poddar, owner of the firm Tarachand Ghanshyamdas, and finally a linseed brokerage firm with Bajaj's brother-in-law and chief accountant Chiranjilal Jajodia.

Business in Bombay did not enrich Poddar, but it helped him in one significant way. The new avatar ensured that the order banning him from entering Bengal was withdrawn. However, Calcutta would never be his home again.

Poddar built up a large social network of friends, admirers and acquaintances in Bombay through the spiritual world of satsang, bhajans and the All India Marwari Aggarwal Mahasabha started by the Bombay

Marwaris in 1919, of which Poddar became the regional secretary in 1920.

Goyandka visited Bombay in 1922 with his entourage for a religious discourse—a defining moment for Poddar. Gradually he became involved with discourses on the Gita. Occasionally, satsangs would take place in the Marwari school where Ram Manohar Lohia was a regular at Gita classes. Goyandka's Satsang Bhavan came up in the wadi (estate) of Shivnarain Nemani, a prominent Marwari businessman, actively involved in the Marwari Aggarwal Mahasabha. Soon, Satsang Bhavan in Kalbadevi became a regular stop for religious men from all over India. Thus began Poddar's tryst with the spiritual world that would become his life. Also, the network he built with gurus and sanyasis would later provide *Kalyan* with ready-made contributors.

One interesting friendship he built in Bombay during his religious discourse days was with Vishnu Digambar Paluskar, the doyen of Hindustani classical music and an exponent of the Gwalior gharana. When Poddar met Paluskar in Bombay the latter was already established as a master vocalist and was running the hugely popular Gandharva Mahavidyalaya, first set up in 1901 in Lahore along with a printing press to publish books on music. Born into a family of kirtankars (singers of kirtans, religious songs) in Maharashtra's Kurundwad, Paluskar met Poddar at one of the religious discourses of which kirtans formed an important part. Paluskar would sing as well as give talks on the Ramayana. Poddar saw Paluskar mesmerize thousands of people at the Ahmedabad Congress in 1921. A regular at Congress sessions, Paluskar would open the proceedings with '*Raghupati Raghav Raja Ram*' and the version popularized by him was Gandhi's favourite.

Paluskar took Poddar under his wing, visiting him regularly to give him music lessons. Though Poddar's involvement with myriad issues left him no time to complete his musical training, his private papers claim that one of the bhajans he wrote—'*Mere To Ram Naam Adhar*'—became a favourite with Paluskar who would begin every discourse with it. Paluskar set up an ashram in Nasik named Ram Naam Adhar. The association between the two continued for a long time, Poddar using his wide Marwari network to help Paluskar tide over serious threats from creditors, attending his concerts and his discourses at the Allahabad

Kumbh Mela of 1930, which also saw the daily presence of Madan Mohan Malaviya and Jawaharlal Nehru's mother Swarup Rani.

Paluskar died in 1931, and in 1956 Gita Press published *Sangeet Ramcharitmanas*, a collection of eighty-nine songs composed by him based on the *Ramcharitmanas*, consisting of khayal, thumri and dhrupad.[34] It is likely that Ghanshyam Das Birla's youngest son Basant Kumar Birla bankrolled the publication. Junior Birla repeatedly wrote to Poddar throughout 1955, requesting him to write the foreword to the book. Initially, Birla had wanted to publish the book in Calcutta and leave the distribution to Gita Press as it 'was famous for making religious and bhakti books available to the general public'.[35] He also requested Poddar to sell the book at a cheap rate. But later, the whole process of publication was left to Gita Press. At Birla's request, Banaras Hindu University had already made the musical notations of the work.

Meanwhile, misfortune continued to haunt Poddar's personal world. His first child with Ramdei, a son born in 1920, passed away after eighteen months. He arranged the marriages of his two younger sisters, Annapurna and Chanda, in 1919 and 1922 respectively. Soon after, Chanda committed suicide by jumping into a well at her in-laws' house in Bombay. Poddar's private papers are largely silent about the reasons for her death, except for admitting that Chanda's in-laws were unhappy with her for some reason. Poddar decided not to pursue the case of his sister's untimely death and told the police that she had slipped into the well by mistake.

Personal tragedies, minor or major, would not deter Poddar from his public role, be it as a prominent figure in the Marwari world—their business, social or even private space—or at the national level on diverse issues like cow slaughter and the Hindu Code Bill. In Bombay, Poddar had acquired some reputation as a spiritual man. In the Poddar Papers there is an interesting set of questionnaire prepared by sociologist G.S. Ghurye and his research assistant R.V. Athaide of the School of Economics and Sociology, University of Bombay. The undated questionnaire 'desired to ascertain the attitude of the educated in Bombay to certain religious and social problems'.[36] Questions ranged from a person's belief in God, relation between God and the universe, reconciliation between infinite wisdom, goodness and omnipotence of

God to the existence of physical, social, moral and metaphysical evil to belief in life after death and relation between religion and science. Poddar's response, if he gave one, is unavailable, but the questionnaire points to his formidable reputation. Thus Bombay became the site of his debut as a successful social and religious entrepreneur as he took up the editorship of the newly launched *Kalyan* in 1926. Poddar's eight-year stint in the city ended in 1927.

Relations with Gandhi

Being close to Jamnalal Bajaj gave Poddar access to leaders like Tilak and Gandhi whom he had met and aspired to interact with while in Calcutta. Tilak became an acquaintance in Bombay, and Poddar mentioned in the interview for his biography that he had attended the Amritsar session of the Congress in 1919 as a Tilak supporter and openly sided with him when the resolution on Congress's response to the Montague–Chelmsford reforms was being debated. Poddar also claimed he was with Tilak when he breathed his last in August 1920. This claim cannot be verified, but one possible reference is found in Dhananjay Keer's highly adulatory biography of Tilak. Keer states that two days before Tilak's death at Sardar Griha in Bombay, among the hundreds of people who trooped in to see the Maratha leader was one Marwari who distributed a thousand rupees among the poor.[37] Poddar's second claim—that Tilak had changed the opinion set out in his book, *Arctic Home in the Vedas* (1903), that the Vedas were composed in the Arctic (the original home of the Aryans, according to Tilak)—cannot be verified either. Poddar said that when Tilak died he had a revised manuscript ready, and that it disappeared.

But the most significant long-term relationship Poddar forged in Bombay due to his proximity with Bajaj was with Gandhi. Since their first meeting in Calcutta, Poddar had gone through a political baptism—joining revolutionaries, being imprisoned, attending Congress sessions and becoming close to the extreme elements within the Congress party. Meanwhile Gandhi had gained in stature—he was already the Mahatma. The relationship built between Poddar and Gandhi in Bombay was entirely on a personal plane; their divergent views on the Gita, Hinduism,

Congress politics and minority and caste questions would occasionally come to the fore, but a degree of civility always existed. It is only in the early 1940s that Poddar's angry disillusionment with the Congress and Gandhi would become evident in the pages of *Kalyan*.

Personally, Gandhi was extremely fond of Poddar. In a 1935 letter from Wardha, Gandhi expressed 'happiness and satisfaction' with Poddar's views. 'Sometimes I feel a man like you should stay with me. Bhai Jamnalal (Bajaj) also wants this. But wherever you are if you are mentally with me it is like staying with me. What you are doing through *Kalyan* and Gita Press is a great service to God. I feel I am part of what you are doing because you consider me your own and I consider you mine.'[38]

The relationship between the two had deepened in 1932 during the second civil disobedience movement, when Gandhi was lodged in Yerwada jail along with close associates Sardar Vallabhbhai Patel and Narayan Desai. His youngest son Devdas, of whom he had high expectations,[39] had sought Gandhi's permission to marry Lakshmi, daughter of C. Rajagopalachari. Soon after, Devdas was arrested and sent to Gorakhpur jail where he fell seriously ill with typhoid. Devdas's deteriorating health put Gandhi through a great deal of stress. Adding to his worry was the fact that his letters were taking inordinately long to reach Devdas, being held up by censors.[40] Poddar, who had moved to Gorakhpur in 1927, was remembered and his help requisitioned. Gandhi sent a frantic telegram on 16 June to Poddar: 'Send Devdas temperature. Do you see him daily. How long suffering.'[41]

Bride-to-be Lakshmi, who eventually had to wait a long time for marriage, would also inquire about Devdas, writing to Poddar in chaste Hindi. She would be coy in her approach to the subject of her fiancé's health, often asking about Devdas only in the last paragraph of her postcards sent from Coimbatore or Tiruchangadu. Poddar also received requests for updates on Devdas's health from G.D. Birla, Narandas Gandhi (brother of Maganlal Gandhi singled out by the Mahatma as his heir),[42] Jamnalal Bajaj (then in London), Brij Krishna (Gandhi's close aide in Delhi), Madan Mohan Malaviya and others.

Poddar did his best. The inspector general of prisons based in Nainital was requested to grant a 'daily interview' with Devdas.[43]

Poddar's request stated that Devdas—'laid up with fever since the last 12 days'—was the son of Mahatma Gandhi. 'I am very intimately connected with his family, and as such it is but natural if I feel anxious for him . . . I am here in Gorakhpur and can be of some service to Mr Devdas as well as to the jail authorities in the treatment of his ailments.' Aware that his past political record could be a deterrent to his meeting Devdas in jail, Poddar assured the authorities in a wire to the IG (prisons): 'Self (Poddar) detached from politics known to authorities.' But the request was rejected in a terse four-word wire from the authorities: 'Daily interview not permissible.' Eventually, Poddar managed to meet Devdas twice in jail, and sent out a press communique to Malaviya's daily *The Leader*, *Aaj* and the Associated Press.[44] Devdas's condition, Poddar said, was 'quite satisfactory'; he was merely suspected of typhoid, but sixteen days of fever had resulted in weight loss of 15 pounds (over 6 kg). *The Leader* carried the news prominently, quoting Poddar extensively.

Gandhi thanked Poddar profusely for taking care of Devdas. 'I shall not feel anxious about Devdas since you are there. Moreover, Devdas had written to me that you treated him in a very loving manner. The doctor is really a good man. I shall always expect to receive letters from you time to time.'[45] After Devdas was released, Gandhi again wrote to Poddar expressing his affection: 'You are finally free from worrying about Devdas. I have received all your letters. Why should I feel obliged? The civilised way is to seek such help in silence. Only God can reward for such selfless service, a human being cannot. I think such help should be taken in silence.'[46] A letter from Narandas Gandhi followed, with more explicit gratitude to Poddar: 'The kind of interest you have shown in our family matters and sense of urgency you have displayed is praiseworthy. Your hard work and anxiety did not fail. Devdas has been released. He must have met you.'[47]

The year 1932, however, proved to be a watershed in the Gandhi–Poddar relationship. On 2 August 1932 Gandhi wrote from Yerwada jail to Poddar amidst growing fear that the British government would accept the demand for separate electorates for untouchables, passionately advocated by Bhim Rao Ambedkar at the Round Table Conference. Gandhi was still in Yerwada when British prime minister Ramsay

McDonald announced acceptance of separate electorate for untouchables. Determined to 'resist the decision with my life', Gandhi decided to go on a 'fast without food save water with or without salt and soda'.[48] The decision to fast had an immediate impact. On the one hand, orthodox elements within the Congress like Malaviya, Rajagopalachari and Hindu Mahasabha's B.S. Moonje sat at the negotiating table with leaders of the untouchable class such as B.R. Ambedkar, M.C. Rajah and P.N. Rajbhoj, resulting in the Poona Pact of 1932. On the other, news of Gandhi's fast caused a huge moral upsurge throughout the country. From conservative Allahabad to cosmopolitan Bombay, temple after temple opened its doors to untouchables. In an unprecedented move, six temples of Bombay took a poll on the issue by placing a box at the entrance, and those in favour of entry by untouchables won by a thumping majority—to be precise 24,979 people were in favour against a hopeless 445 who opposed the move. While Padmaja Naidu called it a 'catharsis' that would cleanse Hinduism of the 'accumulated corruption of centuries', Rabindranath Tagore, who had rushed to see Gandhi after the news of his fast unto death, called it a 'wonder'.[49]

G.D. Birla conveyed news of Gandhi's fast and the subsequent Poona Pact to Poddar who was in his native Ratangarh. For a shocked Poddar, at the helm of a flourishing publishing house propagating a ritualistic form of Hinduism with strong emphasis on the fourfold varna system, the change was far too sweeping, and a huge threat to the existing social order. He immediately wrote to Gandhi, beginning by chiding the Mahatma for thanking him for taking care of Devdas in Gorakhpur jail. 'I do not know why you thought of writing these words. Maybe I am the one feeling too proud of what I have done and wanted to make you feel obliged. Fact is I could not take much care of Devdas. Whatever I could do is nothing more than love and affection for him.'[50] Poddar reminded Gandhi of an incident in Bombay, many years ago, when the Mahatma was unwell in Juhu and *Navjivan* had made a public announcement that no one should come to meet him. Unaware of the statement in *Navjivan*, Poddar had gone to meet Gandhi and was being turned away when Gandhi himself sent for him and made it clear that the newspaper announcement was not meant for family members. 'I still remember your affectionate words . . . From that day I consider myself your family member. In such a context what I did for Devdas is neither unique nor worth talking (about) . . .'

Niceties over, Poddar now raised the issue that had been troubling him. He was careful to tell Gandhi that after much deliberation he had decided to speak out, like a child, and requested Gandhi to read the letter and advise him.

Poddar then came to his point: 'These days a big agitation by dalits is going on in the country that has intensified due to your fast. At various places, people are dining with dalits and they are being allowed inside temples. Outcome only god knows. Just like those believing in god and shastras are accused of blind faith I find that this movement has not only become a victim of blind faith but also there is lack of discernment. Even those in favour of dining with dalits agree (though I do not equate dining with them as a mark of equality) that they cannot be considered pure until they have a pure bath, wear fresh clothes, give up alcohol and meat or at least stop feasting on dead cattle. Only then co-dining makes sense. But your common dining and temple-entry movement is not even checking if they have fulfilled these norms. What is taking place is mere eating together, letting them inside temples, and allowing them to participate in rituals. No one is talking of upliftment of dalits but only reiterating their untouchable status. Is this lack of restraint or reform? Is this enrichment of purity or its destruction? Have you thought of the repercussions of this unbridled disrespect to our body and soul?

'With due respect I would like to reiterate that dining together and equal rights in everything would not lead to love for dalits. That would happen only with pure heart and good behaviour. Even Pandavas and Kauravas used to dine together but it led to a big battle.'

Not sure if his arguments would convince Gandhi, Poddar resorted to the ultimate ploy of holding up a mirror to Gandhi, reminding him that his reformist zeal was out of sync with his past. He extracted a series of Gandhi's writings on caste and untouchability in *Navjivan* in the early 1920s, and made it part of his letter. In these articles Gandhi had said that to remove untouchability it was not important to dine with antyaj (untouchables) or give daughters in marriage: 'I do not ask that you drink from their lota (pots) without cleaning them up';[51] 'If eating together results in friendship then Europe would not have witnessed the great war';[52] 'How can untouchables be allowed in all temples?'[53] Not only does Gandhi's ambiguous position on caste come to the fore in these extracts, they also explain his less-than-enthusiastic follow-up of the Poona Pact.

Poddar was unrelenting in his letter, upbraiding Gandhi, the liberals within Congress and the intelligentsia. 'Today if someone who respects you wants to criticize you or your views and would like to show infirmities of your opinion, then he is attacked and abused. He is called obscurantist, sanatan dharmi, traitor and what not. Recently, in Kashi (Banaras) there was an incident of stone pelting in a meeting. In such a situation many people have suspicion about the state of future swarajya (self-rule).'

Poddar then asked Gandhi a set of questions. 'I know you do not believe in changing someone's view or belief system through force. You have said so many times that an individual should have the freedom of religion. But what is happening? Letting all kinds of people enter places of worship against the wishes of those who run these institutions is against the spirit of freedom of religion or not? It would destroy our temple system. Have we asked if those being let inside the temples even want to go there or not? If they want, why not build separate temples for them. After all, Rama went to the hut of Sabri. But I guess the entire issue is about rights.'[54] Lamenting the role of Ambedkar, who was at the receiving end of severe criticism in *Kalyan*, Poddar told Gandhi that the Dalit leader had already said their movement was not about God but was a fight for social equality and strong presence in government jobs. Finally, Poddar repeated that he was Gandhi's 'partial bhakt': 'I am not your follower but part of your family. I request you to put an end to this unrestrained behaviour of your followers. I have merely given you a glimpse of what is happening. In reality a lot more is taking place. It is an attack on an individual's freedom of religion.'

Gandhi was quick to respond. He stood by every word in *Navjivan* that Poddar had cited. 'To understand what I say one needs to understand my conduct for I try to avoid saying anything that contradicts my conduct and doing anything contrary to what I say. And I admit my own weakness whenever my conduct is inconsistent with the opinions I express.'[55]

Refuting Poddar's allegations, Gandhi said, 'I do not see any inconsistency between my profession and my conduct.' Distancing himself from 'those who taint and slander sanatanists', Gandhi said that 'himsa' or violence would 'undoubtedly injure the cause of the removal of untouchability', and that 'cleanliness and some code of conduct are always desirable'. He continued, 'It is a sin to use coercion in this matter or despise those who refuse to inter-dine. Similarly to force one's way into temples against the wishes of the trustees is an act of sin.' For Gandhi it was clear that 'rather than witness such reform I would prefer death because I am convinced that compulsions can neither remove untouchability nor safeguard Hinduism'.

However, in the same letter Gandhi blamed the followers of sanatan dharma for social ailments like untouchability and barring Dalits from entering temples: 'The caste Hindus having created a class of outcastes, have up to the present day been treating them in a most irreligious and brutal manner. This has caused uncleanliness and other vices to creep in among them. Sooner or later the Hindus have to atone for it.' Gandhi told Poddar he wanted to 'satisfy' him, 'from self-interest, for I expect a great deal of work from you in this cause'.

Gandhi's best efforts to change Poddar's views on untouchability failed. Poddar's diatribe against Gandhi continued in the pages of *Kalyan* till 1948. Thus a relationship that had begun as hero worship on Poddar's part took a stormy turn during the intense phase of the national movement from the 1930s when Gandhi was reformulating his position on various social issues and when the competing interests of Muslims, Dalits and the strong Hindu right were challenging the position of Congress as the sole voice against the British government. As late as 1956, Poddar maintained that 'practising untouchability does not mean hatred for anyone' and 'untouchability is scientific and has the sanction of the shastras'.[56]

Even before 1932, Poddar's reverence for Gandhi had begun to show signs of weakening. Writing to his friend Prabhashankar Gupt in 1931, Poddar said he considered Gandhi 'a western sadhu in Indian dress whose many views I do not agree with and some I even find unacceptable'.[57] The man whose simplicity, self-service, spirituality and love for swadeshi had drawn Poddar so intensely was no longer his hero but the biggest stumbling block and challenge to the traditional Hindu order.

Still, the relationship between Poddar and Gandhi was marked by occasional warmth. In 1937, Poddar wrote to Gandhi about an early-morning dream he had in which someone told him 'Gandhi is not going to live for too long. He should spend rest of his life in praying to god.'[58] Poddar said he rarely had such dreams, but hoped this one would turn out to be false. 'I debated for long whether to write to you or not. Please tear off this letter after reading so that others do not get to know about my insolent behaviour.' Gandhi chose to call Poddar's dream a 'sign of love'.[59] 'As for death, it is a companion of birth and a very faithful one. It never fails. Why should one worship god only when nearing death? What I regard as worship goes on every moment.' Gandhi also asked Poddar why he wanted his dream to be false. 'Even if I live to be a hundred, it will seem too short to my friends. Then what does today or tomorrow matter?'

Again in 1940 when Gandhi set up the Goseva Sangh, Jamnalal Bajaj wrote to Poddar seeking his views on the constitution of the new body. Bajaj requested Poddar to become an ordinary member of the Sangh and shoulder some of its responsibility. Bajaj said the idea to involve Poddar had come directly from Gandhi.[60] Though Poddar opposed Gandhi through *Kalyan*, privately he respected the Mahatma. Writing to Bajaj from Gorakhpur, he said, 'I cannot understand many of Bapu's ideas and works. In many cases my heart openly opposes them. They create problems for me. But then Bapu is Bapu. After all, what has [one's opinion on] Mahatma Gandhi's views to do with bhakti to Bapu.'[61]

Poddar—who had consciously distanced himself from the Congress party since the Ahmedabad Congress of 1921—was now openly working with the Hindu Mahasabha. He was among the key organizers of the Mahasabha's annual convention in Gorakhpur in 1946.[62] This, coupled with *Kalyan*'s virulent attack on Gandhi, was to cause Poddar considerable trouble five months after Independence. Gandhi's assassination on 30 January 1948 in Delhi's Birla House by Nathuram

Godse and others associated with the Hindu Mahasabha and RSS, resulted in the arrest of more than 25,000 people throughout the country—among them Poddar and his mentor Jaydayal Goyandka. G.D. Birla refused to help the two, and even protested when Sir Badridas Goenka took up their case. For Birla, the two were not propagating sanatan dharma but shaitan (evil) dharma.[63]

Strangely, the rich private archives in Gorakhpur contain no reference to Gandhi's assassination. Even the series of monographs and laudatory biographies of Poddar ignore the event completely. The only reference to Gandhi's assassination comes in an unpublished manuscript of Poddar's biography. It says Poddar was in Delhi on 30 January 1948 when the assassination took place. The manuscript squarely blames Mahavir Prasad Poddar, a former manager of Gita Press and close aide of Hanuman Prasad and Goyandka, for spreading suspicion against the two for alleged involvement in Gandhi's killing. 'Due to various reasons Mahavir Prasad is spreading the malicious rumour that Bhaiji (Hanuman Prasad Poddar), Gita Press and *Kalyan* are responsible for (the) assassination. For the past few months he has been writing to many Congress leaders.'[64] According to the manuscript, Hanuman Prasad was troubled for a few months but travelled fearlessly to Lucknow, Allahabad, Calcutta, Delhi, Ratangarh and other places. The district magistrate of Gorakhpur alerted Poddar not to return to the city for some time as an arrest warrant might be issued against him. The revealing aspect of the manuscript is its muted tone in reference to 'the unfortunate incident'. Since Gambhirchand Dujari, the chronicler of Hanuman Prasad's life, was not in Gorakhpur in 1948, his biography does not provide any illumination either.

Gita Press maintained a studied silence on the Mahatma's assassination. The man whose blessing and writings were once so important for *Kalyan* did not find a single mention in its pages until April 1948 when Poddar wrote about his various encounters with Gandhi. Excerpts from his writings would later return to the pages of the journal, but the significant question remains unanswered: Why was there no mention of Gandhi in the February and March 1948 issues of *Kalyan*?

The CID Archives partly answer this question. Poddar was actively involved in defending the RSS that had been banned on 4 February 1948 for its alleged role in Gandhi's assassination. On 15 July 1949—four days after the Nehru government lifted the ban on the RSS—Poddar attended a public meeting at Gorakhpur with Atal Bihari Vajpayee, then editor of RSS weekly *Panchjanya*. Vajpayee criticized the 'government and Congressmen for having allegedly blundered in banning the RSS, the only organization which could really do something for Hindus'.[65] He added that the government 'did not deserve thanks for having lifted the ban as it had taken them one and half years to correct their mistake'. Poddar, the CID report said, also 'delivered a short speech on similar lines'.

Poddar's association with the RSS was not limited to attending this public meeting with Vajpayee. After Golwalkar was released from jail in 1949 and toured important towns of the United Provinces, Poddar presided over a function to welcome him at Banaras. In his speech delivered in fluent Hindi—the CID claimed 30,000 people came to hear the RSS chief at the Town Hall—Golwalkar emphasized the revival of ancient Hindu culture, consolidation of India and the adoption of Hindi as the state language. Golwalkar's speech went on even as 'processions sponsored by Socialists and supported by Communists were taken out with slogans such as *Golwalkar laut jao* and *Bapu Ke Hattiara Sangh* (Golwalkar, go back; RSS, the killer of Bapu). Golwalkar was shown black flags and some hundred protestors were arrested.'[66]

Advisor to the Rich and Powerful

Even after moving to Gorakhpur, Poddar remained connected to the politics of the Marwari Aggarwal Mahasabha, though he did not play any direct role. In 1928 he was invited to preside over its tenth annual meeting in Bombay. The battle between the reformists and revivalists that Poddar had witnessed in the 1926 session of the Mahasabha had now turned intense and ugly. Poddar agreed to preside over the proceedings only if the two groups came to some understanding. However, even as he was about to reach Bombay, there was a tussle between them. Finally, he refused to preside over the meeting and passed the baton to his friend Ranglal Jajodia. To quell speculation,

Poddar issued a statement clarifying his reasons, which was carried by *Aggarwal Samachar* and other newspapers.[67]

Poddar did, however, address the gathering. In an exhaustive speech he made it clear that he himself was on the side of the revivalists or sanatanis. The speech is remarkable as it encapsulates his sanatani vision for Hindu society and is a ready reckoner of the moral universe that Gita Press was proposing to create. From culture, society, Western influence and education, to women and the domestic sphere, rituals and clothing—Poddar left no aspect untouched.[68]

Close as he was to most leading Marwari business families of the time, Poddar's relationship with the Dalmias transcended all. Originally from Rohtak, Ram Krishna Dalmia, the enfant terrible of Marwari business world, was the ultimate success story in the early decades of the twentieth century. Starting as a trader, Dalmia's first flush of wealth came from his speculative trade that was later invested in an industrial conglomerate with interests in sugar and cement. Poddar and Dalmia, who was seven months younger, met in Calcutta, became intimate friends in Bombay and remained so throughout their lives. Poddar would often say he was connected with Dalmia from a previous birth. Dalmia had also introduced his younger brother Jaidayal to Poddar in Bombay, where the three lived together. When Jaidayal woke up in the middle of the night, he would find Poddar absorbed in some religious text.[69] As Ram Krishna Dalmia later wrote, Poddar was like a third brother who even confided in him that there had been an educated Bengali girl who had grown fond of him when he was in confinement after the Rodda Conspiracy. According to R.K. Dalmia, the girl even waited for the already married Poddar for a few years, but could not be traced later.[70] And while the Poddar Papers and hagiographies on him only talk of Poddar's benevolent nature, Dalmia's account indicates that it was he who often helped Poddar. When the latter left Bombay for Gorakhpur to edit *Kalyan*, Dalmia set up a trust with a corpus of Rs 10,000 to take care of the expenditure Poddar and his family would have to incur. On a later occasion, Poddar would ask the Dalmia brothers to settle his debts in Bombay and Calcutta.[71]

According to Jaidayal Dalmia, Poddar was the 'guardian of the Dalmia family' whose opinion carried immense weight even in mundane matters. Be it Ram Krishna Dalmia's insatiable sexual appetite, his eldest daughter Rama's education or the appointment of a private secretary, Poddar advised the family in all matters.[72]

Rama was given modern education and was well versed in Hindi, Sanskrit and English. At a time when even girls of affluent families rarely stepped out without an escort, Rama could cycle, swim, drive a car and ride a horse. This became a problem when in the 1930s Dalmia tried to find a suitable match for her. Poddar wrote to inquire about the matter, and advised: 'Rama is yet to get married. What happened to family from Ferozepur? I think it is not proper to keep the girl unmarried till now. If you come down a bit, marriage will be possible.'[73] An advertisement was placed in the newspaper, seeking marriage proposals to be sent to a particular box number. Many proposals came but none was from a good Marwari family. Eventually, a proposal from Shanti Prasad Jain of Najibabad in the United Provinces was accepted.[74] In later years, the Jain family became owners of *The Times of India*, incidentally one of the earliest newspapers to understand the potential of matrimonial advertisements as a huge source of revenue.

So close was Poddar to the Dalmias, when a man came to their Danapur factory (near Patna) for help after having killed a senior British police officer in Calcutta, he was promptly sent to Poddar in Gorakhpur. The man was given refuge alternately in Gita Press and Gita Vatika.[75]

In 1939, Dalmia Cement, part of R.K. Dalmia's Rohtas group of industries, was caught in a bitter price war with Associated Cement Companies (ACC), a single-product company.[76] Dalmia Cement could sell at below production cost, a business ploy that ACC could not afford. Poddar, who would often spend time in Dalmia's Dadri unit (in present-day Haryana), was in favour of his coming to terms with ACC as the price war would force the government to intervene. Realizing that the individualistic Dalmia could not be easily convinced, Poddar wrote to an ailing Jamnalal Bajaj requesting him to intervene, saying that if the 'two come together it would be beneficial to both'.[77] Less than a month later, once again Poddar requested Bajaj to intervene, reiterating his earlier 'mutually beneficial' argument but also emphasizing that Dalmia Cement was a 'Marwari enterprise' so 'you should see it from this perspective so that it grows well'.[78] Bajaj's refusal resulted, as expected, in government intervention in 1941, when Dalmia Cement and ACC had to sign an agreement that the two would sell cement through the Cement Marketing Company of India on the 'basis of fixed quota and fixed price'.[79]

Ram Krishna Dalmia's life was eventful. He would marry six times, fathering eighteen children, at times almost simultaneously, from five of his wives. A regular at Poddar's spiritual discourses in Bombay, Dalmia had once nearly given up everything to take up the life of a mendicant, only to be overcome by lust again. After 1947, a failing business empire—for which Dalmia blamed Nehru[80]—and increasing family burdens would see the maverick industrialist turn to Poddar for solace and guidance. He, in turn, considered it a personal misfortune that Dalmia led a life that *Kalyan* would have called debauched and a diversion from the tenets of sanatan Hindu dharma. The partially published manuscript of his life shows that while he regretted Dalmia's path of lust, he saw it as divinely ordained. 'It is due to God's wish that his hidden lust is on open display. It will get reversed and he will soon be back at the feet of God. He still has qualities that could impress any neutral person,' Poddar would tell his biographer Gambhirchand Dujari. Poddar was not willing to give up on Dalmia who had in the past provided financial help to whomsoever he had recommended. His younger brother Jaidayal Dalmia too was totally involved with Gita Press.

Grappling with internecine jealousies and intrigues among his various wives, Dalmia would tell Poddar how in the midst of the financial crisis his youngest wife Dineshnandini was 'troubling me so much not even an enemy would dare'. Dalmia alleged Dineshnandini had stolen Rs 8,000–10,000 that she was refusing to return. 'I am tolerating her in silence and atoning for my sins.'[81] A few months later he would repeat the charge against Dineshnandini: 'If she is criticizing me in front of others, she is accumulating sin.'[82] This was the same Dineshnandini Choradiya who, as a liberal feminist poet known for her long verse, used to adorn the pages of prestigious literary journal *Chand*. Her *Shabnam*, published with a foreword by critic-poet Ramkumar Varma, received rave reviews and the prestigious Sekhsaria Award in 1937. But literature would take a back seat after her entry into the Dalmia household, where mutual suspicion, intrigue and one-upmanship reigned.

At times even trivial personal issues would be put before Poddar for intervention. Jaidayal Dalmia, who was involved in the family business as well as the running of Gita Press, would ask Poddar to counsel his son Vishnu Hari against hiring women 'steno-secretaries' in the offices of Dalmia companies. Vishnu Hari would later become head of the Vishwa Hindu Parishad and a front-line leader in the Ayodhya movement that resulted in the demolition of Babri Masjid in 1992.[83]

Nothing revealed Poddar's importance as the 'guardian' of the Dalmia family more than the Report of the Commission of Inquiry (Inquiry on the Administration of Dalmia–Jain Companies) that came out in 1963. The commission had been set up on 11 December 1956, headed by Vivian Bose, to 'inquire into and report on the administration of nine companies,[84] the nature and extent of the control direct and indirect exercised over such companies and firms or any of them by Ram Krishna Dalmia, Jaidayal Dalmia, Shanti Prasad Jain, Shriyans Prasad Jain, their relatives, employees and persons concerned with them'.[85] The delay in finalization of the report was due to court cases filed by the Dalmia–Jain group.[86]

The commission found that the 'funds of public limited companies, banks and insurance companies were improperly used for buying shares of other companies with large accumulated resources and substantial liquid resources in order to obtain control over them'. The commission also found that it was always the public companies that suffered, and the investing public along with them. Companies in which the public had bought shares 'were made to give loans and advances without security and at low rates of interest to companies in which the Group, or Ram Krishna Dalmia, were interested to the advantage of the latter and detriment of the former'. Large advances were even made to Dalmia personally.

Poddar appears in the Bose Commission's report at crucial junctures. Throughout the proceedings of the commission, Shanti Prasad Jain and Jaidayal Dalmia had maintained that the Dalmia–Jain business existed as a group up to 31 May 1948. However, the commission took into account an exhibit, a document in Hindi, executed on 15 July 1946 in Mussoorie. Shanti Prasad Jain told the commission that 'Hanuman Prasad Tauji (uncle), an intimate friend of the family whom all trusted and revered' had drawn up the document.[87]

After translation of the document, the commission came to the understanding that 'at the date of document the three of them jointly held the principal' that consisted of cash and shares 'situated anywhere'.[88] The document prepared by Poddar, the commission said, did 'not divide any property physically' but 'merely defined or re-allocated the share of each'.[89] The document also spelt out the 'exact interest that each was to have' and 'how that interest was to be divided and distributed'. It also specified that dividends from shares would be divided among different charitable trusts as well as the three proprietors in accordance with the shares held by each. The three—Ram Krishna Dalmia, Jaidayal Dalmia and Shanti Prasad Jain—were termed 'maliks' (owners) by the document.

When confronted by the commission, Shanti Prasad Jain dismissed it, saying the document was a 'lot of nonsense executed to humour an old-fashioned friend of the family who was not familiar with the precise legal form' through which the assets were being managed. Jain said he had signed the document because the Dalmia brothers had signed it. His lawyer argued that the document was a 'make-believe document executed just for consolation to make a show' and it was never acted upon.[90] But the commission did not agree; it believed the Poddar-drafted agreement was important and relied upon by the three proprietors.

Another important document that was again drawn up by Poddar consisted of a list of companies that had been partitioned (divided) in April 1948. Bose and other members of the commission found it odd that 'Poddar an old friend of the family was again called in to help settle the basic principles of the partition'.[91] Though Shanti Prasad Jain told the Commission that the 'principles evolved themselves', his elder brother Shriyans Prasad Jain in his cross-examination said, 'These people regard him (Poddar) as one of the elders; though he may not be a blood relation he is more than a blood relation.' He admitted Poddar had helped in 'framing the basic principles of the dissolution'.

Though the Nehru government had appointed the commission, the ordeal continued till the time of Lal Bahadur Shastri. Shanti Prasad Jain and Rama Jain 'rebuffed (R.K. Dalmia's) efforts to resume command' of *The Times of India*, after his release from jail in 1964,[92] and Poddar who had good relations with Shastri requested him to show compassion as 'Ram Krishna Dalmia and Shanti Prasad Jain have suffered enough'.[93]

The Dalmias were not the only ones to involve Poddar in their business concerns. Even Seth Govind Das, who by his own admission had relinquished the family business, would request Poddar to prevail upon Purushottam Das Tandon to become a shareholder of his company before its annual general meeting. Das also asked Poddar to convince the Raja of Padrauna (near Gorakhpur) to buy shares of his company.[94]

Poddar would receive requests for help from all quarters, even from Gandhians for whom he had become an anathema in the wake of January 1948. Dada Dharmadhikari and Vimla Thakkar, senior members of the Sarva Seva Sangh involved in Vinoba Bhave's Bhoodan (land grant) movement who were getting Rs 250 per month from the Dalmia–Jain trust, asked Poddar for help when this suddenly stopped in August 1958. Thakkar wrote to Poddar thanking him for having the monthly contribution restored in January 1959.[95]

Ram Sinh, the Raja of Sitamau (Madhya Pradesh), was enamoured of both Poddar and Goyandka and regularly sought their advice from the mid-1930s onwards. Sinh, considered a progressive ruler,[96] sent his private secretary Shivram Krishna Godbole all the way to Gorakhpur to meet Poddar.[97] In 1935, when Ram Sinh built a small cottage for meditation, Godbole was asked to consult Poddar about the colour that should be used to paint the place.[98] Either directly or through Godbole, Ram Sinh kept in regular touch with Poddar, often prodding him to come to Sitamau and conduct satsangs. His constant concern was about his disturbed mental state and the spiritual solution to it. It is possible Ram Sinh's problem was related to his son Govind Sinh's decision to convert to Christianity in 1936. Poddar had heard the news and inquired about it from Godbole who confirmed it.[99] According to Godbole, Govind Sinh had wanted to convert earlier but was convinced not to take the step before meeting with religious scholars to understand Hinduism's basic ethos. Though he promised not to take any sudden decision, he did exactly that. He went to Indore all alone and informed the family after the conversion rites were over. Godbole said that though Ram Sinh had taken the episode in his stride, he needed mental peace that only a satsang could provide. Poddar was asked to come to Sitamau. In later years, Ram Sinh visited Gorakhpur and Rishikesh to attend Poddar's or Goyandka's religious discourses, and the two Gita Press stalwarts also visited Sitamau.

Jagat Narayan Lal from Bihar was among the senior leaders of the Hindu Mahasabha who switched to the Congress after Independence and became at various points minister of law, cooperatives and animal husbandry. But he kept alive his connections with the conservative elements including Dalmia and Poddar. Incidentally, in the elections to the Central assembly in 1935, Lal had contested as a Hindu Mahasabha candidate against Dalmia as an independent and Anugraha Narayan Singh of Congress. (Lal's deposit was forfeited and Dalmia could barely scrape through).[100]

It was to Gorakhpur that M.S. Golwalkar of the RSS came to meet Poddar for the first time, but the year is unknown. He had heard about Gita Press and its religious publications. 'I was always curious to know about this organization that was making religious texts available at nominal rate. What is this organization? Who runs it?' Golwalkar wrote in an article after meeting Poddar.[101] He recalled meeting a cheerful person of medium height, full of sophistication and sweet language. Golwalkar wrote that any organization could not succeed only through noble goals and money: 'What is needed is a person who to achieve the goal is far-sighted, focused and a good planner. He should also be willing to sacrifice his mind, body, soul and money. Gita Press has the amalgamation of all this in Jaydayal Goyandka and Hanuman Prasad Poddar.'

The conservative section of Congress, led by Hindu revivalists Madan Mohan Malaviya, Kanaiyalal Maneklal Munshi and Sampurnanand, was always close to Poddar. Malaviya's death in 1946 and Gandhi's assassination in 1948 did not change Poddar's equation with the Congress, at least with this section.

In an undated letter, believed to be of the 1950s, to then home minister Govind Ballabh Pant, Poddar referred to Pant's offer of a

Bharat Ratna that he had already refused.[102] Poddar's letter quotes verbatim Pant's reaction to his refusal of the highest national honour: 'You are so great that humanity should be proud of you and therefore I had recommended you for Bharat Ratna' and 'you are far superior than Bharat Ratna'. Strangely, Poddar told Pant that he had 'burnt the letter' in which the offer of Bharat Ratna was made. He also requested Pant that his letter should be 'kept secret'. Destroying letters and other communications was a regular feature of Poddar's life. In fact, the partially published manuscript of his life, based on interviews, quotes him as saying he destroyed letters from Tilak and many others. Several of his letters contain instructions to the recipients to destroy them after reading.

Poddar also told his biographer Gambhirchand Dujari that during the colonial period he was first offered the title of Rai Bahadur by Gorakhpur collector Adhya Prasad, and later knighthood by United Provinces governor Sir Harry Graham Haig. 'When I refused the knighthood, Haig was very happy and told me such honours are akin to putting a collar around a dog's neck.'

Closeness to politicians also meant Poddar had to sometimes get involved in the machinations and take sides during challenging political contests, often at the cost of the high principles that he and *Kalyan* espoused so passionately. When Sampurnanand took over as chief minister of Uttar Pradesh after G.B. Pant was made Union home minister in 1955, Congress's famed factional feud came out in the open and soon assumed serious proportions. Poddar's friend of many years, Sampurnanand, a kayastha, had differences with his revenue minister Charan Singh, who resigned from the Sampurnanand cabinet in 1959. Singh's opportunity to retaliate came when an allegation of corruption was made against Lokpati Tripathi, son of the state's home minister Kamlapati Tripathi. The allegation was that the irrigation department had given a work contract without tender, and this firm had outsourced the work to Hindustan Commercial Corporation, a company allegedly owned by Lokpati Tripathi.

Poddar's letter to Sampurnanand was in defence of Tripathi and against Prayag Narain, deputy chief engineer of the irrigation department, who he said was working in tandem with Charan Singh.[103]

Poddar said the questions on the scam, popularly called the Sarda Sagar dam scandal, raised by Raj Narain, then the Socialist Party MLA from Moti Mahal, Lucknow, had been supplied by Prayag Narain. He called for severe action against Prayag Narain 'lest it may cause a severe damage to the party in power and nation as a whole'. The petitions department of the UP government acknowledged Poddar's letter.

The scandal soon got out of control, forcing Prime Minister Jawaharlal Nehru to intervene. Paul R. Brass brings out the larger story of the scam in which Charan Singh was drawn in, allegedly for fomenting trouble against Sampurnanand.[104] Nehru's intervention did not go in Charan Singh's favour and in subsequent years Singh would become one of the most vocal voices against the dominant Congress.

Poddar's relationship with Kamlapati Tripathi continued, and in 1970, Tripathi made him a key member of the national committee to celebrate 400 years of Tulsidas's *Ramcharitmanas*. Samuparnanand, who had resigned as chief minister in 1960 as a fallout of the Kamlapati Tripathi saga, also remained close to Poddar. Leading a retired life in 1967, he would seek Poddar's help in securing a job for Vidya Bhaskar, former editor of *Aaj*, in Ramnath Goenka's proposed new Hindi newspaper. Bhaskar had already had a meeting with B.D. Goenka, son of Ramnath, but Sampurnanand wanted Poddar to put in a word.[105] Poddar, whose relations with Ramnath Goenka were excellent, obliged, but the project would take several more years, and *Jansatta* started only in 1983.

In the past, Poddar had sought Goenka's help for newsprint and a printing press. With the anti-Congress and anti–Indira Gandhi wave on the rise since the mid-1960s, articulated mainly by Goenka's *Indian Express*, the owner threw his hat in the electoral arena, contesting in the 1971 Lok Sabha elections as the Jana Sangh candidate from Vidisha. For the ailing Poddar, this was an occasion to sacrifice another of his vows, namely to keep away from direct politics. Though only two years before Poddar had advised Goenka to slowly wind up his business and immerse himself in full-time devotion to God, so that he would have less worries,[106] he now issued a public statement in Goenka's support. Poddar underlined that his aim was that 'religion should not suffer in the country since religion is the only way to achieve human welfare'.[107]

Goenka, he said, was not merely an industrialist but also a social worker who was progressive and large-hearted. 'Above everything he is religious. I know him from my childhood and have highest regard for him. I request voters to ensure he wins with highest margin. People would gain from his desire to serve.'

Goenka's first attempt to fight an election in 1951–52 as a Congress candidate from Tindivanam in Madras state had failed miserably, as he had finished second with a paltry 15.5 per cent of the votes. This time he won, garnering 52.04 per cent of the votes. Manibhai J. Mehta of the Congress came a distant second with 41 per cent.

The Devotion of Women

After some tragic setbacks, Poddar's personal life was on an even keel by the 1920s. Following three failed attempts, his wife Ramdei gave birth to a daughter Savitri in 1929, their only child. A chasm existed between what he stood for and passionately advocated in *Kalyan* on issues of marriage and the man–woman relationship, and happenings in his own life.

A few years before his death, responding to a query about his relationships with women, Poddar told an unnamed acquaintance that he did not have permission from the divine to divulge everything. Assuming the role of a man with godlike qualities, he rated the women he had known as his 'devotees': 'Yes, I can give an indicative answer in brief. Among female devotees I have been attracted to three: Ramdei, my wife in this life, Chinmayi Devi of South India and Savitri Sekhsaria. There are other men and women too. But they are much below these three. Among men though Jaidayal (Dalmia) is not considered a devotee and even he does not think himself to be one but consider him the best. He has the highest place among those whom I really like.'[108]

Little is known about Savitri Sekhsaria apart from the fact that she belonged to a well-off Bombay family. Harikrishna Dujari who knew her well told me, 'She was totally devoted to Poddar and used to spend a few months in Gorakhpur every year.' Barring a single reference, Poddar's personal papers do not talk of Savitri, but Chinmayi Devi appears in his personal accounts as a devotee from Bezwada (present-day Vijaywada). On a pilgrimage in 1956 Poddar was staying with an acquaintance in Vijaywada when he met Chinmayi Devi who was living in the neighbourhood. Poddar saw a framed photograph that Chinmayi was worshipping and, immediately recognizing it as a photograph from his Bombay days, asked who the man was. Chinmayi replied that she had read about him in a paper long ago, and had surrendered herself to him though she had never met him. When she finally realized that the man in photograph was standing in front of her, she worshipped him by putting a tilak on his forehead and sandal paste on his feet. Despite Poddar's curiosity to know more about her, she asked him to leave and would not reveal anything. This spiritual encounter, recounted by Poddar ten years later, was in keeping with his status as a man with godlike qualities.[109]

Three other women had an impact in Poddar's life—Sarojini Devi, Raihana Tyabji and Irene Wolfington. They met Poddar at different stages of his life: Sarojini when he was fifteen and already married; Raihana when he was approaching middle age; and Irene, the spiritual seeker from the United States, in the last decade of Poddar's life, causing considerable consternation to him and the spiritual world he inhabited.

The story of Sarojini is replete with twists and turns in which, as always, Poddar comes out morally triumphant despite complete surrender by a woman. He becomes the rishi who cannot be drawn by allurement of any kind, even carnal. Poddar first met Sarojini in 1907 and the relationship, if it can be called one, ended in 1911 with Poddar agreeing to accept the sacred aspect of her love, reminiscent of Radha's for Krishna. She gave him a gold ring, and the two never met again. Sarojini wrote to him many years later telling him she had decided to end her life as her body could not take the pangs of separation any longer. 'Hindu women accept only one man,' she wrote. Poddar's attempts to locate her proved futile. She committed suicide by jumping into the Ganga at Prayag (Allahabad), exemplifying Solomon's words, 'There is death, but death by love is an ecstasy, a sweet martyrdom.'[110] The ring, Sarojini's parting token of love, was given away by Poddar to a talented student of Jalandhar Girls School. Poddar remained silent about Sarojini during his active years but narrated the incident to two of his biographers—Gambhirchand Dujari and Bhagwati Prasad Singh—in the last decade of his life, always drawing a parallel between Sarojini and the self-sacrificing Radha.

In her devotion and passion, Irene Wolfington proved to be unlike any other female bhakt Poddar had encountered before. In India since 1963, she had been with the Divine Life Society and Manav Seva Sansthan and by 1965 was sure she did not belong to the USA any more.[111] Irene, with her Western liberal education, effortlessly straddled the sacred and the profane. She left behind a massive trail of evidence about her thirst for Hindu spiritualism and emotional dependence on Poddar as well as Swami Chakradhar who was then staying at Gita Vatika.

Swami Chakradhar's background is shrouded in mystery. Born in Gaya, Bihar, he was known to Jaydayal Goyandka and came to Gorakhpur in 1936. He was rechristened Radha Baba and became some kind of a cult figure within a few years. He and Poddar would get extremely close and a trust, Radha Madhav Seva Sansthan, would later be set up. Gita Vatika now houses the trust as well as a large memorial to Radha Baba.

In 1941, Poddar wrote to Ghanshyam Das Birla about some case against Radha Baba, and sought his help. No copy of this is available, but Birla's reply reveals that the case related to money: 'I do not understand why there should be a case against Baba. He used to get money himself and spend. Whether he was keeping an account or not should have concerned only those who donated to him.'[112] Birla asked Poddar to provide details but expressed reluctance to get involved, though he said Gandhi should be informed. Poddar promptly sent him another letter that again is unavailable, and Birla wrote back that he had forwarded Poddar's letter to Gandhi but asked him not to be hopeful.[113]

Irene's overwhelming presence in the private papers of Poddar is not reflected in the authorized published works on him. But her relationship with him and Swami Chakradhar is spelt out in a letter Poddar wrote to the then union home minister Gulzarilal Nanda, seeking his intervention to extend Irene's visa. 'Unexpectedly, she feels an attraction towards Swami Chakradhar and me. For the past two weeks she has been insistent that I keep her with me and lead her along the spiritual path.'[114] As in the case of Sarojini, Poddar distanced himself from Irene's desire, writing to Nanda: 'You know I have kept myself away from such things. Neither do I have an ashram nor any special way of sadhana. But I feel this lady's inclination is read and inspired by god. Ever since she has met me she is pleading me with tearful eyes to let her stay with me.'

Poddar's interpretation of Irene's wishes was not quite accurate. In fact, Irene was obsessed with the Swami. Irene had met Chakradhar in Vrindavan and saw in him the perfect guru she was in search of, but her devotion was laden with roadblocks. In March 1965, even as her visa extension was delayed, Irene was more worried about not being able to meet Chakradhar. She wrote to the Swami: 'I feel like a corked bottle full of fruit juice that is getting fizzier and fizzier! When and how it will blow god alone could guess.'[115]

As Chakradhar became more and more withdrawn, Irene would get more anxious and pine for him, seeking Poddar's help. Poddar stepped in, holding out the carrot of visa extension to rein in Irene. In June 1965 he laid out some ground rules for her. 'Upon my request Sri Nanda has accorded permission to you to stay in India for one year or more, i.e., till 9 June 1966 at the most . . . Instead of loitering here and there all the day you will have to chalk out a daily routine for yourself which would include fixed hours for japa (recitation of mantra), dhyan (meditation), study of healthy literature, observance of mauna (silence).' Irene was told she could see Swami Chakradhar at fixed hours along with others, and for fifteen minutes alone. Poddar added that his letter had the approval of Baba himself.[116]

Irene resented Poddar's diktat. Apart from doubting his claim that the letter had the approval of Baba, Irene hit out at Poddar's 'we are conservative' argument against women getting close to Swami Chakradhar. Her ire against Poddar was building up especially as he had divulged her love for Baba to other women. She was particularly angry that Lalita Dalmia, wife of Vishnu Hari Dalmia, had been told about her 'affairs'.[117]

Irene's visa extension did not come through until December 1965. She eventually left Gita Vatika for Vrindavan and Rishikesh and rechristened herself Manjushri and even Mata Irene. She would occasionally write to Poddar and also sent letters for the Baba with a request that he should read them out to him.

Raihana Tyabji's life was a contrast to Irene's, though both were non-Hindus steeped in the Radha tradition. Raihana won a firm place in the hearts of both Gandhi and Poddar. A Sulaimani Bohra Muslim born in Baroda in 1900, she was the daughter of Abbas and Ameena Tyabji. Ameena, the second wife of Abbas, was the daughter of Badruddin Tyabji, president of the Indian National Congress in 1887. The London-educated Abbas retired as chief justice of the Baroda High Court and he and his wife were part of the inner circle of Baroda ruler Sayaji Rao III. Post-retirement, he became an active Congress leader, took to khadi and adopted other aspects of the Gandhian lifestyle. He headed Congress's fact-finding committee on the Jallianwala Bagh massacre of 1919. Abbas played an important role in the salt satyagraha and earned for himself the epithet 'grand old man of Gujarat' from Gandhi. Raihana's sister Sohaila was the mother of eminent historian Irfan Habib.

While Raihana's first meeting with Gandhi in 1915 in Bombay and subsequent intimate relationship are known through scores of letters in the *Collected Works of Mahatma Gandhi*, the Poddar Papers as well as the vast body of hagiographies on him are silent on how Poddar and Raihana met.[118]

Raihana's relationship with Gandhi and Poddar was complex, multilayered and seemingly contradictory. (Interestingly, Gandhi destroyed Raihana's letters to him.) Credited for 'having taught Urdu to the Mahatma and for having encouraged him to incorporate verses from the Qur'an into his prayer meetings',[119] Raihana was also a brilliant singer of bhajans who would perform at Gandhi's ashrams and annual sessions of the Congress. Gandhi acknowledged her beautiful voice: 'But I should prize your presence even if you had not that rich melodious voice.'[120] He addressed Raihana variously as 'Mad Raihana', 'Raihana the Crazy' and at other times 'beloved daughter'.[121] He would often invite her to Sevagram Ashram in spite of the fact that she did not attempt tasks like spinning.[122] Raihana differed with Gandhi on the latter's experiments with brahmacharya (abstinence from sex) but became one of 'Bapu's brahmachari soldiers' by choosing to remain unmarried for life—a decision that was taken either due to the break-up of her 'possible engagement to a first cousin' or because of the leucoderma she suffered from.[123] Gandhi engaged with Raihana at all levels, personal and public.

It is likely that by the time Raihana came in contact with Poddar, her masterpiece *The Heart of a Gopi,* written over three days in 1924 'with sheets of foolscap and poised pen', was already being discussed—even though it was published only in 1936.[124] The stupendous success of *The Heart of a Gopi,* as Lambert-Hurley argues, was in the tradition of Kabir, Bulleh Shah and Raskhan, an attempt to 'inhabit the shifting ground between faith groups' and rejection of 'an exclusively Hindu or Muslim paradigm'.[125]

While her relationship with Gandhi had myriad hues, Poddar was Raihana's Krishna and she his gopi or Meera. She was not alone in her devotion to Poddar: Saroj Nanavati, daughter of Justice D.D. Nanavati, whom Raihana had befriended in the early 1930s during her research at the Bhandarkar Oriental Research Institute, Poona, was equally enamoured, though less assertive. Saroj and Raihana lived for a few years with the Gandhian Kaka Kalelkar in his ashram in Wardha and later the three moved to the Gandhi ashram in Delhi.[126]

Poddar asked Raihana and Saroj to destroy the letters he wrote to them, but the rich cache in the Poddar Papers show that both he and his two 'gopis' wanted their 'sacred relationship' to survive. Though both Raihana and Saroj sought his attention, it was Raihana—full of tantrums, unusually dramatic and exceptionally forthright—who dominated Poddar's heart. For the world, Poddar was simply their elder brother and they his sisters, but there was an undercurrent of mystique, an unknown factor, that ran through their relationship.

Praising an article Raihana had written for *Kalyan,* Poddar expressed admiration of her love for Krishna. 'I know you are a true Muslim. I do not want you to become less of a Muslim. My Krishna is not of Hindus alone. He belongs to a gopi's heart. Wherever there is a reflection of gopi's heart, Krishna exists and he is willing to give everything.'[127]

In this long letter it also comes out that Raihana wanted Gita Press to publish *The Heart of a Gopi*. Poddar came up with a convoluted and unconvincing defence for not having published the book: 'Kakasaheb

(Kalelkar) also explained to me. If there was even a slight possibility of allegation against you of having become a Hindu I would not have liked to publish it from Gita Press . . . You are a true Muslim. I do not want anyone to suspect you after reading The Heart of a Gopi.' Poddar added that though Kalelkar called *The Heart of a Gopi* a literary work, and some other person had said the book was a flight of emotions and had nothing for the nation, he thought the book was beyond literature and emotion.

Raihana's reply reveals a mind totally immersed in Krishna; she saw Poddar as his personification and was in no mood to distinguish between the two. Ecstatic with devotion, Raihana said she had not stopped crying since receiving Poddar's reply. For her, all that mattered was pining for Krishna and living in close proximity to him. Literally and metaphorically, Raihana saw Poddar as her Krishna whose words were those of God. Despite her devotion to Poddar, Raihana defied him on one count, Poddar had asked her to destroy his letter, but she replied, 'Bhai Saheb, I should destroy your letter! Oh god! Shouldn't I kill myself before that? I am able to listen to his voice and you want me to strangulate that. What kind of a cruel order is this? Do not be afraid. Your words inspired by Krishna would not pass through any incompetent or unsuitable person. Bhai Saheb your words are a gift from Krishna.'[128]

Raihana's veneration had its impact on Poddar. In his subsequent letters to her, Poddar told her he was at the mercy of Krishna and totally unaware of what was in store for him. 'By birth I am a varnashrami (one who believes in the four stages of life) Hindu but in reality I am nobody. I belong to my Krishna. If Krishna keeps me as his own I can accept anything . . .' He described, in greater detail than in his previous letter, the various forms of Krishna, his playfulness and the personal and spiritual amelioration that bhakti to him promised. Poddar told Raihana he had been possessed by a kind of magic similar to that which had engulfed her. He thanked his fate for giving him sisters like Raihana and Saroj and trusted in the relationship remaining pure and truthful.[129]

Raihana's reply was more intense than her previous letter. She told Poddar his letter gave her immense succour: 'I cannot do without reading it once daily. Every time I keep thinking of one thing or the other you have written.'[130]

Still at Dalmia's factory in Dadri, Poddar wrote to Raihana about his various experiences of Krishna, in his dreams, in his thoughts and even fantasies. Surprised by the open and fearless tone of Raihana's letter, Poddar admitted he had also never been so free with any of his associates, friends and those who revered him: 'What I write to you is a fact, not my imagination or mere writing skill. I do not know how these things have been revealed to you. Only Krishna knows. I cannot tell you how my love for you is growing. My Krishna is your friend. What kind of pleasure and what kind of relationship is this? The question of Hindu–Muslim is outside the realm of our relationship. What has that got to do with us? I like your unfettered behaviour.'[131]

Poddar's papers are silent on his relationship with Raihana and Saroj after Independence. From the Gandhi ashram in Delhi, Raihana offered 'spiritual guidance as comfort to those with mental difficulties'[132] and corresponded with the likes of Mary Cushing Niles, management consultant from America. Raihana became close friends with Niles who would often confide her problems at work, as well as in her marriage and with her daughters. Their correspondence also shows how Niles reviewed in 'detail several of her own past incarnations as they were "seen" by Tyabji'.[133]

On 18 May 1975 Raihana died, relatively unsung. News of her death was carried as a brief by *The Times of India* that called her 'a sufi' 'who worked for Hindu-Muslim unity and women's emancipation'.[134]

Communion with God

The image of Poddar as a grand seer who could not be distracted from his preordained path of propagating sanatan Hindu dharma was a part of a larger exercise undertaken by himself and those around him, led by Goyandka, to show him as God's chosen one. Though this myth began with the story of his birth, what added lustre to it was Poddar's own claims of having repeatedly experienced communion with God.

G.D. Birla, who had grown close to the Congress, especially to Gandhi, and was a firm believer in secular principles, openly resented such claims. Goyandka had written to Birla about Poddar having 'visions' of God but Birla was not impressed. In a subsequent letter to Birla, Goyandka referred to what Birla had said—'I think it is wrong to encourage talk about such things and even spreading it'—and argued: '. . . one does not know the condition of another person . . . It is up to you to believe it or not.'[135] Goyandka was sure 'Poddar is not a person who would lie'. Goyandka himself claimed to have 'visions' of God, but in the narrative about the two leading figures of Gita Press, Poddar, the disciple, eclipses his mentor.

Both Gambhirchand Dujari's account of Poddar's life (2000) and the earlier biography by Bhagwati Prasad Singh (1980) speak of Poddar's 'visions' that were not only beneficial to him but also to the public. Poddar was seen as God's own messenger who would provide accounts—often even verbatim reproductions of his conversations with God—to the public about what God felt and wanted from believers and how pressing issues of religion should be dealt with. Such 'visions' were not the only way in which Poddar's extraordinary position was extolled; there were a series of simultaneous events, most of them supernatural, which showed the 'pervading presence of god' in Poddar's life.[136]

In one case of 1925 in Bombay, described in Dujari's account, Poddar met a Parsi gentleman at the Chowpatty beach who introduced himself as a 'ghost'. The narrative, entirely in Poddar's words, describes how this Parsi gentleman approached him seeking his help to conduct pind daan.[137] This raised the obvious question of why a Parsi would want to perform a Hindu ritual, and that too in the afterlife. Poddar said that when he asked this question the Parsi replied that he had been an ardent reader of the Gita in life. Poddar sent priest Hariram to Gaya (Bihar) to carry out the pind daan on the Parsi's account.

Poddar listed three other extraordinary events in his life. Whether by divine providence or God's benevolence towards his chosen one, in one case his friend Ram Krishna Dalmia was helped to tide over a serious loss in business, and in the other two cases Poddar himself was saved from being hit by a stone while travelling in a train. On both occasions the stones flew inside the compartment seconds after he had changed his seat.

The Poddar Papers do not specify the year, but talk of a huge loss to Dalmia incurred through speculation. This is said to have been recovered after Poddar conducted a special religious proceeding; however, Dalmia failed to fulfil the vow made during the proceeding, though Poddar warned him that this could result in another loss. The Poddar Papers claim that Dalmia indeed suffered another big loss, though there is no substantiation of this fact.

Poddar's first so-called 'vision' of God in the presence of others was on 16 September 1927 in Jasidih (now in Jharkhand), a mining town with a large Marwari population that controlled the trading business. Jaydayal Goyandka was there for a religious discourse along with his entourage, and Poddar told Goyandka and others about his earlier 'visions' of Lord Rama and then of Lord Vishnu himself in Simlapal where he had been sent for his involvement in the Rodda Arms Conspiracy. His encounter with Lord Vishnu was an aborted one, he said. Later in the day, Goyandka with his followers climbed up a hillock near Marwari Arogya Bhavan for the discourse. Poddar suddenly turned silent, and seconds later told the gathering that God had appeared before him. Someone asked if God was standing or sitting, and Poddar replied, 'He is on a lotus.' There was silence again, then Poddar expressed anxiety that he could not touch the feet of God as he was moving away. After a brief interval, he claimed God was again in front of him, urging the others to look as well. He was touching God's feet, Poddar said, and then fell unconscious. It was Goyandka's feet he was touching.[138]

This experience repeatedly recounted, evolved into a pattern in his accounts of subsequent 'visions'. The most graphic of his visionary experiences was in Gorakhpur on 8 October 1927, just days after his Jasidih encounter. Poddar recounted that God gave him twelve pieces of advice:

- It would be beneficial to keep the experience of your 'vision' of me secret.
- People who fight in the name of religion do not know my influence.
- Full cow protection will take some time to get implemented.
- My incarnation is far away.
- If you want to do good for society, take my name. In this period taking my name is good enough.
- Those who give patronage to sinners in my name cannot be protected even by Yamraj.

- It is wrong to think that my name will help in washing away sins and help in getting material benefits.
- My name is dearer than the name of a beloved. It should be used for love alone.
- Arrogance is on the rise. It is the biggest stumbling block to getting near me. Warn arrogant people that it would destroy them. Arrogance is worse than lust and anger.
- Do not assure anyone that he will have a 'vision' of me.
- Do not make any mention of this experience other than the one in Jasidih.
- I will not come like this again. I have come twice without you even calling me. I had to tell you all this. Remember me and I will appear before you, but do not commit any mistake.

Poddar would have more 'visions' of God in the next few years. In 1936, he claimed to have been met in Gita Vatika by celestial sage Narada and Angiras (the sage who received the Atharva Veda). Poddar claimed that they explained to him concepts that are not part of the shastras.

The news of Poddar's extraordinary powers, some called them divine, spread like wildfire in the Marwari community. When Balkrishna Lal Poddar of the firm Tarachand Ghanshyamdas and an old business associate of Poddar asked him a few questions relating to his 'vision' of God, Poddar's reply was predictable. He said there were many who 'suspect, doubt, give wrong argument and dispute' but 'I do not care even if it is humiliating to my beloved Lord'. As had become a pattern in his life, Poddar asked Balkrishna to return the letter, keep it secretly or destroy it: 'It would be good if others do not read it.'[139]

Though at first Poddar was circumspect about his 'visions' becoming a matter of public knowledge, by the 1950s he freely talked of having God's 'vision' as a commonplace achievement possible for anyone who was devoted to God.

Self-doubt

Despite his life being completely devoted to spiritualism and his proclaimed interaction with the divine in all its manifestations, Poddar was not immune to the emotions and aspirations that drive ordinary men. He suffered long spells of self-doubt coupled with a sense of failure at convincing everyone around him about the supremacy of religion, spiritualism and the path that should be followed. 'Members of my own family despite knowing of my status act in a contrary fashion. They go for movies, eat bread that maybe is made by Muslims or untouchables. They use glass utensils, eat each others' jhootan (leftovers), do not greet elders and do not offer evening prayers. I observe all this and cannot do anything about it.'[140] Poddar's despondency about his own life and the working of Gita Press would continue throughout the 1960s.

Even before he joined the Gita Press, Poddar had wanted to live on the banks of the Ganga. In fact, Goyandka had promised to set him free once *Kalyan* stabilized, but this never happened. For all his protests and threats about leaving, Poddar's association with Gita Press lasted his lifetime. At times he would openly talk about the rot in Gita Press and tell his friends that it should be closed down. Goyandka would then remind him about the Press's mission of societal good. When Poddar requested Goyandka's permission to join Gandhi's Salt Satyagraha in 1930 at Padrauna, near Gorakhpur, Goyandka turned him down, writing that 'joining politics can be an obstruction to the path of bhakti'.[141]

In 1934 Poddar made a request to Goyandka for 'leave from writing, talking and putting his name' to anything in *Kalyan* and by the Gita Press. 'I live here but my mind is not in work,' he told Goyandka.[142] Goyandka's reply in half-Marwari and half-Hindi was a masterstroke that totally disarmed Poddar.[143] Not engaging in argument with Poddar's statement that his mind was always restless and he needed peace, Goyandka replied that he should take it as the will of God against which he or anyone else could do very little. As for Poddar's desire not to write, Goyandka put him in a moral bind: 'Without your writing *Kalyan* would become lacklustre. I would not be surprised if *Kalyan* loses its readers in the future. You did not write for the *Shakti Ank* and the issue does not have the same appeal. If you do not write others will also not write. Some articles have appeared that have produced a negative impact. Try your best to write. The rest is up to God.' Further, Goyandka wrote, 'Without your name *Kalyan* cannot be advertised. It would also be wrong to falsely use your name.'

In response to Poddar's desire to live in isolation and peace, Goyandka offered to build a house for him in the garden of one Sukhdeo where he could work without interference from too many people. In his letter Poddar had expressed regret for his behaviour that he said was akin to an animal's, but Goyandka did not agree: 'Your behaviour is impeccable. I don't understand how you can say that everyone in the world is better than you.' Goyandka finally prevailed upon Poddar to give up his stand of not associating himself with *Kalyan* and the Gita Press.

In 1939 a melancholic Poddar left Gorakhpur and the work of Gita Press to stay at friend Ram Krishna Dalmia's cement factory in Dadri. Though he had taken Goyandka's permission for three months' sabbatical, Poddar did not intend to return. Writing to one Madan Lal, Poddar said he had not taken a vow not to return to Gorakhpur but at the same time he did not know where he would go.[144] A few months later, one Pitambar Prasad Aggarwal sought his help but Poddar curtly told him he had stopped looking after the work of Gita Press and was leading a secluded life.[145] Goyandka finally convinced him to return.

In 1962, citing general inertia, he expressed his helplessness in running the affairs of *Kalyan* and Gita Press. He requested Goyandka that he should be relieved from all responsibilities of Gita Press and *Kalyan*—to the extent that the two should not bear 'my name, signature and advice' and 'I should be considered dead.'[146]

Writing to an acquaintance, Poddar said he was not the person he had been made out to be by others, and neither was Gita Press any more the ideal place to seek spiritual solace. 'Till a few years ago this was a good place for those involved in spiritual exercise . . . This place is not fulfilling, as it is marked by demonic traits like self-promotion, jealously, materialism.'[147] Indulging in self-flagellation, Poddar continued, 'There is no limit to my meanness and misdemeanours. Neither could I become a good person nor could I help my associates improve.' He also gave instance of other organizations, saying that Aurobindo Ashram had become a centre of commerce and education, Ramanasramam was caught in legal wrangles and the Ramakrishna Mission was only involved in running hospitals—all activities far removed from the path of God.

Again in 1967 Poddar moved out of Gita Press and was living in Dadri when Shiv Narayan, a sadhu, wrote to him seeking to work for *Kalyan*. Poddar replied that he had completely left work at Gita Press and was immersed in meditation and other spiritual activities.[148]

Such long absences from Gorakhpur were noticed outside the Gita Press family, and commented upon. In 1939, when Poddar was out of Gorakhpur and Chimmanlal Gosvami was filling in for him, writer Nand Dulare Vajpayee accused Gita Press of becoming a commercial enterprise and Gosvami of being an unworthy replacement, even if for a short while. Poddar was in Bankura when he received Gosvami's letter about Vajpayee's criticism. Poddar dismissed the charge of Gita Press having become commercial but admitted he had been selfish in leaving the work to Gosvami: 'I know you will not have the same place in the Press department and running of the organization but I have deliberately and selfishly passed on the work to you. It will not cause any harm. But I will remain obliged for your favour.'[149]

Growing Stature

Over the years, as Poddar's stature grew, so did his disenchantment with Gita Press. He not only distanced himself from the organization of which he was the pivot, but got more and more involved with other organizations. Besides being closely associated with the movements for cow protection, against the Hindu Code Bill and restoring the birthplaces of Rama and Krishna, he was roped in as a delegate for the All India Cultural Conference organized by Indian Cultural Academy (ICA) in March 1951. With President Rajendra Prasad as chairperson and the official historian of Congress Pattabhi Sitaramayya as working chairperson, the ICA was filled with other senior Congress leaders like Zakir Husain, Rameshwari Nehru and M. Ananthasayanam Ayyangar.

Held in the Diwan-e-Khas of Red Fort, the conference consisted of freewheeling discussions amongst writers, artists, musicians, dancers and philosophers on strengthening the foundations of Indian culture. Poddar was invited for his contribution to the Indian culture.[150] This invitation, within three years of Gandhi's assassination, by a body dominated by Congress leaders, demonstrated their acceptance of

Poddar despite his bitter, often brutal, criticism of Gandhi in the years before Partition and his vocal prescription for turning India into a Hindu Rashtra.

Poddar found similar acceptance when the Bharatiya Chaturdham Veda Bhawan Nyasa (BCVBN) was set up in the early 1960s. The principal objective of BCVBN was to build four Veda Bhawans at the four dhams (pilgrim centres): Badrinath, Jagannath Puri, Rameshwaram and Dwarka. The BCVBN also proposed to propagate vedic culture; conduct research on the Vedas; publish vedic literature; arrange recitation of Veda mantras and rituals; arrange the teaching of the Vedas and allied literature; start a printing press; publish newspapers, periodicals, pamphlets, books, articles, leaflets, booklets, etc., and 'do all such other things as are incidental or conducive to the attainment' of its objectives and 'as are considered necessary for the welfare and happiness of the people'.[151]

The BCVBN brought together leaders of the Congress and Hindu Mahasabha, industrialists and religious figures. Its list of trustees was a reminder of the clout the conservative section within the Congress still wielded. Not only were they ready to collaborate with those whom they opposed politically and electorally, but some of them even did not find it improper or unconstitutional to become a part of a religious cause even while occupying a constitutional post such as the governor of a state. The trust consisted of people like Biswanath Das, governor of Uttar Pradesh; M. Ananthasayanam Ayyangar, governor of Bihar; Sampurnanand, governor of Rajasthan; Sri Prakasa of Seva Ashram, Banaras; K.M. Munshi of Bharatiya Vidya Bhavan, Bombay; Mahant Digvijaynath of Gorakhnath temple, Gorakhpur and also a Hindu Mahasabha leader; Sir Surendra Singh Majithia, a businessman; Jugal Kishore Birla, elder brother of G.D. Birla; Ramnath Goenka, industrialist and owner-publisher of *The Indian Express*; Mungturam Jaipuria, industrialist; Hanuman Prasad Poddar, editor of *Kalyan* and many others.[152]

Culture and religion alone would not engage Poddar. A few months after the famous Naxalbari incident in Bengai Jote village in Siliguri subdivision, in which nine people died in police firing over their demand for fair price for crops, West Bengal witnessed statewide incidents of leftist violence—the start of the Naxalite movement. It had the business community and votaries of Indian culture worried about what they claimed to be the impending danger of rising communism. Poddar was roped in by an organization called the Indian Culture Defence Council run by Purshottam Dass Halwasiya. Realizing that communists were propagating their ideology through cheap literature, Halwasiya would tell Poddar about his plan to counter them by the collective and coordinated effort of outfits like the Jana Sangh, Akhil Bharatiya Vidyarthi Parishad (ABVP), Swastik Prakashan and other bodies closely associated with the RSS.

Poddar wrote for an Indian Culture Defence Council pamphlet, calling communism a devilish ideology that was spreading due to Western views and education, and pleasure-seeking literature. 'What is happening in West Bengal portends a bleak future. This kind of lawlessness, indiscipline, cycle of violence and counter-violence has never been witnessed before. This is not confined to politics alone but has spread to education, industry, trading and women. Everyone is scared. In the name of poor people, only poor are being exploited . . . It should not be allowed to spread. There is a need to come together, form defence committees, provide financial help and desire to give life at the right time.'[153]

Tributes and Tribulations

In the 1960s, as Poddar's mood fluctuated between total withdrawal from, and reluctant participation in, the affairs of Gita Press, his friends and admirers were planning a big celebration on the occasion of his hirak jayanti. Though hirak jayanti, or diamond jubilee, celebrates a person's sixtieth birthday and Poddar had turned sixty in 1952, earlier attempts to felicitate him had been unsuccessful.

In 1953, a committee consisting of leading Hindi writer Hazari Prasad Dwivedi, Rajbali Pandey who was principal of the College of Indology, Banaras Hindu University, littérateur Sitaram Chaturvedi and many others had planned a commemorative volume in Poddar's honour. This volume was to have contributions from 101 front-ranking writers, politicians and intellectuals—from the Shankaracharyas (the custodians of orthodox Hinduism) to President Rajendra Prasad. Surprisingly, even Mahadevi Varma, a rebel who challenged sanatan Hindu dharma, was approached and agreed to be one of the contributors.[154]

But Poddar killed the elaborate venture. When the felicitation committee convenor Nageshwar Dixit approached him to write a message for the commemorative volume, Poddar flatly refused: 'The principles that I adhere to and advocate never sanction any such undertaking aiming at self-praise whatsoever. May God bless me to be true to them to my last breath, and if so—I am afraid I may hurt your feelings—I must wholeheartedly discourage all such efforts.'[155]

The committee was shocked. Vishwanath Kumar Varma, another convenor, tried his best to convince Poddar. He said the 'contents' for the volume had been received from many people and 'letters have already been issued to many personalities in the field of education and learning, religion and philosophy, politics and culture, etc'.[156]

This renewed appeal cut no ice with Poddar. He firmly told Varma to give up the project since it would 'sadden and harm me'. Poddar said any attempt to honour him would be a sign of a decline in his principles. 'I can neither support this venture nor cooperate or ask anyone else to cooperate,' he explained. To ensure that the venture did not take off at any cost, Poddar issued a threat: 'If you do not listen to me I will have to publicly oppose it.'[157]

So, in the last quarter of 1967, when Poddar was seventy-five years old, his friends and admirers got together again to commemorate his 'diamond jubilee'. The group included film-maker S.N. Mangal who was close to Morarji Desai of the Congress, along with a section of Hindu nationalists, and old friends like Omkarmal Saraf, Jaidayal Dalmia and Ramnivas Dhandaria. Mangal conceived the proposal for a commemoration volume running into 300 to 350 pages. Writing to Jaidayal Dalmia, Mangal said that earlier the plan was for a volume of 1,000 pages, but it was decided that such a book would only adorn bookshelves.[158] Mangal had spoken to Desai and elicited his support for the venture.

Mangal considered Poddar's life to be a 'civilisation in itself' and proposed a building in his name. He also wanted a literary and religious week to be celebrated throughout the country in honour of Poddar. However, all the plans were soon scuttled, as Krishna Chandra, who must have consulted Poddar, wrote against holding any event or bringing out any book. Mangal wrote to Dalmia for support. He argued that the idea behind the programme was to highlight Poddar's contribution to inspire the youth. 'It is important to highlight his contributions in his lifetime. There is no point doing it after his death. If it does not happen now it will never happen. We will not have the presence and help of a daring personality like Saraf.'[159]

In the midst of all this, fissures within the organizing committee began to come out in the open. Meanwhile, Krishna Chandra continued to faithfully report Poddar's disapproval of the event.

As uncertainty loomed over the commemoration volume, Mangal and Dalmia began discussing the possibility of a documentary on Poddar that could be distributed through the Films Division, an offshoot of the government's information and broadcasting ministry.[160] Mangal wanted the idea for the documentary to be approved in Swargashram, Rishikesh (run by Gobind Bhawan) where a major meeting of the trustees of Gobind Bhawan was planned for the end of April 1968. Meanwhile, Shanti Prasad Jain, Ramnath Goenka and Omkarmal Saraf made a public appeal for cooperation to celebrate the contribution Poddar had made.[161] Poddar, ignoring the appeal, wrote to them not to persist with the idea of bringing out a book. Finally, when the meeting in Rishikesh took place, Saraf could not attend it due to ill health.[162] Dalmia too was absent because of some family commitment.[163] At the meeting it was decided to bring out a book tracing Gita Press's contribution rather than Poddar's.[164] The idea was to celebrate the institution rather than an individual, and thus overcome Poddar's opposition. The meeting also decided that a documentary on Poddar would be made after the volume on Gita Press and, thereafter, a separate volume on Poddar could be planned. Dalmia wrote to say he would accept whatever was decided in Rishikesh.[165] So, yet again, Poddar had his way.

Between 1968 and 1970, Poddar would resign from many trusts like Krishnajanam Sthan Trust, Mathura, and Swargashram, Rishikesh. In his resignation letter from Swargashram, Poddar would refer to mutual distrust among the members of Gita Bhavan and unnecessary litigation with other religious trusts on matters of construction.

By 1970 Poddar's health had deteriorated sharply. A diabetic, he refused to take insulin on the grounds that it contained substances derived from animal parts. In addition, multiple ailments of heart and stomach cancer rendered him almost permanently bedridden. While the plans of Poddar's admirers to celebrate his diamond jubilee had not materialized, newspapers and magazines would not forget him, and neither would old friends.

From Los Angeles, Swami Prabhupada wrote wishing him good health.[166] An effusive Teji Bachchan, wife of noted Hindi writer Harivansh Rai Bachchan, would send a telegram to Poddar citing a couplet from the Ramayana.[167] She called him the fountainhead of knowledge and wished him immortality and life at the feet of God. Poddar was Teji Bachchan's rakhi brother; she not only called him brother but also considered him to be God incarnate.

Controversy would not leave Poddar even at this stage. In 1970, Prabhudatt Brahmachari, Poddar's comrade-in-arms during the cow-protection movement, warned him about the impending investigation into his alleged role in the theft and illegal transfer of ancient idols to foreign countries. Brahmachari wrote to Poddar on the basis of a tip-off received from a police officer in Patna. Aware of deterioration in the affairs of Gobind Bhawan, Brahmachari told Poddar it could be the handiwork of some businessman who had close links with the Bhawan. Poddar thanked Brahmachari for the information and termed the allegations as 'fictional' and without basis, daring the CID officers to go to court.[168] He also said the issue had been brought to the notice of the Gobind Bhawan authorities who had denied the allegations.

While the allegations of theft of idols remained unsubstantiated, it is a fact that Poddar, Jaidayal Dalmia and the latter's associate Hitsharan Sharma were persistently requested by the International Society for Krishna Consciousness (ISKCON) to arrange for idols of Krishna from Gorakhpur and Vrindavan to be sent to the UK and USA. In 1968, when Sharma had refused to return Rs 2,000 he had taken from ISKCON to organize paper for printing a book by its founder Swami Prabhupada, Prabhupada, then in Seattle, asked two of his disciples, Achyutananda and Jaya Govinda, to realize the money through the influence of Ram Krishna Dalmia and Poddar and use it to 'purchase deities'. He said ISKCON needed '100s of pairs of Deities of different sizes'.[169]

Prabhupada had requested Poddar to 'recommend some of your Vaisnava (sic) friends to contribute such murtis'[170] and the Dalmia–Jain Trust and Birla Trust had donated five pairs of Radha–Krishna murtis (idols) for installation in different ISCKON centres. The job of dispatching the murtis was left to Hitsharan Sharma; Sumati Morarji of the Scindia Steam Navigation Co. had agreed to carry them.

Poddar's Legacy

Hanuman Prasad Poddar breathed his last in Gita Vatika on 22 March 1971 amidst his family members and admirers who had started trooping in on hearing about his deteriorating state.

His will, finalized in January 1970, contained a large dose of confession about his attitude towards minorities—Muslims in particular. Admitting that for a long time he had been against Muslims in general, he said, 'It was not against any individual.' Poddar listed Muslims like Mohammad Syed Hafiz of Allahabad University and Christians like C.F. Andrews and Arthur Massey as his friends. He also talked of his involvement with extremist politics in his youth and hatred for certain British officials, saying, 'This feeling disappeared as I came closer to Gandhiji.' But Poddar did not discuss the various hues of his relationship with Gandhi, from deep reverence to visceral hatred.

More incisive than Poddar's will was his long article for *Satsang Sudha*, a monthly publication of Gita Vatika, written the previous year. Titled 'Clarification of My Position', it played down his achievements and the myths associated with him. 'I am neither a Yogi nor a Mahatma. I do not have divine or magical power. Those who see such power in me do so out of mistake . . . I have also not started any new religious sect nor do I boast of having given birth to new tenets of spiritualism.' While denying all the qualities that his admirers never tired of talking about, Poddar was liberal in his praise of the Radha Madhav Seva Sansthan and its various activities. However, he clarified that he was not directly involved with the organization.[171]

The legacy of Poddar was forgotten within a few months of his death as a power struggle ensued between his family and members of the Gobind Bhawan Karyalaya. The battle was over control of the sprawling Gita Vatika complex that Poddar had made his home. Gobind Bhawan Karyalaya wanted to make it clear that the rights over the property did not vest with Poddar's family. On 13 May, less than two months after Poddar's death, the trustees of Gobind Bhawan met and passed certain resolutions, the main one being that no memorial should be erected at the site of Poddar's last rites in Gita Vatika. Ishwari Prasad Goenka, trustee of Gobind Bhawan, wrote on this matter to Parmeshwar Prasad Fogla, who had married Poddar's daughter Savitri in 1941.[172]

Fogla was informed that the trustees felt the decision to allow Poddar's cremation at Gita Vatika had been wrong and against the principles set by Jaydayal Goyandka. Two trustees—Bihari Lal and Ram Das Jalan—were blamed for the decision allowing the cremation. It had been decided that nothing should be kept at the site where Poddar was cremated. 'Respected Sethji (Goyandka) and Bhaiji (Poddar) were against the idea of building a memorial, therefore nothing should be kept there. Trustees had only given permission for cremation not to build a memorial,' Goenka told Fogla. Goenka also said all sorts of rumours were emanating from Gita Vatika, all of which were against the values propagated by Goyandka and Poddar. 'Officials of the Gita Vatika should be warned not to vitiate the atmosphere.'

Fogla was asked to ensure that no construction, makeshift or permanent, came up in Gita Vatika. The trustees also made it clear that the rights to the property did not vest with Poddar's daughter Savitri or anyone else. However, Gobind Bhawan Karyalaya Trust exempted the family from the rent of Rs 100 per month that Poddar had been paying.

Within days, Gita Vatika was rife with rumours that Poddar's family would be asked to vacate the premises. Ishwari Prasad Goenka was asked to allay the fears of Poddar's family: 'Trustees have not taken any decision to get the bagicha (Gita Vatika) vacated. We view Bhaiji's family with the same respect we accorded to him. If you make enquiries you will know what is right and what is not.'[173]

Not even a year after Poddar's death, Jaidayal Dalmia, who had been one of his closest aides, levelled a series of serious allegations against Radha Baba, Poddar's daughter Savitri Devi and Radheshyam Palriwal whom Poddar had brought up as a son. Among other allegations, Dalmia hinted at a relationship between Savitri and Palriwal and demanded the latter's removal from the Poddar family and Gita Vatika on grounds of moral turpitude. Dalmia had distanced himself from Poddar's first death anniversary function and even alleged that the commemorative volume brought out on the occasion was guided more by commercial interest than reverence. Dalmia went public with his allegation of debauchery in Gita Vatika and even threatened to go on a fast should Radha Baba refuse to expel Palriwal.

It took another of Poddar's acolytes Chimmanlal Gosvami to defend Radha Baba, Savitri and Palriwal. A former personal assistant to Madan Mohan Malaviya, Gosvami was a Sanskrit scholar who had quit his job as a senior official of Bikaner state to join Gita Press as the first editor of the English-language *Kalyana-Kalpataru*. After Poddar's demise he took over as editor of *Kalyan*, and was instrumental in organizing the nationwide commemoration of Poddar and publication of a mammoth volume on him on his first death anniversary.

In a lengthy public statement, Gosvami dismissed all the allegations and reminded Dalmia of the benevolence Poddar had always shown him. Gosvami made it clear that the expulsion of Palriwal from the family was a decision that could be made only by the head of the family and not Radha Baba. Gosvami said there was no evidence, as alleged by Dalmia, about Palriwal trying to defame Poddar after his death, and that if Dalmia had doubts about Palriwal's character he should encourage him to reform instead of defaming him and maligning Poddar's family in public. Gosvami also denied other allegations—that Savitri had bequeathed all her property to Palriwal, or that Baba had ever told Savitri to commit suicide to atone for her alleged relationship with Palriwal.[174]

Gosvami's emotional defence and subtle attack on Dalmia helped resolve the matter in the Poddar household and Gita Vatika, but the damage had been done. Though Gita Press kept aloof from these machinations, confining itself to republishing Poddar's huge body of work in *Kalyan* and *Kalyana-Kalpataru*, a trend that continues till today, Gosvami could feel a new wind blowing in the publishing house.

More than two years after Poddar's death, when Seth Govind Das requested that one of his plays being serialized by *Kalyan* should also be published as a book by Gita Press, Radheshyam Banka, on behalf of Gosvami, told him: 'After the death of Babuji (Poddar) situation has undergone a big change. In the present circumstances publishing a book is nearly impossible. We will try but circumstances look adverse.'[175] Still, Poddar's formidable legacy endures. He is Gita Press's very own saint and remains Nityalilalin, ever-present.

Jaydayal Goyandka: A Shadowy Presence

Written literature about Goyandka, even hagiographic, is scarce. For a founder of the most successful religious publishing enterprise of the colonial period, whose success continues unabated, Goyandka has received less than his due. Even in the copious literature about the founding duo published from Gita Vatika, a conscious effort to talk up Poddar over Goyandka is apparent. Accounts of Goyandka's life are brief—mere appendages to the detailed writings on Poddar.[176] They appear more as apologies or afterthoughts to avoid the raising of eyebrows their omission might occasion. Unfortunately, because of the dearth of sources, this chapter is constrained to make that very same discrimination between the two colossi of Gita Press in terms of the space given to accounts of their lives.

Stories about Goyandka's birth are less spiritually oriented than those about Poddar. Jaydayal was born in 1885 in Churu, Rajasthan. His father Khubchand Goyandka had lost his parents at an early age, and the burden of raising Khubchand and his two siblings, brother Lalchand and sister Lakshmi, fell on their grandfather Shalagram Goyandka. The family was God-fearing, but action mattered more than knowledge of religious texts. As was the tradition among Marwaris, Khubchand's grandfather put him through the paces of business at a young age. But his very first foray resulted in a huge loss, and the young Khubchand was barely able to recover a part of his investment. Next he dabbled in brokerage and became a commission agent. Younger brother Lalchand was sent to Calcutta from where he would send handcrafted garments to Churu for sale at a small profit.

Accounts of Jaydayal Goyandka's early years and education in Churu are vague, but abound in tales about his innate qualities of selfless love for his father and other elders of the family. Married at the age of twelve, Jaydayal is believed to have not consummated the marriage for many years. Also, a bottle of perfume gifted to him by his friend named Hanuman Prasad Goyanka (at the behest of Khubchand) was never opened, signifying his reluctance to enjoy marital life. At the age of sixty, Jaydayal would joke that the bottle was still intact in Churu.

Jaydayal's story starts assuming mythological overtones when, at the age of fifteen, he is believed to have become a follower of Lord Hanuman and had a darshan of the monkey god. Thereafter, Goyandka worshipped a series of gods—Surya, Shiva, Rama—claiming to have 'visions' of each of them in turn. As in the case of Poddar, Goyandka's 'visions' were often accompanied by conversation with the god/goddess.

In 1899, an encounter with Mangalnath Maharaj of the Nath Sampradaya in Churu further changed the course of Goyandka's spiritual quest. In Mangalnath, Goyandka saw a role model to emulate. In 1907, Goyandka claimed he had his first 'vision' of Lord Vishnu who invested him with magical power. That year Goyandka's childhood friend and spiritual fellow-traveller Hanuman Prasad Goyanka was afflicted with syphilis. Goyandka's hagiographers claim he cured the disease, taking away half of his friend's pain. No moral comment is made on the friend's contracting of syphilis—common among the rich but not among the spiritual.

For a decade beginning 1910, Goyandka pursued business but still kept ample time for his satsangs and spiritual discourses. After gaining experience at his maternal uncle's business in Bankura, he branched off on his own in Chakradharpur. His reputation as a god-man gained ground around the same time. Every day after work, he would travel to nearby Kharagpur where he had a group of friends and acquaintances keen on religious discourse. In Calcutta religious congregations would take place at 174, Harrison Road and Goyandka would spend the night at his friend Atmaram Khemka's house. As Goyandka's discourses began attracting more and more people, Gobind Bhawan was started. His old friend Hanuman Prasad Goyanka, then working with Khemka, would be by Goyandka's side during his discourses in Calcutta. It was here that Goyandka would also get closer to Hiralal Goyanka and his father Surajmal Goyanka. Later, as kathavachak at Gobind Bhawan, Hiralal would be at the centre of a sex scandal involving Marwari women that would shake the foundations of Gita Press and erode Goyandka's standing as a mystic, divine healer and grihasta sadhu.

In 1923, Gita Press was registered as a subsidiary of Calcutta-based Gobind Bhawan Karyalaya under the Societies Registration Act of 1860, now known as the West Bengal Societies Act, 1960. Gita Press was first located in Urdu Bazaar in a rented accommodation where a hand press was installed in September 1923. Because of poor production quality it was replaced within a month with a treadle machine acquired for Rs 2,000. This failed too, leading to the acquisition of a pan flat-bed cylinder machine for Rs 7,000, an exorbitant price in those days. As the publication of the Gita progressed, the place was found to be too small and a piece of land was bought for Rs 10,000 in July 1926. In the next few years, as work expanded and *Kalyan* moved to Gorakhpur, successive adjoining plots were bought. Gita Press also kept pace with technological changes that had become necessary to meet the rising demand for the new journal.

As Gita Press found a firm foothold and its finances were worked out, Goyandka, the incessant traveller, resumed his forays into the spiritual world. At times, warring Marwari families would invite him to preside over the division of their assets and business, often giving him the final say. Goyandka's moral authority in the community ensured that his verdict was rarely violated.[177] The economics behind having a community elder like Goyandka as arbiter was not lost on Marwaris—it saved lakhs of rupees and precious business time that would have otherwise been spent in litigation.

Goyandka's services would also be requisitioned to settle social debates within the sanatan Hindu dharma fold, as evident from Gita Vatika's account[178] of Goyandka mediating between Congress and Hindu Mahasabha leader Madan Mohan Malaviya and Swami Karpatri Maharaj, 'the most influential ascetic of Banaras and later founder of Ram Rajya Parishad',[179] on the issue of allowing untouchables to be given diksha (initiation through Vedic verses), thus far the sole preserve of brahmins and a few other castes.

Jaydayal Goyandka had three brothers and three sisters. His younger brother, Harikrishna Das translated many Sanskrit texts into Hindi, later published by Gita Press. A better part of Jaydayal's life was spent in religious work, leaving little time for business. The youngest of the Goyandka brothers was Mohanlal, whom Jaydayal adopted. A graduate from Rishikul Ashram in Ratangarh, Mohanlal lost his wife early and remarried at Gandhi's behest. According to Dujari's account Mohanlal was highly influenced by Gandhi from an early age and had met him several times. But remarriage did not help Mohanlal; he soon left his home and his khadi business. He returned eventually, once again on Gandhi's request, and joined his maternal uncle's grain business in Bankura. By 1930, Mohanlal and Harikrishna had branched out on their own, and in 1932 registered a cotton-trading firm called Jaydayal Harikrishna. Within a few years, the company expanded—first a dyeing unit came up and then a vest-manufacturing factory. A series of family tragedies in the late 1930s resulted in their business being run through the Goyandka Trust. A major share of the profit was ploughed into the running of schools and bridge-building.

Jayadayal Goyandka grew distant from his family, involving himself in meditation, satsang and spiritual writing. Influenced by his interpretations of the Gita, Ramsukh Das, an eminent exponent of the Gita, and Swami Chakradhar persuaded Goyandka to pen a comprehensive commentary on the text. Through an elaborate exercise that entailed intense debate with scholars and swamis on various interpretations, Goyandka began work on his commentary in Gorakhpur in 1936, and completed it in 1939 at Bankura. The first version came out as *Kalyan*'s annual number of 1940 and later as a book *Gita Tattva Vivechani*, one of the highest-selling titles from the Gita Press stable.

A substantial part of Goyandka's time would be spent at Swargashram in Rishikesh. He had started visiting the town in the early 1920s, and when he was not travelling, most of his time was spent there. He was visiting Gorakhpur less and less frequently, partly on account of growing differences with Poddar on various issues; and Swargashram became Goyandka's second home, the place where he would breathe his last.

Poddar acknowledged that his relationship with Goyandka was multilayered, but wished this to remain private. He would tell

Gambhirchand Dujari: 'You should not discuss with anyone my spiritual relationship with him or the fact that we are like a brother-sister. Also do not mention that his poems are not getting published in *Kalyan*. You should maintain silence. You and (Chimmanlal) Gosvamiji should pay attention to my request.'[180]

Run by Gita Press, Swargashram is still among the largest ashrams in Rishikesh, with close to a hundred rooms for visitors and year-round religious congregations. And Gobind Bhawan, the parent organization that originally operated from rented accommodation in Calcutta's Banstalla Street, got land of its own on Mahatma Gandhi Road (erstwhile Harrison Road) in 1949.

When Goyandka was busy brainstorming for his *Gita Tattva Vivechani*, his brother-turned-adopted-son Mohanlal lost his youngest son, a loss that shook Goyandka. No longer in fine health himself, though he remained engaged with various religious and philanthropic activities, Goyandka could not stay aloof from family affairs. His wife passed away in 1960 in Bankura, and then came news of Mohanlal's arrest in 1964 in Calcutta. It could not have happened at a worse time. Poddar's letter to Prime Minister Lal Bahadur Shastri requesting his release indicates that Mohanlal had been arrested under the Defence of India Act. Poddar told Shastri that Mohanlal was an old acolyte of Gandhi's who had rendered selfless service to the people of Bankura and worked all his life to popularize khadi. Poddar blamed the West Bengal government for not taking account of this. 'Please exercise your influence and get an innocent man free,' Poddar pleaded with Shastri, adding that Mohanlal was being deprived of caring for his father who had no one else to look after him.[181]

With Mohanlal still in jail, Goyandka requested Poddar and others to shift him to Rishikesh, which they did. At the end of March 1965, Poddar came from Gorakhpur to Rishikesh and even Mohanlal got parole to visit his father. Bedridden by now, Goyandka had refused 'English' (allopathic) medicine of any kind. Over the next few days, more and more of his followers gathered in Rishikesh. Goyandka would still dictate letters and ask Poddar to recite his favourite religious verses while he waited for the inevitable end. On 17 April, Goyandka was laid outdoors for followers to have a last darshan; by four in the evening, he was no more. His followers refused to believe he died in the conventional sense—for them Goyandka's body and soul had merged with Brahman (the absolute reality which includes the divine). Thus, he became Brahmalin Jayadayal Goyandka.

The following month, *Kalyan* carried several tributes to its founder. Trustees of Gobind Bhawan appealed to Goyandka's disciples not to mourn his death but follow his divine lessons and model their character on him. Poddar wrote that though the world had been deprived of Goyandka's physical presence, sermons and exemplary character, he continued to live in the minds of everyone.[182]

Gita Press would now be the sole concern of Poddar, a responsibility he had already been shouldering despite repeated attempts to relinquish it. So overwhelming was the influence of Goyandka and Poddar on Gita Press that even today the two names continue to grace the pages of *Kalyan*, month after month.

२: The World
of Gita Press

The idea of a journal to promote the principles of sanatan Hindu dharma had been crystallized in the course of a half-hour train journey. Returning to Bombay from Delhi after the meeting of the All India Marwari Aggarwal Mahasabha in 1926, Hanuman Prasad Poddar alighted at Rewari in Haryana and journeyed to nearby Bhiwani where Jaydayal Goyandka was to give a religious discourse. The next day, Poddar and Goyandka were returning to Rewari by train, from where Poddar would leave for Bombay and Goyandka for Bankura in Bengal. Lakshmi Narayan Murodia, a prominent businessman from Pilani and an influential figure in the community, was also on the train. During the half-hour journey, they discussed G.D. Birla's remark that the Marwari Aggarwal Mahasabha should bring out a separate journal on Hindu religion rather than mixing it with community issues. Murodia urged Poddar to take on editorship of the proposed journal. Though Poddar protested feebly, Murodia's seniority in age and standing in the community probably silenced him into acceptance.

The question of a name for the journal came up, and Poddar suggested *Kalyan* (which could mean beneficence, welfare or good fortune). The other two wholeheartedly agreed and it was decided that the first issue of *Kalyan* be out by Akshaya Tritiya, an auspicious day in the Hindu calendar. The magazine would be published by Goyandka's Gita Press, already established in Gorakhpur but languishing; in the coming years, *Kalyan* would catapult Gita Press to new heights and unrivalled success.[1]

The First Year

Once back in Bombay, the *Kalyan* project slipped out of Poddar's mind, but coincidence lent a helping hand. He happened to meet Khemraj Krishnadas, owner of Sri Venkateshwar Press, who offered to help with the registration and printing of the magazine. A prominent name in the printing business, Khemraj's patronage meant that *Kalyan* never faced the teething troubles encountered by most other contemporary publications. Also, its avowed mission of reinstating the ancient glory of sanatan Hindu dharma put the journal beyond the colonial government's strict political surveillance.

With most practical concerns taken care of, Poddar was left with the editorial responsibility of requisitioning articles for the journal from his wide network of contacts—spiritual men, politicians and writers he had met in his various avatars as a revolutionary, businessman and acolyte of Jaydayal Goyandka. The first issue of *Kalyan* came out in August 1926, published by Venkateshwar Press under the aegis of Goyandka's Bombay-based Satsang Bhavan. Offered at an annual subscription of Rs 3 in India and Rs 4 overseas, the monthly magazine claimed to represent bhakti (devotion), gyan (knowledge), vairagya (asceticism) and dharma (religion).

The cover of the inaugural issue was plain but tastefully designed. The inside cover had a colour painting of young Lord Krishna with his flute at the centre of the page with stanzas from the Gita all around. The journal also spelt out its nine rules, the most prominent among them being publication on Krishna Ekadashi that falls in the first fortnight of each month, not accepting any commercial advertisement, and restricting the contents to devotion, divine power and tales of gods.

The thirty-four-page inaugural issue of *Kalyan* had two articles by Goyandka, one on ways to achieve kalyan and the second his replies to a series of questions from devotees. He wrote in Marwari that was translated into highly Sanskritized Hindi. Both Goyandka and Poddar would don the mantle of religious/social agony columnists throughout their life. The inaugural issue also carried an excerpt of M.K. Gandhi's article from *Navjivan* on the meaning of the innate or natural, and a very short 'filler' piece by Rabindranath Tagore on the pitfalls of desire, both material and physical. Gandhi's influence would be more prominent in subsequent issues that very first year.

The method and mission of *Kalyan* was explained through two separate comments by Poddar, who preferred to write under the generic title of editor. The first of these editorial comments—'*Kalyan Ki*

Avashyakta' (Need for Beneficence)—dwelt on the multiple connotations of kalyan: 'It assumes different meanings for different people . . . For some having a woman, a male child, wealth, honour and prestige is kalyan and for others abandoning all these and leading a life of isolation is kalyan; for some usurping the wealth of others is kalyan but for many others abandoning wealth is kalyan.' Further, 'The person entrusted with the task of editing *Kalyan* acknowledges he does not have the qualification or the ability to carry out the task. He is yet to achieve the quality of beneficence but he believes in being good to people. Working for *Kalyan* will inspire him further to be good to people.'[2] Such self-deprecation was to become a hallmark of Poddar's writing.

But the true goal of *Kalyan* was expressed in the editorial comment on the last pages. In his observations on the state of international affairs, Poddar lamented the direction in which Europe was headed, with constant news of death and devastation; nor was the United States spared as Poddar specifically mentioned the fire in the ammunition depot in Dover, New Jersey, that had killed many. 'Everyone is unhappy and there is mutual distrust. In some places there are instances of rebellion, political assassination and oppression of the poor, and at other places an unsuccessful attempt to foist equality by robbing the rich. In a nutshell, people in Europe and the USA are facing a severe crisis: spiritual, divine and material.'[3] Shifting his gaze towards Asia, Poddar noted the violent civil war in China between the ruling Kuomintang or Chinese Nationalist Party and the Communist Party, the uncertainty in Iran where the Pehlavi dynasty had assumed power in 1926, and the political instability in Japan. Poddar's first editorial was reflective of the man: sweeping historical narrative and grand designs to save Hindu society. Concerned by the rise of socialism and communism, Poddar declared that the idea of robbing the rich to feed the poor was a near-failure. He might have been an unsuccessful businessman, but throughout his long public life he always defended the free market and the running of industry and business minus state intervention.

Turning to India, Poddar wrote that the foremost problem facing the country, along with ever-existing ones like malnutrition and unemployment, was the fact that 'two big communities are out to finish each other'. He referred in general to the destruction of temples and mosques, and killings in the name of religion. His views did not project any false objectivity, however, as the particular injustices he spelt out were always ascribed to Muslims. Poddar mentioned how attacks on the poor and defenceless (abala) and on pure unsuspecting women were misguidedly seen as furthering the cause of religion; in the same breath, without directly referring to the cow, he raised the issue of slaughter of beneficent (upkari) animals that had turned the land red. Poddar ascribed the decline in values to materialism and disbelief in the existence of the supreme lord. 'We are aspiring to be happy by worshipping sins. If we do not remove ourselves from this path of decline, the consequences will be even more severe.'

Having set the tone, Poddar explained and interpreted the communal climate of early twentieth-century India marked by deep distrust and violence between the two communities. Under the subheading 'Hindu–Muslim Problem' he wrote: 'It (violence) neither helps in the propagation of Hinduism nor is beneficial to Islam.' Again, this objective tone was momentary, for he ended with an invocation to his co-religionists to 'conserve strength and power' and not use them against the poor and helpless, not even against people of the other religion, but to protect their own religion and the sanctity of their women against oppressors. 'Such self-defence will have divine sanction.' Poddar's prescription was that if attacks on places of worship or on women were born out of ignorance, the perpetrators of such violence should be counselled, but in case that failed, physical means should be used. Physical strength was important, he said, but it needed sanghbal (unity of strength). Also, 'We should remember ahimsa (non-violence) is not cowardice. Non-violence and absolution are the qualities of the fearless and brave, and not of cowards and the faint-hearted who hide in their homes.' As the flag bearer of Gita Press, *Kalyan* had thus spelt out its concerns as well as prescribed the recipe of self-defence for Hindus.

The second issue of *Kalyan* relied mainly on the speeches of Jaydayal Goyandka and his replies to followers. There was a short article by Gandhi—whether it was extracted or exclusively written for the new journal is not clear. Stressing the importance of reciting the name of

Rama, the article titled '*Naam Mahatmya*' (The Greatness of God's Name) dwelt on how in the Ramayana, by taking Rama's name a bridge was built to reach Ravana's Lanka. In his personal life, Gandhi said, Rama saved him from turning into a debauch. 'I have made tall claims but if I did not have the name of Rama to recite I could not have addressed three women as my sisters.'[4]

In contrast to Gandhi's emphasis on purity in private life was Goyandka's concern about the public sphere in which Hinduism, he felt, faced severe threat. Replying to a devotee's query about ways of personal salvation, Goyandka gave first priority to salvation for Hinduism and advocated a fourfold path: propagation of religious education; religious discourse by saints and scholars; distribution of religious texts at low prices; and setting up orphanages to secure the religious identity of orphaned boys.

Simultaneously, Satsang Bhavan, the publisher of *Kalyan* in Bombay, was taking the first tentative steps towards the distribution of cheap religious texts being produced at Gita Press in Gorakhpur. With sales counters limited to Bombay, Gorakhpur, Bikaner and Delhi, Satsang Bhavan solicited agents in other places promising them 'appropriate commission' on the books they sold. By now thirteen titles had been published, five of them noteworthy. The first was a summary of various chapters of the Gita, the second a volume titled *Stri Dharma Prashnottari* (Questions and Answers on Women's Dharma), the third an illustrated volume on ways to control desire and the fourth a booklet of devotional ghazals sold at two copies for one paisa (sixty-fourth of a rupee). The fifth and most expensive book was the complete Gita, priced at one rupee. All this was just the beginning; the shifting of *Kalyan*'s editorial staff to Gorakhpur in 1927 would lead to a jump in the number of religious titles published.

Yet to enlist regular contributors and find its bearings, the third issue of *Kalyan* published Jaydayal Goyandka's reply to a year-old spiritual query by G.D. Birla. Of all the seekers of Goyandka's wisdom, Birla was the only one identified by name. His question was related to achieving salvation, a task he said he found more insurmountable than climbing Mount Kailash. Birla wanted to know if his affluence, though put to use in the service of Gandhi and his philosophy of truth and ahimsa, was an impediment to his salvation. Goyandka agreed that wealth could be a stumbling block but said that it could be used wisely too. Praising Birla's devotion to Gandhi, Goyandka added bhakti (devotion) to ahimsa and truth as a way out. Birla should not limit himself to reciting the name of God but should see God in everything, and with God as witness take the decision to avoid the path of sin. From the published reply it emerges that Birla had refused to accept Goyandka as his spiritual mentor, a fact Goyandka took in his stride—thanking the leading industrialist for recognizing that he lacked the qualities to be his mentor.

By the fourth issue, the distribution network for *Kalyan* and Gita Press books had slowly expanded, with new agents in Bettiah (Bihar), Bikaner, Ratlam (Central Provinces), Delhi and Tinsukia (Assam). All individual distributors were Marwari businessmen. By the beginning of the second year, Gita Press was looking to appoint thousands of agents for *Kalyan* and its other publications. Today a mammoth distribution network exists, with Gita Press bookshops in twenty cities, retail outlets in four and stalls at thirty-five railway stations across India. In recent years, Gita Press publications have become available online.

With passing months, *Kalyan* became more focused on the Hindu religion and the threat of what Poddar and others likened to a dark age. The magazine gradually began to attract big names to write articles exclusively for it. Bhupendranath Sanyal,[5] who had contributed short articles to the first four issues of *Kalyan*, penned a longer piece—'*Hamara Param Lakshya*' (Our Ultimate Destination)—lamenting the demise of religiosity among Hindus and how religion was the sole way out of the current crisis. This piece by Sanyal, who would go on to write forty-five articles (according to a catalogue in Gita Vatika) for *Kalyan* in coming years, was the earliest and strongest defence of sanatan Hindu dharma and articulated the larger vision of Gita Press. Sanyal, who had briefly taught at Santiniketan,[6] argued that the distinguishing mark of a nation was its soul that gave definition and meaning to its existence. Sanyal's narrative was dependent on the 'singularity of national history' that by implication took him to a 'single source of Indian tradition viz. ancient Hindu civilization'.[7] Sanyal said India—for him a country solely of Hindus—was known for its religiosity that defined the personal behaviour of Hindus, their social customs, politics and administration. 'Religion is at the heart of India's inception and character. It is not an imaginary entity for India but has material and organic form. If we do anything disregarding religion it would not be beneficial,' Sanyal wrote, at one point countering Karl Marx's 'religion is the opiate of the masses' with 'religion is the medicine of masses'. Sanyal talked of an attack by 'virodhi sabhyata' (adversarial or foreign civilizations or religions, implying Islam or Christianity) that corrupted the tenets of sanatan Hindu dharma. As a result, he said, Hindus were looking at bijatiya (alien) culture and its material aspects with admiration and aspiration. 'The path of eternal Hindu religion might not promise the prosperity and material comfort of European civilization but it will ensure peace, love and happiness in India.'[8]

Sanyal's construct of Indian history as Hindu history, denying even a mention to centuries of Muslim and British rule and influence, was in line with the view of Hindu nationalism as representing Indian nationalism. In this view, both Muslims and the British would bear the tag of foreigners and polluters of sanatan Hindu dharma that had resulted in the 'dark age' of the late nineteenth–early twentieth century. Partha Chatterjee contends that this 'notion of Hindu-ness' should not be seen as a religious construct alone, since there are 'no specific beliefs or practices which characterize this "Hindu" and the many doctrinal or sectarian differences among Hindus are irrelevant to this concept'.[9] The only distinction that the Sanyal kind of history made was between what happened in India and what came from outside. In the process, as Chatterjee points out, even the most vocal opposition to brahminical Hinduism, as posed by Buddhism and Jainism, finds place in the Indian history while Islam and Christianity are left out.

The novelty of a religious journal upholding sanatan Hindu dharma meant many readers would turn to *Kalyan* for spiritual solace and even for advice on direct communion with and darshan (vision) of God. Poddar concealed the identity of one such reader from Gujarat who wanted a categorical reply about whether it was possible to have darshan of God.[10] For someone like Poddar, who for the next few years would claim to have several visions of gods and conversations with them that became part of the carefully cultivated folklore around him, there was nothing outrageous or unrealistic about the question. The crux of his long reply was a resounding yes, provided the devotee had supreme longing to see God, almost akin to a lover's pining for his beloved.

Gita Press benefited greatly from its new vehicle *Kalyan*. Its activities were not limited to the print arena. Regretting that India had slipped into a dark age as people had stopped thinking about God, Gita Press through *Kalyan* appealed to Hindus to recite *Hare Ram, Hare Ram; Ram, Ram, Hare, Hare; Hare Krishna, Hare Krishna; Krishna, Krishna, Hare, Hare*—a mantra that has the name of God sixteen times. A similar attempt in 1925 by Satsang Bhavan had not been very successful, but a year later the power of *Kalyan* was on display.[11]

Kalyan asked its readers to recite the mantra three-and-a-half crore (35,000,000) times within a Hindu calendar month, which would mean that God's name would be repeated a total of fifty-six crore times. Readers were asked to spread the message to every nook and corner of the country. Participants in this exercise were to report the number of times the verse was recited but not name those who recited it. A new department called Naam Jap Vibhag was set up in Satsang Bhavan to maintain a record of the recitations being reported. This continues as a department of Gita Press in Gorakhpur today.

The striking feature of this initiative was its comprehensive nature, belying Gita Press's firmness on matters of ritual, varnashram dharma (the four stages of life) and gender. One, it made clear that while each individual should recite the verse at least 108 times daily there was no harm if the process was interrupted. Further, the appeal was to Hindus of all castes, men, women and children. This ran counter to Gita Press's dominant discourse on upholding the fourfold caste system and prescribing strict rituals and moral and public rules for women—most significantly the need for them to be segregated from God and their husbands during the 'impure' period of menstruation.

Gita Press used *Kalyan* in its first year as a testing ground for issues that it would later take up on a sustained basis—cow protection being chief among them. Ganga Prasad Agnihotri, a leading voice on cow protection, lamented the practice of cow slaughter and advocated the spread of literature on the cow as an auspicious symbol representing good fortune.

One of the first letters to the editor in *Kalyan* was from Lajjaram Mehta, author of *Adarsha Hindu* (The Ideal Hindu), published in 1915. Mehta was a prominent writer of the pre-Premchand era and his work exemplified 'resistance to the social transformation' taking place in India at the time. In *Adarsha Hindu*, Mehta had attempted to 'emphasize the significance of Hindu religion, eradicate the evils in Hindu society and to create a healthy and virtuous society based on the beliefs of sanatan dharma'.[12]

In his letter to *Kalyan*, Mehta praised the initiative 'especially at a time when, intoxicated with the dream of Swaraj (self-rule), sanatan dharma is being attacked'.[13] He continued, 'There is need for a journal that would explain issues like untouchability and widow remarriage from the point of the shastras (traditional texts) and save varnashram dharma from our friends who are advocating a mixed-varna (caste) system.' His ire was directed at political leaders who 'don't have knowledge of Sanskrit and the shastras, are not leaders of sanatan dharma nor have the right to enter the provincial council or rule the country'.

The letter was given a place of prominence in *Kalyan*, and in his editorial response, Poddar entirely agreed with Mehta. Poddar justified untouchability but urged upper castes to be benevolent and kind towards lower castes—without coming in contact with them, just the way 'we do not come in contact with our respectable mother and beloved wife when they are menstruating'.

Further, he termed widow remarriage a sin. In his view, one who enticed a widow into marrying again denied her the virtue of spending the rest of her life in remembering her husband. 'A fear is being created among widows that suppressing their physical urges will torment them. Invoking passion amongst widows is the biggest threat to Hinduism's holy and glorious tradition of virtuous women.'

Gita Press in general and *Kalyan* in particular claimed to uphold Hindu tenets delineated in the shastras. Gender segregation was prescribed even during Holi, the popular north Indian festival of colours that saw temporary suspension of gender and caste barriers. For *Kalyan*, a man playing Holi with 'other women' was a form of sexual union and even playing with 'apni stri' (one's own woman) would cause loss of virility. Instead, it said, Holi should be spent propagating stories of Prahlad and reciting devotional songs.[14]

The early issues of *Kalyan* were defining ones: their broad sweep of contents and various columns would remain more or less unchanged for decades. Though new columns were added and some columns became irregular, the template of the inaugural year endured in spirit. Several special columns appeared in *Kalyan* over the years.

The column '*Kalyan*' was written by Poddar under the name Shiva. After Poddar's death, the column continued, with his articles and speeches being republished. Though rechristened '*Kalyan Vani*' for a while after he died, it soon reverted to '*Kalyan*'. '*Padho, Samjho Aur Karo*' (Read, Understand and Practise) appeared in 1958 for the first time and was aimed at inculcating high moral values among readers by citing real-life incidents to prove the existence of a supreme power. In another early column, '*Paramhans Vivekmala*' (Moral Tales of the Supreme Seer), Swami Bhole Baba's discourse appeared in question-answer format. '*Vivek Vatika*' (Garden of Conscience) consisted of sayings and writings of seers and extracts from religious texts. Through '*Parmarth Patravali*' (Letters on Salvation) Poddar and Goyandka replied to the religious and spiritual queries of readers, while '*Parmarth Ki Pagdandiyan*' (Roads to Salvation) carried notes and advice for devotees. '*Sadhakon Ke Prati*' (For the Devotees) was a column by Swami Ramsukh Das, a trusted friend of Poddar's, and dealt with questions from people caught in spiritual and religious dilemmas. After the Swami's death in 2005 the column continued, using views from his discourses. '*Satsang Vatika Ke Bikhre Suman*' (Scattered Flowers of the Garden of Discourse), since discontinued, contained nuggets of advice for those involved in prayer, meditation and devotion to God. In '*Kaam Ke Patra*' (Meaningful Letters) Poddar replied to the devotional, moral, practical, social, political, familial and personal questions of readers. This was one of the most popular columns of *Kalyan*. The column '*Bhakt Gatha*' (Tales of Devotees) has been in existence since 1926, though it is not as regular now as in earlier years. '*Vratotsav*' (Joy of Keeping Religious Vows) is immensely popular among those who keep fasts or perform other rituals on certain festivals or on the basis of the celestial positions of planets. '*Sadhnopayogi Patra*' (Useful Letters on Devotion) is similar to '*Kaam Ke Patra*'.[15]

Kalyan's leading light, Jaydayal Goyandka, suffered from stomach ailments, and towards the end of 1926 was taken from his hometown

Bankura to Banaras for treatment under the prominent city vaidya (Ayurvedic practitioner) Trimbak Shastri. The journal would regularly carry updates on his health and continued to publish his replies to readers, many given during his discourses and speeches.

At the end of the first year, *Kalyan* had done exceedingly well, with a circulation of 3,000 copies each month, an unbelievable figure for a genre-based journal. In fact, as was customary in India, most copies were read by more than one individual, being passed from hand to hand, so the actual readership may have been five or six times more. There were instances of rich Marwari businessmen buying *Kalyan* in bulk: Kasturchand Goradia of the firm Shaligram Kasturchand took fifty subscriptions, another reader took ten and some promised to pay double the cover price if the publishers doubled the number of pages. Enthused by the response, a publisher's note in the seventh issue of the first year promised a change in format and size of *Kalyan*.

Satsang Bhavan's venture of publishing cheap but high-quality religious texts and commentaries on them had also grown within a year to eighteen titles, most of them related to the Gita. Then there were titles that adhered to Gita Press's mission of pulling the Hindu society out of the darkness that threatened sanatan dharma. Texts like *Stri Dharma Prashnottari* prescribed how women should conduct themselves, and *Sarva Tantra Siddhant Padarth Sangrah*, a collection of Sanskrit texts selected by Gaurishankar, a sanyasi (monk), was brought out to educate school-going children.

From Bombay to Gorakhpur

What was supposed to be a short-lived printing arrangement for four or five months between Satsang Bhavan and Sri Venkateshwar Press continued for a little over a year. *Kalyan* shifted to Gorakhpur in 1927 only after the year's first special issue—*Bhagwan Naam Ank* (Issue on God's Name)—had been published from Bombay with a print run of 6,000. The issue, devoted to a specific aspect of religion, was a great success and became a trend that still continues. In its review of *Bhagwan Naam Ank*, the popular weekly *Hindu Panch* prayed for the success of *Kalyan* from its heart.[16]

Within a month, the *Bhagwan Naam Ank* saw a reprint of 2,000 copies that came out from its new abode, Gorakhpur. One 'Gujarati gentleman from Bombay' bought 1,000 copies and another reader from Banaras bought 500 copies for free distribution.[17] Gita Press and *Kalyan* were no longer staring at success—they had achieved a feat unparalleled by any other journal of that era.

Later special issues of *Kalyan* on *Nari* (Woman, 1948), *Hindu Sanskriti* (Hindu Culture, 1950), *Balak* (Male Child, 1953) and *Shiksha* (Education, 1988) are still in huge demand and keep getting reprinted. While the special issue of 1927 had 110 pages, subsequent years saw annual issues running into 700 to 800 pages covering various aspects of sanatan Hindu dharma.

In 1927, when *Kalyan* shifted to Gorakhpur, this eastern district of the United Provinces was known for sugar-cane farming, sugar factories and a railway junction in the district headquarters that facilitated trade. At the height of the non-cooperation movement, on 5 February 1922, peasants had burnt twenty-two policemen alive in Chauri-Chaura village of Gorakhpur district, leading Gandhi to suspend the movement.

Chauri-Chaura and Gorakhpur became known nationally and internationally because of this deplorable incident. However, Gorakhpur had also been home to other movements. Through the Nagari movement, Hindi was introduced as a court language in 1900 along with the already existing Persian.[18] In 1913, Gorakhpur's Nagari Pracharini Sabha managed to get judicial forms printed in Hindi. The next year came *Gyan Shakti*, 'a literary journal devoted to Hindi and Hindu *dharma prachar* (propagation) published by a pro-government Sanskrit scholar with financial support from the rajas of Padrauna, Tamkuhi and Majhauli as well as some from the *rausa* (notables) of Gorakhpur', and in 1915, Gauri Shankar Mishra, later a prominent leader of the UP Kisan Sabha, launched *Prabhakar*, the aim of which was to 'serve the cause of Hindi, Hindu and Hindustan'.[19] While *Prabhakar* closed down within a year and even *Gyan Shakti* was suspended for nearly a year in 1916–17, two other journals, the weekly *Sandesh* and monthly *Kavi*, played an important role in spreading Gandhi's message in Gorakhpur.

As for the cow-protection movement, like other towns in the United

Provinces, Gorakhpur took part by setting up gaurakshini sabhas. In Gorakhpur the most notable intervention was the meeting of gaurakshini sabha in 1893 where 'sixteen rules were drawn up' including the 'explicit message that chamars and others buy cows and sell them to butchers; and Musalmans and others are the very cause of the slaughter of cows. Cows shall not be sold into the hands of any such persons, and if any kind of cow dies the owner shall sell its skin to a proper person, and apply the money to cow-protection.'[20]

In purely religious terms, as spelt out in Francis Buchanan's account of his travels across Patna, Gaya, Shahabad and Gorakhpur, 'higher percentages of Brahmin gurus in Shahabad and, more especially, Gorakhpur districts were vaishnava in their religious outlook'. The rising influence of vaishnavas, as pointed out by Buchanan in the nineteenth century, would be ratified by 'Jogendra Nath Bhattacharya, president of the college of Pandits in Nadia (Bengal)' when he said, 'Vaishnavas are very fast extending the sphere of their influence, and many of the *tantriks* are now espousing vaishnava tenets in order to have the advantage of enlisting among their followers the low classes that are becoming rich under British rule.'[21]

This was the political and religious setting when *Kalyan* shifted to the sugar-cane town where Gita Press was located. In existence since 29 April 1923, Goyandka's brainchild Gita Press had been set up at the insistence of his friend Ghanshyamdas Jalan.[22] Before the press started, copies of the Gita would be brought from Gobind Bhawan, Calcutta, for distribution in the United Provinces. Sabhapati Mishra was appointed to take the text to villages and schools. This was when the system of rewarding any student who could recite a chapter of the Gita began. Mahavir Prasad Poddar, a business partner of Jalan's who had some experience of publishing, joined the venture and took care of its accounts. One of the earliest associates of Goyandka, Mahavir Prasad was slowly marginalized as Hanuman Prasad took over the affairs of Gita Press.

One of the first changes that the Gita Press witnessed after *Kalyan*'s move to Gorakhpur was the inculcation of missionary feeling among the editorial staff. They were mandated to live as a family and follow the strict regimen of devout sanatanis. The remuneration and perks were not attractive, a fact Goyandka would make bluntly clear to

Nandlal Joshi, a prospective employee, telling him that his salary could not be more than Rs 40 or Rs 50 per month. 'It is impossible to imagine a life without debt working for *Kalyan* and Gita Press. If you want a debtless life think of starting a business,' he advised Joshi.[23]

The idea of working for spiritual gratification at Gita Press was not without attraction. Even in 1968, an appeal to join *Kalyan* drew a number of applications from a wide range of people; some like V.K. Roy, a retired store purchase and supplies officer of Indian Airlines, offered his services gratis but with the rider that he and his wife be given a furnished flat and free supply of tea and milk. Nemani Kameswara Rao, retired from the Cooperative Land Mortgage Bank in Yellamanchili, Andhra Pradesh, also demanded a 'simple and heartfelt cottage and simple food twice a day, fit for a recluse'. Both were old subscribers of *Kalyan* and in the autumn of their life wanted to do something good for religion.

The relatively younger Upendra Nath Jha from Bihar was also vying for the same job, hard-selling his qualifications, the foremost of which, he claimed, was his brahmin origin and full knowledge of the working of Gita Press. Two men in their twenties, Madan Gopal, a postgraduate in English from Delhi, and Bhagwandhar Diwan, a history lecturer from Raigarh, Madhya Pradesh, were willing to give up their well-paid jobs to work for Gita Press.

Those who came to work for *Kalyan* and Gita Press in Gorakhpur lived as a family; even those who left kept the relationship alive either by writing for *Kalyan* or through a continuing friendship with Poddar.[24] The editorial staff of *Kalyan* and Gita Press were not only ill-paid but were also required to lead an austere life, following the rituals and regimen of ideal sanatanis. In the early days, the editorial office was situated in a building that had a large garden to the west of the famous Gorakhnath temple. The day would start at six with the editorial staff participating in a kirtan followed by Chimmanlal Gosvami, Poddar's second-in-command, reading from religious texts. Work would begin after a short discourse from Poddar. The staff was expected to spend their time, even working hours, in practising the principles of the Gita and Ramayana, reciting the name of God in their mind, talking less and always speaking the truth.

A community kitchen with a variety of food was set up to cater to the taste buds of the editorial staff drawn from all over the country. The first group consisted of Shantanu Bihari Dwivedi, Nand Dulare Vajpayee, Bhuvaneshwar Nath Mishra 'Madhav', Chimmanlal Gosvami, Dulichand Dujari, Deodhar Sharma, Rajbali Pandey, N. Ramachandran Brahmachari, Gopal, Krishna Das Dada, Munilal Gupt (later Swami Sanatan Dev), Hajari Lal Maheshwari and Chandrasekhar Pandey.

Gopal's job was to edit and rewrite long articles. Vajpayee assisted with edits and with replying to letters to the *Kalyan* editor, and edited the Ramayana, one of Gita Press's best-sellers. A postgraduate from Banaras Hindu University, Vajpayee was a favourite of Shyamsundar Das, a founding member of the Nagari Pracharini Sabha. Vajpayee retired as head of the Hindi Department, Sagar University and was made vice chancellor of Vikram University, Ujjain (Madhya Pradesh).[25] He was considered a worthy successor to noted Hindi critic Acharya Ramchandra Shukl. Ramachandran was an itinerant spiritual seeker. He had spent time with Swami Sivananda in Rishikesh and been a part of the Ramakrishna Mission. He was in Gorakhpur to be in the company of Poddar. Ramachandran's typing skills were put to good use by Gita Press for which he was paid a small amount.[26]

A Proposal to Shift to Banaras

In 1936, less than a decade after *Kalyan*'s move to Gorakhpur, Jiwanshankar Yagik of Banaras Hindu University, a close friend of Poddar and a regular contributor to *Kalyan*, began to push for shifting the entire Gita Press operation to Banaras. Yagik was so consumed with the idea that in early 1937, when news of a meeting of the Gobind Bhawan Trust in Bankura reached him, he wrote to Poddar spelling out seventeen reasons why the shift should take place and requesting him to lobby with the trustees for the relocation of Gita Press. Besides mentioning that Poddar's own family was desirous of moving to Banaras and that those loyal to Gita Press and *Kalyan* in Banaras would do everything to help it in the new place, Yagik gave more substantial reasons. He believed that as the work of Gita Press and *Kalyan* expanded, being in Banaras would help it wield greater influence. 'It would add to the prestige of Banaras as well as Gita Press. Sadhus and mahatmas are easily available in Banaras and need not be invited the way it is done in Gorakhpur.' Banaras, he said, was also ideal for research on the Gita and Ramayana. Yagik said that if the views of *Kalyan* readers were taken, a majority would be in favour of the shift and would even offer monetary help.[27]

Poddar did not inform Yagik about the outcome of the trustees' meeting, neither did he reply to two of the letters sent to him. An upset Yagik alleged that Poddar was suffering from a trait common among 'big modern men', namely, not answering mail. Yagik said he had expected Poddar to come to Banaras from Bankura, instead news came that the press building in Gorakhpur was being expanded. 'Why cannot you put it on hold until a decision is taken on the shift?' he asked Poddar.[28]

Poddar's reply to Yagik is not available, but going by Yagik's next letter it seems that Poddar had expressed reluctance, saying, 'God is not willing,' which further infuriated Yagik.[29] Apart from the financial burden that a shift would have placed on Gita Press, Poddar's total lack of enthusiasm could have stemmed from disinterest; by 1930 he had wished to leave Gita Press.

Although the move to Banaras did not happen in his lifetime, Yagik's dream would come partially true—it would take another six decades, but Gita Press would shift the editorial office of *Kalyan* to Banaras in 1999–2000.

Criticism and Controversy

As editor of *Kalyan*, Poddar would select and edit the main articles, being occasionally helped by Gosvami and later by Radheshyam Banka, another trusted aide. Poddar and Gosvami did the proofreading themselves, and would cross-check each reference with the original text and even delay publication till everything was cleared. But even such a regimen was no guarantee against mistakes. *Kalyan* learnt this the hard way with its annual number of 1935, *Yoga Ank*. An article devoted to the lives of 'famous yogis and swamis' described 'Ramanand as a follower of Ramanuja who had been excommunicated for a careless commensal behaviour while on pilgrimage'.[30]

Avadh Kishor Das, a scholar of the Ramanandi sect, took on *Kalyan* for getting its facts wrong: 'We have nothing whatsoever in common with the Ramanuji sampraday (cult). We disagree with them on every point . . . The editor and author of *Kalyan* should realize that jagat-guru (lord of the world) Shri Ramanandacharyaji was never a follower of the Ramanuji sampraday . . .'[31] *Kalyan* had to accept its mistake.

Every now and then, there would be objections to claims made by contributors. Viyogi Hari, a founding member of the Hindi Vidyapith, Hindi Sahitya Sammelan activist and close confidant of freedom fighter Purushottam Das Tandon, objected to Bhakt Ramsharan Das's style of reiterating that his article told a true story. Viyogi Hari, who had himself taken sanyas in 1921 and given up his real name Hariprasad Dwivedi (he later became an active member of the Bhoodan movement),[32] wrote to Poddar: 'What does it prove by writing repeatedly that it is a true story?'[33] Viyogi Hari was a regular contributor to *Kalyan* in its early days, having contributed thirteen articles between 1927 and 1933. Poddar would, however, regret the transformation in Viyogi Hari: 'Don't know if he has become an atheist. But he has definitely changed.'[34]

The 1935 *Yoga Ank* also had an article on Dharam Das as the spiritual leader of Kabirpanthis (followers of Kabir). It was pointed out by the Kabirpanthis of the United Provinces that Dharam Das was a resident of Bandho village near Jabalpur and had two sons, Narayan Das and Chudamani Das, who were the leading disciples of the Kabir sampraday but were grihastas (householders or family men). The Kabirpanthis of the United Provinces said a disciple of the two brothers, Gopal Das, was the head of Kabir's seat in Kashi (now Banaras). Poddar published this information and apologized for having hurt the sentiments of the Kabirpanthis.[35]

Kalyan also could not escape allegations of plagiarism. An article on alchemy in the 1940 *Sadhana Ank* (Issue on Meditation) by Narayan Damodar Shastri was alleged to 'be a verbatim translation' of certain sentences and paragraphs from a Gujarati book *Yoginikumari*, Part I, by the late Chhotalal Jivanlal, editor of *Mahakal*. The complainant wanted to know how the writer of the article and editor of *Kalyan* 'propose to rectify the said trespass of our rights at an early date'.[36] In

1960, an article on Lord Krishna by Mangal Dev Shastri Aryopadesh was challenged by one Jagdish Chaturvedi as having been plagiarized from his article that had appeared in the journal *Ved Prakash*. In its defence, *Kalyan* said it had not seen the article in *Ved Prakash*, but it apologized to Chaturvedi: 'No editor is omniscient to know if an article is original or lifted. Anyway we apologize to the original writer. It is a shameful act. We request Mangal Dev not to repeat such acts in future. He should also apologize to the writer of the original article.'[37]

In 1960, *Kalyan* was thirty-four years old, firmly established and immensely popular across the Hindi heartland. Writing for the journal was considered prestigious. A devious mind even exploited this success to his advantage. Gita Press started receiving letters from Delhi, Chhindwara and other places that one Balram Sharma of Indore who claimed to be an astrologer and a contributor to *Kalyan* was duping people. *Kalyan* had to clarify that their writer Balram Sharma was not Indore-based but from Rae Bareli, and appealed to its readers not to fall prey to such tricksters.[38]

While instances of plagiarism and misrepresentation are not uncommon in the life of a journal or publishing house, the ignominy of a sex scandal was a different matter. In late 1927, when *Kalyan* was only a year old, its father organization Gobind Bhawan would witness one of the seamiest sex scandals of the first half of the twentieth century, shaking the Marwari community across India.

A section of the fast-growing space of Hindi journals led the campaign, not only exposing the scandal but raising questions about the private world of Marwaris, of men engrossed in business and profit, and women left to the care of servants, attendants and god-men like Hiralal Goyanka (to whom Goyandka had handed over the reins of Gobind Bhawan in the early 1920s), resulting in them becoming victims of sexual predators.

The weekly *Hindu Panch* was relentless in its coverage of the issue. For weeks it raised questions about the silence of Marwari-run newspapers and journals, and the community's attempt to put a lid on the scandal and let Goyanka go unpunished. While Poddar came out unscathed, Goyandka could not deny his association either with Gobind Bhawan or his handpicked man, Hiralal Goyanka, who had even written for *Kalyan* in the first two years in a moralistic and high-sounding tone. *Hindu Panch* equated Goyandka and Goyanka as 'brothers' with a 'strange past'. Goyandka had started out as a cloth merchant in Bankura and had become an expert on the Gita, claiming divine powers as 'god had entered him'.[39] This bolstered his image among the Marwaris of Calcutta who helped in the establishment of Gobind Bhawan. *Hindu Panch* stated that even while Goyandka was at the helm of Gobind Bhawan, rumours had begun about the place being a den of decadence, and the daily *Swatantra* had even carried some cartoons depicting this, but to no avail. When Hiralal took command and proclaimed himself an impersonation of God, more Marwari women began flocking to Gobind Bhawan, attending his lectures and showering him with the love reserved for gods. This included eating food left over by Hiralal, and drinking the water in which they had washed his feet.

The prestigious Hindi journal *Chand* came out with a special issue on Marwaris in November 1929, talking about their philanthropy and their private life in equal measure. Questioning the virility of Marwari men, *Chand* depicted a highly immoral world where the sexual desires of Marwari women were fulfilled at home by close male relatives or domestic help, and by religious men outside.

According to *Chand*, Hiralal (now called Bhaktraj) had become an expert on the Gita and his sermons were day-long affairs. He had won the confidence of Marwari men with his campaign against sending Marwari women to Muslim shamans for treatment of infertility. As his popularity grew, Hiralal added raslila (enactment of the dalliance of Krishna with gopis) to his sermons, with himself in the role of Lord Krishna and the women devotees as his gopis. Abetted by a few close women aides, Hiralal found easy prey among these devotees who so believed in his divine qualities that they would wear his photograph in amulets round their necks.[40]

Without mentioning the date, *Hindu Panch* said Hiralal's exploits were first brought to light in Rishikesh where Goyandka had gone to give a religious discourse. Even as he was holding forth on ways of achieving salvation, a widow in the audience stood up to ask him what was the way out of a pregnancy for which Bhaktraj was responsible. Her revelation caused a major storm in Rishikesh, with many other similar cases coming to the fore. Newspapers took up the issue and came out with special supplements. Realizing that the matter was getting out of hand, Goyandka went to Calcutta to hold a meeting.[41]

In his statement, Goyandka admitted he had been aware of certain wrongdoings in Gobind Bhawan but had chosen to ignore them as he considered Hiralal a man of integrity. Goyandka said that when he had come to know about women worshipping Hiralal's photograph, 'I had objected to it in strong words but women continued to worship him.'[42] He further stated that non-cooperation with Hiralal would be the best punishment for his sins. 'Hiralal should go to a place of pilgrimage, make his body suffer and never show his face to people.' Goyandka cautioned his own followers who believed him to be an avatar (incarnation) of God: 'I have said so many times, I am neither God nor a beneficent human being. God and such a human are flawless. I am not.' He was also reported to have requested the husbands of the women victims to forgive their wives since they had surrendered themselves before Hiralal out of ignorance and genuine belief that he was an incarnation of God.[43]

No police case was registered against Hiralal who disappeared from Calcutta. *Hindu Panch* said the incident was not only shameful for Marwaris but for all Hindus. 'Why is no Marwari child demanding the arrest of Hiralal Goyanka? What shame. Why are sanatanis and reformists not exhibiting their power and intelligence? A community that should have been outraged and gouged out the eyes of whoever looked at an Aryan woman is not in the least bothered about the loss of their modesty.'[44] The weekly demanded that Gobind Bhawan be handed over to the Hindu Mahasabha, 'which would be some atonement for the sin'.

Hindu Panch took to task newspapers and community elders like Jamnalal Bajaj and G.D. Birla who wanted to put a lid on the incident. Uncomfortable with the media campaign against Marwaris and their philanthropic initiatives, Birla had already written to Gandhi's associate Mahadev Desai about how 'local vernacular papers and magazines were full of dirty literature . . . It has become difficult for one to allow young boys and girls to read such Hindi papers.'[45] Birla alleged the incident was being used by many journals to 'blackmail' community leaders. He also sent Desai a copy of *Hindu Panch* of the week ended 17 May 1928 that not only devoted many pages to the Hiralal episode but even alleged the involvement of a lady teacher in a school run by Birla, and others, as accomplices in the sex scandal: '. . . the paper has tried to vilify a girls' school which is being conducted by some of us here. Of course, every word written in it is false. The sole object of the editor of the paper is to harm the institution.' Birla wondered 'whether it would not be advisable if Gandhiji put in a word or two in *Navjivan*'.

Gandhi wrote immediately in *Navjivan*. In the issue of 24 May 1928, *Hindu Panch* reproduced the article and *Kalyan* carried it with a footnote from Poddar that thanked the Mahatma for his article and stated that Gita Press and *Kalyan* had always stood for selfless devotion to God and had warned devotees about the consequences of misusing God's name.[46] Hiralal was condemned as 'that worker' and advised to take resort to God and atone for his sins. The gist of Gandhi's article was that it was 'a regrettable incident but does not surprise me', as there were people all around who used religion for material and physical ends. 'Those who think the name of Rama would help them get over their imperfections and desires are always successful. But those who use the name of Rama to further their physical passion are doomed.' He also advised women never to worship a living person: 'No living person can be called ideal. Those considered good today have turned out to be evil later. Therefore, God is worshipped. If you want to worship a human being, do that after he is dead. Worship is about devotion to qualities, not form.'[47]

Gandhi's words had no effect on *Hindu Panch* that had taken upon itself the task of protecting the interests of sanatan Hindu dharma, whether from the rot within or from the external Muslim threat. The journal particularly condemned the conspiracy of silence within the media in Calcutta and the attempt by the Marwari leadership to brush the Hiralal episode under the carpet. It pointed out how *The Statesman* had criticized Hiralal but left out Gobind Bhawan while *Vishwamitra* had stopped accepting any article about the episode. It also bemoaned the 'false campaign by Marwaris against monthly *Chand* and its special publication *Ablaon Ka Insaf* (Justice for Women)'.[48] In a scathing attack on reformists and the media world, writer Satyadev Vidyalankar further argued that the Hiralal episode should have been used to usher in reforms. The job of the media, he said, giving instances of the role played by it in the USA against slavery and by writers like Tolstoy before the Russian Revolution, was to ensure that truth does not perish. 'Editors should be able to create a feeling of anger and hatred against such incidents in the minds of the readers.'

In the face of this attack, Gita Press and *Kalyan* did something surprising. A full-page advertisement was placed in the 21 June 1928 issue of *Hindu Panch* asking readers to book the *Bhakta Ank* (Issue on Devotees), the annual number of *Kalyan* in its third year. The advertisement carried statements by Mahavir Prasad Dwivedi and Gauri Shankar Hirachand Ojha praising *Kalyan*'s contribution to the Hindu religion and to Hindi. The advertisement appeared for two consecutive weeks but was not enough to buy peace, as *Hindu Panch* continued to serialize '*Vyabhichar Mandir*' (Temple of Immorality), an article on Gobind Bhawan.

The high-profile sex scandal in Calcutta had its repercussions in far-off Gorakhpur on the functioning of Gita Press and *Kalyan*. Mahavir Prasad Poddar, who had been a key person managing the affairs of Gita Press, quit soon after news of the scandal broke.[49] A Gandhian and an important figure in Gorakhpur, he had never got along with Hanuman Prasad Poddar; however, Mahavir Prasad seems to have renewed his relationship with Gita Press later. In 1937, the United Provinces government appointed him along with Baba Raghav Das as non-official visitors to Gorakhpur jail for a period of one year,[50] and in the records, Mahavir Prasad Poddar's address is that of Gita Press.

The scandal had scarred Hanuman Prasad Poddar as well. He admitted to his close aide Gambhirchand Dujari, who also faced allegations of moral turpitude, that many people had turned away from Gita Press out of disappointment. He warned Dujari to be careful as 'these are bad times and anything can happen'.[51] Poddar had also advised Dujari earlier to come to Gorakhpur alone and leave his wife with his mother: 'I have no desire to allow any woman in Gita Vatika (Poddar's office-cum-residence).'[52]

As such, Gita Press dealt with the controversy by brazening it out. The public outcry, media campaign and moral questions were met with silence and total disengagement. The fact that the scandal had taken place in Calcutta helped Gita Press to maintain a distance, even if Goyandka could never wash off the stigma.

The irony was that, a few months before news of the Hiralal sex scandal broke, *Kalyan* had severely criticized *Hindu Panch* for carrying an article eulogizing Lord Krishna's uncle Kamsa, who had killed the earlier children of his sister Devaki and had tried to kill Krishna as well. In his editorial comment, Poddar said it was heart-wrenching to read such an article by a Hindu denigrating Lord Krishna whose name 'is uttered by every Hindu child', and further that 'it is a misfortune of Hinduism that such writers gain in stature'.[53] He also referred to a little-known book *Hindustan Na Devo* (Gods of Hindustan) by a European lady, translated by an Indian, which 'heaped abuse on Lord Krishna'. Poddar lamented the new genre of book review and literary criticism that gave credence to such writings. However, he gave the benefit of the doubt to his friend Ramlal Varma, editor of *Hindu Panch*, for having made a mistake out of ignorance. Poddar said Varma had already regretted the article, calling it worse than death, and had printed two supplementary pages that had been dispatched to subscribers with a request that they burn the earlier article. While Poddar wrote that 'Varma has done the right thing', he also suggested that the editor make special amends by reciting God's name.

Popularizing the Gita

Even at the height of the storm created by the Hiralal episode, Gita Press did not lose sight of its 'save the sanatan dharma' mission. *Kalyan*, of course, was the main vehicle but it was not sufficient—there was need for its readers to be actively involved in the mission. Two important initiatives were taken with this in mind: in 1929, Gita Examination Committees were set up to spread knowledge of the text throughout the country, followed by the Gita Society in 1934 for further propagation of the text.

No Indian publishing house so far had donned the mantle of moral, religious and spiritual activist and pedagogue. Both Goyandka and Poddar considered the Gita an impartial, meaningful religious text without parallel in the world. As Monika Freier states, they wanted the Gita to be 'made accessible to a broad audience who could read the translations in their own mother tongue, but also rely on the interpretation offered simultaneously'.[54] Goyandka's translation of the Gita helped it become a 'central religious text for a Hindi-speaking audience'. Freier observes that the duo were against 'the metaphorical reading' of the Gita; for them the text was 'a faithful reproduction of the dialogue between Lord Krishna and the epic hero Arjuna right before the great battle of Mahabharata'—not an 'allegory but the ultimate gospel'. She further describes how, in order to deal with passages of the Gita that needed further interpretation after translation, Poddar and Goyandka brought out pamphlets on 'religious and social questions' that 'translated the scriptures into guidelines for everyday practices'.

While hard-selling the concept of Gita examinations, Poddar vehemently argued that it was through the study of the Gita and imbibing its values that a person could achieve salvation even while engaged in worldly pursuits.[55] He believed that the Gita alone had the solution to the social, political and religious degradation of India caught in colonial rule. He traced the nation's inertia to it having strayed from the path of the Gita. 'What does one say of the Gita? It is the personification of God. Therefore, it should be popularized in each household and taught in each school. By simply relying on Gita one can learn to be responsible.'

The idea of Gita Examination Committees was conceived on 1 July 1927 in Barhaj. Situated on the banks of the River Sarayu, in Uttar Pradesh's Deoria district, Barhaj is the birthplace of Deoraha Baba, considered by his devotees as an avatar of Hanuman.[56] Politician-sadhu Baba Raghav Das also built his ashram in Barhaj. Both Deoraha Baba and Raghav Das were among the large number of religious personalities who wrote for *Kalyan* and supported Gita Press. Touted as the Gandhi of the eastern districts, Baba Raghav Das, a Maharashtrian brahmin who had come to Deoria in spiritual quest after his entire family died of cholera,[57] was the convenor of the Gita examinations. (Post-Independence, the Congress successfully pitted him against Acharya Narendra Dev of the Congress Socialist Party in the assembly election from the Faizabad constituency.)

In the Barhaj meeting, the syllabus for the Gita tests was prepared and sent all over the country. It was also decided to conduct the tests on 5 November and declare the result a month later. Despite the paucity of time, examination centres were established in Rajasthan's Churu and Ratangarh; Bada Rajpur and Ara (Bihar); Barhaj, Ghusi, Basantpur, Mahuadabar, Pakardiha, Kubernath, Padrauna and Tamkuhi (all in Gorakhpur district); Banaras and Ghazipur. Outside the Hindi heartland, the Gita Dharma Mandal of Poona approved the syllabus and examination system and even set up two test centres at Poona and Miraj and translated the course material into Marathi. Only seventeen students took the Marathi test but G.V. Kelkar, head of the Gita Dharma Mandal, promised more students would appear from the next year.

In the Hindi region, twenty-two students appeared for the second-level Madhyama test and 170 for the first-level Prathama test. Drawing on his strong network, Poddar created a prestigious board of examiners that included himself, Goyandka and big names of the Hindi literary world like Makhan Lal Chaturvedi, editor, *Karmayog*, Khandwa; Baburao Vishnu Paradkar, editor, *Aaj*, Kashi; Laxman Narayan Garde, editor, *Krishna Sandesh*, Calcutta; Ramdas Gaur, author of *Hindutva*, the one-volume encyclopaedia published in 1938, and among the earliest to write scientific articles;[58] Gaurishankar Mishra of Banaras; and Swami Sachchidanand Maharaj of Gorakhpur. Seventeen of the twenty-two students cleared the Madhyama test and eighty-three of the 170 passed Prathama. Madhyama and Prathama toppers Shiv Prasad of Churu and Ambika of Ghazipur, respectively, were given silver medals and cash prizes of Rs 24 and Rs 16. Cash incentives of smaller amounts (Rs 2–5) were given to other successful candidates.[59]

Taking its role of 'religious pedagogue'[60] seriously, Gita Press formalized the rules of the Gita examination in the next few months. It was decided that, instead of two, there would be three tests—Prathama for beginners, Madhyama for mid-level students and Uttama for the highest level. Tests were to be conducted in the month of September and the results would appear in *Kalyan* after three months. Centres were to be established in places with a small post office and where there were at least sixteen candidates appearing for the test. The test fee was waived for female candidates, while male candidates had to pay a nominal amount. To get a first division in Uttama and Madhyama tests a candidate had to score an aggregate 65 per cent or more, for a second division 50 per cent or more was required, and to pass in third division a student had to get a minimum of 40 per cent. In case of the Prathama test, a candidate had to get 60 per cent for a first division, 45 per cent for a second division and 34 per cent to pass in third division. Candidates could request re-evaluation of their papers within a month of declaration of the results; answer sheets were to be retained in the Gita test office for six months.[61] The examination committee also reserved the right to let students who had not cleared Prathama sit for the Madhyama test.

News about the Gita tests appeared in issues of *Kalyan*, on one occasion correcting the first year's results and even arguing for a truncated test that would fetch candidates a certificate. In 1939, *Kalyan* claimed that Gandhi had endorsed the Gita tests: 'A gentleman who is a great lover of the Gita asked Gandhi's permission to take Gita tests. The gentleman wrote that Gandhi wanted parts of the Gita to be incorporated in the school syllabus as a compulsory subject. Gandhi was also of the view that the Gita test committee should make memorizing the text part of its rules.'[62]

Not content with the Gita tests as a tool to prepare a critical mass of people well versed in the tenets of the text, in 1934 Gita Press started the Gita Society 'for the propagation of Gita literature here as well as abroad and to popularise it amongst schools and colleges of India and other countries, so that people of different faiths, while adhering to their own religions, may mould their lives according to the teachings of the Gita'.[63]

Poddar's network once again came in handy as leading public figures throughout the country lent their name to the venture. Sir Manmatha Nath Mukherjee, a judge at the Calcutta High Court, was president of the Gita Society. Considered close to Hindu Mahasabha, Mukherjee was one of the three names recommended by Veer Savarkar for membership of the Viceroy's War Council in 1940, along with B.S. Moonje and Syama Prasad Mookerjee.[64] Earlier, Mukherjee had made a name in the celebrated case related to *Anand Bazar Patrika*. The paper had come under the scrutiny of the dreaded Indian Press

(Emergency Powers) Act that caused a vernacular newspaper to forfeit its deposit if it published anything against the government. Mukherjee and the other Indian judge, Sarat Kumar Ghosh, had set aside the order of forfeiture.[65]

Baba Raghav Das, now at the helm of the Gita tests, was made secretary of the Gita Society. Members of the Society were drawn from all walks of life—politics, academics and business—and even included non-Hindus. Among others, there was Syama Prasad Mookerjee, then vice chancellor of Calcutta University; S. Radhakrishnan, vice chancellor of Andhra University; industrialist turned right-wing politician Jugal Kishore Birla; historian Radha Kumud Mookerji; Sir Badridas Goenka, the first Indian chairperson of the Imperial Bank of India (1933); Gouri Shankar Goenka who was involved in an intense legal battle over the reduction of share capital of Marwari Stores Private Ltd.,[66] and Krishnalal M. Jhaveri, ex-chief justice, Bombay High Court and author of *The Present State of Gujarati Literature* written in English.[67] Taraporewala even wrote to Poddar suggesting the names of six people who could be requested to become members of Gita Society: K. Dadachandji, author of *Light of the Avesta and Gathas*; industrialist Mavji Govindji Seth; R.P. Bakshi, principal of Anandilal Poddar High School, Santa Cruz, Bombay; Khurshed S. Dabu, principal of the Parsi Orphanage, Surat; theosophist and writer K.J.B. Wadia; and Hirendra Nath Datta, an attorney from Calcutta.

An equally formidable list of people supported the venture from the outside, including Madan Mohan Malaviya, Sanskrit scholar Gopinath Kaviraj, Carmichael professor of ancient history and culture at Calcutta University Devdatta Ramakrishna Bhandarkar, and Sadhu Thanwardas Lilaram Vaswani, founder of the Mira movement in education and the Sadhu Vaswani Mission (also a regular writer in *Kalyan*).

Among foreign scholars, F. Otto Schrader, former director of the Adyar Library, Madras, and professor of divinity at the University of Kiel, Germany, who was already a known name to *Kalyan* readers, agreed to join the Gita Society. But the most enthusiastic was Ernest P. Hortwitz of Hunter College, New York, who found the Gita Society a 'fine and feasible idea'.[68] Hortwitz was no ordinary Gitaphile. He had taught the text in Hunter College for twelve years 'as part of world literature' and was convinced 'no world scripture teaches more clearly and sublimely self-realisation and cosmic consciousness than Gita, which is a unique platform where all the major and minor creeds of the whole universe can seek and cooperate for the advancement of the world's spiritual culture'. With Hitler ruling Germany, Hortwitz talked of how the Nazis were 'deeply impressed by the heroic aspect of the Gita, represented by the kshatriyas, those dauntless defenders of *advaita*'. Addressing Poddar as brother, Hortwitz said he was off to the Pacific coast, Portland or Seattle, but would not mind sparing time for the Gita, though it would not be possible to help the initiative financially. 'But wherever I stay if you have friends and supporters in that place, who would like to establish a Gita Society branch or Gita class, I shall only be too happy—if you want it—to conduct it.'

On the other hand, there were some who declined to be a part of the Gita Press pedagogy. Firoze C. Davar, a plain-speaking Parsi writer with strong views on religious identity, declined membership of the Gita Society in 1934: 'I am a man of very limited means. By that account I have refrained from becoming a member of some worthy Zoroastrian societies, which I think, in fairness, must have a prior claim over me.'[69] Davar also talked of being 'innocent of Sanskrit' and though, he said, he admired Hinduism, particularly the Gita, he was 'but a very indifferent student of the same . . . This is not mere mock-modesty on my part nor a pretext to evade future trouble.'

The secretary of leading industrialist Sir Purshottamdas Thakurdas wrote on his behalf regretting 'inability to comply with the request'.[70] Eminent Sanskrit scholar Sir Ganganath Jha also opted out on the ground that his health did not permit him to add to his activities and he did not 'relish the idea of being a sleeping member of any society'.[71] Edwin Greaves of the London Missionary Society and an established figure of Banaras's literary world, having authored a book on Hindi grammar, wrote for *Kalyan* but was circumspect about the Gita Society. Greaves said he could not 'pretend' to understand the Gita and 'in the second place so far as I do understand the general outlook taken I do not agree with it. The conception of the meaning of life, its conditions and purpose as unfolded in the Gita, differs widely from those which commend themselves to me as the soundest and the best.'[72]

And then there was Ragbans Kishore Balbir from an elite kayastha family of Delhi, studying philosophy in St Stephen's College. For his age, Balbir expressed unusual anguish about people's ignorance of their religion. He asked how any 'gentleman of today, gentleman in the most modern sense, can very easily claim to be an atheist'. Having read many translations of the Gita, Balbir had concluded that the text was the sole path to self-realization and could well be the sole marker of nationalism: 'If every Hindu, Muslim, or Christian takes up this principle and begins to realize himself, we can very easily get Swaraj, we can easily get that Independence for which we all have been trying for so long'.[73] Balbir suggested two people who could help further the cause of the Gita Society, Rai Sahib Azmat Singh, headmaster of Sanskrit High School and Professor N.V. Thadani, principal of Hindu College. Of course, he offered to do 'any work, any service' himself. Curiously, this very Balbir, the passionate youth worried about spiritual decay and elusive Swaraj, was on the list of people awarded 'honours, decorations and medals' by the British Empire in 1947, the year the elusive Swaraj became a reality.[74]

In the troubled aftermath of Independence and Partition, Gita Press came up with the Shri Gita-Ramayana Prachar Sangh (Gita-Ramayana Propagation Society), asking people to recite the two texts in a regimented fashion for peace, succour and tranquillity. Simultaneously, it was decided to revive the Bhagwan naam jap introduced in *Kalyan*'s first year. Since it was a Gita Press initiative, a general appeal was not enough; it had to be formalized and turned into collective action in mission mode. In a well-publicized statement, Poddar talked of widespread disturbance, oppression and pain.[75] In such a situation, he said, it was important for the peace and welfare of our motherland India and the entire world, that people should resort to the naam jap as had been done in 1926. Again, there were none of the strict sanatan dharma restrictions of gender, caste or age; everyone was asked to participate in the chanting. While women were allowed to chant Hare Ram during menstruation, they were asked not to use tulsi (sacred basil) beads to keep count. Instead, they could use wooden beads. The duration of this chanting mission was from 16 November 1948 to 13 April 1949. Participants had to report their chanting count to the Naam Jap Vibhag of Gita Press.

The rules of Shri Gita-Ramayana Prachar Sangh were more elaborate.[76] Membership of the Sangh was open to anyone—disregarding barriers of caste, class and gender—who believed in the tenets of the two texts. Applicants for membership were expected to fill in forms; those members who could get others to join would be made associates. Monitoring of the membership was to be done through two departments dealing with the Gita and the Ramayana.

Four kinds of membership were on offer for the Gita department. The first included those who read the entire Gita (eighteen chapters) once every day, i.e., 365 times in a year. The second type of members could finish all the chapters over two days, and the complete text 180 times in a year. The third category of members read six chapters in a day, thus reading the Gita 120 times in a year. The last category of members could read as much of the Gita as they wished daily as long as they completed at least forty-two readings in a year. Members were also advised to devote an hour daily to observe the teachings of the Gita.

It was expected that a member of the Ramayana department would read Tulsidas's text twice a year. Gita Press's insistence on the *Ramcharitmanas* of Tulsidas and not any other version was with good reason—promotion of the 1938 *Manas Ank* of *Kalyan*. Poddar had realized early on that for a religious publishing house aspiring to become the sole mouthpiece of sanatan Hindu dharma it was important to make texts like the Gita and Ramayana available to the public at low prices. He had issued an 'appeal for manuscripts of Ramayana in the hope of obtaining a complete one in Tulsi's own hand'.[77] Receiving no positive response, Poddar with the help of Anjaninandan Sharan, a scholar-sadhu of Ayodhya, 'began to assemble an edition based on the oldest available manuscripts'. After working for years, the annual issue of *Kalyan* devoted to *Ramcharitmanas* was published in 1938. The 900-page *Manas Ank* was considered a 'milestone in popular Hindi publishing'. 'Lavishly illustrated with specially commissioned paintings embellished with gold and protected by waxed slipsheets, it looked less like a journal than like a family heirloom.' It contained a 'verse-by-verse prose translation by Poddar, as well as extensive front and back matter'. The very first print run was of 40,600 copies and by late 1983 a total of 5,695,000 copies had been printed, a record unparalleled in the world of Indian publishing. In time, pocket-size versions of the *Ramcharitmanas* were brought out by Gita Press.[78]

Manas Ank's impact was far-reaching. The doyen of ancient history at the University of Madras, K.A. Nilakanta Sastri, had no direct contact with Poddar, but S.S. Suryanarayana Sastri of the university's department of Indian philosophy wrote on his behalf: 'The first part containing Tulsi Das' Ramacaritamanasa is so valuable that there is a special demand for it from my friend K.A. Nilakanta Sastri of the Indian History department.'[79] Poddar immediately obliged.

One could become a member of both Gita and Ramayana departments of the Shri Gita-Ramayana Prachar Sangh, but had to be sure to read the texts oneself, after a bath. However, if one was unwell or travelling there was no need to take a bath—reading was more important. During menstruation, women members were advised not to touch the text but to request someone else to read it out to them. Gita Press also made it clear that members would not be given free copies of the Ramayana or the Gita.

Meanwhile, individual efforts related to the Gita, whether translations or fresh commentaries, were being sent to the Gita Press for endorsement. For instance, in 1939 a request was sent to Gita Press to publish a Marwari translation of the Gita with commentary by Gulab Chand Nagori, that, it was said, would not only help in the development of the language but would be beneficial to less-educated Marwaris, especially women, who would be able to read the text easily.[80]

Over the years, as Gita Press gained a reputation as the country's biggest religious publishing house, even the Indian Army would request it for free copies of the Gita to present to jawans at the end of their training. The request in the 1960s was for an average of 1,000 copies every year of the Gita in 'Hindi script without commentary'.[81] Gita Press's response is not known, but it aggressively pushed pocket-sized Gitas for free publicity. Helping the army would have suited its ideological belief in a strong nation.

In 1967, a year after the army's request, the Indian government sought the assistance of Gita Press. As part of the preparations to celebrate Gandhi's birth centenary in 1969, Deputy Prime Minister Morarji Desai proposed that documentaries be made on Gandhi and the Gita. S.N. Mangal of the Indian Cultural Defence Council, an organization set up with the help of Jana Sangh and Omkarmal Saraf, Poddar's comrade in the Rodda Arms case and 'promoter of the short-lived Calcutta Industrial Bank',[82] was approached. Mangal consulted Poddar who called the Gita documentary proposal 'revolutionary' and referred him to spiritual gurus for further guidance. Mangal said the documentary would cost Rs 10 lakh but this could be brought down if he (Poddar) helped.[83]

Kalyana-Kalpataru

Poddar regularly sent out issues of *Kalyan* to selected scholars and religious leaders abroad who were doing their bit for the cause of sanatan dharma; however a need was felt to reach out to the non-Hindi-speaking public, especially the Hindu diaspora in the West, and in former plantation outposts like Mauritius, Trinidad and African countries. Thus was launched the English-language journal *Kalyana-Kalpataru* in 1934.

The Western world's relationship with Indian spirituality and scholarship was built through 'the availability of the Indian classics and the commentaries and histories being written by the Orientalist scholar-bureaucrats and missionaries'.[84] Mauritius, on the other hand, with a large population of Indians whose forefathers had gone as plantation workers, was witnessing an identity crisis of two kinds—Hindu–Muslim fragmentation on the one hand, and Tamil self-assertion on the other. An assertive 'Hindi-speaking Hindu elite' had floated the idea of Chhota Bharat and matters came to a flashpoint in 1935 when this group celebrated the 'centenary of the beginning of Indian immigration', creating a clear division between the post-abolition (1835) Indian population, originating mainly from Bihar, and of Indians who had come much earlier, mainly from the French *comptoirs* (trading posts) in south India.[85]

The launch of *Kalyana-Kalpataru* helped Gita Press in its attempt to don the mantle of being the sole spokesperson for the Hindu cause. Scholars or spiritual seekers, everyone knocked on the doors of Gita Press. Within a year of *Kalyana-Kalpataru*'s launch, Gita Press could feel the change.

Cultural philosopher Tarachand Roy, teaching in Berlin, 'serving the cause of my motherland', asked for a regular supply of books, *Kalyan* and even Poddar's photograph to be used as 'a slide in my lectures on India and her culture'.[86] Impressed with cheap editions of the Quran being distributed free, Roy asked if Gita Press could also bring out an English edition of the Gita for free distribution in Europe. He even suggested seeking help from 'well-known Hindu families and Rajas'. Roy was also instrumental in Poddar's contacting of leading Indologists like Helmuth von Glassenapp, W. Kirfel, Ludwig Alsdorf and Ernst Waldschmidt.

The English journal had several readers in India as well. One of them, G.A. Bernand, an employee of American Express in Calcutta, wrote with many requests, from publication of an illustrated *Yoga Ank* in English to help with finding someone who had 'practiced Tantrik yoga, especially pranayam and kundalini yoga' and could help him in this art.[87]

One of the biggest patrons of Gita Press and *Kalyana-Kalpataru* was Shanti Sadan of London. Established in 1929 by Hari Prasad Shastri of Bareilly, Shanti Sadan claimed to have introduced Adhyatma Yoga (yoga of self-knowledge) in Britain. Before settling down in London, Shastri had taught in Japan and in China where he befriended Sun Yat-sen and lived for eleven years translating Buddhist classics, supervising translation of the Quran into Chinese and the works of Confucius into Hindi.[88] Inspired by *Kalyana-Kalpataru,* Shastri had introduced 'repetition of the sacred mantram *Hare Ram*' in Shanti Sadan and asked his close aide Uttama Devi to inform Poddar about it and thank him.[89] *Kalyana-Kalpataru* had suspended publication in 1942 due to short supply of newsprint and when it resumed after a year, Uttama Devi wrote to Poddar about resuming her subscription as well as those of two friends Ms Robley and Mrs Barnard. 'A great deal of use is made of the *Kalyana* by our groups, who appreciate it enormously. We are very glad that it has been possible to produce it again,' she wrote to Poddar.[90]

Kalyana-Kalpataru's year-long suspension evoked disappointed reactions among several of its patrons. Subscriber Louise Wilding on getting the news wrote: 'The English speaking section of your readers will experience a loss by the stopping of your English publication.'[91]

She also asked that the copy of her husband H. Wilding's book *Cosmos* loaned to Gita Press for carrying an extract be returned immediately, promising to send the book again when publication was resumed. Louise told Poddar it was important that *Kalyana-Kalpataru* should start again as it 'breathes the very spirit of India'—'That spirit, which we believe, will come as a rejuvenating force for the whole world, when India shall realize her full significance in the world's life.'[92]

Premel El Adaros, later Swami Brahmavidya, and founder of the Society of Transcendent Science in Chicago, was a friend of Poddar. He had plans to popularize *Kalyana-Kalpataru* as well as other publications of Gita Press in the United States and was saddened by the news of the suspension. However, by the time Adaros wrote to Gita Press, publication of *Kalyana-Kalpataru* had resumed. Adaros requested regular supply of *Kalyana-Kalpataru* as well as other publications. He said sending him these 'would be well worth your while as we could besides paying you for same, the costs, add extra as a gift for your time, trouble and trust'.[93]

The life story of Henry Thomas Hamblin from Sussex was similar to Poddar's in many respects. Born into a poor family, Hamblin became a successful optician by dint of hard work and dedication. But Poddar-like 'visionary experiences where he came in contact with a divine presence'[94] turned him into a mystic. He started the instantly successful magazine, *The Science of Thought Review*, which was based on the principle of 'Applied Right Thinking'. Poddar and Hamblin corresponded in the mid-1940s. Hamblin was aware and appreciative of *Kalyan*. Poddar had ordered many books from Hamblin, but some of them were out of print as the government had put restrictions on the use of paper that was in short supply. Hamblin sent the available books at half the price and even bore the postage.[95]

Growing irreligiosity among people bothered Hamblin too. He wrote to Poddar of how in post-war Britain 'churches are becoming empty, except the Roman Catholic, and their people of course accept all the old Theology and Doctrine and Dogma . . . They swallow it all whole, like a fish swallows a bait. Although there are thinkers among them, their followers are generally gullible people.' Hamblin believed that 'materialism has reached its limit in this country and now the tide has turned'.[96]

Jean Herbert, a high-profile French Indologist who was among the founders of the interpretation service in the United Nations, travelled to India and other parts of Asia in search of knowledge on Buddhism and Hinduism. He took to *Kalyana-Kalpataru* in a big way, translating two of its articles for his mammoth *Mélanges sur l'Inde* (Vignettes from India). Herbert told Poddar that, for his next book on Hindu spirituality, *La Mythologie Hindoue, Son Message*, he had quoted *Kalyana-Kalpataru* 'with full references and acknowledgement about 50 times'.[97] The war years had resulted in irregular delivery of the journal in Europe and Herbert hoped its circulation would rise once normalcy was restored, as it was 'gradually becoming known in France'.

As *Kalyana-Kalpataru*'s reach and impact spread through the Western world, Gita Press was approached with all kinds of requests. W.D. Padfield, based in Delhi, wrote to the editor on behalf of her friend in Paris, a reader of *Kalyana-Kalpataru* who had gone through a 'few articles on authentic cases of re-incarnation' and urgently requested 'relevant back numbers'.[98] When Y.G. Torres, a Mexican girl, came to India on a scholarship to study Indian culture at Delhi University, her Indian contact Krishna Dutt Bharadwaj, a teacher in Modern School, wrote to Poddar on her behalf requesting a subscription to *Kalyana-Kalpataru*. Bharadwaj mentioned that Torres had decided to turn vegetarian during her stint in India.[99]

Within India, *Kalyana-Kalpataru* attracted the attention of Sri Chitra Central Hindu Religious Library, Trivandrum, when it decided to launch a religious quarterly *Chaitra Prabha* under the auspices of the Devasom department, for the uplift and promulgation of the Hindu religion. After the first issue of *Chaitra Prabha* came out on 12 November 1945, Temple Proclamation Day, the curator of the library wrote to Gita Press requesting 'general permission' to translate articles from *Kalyana-Kalpataru* for the 'benefit of the public in Travancore and outside'.[100]

Epic as a Journal: The Short Life of Mahabharata

In November 1955, Gita Press launched another monthly journal, *Mahabharata*, to be published for three years. In its first issue, Poddar's editorial comment, titled '*Namra Nivedan*' (Humble Submission), explained the rationale for a limited-period journal devoted exclusively to one religious text. He said there were many Hindi translations of the Mahabharata as well as commentaries on it, but all of them came separately and were expensive; the thirty-six issues of the journal would provide the complete original Sanskrit text and its Hindi translation.

In the inaugural issue, Poddar explained the Herculean task of putting together the Mahabharata because of the variation in texts prevalent in different parts of India. Referring to the evolution of the epic, Poddar said that over the centuries additions had been made that sometimes led to mutually contradictory contents. Even the complete and revised Mahabharata in over 89,000 verses brought out after years of research by the Bhandarkar Oriental Research Institute in Poona, in Poddar's opinion, could not be said to have been born out of consensus or to be true to the original.[101] After much deliberation Poddar decided to follow the commentary on the Mahabharata by Nilakantha Chaturdhar since it also included verses recited in south India. The job of translation was entrusted to Ram Narayan Dutt Shastri Pandey and Swami Akhandanand Maharaj. The annual subscription for *Mahabharata* was fixed at Rs 20, a fairly low price even in the mid-1950s.

The task of publishing the Sanskrit text and the Hindi translation was accomplished by the ninth issue of the third year, but it was decided to carry related articles on the Mahabharata as well as the procedure for reciting and listening to the text in the last three numbers. In the penultimate number, Gangashankar Mishra wrote a long essay on Western scholars' fascination with the Mahabharata, presenting an exhaustive account of works by scholars like Charles Lawson, Alfred Ludwig, Albrecht Weber, Ludwig von Schroder, Max Müller, Edward Washburn Hopkins and G.A. Grierson.

Poddar wrote in the final issue of *Mahabharata* that the entire effort of serializing the epic was part of Gita Press's larger objective of standardizing religious texts. He stated that the Mahabharata of Veda Vyasa had one lakh verses and these had been presented in the journal.[102] The Hindi translation was later issued in six volumes that are still in print.

The Annual Issues of Kalyan

In the more than eight decades of *Kalyan*'s life so far, nothing has been more meticulously planned than its annual numbers. Called *varshikank*, these issues have been vision documents for Gita Press, ready reckoners of Hindu identity and indicators of what is correct and what is wrong with Hindu society, culture, religion and even politics. In short, these annual issues have spearheaded the mission of Gita Press both in letter and in spirit.

What marks them out is not just their diverse choice subjects—from God, Cow and Hindu Culture to Woman, the Male Child, Education, Good Behaviour and Humanity, besides scores of issues exclusively devoted to the Ramayana, Mahabharata, Gita, Puranas, Upanishads, etc.—but also the manner in which traditions were 'invented' on each subject by Gita Press to 'establish continuity with a suitable historical past'. These traditions became a 'process of formalisation and ritualisation, characterized by reference to the past, if only by imposing repetition'.[103] Politically, such invention of Hindu traditions, both religious and cultural, became a tool for national integration and self-assertion.[104]

Considering the mammoth size of each annual issue, running into no less than 500 pages even during times of control on newsprint, planning had to begin at least six to eight months in advance. The topic would be decided by Poddar after long deliberations with scholars, sadhus and senior members of the editorial team. Then, Pandit Gopinath Kaviraj, a Sanskrit scholar in Banaras, was roped in to suggest various aspects of the subject on which articles could be sought as well as persons with domain knowledge. Poddar had two point persons in Banaras, Shivnath Dubey and Ram Narayan Dutt Shastri, who would work closely with Kaviraj to give final shape to the idea. Poddar had even arranged for someone from Bengal to take dictation from Kaviraj of his articles in Bengali.[105]

Kalyan would then publish the proposed contents list and Poddar would himself write a letter to important contributors explaining the theme and the rationale behind its selection. This printed letter of invitation for each year's annual issue begins with *Kalyan*'s circulation figure, which gives us an idea of the journal's steady rise. At the end of the sixth year of *Kalyan* in 1931, its circulation was 16,000.This grew to 27,500 by the end of the ninth year (1934), a more than 50 per cent rise in three years.

The letter for the *Hindu Sanskriti Ank* (1950) stated: '*Kalyan* is striking off over a hundred thousand copies each month', a figure that could 'have been easily double had we not been compelled to disappoint about twenty thousand prospective subscribers annually for the last three or four years'.[106] The objective of the issue would be to 'bring to light the true nature of Hindu culture, its wide range and influence, those who inspired and preserved it, its degeneration and the factors contributing to the same, how to revive it, in all its aspects—religion, politics, social organization, art and literature, etc.' Poddar also requested contributors or their friends to send any 'printed copy or manuscript of some old cultural or religious book, or some old painting or image' they might possess. He promised to return these after use.

Articles were solicited in Hindi as well as in English, Sanskrit, Bengali, Gujarati or Marathi, which would then be translated for *Kalyan*. Poddar claimed that 'people speaking different languages have started learning Hindi just to read *Kalyan*'.[107] His letters changed in tone and tenor according to the subject of the annual issue, and often made a passionate plea, citing various threats that the Hindu religion faced. The letter requesting articles for *Gau Ank* (1945)—unlike other annual editions it appeared in October and not in January—articulated the 'woeful predicament' the revered domestic animal faced. The annual issue, Poddar said, would discuss the subject of cow protection in all its aspects—religious, social, economic and scientific—as well as measures for the amelioration of the condition of cows.[108] Like the *Hindu Sanskriti Ank* five years later, *Gau Ank* had a print run of over 100,000 copies, though the number of pages was less than planned because of the tough paper control measures in force.

While working on an annual issue, Poddar and his team spent a lot of time and energy in research with the aim of highlighting the importance of the specific aspect of Hindu religion to which the issue was devoted. In *Gau Ank*, for instance, Poddar relied heavily on government statistics to make his point about the dwindling number of cows and by implication their waning importance in the life of Hindus and the threat cows faced from Muslims. The director of commercial intelligence and statistics in Calcutta and the director of farms in Simla were approached for statistics on dairy farms.[109] Sardar Bahadur Sir Datar Singh, cattle utilization adviser to the Government of India, was requested to provide lists of gaushalas (cow shelters) and pinjrapoles (homes for old cows) in various provinces and states.[110] Similar requests for information were made to individuals and organizations all over the country.[111]

To enhance the aesthetic and visual appeal of the issue, Poddar wrote to the secretary of the Imperial Council of Agricultural Research seeking photographs published in its bulletin and in *Indian Farming*.[112] Noted director V. Shantaram's Prabhat Film Company was asked to send stills from its 1939 production *Gopal Krishna*. Poddar promised to pay for the stills as demanded by the film company or return them after use.[113] Sri Ramanasramam situated in Tiruvannamalai, Madras Presidency, sent Gita Press what it claimed was the only 'available photo of the cow Lakshmi with Sri Bhagvan'. Niranjananda Swamy, sarvadhikari of Sri Ramanasramam, told Poddar that in 'pre-war times any number of even bigger size photos were available . . . It would be well if you can kindly arrange for an enlarged picture from which a bigger size block can be made. Since Gita Press illustrations (especially in colour) are exemplarily good, we trust a suitable big block can be made.'[114]

For *Ishwar Ank* (Issue on God, 1932), Poddar devised five questions about God that were put to prominent individuals:

1. Why should we believe in the existence of God?
2. What are your arguments in proof of the existence of God?
3. What is the harm in not believing in Him?
4. How can one realize God?
5. Can one live by having faith in God?

Gandhi sent detailed answers ranging from 'we must believe in God if we believe in ourselves' to 'denial of God is injurious in the same way as denial of ourselves' and 'truly, no one in the world is an atheist; atheism is merely a pose'.[115] Poddar followed these questions with a letter asking Gandhi to narrate an incident that may have strengthened his belief in God. Gandhi candidly replied that there was no such incident; initially, he had not had faith in God but it happened as he 'started thinking and reflecting about religion'.[116] Sensing that Poddar wanted to use his replies in *Kalyan*, Gandhi cautioned him this would be futile; even if it was for Poddar's 'own guidance', it would not be of much use since 'in this matter another man's experience will not help you'. On learning the purpose, Gandhi wrote, 'My mind has turned almost blank upon learning that you have asked the questions with a view to publish them in *Kalyan*.'[117]

In 1935, Poddar posed four questions of a similar nature to a range of people. One of them, C.F. Andrews, declined to reply: 'I am afraid it is quite impossible for me in the overwhelming stress of things, with ill health critically to combat, to answer your questions. I am so sorry to have to refuse in this manner.'[118]

On the advice of Gandhi, *Kalyan* did not review books or journals lest it be accused of bias. However, the annual issues of *Kalyan* were reviewed regularly by other journals. The highly successful *Manas Ank* of 1938 received rave reviews. The periodical *Arya Mahila* said praising *Kalyan* would be akin to throwing light on the sun, and asked every 'Hindu man and woman to possess a copy of *Manas Ank*'.[119] *Bharata Dharma*, a periodical from Banaras, had this to say: 'At a time when the whole nation desires a common language and a common script, this publication is both timely and serviceable.' Welcoming the prospect of Hindi getting a major fillip thanks to the simple translation of Ramayana along with a commentary, *Bharata Dharma* praised *Manas Ank* for doing 'justice to the grandness of the theme, the greatness of Tulsidas and to the popularity of the book' and commended it to 'all who love Hindi and the Ramayana'.[120] The journal *Sudharak* from Lahore was also effusive in its praise of *Manas Ank*.

Similarly, *Yoga Ank*, *Kalyan*'s annual issue of 1935, had received praise from varied quarters, including Kanpur-based Hindi daily *Pratap*, English daily *Bombay Chronicle* and *Cherag*, the Parsi periodical. *Bombay Chronicle* praised *Kalyan* in general for the 'non-sectarian character of contributions'[121] and *Cherag* exhorted Parsi intellectuals to subscribe to *Kalyan* or to the English *Kalyana-Kalpataru*: 'We make bold to say, if many of our Parsi writers just peeped into this volume, they would find the insignificance of their intellectual and spiritual progress.'[122]

Naturally, there were also occasions when *Kalyan*'s annual issue came in for criticism. While reviewing *Shakti Ank* (1934), the weekly *Abhyuday* and monthly *Saraswati* criticized Poddar. Noted Hindi writer Ambika Prasad Vajpayee brought this to his notice, requesting him to write a rejoinder, but Poddar refused. First, he said, he acknowledged that he was not competent to edit even a literary journal let alone a religious and spiritual one. Second, he told Vajpayee, 'There will be no reply to anyone's criticism of *Kalyan* and its editor. Whatever is good in *Kalyan* is due to the grace of god and whatever is wrong could be ascribed to me. Praise makes one arrogant. Criticism should be considered truth.'[123]

Art and Artists

One of the biggest tasks before the editor of *Kalyan* from its inception was to make it lively for the reader, and this was in part achieved by the use of illustrations. Gita Press paid a great deal of attention to the visual representation of gods and goddesses in all its publications, also selling the pictures separately. Two significant developments helped: the introduction of chromolithographs from the 1880s with 'their bright and large range of colours, strong clean lines, subtle shading and high finish';[124] and the success of the monthly journal *Modern Review*, published from Calcutta since 1907 and edited by Ramananda Chatterjee, Poddar's friend and president of Hindu Mahasabha in 1929, in bringing 'art to the reading public as part of the nationalist agenda'.[125] Partha Mitter argues that through mechanical reproduction 'Hindu religious themes became enmeshed in exhuming the nation's past'.[126]

The popular growth of chromolithography in Bengal and Maharashtra was an advantage for *Kalyan*. In its first year the journal sourced images of gods and goddesses from Lakshmi Art Printing Works in Bombay. Established in 1910 by pioneer film-maker Dhundiraj Govind Phalke in his earlier avatar as a printer, the press was known for printing 'illustrated booklets *Suvarnamala* coinciding with festivals like Shivratri, Ram Navami, Krishna Ashtami, Ganesh Chaturthi and Divali' consisting of 'single-colour illustrations' by noted artist M.V. Dhurandhar, which were available on subscription.[127] After *Kalyan* shifted to Gorakhpur in 1927, the illustrations were sourced from Laxmibilas Press in Calcutta. Soon, Gita Press began employing full-time artists as well as freelancers. The bulk of its artists would be drawn from Bengal—some of whom had trained under Abanindranath Tagore.

Kajri Jain contextualizes the birth of Gita Press and *Kalyan* in the larger 'ethos of the bazaar'.[128] Bazaar for her is a 'shorthand term for the extensive informal economic and social networks of indigenous trading communities on the subcontinent, which persisted through the colonial era and interfaced with colonial trade in mutually profitable ways'.[129] The bazaar, she argues, placed a premium on the creditworthiness of an individual that was not solely dependent on economic performance but also on factors like moral qualities of piety, thus creating a world 'where moral, sacred and commercial realms were deeply interconnected' and in the long run giving rise to a 'moral community' that would form the support base of the Hindu Mahasabha and later Jana Sangh.[130]

The devotional aspect of the bazaar was articulated through texts and printed images of gods; what added to this process was the dominance of Vaishnavites among the north Indian trading communities and an overlapping discourse of sanatan dharma emphasizing the use of images for worship.[131] Gita Press's mission was drawn from the 'socially reformist but religiously conservative culture of urban Vaishnava community organizations'[132] and propagated through *Kalyan* and other publications. Poddar believed it was neither advisable nor possible for everyone to attain nirguna Brahman, the 'formless, nameless, indefinable highest reality'.[133] Instead, he advocated attainment of saguna Brahman through devotion to 'particular deities with particular attributes'.[134] The mechanically reproduced illustrations of gods and goddesses in *Kalyan* and in religious and pedagogic texts provided a medium for such devotion. Since 'access to temple or other forms—stones, precious metals—worshipped as manifestation of god' was not always easy because of control of these by the priestly class, the 'printed image of god fills that gap'.[135]

'Mechanical reproduction,' as Walter Benjamin points out, 'emancipated the work of art from its parasitical dependence on ritual.'[136]

Ironically Gita Press, while propagating the fourfold caste system and openly supporting untouchability, made these mass-produced colourful images of gods/goddesses accessible to any Hindu home irrespective of caste. However, the visuals often expressed the superiority of brahmins, on which the entire basis of sanatan dharma rested. For example, one image depicted a brahmin having a vision of God while a semi-clad chandala was shown bewildered and struggling below. Sourced from Laxmibilas Press, Calcutta, the picture's caption spelt out what could have been left for the reader to decipher: '*Brahmin Aur Chandala: Brahmin Ko Pehle Bhagwat Darshan*' (Brahmin and Chandala: Brahmin gets darshan of God first).[137] Gandhi, replying to a letter from Poddar in 1935, incidentally wondered why there was need for so many images of gods in the pages of *Kalyan*. Gandhi mentioned that he had also raised this issue with Raghav Das,[138] known as the Gandhi of the east, who had worked for the journal.

While, Poddar does not seem to have responded to this aside, Gita Press had always claimed that the images of gods and goddesses in their publications brought peace and salvation to the reader. Years later, arguing that human consciousness was like the lens of a camera with the power to capture and store even the minutest of details, Ramcharan Mahendra, who penned many books for Gita Press, said posters of films, film journals and mainstream magazines were full of images that drove sexual desire and encouraged immorality, but keeping the images of gods and goddesses in the house fostered positive thinking and warded off dark thoughts and mental illness. 'Pictures and images of gods are a kind of symbol. For an ordinary person, these are the easiest means to understand the complexities associated with gods. Each picture and statue carries innumerable divine secret messages. They open the door to experience divinity. The mind gets the support of ears, eyes and other organs.'[139]

Mahendra took readers on a journey through Hindu images, from goddesses like Lakshmi, Saraswati, Durga—symbols of three kinds of power—to gods like Ganesh, the remover of all obstacles, Hanuman, the fearless monkey god, and the most venerated Rama and Krishna. Pictures of gods and goddesses, he said, acted as spiritual gurus and kept the mind, body and soul in control.

For Mahendra the images' significance lay in the colours, the science of which, he lamented, was lost on present-day Hindus.[140] Red, Mahendra said, was the holiest of the colours and carried the greatest significance. 'Red is used during all auspicious occasions. Normally, red tilak is applied on all gods and goddesses. Red sandal paste is considered a symbol of moon. It also signifies valour. By applying a red tilak a man gains energy, becomes brave and proud.'

In case of women, Mahendra stated, the red sindoor (vermilion powder applied by married Hindu women in the parting of their hair) not only enhanced their beauty but signified how fortunate they were. He extended the argument to claim that women with sindoor did not become victims of sexual crimes as even a criminal considered them 'pious and chaste . . . the red line creates the boundary of a married woman's dignity'.

Saffron was considered a symbol of renunciation, meditation and asceticism. Mahendra said saffron resembled the flame of fire and had the power to extinguish bad thoughts. By wearing saffron robes seers got closer to God and imbibed qualities of self-control and selflessness.

Green, he argued, was the symbol of nature, peace, tranquillity and life. He pointed out that, apart from red, goddess Lakshmi is also decked in green clothes. 'The mixture of red and green lends truthfulness, serenity and fortune to goddess Lakshmi. The mix of these two colours is a symbol of enterprise. Therefore, Lakshmi stays with men who are industrious, hard-working, energetic and confident.' The significance of green in Indian mythology and religion was also illustrated through examples of sadhus going to forests for meditation, and their gurukuls being in verdant settings.

According to Mahendra, yellow was the symbol of knowledge, wisdom and conscience and thus the colour favoured by students and other seekers of knowledge. Two gods—Vishnu and Ganesh—signifying knowledge and wisdom, Mahendra said, were also dressed in yellow.

Blue was the symbol of valour and strength; therefore, Mahendra said, Rama and Krishna—who fought demons—were depicted in blue to signify their heroic deeds. 'Like the all-encompassing blue sky, Rama and Krishna are known universally. The blue colour highlights their tolerance and stable mind.' Finally, white, born out of the mixture of seven colours, was the symbol of peace, purity and knowledge, while black signified death and inauspiciousness.

With so much significance invested in the dialectics of colours and their inherent spiritual power, Poddar was often consulted by friends on what colour they should paint their puja rooms. As we saw earlier, Raja Ram Sinh of Sitamau asked his private secretary Shivram Krishna Godbole to inquire about the colours to be used for a meditation centre, on walls, door and windows. Godbole also asked if varnish paint could be used.[141] While Poddar expressed the opinion that colours were not so important as to impede true devotion to God, different colours were used to depict each god. The basic colour of Lord Rama was blue and shades of green and since Ram Sinh was a devotee of Rama, Poddar told Godbole, 'You can paint the door and windows green. The inside walls should be yellow to depict God's manifestation as pitambara. Blue could also be used, but ultramarine must be avoided.'[142]

The response to Gita Press's religious imagery was largely positive. One criticism, however, came from Goyandka himself. Writing from Vrindavan, he cited a particular illustration in *Shrimad Bhagvat* of a person having a vision of God, in which God's gaze was directed downwards. Baba Sukhram Das of Vrindavan had disapproved of this portrayal, so Goyandka requested Poddar to have the illustration altered so that God would look upwards.[143] Earlier, in 1952, Ranganath Ramachandra Diwakar from Karnataka, an old reader of *Kalyan* and contributor to various special issues, agreed to write for the *Balak Ank*, but pointed out to Poddar the need to 'attend to the art side of the magazine' as 'the pictures are practically devoid of bhava (emotion)'.[144]

Such occasional criticisms apart, Gita Press had evolved a conscious policy on the art to be published and the manner in which gods and goddesses were to be depicted. The larger idea was propagation of Hindu nationalism. Rama and Krishna were always shown as protectors of humanity and very often paintings of Krishna's raslila were carried in *Kalyan* or other publications.[145] Pictures of goddesses evoked feelings of the mother among devotees; they were often shown in their protective roles slaying demons. Artists were asked to ensure that their depiction of deities conveyed power, dignity and beauty. Also, the concepts of karma, rebirth and heaven were propagated through pictures, along with images of what awaited a person in hell, so as to make sure people chose the path of devotion and morality.[146]

When Gita Press began to commission original works for its publications, one place where Poddar looked for artists was Nathdwara, seat of the Shrinathji temple, in his home state Rajasthan. Nathdwara's Pushtimarg sect had 'supported its own dedicated community of painters since around the eighteenth century' to 'paint murals, *pichhavais* (decorative cloth backdrops) and other ritual decorations, portraits of the order's high priests, manuscript illustrations and various types of miniature paintings'.[147] The work, mainly souvenirs for pilgrims, by these brahmin painters belonging to the Gaur and Jangir sub-castes, was popularized by 'mercantile communities poised along the busy western and northern trade routes, particularly the Marwaris', and from 1927 onwards further popularized as 'framed pictures by S.S. Brajbasi and Sons'.[148]

The Poddar Papers contain three letters from Nathdwara-based artist Prem Narendra Ghasiram Sharma, son of the most famous Nathdwara painter Ghasiram Hardev Sharma.[149] The senior Ghasiram Sharma was the 'chief painter (*mukhiya*) in the Shrinathji temple'[150] who also did oil and tempera paintings on the walls of Garh Mahal, Jhalawar. He died in 1930 as a result of which Prem Narendra was unable to fulfil his commitments to Gita Press. He wrote to Poddar apologizing for the delay and promised that despite the 'uncertainty of the physical state, his (Narendra's) art would continue to serve *Kalyan*'.[151] However, three months later, Prem Narendra again regretted not being able to send 'pictures according to the order'. He ascribed the delay to his poor health and subsequent recuperation at a hill station. 'Now I am able to work properly. My shop is also doing well. Of the two paintings sent to you, *Balakrishna* is priced at Rs 20 and *Pushp Vatika* Rs 10. If you do not like them please return them as they were sent as samples from the shop.'[152] There were delays on new orders as well[153] but Poddar bore these patiently out of respect for the artist's stature.

In 1932 Gita Press advertised jobs for artists, in *The Leader*

(Allahabad) and *Amrita Bazar Patrika* (Calcutta). This attracted a flood of applications from all over the country, from artists steeped in modernity with their training in new art colleges of Calcutta, Bombay and other places, to those who had learnt painting as a craft within the family.

Satyendranath Banerjee of Calcutta had trained under Nandalal Bose and Asit Kumar Haldar in Kala Bhavan, Santiniketan for six years.[154] He had testimonials from Bose and C.F. Andrews (who had taught him at Santiniketan) from way back in 1923 when Banerjee was applying for a job in Karachi.[155] With his experience of working for two institutions, Prem Mahavidyalaya in Vrindavan and Daya Ashram in Karachi, Banerjee was asked to come to Gorakhpur in 1932. Not sure about 'the nature of work' he would have to do there, Banerjee demanded a minimum salary of Rs 75 and that he be allowed to do some private work as well.[156] He agreed to send a few more prints as specimens of his work. Finally, Banerjee was accepted as a freelance artist who would send work from Calcutta from time to time on themes suggested by Poddar and others at *Kalyan* and Gita Press.

Unknown to Banerjee, he had been competing for the job with a senior artist from Santiniketan, Mohammad Hakim Khan. Hakim, along with Banerjee's teachers Bose and Haldar, were among Abanindranath Tagore's first batch of six students. Little was known of Hakim as he had disappeared from the Calcutta art scene.[157] But as the Poddar Papers reveal, Hakim had moved to Lucknow where he worked on illustrations for a host of Hindi literary journals like *Madhuri* and *Sudha*. That may be how he was known to leading Hindi writer Premchand who recommended him to Poddar. Premchand, writing under his real name Dhanpat Rai, said he had known Hakim, who earlier worked for *Saraswati* for eight years. Significantly, Premchand emphasized that Hakim, despite being a Muslim 'does a successful depiction of Hindu gods'. Recently, Premchand wrote, Hakim had illustrated scenes from the Valmiki Ramayana that were soon to be published in *Sudha*. 'He is also doing an oil painting of Krishna that has been priced at Rs 1,000. There is no element of religious animosity in him. He is a gentleman.'[158] In his application Hakim also reiterated, 'although a Mohammedan I can illustrate Hindu characters successfully'.[159] These references to Hakim's faith may have been a result of the intense communal tension in the United Provinces at the time; in 1931, serious riots in Kanpur had led to widespread vandalism of mosques and temples, and the killing of leading journalist-politician Ganesh Shankar Vidyarthi.

Though drawing a salary of Rs 140 in *Sudha*, Hakim was willing to negotiate since his job there was soon coming to an end. He was invited to Gorakhpur immediately but could not make it because of his child's illness. When, he went there a month later, it was decided he too would be commissioned on a freelance basis. It seems Poddar did send Hakim some assignments at his *Sudha* office address, but Hakim could not deliver in time owing to various difficulties—his dues from *Sudha* had not come through, his children were not keeping well and he could not work due to the 'hot and rough' weather. Requesting Poddar not to think he was 'careless', Hakim promised to send the pictures after carrying out the suggested 'corrections'.[160] By July 1932 Hakim started sending his work to Gita Press and sought more assignments.[161]

Another of Abanindranath's first pupils at Santiniketan, Sarada Charan Ukil, also sought work at Gita Press. The eldest of three artist brothers who were contemporaries of Amrita Sher-Gil, Sarada had set up Delhi's first art school in 1918 teaching a 'watered down version of Bengal school'.[162] During his early years Sarada painted 'oil portraits of wealthy patrons' and later made a name with his 'Indian-style paintings'.[163]He had also dabbled in films, playing the role of King Suddhodhana in Franz Osten's 1925 adaptation of Edwin Arnold's 1861 classic *Light of Asia*.[164]

The beginning of Sarada's association with Gita Press is not certain but his earliest letter in the Poddar Papers dates to 1935. In response to a telegram from Poddar, Sarada sent three of his original works—*Krishna & Radha, Shiva in Meditation* and *Guru Nanak and Origin of Panja Saheb*—with the clear instruction that the 'honorariums and the cost of sending the pictures' be sent to him on receipt of the parcel.[165] Conscious of his standing as a student of Abanindranath Tagore, though he did not mention Tagore's name, Sarada offered to contribute pictures for the 1936 *Vedanta Ank*, and requested Poddar to send him some literature on the subject. 'I do not want to produce too common and ordinary pictures for fear of my reputation. Hence I am so very anxious for some themes on the subject.' In the next breath he raised the issue of payment, saying the Rs 75 sent for the last three pictures—probably the ones just mentioned—was less than the earlier rate of Rs 30 for each picture. Asserting his standing, Sarada also said unlike in his 'former days' he had stopped giving pictures to monthly magazines but made an exception for *Kalyan* out of 'personal regards' for Poddar.[166]

By 1939, one sees a different Sarada. Desperate to sell his works he was no longer talking of exclusivity and reputation. He had painted the life of Buddha in thirty-five pictures for Digvijaysinh Ranjitsinh, Jamsaheb of Nawanagar, who had given him permission to get them published in book form with the condition that the size of the pictures should not exceed 7 x 5 inches and a minimum of 2,000 copies be published. Sarada had also done the life story of Krishna in thirty pictures and wanted to publish them as a book.[167] He put both proposals to Poddar who agreed in principle to publish the Buddha's life. He also showed interest in the Krishna pictures and selected most of them for reproduction in the 1939 *Gita Tattva Ank* (Issue on the Principles of Gita) of *Kalyan*, saying Gita Press would like to keep some of the 'pencil paintings'. And then came the subject of price: 'I know it is so ugly to talk of prices and remuneration for a thing of art which is always priceless, but we have to see to this aspect also in this matter-of-fact world.' He reminded Sarada of the larger mission of Gita Press which was a 'religious institution with an ideal to propagate spiritual ideas through publication of journals, books, pictures, etc'.[168]

Negotiations between Sarada and Poddar stretched over a year, both being hard bargainers. While standing out for better terms for the Buddha and Krishna books, the artist acceded to Poddar's request for permission to reproduce some of the Krishna drawings in *Gita Tattva Ank*: 'By publishing some of the pictures, I think, I shall be able to secure the opinion of the members of my committee.'[169] Sarada agreed to charge Rs 80 (rather than Rs 100 quoted earlier) per picture for reproduction of the pencil drawings as a 'special concession' only for Gita Press.[170]

A long silence after this from Poddar, possibly a ploy to draw out Sarada, worked. In March 1940, a desperate Sarada revised his earlier terms, asking for a lump sum of Rs 3,000 for the Krishna book instead of Rs 5,000; and Rs 2,000 for the Buddha rather than the previous demand of Rs 3,000. Sensing that Sarada was vulnerable, Poddar drove an even harder bargain. He used the pretext of World War II and the consequent rise in paper prices and non-availability of art paper and ink to tell Sarada that the printing of the books would be delayed, also stating that the terms were still too high. At the same time, he asked Sarada to draw for the *Sadhana Ank* (1940).[171]

Sarada immediately brought down his demand by Rs 500 for each of the two books. 'Immediate publication of the volumes is what I am really anxious of [for] . . . I hope you will now understand my point of view and will leave no stone unturned for the spread of our spiritual culture and love of god, for which you and I are both struggling hard.'[172] Three days later, Poddar wrote back, first asking Sarada to send six paintings on the lives of Krishna, Buddha and Chaitanya Mahaprabhu for the *Sadhana Ank,* and then dropping a bombshell—expressing his helplessness and inability to publish the books in the immediate future though agreeing to place the reduced terms before the publication committee of Gita Press.[173] His hopes dashed, Sarada sent the six paintings for the *Sadhana Ank* and pleaded for remuneration of Rs 150 as he was in 'bad need of money'.[174]

The paintings sent for *Sadhana Ank* were returned to Sarada after use and to his dismay he found some of them were 'injured' and one painting had been 'retouched and disfigured by your press artist which is objectionable'.[175] He also complained that the 'pictures were badly packed with the result they got defaced'. Sarada took 'strong exception to the negligence', asked Poddar to warn the in-house artist and claimed damages of Rs 150. He sent back the paintings so that Poddar could see the damage for himself. Poddar's reply that he did not find anything wrong must have upset Sarada greatly; however, he was in no mood to further spoil a relationship that was already strained. He did not repeat the demand for damages, but wrote in a conciliatory tone: 'I was much surprised and sorry that you misunderstood me, for the retouched picture had no connection with you; it was only a sort of information for you that your block maker may not do such sort of things at all, in future. You very well know my relations are different with you . . .'

However, he held his ground that the 'face of the picture was badly retouched and in the background too there were spots of blue colour which have definitely reduced the quality of the picture'.[176]

While Sarada Ukil was busy carving a niche for himself in far-off Delhi, the Calcutta art scene that he had left behind was witnessing a fervent debate between revivalists and those steeped in the Western art idiom. At the centre of the debate was Ordhendra Coomar Gangoly, editor of the highbrow art magazine *Rupam* and an ideologue of the Bengal School.[177] He was a firm believer in the 'existence of a specific national and race ideal in all great art', and argued that 'nationalism was of far greater value and significance than cosmopolitanism in the artistic development of a country'.[178] Gangoly's idea of cultural nationalism tied in with that of Gita Press.

In the 1930s, in the midst of intense debates that had ramifications in Calcutta, Bombay and London,[179] Gangoly, also an artist, was contributing paintings to *Kalyan*. A representative of Gita Press picked up the works from his Calcutta residence. Gangoly was fond of giving detailed instructions to Poddar on the manner in which his paintings were to be displayed and their identification.[180] He also demanded two sets of colour blocks as soon as copies of *Kalyan* were printed. Gangoly prepared and sent blocks of his paintings for the *Hindu Sanskriti Ank* in 1950, but these were received so late they could not be included in the special number. Poddar promised to use his works in the subsequent number but not before making it clear that the Rs 170 that Gangoly had spent on getting the blocks made was higher than the estimated cost of Rs 140, which itself was more than what Gita Press generally paid for such blocks.[181]

For the *Hindu Sanskriti Ank,* Poddar also contacted the superintendent of the Archaeological Survey of India requesting rights to 'reproduce some photographs that had already appeared in several books and periodicals'. A substantial request was made to the chief secretary of Travancore state, for the reproduction of twenty photographs and plates from T.A. Gopinatha Rao's *Elements of Hindu Iconography* (1914).[182] The permission came just in time for the pictures to be included in the annual number.

The most intriguing of the artists contributing to *Kalyan* was

Dattatreya Damodar Deolalikar. A graduate from Holkar College, Indore, Deolalikar went to the Sir J.J. School of Art, Bombay, on a state scholarship, where he trained under Cecil Burns, A.K. Trindade and Gladstone Solomon. Considered a master watercolourist, he later taught at the J.J. School and his influence could be seen in the works of his star students, including N.S. Bendre and M.F. Husain. Deolalikar returned to his hometown to become the principal of the Indore School of Art in 1929. Though honoured by the Holkar rulers of Indore, Deolalikar went through a serious financial crisis during the recession of the 1930s, as his salary was not increased for many years, forcing him to give private tuitions. After a stint as professor emeritus in the Gwalior School of Art, he settled down in Delhi with government help.[183]

It was during the period of financial distress that Deolalikar knocked on the doors of Gita Press for work. He communicated with Poddar mostly through telegrams showing the acute urgency of his need. Frustration had set in within a year of his becoming the principal of Indore School of Art. Deolalikar wired Poddar about the possibility of getting six months' leave in 1931 and sought his advice. Then even before Poddar could reply, Deolalikar sent another telegram to say he would be in Gorakhpur within a week.[184] Gita Press wired back asking Deolalikar to wait, and Poddar wrote to him that it had been decided not to spend too much on pictures, so 'we had to give up the idea of giving you work throughout the year. Please do not proceed on long leave. You can take a month's leave and come here. Right now our desire is to spend little and get little work from you.'[185] Deolalikar did not lose hope. He began sending paintings and drawings from Indore and seeking more assignments; he would also ask for some kind of interim payment to meet his expenses.[186] He kept Poddar posted of even the minutest progress in the assignment—for instance, the number of days it took for an oil painting to fully dry.[187] Deolalikar got regular assignments from Gita Press throughout the 1930s, which supplemented his income; he occasionally demanded money on an urgent basis. He also did not give up the desire to visit Gorakhpur, applying for six months' leave in 1932,[188] and it is likely he made the trip to Gita Press.

Kanu Desai of Ahmedabad was another prominent artist who contributed to the corpus of Hindu iconography at Gita Press and

Kalyan. He was a student of Ravishankar Rawal—artist, editor of the iconic art magazine *Kumar*, political activist who along with Nandalal Bose decorated the pandal for the Haripura Congress,[189] and also a first-rate teacher. Desai's work is today housed in the Baroda Museum, as curated by the art historian and Indologist Hermann Goetz.[190]

Desai's association with Gita Press began in the early 1930s, and by 1938 he was asked to do cover illustrations for *Kalyana-Kalpatraru's Dharma Tattva Ank*. He also offered to prepare illustrations on a list of subjects that included such abstract themes as dharma of humanity, dharma and war, value of faith in God and many others, so that they could be used throughout the year.[191] Asked to contribute drawings for the annual number of *Kalyan* on *Gita Tattva* (1939), Desai sought Poddar's help for ideas as he felt it was 'not easy to draw and give the most suggestive, proper and symbolic ideas in pictures on Gita unless one has properly studied it and taken it to heart'.[192]

Daughter of a Hungarian father and a Russian mother, both teachers in Geneva, Eve Yvonne Maday de Maros came to India in search of her love, army officer Vikram Ramji Khanolkar of the Sikh Regiment, whom she had met while he was holidaying in Europe after his course at the Royal Military School, Sandhurst. Once in India, she married Vikram, imbibed the Indian way of life and culture and took a new name, Savitri. A painter with a deep passion for Indian mythology, when asked by Hira Lal Atal, adjutant general, to design the Param Vir Chakra, independent India's highest medal to be given for wartime bravery, she used the image of a double vajra (thunderbolt). Coincidentally, the first Param Vir Chakra was awarded to the late Major Som Nath Sharma, brother-in-law of Savitri's elder daughter.

Savitri's husband was posted to Nowshera in the North-West Frontier Province in 1939 when she contacted Gita Press for the first time with her paintings. She sent two pictures for publication in *Kalyana-Kalpataru*. One was a watercolour representing 'the essence of worship' or 'adoration' and the second was a 'china ink silhouette representing Sankar or Natraj, the lord of destruction at play'.[193] Gita Press accepted her works and Poddar, as it emerges from another of Savitri's letters, sought her permission for 'retouching' the 'adoration' painting. Savitri agreed but demanded, like other artists, that the originals be returned once the block was ready.[194]

The most successful and prolific artist for Gita Press was Binay Kumar Mitra from Allahabad. Along with Jagannath Chitrakar and Bhagwan Das, Mitra became a resident artist at Gita Press. A Bengali from Allahabad, Mitra's work continues to adorn the pages of *Kalyan* even today.

By the late 1960s, Gita Press had built a huge bank of art works but had begun losing its artists mainly to age and illness. In their editorial comment in the *Upasana Ank* (Issue on Worship, 1968) of *Kalyan*, editors Poddar and Chimmanlal Gosvami spelt out various reasons for the special number having fewer illustrations: 'Our old artist B.K. Mitra has lost his vision and cannot draw any longer. Jagannath Chitrakar, our second competent artist, has passed away. Bhagwan Das is a good artist but does not keep good health these days. Therefore, we could not give as many illustrations as we wanted. But those that are given are beautiful and soulful.'[195]

In 1955, President Dr Rajendra Prasad inaugurated two artistic innovations at Gita Press in Gorakhpur—Gita Dwar and Leela Chitra Mandir. According to Poddar, the elaborate architecture and sculpture of the new gateway, Gita Dwar, represented the confluence of Indian art, culture and devotion. The gateway has figures of five deities—Narayan (Vishnu), Shiva, Ganesh, Surya and Maha Shakti—considered the soul of sanatan dharma. Then there are two statues of incarnate deities, Rama and Krishna, along with seven symbols as well as architectural elements from seventeen places of worship across the country integrated into the design of the dwar. The choice of the places of worship is interesting not only for its geographical spread but also for its attempt to integrate home-grown religions like Buddhism, Jainism and Sikhism with sanatan Hindu dharma—Ellora, Ajanta, Dakshineshwar, Dwarka, Mathura, Sitamarhi, Konark, Madurai, Amritsar, Khajuraho, Sanchi, Mount Abu, Kedarnath and Bodhgaya among others.[196]

Leela Chitra Mandir was equally grand in design and intention. Spread over an area of 800 square metres, with ceilings over 6 metres high, the complete Gita is inscribed on its walls along with 700 selected couplets of Kabir, Rahim, Tulsidas, Sundardas, Paltu and Narayan Swami. The pictures, 684 of them, represent varied influences on

Indian art. Paintings from the Mughal, Rajput, Kangra, Mewari, Bombay, Bengal and south Indian schools are displayed. Gita Press specially invited artists of these different schools to execute the task. The pictures depicted Krishna Lila, Ramlila and various reincarnations of god and sages.[197]

In his speech, the president stressed the immortality of Indian culture and the tolerance of sanatan Hindu dharma that was an amalgam of many religions. 'Whereas other religions differentiate one from another, the Bhagavadgita is an example of integration,' Prasad said. He asked Gita Press to open its doors to ordinary citizens so that the values of sanatan Hindu dharma could spread further and help transform people's lives. Prasad said institutions like Gita Press for which 'I have great regard are engaged in translating the vision of sanatan Hindu dharma into reality and I want them to succeed further'.[198]

Chronicle of the Dead

Though it may seem insignificant, one curious way in which *Kalyan* exhibited its catholic nature was by according respect to the dead, howsoever opposed the person might have been to the cause of Hindu nationalism in general and to Gita Press in particular. Following the principle of not talking ill of the dead, *Kalyan* built up an interesting collection of obituaries of a mix of people ranging from Keshav Baliram Hedgewar to King George V, Motilal Nehru, Jawaharlal Nehru, M.S. Golwalkar, Sampurnanand, S. Radhakrishnan, Jugal Kishore Birla, Indira Gandhi and Rajiv Gandhi. The greatest tribute however was paid to Pandit Madan Mohan Malaviya as *Kalyan* brought out an extra issue on his death in 1946; no other obituary came close to such an expression of reverence.

Of course, there were some significant delays and deliberate omissions as well. The assassination of Mahatma Gandhi was never mentioned, though much later, in 1948, several articles were carried about the life and teachings of the Mahatma. B.R. Ambedkar, who remained an anathema to Gita Press's world of sanatan Hindu dharma, was completely ignored after his death.

Gita Press was into its third year when Lala Lajpat Rai succumbed to the injuries received during a lathi charge in Lahore while protesting against the Simon Commission in 1928. Poddar described Lala Lajpat Rai as a martyr to the cause of the nation and expressed the need to emulate his life of dedication and service, and fill the void left by him.[199]

The Nehrus, Motilal and his son Jawaharlal, were not among the favourites of Gita Press. Jawaharlal especially had kept a safe distance from *Kalyan* and the activities of Gita Press. Motilal too maintained a secular image despite his occasional trysts with religion to satisfy the conservative section within the Congress led by Malaviya. After Motilal's death in 1931, Poddar wrote appreciatively of how he had taken to religion in the last days of his life by reciting the Gayatri mantra and Rama Naam.[200]

The Delhi Durbar of 1911 to commemorate the coronation of King George V had made the king a household name in India. His death in 1936 came at a time when *Kalyan* was still finding its feet, and for a journal that counted Hindu nationalism as the sine qua non of the freedom movement, paying tribute to King George V was possibly a calculated act to win the goodwill of the colonial government. Poddar called George V an ideal husband, father, son and friend, and justified the gloom his death had brought to his subjects, family and friends.[201]

Hindi literary don Premchand was an old friend. A few months before his death in October 1936, Premchand had visited Gita Press and promised to come back and stay in Gorakhpur for two months. Poddar wrote with regret that Premchand had not been able to fulfil his promise, philosophizing that this was how destiny worked.[202]

RSS founder K.B. Hedgewar died in June 1940 but Gita Press honoured him a decade later. In a short tribute in *Kalyan*'s mammoth *Hindu Sanskriti Ank* of 1950, Shivnath Dubey wrote in gushing terms of how Hedgewar was cut out for bigger things right from childhood. Describing Hedgewar's daredevilry during his days as a medical student in Calcutta, his founding of the RSS in 1925 and his decision to remain a bachelor, Dubey concluded 'you will be alive till Hindus exist', summing up the deep respect Gita Press had for Hedgewar.[203]

Unlike Gandhi and many of his colleagues in the Congress, Nehru had never patronized Gita Press. His Western education and views, coupled with his left-of-centre policies were antithetical to the Hindu nationalists of the new India. Therefore, *Kalyan*'s glowing tribute to Nehru after his death in 1964 seemed more an act of compulsion—Gita Press was aware of Nehru's popularity and the moral cost if they omitted to pay tribute to the country's first prime minister. Poddar's obituary acknowledged Nehru's stellar role in working for international peace and solidarity. He said there was enough in Nehru to be followed by people across the ideological spectrum.[204]

Nehru's successor Lal Bahadur Shastri and his wife Lalita were personally close to Poddar and Gita Press, and contributors to *Kalyan*. Shastri's sudden death in Tashkent in 1965, Poddar wrote, had sadly caused his victory procession (after the war with Pakistan) to metamorphose into a funeral procession. Calling Shastri the beacon of world peace, Poddar equated his death, still a matter of great speculation, to martyrdom. He said the Shastris were part of the Gita Press family,[205] and that Shastri's sudden demise was a lesson that, since life is uncertain, people should never give up devotion to God.

Poddar himself died in 1971 and Chimmanlal Gosvami became the editor of *Kalyan*. Instead of confining Poddar's memory to one issue of *Kalyan*, the journal remembered its founder editor over several issues, his articles being reprinted even today.

Golwalkar's death in June 1973 was another big jolt to Gita Press. An exhaustive tribute was written by Bhimsen who had been loaned by the RSS to the Gita Press so that he could serve Poddar in Gorakhpur. In fact, Golwalkar and Poddar had run a mutual admiration society. Golwalkar had always said that though many great men spread the message of patriotism, social unity and social service, it was only Poddar who could successfully turn people into believers on such a large scale and make fundamental religious texts so popular. Bhimsen wrote of how happy Golwalkar had been to send him to work for Poddar. He recalled Golwalkar's early training in spiritualism under Swami Akhandananda, one of the sixteen direct disciples of Ramakrishna Paramahamsa, at the Ramakrishna Mission ashram at Sargachhi. It was on Akhandananda's advice that Golwalkar had maintained a beard and long hair throughout his life. [206]

Bhimsen particularly appreciated the way Golwalkar had not let politics influence the running of the RSS despite the fact that the swayamsevaks took a keen interest in politics. He recounted an interesting encounter between Golwalkar and Atal Bihari Vajpayee in an RSS camp, also attended by senior RSS/Jana Sangh leader Deendayal Upadhyaya, near Wardha in the 1950s. During the question-answer session, Vajpayee asked Golwalkar, 'The nature of power is such that the moment it gets centralized it generally turns into brute power; what is the guarantee that your theory of intense power culled from ancient Indian philosophy and religion will not become brutal?' Golwalkar replied, 'Any power that is fundamentally spiritual will never become pashvik (brute power). One should worry only about the fundamentals.'

Indira Gandhi had endeared herself to Hindu nationalists at various stages of her prime ministership. Her action in East Pakistan that led to the creation of Bangladesh in 1971 had made her a heroine, with some equating her to goddess Durga, the ultimate personification of shakti (power). Her assassination in 1984 at the hands of her own security personnel, *Kalyan* said, would forever be classified as a black spot in Indian history. The obituary continued in glowing terms: 'Mrs Gandhi was India's biggest leader who was working fearlessly to solve the nation's problems. Her sole aim was the nation's unity, integrity, peace and progress for which she gave up her life. Though some antisocial elements have eliminated her physical self, her soul will be impossible to kill.'[207]

Less than seven years later, Rajiv Gandhi, Indira Gandhi's elder son and former prime minister himself, was assassinated in Sriperumbudur, Tamil Nadu. *Kalyan* editor Radheshyam Khemka equated the killing of the leader to tandava, 'a dance of world destruction, the dance of the enamoured Shiva',[208] citing it as an example of how violence had taken over society. Equally shocking for the journal was the new instrument of assassination used—a human bomb.[209]

Economics and Workforce

Sustaining an initiative like Gita Press, not based on profit, was always a challenge—something Poddar foresaw a few days after the first issue of *Kalyan* came out. Writing to Gambhirchand Dujari, Poddar said that until *Kalyan* had 2,000 subscribers, publishing from Bombay would be a loss-making proposition and 'efforts should be made to increase the subscription base'.[210]

With some leading Marwari industrialists associated with the publishing house, Gita Press sought to create a new business model that could straddle the worlds of no profit and huge capital input. A solution was found: Gobind Bhawan Karyalaya, the managing trust of Gita Press, would diversify into the highly profitable newsprint business. It was also decided to start small-profit ventures such as making khadi clothes, sacred thread (janeu), soap, glass bangles, shoes (without leather), ghee and ayurvedic medicines. It was expected that the profits from these diversified products would not only subsidize low-price publications but also provide Gita Press with enough liquid cash. Gobind Bhawan also ran an ashram in Churu, Rajasthan to teach Sanskrit and the Vedas to male students.

But the alternative business model lacked consideration for the workforce that multiplied as circulation of *Kalyan* increased and other publications were regularly reprinted. Poddar, Goyandka and other promoters were so consumed with their idea of defending and popularizing sanatan Hindu dharma, they assumed that whoever came under the umbrella of Gita Press would make their personal ambitions and family commitments subservient to the larger cause of religion. Gita Press soon realized its mistake. Beginning in 1932, it faced five major strikes by press workers in less than twenty years.

The 1932 strike was initially met with strong disciplinary action by the Gita Press administration but this did not quell it. Poddar was in Ratangarh and had to intervene to stitch up a compromise, but this was short-lived as workers under Gauri Shankar Dwivedi struck work again the next year. This strike was contained again without fully settling the demands of workers. The strike had started after Gobind Bhawan Karyalaya decided to cut staff salaries by Rs 15 per Rs 100. Poddar protested against the decision and defended the workers. He said, unlike other press workers, those of Gita Press had no fixed office hours or holidays. 'When there is work they are in press from six in the morning to eleven in the night . . . There are workers who are barely able to run their households on Gita Press salaries. I do not know how in such a situation the decision to cut salary can be justified.'[211] Poddar said he would take up the matter with Goyandka as well.

The growing discontentment among Gita Press workers was exploited by the emerging ideologies of communism and socialism.[212] By the 1920s and '30s, trade union culture had made its presence felt in Gorakhpur. Local Congress leader Vindhyavasini Prasad Varma was organizing railway workers, protests and demonstrations in the city.[213]

Another strike took place in 1936, when Poddar was again in Ratangarh. Aware of the change in the political climate and the dominance of Congress in the politics of the United Provinces, Poddar tried to convince Ganga Prasad, senior administrative official of Gita Press, to adopt a lenient approach: 'This is the time of Congress governments in the provinces. Naturally, workers and peasants are feeling empowered. We also want to see poor and depressed classes live in peace and happiness. We should not be surprised with whatever we are hearing from our employees. Looking at the changes we should know the age of workers and peasants is about to come that would lessen their pain and struggle to some extent. But I think growth acquired through hatred and violence is not going to last.'[214]

Poddar advised Prasad to talk to the union leaders and provide them with all the facilities possible. He suggested that if need be the opinion of Gandhi and Malaviya should be taken. 'Our institution should foremost be known as an organization for poor people. I kept quiet and am still not saying anything as I did not see my purpose getting fulfilled . . . There is no need to threaten anyone . . . I do not consider Gauri Shankar Dwivedi a leader of workers. Whatever he is doing is out of hatred. Sampurnanand, Narendra Dev, Rajaram Shastri and Purushottam Das Tandon should also be consulted.'[215] But Poddar himself had to come to Gorakhpur and talk to the union leaders before the strike was called off. While most of the workers were reinstated, the Gita Press authorities sacked a few.

One of the major demands in 1937 was the setting up of a provident fund for workers. This demand was finally met in 1939 when the Gita Press Gorakhpur Provident Fund was formed. The notification was issued by the industries department on 3 April 1939 after the board of trustees of Gobind Bhawan Karyalaya approved the provident fund rules.[216]

In 1945, when a strike notice by the workers was met by partial acceptance of their demands, the strike went ahead. Despite Poddar's best attempts, a lockout had to be declared in Gita Press for one-and-a-half months in 1946. Then again in 1948 the workers went back on the warpath. The Criminal Investigation Department in several reports to the government pointed out that 'labourers of the Gita Press contemplate striking should their demands not be fulfilled'. At one point the workers suspended their strike, but realizing that their demands were not being fulfilled, they gave notice to strike again.[217]

One factor that impacted the finances of Gita Press was its interventions in times of public distress, almost on the lines of the RSS, providing flood and famine relief as well as running free Ayurvedic dispensaries. Though these activities aimed at building social capital were carried out largely through contributions from its rich Marwari patrons and partial help from the government, over the years Gita Press had to dip into its own coffers to sustain them. The Gita Press Seva Dal started by Poddar during the 1936 flood in Gorakhpur and neighbouring areas still continues as an important department of Gobind Bhawan Karyalaya.

The Poddar Papers have a chronicle of Gita Press's work during the 1936 and 1938 floods as well as the 1942 famine, and the rich dividends it earned in terms of accolades and appreciation from the local administration, politicians and the press. The iconic journal *Saraswati* carried Poddar's appeal for foodgrains and clothes.[218]

The collector of Gorakhpur, J.E. Pedley, ICS, was so enamoured of the work done by Gita Press during the 1938 flood that he left a testimonial praising the 'selfless generosity of Hanuman Prasad Poddar and of the Press', without whom it 'would have been quite impossible to extend any relief at all to thousands of persons in the flooded villages in this and in other districts'.[219] At the time of 1942 famine it was the turn of Gorakhpur commissioner H.S. Ross to sing paeans of Gita Press's work in making foodgrains available at the cheapest possible rates, 'a work of real philanthrophy'.[220] When permission for the supply of rice bought by Gita Press in Muzaffarpur was delayed, Ross intervened and wrote to the Bihar government's controller of prices to grant permission for export of grain from the state as it was a 'purely philanthropic undertaking'.[221] He pointed out that Gita Press had their own wagons for transporting the grain. A host of other British officials, from those in the administration to those in the railways, praised Gita Press for its relief work.

In the 1950s, as independent India's first government got down to business, Gita Press faced the heat of new regulations. The first decision to directly affect Gita Press related to a hike—almost 100 per cent—in the postal rates for book packets. Gita Press protested and sought the intervention of sympathetic members of parliament like Seth Govind Das, a veteran Congress leader and conservative who was a close friend of Poddar's.[222] Arguing that the hike in postal rates 'directly concerns the vast population of the country and indirectly the finances of the country and the growing unemployment' and 'is also working as a brake against the spread of education and knowledge', Gita Press sent a brief to Seth Govind Das with a request to raise the issue in parliament. It claimed that the postage charge on some of its popular publications—Bhagavadgita, Ramayana and Durga Saptashati—was equal to the price of the book, and accused the postal department of misusing its monopoly. The government refused to relent.

In 1956, when news came about the possibility of government extending the Employees' Provident Fund Act XIX of 1952 to the printing industry, Gita Press was the first to petition the labour commissioner, Uttar Pradesh, seeking exemption. One reason offered was the reluctance of workers to join a government-run PF scheme. B.L. Chandgothia, manager, Gita Press, argued that the press already had its own provident fund with 'rules no less favourable to the employees than the provisions in the government employees' provident fund'.[223] He agreed to amend any rule that was found less favourable to the workers. Chandgothia also volunteered to have the accounts of Gita Press examined to prove its 'sound financial position'.

The provident fund issue was simple compared to the recommendations of the wage board for working journalists in 1967. Alarmed at the prospect of *Kalyan* and *Kalayna-Kalpataru* falling under the definition of newspapers, Jaidayal Dalmia, who was closely associated with Gita Press through the 1960s, sought the opinion of the legal department of his Dalmia enterprise. The legal opinion was clearly that the two journals did not fall under the category of newspapers as the articles appearing in them 'do not contain any public news or comments on public news', but Gita Press was cautioned to cross-check if other printed periodicals of the same type were classified as newspapers by the wage board.[224] Dalmia also advised Gita Press to seek legal opinion from the advocate general of Uttar Pradesh so that in case there was any future complication, the state government would find it hard to dismiss the opinion of its highest law officer.[225]

By the late 1960s, Gobind Bhawan Karyalaya was faced with a steady decline in income without any curtailment of expenditure. To add to this, the price of newsprint was slated to increase by 25 to 30 per cent and press workers were to get the new salary fixed by the government, leading expenditure on salaries to go up by Rs 3 lakh annually. Poddar said there were two ways to deal with the situation: either increase the income or scale down Gita Press's work. Though the price of *Kalyan* had been increased, it would not be enough to offset the losses. Various measures had failed: the decision to rent out the ground floor of Gobind Bhawan Karyalaya in Calcutta had proved a non-starter; similarly, the manufacturing of ayurvedic medicines for sale to government hospitals at a commission of 20 to 25 per cent had not taken off. Poddar suggested that the ayurvedic unit could be restarted for extra income. Another proposal mooted by Mohanlal Patwari, a follower of Goyandka, was to start a business in handloom clothes to be run by Gita Press, which could bring an annual income of Rs 150,000. Poddar was agreeable and, to elicit support, he requested Ishwari Prasad Goenka to attend the meeting of the Gobind Bhawan Karyalaya trust. 'There are issues that cannot be settled through circulars without discussing them in the meeting.'[226]

In 1969, workers of the shoe unit in Calcutta, possibly influenced by the rising tide of trade unionism in the city in the late 1960s, represented to Gobind Bhawan Karyalaya protesting against the policy of showing them as contractors and deducting Rs 5 per month per worker as licence fee. The workers demanded a 25 per cent increment in shoe-making rates, an end to licence fee, an annual bonus of one month's salary, festival leave with full wages and introduction of provident fund with contribution of 10 per cent of wages from both employer and employee.

Unlike the press, the shoe business was a diversification for Gobind Bhawan Karyalaya and could easily be closed if the workers persisted with their demands. Matters came to a head in December 1969 when the workers laid siege to the Gobind Bhawan office. Many senior functionaries were held hostage for many hours and the police had to intervene. Even before the hostage incident, a decision had been taken to close the leather unit as Gobind Bhawan was clear that giving its workers permanent jobs would not only eat into its marginal profits but lead to further complications. In addition, the state government was not cooperative. A Gobind Bhawan official would rue the growing power of workers: 'No one can think of doing anything against workers . . . Looking at the situation in Bengal it is impossible to have any favourable settlement.'[227]

Gobind Bhawan got a shot in the arm when the office of West Bengal's labour commissioner, after investigation, concluded that 'the persons worked under contract agreements and acted not as "workers" defined under the provisions of the Industrial Disputes Act'. The labour commissioner's office also pointed out that thirty-seven persons had already settled their dues as 'suppliers'. 'In the circumstances, the suppliers cannot be treated (as) workers under the Industrial Disputes Act and as such the dispute cannot be deemed to be an industrial dispute.'[228]

The Bhawan's annual statement of accounts for 1968-69 showed a drop in the sales of all varieties of shoes except fancy slippers. The sale of velvet shoes had gone up on paper; however, a year earlier (1967-68) they had not been sold at all. The report noted a rising tendency among the staff of the shoe department to steal goods. There were similar stories of financial loss from other departments.[229]

Finally, when the trustees of Gobind Bhawan met on 7 March 1970 at Poddar's residence in Gita Vatika, the first item on the agenda was to close the shoe business forever. It was also proposed that the house where the workers lived should be vacated and the property sold.[230] The trustees also decided that the Rishikul Brahmacharya Ashram in Churu would not admit new students till certain rogue elements among them had been expelled. Even the annual function of the ashram was put on hold.

Gobind Bhawan Karyalaya was constantly confronted with reconciling the conflict between commerce and religion, profit and charity. While the newsprint business brought in huge profits, mounting losses in Rishikul Ashram, Gita Press, *Kalyan* and Gobind Bhawan were a cause of great worry. The running costs of Gita Press were also met through interest on contributions people had made.

After much discussion and internal bickering, the cover price of *Kalyan* and other publications was increased. The first price rise in Gita Press publications, to the extent of 50 per cent, had taken place in 1942 when newsprint prices increased, but the prices were reduced again when the cost of newsprint stabilized. Poddar realized that price increase was the only way the venture could be sustained and the anger of employees quelled. He justified the increase in the 1960s, arguing: 'Why would seeking to recover one rupee on expenditure of the same amount be considered against religion?'[231]

Taking full responsibility, Poddar stated that Gita Press's prices were still lower than those of other organizations selling religious texts. 'The last hike took place when the price of newsprint was three rupees per pound and monthly staff salary began at six rupees.'[232] Like an ace businessman out to revive a failing business, Poddar explained how despite input costs having gone up by five to seven times, the publications had continued to be sold at the earlier prices, losses being offset by high profits of the newsprint business. However, the profits from newsprint were now almost at an end. 'Last year the overall loss (of Gita Press) was two lakh rupees. We will have to hire more people this year and the next. Along with the all-round rise in prices we have to deal with government rules and the trade union. I do not think workers are unjustified in demanding better salaries. If we do not increase the prices, losses would mount, our capital would deplete and work would stop.'

Poddar highlighted the fragile state of Gita Press's finances: '. . . capital is invested in the press and in real estate, book stock has been built through deposits from people and for newsprint bank loans have been taken'. He dismissed a suggestion that Gita Press should ask for contributions to run its affairs, wondering who would give money every year. 'Not all trustees are crorepatis. With contributions we can undertake work during emergencies like drought, not manage an institution that runs on sales. The matter is different in the case of Christians as they have funds running into crores for religious propagation. Forget contributions, no trustee has even a lakh or two to cover running costs. We had to borrow from two trusts. In such a situation we cannot run the operation on emotions. One has to deal with the situation in a realistic manner.'

Despite the financial hardship Gita Press was undergoing, it was decided in 1968 to publish an English translation of the Bhagavadgita in book form. The translation had appeared continuously for six years from 1952 to 1957 as the annual numbers of *Kalyana-Kalpataru*. Running into 1,728 pages, this was a mammoth task. Jaidayal Dalmia approached *The Times of India* and *The Indian Express* to give cost estimates for 3,000 to 5,000 copies without factoring in profit, since 'the aim of Gita Press is to supply religious books as cheap as possible'.[233] *The Times of India* gave an estimate of Rs 67,392 for 3,000 copies if printed on white paper and Rs 91,584 for printing the same number of copies on Bible or thin paper.[234] Goenka said *The Indian Express* did not have an 'offset press in Delhi' but only a 'rotary press'. He, nevertheless, offered to 'do any work for [Gita Press] in Delhi . . . free of cost'.[235]

In 1970 Gita Press faced a major crisis when newsprint supply was stopped. In those days newsprint was in short supply, with each newspaper having a quota of indigenous and imported newsprint fixed by the government. Many newspapers tried to fudge their circulation figures so that they could get more newsprint which they could sell in the black market.

What could have been merely an escalation of its financial woes turned out to be a murky episode as it was soon revealed that Gita Press had been selling the newsprint allotted for publication of *Kalyan*, *Kalyana-Kalpataru* and religious texts in the open market. Its supplier Orient Paper Mills, owned by Ganga Prasad Birla, immediately suspended the supply. Poddar was not in the best of health, and his complicity in this affair is not clear. The incident caused immense damage to the reputation of Gita Press that was not only engaged in publishing religious texts upholding the tenets of sanatan Hindu dharma, but had always advocated high moral standards and honest dealings in private and public.

When G.P. Birla agreed to resume supply of newsprint, he made note of Poddar's assurance that the 'paper supplied to them for publication work would not be resold in the market'.[236] But Shyam Sundar Goenka, G.P. Birla's aide, was blunt, telling Poddar that the 'difficulty being faced by Gita Press is due to their own deeds'.[237] He assured Gita Press that 'an institution working for a good cause' would not find difficulty in the matter of getting supplies required for their own consumption. In what seemed to be an acknowledgement of Poddar's growing disenchantment with the functioning of Gita Press, Goenka asked him if the press would sincerely act as per his assurance.

Within a few months Gita Press faced another major shortage of newsprint. While the monthly allotted quota was of 150 tonnes, it was getting merely 30 per cent of this. Poddar had to intervene again and take up the issue with G.P. Birla so that Gita Press could continue to 'carry out its work of producing noble literature'.[238]

When in 1970 Ramnath Goenka found a text called *Narayanam* consisting of 1,008 Sanskrit shlokas (verses) rendered in Devanagari, he sent the text to Poddar with a request that it be published along with a translation. However, on discovering from Jaidayal Dalmia that Gita Press was facing a newsprint crunch and was even outsourcing some of its own work, Goenka offered to get it published from Delhi.[239]

As the losses piled up, Gita Press had to consider hiking the prices of its publications. Gobind Bhawan incurred a loss of Rs 34,000 in 1970, whereas the previous year it had made a profit.[240] Rising input costs—paper, postage and salaries of employees—were making it difficult to run the operations. This time, however, Poddar resisted the price rise. He said any hike would go against the basic ethos of Gita Press to provide high-quality books at cheap rates. Poddar convinced trustee Ishwari Prasad Goenka that the hike, if any, should take place only after the preparation of the balance sheet for 1970. Keeping the rising Naxalite violence in Bengal in mind, Poddar also argued that any hike in the price of books leading to extra income would not be advisable in the prevailing political circumstances. He was worried about the spread of violence from Bengal to other provinces.[241]

At the same time, Poddar expressed the fear that mounting losses could result in the suspension of publication of religious literature. He cited the instance of *Ramcharitmanas Gutka* (handbook) that was sold at 90 paise though it cost Rs 1.25 plus the commission to booksellers.

The price of *Ramcharitmanas Gutka* was intensely debated within Gita Press as it had received a bulk order for 100,000 copies from Mauritius in 1970. Caught in the dilemma of charging just the cost price or weaving in a marginal profit, Poddar and Jaidayal Dalmia considered various options. One was not to mention the cover price and to put the name of Indo-Mauritius Maitri Sangh (India-Mauritius Friendship Federation) as the publisher instead of Gita Press.[242] After much discussion each copy was priced at Re 1. It was proposed that the cost of Rs 3,500 for preparing the negatives for offset printing be contributed by Vishnu Hari Dalmia, son of Jaidayal Dalmia and a senior member of Vishwa Hindu Parishad (VHP). The objective of this right-wing organization with members drawn from the RSS and other Hindu groups, established in August 1964, was to create a large network of Hindus across the world. Mauritius with more than 50 per cent Hindu population and a large number of religious organizations was an ideal hunting ground, and it is possible that the VHP had a role in this bulk order.

Around the same time, Gita Press approached the Reserve Bank of India for issuance of a blanket permit for export of religious literature.[243] The permit was probably being sought to meet the order from Mauritius. Gita Press already had an export permit that was sanctioned on a monthly basis. The extension of this permit every thirty days, Gita Press argued in its application, usually took a long time, as a result of which the shipments regularly missed the Scindia Steam Navigation Company vessel that used to carry them free of cost. Gita Press, therefore, sought an annual permit for the 'export of religious books free of charge to various countries except China, Portugal and Pakistan'.[244] It was pointed out to the RBI how the export of such literature was helpful 'for developing better religious and cultural ties with other countries of the world'.

Over the decades since Poddar's death, Gita Press has seen further financial highs and lows. However, it remains a phenomenon in India's publishing world and has moved with the times, at least technologically speaking, with its user-friendly website offering copies of its publications as well as online subscriptions to *Kalyan* and *Kalyana-Kalpataru,* still at surprisingly low prices.

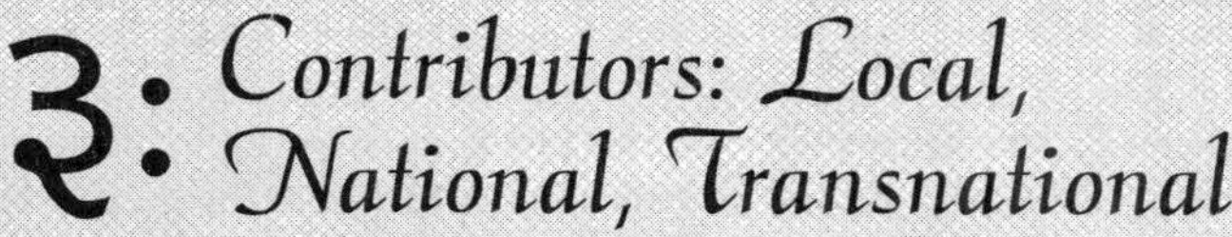

३: Contributors: Local, National, Transnational

Hanuman Prasad Poddar would often claim that the editorial policy of Gita Press in general, and of *Kalyan* in particular, was to follow the middle path, not attacking other religions and not advocating reconversion to Hinduism. This statement of respect for all religions ran somewhat counter to their position that, as all religions were different, there could not be unity among them.[1] In fact, *Kalyan* and other Gita Press publications often presented opinions that polarized communities during periods of tension and violence.

Besides the epics and historical texts, Gita Press publications drew on Shruti, Smriti and the Puranas for their form and content.[2] Shruti, 'the most sacred part of the scriptures of Hinduism, is considered an ultimate authority in matters of faith and practice; it can be interpreted, but not superseded or bypassed'.[3] It is believed, as historian A.L. Basham points out, that Shruti was 'directly revealed to its authors'.[4] The Samhitas, Brahmanas, Aranyakas, Upanishads come under this category. Smriti, 'what has been revealed', consists of Hindu religious texts written in the post-Vedic period; these texts 'deal mainly with law ascribed to inspired lawgivers, such as *Manusmriti* and *Yajnavalkyasmriti*'.[5] Smriti is a few notches lower than Shruti in sanctity.[6] Without getting into the larger philosophical, religious and social conflict of Shruti vs Smriti, Gita Press straddled the two worlds, taking from texts of both the genres. The larger idea was to educate the masses about India's golden past as a point of reference for the current dark age. In an enterprise that looked at the 'entire nation as a classroom' and its publications as tools of pedagogy,[7] making any distinction between Shruti and Smriti would have meant digressing from the larger mission of defending sanatan Hindu dharma and restoring its glory.

The editorial policy aimed at inculcating six qualities in human beings through two means—conscience and detachment. The six ultimate goals were listed as titiksha (forbearance), sam (equilibrium), dum (vitality), uprati (freedom from physical desires), shraddha (faith/

respect) and samadhan (resolution).[8] However, these lofty goals were diluted by ambivalence when the journal stated that it recognized the importance of money and carnal desire in the life of human beings while stressing that the yearning for these two should be moderated by religion.[9]

Seeking contributions for *Kalyan* and other publications was a secular exercise. Poddar would knock on each door, regardless of the writer's religious or political affiliation. The contributors to *Kalyan* were a mix of Hindu, Muslim, Christian and Parsi mendicants and spiritualists, academics and Indologists (both Indian and foreign), poets and writers, community or political leaders. The idea was to create a wide consensus on the need for Hinduism's revival and to make this a collective exercise.

Sadhus, Sanyasis, Sanatanis

Accounts of Gita Press are full of stories of how contributions were extracted from sadhus and sanyasis. Gopinath Kaviraj, principal of Government Sanskrit College, Banaras, and a leading scholar of the city, is believed to have forced maverick Swami Jyoti (Kshirodnandan Dutt Roy) to write for *Kalyan*'s annual number of 1933 by locking himself in with the Swami for six hours even while devotees waited outside. Sri Narayan Swami, deputy-collector-turned-sanyasi, after much cajoling by Poddar to write about his life's journey, agreed to write in Urdu, and the text was later translated. Swami Sivananda wrote in English. Another contributor was Meher Baba, a swami of Parsi origin, severely criticized by journalist Paul Brunton for his tall spiritual claims but also credited with 'introducing yoga and meditation to the West'.[10] C.D. Deshmukh, lecturer of philosophy at Morris College, Nagpur, and one of Meher Baba's closest aides, visited Gorakhpur in 1941 as part of his lecture tour in north India. Days before he reached Banaras from where he was to travel to Gorakhpur, Deshmukh wrote to Poddar expressing an interest in delivering a lecture on the Gita or participating in a satsang, however small.[11]

Sri Aurobindo Ghose and the Mother (born Mirra Alfassa in Paris) together contributed more than fifty articles to *Kalyan*. Poddar and

Aurobindo had known each other from Calcutta. Poddar claimed that the Ghose-edited newspapers *Bande Mataram* and *Dharma* that later became *Karmayogin* influenced him as a young man to take to revolutionary activity, join the Swadesh Bandhab Samiti and Anushilan Samiti. Poddar's relationship not only with Ghose, but also his followers at the Pondicherry ashram, was to last a lifetime. Many of the ashram inmates were associated with the various departments of Gita Press.

Preparing an exhaustive list of the sadhus/sanyasis who wrote for *Kalyan*, and the stories associated with their contributions, is an exercise in itself. Based on an index of authors in the Poddar Papers, one may state with a fair amount of conviction that a majority of India's godmen wrote for Gita Press. After all, it was a religious journal, the first of its kind, and captured the imagination of readers, particularly those involved in the Hindu religious world.

There was, for instance, the contributor Madhava Ashish, born as Alexander Phipps to Protestant parents. He went from a public school to the College of Aeronautical Engineering at Chelsea, London, but could not finish his course. Phipps came to India during World War II as an aircraft engineer, and a chance meeting with Ramana Maharshi took him to Uttar Brindavan Ashram in Mirtola village of Almora district. Phipps was rechristened Madhava Ashish by his guru Sri Krishna Prem, and became Krishna Prem's closest aide. In 1959, Madhava wrote to Poddar expressing his guru's inability to write for the *Manavta Ank* (1959) since he 'had completely given up writing'.[12] Madhava also declined to write himself. However, seven years later he wrote for the *Dharma Ank* (1966).

Other sanatan dharma organizations sometimes sought Gita Press's collaboration. Bharat Dharma Mahamandal founded in 1902, in which Madan Mohan Malaviya had played an important role, was one of the first such organizations. By 1934, the Mahamandal, which claimed to be an 'all-India socio-religious association of the sanatanists recognized by the Imperial government, Hindu ruling princes, all religious heads and all Hindu communities' realized that, despite its experience, its publications were not reaching the public in the same manner as those of Gita Press. The Maharaja of Darbhanga, who headed the organization, wrote to Poddar that its publications were not doing well since it was run by brahmins who did not have knowledge of commerce. Poddar was requested to take over the entire range of Mahamandal publications and print them the way he wanted. 'You are also doing the work of Bharat Dharma Mahamandal. It is not only for the welfare of Hindus but you have been entrusted this task by gods themselves to spread the light of knowledge in the world.'[13] However, for reasons unknown, Gita Press could not oblige.

Similarly, there was yoga teacher Swami Dev Murti, who had taken yoga to Europe in a big way and operated out of his headquarters in Lauf, Germany. In 1968, the Swami was visiting India after a decade, with thirty European disciples. His contact person in Delhi, one Shyam Swarup Sharma, wrote that Gita Press and Swami Dev Murti were on a similar mission to propagate Indian civilization, culture, philosophy and religion; that the Swami had deep appreciation for the work being done by Gita Press and desired that all its publications be kept in his ashrams in Europe. Sharma said during his one-day visit to Banaras, Swami Dev Murti would like to visit the office of Gita Press there.[14]

Towards some god-men Gita Press was not so positively inclined, for example Mahesh Yogi whose new form of yoga and philosophy of transcendental meditation—loosely explained, it involved the merging of the conscious and the subconscious mind—had become a sore point with Poddar. The Beatles had visited Mahesh Yogi in his Rishikesh ashram in 1968, bringing him and his meditation technique under blazing international media spotlight. Gita Press saw Mahesh Yogi's practice as a deviation from the well-laid-out shastric path and a threat to sanatan Hindu dharma.

Poddar chose to ignore him, calling his principles 'blatantly against the tradition of sanatan dharma devotion'. Ruling out any article on Mahesh Yogi in *Kalyan*, Poddar said even criticism would amount to giving him publicity: 'Readers of *Kalyan* who do not know about him will also become aware of him.'[15] However, in his column where he replied to readers' queries, Poddar did refer to Mahesh Yogi, though not by name, questioning the interpretation of a stanza from the Gita in support of transcendental meditation: 'Popularity and large crowd is not an index of being truthful . . . These days there are many non-shastric sects in existence. This is also one of them.'[16]

With the International Society for Krishna Consciousness (ISKCON) in the USA, and its founder Swami Prabhupada, Poddar and Gita Press shared a more gentle relationship at both personal and institutional levels. Though at times Prabhupada would be highly critical and even dismissive of Poddar—calling him a 'mundane type',[17] 'not so formidable rascal' and 'impersonalist'[18]—he held Gita Press in high esteem for popularizing the Gita and the cult of Krishna. He was also appreciative of the fact that Gita Press did not accept any advertisement or review books in *Kalyan* and *Kalyana-Kalpataru*.[19] In 1961 or 1962, Prabhupada visited Gorakhpur as the guest of Poddar, and in February 1971, Prabhupada and forty of his students from ISKCON were the guests of Gita Press.[20]

In January 1970, Poddar wrote to Prabhupada for information as he wished to carry a comprehensive article on him and the growth of ISKCON in *Kalyan*. Since Prabhupada was travelling, he replied to Poddar only in the beginning of February, sending a long autobiographical sketch, beginning with his days as a manager in Calcutta's Dr Bose Laboratory and the life-changing experience of his meeting with his guru Srila Bhaktisiddhanta Sarasvati who asked him to preach the message of Lord Chaitanya in the Western world. Prabhupada thanked Poddar for helping him and ISKCON in the publication of the first volume of *Srimad-Bhagavatam* (1960–61) and explained in great detail the working of ISKCON, rules of the sect, etc.[21]

Even as Prabhupada was preparing to send material for the *Kalyan* article to Poddar, the latter sought permission to also publish the ISKCON account in a book form. Prabhupada agreed. He told Poddar that ISKCON's London office would send more pictures and newspaper cuttings for the book, writing: 'This book will enthuse me as well as the whole Vaisnava society . . . So in India also we have to do many things because very recently, by the propaganda of the politicians the younger generation has become victimized to become Godless.'[22]

The article appeared in *Kalyan*'s April 1971 issue. Prabhupada wrote a thank-you letter, asking Poddar to send a specimen copy by airmail.[23] Prabhupada also informed N.C. Chatterjee, independent member of the fourth Lok Sabha and former president of the Hindu

Mahasabha, about the *Kalyan* article which, he said, had 'very nicely presented news' about ISKCON's activities. 'As a result we are getting many inquiries from India,' Prabhupada told Chatterjee.[24]

Conservatives, Traditionalists, Liberals

In 1926, when Poddar went with Jamnalal Bajaj to Gandhi to seek his blessings for *Kalyan*, he was given two pieces of advice by the Mahatma: do not accept advertisements and never carry book reviews. Gandhi argued that advertisements often made tall claims that were untrue and once they started coming they would generate a lot of revenue so it would be impossible to stop them. As for book reviews, Gandhi held that most writers would expect laudatory remarks and one would have no choice but to praise every book or else risk offending the writer. Poddar accepted this advice and even today *Kalyan* and *Kalyana-Kalpataru* do not carry advertisements or book reviews.[25]

Though early issues of *Kalyan* carried several pieces by Gandhi, who also blessed the journal with a handwritten note carried in *Bhakta Ank*, the annual issue of *Kalyan* in 1928, Poddar was not willing to publish Gandhi's translation of the Gita—*Anashakti Yoga*—as he felt that Gandhi's refusal to accept the Gita as a historical text was not in consonance with the views of Gita Press.[26] *Kalyan*'s disagreement with Gandhi on the question of Gita spilled over to other journals as well. Reviewing *Kalyan*'s *Shri Krishna Ank* (1931), journal *Saraswati* highlighted Padam Singh Sharma's critique of Gandhi. Sharma had mocked Gandhi for calling the battle of Mahabharata an imaginary tale but still lifting lessons on ahimsa from the Gita—Arjuna at the beginning of the battle had already articulated the ideals of peace and non-violence.[27]

The relationship between Gita Press and the Mahatma grew tempestuous after a series of deep disagreements on caste and communal issues, such as temple entry for Harijans and the Poona Pact. Still, *Kalyan* carried a total of fifty-four articles by Gandhi going by index of writers in Poddar Papers, some extracted from *Navjivan* and *Harijan*, but most others specially commissioned and a few even carried posthumously. Poddar would often contact Jamnalal Bajaj or Mahadev

Desai for a contribution from the Mahatma. At times, Pyarelal, another of Gandhi's aides, would select the piece and send it to *Kalyan* with Bapu's approval.[28] Gandhi wrote on a whole range of issues, from the importance of God in one's life to the influence of Western culture, the status of Hindu widows and the merits of cow protection. Interestingly, Gandhi's articles appeared even during the tumultuous 1940s when *Kalyan* was severely critical of him for his stand on Muslims.

Jamnalal Bajaj, among the closest to Gandhi and called his fifth son, did not exhibit the same enthusiasm as his mentor when it came to writing in *Kalyan*, though he had contributed to its predecessor *Marwari Aggarwal*. Bajaj wrote only one article for *Kalyan* on how taking God's name helped him.

Another of Gandhi's followers, G.D. Birla also did not write for *Kalyan* despite being close to Poddar and Goyandka. After Gandhi's assassination, he distanced himself further from Poddar and what Gita Press stood for. In 1958, Poddar asked him for a contribution but G.D. Birla regretted on the ground that he was 'soon going abroad'.[29]

Jugal Kishore Birla was G.D. Birla's elder brother. After amassing a fortune from opium, gold and silver trades he had relinquished everything and taken to religion, hobnobbing with leaders of the Hindu Mahasabha. A close associate of Poddar in the cow-protection movement and against the Hindu Code Bill, Birla wrote a few articles for *Kalyan*, including one in the 1950 *Hindu Sanskriti Ank* that Poddar especially liked. Thanking Birla, Poddar discussed the continuing violence in various parts of the country. 'Situation in the country is adverse. It is expected to get worse.'[30] *Kalyan*'s policy of publishing profiles of saints from Islam and Christianity invited criticism from Jugal Kishore Birla, who would often ask, 'Does Hinduism not have enough saints that you keep publishing about Islam and Christianity?'[31]

Gandhi and Malaviya represented two ends of the spectrum within the Congress. Both were considered important by Gita Press, though Malaviya was its vocal supporter and was thus seen as its true patron. Yet, compared to Gandhi, Malaviya was not as keen when it came to writing for *Kalyan*. Poddar would later admit, 'He never used to give a categorical answer to requests for contribution. He was very good at talking, not so much at writing.'[32] Malaviya contributed fifteen articles in all, many of them published after his death in 1946.

Others of the political class who were wooed by Gita Press included theosophist and Congress leader Annie Besant. Author of *Sanatana Dharma: An Advanced Textbook* along with Bhagwan Das, Besant died in 1933 and did not see Gita Press prosper, though Poddar had convinced her to write an article on Krishna Lila for the *Shri Krishna Ank* of 1931. Besant's life story would be showcased by Gita Press as that of an 'adarsh bharatiya nari' (ideal Indian woman). Her writings would find place in *Kalyan* even after her death.

S. Rajaram, editor of *Bharata Dharma*, 'a magazine of liberal Hinduism'[33] and the official organ of Bharat Samaj, also wrote on Krishna for the 1931 *Kalyan* annual. In 1939, S. Satyamurti, firebrand Congress leader from Madras Presidency and one-time London correspondent of *The Hindu*, contributed an article to *Kalyan* on the Ramayana as the source of human life. Then there was M.S. Aney, a prominent Tilakite, founder of the Congress Nationalist Party and member of the Constituent Assembly, who in 1949 during his stint as governor of Bihar would write on the spiritual impact of the Upanishads. Socialist Acharya Narendra Dev, as vice chancellor of Banaras Hindu University, would write on children's education for *Kalyan*.

C. Rajagopalachari, a leading light of the Congress who would later found the Swatantra Party, contributed five articles to *Kalyan*, the first of which appeared in 1928 on Bhakta Kanappan, the legendary tribal chief in Tamil literature who gave away both his eyes to Shiva out of devotion. In 1935, Rajagopalachari was requested by Poddar to write on God, but politely declined. Instead, Rajagopalachari sought Gita Press's help in printing the 'condensed Gita' that he had written in English for publication by the Inter-Religious Student Fellowship, a Madras-based institution that had brought out a similar condensed Bible by Verrier Elwin.[34] Gita Press, however, did not oblige, possibly because Rajagopalachari made it clear that Gita Press would have to bear the 'entire financial responsibility and loss or gain'.[35]

The controversial *Hindu Sanskriti Ank* of 1950, that represented Hindu culture as the epitome of world culture, included an article by Rajagopalachari. But two years later, as chief minister of Madras, he would regret his inability to contribute to the *Balak Ank* (1953): 'I send my best wishes, but feel sorry I am not able at present to do what I like.'[36]

Five articles by philosopher-politician S. Radhakrishnan appeared over three decades in *Kalyan* on a range of topics, including the concept of God in Hinduism and the importance of religion. On occasion he would decline to contribute but not without lauding *Kalyan* 'which has been doing good work all these years'.[37] Poddar roped in Radhakrishnan for other initiatives like the Gita Society.

Pattabhi Sitaramayya, authoritative biographer of the Indian National Congress, would bring his scholarship to bear on the relevance of Ramayana and the role of parents in the life of children. Then there were conservative Congressmen like Purushottam Das Tandon, K.M. Munshi and Sampurnanand. Tandon wrote a piece on the tradition of Hindu women worshipping their husbands. Munshi, a lawyer and educationist opposed to conversion, had traversed the entire spectrum of politics from Congress to the Swatantra Party to Jana Sangh, and endeared himself to right-wingers by playing a key role in the rebuilding of Somnath Temple in Gujarat. Though he contributed only four articles to *Kalyan*, Munshi, also president of Bharatiya Vidya Bhavan, used the vast resources of Gita Press for his religious writings. On one occasion he asked Poddar for a 'Sanskrit-Hindi translation of Hari Vamsa' as he was writing 'the romance on the life of Sri Krishna based on Puranas'.[38] On another occasion he would thank Poddar for sending 200 copies of the Gita for free distribution to visitors and students at Bharatiya Vidya Bhavan.[39]

Sampurnanand's writings in *Kalyan* varied from Christianity to Hindu culture, women and children. One-time education minister of the United Provinces, chief minister of Uttar Pradesh and later governor of Rajasthan, Sampurnanand was so close to Poddar that the *Kalyan* editor felt free to write: 'A request was sent to write for *Hindu Sanskriti Ank* but we have not received any reply. I presume it is due to your hectic schedule and priority to official work. But *Kalyan* also belongs to you. You have always blessed us. Moreover, the topic is such that only competent people like you can write.'[40] Poddar further mentioned that 125,000 copies of the issue were to be printed. When Sampurnanand had still not delivered, Poddar shot off another letter though the issue had already gone to press: 'Your article should appear. It's being eagerly awaited.'[41] Sampurnanand obliged with an article titled '*Hindu Sanskriti*' that had to be added to the issue in its final stages. Sampurnanand in turn exercised his right over Gita Press. Any delay in getting a copy of *Kalyan* would result in an immediate reminder being sent to Goyandka.

There was a history to this relationship. In 1937, a highly depressed Sampurnanand, who had been unwell for more than a month in Banaras, unburdened himself to Poddar about his failing health and lack of money: 'I am an ordinary worker who is always short of money. Every thing is disorganized.'[42] Poddar sympathized and promptly sent Sampurnanand some money. An overwhelmed Sampurnanand wrote: 'The words with which you have sent the money have not only made it impossible to pay the debt but also made it difficult (for me) to thank you.'[43]

During his term as chief minister of Uttar Pradesh, Sampurnanand contributed to the *Bhakti Ank* (Issue on Devotion, 1958). Poddar had problems with the chief minister's views on devotion and wrote to Sampurnanand explaining that though he disagreed with the views expressed in the article, 'it has been decided to publish it with editorial comment . . . Hope you do not have any problems with that.'[44] In his editorial comment, Poddar disagreed with the oversimplified path of the devotion or 'bhakti marga' that Sampurnanand advocated, saying that simplification did not mean there was no need to follow rules.[45] Significantly, considering that the UP chief minister was the author, Poddar made it clear the article was not open to further debate.

Lawyer-politician Kailash Nath Katju was also a keen patron of Gita Press and would always find time to contribute. When Poddar's request for a contribution to *Hindu Sanskriti Ank* came in June 1949, Katju at first declined. However, persuasion and persistence, as was the editor's practice with big names, worked. In August, Katju, then governor of West Bengal, suggested that his piece 'Bhagwat Gita and Communism' written for the Independence Day special issue of the Allahabad newspaper *The Leader* be carried in *Kalyan*'s special number. Katju reasoned that while *The Leader* 'has, like the present day daily newspapers, a limited circulation in a limited area', *Kalyan* would go 'far and wide throughout the length and breadth of the country'.[46] Poddar acquiesced.

Katju's article was suitably inimical towards the communist ideology that was seen by Gita Press as a threat to the Hindu social, religious and economic order. In fact, articles on samyavad (communism) as a cause of concern for the new nation would appear at regular intervals in *Kalyan*, and Gita Press would publish Swami Karpatri Maharaj's '*Marxwad Aur Ram Rajya*' (Marxism and the Ideal State) in 1957.

Though he contributed other articles to *Kalyan*, by the time of *Balak Ank*, while keen to contribute, Katju would say he did not 'know what to write . . . The daily work seems to have made me completely dry.'[47]

Purshottamdas Thakurdas, one-time director of Tata Sons, cotton magnate, politician and editor of the Bombay Plan, wore many hats. An active campaigner for the protection of the interests of Indian industrialists, he was at the same time a member of the central board of the All India Anti-Untouchability League and the Hindu Sanrakshan Mandal in Bombay. He had already vociferously defended the role of Hindu Mahasabha and Arya Samaj in the Bombay riots of February 1929.[48]

Thakurdas had an abiding interest in Gita Press and *Kalyan*. An article on the importance of Gita in the April 1942 issue of *Kalyan* by Mohammad Hafiz Syed, a regular contributor who was teaching in Allahabad University, interested Thakurdas so much that he would congratulate Poddar for carrying the piece and even ask for Syed's address.[49]

When Poddar requested him to write for the *Gau Ank* of 1945, Thakurdas convalescing in Nasik would reply through his secretary that though he did not 'ordinarily take up any additional work', an exception would be made since it involved cow protection. Thakurdas agreed to write an 800-word article in English on the importance of cows, on the condition that it would be translated into Hindi for wider dissemination. He hoped the cow number of *Kalyan* 'would awaken the conscience of the Hindu public'.[50] But advanced age and failing health forced him to turn down the request to write for the *Hindu Sanskriti Ank*. He also plainly stated that he was not sufficiently a scholar to write on any of the subjects listed in Poddar's letter.[51]

A fellow Marwari from the Central Provinces, Seth Govind Das, had relinquished his share of fortune to become a full-fledged politician, playwright, poet and a strident advocate of Hindi and cow protection. His grandfather Seth Gokuldas of the banking firm Sevaram Khushalchand had been a 'big help to the East India Company in the Central Provinces'; he owned 158 villages and had the 'title of raja prefixed to his name'.[52] A lifelong Congressman, Seth Govind Das would later collaborate with M.S. Golwalkar and Poddar for the Krishna Janmabhoomi movement in Mathura.

Das identified himself with the mission and method of Gita Press. For him, the contribution of Gita Press to 'religion and culture was unrivalled'. He coaxed Poddar to publish his writings in *Kalyan*, mostly travelogues to present-day Uttarakhand and south India and a five-part play on Vallabhacharya (he would even insist that Gita Press should publish them as books).[53] Das felt it was an honour to help Gita Press; as a member of parliament, he had taken up the matter of the steep hike in postage.[54]

In the almost endless list of politician-writers for *Kalyan*, the name of Jawaharlal Nehru is notably absent. Poddar and Nehru had met briefly when the latter visited Gorakhpur during the 1936 floods. In various accounts, Poddar claims that he had offered Nehru his car to travel for a meeting to Barhaj, close to Gorakhpur.

Let alone an article, Nehru refused to send even a short message when requested by Poddar for the *Hindu Sanskriti Ank*, and again for the *Manavta Ank*.[55] Nehru's home minister G.B. Pant was more enthusiastic and sent a short message for the *Manavta Ank*. Poddar and Pant had known each other for a long time. Pant contributed to *Kalyan* and supported Gita Press in all its initiatives. As home minister, he wrote to Poddar that during an official trip to Gorakhpur he would find some time to visit the Gita Press office.[56] Nehru's aloofness towards religion in general and Gita Press in particular would come up for discussion between Poddar and Pant, who shared the opinion: 'Whatever Jawaharlal might say publicly, I think he is a believer.'[57]

Lal Bahadur Shastri presented a perfect contrast to Nehru's liberal Western upbringing and education. Educated at Kashi Vidyapith, Shastri was steeped in Hindu traditions. He wrote two articles for *Kalyan* in 1965 (he was prime minister then) on the power of God's name and the message behind religion.

With Dr Rajendra Prasad, Gita Press, especially Poddar, had a relationship marked by a high level of mutual admiration. A 'sanatani Hindu' who believed in idol worship and even observed fasts during solar and lunar eclipses, Prasad was closely associated with the cow-protection movement and the propagation of Hindi. As a contributor to *Kalyan*, he always found the time to deliver. Even as president, when asked to write for *Balak Ank*, he sent word through his personal secretary: 'President always has the best wishes for *Kalyan*. He respects the work done by Gita Press.' It was suggested that the journal carry an extract of his speech delivered at Birla Vidya Niketan, Nainital, as 'President has stopped writing for journals'.[58]

The president inaugurated Gita Press's new building in 1955. He saw the Press as doing great service to Hindus; he was an ardent reader of its publications and would even have them read out to him.[59] When Prasad did not receive the sixth issue of the short-lived *Mahabharata*, his personal secretary wrote to Poddar so that his collection would be complete.[60]

One episode indicates the care with which he read *Kalyan*. In 1956, an article in the *Satkatha Ank* (Issue on Stories from the Scriptures) referred to 'Jeera Deyi' (Zeradei), Prasad's birthplace near Chapra in Bihar. Prasad immediately asked his personal secretary Gyanwati Darbar to ask for the book *History of Persia* by V.A. Smith that was cited by the writer in *Kalyan* as referring to 'Jeera Deyi'. The Rashtrapati Bhavan librarian visited Delhi University library but could not find the book there. A desperate DU librarian wrote to Poddar requesting him to find out from Janaki Nath Sharma, writer of the *Kalyan* article, 'whether the reference *History of Persia* by V.A. Smith is correct; whether the author can send a typed copy of the pages from which this reference on Jeera Deyi has been taken and whether the author has got a copy of the book'.[61]

J.B. Kripalani, Rajendra Prasad's predecessor as Congress president in 1947, later a socialist and steeped in the Gandhian tradition, refused to write for *Kalyan*'s *Hindu Sanskriti* number. His assistant N. Krishnaswamy wrote to Poddar expressing 'regret' due to Kripalani's 'preoccupations'.[62] But the prominent names among the second-rung Congress leaders were not so lukewarm towards Gita Press. If Sri

Prakash, as governor of Bombay in 1957, wrote to Poddar seeking copies of the journal *Mahabharata* that he felt would help him cope with the untimely demise of his second son, Sriman Narayan, a Gandhian economist, member of parliament, ambassador to Nepal and governor of Gujarat, offered to write on any topic suggested by Poddar.[63] In fact, as ambassador to Nepal, Narayan helped forge a larger network of Hindu organizations involving the king of Nepal and prominent Hindu leaders like Poddar.

The Far Right

The story of Gita Press would be less than half-told without reference to the political and religious leaders belonging to the far right who not only contributed as writers but at crucial junctures used Gita Press and *Kalyan* to deepen religious polarization in India, especially during the communal flashpoints of the 1940s. The mix of writers reflected differing viewpoints. For instance, the animosity between the Arya Samaj and Sanatan Dharma Sabha did not come in the way of Swami Dayanand's speeches and writings being carried in *Kalyan* along with those of other prominent Arya Samajists like Nardev Shastri Vedtirth, Chandkaran Sharda and Yudhishtir Mimasa. Sharda had been actively involved in the Congress and became an important member of the Rajputana Madhya Bharat Sabha when it was established during the 1918 Congress session in Delhi with Jamnalal Bajaj as president and Ganesh Shankar Vidyarthi as vice-president.[64] In his speech, Sharda used harsher words than Poddar, saying Hindus had become 'cowardly, weak and lazy'.[65] For *Kalyan*'s *Hindu Sanskriti Ank,* Sharda wrote on what constituted Hindu culture. The running theme of his article was a comparison between the Hindu culture exemplified by Rama and Bharat, each stepping aside for the other to rule, and the Muslim example of Aurangzeb killing his siblings to grab power.[66]

Madhav Sadashiv Golwalkar of the RSS made his presence felt in the pages of *Kalyan* in 1947 through his article '*Sachcha Rashtravad*' (True Nationalism) and also excerpts from his speech '*Hamari Sanskriti Ki Akhand Dhara*' (The Continuum of Our Culture) made to RSS cadres in Delhi. Responding to Poddar's invitation to contribute to the

Hindu Sanskriti Ank, Golwalkar sent a short piece giving the editor the freedom 'not to publish if you do not like it . . . I am not a writer nor very educated. But I am writing simply because of the respect that I have for you and your love towards me. The subject is too vast but it became easier for me to write since you had defined the broad contours of the article. Today people are ashamed to call themselves Hindus.'[67] Five years later, Golwalkar wrote effusively: 'The off-tracked Hindu . . . of today should study this (*Hindu Sanskriti Ank*) and realize the greatness of his life. Once the realization sets in he would discard [his] un-Indian belief system.'[68]

In all, Golwalkar wrote seven articles for *Kalyan*. He was such an ardent reader of the journal that when he went to Pattambi (Malabar) in Kerala for oil therapy and recuperation, his associate Aaba Thate requested a copy of the *Satkatha Ank* to be sent there by parcel post.[69] When Golwalkar received the copy at the residence of A.K. Warrier, the RSS karyavah (in-charge) of Pattambi tehsil, he praised the issue, saying it had 'nursed my mind'.[70]

Thus, in just over two decades, Gita Press became an attractive platform for the liberal and orthodox Congress elements as well as those preaching and practising strident Hindu nationalism. The colossus Gandhi still featured in the pages of *Kalyan*, but his authority was clearly being challenged and his tools of passive resistance, tolerance and non-violence severely attacked and mocked as helping only Muslims. Poddar, incidentally, presided over the reception held for Golwalkar in the Town Hall of Banaras in 1949, on his release after being arrested for his alleged involvement in the Gandhi assassination.

An old acquaintance of Hedgewar, Veer Savarkar and Golwalkar, Syama Prasad Mookerjee quit the Congress and joined the Hindu Mahasabha in 1939. Belonging to an elite Bengali family, Mookerjee was 'brought up in an erudite atmosphere' with the best of liberal education in India and Britain.[71] A growing disillusionment with the Congress, on whose ticket he had been elected to the Bengal legislative council in 1929, brought him to the welcoming arms of the RSS and Hindu Mahasabha. In 1951 he formed the Bharatiya Jana Sangh, the political arm of the RSS. Poddar courted him for long, requesting him to write articles for the special issues on *Gau* and *Hindu Sanskriti*, and

Mookerjee would oblige on both occasions. In 1952, a year before his death in Kashmir, Mookerjee, by then out of Nehru's cabinet on the issue of the Nehru–Liaquat pact and immersed in opposing the government's Kashmir policy, would express his inability to write a long article and instead offer to pen a short one for *Kalyan*. However, he continued to subscribe to *Kalyan* and informed Poddar, 'I do not get your magazine regularly every month.'[72] Poddar's handwritten remark on this letter, marked 'urgent', instructed his staff to ensure that Mookerjee got copies of *Kalyan* and *Kalyana-Kalpataru* without fail.

Mookerjee was not alone among the Bengali elite who gravitated towards the Hindu Mahasabha and its politics. Nirmal Chandra Chatterjee, an eminent lawyer and judge, joined the organization around the same time as Mookerjee and became a leading conservative voice during the tumultuous 1940s and in independent India. He remained with the Mahasabha, declining invitations to join the Jana Sangh when it was formed in 1951. A three-term Lok Sabha member and an eminent lawyer of the Supreme Court till the early 1960s, Chatterjee, father of former Lok Sabha speaker and leftist leader Somnath Chatterjee, was effusive when asked to contribute to *Kalyan*. 'You do not know my respect for you and my admiration for the great work you have done for Hindu religion and culture,' he told Poddar.[73] He wrote on the future of Hindu jati (race) in the annual number of 1953.

In the same annual issue, one-time Congressman, former premier of the Central Provinces and Berar and later chief minister of Alwar, Mahasabha leader Narayan Bhaskar Khare wrote on the need to revive religious principles among people. In his speech as Mahasabha president in Calcutta, 1949, Khare had given a call for the formation of a 'cultural state of Hindu Rashtra'.[74] A known Gandhi-baiter, Khare was among those arrested in connection with the assassination of the Mahatma in 1948.[75] Among the other leading Mahasabha contributors to *Kalyan* were Mahant Digvijaynath (head of the Nath sect based in Gorakhpur), N.C. Kelkar (Hindu Mahasabha president during the Kanpur session, 1925) and sadhu-politician Baba Raghav Das who was the most prolific.[76] As many as forty-five articles by Das appeared in *Kalyan*. Interestingly, he contested and won as a Congress candidate, fully supported by Hindu Mahasabha, during the 1948 by-election to the

Faizabad assembly constituency against Acharya Narendra Dev, another prominent *Kalyan* contributor.

Sanskrit scholar, Indologist and an expert on languages, Raghuvira was among the earliest Congressmen to leave the party in 1961 over differences with Nehru on government's China policy. He joined the Jana Sangh that elected him party president in 1962. Raghuvira turned his International Academy of Indian Culture (Sarasvati Vihar) into a centre for research on Hindu culture, religion and languages. An activist for Hindi and other Indian languages, Raghuvira was behind the compilation of the *Greater English-Hindi Dictionary* (1969), among other lexicographical works published by Sarasvati Vihar. The Hindi literary world was critical of his efforts, especially his excessive stress on Sanskritized Hindi. A majority of Raghuvira's six articles in *Kalyan* dealt with national language and formation of a national identity. Later, his son Lokesh Chandra, scholar of Buddhism and Indian art, would also write for *Kalyan*. Poddar was Raghuvira's benefactor. Raghuvira offered to make him a member of Sarasvati Vihar since 'there is no one who understands our mission better than you'.[77] It was rather unusual that Raghuvira would refuse to take money for ten books sent to Poddar and, in the same letter, ask for Rs 70,000–80,000 to run his institute as it did not have enough cash for its monthly expenditure.[78]

Then there were the sadhu-politicians who took time out to write for Gita Press. Swami Karpatri Maharaj and Prabhudatt Brahmachari hogged the political limelight in the years immediately after Independence for their role in the cow-protection movement and protest against the Hindu Code Bill. These two sadhu-politicians, with considerable following and the stout backing of the RSS and Hindu Mahasabha, were part of the first-generation, slowly forming opposition to the Nehruvian socialist and secular order.

Born in 1907 in the Pratapgarh district of the United Provinces, by the time of Independence, Karpatri had acquired a reputation as a rabble-rouser who had strong views on the course India should chart. His life story followed the familiar god-man trajectory—gravitating towards God from a young age, he renounced domestic life at sixteen (he was married at the age of nine). His spiritual quest took him to various gurus and he is said to have gone to the Himalayas to lead the life of an ascetic before joining the Dandis, an order of sanyasis established by Shankara. As communal polarization hardened in the late 1930s, Karpatri Maharaj formed the Dharma Sangh in 1940 and started the paper *Sanmarg*.[79] In many ways it was a new coalition of various sanatan Hindu religious organizations to speak in one voice and work unitedly for the defence of Hinduism.

Apart from raising the bogey of threat to Hinduism, the Dharma Sangh coined slogans in defence of religion that are still part of sanatan Hindu religion congregations, private or public. For example, '*dharma ki jay ho*' (may religion conquer), '*adharm ka nash ho*' (may irreligiosity be destroyed), '*praniyon mein sadbhavna ho*' (may there be goodwill among living creatures) and '*vishwa ka kalyan ho*' (may there be welfare in the world).[80] By 1948, Swami Karpatri had formed his own political party, Ram Rajya Parishad. '. . . certainly the most orthodox of all the rightist parties which have achieved any renown', the Parishad stood for a 'rural economy based on traditional jajmani system and barter, traditional system of medicine such as ayurveda, prohibition of alcoholic drinks and cow slaughter'.[81] Karpatri's insistence that the Jana Sangh should be based on a holy Hindu text, a suggestion rejected by Deendayal Upadhyaya,[82] resulted in right-wing parties failing to put up a united front in the early 1950s.

Karpatri wrote thirty-nine articles for *Kalyan*, a majority of them communal in nature. Held in high esteem by Poddar and Gita Press, Karpatri Maharaj's role in the movements for cow protection and against the Hindu Code Bill would be of great significance in a comprehensive assessment of his contribution to the Hindu cause.

On the other hand, Prabhudatt Brahmachari, 'the saint of Jhusi',[83] was more open to political manoeuvring. Unlike Karpatri, Prabhudatt took to religion after being a full-time political activist. Born in Aligarh, he was among the earliest sadhu-politicians to participate in the national movement. He edited the newspaper *Aaj* in Banaras[84] before giving it all away and setting up an ashram in Jhusi near Allahabad.

He had developed a close relationship with front-line RSS leaders, and Golwalkar and others convinced him to contest against Jawaharlal Nehru in the first general election of 1952.[85] Despite a strong campaign by the RSS network and other right-wing groups on issues like cow protection and the avowed threat to Hindu family values by the proposed Hindu Code Bill, Prabhudatt could garner only 56,718 votes against Nehru's 233,571. Still, overnight, Prabhudatt became the darling of the conservative set. In the next few years, he joined a galaxy of right-wing political groups and leaders that included Poddar and Gita Press, to make common cause on cow protection and against the Hindu Code Bill. A contributor to *Kalyan* from its second year on, Prabhudatt wrote fifty-four articles. He and Poddar shared a great personal rapport.

Kaka Kalelkar and Vinoba Bhave not only contributed to *Kalyan* but also became fellow-travellers of Poddar and Gita Press in their campaigns for cow protection and the popularization of Hindi and the Gita. However, despite their closeness to the Hindu Mahasabha and later Jana Sangh leaders, both of them retained their inclusive core and Gandhian values. Bhave, spiritual inheritor of Gandhi, an expert on Gita and leader of the Bhoodan movement, wrote on a range of subjects—from Gita to Hinduism to family planning—from *Kalyan*'s early days to the time it turned forty and beyond.

Kalelkar, who headed the Backward Classes Commission in 1953, was also a contributor to *Kalyan* from its early years but would not mince words when he felt the need to disagree with the editor. In 1968 he was invited by Poddar to contribute to *Kalyan*'s 1969 annual number on *Parlok Aur Punarjanam* (Next World and Rebirth). Critical of the '200 to 250' topics that Poddar had listed for the issue, Kalelkar wrote that though he believed in the concept of rebirth, it made him angry whenever he heard that a person could be released from the cycle of rebirth if he/she bathed in a particular river or had a darshan of a particular statue of a god.[86] He believed in the importance of karma (deeds): 'One's deeds in this life are based on actions of the previous life. At the same time, a person is also guided and inspired by resolutions made in this life.' Kalelkar warned Poddar that he would end up collecting garbage from innumerable belief systems that would be difficult to review. He said detractors of sanatan Hindu dharma would immensely enjoy a special issue of *Kalyan* on a topic like rebirth: 'They would be able to say that the followers of sanatan Hindu dharma believe in concepts that are idiotic and make no sense.' Kalelkar nevertheless complimented Poddar for his effort, and requested him to carry his letter in the special issue of *Kalyan*.

Poddar carried Kalelkar's letter of criticism in full, but with his own rebuttal. To claim that whatever was logically acceptable was the sole truth, Poddar said, would be a daring act. 'There are things beyond our understanding that are considered to be true. Belief and logic do not coexist . . . Even if it is considered a sign of our poor knowledge we consider historical Krishna and Lord Krishna to be indistinguishable. When Kaka talks of garbage I take it as a compliment, as his style of humour. It is possible that from the mountain of garbage some of us would be able to find a pearl or two.'

Kalelkar liked the manner in which his letter was reproduced with Poddar's reply. Later, Kalelkar told Radheshyam Banka, a key Gita Press functionary, 'If Poddar is agreeable *Kalyan* can be used to debate differences of approach on sanatan dharma.'[87]

Intellectuals, Academics, Journalists, Artists

Historian Radha Kumud Mookerji had cut his teeth in politics during the Swadeshi movement against the Partition of Bengal. Associated with the Dawn Society, Mookerji along with a few others was instrumental in leading the boycott of university examinations. Later, he became a part of the National Council of Education, designing the syllabus and teaching in Bengal National College, the Swadeshi movement's initiative in higher education in Calcutta.[88] His involvement with what is called the national education movement did not last long, but the historical research conducted by him and others of his group had a 'swadeshi wind' about it.[89] Mookerji researched and produced works on Chandragupta Maurya and ancient Indian oceanic trade and shipping.[90] He relied on 'classical Hindu texts and scriptures' to argue for India's fundamental unity, an attempt to counter the 'colonial notion' that Indian unity had been brought about by the British. Mookerji's thesis endeared him to Hindu nationalists, whether in the Hindu Mahasabha or at Gita Press.

As the clouds of Partition darkened, Mookerji presided over the 7–8 October 1944 meeting of the Akhand Hindu Conference, a brainchild of Veer Savarkar, that saw the coming together of adversarial groups representing sanatanists, lower castes, Sikhs, organizations like the Arya Samaj and political parties like the Democratic Swaraj Party, Congress Nationalist Party and a few others. The idea was to present a united front against Partition. In his speech Mookerji said, 'A crisis of the first magnitude has been created in our national history by some great leaders who have convinced themselves that it is impossible for our mother country to attain her independent status which is her birthright, except on the basis of Hindu-Muslim unity.'[91]

For Mookerji, Poddar was a reverential figure: 'I regret I do not know how to address an exalted personality like yourself. I am unable to express my feeling of greatness towards you which has increased all the more as you have made me look small by addressing me as His Highness.'[92] Mookerji wrote for *Kalyan* and in turn invited Poddar to write for a publication with which he was involved. In 1954, when Mookerji's article on Vedic thought was accepted for publication in *Kalyan*, the happy author asked if it would be possible to 'print the Sanskrit terms, with which the article bristles, with necessary diacritical marks and accented types, as prescribed for their transliteration'.[93] However, his request could not be granted.

Radha Kumud's brother Radha Kamal Mukerjee was a sociologist, economist, ecologist, spiritualist and institution-builder. Radha Kamal lived for some time with Benoy Kumar Sarkar who was a friend and colleague of Radha Kumud at Bengal National College.[94] A brilliant student, successful teacher and a polyglot, Radha Kamal, as historian Ramachandra Guha points out, 'anticipated, by decades, the methodological alliance recently forged in American university departments between ecology and the social sciences'.[95] Drawn to the Ramanandi sect very early in life, in his later years, Radha Kamal held discourses on the Gita in Lucknow where he taught sociology and economics at Lucknow University after stints in Calcutta, Gwalior and other places. For him, the study of history was important to 'recover the glory of his motherland',[96] an argument that must have endeared him to Gita Press. A contributor to *Kalyan* from its early years, Radha Kamal wrote four articles on topics as varied as religious mystique, science and power, and the relationship between forests and pastureland.

Radha Kamal shared a warm relationship with Poddar, addressing the *Kalyan* editor as 'Poddar Mahashaya', and expressing 'surprise' that

Poddar had not met him when visiting Lucknow. In future, he requested Poddar, 'kindly stay in my house'.[97] Theirs was not the usual editor–contributor relationship. In one communication, Radha Kamal asked Poddar if he had 'sent Rs 100 to Messrs Longmans', but there is no reference in the Poddar Papers that explains this transaction. Both brothers often wrote for *Modern Review* published from Calcutta.

Also among the contributors were academics such as Satyendra Nath Sen, professor at City College, Calcutta, former member of the Bengal legislative assembly and a political activist working for the rights of Hindus. In the index of writers maintained by Gita Press, the title Dharmaratna (jewel of religion) is prefixed to Sen's name. Sen wrote for both *Kalyan* and *Kalyana-Kalpataru*. When asked to contribute an article on 'dharma and politics' for *Kalyana-Kalpataru*, he agreed but requested more time as he was 'awfully busy these days in connection with an agitation for counteracting government's interference with the civic and religious rights of the Hindus as manifested by the immersion tangle in many places in Bengal'.[98] The government had banned the passing of Durga Puja immersion processions with music through areas that had mosques, resulting in protests throughout Bengal. Hindu Mahasabha leaders were actively involved in the movement that led to widespread communal tension.[99] In 1945, when asked to write on the cow, Sen told Poddar he was busy and instead asked him to carry his review of *Kalyan*'s *Gau Ank* that had appeared in *Voice of India*,[100] a monthly published by the National Committee for India's Freedom based in Washington DC.

Lending diversity to Gita Press's corpus of contributors was Kshitimohan Sen, eminent scholar of Sanskrit and a Santiniketan don (grandfather of Nobel laureate Amartya Sen). With a life spent studying Hindu religious texts and social institutions, Sen's interpretation, whether of the Islamic influence on Hinduism, the caste system among Hindus or the position of women, was fundamentally different from the tenets of sanatan Hindu dharma. However, Sen was an 'unusual combination of consummate scholarship and undogmatic open-mindedness',[101] and his stature as a scholar seems to have brought him into *Kalyan*'s fold of contributors. He wrote four articles, including one on Kabir and the unity of Hinduism. Medieval poets of both bhakti and Sufi traditions were Sen's area of expertise, as is proven by the continuing publication of his 1929 classic *Medieval Mysticism of India*. Sisir Kumar Ghosh, translator of Sen's *Hinduism*, was also a regular in the pages of *Kalyan*.

Many articles by Rabindranath Tagore, who had managed to get Kshitimohan Sen to Santiniketan after much persuasion,[102] were extracted in *Kalyan*. Though early issues of *Kalyan* carried Tagore's writings, by 1936 his staff were citing his age in reply to requests for contributions from him: 'Rabindranath Tagore has reached the age when it is finally necessary for all people to retire from public activity. Ominous physical signs are becoming manifest and his medical advisers and relatives have been able now to persuade him to make himself free from all work which may be avoided . . . Will you therefore kindly forgive him his inability to comply with your request?'[103]

Four years before the publication of *The Position of Women in Hindu Civilisation* in 1938, a shastric defence of how women were protected and respected in ancient India, historian A.S. Altekar of Banaras Hindu University was requested to write for *Kalyan*'s *Shakti Ank*. Altekar sent a letter of regret, his tone and tenor suggesting familiarity with Poddar and *Kalyan*. After thanking Poddar for the invitation, he wrote: 'I am, however, extremely sorry that owing to my present literary commitments, it would not be possible for me to send any contribution for the number.'[104] It is likely that Altekar was already working on his magnum opus on women.

India's best-known linguist and an authority on Indo-European languages, Suniti Kumar Chatterjee took the time to write on the concept of Shiva in India for *Kalyan*'s annual issue on Shiva in 1933. When the *Hindu Sanskriti Ank* was being planned, Poddar wooed Chatterjee again. Thanking him for his 'valuable' article on Shiva, Poddar requested him to 'contribute an article on the glory of greater India in the days of yore' that would present an account of 'all the important aspects of Indian culture as it existed and is still found in greater India'.[105] Chatterjee did not write this time.

The father-son duo Sir Ganganath Jha and Amar Nath Jha were scholars of repute in Sanskrit and English respectively. The two had long dominated the academic world of Allahabad and Banaras and could not escape the attention of Poddar, always in search of reputed contributors. Jha senior wrote eleven articles for *Kalyan* on various aspects of yoga, Vedanta, Gita and God. Unlike many scholars of his time, he stands out for confining himself to his subject. On the occasions that he failed to write on the topic requested by Poddar, he would send an alternative piece, giving Poddar the freedom to take the editorial call: 'I hope this might be acceptable. If not please do not hesitate to tell me so. I shall then try to send something else.'[106] Jha's son Amar Nath wrote for the *Balak Ank* in 1953.

Three eminent foreigners who came to India in search of spirituality, peace and love, and made it their home, were pursued by Poddar and convinced to write for *Kalyan* and *Kalyana-Kalpataru*. During the first quarter of the twentieth century, C.F. Andrews, Nicholas Roerich and George Arundale had made their home in Delhi, Himachal Pradesh and Madras respectively, and contributed immensely to India's intellectual enrichment.

Andrews, a British clergyman and lecturer at St Stephen's College in Delhi since 1904,[107] became a key person in Gandhi's inner circle and played a crucial role in the national movement as a passionate advocate of the Indian cause. The period Andrews was coming close to Gandhi is also the time Poddar was deeply enamoured of him, and it is likely the two disciples had formed a bond. A certain degree of comfort must have existed early on between Andrews and Poddar as we find a 1923 letter from Andrews, then in Santiniketan, recommending Satyendranath Banerjee for an artist's job at Gita Press.[108] Gita Press had just come up in Gorakhpur, publishing religious texts in small numbers, and *Kalyan* had not yet been conceived, though Poddar was already close to Goyandka. Andrews' first article appeared in the third issue of *Kalyan* in the first year. It was on St Francis of Assisi. Fourteen years later, he contributed another one on the worldwide propagation of the Gita.

Cambridge-educated Arundale was principal of Central Hindu College, and tutor to J. Krishnamurti and his brother Nityananda who succeeded Annie Besant as president of the Theosophical Society. First asked in 1935 to send an article, Arundale refused: 'I am afraid that with my innumerable preoccupations, especially just now, it is quite impossible for me to send you any article.'[109] In 1940, Arundale wrote an article on the Gita, his sole contribution to *Kalyan*.

Sophia Wadia of the United Lodge of theosophists, shot to fame with her *Brotherhood of Religions*, a compendium of essays that showed the 'similarity in the fundamentals'[110] of all religions. Her quest for knowledge of all religions had brought her in touch with Gita Press. In 1934, when the Gita Society was floated, Wadia 'greatly approved of the idea'[111] and 'gladly' joined. In *Kalyan* she wrote on the concept of God in theosophy. Like Wadia, Sir S. Subramanya Iyer, founding member of Theosophical Society of India and a close associate of Annie Besant during the time of the Home Rule League, wrote a lone article for *Kalyan* on the lifeline of 'Aryans'.

In 1928, after a long journey throughout the country, painter Nicholas Roerich had made his home in Naggar, Kulu, in the then state of Punjab. Here he ran his Urusvati Himalayan Research Institute 'to study the results of their (the Roerichs') expedition, and of those explorations that were yet to come'.[112] A keen observer impressed with Indian spiritualism, 'philosophical concepts were turned into visual images' by him. (His son Svetoslav, also an artist, married noted Indian actor Devika Rani.) Within few years of Roerich's settling in India, he and Poddar were communicating with each other. In 1932 Poddar was informed about 'spare leaflets of Prof. de Roerich's book *Realm of Light*' and the 'possibility of including these with your magazine (*Kalyan*) to your closest subscribers'.[113]

Roerich himself was excited about writing for *Kalyan*. A request in 1932 from Poddar to contribute for the *Ishwar Ank* met with an enthusiastic response. Roerich promised not only to write the article '*Raj Rajeswari*' but also to send a photograph of one of his paintings. Along with this he also sent a 'coloured reproduction of the same painting amongst a set of coloured postcard reproductions of paintings' housed in his museum in New York. He had fulsome praise for Gita Press and *Kalyan*: 'I greatly rejoice seeing your sincere enlightened strivings towards the highest principles of Existence and I certainly wish your journal full deserved success.'[114]

Yet another novel contributor to *Kalyan* was C.Y. Chintamani. Born in a family of priests that served the royal family of Vizianagaram, he made the United Provinces his karmabhumi (place of work)—first as the editor of *Indian People*, promoted by Motilal Nehru, and later as the editor of Madan Mohan Malaviya's *Leader*. A one-time Congressman, Chintamani left on grounds of corruption within the party and floated his own National Liberal Federation with the likes of Tej Bahadur Sapru, Chimanlal Setalvad, Dinshaw Wacha and S.N. Banerjea. An eccentric follower of Gopal Krishna Gokhale—to the extent that he would book an extra train berth and keep it vacant for his idol (who died in 1915)—Chintamani became a member of the UP legislative council and the province's first education minister.[115] On Poddar's insistence he wrote two articles for *Kalyan* in the late 1930s, on Tulsidas's *Ramcharitmanas* and on the Gita.

Then there was journalist and writer Shripad R. Tikekar of Poona, who proved to be a tough negotiator and remarkably blunt about money. In 1927, Tikekar had written for *The Crisis*, the journal of the National Association for the Advancement of Colored People, edited by African–American civil rights activist W.E.B. Du Bois.[116] When this article was offered for publication in *Kalyana-Kalpataru*, Poddar refused to pay for it—which was unacceptable to Tikekar. In 1935 Tikekar wrote again, this time with an offer Poddar could not resist. Tikekar said he had the full text of Warren Hastings's 40,000-word note on the first English translation of the Gita published in 1784. After stressing the novelty of what he had, Tikekar told Poddar: 'You can imagine the difficulty in securing such an old copy of the original, let alone the trouble and cost of typing. To you I need not request to consider the worth or importance of the note, especially when it comes from the pen of so known a personality as Warren Hastings. May I therefore know what terms you would offer me for the contribution if at all you care to have it?' Further on, Tikekar descended to his blunt language: 'Let me plainly say, that whatever high your ideals, and howsoever laudable the objects for which you work, you cannot and I am sure, will not expect others to work for you for the mere love of labour.'[117]

From Tikekar's next letter it is clear Poddar had shown some interest and made inquiries about the payment expected. Tikekar demanded Rs 20 for the full text, and repeated: '. . . under no circumstances, will it be allowed to be published gratis'.[118] Finally, Poddar asked Tikekar to edit Hastings's note to 5,000 words. This Tikekar sent to Gorakhpur in April 1935, reminding Poddar that what he was charging was not a fee but money that he had spent from his own pocket. As their relationship had thawed a bit, Tikekar asked for more work, 'Will you please allow me to be of some use to your magazine? But you will have to allow little considerations for the expenses which I have to suffer.'[119] He offered an entire list of Hindu temples in Afghanistan, and requested that he be sent a copy of the issue of *Kalyana-Kalpataru* in which the Hastings note appeared.

Response of the Hindi Literary World

For *Kalyan* it was not enough to have gathered the mightiest, the best and the holiest among its writers; this first-of-its-kind religious genre journal needed to be noticed and patronized by the Hindi literary world. Poddar's legendary networking skills and almost dogged perseverance were on full display here. The Hindi Sahitya Sammelan, that started as an offshoot of the Nagari Pracharini Sabha in 1910 and became an independent body with headquarters in Allahabad, held annual meetings at various venues in north India. In 1930, the meeting was held in Gorakhpur and Poddar hosted stalwarts like Banarsi Das Chaturvedi, Thakur Shivmurti Singh and others. Poddar's aide Ramjidas Bajoria was entrusted the task of taking care of the writers, prompting Chaturvedi to remark: 'If ever a school of care and hospitality is opened Bajoria should be made its principal'.[120]

Poddar also got involved with the Dakshin Bharat Hindi Prachar Sabha started by Gandhi in 1918 to popularize Hindi as the national language.[121] He participated in literary politics from the margins and made *Kalyan* a forum for articles on Hindi as the keystone of nationalism. Most of these articles were one-sided, glorifying the spread of Hindi as a unifying force, a kind of cultural glue. The Hindi Sahitya Sammelan would appreciate Poddar's initiative and efforts in 1967 by honouring him with its highest award, Sahitya Vachaspati.

However, Gita Press's mission of defending and disseminating sanatan Hindu dharma and addressing the question of cultural and political identity failed to cut much ice with the leaders of the Hindi movement. As a result, despite its vast body of work, Gita Press failed to find a place in authoritative accounts of twentieth-century Hindi literature. Two exceptions were *Mishrabandhuvinod* and *Hindi Bhasha Aur Uske Sahitya Ka Vikas*.

Mishrabandhuvinod (Delight of the Mishra Brothers), a monumental four-volume history of Hindi literature and a passionate defence of Hindi as a language of independent standing with its own grammar, was the first 'comprehensive attempt from within the Hindi community to craft a historical narrative for their own literature'.[122] 'Those who depend on Sanskrit grammar to write Hindi language are the ones who do not recognize the existence of Hindi. We consider them enemies of Hindi,' *Mishrabandhuvinod* stated.[123]

A collaborative exercise of three brothers—Ganeshbihari, Shyambihari and Sukhdevbihari Mishra—*Mishrabandhuvinod* was a raging success when it appeared in 1913. Sold out immediately (black marketeers seem to have made a killing),[124] the book was updated with subsequent editions including new writers, those omitted in earlier editions and those on the horizon.

The novelty of *Mishrabandhuvinod* was its chronicling of the major, minor and even minuscule initiatives that helped Hindi find its feet. The mammoth exercise was inclusive in intent, lending space to all kinds of writers and all genres of writing without discrimination, but with critical analysis of the potential of each one of them.

In the 1934 edition of *Mishrabandhuvinod*, Poddar finds a brief mention with 'Marwari' suffixed to his name as *Kalyan*'s editor whose articles are full of 'scholarship'. *Kalyan*, the book states, 'has a circulation of 20,000 per month; among all Hindi journals it has special importance but the articles are ordinary'.[125] Call it a reflection of Poddar's ability or his considerable networking skills, his persona had subsumed both Gita Press and Jaydayal Goyandka, the prime mover behind the initiative.

Hindi Bhasha Aur Uske Sahitya Ka Vikas (The Origin and Development of the Hindi Language and Its Literature) was a compilation of lectures delivered by Ayodhya Singh Upadhyay 'Harioudh' at Patna University, published by the university in 1934. A former kanungo (land registrar) from Nizamabad in Azamgarh district of Uttar Pradesh and a sanatani (traditionalist) in his religious beliefs, Harioudh wrote during his years in service and later took to teaching at Banaras Hindu University and elsewhere.[126] An acquaintance of G.A. Grierson who conducted the Linguistic Survey of India (1898–1928), Harioudh was also a contributor to *Kalyan*, mostly of poems. His book, less ambitious than *Mishrabandhuvinod*, contextualized the growth of Hindi more cogently. It did not go into reporting each personality and every change. While admitting that Urdu literature had reached a level of sophistication, Harioudh vehemently argued that the two languages were not only different but 'Hindi is the mother of Urdu . . . I do not agree that Hindi is based on principles of Urdu language'. He praised Gita Press for its publication of religious books, but reserved the credit for Poddar: 'His enthusiasm is not only praiseworthy but worthy of even superlative commendation. He not only writes religious books but also gives the task to others. He is seriously involved in popularizing these religious books.' Harioudh placed *Kalyan*, clearly a religious journal, along with Hindi mainstream and literary magazines like *Madhuri*, *Chand*, *Sudha*, *Saraswati*, *Vishal Bharat*, *Vina*, *Hans* and *Vigyan*, that in his opinion were not only well edited but considered prestigious in the Hindi literary world.[127]

Between *Mishrabandhuvinod* and Harioudh's *Hindi Bhasha Aur Uske Sahitya Ka Vikas*, appeared Ramchandra Shukl's *Hindi Sahitya Ka Itihas* in 1929, the most authoritative account of Hindi literary history. Though Shukl's work would later be comprehensively criticized, it still retains its seminal position. Shukl laid stress on including only important writers and major literary trends to place the growth of Hindi in a historical context, and this may account for his omission of Gita Press, *Kalyan* and even Poddar. Interestingly, Shukl wrote on '*Manas Ki Dharmbhumi*' (Spirituality of Mind) for *Kalyan* in 1938. Omission from Shukl's influential book presumably played a role in the lack of critical attention paid by modern historians of Hindi nationalism and public sphere to Gita Press's contribution.

Poddar with his extraordinary zeal disregarded the lukewarm reception given to him by the chroniclers of Hindi's history. As was his style, he worked on personal terms with contributors and waded through the vast Hindi literary world inviting everyone who cared about the perceived danger to sanatan Hindu dharma or Hindu nationalism to write for Gita Press. Even those keen to give their views on the secular aspects of religion were welcome to do so. In the end Poddar collected a perfect blend of traditionalists, ultra-conservatives and progressive Hindi writers. Many Hindi writers who contributed to *Kalyan* in its early decades, and did not live to see the journal's journey through the communal cauldron of the 1940s and '50s, would have regretted their association with it.

A list of contributors, a veritable who's who from the Hindi world, illustrates how everyone partook in the Gita Press project in its early years. Babu Shyamsundar Das, one of the founding members of the Nagari Pracharini Sabha in 1896, spent his life teaching Hindi in school and at Banaras Hindu University, and propagating the language as the lingua franca of the masses. Das's biggest contribution was as editor of the sixteen-volume *Hindi Sabdsagara,* a Nagari Pracharini Sabha publication. His single piece in *Kalyan* appeared in 1929 on the poetics of Tulsidas.

The oeuvre of Mahavir Prasad Dwivedi is synonymous with an age in Hindi literature called the Dwivedi Yug (Dwivedi Era) that inspired many generations of writers. Editor of the highbrow *Saraswati* for seventeen years, Dwivedi was a language scholar and a pioneer of Khari Boli (standard Hindi dialect shorn of both Sanskrit and Urdu words). He had met Poddar in Calcutta,[128] and wrote four original pieces for *Kalyan* in its first decade on the themes of compassion, Ganga and prayer. One more article was extracted from his published work.

Dwivedi had the highest regard for Poddar and *Kalyan* and missed no opportunity to praise him. Even when he expressed his inability to send an article, Dwivedi would give Poddar permission to extract from his published works. He was also a regular reader of *Kalyan* and at times, overwhelmed by Poddar's writing, would send a postcard of appreciation. After reading *Ishwar Ank* he wrote: 'My eyes are full of tears and some of them have fallen on the postcard. You are great, your work is great . . .' A few years later, on receiving a copy of *Kalyan*'s *Sant Ank* (Issue on Saints, 1937), Dwivedi effusively thanked Poddar for 'doing good to my materialistic life'.[129]

Editor, writer, activist—and post-1947 a nominated member of parliament—Banarasi Das Chaturvedi was the Hindi literary world's most influential figure for a long time, with excellent networking skills across the political–literary divide. Wearing multiple hats, Chaturvedi's lifelong mission was to work for indentured Indian labour in Fiji, which brought him close to C.F. Andrews and a large number of political leaders across ideologies.

As editor of *Vishal Bharat* owned by Ramananda Chatterjee of the Hindu Mahasabha who was also owner-editor of *Modern Review* in English and *Prabasi* in Bengali (all three published from Calcutta), Chaturvedi was in the thick of Hindi literary politics. He ran a concerted campaign against *Chocolate*, (1927), a collection of stories by Pandey Bechan Sharma 'Ugra'. The collection was an instant best-seller, but was not to the liking of the 'literary establishment' as it not only dealt with the forbidden subject of homosexuality but 'depicted homosexuals not as slum or prison dwellers, but as respectably married middle-class men, both Hindu and Muslim, with flourishing social networks of their own, engaging in liasions in their homes and in public spaces'.[130] From Premchand who disapproved of the book to Gandhi who Ugra claimed was supportive,[131] virtually everyone of note got embroiled in the controversy, but it was Chaturvedi who termed such work 'ghasleti sahitya' (inferior literature). Chaturvedi and Ugra corresponded with each other, the former insisting that 'chumban-pratha' (practice of kissing) according to medical science led to various diseases.[132] Still, Chaturvedi published a story by Ugra in *Vishal Bharat*, though the two sparred on the kind of drawing that should accompany it.[133]

Poddar and Chaturvedi were old acquaintances. In 1931 Poddar, while condoling with Chaturvedi on the death of his son, praised his work among indentured labour and advised him to 'pray to the supreme God and see for yourself if your worries get translated into happiness or not'.[134] Chaturvedi contributed three articles to *Kalyan*—a relative study of Gandhi and Lenin, on children's literature and on bhakti. In 1941, he suggested to Poddar that *Kalyan* should bring out a special *Matribhumi Ank* (Motherland Issue): 'Not only would it educate the masses, even the topic would be contemporary.' Chaturvedi volunteered to help bring out the special edition and promised to come to Gorakhpur to plan it. Acknowledging that 'our world view does not match on many issues', Chaturvedi said the two could 'work together on issues where they agreed'.[135] But the issue never materialized.

Occasionally, Chaturvedi sought financial help from Poddar for people and causes dear to him, a fact he admitted in a letter of 1958 written to wish Poddar a quick recovery from illness. Asking 'how can I forget the help you gave me from time to time?' Chaturvedi listed the monetary help Poddar had given him on various occasions (amounts between Rs 80 and 150) as well as timely payments for contributions to *Kalyan*. Significantly, in the same letter, Chaturvedi explained that because he was a brahmin he did not write 'pranam' (a form of greeting to elders) to Poddar, but instead wrote 'ashish' (blessing to someone younger)—revealing Chaturvedi's deep-seated sense of his caste superiority.[136]

Munshi Premchand, the greatest writer of his time, was an influential voice in the Hindi public sphere when Poddar began prodding him for contributions for *Kalyan*. The choice of Premchand for a journal like *Kalyan* was curious, for the writer not only depicted the diminished role of religion in lives of his characters but publicly took a stand counter to that of Gita Press and the Hindu Mahasabha in their open opposition to Urdu as the language of Muslims. In 1934 he had stated at a meeting of the Dakshin Bharat Hindi Prachar Sabha: 'The name Hindi was given by the Muslims, and until just fifty years ago, the language now being described as Urdu was called Hindi even by Muslims.'[137]

After consistent persuasion by Poddar, Premchand wrote on Sri Krishna in 1931. But he made his reluctance apparent: 'I received your kind letter. You are right I have not written anything for *Kalyan* in three years. The reason is it is a religious magazine and I have no knowledge of religious matters . . . You are an authority and yet you request a novice like me to write. I will have to follow your command. I like the topic of Sri Krishna and the Future World and I will write something on it.'[138] In 1931, Premchand's first article appeared in *Kalyan* on this topic.

In asking Premchand to write for *Kalyan*, Poddar seems to have turned a blind eye to the dialectics of language politics in which the writer played a key role. Premchand's stature was possibly the reason; besides, he and Poddar were comfortable with each other. As we saw earlier, Premchand even recommended a Muslim artist, Mohammad Hakim Khan, for a job in Gita Press. In 1948, twelve years after the writer's death, *Kalyan* published an extract of Premchand's article on the true calling for women in its annual *Nari Ank*.

Gita Press's policy of indifference to conflicting viewpoints being held by their writers was not limited to Hindi language politics but extended to new literary trends as well. For Poddar, the literary and personal predilections of writers meant little, as long as the contributions followed the Gita Press template. The biggest challenge to the established literary norms of the Dwivedi Yug came from three poets, unknown to each other, working in different places. It was the beginning of a new era of irreverence that would shake the world of Hindi literature. The poetry of Jayshankar Prasad, Suryakant Tripathi 'Nirala' and Sumitranandan Pant was uniformly derided by the literary establishment and labelled 'chhayavad' (literally, of the shadows), which came to denote neo-romanticism in Hindi poetry or an 'allegedly mystical-ethereal-escapist school of poetry'.[139] Dwivedi himself led the onslaught and was most disparaging towards chhayavad: 'Perhaps what is meant by chhayavad is poetry that is the shadow (chhaya) of poetry being written elsewhere.'[140] What rankled the Hindi public sphere was not only the chhayavadis' complete disregard for rules of 'language, meter, prosody, etc., but their choice of subjects like love, loss, romance, nature, beauty', and their emphasis on 'broadening the social context of individual'—these ran counter to the dominating theme of nationalism 'at a time of intense political and social ferment, a time of alternately soaring hopes and sinking despair about the future for independence'.

Prasad from Banaras, Pant from Almora (later settled in Allahabad) and Nirala the quintessential yayavar (itinerant) originally from Unnao in Uttar Pradesh, but born in Mahishadal (part of East Medinipur), a princely state in Bengal,[141] formed their own literary space and got their works published. In the case of Prasad and Pant, breaking the rules was limited to literary style and world view, but Nirala (which means unique), the most talented of the triad, was irreverent to the core, out to destroy all the institutions of sanatan Hindu dharma that Gita Press so zealously championed.

The high watermark of Suryakant Tripathi's career was his stint at *Matwala* (the intoxicated; the wayward or free spirit).[142] Launched in Calcutta on 26 August 1923 by Seth Mahadev Prasad, *Matwala* was a journal with disdain for institutions, individuals, organized religion, politics and politicians, but respect for the progressive ethos. *Matwala*'s attack on sanatan dharma was so scathing that a journal called *Dharma-Rakshak* was brought out in response.[143] 'Nirala' was added to Tripathi's name by what came to be known as the *Matwala* gang. A motley group of immensely talented writers—satirist Munshi Navjadiklal Srivastava, writer of beautiful prose Shivpujan Sahay, and the head of the group Nirala—formed the core of *Matwala*, in which leading names of that time wrote. Nirala, who eventually quit *Matwala* over the magazine's failure to defend him against charges of plagiarizing Tagore and later not publishing his poems, was known for his magnanimity to all even while he himself suffered financially. A kanyakubja brahmin, Nirala discarded the sacred thread, mixed with Muslims, drank alcohol, visited a 'very unwell' prostitute in Calcutta's Sonagachi brothel—he was taken there by Ugra as revenge for Nirala having served him country liquor mixed with colour—and contracted a serious disease. Eventually, Prasad got Nirala treated in Banaras: one chhayavadi to the aid of another.

For *Kalyan*, Nirala chose to write on contemporary literature and religion, a theme that must have nagged him in the midst of the all-round attack that he and his chhayavadi fellow-travellers were facing at the hands of the literary establishment enmeshed in the language of Hindu nationalism. Nirala's article appeared in 1931, when he had left *Matwala* and was freelancing. Again, it was the result of Poddar's constant persuasion. Embarrassed by the reminders, Nirala explained he had been caught up with domestic affairs: 'What should I write? I am ashamed of my behaviour towards a gentleman like you. For the future issues of *Kalyan* I will keep sending something. One article will reach you soon.'[144]

Poddar had requested Pant to write on the importance of Hindu religion for the *Hindu Sanskriti Ank* of 1950.[145] While this stage of Pant's career was marked by the 'culmination of the *chhayavad* phase' and beginning of 'ideological poetry inspired by Gandhism and Marxism', he later took to 'philosophical poetry inspired by Aurobindo'.[146] For the *Hindu Sanskriti Ank*, he wrote a poem '*Stavan*' (Praise), a highly Sanskritized eulogy to God.

Prasad, a tobacco merchant from Banaras, began as a poet in Braj Bhasha (dialect of Hindi spoken in western UP), took to Khari Boli and later emerged as the fountainhead of chhayavad poetry. After *Saraswati* declined to publish his poetry, he started his own journal, *Indu*.[147] Like Nirala and Pant, Prasad also chose to write on the relatively safe topic of 'mysticism' for *Kalyan* in 1937, the year he died. Mahadevi Varma, a late entrant to the chhayavad school but a prominent voice of the Hindi literary world, never wrote for *Kalyan*.

Gita Press's eclectic mix of contributors from the world of Hindi literature included Maithilisharan Gupt, the most influential nationalist Hindi poet of the Dwivedi era, christened 'rashtra kavi' (national poet) after 1947 and also nominated to the Rajya Sabha for two terms from 1952. He had shot into fame with *Bharat-Bharati* published in 1912, a 'rousing nationalist survey of the state of the nation and Hindus'[148] and simultaneously a eulogy to British rule: 'It is not possible that foreign rule by even the noblest soul would be fair; even if it's true, British rule is acceptable to us. It is better organized and full of hope.' Gupt even 'doled out a certificate' to the British government for its work during famines.[149] The irreverent *Matwala* would take a swipe at Gupt when news of his poem '*Ish-Vinay*' (Prayer to God), part of *Bharat-Bharati*, came: 'Prayer to British rule! Taking the name of Rama in Lanka. He should be interned somewhere to justify the name Gupt (secret).'[150]

Bharat-Bharati's larger significance was its contribution to sharpening of Hindu–Muslim identities and the effortless ease with which the terms 'Hindi', 'Hindu' and 'Indian' were used interchangeably among writers, journalists and a section of politicians. When Gupt and Poddar met in Calcutta, *Bharat-Bharati* was already the rage and the poet had acquired cult status. Poddar would not forget Gupt when planning the *Hindu Sanskriti Ank* of 1950—knowing full well that Gupt was not in good health, Poddar insisted that he write at least a page. 'You are the tallest among the virtuous poets of the Hindi literary world who is also a big devotee of Hindu culture. Therefore, I am making a special request. Take care of your health but please send something.'[151] Finally, a small poem '*Apni Sanskriti*' (Our Culture) was extracted from Gupt's

Hindu, a collection of poems published in 1927 where he took an anti-British stance and in which the notion of Hindi/Indian nationalism got sharper.

Earlier, in 1945, Gupt had disappointed Poddar by not writing for the annual *Gau Ank* on grounds of ill health. Convalescing in his village Chirgaon in Jhansi district, Gupt told Poddar that both he and his younger brother Siyaram Sharan Gupt, also a poet, were very unwell, with some breathing problem. But he told Poddar to 'extract poems on gau-badh (cow slaughter) from *Bharat-Bharati*'. Gupt added that he had not had a 'darshan of *Kalyan* for a long time but news of its growth and widespread circulation keeps coming to me. If not for anything, I am happy for Hindi.'[152]

Shivpujan Sahay, 'the typical, impecunious, and itinerant freelance Hindi journalist'[153] from Bihar commanded immense respect in the Hindi literary world across factions, for his chameli or flower-like prose.[154] He was also the Hindi world's Mr Congeniality. If Nirala, the irreverent, was so fond of him as to take care of Sahay's wife's serious illness in Calcutta,[155] Poddar, the dogged editor, would pursue him relentlessly to contribute to *Kalyan*, and the entire galaxy of Hindi writers, poets and critics would trust him for his honesty. An institution builder who single-handedly managed the Bihar Hindi Sahitya Sammelan in its formative years after 1947, Sahay had been editor of the weekly *Jagran* in Banaras in the early 1930s. Poddar had praised the work of *Jagran* and requested Sahay to write for the *Ishwar Ank*, *Kalyan*'s 1932 annual number.

No letters from Sahay are to be found in the Poddar Papers, but it is clear that he did make a promise to write. This is evident from Poddar's letter thanking Sahay for accepting the invitation, and even requesting him to remind Jayshankar Prasad, who lived close by in Banaras, to send the article he had promised.[156] Though ill health prevented Sahay from writing for *Kalyan*, he was a keen reader of the journal and would request copies of issues he had missed. Poddar obliged whenever he could.[157]

Poddar was consulted on religious articles published in *Jagran*. For instance, asked to provide a list of books on Tulsidas, Poddar replied to *Jagran* staffer Pravasi Lal Varma that the existing books on Tulsidas were of doubtful authenticity and the poet had written only a very brief profile of himself.[158] The hagiography *Gosai-charit*, believed to have been written seven years after Tulsidas's death by his disciple Benimadhav Das, was considered the most authentic account but no copy of it existed. In 1926, when a manuscript said to be of Das's work had been found in Bihar, the event had caused both 'excitement and scepticism', with many scholars dismissing it as a 'nineteenth-century fabrication'.[159] However, Gita Press published it in 1934.

The lives of Baburao Vishnu Paradkar and Poddar converged for a certain length of time. A Maharashtrian, born in Banaras and educated in Bihar, Paradkar came to Calcutta for work and part-time study. He joined the newspaper *Bangavasi* and later *Hitvarta*. Impressed by Aurobindo Ghose (then head of Bengal National College) and his brother, Paradkar became involved with the revolutionary movement.[160] Paradkar translated the Gita into Hindi at the behest of the Sahitya Samvardhani Samiti set up by young Marwaris in Calcutta, which is when he got to know Poddar. The translated text's cover of Bharatmata with the Gita in one hand and sword in another, a standard depiction of India as a Hindu nation used by the RSS and other right-wing organizations, brought Paradkar to the notice of the British government. Poddar claimed Paradkar was also party to the Rodda Arms Robbery case, tasked with hiding ammunition.[161] Paradkar was externed from Bengal and came to Banaras where he eventually edited the Hindi *Aaj*, turning it into a leading newspaper of the United Provinces. Ugra, still in his teens, had his first article published in *Aaj*, thanks to Paradkar whom he considered his guru. Paradkar contributed a single article on goddess Bhagawati to *Kalyan* but, more significantly, was sought by Gita Press to translate Marathi articles into Hindi.

Laxman Narayan Garde was another translator of Marathi articles into Hindi and English for *Kalyan* and *Kalyana-Kalpataru*. Coming from the same small but intellectually significant Marathi brahmin population of Banaras as Paradkar, Garde worked at *Kalyan* in the initial years but, like many of his journalistic stints, this was a short one. An admirer of Tilak, a Gandhi-baiter and a known 'votary of Hindutva', Garde translated Veer Savarkar's 1923 text *Hindutva* from Marathi to Hindi with the title *Hindupad Padshahi*. Ideologically rigid, Garde at one point used to give discourses on Tilak's *Gita Rahasya* in Calcutta where he worked with *Bharatmitra* and later *Shri Krishna Sandesh* financed by Dr S.K. Barman of the Dabur family.[162]

For all his ideological firmness, Garde's life was somewhat complicated and even at odds with all he stood for publicly. He would constantly consult Poddar, whom he considered his conscience-keeper along with Sri Aurobindo and the Mother, for a way out of the 'constant sins he committed'—he mentioned one instance when he returned from a cinema hall in Banaras on having visions of Poddar, and asked him to recommend someone who would morally guide him in Banaras.[163] Though the only sin he referred to was watching a movie, going by the drift of the letter it seems that Garde had committed more sinful acts.

In his later years, Garde would write to Poddar of a court battle with his wife who insisted on her 'swatva' (own identity).[164] Going by Garde's account, his wife had left him and demanded monetary compensation, something he was finding difficult to fulfil despite sending her Rs 300 every month. He would also bemoan to Chimmanlal Gosvami, co-editor of *Kalyan*, the time he had to waste in courts, his inability to write and financial troubles.[165] He contributed nineteen articles on various religious and cultural issues to *Kalyan*, including a highly critical one on Gandhi and Hinduism for the *Hindu Sanskriti Ank*.

In the 1930s when *Kalyan* and Gita Press were trying to find a foothold in the United Provinces and outside, Harivansh Rai Bachchan had already become a household name in the Hindi world with his *Madhushala* inspired by Omar Khayyam's *Rubaiyat*. It seems that Poddar and Bachchan got close after Bachchan wrote an invocation to God in the form of a geet (poem) for *Kalyan* in 1960.[166] Poddar's personal relationship with Bachchan may have been a result of the deep and lasting impression that Radha Baba, Poddar's friend and associate, had made on Bachchan. Bachchan had met Radha Baba in Delhi in the 1950s through Ramnivas Dhandharia, an industrialist from Calcutta who was also a friend of Poddar. In letters to Poddar from Bachchan and his wife Teji, Radha Baba was always referred to with great reverence. Bachchan claimed that the Baba 'through a dream gave me the inspiration to translate the Bhagavadgita' into the Awadhi used in *Ramcharitmanas*.[167] Thus was published *Jan Gita*. In 1958, on his younger son Ajitabh's twelfth birthday, Bachchan went to Gorakhpur to recite the text to Radha Baba. After two editions of *Jan Gita* had come out, Chimmanlal Gosvami, Ram Bhai and Madhav Sharan (all associated with Gita Press) pointed out certain inaccuracies, and Bachchan made the corrections. When he went to gift the revised *Jan Gita* to Radha Baba in 1964, the latter told him to prepare a Khari Boli version of the Gita. Bachchan took up the challenge and completed the translation in January 1966.[168]

The story of Hindi would remain partially told without reference to Shivprasad Gupt, magnanimous publisher of Gyanmandal Press who also launched newspapers and journals like *Aaj*, *Maryada*, *Swarth* and (when the colonial government was on his trail) the cyclostyled *Ranbheri*. At the time of Independence, he published *Samaj*, edited by Narendra Dev. Gupt was something of an enigma in Banaras, bankrolling institutions like Kashi Vidyapith with a grant of Rs 10 lakh, providing funds to the Nagari Pracharini Sabha, financing Congress workers and revolutionaries in equal measure and establishing the Bharat Mata Mandir.[169] Through all this, Gupt maintained an unflinching loyalty to Gandhi. He also found time to write for *Kalyan*.

Ramnaresh Tripathi was a Braj Bhasha and Hindi poet, and a political activist who participated in the non-cooperation movement and was closely associated with an assortment of bodies like the Tilak Swaraj Fund and later the Nagari Pracharini Sabha. Tripathi's contribution to the cause of Hindi was immense: a three-volume compilation of rural folk songs *Gram Geet* and a seven-volume collection of poetry *Kavita-Kaumudi*. Tripathi established his own publishing house, Hindi Mandir, and edited the children's magazine *Banar*, only to later give it all away to Sasta Sahitya Mandal. He retired to Basant Niwas, the house he had built in Sultanpur, but his later years were troubled ones, as the railways claimed the land on which his house was built.

A staunch patron of *Kalyan*, when he was asked in 1952 to write for the following year's *Balak Ank*, an effusive Tripathi told Poddar: 'The service you are doing to Hindus is unparalleled in history. To some extent it can be compared to King Ashoka's service to Buddhism . . . I love children's literature. But I do not have my own press or journal. Whom should I write for? Whenever you need an article please write to me. I am your friend.' Tripathi praised Poddar for his commentary on *Ramcharitmanas*. 'I was enthralled with your ability to explain Awadhi and its uses by Tulsidas [though] your language is Marwari. Even those whose mother tongue is Awadhi commit mistakes.'[170]

Jainendra Kumar participated in the national movement and was arrested during the flag satyagraha of 1923. He made his literary mark with the novel *Parakh* that fetched him a Hindustani Academy prize.[171] Considered close to Premchand and a supporter of Hindustani, Jainendra Kumar was asked to write for *Kalyan*'s *Manavta Ank* of 1959 but he seems to have missed the deadline for which he apologized to Poddar. Aware of Poddar's growing reputation as a spiritual guru, Kumar, in the same letter, expressed his 'keen desire' to meet him. 'At times I get very worried with myself. Hope I get some reply.'[172]

In an era when the distinction between Hindu identity and nationalism was hazy, journals like *Kalyan* became an attractive proposition for an entire generation of Hindi writers who were yet to make a mark for themselves but were keen to engage with the nationalist discourse. So we find a host of writers drawn to Gita Press and its vehicle *Kalyan* with no pretence of being highbrow or even literary. All Gita Press demanded from its contributors was adherence to their stated discourse of 'Hinduism in danger', and in return promised a massive circulation and reach outside literary circles.

These writers included Pitambardatt Barthwal, originally from Garhwal and the first D.Lit. in Hindi from BHU; Ramdas Gaur, among the earliest science writers in Hindi who also dwelt on scientific advaita; Badrinath Bhatt, writer from the Dwivedi era and editor of journals like *Balsakha* and *Sudharak*; Gulabrai, minister of literary affairs with the royal family of Orchha; self-taught Ilachandra Joshi who took on the Hindi literary establishment in *Modern Review*; Gaya Prasad Shukla 'Sanehi' who made equal contributions to Braj Bhasha and Khari Boli and wrote nationalist poems under the pseudonym Trishul; Hazari Prasad Dwivedi, essayist, novelist and Santiniketan don who wrote an authoritative volume on Kabir; Padam Singh Sharma, eminent literary critic known for his brutal but honest writings; Dineshnandini

Choradiya, a talented young woman writer and later wife of industrialist Ram Krishna Dalmia; Ambika Prasad Vajpayee, editor of *Swatantra*; Jhavarmal Sharma, editor of *Calcutta Samachar* and a close associate of Poddar during his revolutionary days; critic Kishori Das Vajpayee; Damodar Sahay 'Kavikinkar', a school inspector and eminent poet; and Gaurishankar Hirachand Ojha, a historian from Rajasthan.[173] Many of them cut their teeth in *Kalyan* and though they later found firm footing elsewhere, they retained the vision of cultural nationalism that Gita Press and the entire gamut of right-wing groups claimed to profess and cherish.

Non-Hindu Contributors

Poddar always claimed that people of all faiths were attracted to *Kalyan* since it followed the middle path, and his persuasive skills did help to give *Kalyan* a semblance of diversity. The journal, being the first of its kind devoted to religion, attracted people from other faiths who were keen followers of Hindu philosophy and religion, more as scholars than believers. It is unlikely that many of them were associated with Gita Press beyond their occasional writing for *Kalyan* or other journals.

It needs to be stressed that the inclusion of writings by non-Hindus in *Kalyan* did not in any way dilute the soul of Gita Press's belief system. The public image of an open-house press did not stand the test of tolerance at times of religious antagonism and violence, a common occurrence from the 1920s onwards. On such occasions it was always Hindus versus the rest—or, to put it bluntly, the Muslims. By the 1940s, the language and discourse became harsher and often crude.

Prominent among *Kalyan*'s non-Hindu writers was Allahabad University professor of philosophy Mohammad Hafiz Syed. From the mid-1930s onwards Syed would write sixteen articles for *Kalyan*, on various aspects of Hinduism, the relationship between Islam and Hinduism, devotion in Islam, Sufism, cow protection and the Gita. In 1934 when the Gita Society was floated Poddar asked him to become a member and to recommend others who could join as well. Syed came up with the names of R.D. Ranade, professor of philosophy at the university, and Hirendra Nath Dutta, a solicitor based in Calcutta, both of whom were 'distinguished scholars and love Gita'.[174] As for himself, he did not reject the proposal outright, but argued against his becoming a member 'as I am not a Sanskrit scholar . . . If, however, you insist I can give you only my reluctant consent. It will be better if you drop me out,' he told Poddar. (Eventually he did become a member.) In the same letter, he said he would 'try to write an article on Gita for your Gita number'. Syed, who continued to contribute to *Kalyan* till the late 1950s, would often complain about being asked to write at short notice, which annoyed him no end.

Syed was something of a spiritualist, for he wrote to Poddar of having gone to Tiruvannamalai to spend a fortnight with Ramana Maharshi. There he encountered one Major Chadwick who had translated some of the Maharshi's unpublished works from Tamil into English verse and prose. Syed had persuaded Chadwick to let him have these for publication in *Kalyan,* and offered to hand them over to Poddar for a fee of Rs 30.[175] However, Chadwick's translation could not be published.

On one occasion Poddar apparently returned Syed's piece '*Nara Aur Narayan*' (Man and God) as it was 'not up to mark', requesting him to write another article. Syed replied that he had shown the rejected piece to Bankey Bihari, a lawyer from Allahabad and the author of *The Persian Mystics,* Ramanathan, assistant editor, *Leader* and others, all of whom 'approved of it . . . I also find it in proper order. I have retouched it. If you care to have it, I may send it on to you again. I am sorry, I have no time to write a fresh article.'[176] Yet he complained if Poddar failed to ask him to write for a special issue of *Kalyan,* as in the case of the journal's 1939 *Gita Tattva Ank.* While expressing his willingness to oblige, Syed carped: 'You ask me at the eleventh hour to contribute an article for your special number, which I find rather hard to comply with as I am a very busy person and keep indifferent health.'[177]

Occasional outbursts and unreasonable demands apart, the Syed–Poddar relationship was typical of an overzealous admirer and his role model. It was not enough for Syed that his articles were being published in *Kalyan*; he wished to meet the editor. Poddar was in Ratangarh in January 1943, and Syed wrote impatiently: 'If you cannot come to UP in the near future where we can meet, I shall do my best to visit you in

Ratangarh some day when I get leave from the university. I am really desirous of meeting you in physical form before I lay down my body.' What had added to Syed's impatience was news of the temporary suspension of publication of *Kalyana-Kalpataru*. Syed wanted his article on the 'Aryan View of Life' to be published in the English journal.[178]

In June 1944, Syed wrote to Poddar again lamenting the physical distance between them but drawing solace from the fact that 'in spirit we are always one . . . I often think of you and feel that I am not away from you, I really do not know when my desire to meet you would ever be fulfilled.' Syed had taken a year off from Allahabad University in preparation for retirement and had more time for *Kalyan*: 'I am glad to tell you that I get more leisure to occupy myself in the services of our Lord more earnestly than before.'[179] By the late 1950s, Syed had met his role model. Poddar would describe how Syed had taken him to his house in Allahabad and shown him a photograph of Krishna with sandalwood paste on the forehead.[180] In 1958, bedridden but still enthusiastic about writing for *Kalyan*, Syed was anxious to meet Poddar once more because 'my life has become so uncertain'.[181]

Syed Kasim Ali from Jabalpur was a journalist with a Sahityalankar (Ornament of Literature) degree to boot. Enthusiastic about writing in *Kalyan*, he considered Poddar a 'dharmatma (religious soul) whose benevolence acts as a big encouragement'.[182] He wrote nine articles for *Kalyan* on the concept of God in Islam, harmful effects of eating meat, humanism in Islam, Baba Tajjudin and other subjects. Kasim Ali even attempted to match couplets from the Ramayana with verses from the Quran.[183] Little is known about another Muslim writer, Mubarak Ali, whose eleven articles in *Kalyan* were of diverse nature, including profiles of Abraham Lincoln and Horatio Nelson.

Another enthusiastic writer for *Kalyan* was Syed Afzal Hussain from Faizabad who considered it an honour to be invited to contribute to the 'most praiseworthy enterprise'. Asked to write on 'that great book' (Gita), Hussain expressed his doubts about being qualified enough but told Poddar he would try his hand on the 'conception of God in certain Islamic sects' and also on the 'ethics of Gita'.[184]

I have earlier described the close relationship between Raihana Tyabji and Poddar. The pages of *Kalyan* were always open to Raihana, who being a Krishna bhakt wrote on various manifestations of Krishna, nine articles in all.

Firoze Cowasji Davar was a lecturer in English in the prestigious Gujarat College, Ahmedabad, where he had been a student. An ardent votary of Parsi Zoroastrians retaining their racial purity, Davar wrote against mixed marriages, arguing: 'Larger communities lose little or nothing by mixed marriages. It is the smaller one that is swamped or overwhelmed so as to lose its communal identity.'[185] Davar did not mind calling himself a 'communalist' and it was little wonder that his plainspeak was often misunderstood. In 1935, clarifying a statement he had made about his lack of knowledge about Hindu lore, Davar wrote to Poddar: 'It is my misfortune that I fail to carry conviction in some of my most serious statements which are misunderstood by my kind and well-meaning friends as representing only modesty on my part. My knowledge of Hindu lore, I beg to repeat, is strictly limited; and my ignorance of Sanskrit makes my adventure into that region not only precarious to me but damaging to the prestige of the paper to which I may have the temerity to contribute.'[186]

In 1936 Davar was again in the news for alleged remarks against Krishna's teachings and the Gita. Once again he wrote to Poddar with an explanation: 'I have never doubted or disputed the universality of Sri Krishna's teaching or of the gospel of the Gita. Nor do I maintain for a moment that the Gita should be confined to Hindus only. They belong to all who choose to profit by them . . . Ignorance of anything, except law, must be admitted as a valid reason. I only hope it is not interpreted as disrespect for Sri Krishna and the Gita.'[187] He need not have worried; requests for contributions to *Kalyan* continued to come to him. For the journal's *Gita Tattva Ank* (1939), Davar wrote an article on the essentials of Zoroastrianism. In 1958 he sent another one on the religion of humanity. By then he had a 'shaky hand' but he considered writing articles for *Kalyan* as a 'debt of honour to the esteemed journal, which aims to disseminate the gospel of love, peace and goodness in society'.[188] Davar's association with Gita Press began in 1932 and resulted in eleven articles.

Most of the international writers who contributed to *Kalyan* and *Kalyana-Kalpataru* belonged to the Christian faith. Ralph T. Templin from the United States was no ordinary missionary. In the fifteen years that he lived in India he pushed the boundaries of his work—from 'creating a cooperative education method that allowed senior boys to help build various structures for local villages' to setting up the 'Peacemakers' movement after the assassination of Mahatma Gandhi'.[189] Templin experimented with Gandhian methods after his return to the US where he first took up the job of director of the School of Living, Suffern, New York, and later was the first white faculty member teaching sociology at the all-black Central State University, Wilberforce, Ohio. He refused to pay tax, did not enlist at the time of World War II, protested against American suppression of the independence movement in Puerto Rico and failed to appear before the House Committee on Un-American Activities during the McCarthy era. Templin contributed articles on human relations for *Kalyana-Kalpataru* long after he had left India—showing the thought and work that went into the search for suitable contributors. His life would be an interesting subject for study, considering that he left behind a rich archive of his India years, now made accessible by the General Commission on Archives and History, United Methodist Church at Drew University, New Jersey.

Christian D. Larson was not a priest but as a New Thought teacher exercised considerable influence. Though sent to the Lutheran seminary at Minneapolis, he switched over to the liberal Unitarian theological school and established a New Age temple. Larson believed each person had a 'latent power which can be put to use for success with the proper attitude'.[190] Widely quoted even now by self-help books, Larson's reputation must have brought him to the notice of Poddar. Larson wrote in *Kalyan* on the need to take refuge in God in times of crises.

Edwin Greaves, a priest belonging to the London Missionary Society based in Banaras, had made a name with his *Grammar of Modern Hindi* that was first published in 1896 and completely revised in 1921. The book did not include any Urdu words. Aware of the intense debate around Hindi and Urdu, Greaves admitted that 'the language dealt with is modern Hindi in the form that many of its best friends are endeavouring to standardize it, a self-respecting Hindi which is not forever parading its aristocratic ancestry by filling its pages with Sanskrit words, nor affecting modernity by the cultivation of Persian vocabulary and idioms'. At the same time, he argued that 'purism in Hindi is sheer folly . . . Words of Persian and Arabic origin, and words imported also from English and other languages, have made their home in Hindi, and it is futile to try and oust them from their place.'[191] Though never considered a serious player in the Hindi–Urdu conflagration, Gita Press had joined the debate following in the footsteps of Hindu Mahasabha, and did its bit associating Hindi with Hindu nationalism.

Greaves wrote four articles in *Kalyan*, though on topics unrelated to Hindi, such as the place of yoga in Christianity and the lives and works of great poets and great men. Also a writer for *Kalyana-Kalpataru*, he was insistent that his article be 'allowed to appear as it is, in its English dress', as 'ninety per cent of readers know English as well as they know Hindi, some of them probably better'.[192]

Three other priests—Arthur E. Massey, George Chaney and E.T. Price—had studied Indian culture and religion closely. They suited Gita Press—having foreigners appreciate various aspects of Hindu religion furthered its mission of taking sanatan Hindu dharma to each nook and corner of the globe.

Carrying excerpts from the works of known writers was a common feature of Hindi journals of the time, and *Kalyan* was no different. It was catholic in its selection: political theorist and philosopher Edmund Burke; priest, historian and proponent of the filling theory of Christianity as the crown of Hinduism, J.N. Farquhar; writers George Bernard Shaw, Robert Louis Stevenson and Oscar Wilde; leading Urdu poet Josh Malihabadi; medieval historian Abul Fazl; the man behind the Linguistic Survey of India G.A. Grierson—*Kalyan* carried works by all these great men, of course carefully selecting those that had a suitable message or a moral.

The English-language *Kalyana-Kalpataru* generated wide interest among European and American scholars of religion, philosophy and Indology, all of whom vied to write for the new journal. With Poddar's relentless scouting of universities and religious institutions for contributors, an enviable mix was achieved.

F. Otto Schrader was an old India hand when he began writing for *Kalyana-Kalpataru* in its early years. A doctorate in divinity from Strasbourg, Schrader had spent eleven years in Madras as director of

Adyar Library before returning home. Having already earned a name as author of *Introduction to the Pancaratra and Ahirbudhnya Samhita,* a 'fit conclusion to his tenure of office as director of Adyar Library',[193] Schrader became good friends with Poddar. From Kiel University, where Schrader was teaching, he would write in German for *Kalyana-Kalpataru.* Satisfied with his article for the *Yoga Ank,* Schrader told Poddar: 'I think you will like it and find no difficulty in translating it.'[194] Schrader was among the few contributors given the freedom to substitute a topic of his choice for the one assigned to him by Poddar. He was also a keen reader of *Kalyana-Kalpataru,* seeking further edification from Poddar whenever he found anything interesting or unknown. When an article in *Kalyana-Kalpataru* of July 1937 referred to the *Brahma Samhita,* Schrader immediately wrote to the editor seeking a copy of the text since he was 'not aware of an edition of that work'.[195]

Oxford-educated John George Woodroffe was just the kind of spiritualist Poddar had in mind when he argued about the supremacy of Hinduism. Here was an upper-class Britisher—son of James Tisdall Woodroffe, advocate general of Bengal—and an academic, lawyer and judge who had taken to Hindu philosophy and religion and become its staunch ambassador, translating Sanskrit texts and entering into polemical debate with detractors of Hinduism and India. When Australia-born Scottish-origin literary and drama critic William Archer in his *India and the Future* pronounced 'India as a whole to be in the state of barbarism', Woodroffe countered with a series of essays, later published as *Is India Civilised?: Essays on Indian Culture,* celebrating 'the principles of civilization of old India with its *dharma, devata* and *Gomata*—a civilization in its depths profound, on its surface a pageant of antique beauty—the civilization of India of the Hindus'. Woodroffe was confident that the 'inherited ideas and instincts (samskara) of a thousand years will assert themselves' and if properly spread Indian culture will have a beneficial effect on men at large.[196] In 1910, Woodroffe was 'initiated' by tantra guru Shivachandra Vidyarnava. He continued to write books—*Shakti and Shakta,* a commentary on the Shakta Tantra Shastra, under the pseudonym Arthur Avalon; and *The Garland of Letters,* a commentary on the Mantra Shastra, under his real name.[197]

Poddar was well aware of Woodroffe's scholarship, especially his translation of texts on tantra, when he invited him to write for *Kalyan* and *Kalyana-Kalpataru* in January 1934. The first letter to Woodroffe in London was returned to Gorakhpur, so Poddar wrote again requesting him to contribute to the *Shakti Ank*. Stating that *Kalyan* with a monthly circulation of 22,000—'a figure not yet reached by any vernacular magazine'—was keen to publish Woodroffe's articles, Poddar told him about the plans for publishing *Kalyana-Kalpataru* in English and that his article would also be carried in the new journal when it came out. 'We know you have made a life-long study of the tantras and the sakta cult and feel sure that you will gladly and readily respond to our call . . . You will be placing not only *Kalyan*, but its numerous readers and sympathisers as well, under a deep debt of gratitude.'[198]

Arthur Berriedale Keith, the 'chief ornament of Scottish learning',[199] was a polymath in the classical sense of the term. A barrister from the Inner Temple and Regus professor of Sanskrit and comparative philology at the University of Edinburgh, Keith straddled many worlds with ease—constitutional law, Indian culture, religion and philosophy—leaving behind a huge corpus of work. A contemporary of Otto Strauss, a German Indologist and also a writer for *Kalyana-Kalpataru*, Keith (like Schrader) could not be easily convinced to write on a topic suggested by the editor. Asked to write for the *Sri Krishna Number* of *Kalyana-Kalpataru*, Keith wrote: 'I do not think that there is any subject on which I could contribute an article which would be wholly acceptable to devotees of Sri Krsna.' Citing the occidental–oriental clash of vision, Keith told *Kalyana-Kalpataru* editor Chimmanlal Gosvami that the 'topic presents itself in a different aspect to occidental minds, and I should not care to present views which might not be in harmony with those of the great majority of your writers and your readers'.[200]

Otto Strauss was also approached to write for the *Sri Krishna Number* but he was too preoccupied to complete the article at short notice. Instead, he requested the editor to carry his 'pending piece, a new interpretation of Bhagvad Gita'.[201] Schrader too did not contribute to the issue on Krishna 'owing to indifferent health' but sent his wishes that the issue would 'prove no less successful than were the preceding ones'.[202]

Renowned mystic Richard Whitwell, author of the popular *Life of Francis of Assisi* and *In the Desert a Highway*, wrote for both *Kalyana-Kalpataru* and *Kalyan* in the late 1950s on the theme of choosing the path of truth in life. In 1958 Whitwell sent an article—he does not specify the topic—'some ways perhaps a little different' from what he had 'usually sent'.[203] Whitwell's only article, on conversing with love, appeared in *Kalyan* in November 1954.

Giuseppe Tucci was among the world's foremost orientalists, a master of Sanskrit, Japanese, Chinese and the religions of the East. Sent to Santiniketan by Mussolini, Tucci taught Italian and Chinese there for many years, as well as initiated the study of Buddhist texts and inscriptions. A supporter of Mussolini and a staunch votary of purity of race, Tucci would often joke that in his 'past life he must have been a Brahmin and then, due to some sin committed, he was born again in a barbarian land'.[204] Along with his reputation as a scholar, such thoughts must have endeared him to Gita Press. Tucci had already become the toast of the Indian press when he joined Santiniketan in 1926. A reputed journal like *Modern Review*, praising Tucci's academic achievements, had said, 'We are thankful to Signor Mussolini for having sent such a versatile scholar to represent the Italian science in the republic of Indian letters.'[205]

In 1958 Tucci was invited to write for *Kalyan* and *Kalyana-Kalpataru*'s forthcoming issue on Humanity. However, by the time Chimmanlal Gosvami's request reached Tucci, he had left Rome for East Asia. His assistant Antonio Gargano wrote to Gosvami that Tucci 'is well aware of the work you are carrying on for the propagation of spiritual ideas, the only means of serving the cause of culture and therefore of peace and understanding among men . . . His return is not contemplated before next year. There is therefore no possibility of his writing a message such as you would like to have for your paper.'[206]

F.D. Lessing of the University of California at Berkeley earned an international reputation for translating several Buddhist tantric texts into English, a task that would be completed by Alex Wayman after his death. Also behind the compilation of an English-Mongolian dictionary, Lessing, like Tucci and others, was aware of *Kalyan*, but could not contribute to the *Manavta Ank*: 'Unfortunately, I am so tied up with my own research which involves various deadlines I have to meet that I have no time to take upon me additional obligations. It is physically impossible to make any promises.'[207]

In its endeavour to make Gita Press and its two journals the sole authority on Hindu spirituality, rituals and culture, Poddar and others at the helm went all out to rope in the best minds of that time. Through his acquaintance Shiv Sharan, Poddar even got in touch with French metaphysicist Rene Guenon who had taken the Islamic name Sheikh Abd al-Wahid Yaha after being exposed to Sufism and various Islamic traditions. A prolific writer, Guenon had also written on Hinduism and Vedanta apart from a severe critique of theosophy that was taking root in India at the time. While in Paris, Shiv Sharan had written to Guenon and was awaiting his response. Poddar was interested in publishing the Hindi translations of Guenon's works, but it seems that Guenon did not respond favourably.[208] The Poddar Papers do not have any follow-up correspondence on Guenon, neither is there any reference to any article by him being published in *Kalyan* or *Kalyana-Kalpataru*.

Ruth Fuller Sasaki was instrumental in popularizing Buddhism in the United States. Having trained in Zen Buddhism in Japan for many years, Sasaki also took up the task of translation and dissemination of Zen texts into English. In the years when she was flitting between the USA and Japan, *Kalyan* approached her for an article, a 'repeated request' which failed to elicit a positive response.[209]

But there were successes too. Asked to write for the *Humanity Number* of 1959, Indologist K. De Vreese responded saying that despite the choice of subjects offered by Gita Press he did not 'find one that is exactly in the field and scope of my life and character'. Instead, he suggested a new subject—'Humanity and Scholarship'—and offered to write on his 'guru', the late J.Ph. Vogel, professor of Sanskrit at the University of Leyden, who had written on Mathura art and been associated with the Archaeological Survey of India. 'Vogel was and will for ever be to me an example of real humanity,' Vreese told Chimanlal Gosvami.[210]

In the vast volumes of Poddar Papers, there are a series of letters in the 1940s from a contributor with initials W.K. whose signature cannot be deciphered. Living in Villa Grussida, Switzerland, W.K. was an enthusiastic reader of *Kalyana-Kalpataru*, often reminding Poddar that some issues had not reached him. Speaking of the ongoing world war, W.K. said: 'This poor Europe of ours is in a chaotic state. No one knows where and when all this is going to end, and one cannot even hope that these are the birth pangs of something better to come.' In the midst of all this, he told Poddar about the poem he was sending for *Kalyana-Kalpataru* and wanted to know why extra copies of the journal in which he wrote were not being sent to him.[211]

At the end of the war, when *Kalyana-Kalpataru* resumed publication, W.K. wrote again with three-fourths of an article he had written based on a class he had attended by Swami Yatishwarananda, a prominent swami from the Ramakrishna Mission. On a personal note, he confided in Poddar that eight weeks ago his sister had been in an area that was bombed, and 'I am anxiously expecting news of or from her'. Three days later he sent another letter, accompanying the rest of the article, mentioning that all his sister's belongings 'are destroyed but hope still lingers that she will be found'.[212]

Contributors came from various backgrounds—some were ICS officials like Otto Rothfeld, author of *Indian Dust*, and Charles Johnston, author of *Yoga Sutras of Patanjali*; then there was H.G.D. Turnbull who wrote books on Shakespeare and Ibsen; Otto Maria Saenger of the German League for Human Rights; H.W.B. Moreno, author of *Palikpara and Kandi Raj*, an account of a zamindar family in Murshidabad; A. Cressy Morrison, chemist, former president of New York Academy of Sciences and author of books like *Man Does Not Stand Alone* and *Seven Reasons A Scientist Believes in God*; Jean Delaire, who set up the first Christian lodge of the Theosophical Society and was a vocal advocate of health reform; transcendental scientist P. Adaros who took the name of Swami Brahmavidya and who was a friend of Poddar; Lowell Fillmore of Unity School of Christianity; and Arthur Mckay, a Christian priest who often interacted with Poddar.

Letters and Requests

Over the years, Gita Press attained a reputation as a one-stop shop for everything about Hinduism, at least for foreign scholars and spiritual seekers. Requests varied from recommendation of a Vedanta teacher to location of 'leaders in the Kabirpanthi movement' and help in securing copies of *Bijak*.[213]

An unusual correspondent was Enzo Turbiani from Genoa, Italy, who first wrote to Poddar as a young boy who had already learnt Hindi because he 'liked India very much'; his letter written in Hindi contained some grammatical errors but made perfect sense. Of the texts he had read in search of Indian philosophy, the Gita had impressed him the most—he called it the 'world's most beautiful creation'. Like many westerners, Turbiani believed that only India could 'teach the world about satya (truth) and mithya (falsehood)'.[214] He forged a long relationship with Gita Press and regularly corresponded with Poddar, often distressed by the glorification of materialism in his home country, and writing that 'wise people are not satisfied with Christianity'.[215] His criticism would get more intense, saying that Christianity only sought salvation for Christians whereas a text like the Gita promised salvation to everyone—man, woman, child, untouchable—who believed in God.[216] Two months later, Turbiani clarified: 'I am not against any religion. I am against injustice. There are many great men among Catholic priests though a large section of them only knows politics.'[217]

Turbiani had discovered similarities between the Gospel and the Gita. He also began writing a book of Hindi grammar in Italian. Hindi, he said, was a beautiful language with a great future.[218] Turbiani would present even his minor worries to Poddar. For instance, after having read Yogi Ramacharaka's *Hatha Yoga or the Yogi Philosophy of Physical Well-Being*, he read another book that severely criticized Ramacharaka and accused him of writing on hatha yoga without practising it. He asked Poddar to suggest the next step.[219]

By the early 1960s Turbiani's quest for spiritual knowledge had taken him to religious texts of Islam, Christianity and Hinduism—and to the conclusion that 'Gita is the greatest and all men should read it'.[220] He further said that, in his view, 1961 was the year when India and Pakistan had again become friends. Unconsciously echoing what the extreme right-wing elements of Indian politics had always advocated, Turbiani hoped that 'one day the two nations would become one'. His hope was drawn from an article in an Urdu magazine that talked of

Urdu being a branch of Hindi, as well as the cultural similarity between the two nations. Turbiani's prayer for peace and integration of the two nations was dashed four years later when India and Pakistan were locked in a battle over Kashmir.

In later years, Turbiani authored two books—*La Vairagya: Sandipani di Gosvami Tulsidas* (1977) and *Il Sikhismo: la religione dei divini maestri* (1987)—and contributed an article on the Ramanandi sect in a Cambridge University Press compendium on devotional literature.[221]

Like Turbiani, Vladimir Miltner got in touch with Poddar and Gita Press as a student. Based in Prague, then capital of the former Czechoslovakia, Miltner was studying 'Indo-Aryan languages but had special interest in Braj and Awadhi languages'. He had many works of Tulsidas but not *Hanumanbahuk*, and requested Poddar to send him a copy, promising to send in exchange some Czech books translated into English. The book arrived and Miltner requested a few more by Tulsidas and Surdas so that his collection of works by these authors would be complete. He started using 'Jagannath' (lord of the world) as his middle name.[222] Later, Miltner became a leading Indologist, authoring many books such as *Folk Tales from India, The Mahabharata, The Hindi Sentence Structure in the Works of Tulsidas* and *Theory of Hindi Syntax: Descriptive, Generative, Transformational*.

Karl G. Gesh was a scientist from Germany who was familiar with Gita Press and *Kalyan*. His letter to the editor had already been published in *Kalyan* when he decided to visit India in 1957 on what he called a 'pilgrimage' for a few months—travelling to Bombay, Wardha and Gorakhpur. Well versed in Hindi, Gesh faced problems with his travel plans but went around in search of knowledge. Years after his visit he continued to write to Poddar, talking of getting invited to deliver lectures on Hinduism.[223]

Philosopher Raymond F. Piper of Syracuse University wrote for help in locating a painting of Shiva by B.K. Mitra, earlier an artist for Gita Press publications. He had written to Mitra, then working with Lalit Kala Akademi (Fine Arts Academy under the Indian government), and also taken the help of the Self-Realization Fellowship of Los Angeles in approaching him, but had received no reply.[224]

The Hindu Centre in East London established in 1967 had built a temple and a large resource centre complete with library. The Centre's founding member B.K. Goyal contacted Gita Press for its publications, including *Kalyan* and *Kalyana-Kalpataru.* Delay in the delivery of books worth 30 pounds sterling, despite repeated reminders, forced Goyal to write directly to Poddar, who was unwell, and even allege that 'someone in the office has misappropriated the draft money'.[225] Within days of Goyal's letter reaching Poddar, the manager of Gita Press confirmed receipt of the money and the dispatch of twenty-two bundles of books. Possibly irked with Goyal's allegation, the manager promised to take up the 'matter with postal authorities'.[226]

Outside the scholarly and religious world, there were ordinary expatriate Indians who looked to Gita Press and Poddar for spiritual sustenance and wrote with personal stories and suggestions. One G.P. Mishra from Mauritius would praise Poddar and Gita Press for helping people like him, living away from home, to remember and talk of God through their writings. He asked Poddar to spare time for his father-in-law, also a resident of Mauritius, who would be visiting India.[227] R.K. Srivastava who lived in Rhonda, Britain, would inform Poddar how he had successfully managed to remain a vegetarian despite his friends telling him how difficult it was to survive on vegetables in a cold country.[228] Ramesh Kumar Prasad from British Guinea (now Guyana), South America, would suggest that Gita Press should bring out Tulsidas's Ramayana with its commentary, predicting it would be a 'money spinner'.[229]

The Ramakrishna Mission Sebashram, a charitable hospital in Rangoon, would request the *Kalyan* editor to send free copies of the journal for its newly opened library in the hospital. It was felt that a journal like *Kalyan* in the library would not only help patients to spend their time well but also promote their speedy recovery.[230] Being helped financially by the Indian government, the managing committee of the hospital regretted that exchange control regulations did not allow even remittance of postage costs. Gita Press agreed to send copies gratis.

Fitting into the Template

In the first four decades, the universe of Gita Press writers was constantly expanding, giving space to anyone who chose to care about sanatan

Hindu dharma. It did not matter what aspect of sanatan dharma was being addressed as long as the writer agreed, even partially, that it was under multiple threat—from colonial rule, the competing interests of Muslims, and the rising culture of material consumption that Gita Press felt had a direct bearing on the moral fibre of individuals. The press's rescue-cum-resurgence mission needed a wide range of contributors inhabiting several spheres: sacred, secular, communal, cosmopolitan, local and transnational.

Careful analysis reveals that, in the catholic world of contributors gathered by Poddar, there was a distinct pattern. He would reach out to anyone who might fit some aspect of the well-designed template. Each contributor was selected with a specific purpose. Mendicants, sadhus and Sanskrit scholars representing various sects and schools of philosophy built the sanctum sanctorum of *Kalyan*. They consistently delved into sacred texts, deconstructing complex concepts for ordinary readers in the simplest of language. Simultaneously, these writers, who included Poddar and Goyandka, worked hard to explain to readers the importance of rituals in the private, domestic and public aspects of one's life. It is a different matter that the burden of these rituals with shastric sanction fell more on women who usually had very little or no say in matters concerning their space. The ideal world of a Hindu nari (woman) followed the narrow path of daughter, wife and mother. It was a task Gita Press took extremely seriously, as expressed not only through the pages of *Kalyan* but also in scores of pamphlets on women, the first one *Stri Dharma Prashnottari* having made its appearance way back in 1926.

Non-experts who had a fair knowledge of sacred texts and were practising sanatanis formed another ring. This group consisted of scholars, both Indians and foreigners; Indophiles, orientals and occidentals; the odd politician such as K.M. Munshi, Govind Das or Sampurnanand; poets, writers, businessmen and school and college teachers. Poddar always walked the extra mile to get the best names to fill this category. They not only lent heft to the journal, their lives were often showcased as success stories of those following the path of sanatan Hindu dharma.

Those involved in the cause of Hindu and Hindi nationalism, cow protection, Hindu Code Bill and other contentious issues inhabited the next ring of contributors. It consisted of leaders of the Hindu Mahasabha, RSS, a section of Congress conservatives like Malaviya, and politician-sadhus like Karpatri Maharaj, Raghav Das and Prabhudatt Brahmachari. Additionally, sections of the Hindi literary world also wrote in *Kalyan*, and representatives of a large number of short-lived organizations that came up during the intense communal phase from the 1930s added to the atmosphere of distrust and disharmony, contributing some of the worst language to the communal discourse.

Finally, there were the scholars and philosophers who did not see the crisis in Hinduism through the highly debatable and translucent prism of Gita Press, but still wrote in *Kalyan*. Writers like Rabindranath Tagore, Kshitimohan Sen, C.F. Andrews, S. Radhakrishnan, as can be discerned from their response to Poddar, genuinely considered Gita Press and *Kalyan* as a spiritual, cultural and religious intervention without subscribing to its communal agenda. But this interpretation has room for scrutiny, as some of these writers also associated themselves with other initiatives of Gita Press aimed at the creation of its ultimate vision of a Hindu rashtra (nation).

४: *Foot Soldier of the Sangh Parivar*

The Hindu revival and reform movements that had begun in the nineteenth century with the Brahmo Samaj (1828) and Arya Samaj (1875) crystallized by the first quarter of the twentieth century into strident Hindu nationalism that used the narrative of Hinduism as a single religion with a hoary past as the basis for its political and social ideology. Romila Thapar calls it 'syndicated Hinduism', projected as the 'sole claimant to the inheritance of indigenous Indian religion'. A facet of syndicated Hinduism is its over-reliance on the interpretation of brahminical texts like the Gita and dharmashastras in such a way as to 'underline a brand of conservatism in the guise of a modern, reformed religion'.[1]

After the lull in the activities of its forerunner, the Hindu Sabha, formed at Lahore in 1909 at the initiative of Lala Lajpat Rai, the Hindu Mahasabha was born in 1915. 'Syndicated Hinduism' became its staple diet; such invention of a singular history was justified on the grounds of creating a counterpoint to 'the enemy image of similarly conceived Islam'.[2] In the aftermath of the Khilafat movement (1919–24) and the Moplah massacre of 1921, Hindu mobilization of this kind was deemed acceptable, with its accompanying stridency of tone and sharpening of religious identities.

Two other events—the publication of Vinayak Damodar Savarkar's *Hindutva: Who is a Hindu?* in 1923 and the formation of Rashtriya Swayamsevak Sangh (RSS) in 1925—contributed in making the 1920s the most productive and significant decade for Hindu nationalism. Savarkar's book, originally titled *Essentials of Hindutva,* was an attempt to historicize the origin of Hindutva (the quality of being a Hindu) of which Hinduism was only a 'derivative and a part'.[3] Savarkar not only made a 'distinction between Hinduism as a culture and as a faith' but also (through liberal citations from works of Darwin, T.H. Huxley and Herbert Spencer) attempted to 'fashion an ethnic nationalism'.[4] He used the word Hindu and Sindhu (the Sanskrit name for the Indus river from which the name India is derived) interchangeably, arguing that the letter S in Sanskrit was changed to H in some of the Prakrit languages.

The founder of the RSS, K.B. Hedgewar, put forward his own concept of nation: 'It is not merely some piece of land that is called a Nation. A Nation is formed by people who have held the same thoughts, the same customs, the same culture and the same traditions since long time past.'[5] This definition led the RSS and its affiliates like the Vishwa Hindu Parishad (VHP) to consider Nepal as part of the 'Hindu Nation'.[6] The RSS, VHP and other organizations inspired over the years by RSS ideals together form the Sangh Parivar—or RSS affiliates.

Parallel to the ideological formulation and sharpening of religious identities, the 1920s saw Hindus and Muslims slugging it out in the open through a series of communal riots 'marked by increasing violence and cruelty'—a 'casual list' puts the number of riots in this decade at twenty-nine through the length and breadth of the country,[7] from the Moplah riots in Malabar (1921), to Ajmer and Sindh (1923), Delhi and Lucknow (1924), Allahabad, Calcutta and Sholapur (1925) to Lahore and Nagpur (1927) and Bombay (1929).

In Defence of Hindu Dharma

Born in the middle of this surcharged decade, *Kalyan* was clear from the start about its stand on the Hindu–Muslim question. Poddar's editorial in the inaugural issue put the blame for the riots squarely on the Muslims, bemoaned Hindu inaction, called for sanghbal (unity of strength) and invoked co-religionists not to turn the principle of non-violence into cowardice.[8]

Hindu involvement in the riots was considered an act of defending the religion. In 1927, when a worried reader of *Kalyan* sought the advice of Jaydayal Goyandka since a warrant had been issued against him for involvement in a riot, Goyandka told him to be prepared for punishment if he was guilty, and not to behave like a coward, as he had acted in defence of the Hindu religion: 'In case you are facing the problem for doing public service then go to jail like a brave man and prove your innocence through evidence . . . Why worry about arrest?

It should be a matter of joy if you are hanged for a public service like this.'[9]

In its early years, *Kalyan* slowly but surely bared its ideological wares to readers. It not only talked of how the decline in religious faith had adversely affected sanatan Hindu dharma, but also presented a new model of faith and devotion that promised instant results. It was a bania model of profit from bhakti. Steeped in the Vaishnava bhakti traditions, initiatives like bhagwan naam jap called on readers to recite God's name to accumulate punya (moral or spiritual merit) that could translate into the benefits of good health, wealth and mental peace. A similar emphasis was placed on charity—including donations to or help in expanding the subscriber base of *Kalyan*—especially from Marwari businessmen.

The innovative model of promising instant shakti (strength in all respects) in exchange for bhakti was strongly promoted by Gita Press through a series of illustrative stories from the lives of prominent individuals like Gandhi and Malaviya as well as of ordinary readers. If the repetition of Narayan had brought constant success to Malaviya,[10] Rama naam was the ultimate talisman that had shown Gandhi the way.[11] One reader wrote about his acquaintance, a devout man who had the surreal experience of receiving an unexpected money order on the eve of his daughter's wedding.[12] In fact, the chronicling of such instances of worldly benefits born out of bhakti has been a constant feature of *Kalyan* throughout its existence.

For Poddar, bhakti through the recitation of God's name was the ultimate recipe to deal with the trials of life and ensure continued divine beneficence. When a woman who had been raped at a family wedding sought his advice, Poddar lamented the decline in morality among men and told her not to reveal the fact to her husband. For herself, she should recite the name of Rama at the rate of a hundred malas (108 rosary beads make one mala) daily for a year.[13]

Kalyan also became the most influential advocate of varna system (fourfold caste system) as the divine order on which the society, politics and economy of the country ought to be based. In this regard, Gita Press was significantly different from fellow-travellers like the Arya Samaj and Hindu Mahasabha who advocated bringing untouchables within the Hindu fold. While issues of *Kalyan* lent space to both

Hindu Mahasabha and Arya Samaj leaders and avoided any direct confrontation on ideological issues despite clear differences, Gita Press was unwilling to dilute its position on the birth-ordained caste system.

This inherent contradiction shadowed Gita Press's endeavour to put up a united Hindu face and become its sole spokesperson. The only concession it made was to include Hindus of all castes, including untouchables, in its call to recite the name of God at a time of their convenience and location of their choice.

In December 1939, Gorakhpur was sharply divided after a spate of incidents of communal violence that directly involved Gita Press and even threatened its existence. Poddar, who was unwell then, was at his native place Ratangarh. Muhammad Ali Jinnah had declared 22 December 1939 Deliverance Day for Indian Muslims, as Congress leaders had resigned from government offices in protest against the British decision that India would enter World War II, a commitment made without consulting them.

The annual Gita Jayanti procession taken out in Gorakhpur on the same day was attacked, resulting in widespread violence across the city. The riot occurred as the procession was passing a mosque in Sahibganj, and lathis and brickbats were used. The incident was serious enough for *The Times of India* to carry an Associated Press report. The Gorakhpur district collector clarified that the violence had 'nothing to do with the Deliverance Day celebrations' as 'the only meeting held in this connection had already dispersed from the Juma Mosque'.[14]

Going by Poddar's letters to his associates in Gorakhpur, many Gita Press employees were injured and detained by the police for attacks on Muslims and mosques. What made it tough for Gita Press was the Muslim rejection of peace through negotiation. The community wanted action taken against Gita Press.

As tension prevailed and the investigation began, Poddar was informed of developments. His reaction was typical—that the incident was the will of God and whatever followed would also be divinely ordained. He wrote to Chimmanlal Gosvami: 'Our heart knows that we did not have any bad intention to attack Muslims or mosques. And no one attacked them. Even then if they (Muslims) are making a fictional case against us, we should see it as the will of God. God does everything. It is God's will that led to the attack on the Gita Jayanti procession and God will also decide what happens in the future. We did not attack them but if the collector considers us to be guilty, it is the will of God. We are innocent before God.'[15] At the same time, the possibility of police action against Gita Press employees made Poddar see the need for legal recourse. He told Gosvami to engage a good lawyer and ensure that all the arrested employees of Gita Press were released on bail and their families taken care of. Recognizing that the matter might not end so quickly, Poddar continued, 'At the most the Press would have to be moved out and we would suffer. If this is what is in our fate it cannot be changed. There is no need to organize false witnesses but we should argue our case well.' He also advised Gosvami to take the help of leaders like Purushottam Das Tandon and others so that 'sympathy stays with Hindus and no one is against us'. He also suggested the names of a few prominent Muslims of Gorakhpur, like Zahid Ali and Murtaza Hussain, who could be approached to help reach some settlement.

However, no compromise was reached; the situation in the town remained tense and the police was on the alert, though the collector sent a telegram in response to Poddar's inquiry stating 'all quiet no cause for anxiety'.[16] Poddar was unwilling to return to Gorakhpur as he had not yet fully recovered from his ailment; also he did not wish to disturb his spiritual programme in Ratangarh. Citing the collector's response as reassurance, Poddar told Gosvami to take the help of Baba Raghav Das and ensure that the staff stayed together at one place for security.

Three days later, Poddar received a frantic telegram requesting him to come to Gorakhpur, as four employees of Gita Press had been arrested. Though Poddar did not go to Gorakhpur immediately, he wrote: 'I do not want press people to think I was not with them at the time of distress.'[17] With Jaidayal Dalmia's help, he hired a lawyer called Shyam Lal to defend the arrested employees. Realizing that the battle should now be fought at both political and communal levels, Poddar raised the question of why the Muslims who reportedly initiated the violence had not been arrested, and also criticized the Hindus of Gorakhpur for their inaction. He said that since Muslims had attacked the procession they should be punished so that such an act was not repeated in future. He floated the idea of approaching Veer Savarkar, the Gita Dharma Mandal and Gita Society to launch a nationwide campaign criticizing the attack on the Gita Jayanti procession. As Poddar did not want to let down the Gorakhpur collector with whom he had cordial relations, he left the decision on approaching pro-Hindu organizations and individuals to Gosvami.

By the end of 1939, a panel of lawyers was in place to defend the press employees and, in early January 1940, Baba Raghav Das arrived in Gorakhpur at the request of Jugal Kishore Birla.[18] Poddar suggested to one Shukla, who was injured in the riots and whose first name is not known, that a third party—the Hindus of Gorakhpur or Hindu Mahasabha or an independent inquiry committee—prepare a report on the riots. He, however, provided the broad outline of the proposed report that should include Muslim complicity in attacking the procession, indulging in rioting, spreading rumours about the recovery of arms from Gita Press and the charging of its employees under Section 144 (joining unlawful assembly). The collector was to be praised in the report. Poddar demanded a copy of the report which he promised to forward to senior government official Pannalal, ICS, 'so that he would know in advance what happened and it would be of help later'.[19] But Poddar advised against sending any telegram to the viceroy, governor, Gandhi or Nehru since this would not be of much help. 'The view of Gandhi and Nehru would be to surrender before the Muslims. Though we want peace we do not support surrender.'[20] It was planned that many religious and social organizations would carry out nationwide protests against the attack on the procession, but that Gita Press's role in organizing such a protest should remain a secret.[21] This entire effort came to naught, and as the Muslims refused any offer of peace, the matter finally went to court. However, the cases were withdrawn after a few months.

Interestingly, the December 1939 issue of *Kalyan* carried a piece by leading Hindi writer Ramnaresh Tripathi, where he recounted his personal encounter with a Muslim tongawala (horse carriage driver) of Bareilly in January that year.[22] The UP town was rife with communal tension when Tripathi landed there in the middle of the night. The writer deliberately hired a tonga whose driver had a moustache: 'During communal riots Muslim tonga drivers become merchants of death. So I hired someone who had a moustache thinking he would be a Hindu.' Tripathi's story then descends into the usual stereotypes about Muslim looks and character. He talks of the tonga driver having a whispered conversation before starting off. As his tonga proceeded in the darkness of night it passed two men, one of whom was an acquaintance of Tripathi from Allahabad. This friend stopped the tonga and Tripathi then discovered that the driver had been taking him to a Muslim-dominated area, where it would have been easier to kill him. The incident narrated in *Kalyan* was meant to show how God had saved the writer, but the underlying communal tenor in the unverifiable tale is unmissable. Similar stories that raised questions about the personal integrity of Muslims appeared in various issues of *Kalyan*.

There was also a patronizing tendency towards 'newer' religions, something that Poddar admitted much later: 'They are all Hindus, whatever be their path to salvation. Buddhists, Jains, Sikhs are various branches of the giant Hindu tree.'[23] Gita Press considered religions born within India as part of the Hindu culture. While this notion, part of the larger narrative popularized by the Hindu Mahasabha and RSS, never brought Gita Press into conflict with Buddhist, Jain or Sikh leaders, in 1934 the Shiromani Gurdwara Prabandhak Committee (SGPC) had to intervene when an article '*Devi Aur Sikh Dharm*' (Devi and Sikh Religion) was proposed for *Kalyan*'s *Shakti Ank*. The SGPC got to know about the topic and wrote to Gita Press saying 'there is a great difference of opinion among the historians as to whether the Sikh gurus especially Guru Gobind Singhji had worshipped Durga (Devi) or not'.[24] While 'some writers who were under the influence of Hinduism' had propagated the view that the Sikh gurus worshipped Durga, the majority, SGPC argued, did not believe in that theory. 'The former view that the Gurus really worshipped Devi goes against their own teachings and the Sikh doctrine.' The SGPC warned Gita Press not to 'deal with this controversial subject at this stage, as its publication is sure to cause great excitement among the Sikh community'.

The office of the Chief Khalsa Diwan, a representative body of the Sikhs in Amritsar, also got wind of the article and asked Gita Press 'which is well esteemed and has become popular in the public in every corner of Hindustan' not to purvey any wrong facts about Sikh history; in case Gita Press wanted to publish the article it should be prepared to carry another one as well, giving the true facts on the subject.[25] Another letter from the SGPC, urging Gita Press not to enter into this controversy worked, and the plan to carry the article in the *Shakti Ank* was dropped.[26] In tune with its principle of non-aggression, especially towards sects and religions it considered within the pale of Hinduism, Gita Press chose to avoid the issue.

Prelude to Partition

In the 1940s, as the prospect of Independence and subsequently Partition became real, the focus of Gita Press and *Kalyan* turned entirely political, reporting and interpreting events through the communal prism. Forgotten during this period was *Kalyan*'s avowed spiritual mission and emphasis on compassion, tolerance and brotherhood. This was also the period when the Gita Press took its cordial relationship with the RSS and the Hindu Mahasabha to another level, that of open collaboration.

On Direct Action Day, 16 August 1946, killings began in Calcutta—'for three days and nights, British India's former capital, still its most populous city, became a free killing field for thugs and thieves, first Muslims, then retaliating Hindus, murdering, plundering, butchering whatever attracted their eyes',[27] leaving 4,000 killed and 10,000 injured. The killings in Calcutta had the blessings of chief minister Suhrawardy who at a rally on Direct Action Day 'promised immunity from police and army interference', though more Muslims seem to have died than Hindus, a point made by both Wavell and Sardar Patel.[28] By October, riots had spread to Noakhali and Tippera. The violence in Noakhali was marked by widespread attacks on property and incidents of rape rather than killings.

The Hindu Mahasabha, which had dispatched senior leaders like Ashutosh Lahiry, Syama Prasad Mookerjee, N.C. Chatterjee and Pandit Narendranath Das to Noakhali for relief work, did not fail to see the long-term gain for the community: 'Notwithstanding this great catastrophe it is a matter of satisfaction to the members of the Relief Committee to see a keen sense of fellow-feeling now awakened amongst all Hindus in every province of India.'[29] The violence soon spread to Bihar, the United Provinces, Bombay and other parts of the country.

For Poddar it was time to throw caution to the winds and exchange Gita Press's stated mission of spreading bhakti (devotion), gyan (knowledge) and vairagya (renunciation) for the language of violence, intimidation, reprisal and everything else that contributed to the uncertainty of the 1940s. Under the title '*Vartaman Vikat Paristhiti Aur Hamara Kartavya*' (Present Troubled Times and Our Duty),[30] *Kalyan*'s November 1946 issue presented a compendium of communal violence from reports in *The Statesman*. Peppered with pejorative words used for Muslims, the article carried graphic tales of rape and torture of Hindu women, and pointed at the complicity of both ordinary Muslims as well as mullahs (Muslim clerics).

Poddar did add that it was not just Hindus who were getting killed in riots; Muslims were dying too. Since Muslims were the aggressors, more Hindus were getting killed initially, 'but ever since Hindus started retaliating the number of Muslims killed is no less'. Poddar blamed Muslim politicians for creating animosity between the two communities: 'If there was one Gandhi-like leader among Muslims instead of Jinnah, peace would have prevailed throughout the country and the two communities would have been helping each other rather than taking the nation on a suicidal path.' Poddar called on each reader to act in the cause of humanity at such a juncture.

Poddar severely criticized the Muslim League for attacking nationalist Muslims like Sir Shafat Ahmed. 'Even nationalist Muslims are Muslims first and nationalists later as is evident from the speeches of Maulana Abul Kalam Azad, but the Muslim League is angry with him. It seems love, sympathy, affection, generosity and a sense of service is disappearing from the world.' Meandering through various themes, Poddar blamed the Communist Party of India (CPI) for taking the side of Muslims, besides claiming that contact between untouchables and caste Hindus had caused people to attack Gandhi and other Congress leaders. He also stated that the interim government did not represent Hindus, as Nehru and the five Congress representatives claimed to represent the nation rather than the Hindu community. He further blamed the English education system for the decline in moral values of educated Hindu youth. However, he said, Hinduism would survive the onslaught, just as it had in the past.

Poddar proposed a twelve-point solution that included formation of a Raksha Dal (defence force) in each city and village to instill a feeling of confidence and security among the Hindu community, and to augment its strength so that the other side would not think of attacking. He also advocated the creation of first-aid facilities in each locality and in homes so that when the time came, people would be in a position to take care of the injured. He suggested that each household keep aside a share of foodgrain for times of emergency. Women should be trained to defend themselves, so that they would have the power of great women warriors. Elsewhere in the same article, Poddar even asked women to be prepared to commit sati like the Rajput women of the yore who preferred to sacrifice their own lives rather than lose their virtue.

Ambivalence and contradiction, so much a part of Poddar's personality, resurfaced again here, as he wrote of Hindu–Muslim solidarity, saying followers of all religions are children of the same God and refuge should be provided to whoever sought it, including Muslims.

Of course, there was Poddar's ultimate recipe for all situations—recitation of God's name, study of the shastras, Gita and Ramayana, and conducting yagnas (sacrifices). Throughout the 1940s and for some years in the next decade, a militant approach in public coupled with recitation of God's name (jap) in private and at community level would be Gita Press's prescription for the problems of rapidly changing politics and society.

Poddar's November 1946 article evoked sharp and varied responses from readers. He chose to publish the gist of these in the December issue.[31] The names of the readers were kept secret, but Poddar admitted many of his 'respectable friends' had found portions of the article objectionable and had requested him to not repeat such remarks in the future. Some of Poddar's friends from Calcutta pointed out that many of the incidents of violence mentioned in the article had not taken place, but Poddar stated that all the incidents mentioned by him were taken from newspapers and offered to show the cuttings in his defence: 'It is good news if some of the incidents were exaggerated and did not take place'. A few others were of the opinion that even if some incidents had taken place, it was better not to talk about them since it bred animosity, to which Poddar replied: 'I agree, but some cases of oppression were intolerable. Not to oppose them would be a sign of cowardice.'

To one friend who argued that 'Hindus were no less (to blame) and there was an active competition between the two communities', Poddar justified the Hindu violence as having been in retaliation to that by the Muslims who had held sway on the first two days in Calcutta while the Muslim League government looked the other way. He also said that, from Calcutta to Bombay, Muslims were known for using knives to kill people and most of their victims were Hindus.

A very prominent and elderly scholar, again unnamed, agreed with Poddar about different religions being manifestations of one God. However, he stressed, the need of the hour was unity among Hindus: 'The moment Hindus wake up, Muslims will be their friends. Congress still does not want Hindus to be united.' For Poddar this letter was an endorsement of his views.

The December 1946 issue of *Kalyan* also carried a further bulletin of communal incidents, now more intense and widespread. Titled '*Hindu Kya Kare*' (What Should Hindus Do?), it expressed a mix of extreme anger against the Muslims together with token avowal of the need to maintain communal amity.

There was a great demand for reprints of the two articles '*Vartaman Vikat Paristhiti Aur Hamara Kartavya*' and '*Hindu Kya Kare*'. Gita Press published them as separate tracts priced at two paise each, and also allowed readers to print and distribute copies themselves. One Pandit Ghasiram Sharma of Agra published and freely distributed 4,000 copies of '*Vartaman Vikat* . . .'[32]

The year 1946 brought another misfortune for Gita Press—the loss of its guide and beacon of hope, Madan Mohan Malaviya, on 12 November 1946. His death could not have come at a more inopportune time for the conservative political set, as the possibility of Partition became increasingly real. For Poddar personally, Malaviya had always been the ideal politician steeped in sanatan Hindu dharma tradition.

As a tribute to Malaviya, Gita Press decided to bring out an additional issue of *Kalyan*. In its entire existence so far, it had not bestowed such an honour on any individual. The rationale was that since the publishing house had faced a strike in September–October 1946, it had been decided to publish an extra issue at the first opportunity. Gita Press chose to call it the October issue, an error since Malaviya had died in November. For Poddar, the more important reason was Malaviya's stature in the sanatan Hindu world. In his view, Malaviya had died a dejected man, witness to an all-out onslaught against the Hindus.

Poddar was aware that spiritual-minded readers might ask why *Kalyan* was devoting so much space to current political events. He argued that *Kalyan* had not strayed away from its spiritual mission, as in sanatan dharma spiritualism was part of action (karma) and karma was in turn part of spiritualism. He said the 100,000 copies of *Malaviya Ank*, published at an extra cost to Gita Press, showed the importance of the special issue.[33]

Malaviya Ank claimed to have scooped the last public statement by the late leader. One of *Kalyan*'s regular contributors, Bhuvaneshwar Prasad Mishra 'Madhav', had been in Banaras to seek Malaviya's help to secure the release of Prabhudatt Brahmachari who had been arrested in a case related to a Ramlila procession. On 28 October, Malaviya dictated a telegram to Govind Ballabh Pant and Rafi Ahmed Kidwai, saying that Brahmachari was a 'first rate spiritual person' who had been falsely implicated in the case.[34] Demanding his immediate release, Malaviya said Brahmachari had been maintaining a vow of silence for a decade and was engrossed in the study of scriptures. 'He remains aloof from politics and communal issues. His arrest has caused immense pain to spiritually inclined people and could further sour Hindu–Muslim relationship.' Eventually, Brahmachari was released.

Malaviya also issued a public statement that Poddar published in the special issue as the last ever made by the leader. Provocative and strident, the statement was an endorsement of what Poddar had been writing in *Kalyan* at the same time.

Coming from a man who was nearing his end, the statement reflected Malaviya's unflinching belief in militant Hindu nationalism. He said Hindu politicians should realize that, apart from the motherland, they also had a duty towards their own religion, culture and co-religionists.

He said his call for unity among the Hindus was necessary due to the action of the Muslim world. He cited 'fiery speeches by Muslim leaders, secret literature of secret Muslim organizations, aggressive attitude of the Muslim League, Calcutta killings and misdeeds of organized Muslim gangs in East Bengal that have created a riot-like situation throughout the country, forcible conversion of Hindus, brutal behaviour towards Hindu men, women and children, rape of Hindu women and desecration and plunder of Hindu religious places' as some instances of Muslim excesses.[35]

Resorting to the standard right-wing narrative, Malaviya regretted the fact that though the Congress was a nationalist organization and the Muslim League communal, the two parties had been treated equally. 'Hindu aspirations are trampled upon even before they blossom and in the name of Indian nationalism, the culture and religion of Hindus are being ignored.' Malaviya said the Congress was only the political custodian of Hindus and other communities, and on matters of communal, religious, cultural and social development, the final decision would rest with Hindus themselves or any organization representing them. Conversion should stop and special facilities be provided to those who were forcibly converted to Islam.

Malaviya exhorted the 'majority Hindus' to adopt a militant outlook: 'Those who do not let Hindus live in peace do not deserve any compassion. If this is the call of religion it should be evident. Hindus should help each other. Hindus do not want their religion to die nor do they want their culture to fade away. If Hindus do not protect themselves they will die.'

Malaviya blamed scores of Muslim leaders for their inflammatory speeches and writings. Many Muslim League leaders like Ghazanfar Ali Khan and others, he said, had challenged Hindus through their wild and irresponsible articles. He pointed out how not a single Muslim League leader had criticized the incidents in Bengal. Malaviya's ultimate message was for Hindus to unite not only for their religion and culture but also in the name of India, their motherland. The message to Muslims was: 'As in the past, Muslims can live peacefully together with Hindus only if they respect Hindu religion and promise not to attack their places of worship, ensure religious freedom, purity of life and chastity of women.'

Malaviya's statement paled beside that of Swami Karpatri Maharaj, who would in 1948 found the Ram Rajya Parishad, one of India's most obscurantist[36] political parties that finally merged with the Jana Sangh. Karpatri's piece in *Malaviya Ank* was a diatribe against the political class for turning the masses away from traditional solutions. He more forcefully condemned Hindu inaction: 'It seems our blood has stopped boiling. How come the descendents of Aryans are tolerating torture and injustice? Our religion, civilization and culture are under attack. Attempts are being made to turn us irreligious and foreigners in our own country.'[37]

Poddar contributed further to these calls for action. Though a firm believer that sanatan Hindu dharma would never die, Poddar felt it had to undergo many agni parikshas (trials by fire) for survival. He contrasted the lack of unity among Hindus with the single-minded force of Islam. He wondered why the Congress with 99 per cent Hindu membership chose to call itself a nationalist rather than a Hindu organization. What further infuriated him was the Congress attempt to undercut the Hindu Mahasabha, with its public promises to abolish the zamindari system, nationalize private enterprises and end all forms of caste discrimination including untouchability, rules of marriage and inter-dining. Such promises, according to Poddar, had fractured Hindu unity. English education was also to blame for fostering the spirit of individualism.

According to Poddar, the creation of the Adi Hindu Mahasabha in 1927 had been the handiwork of politicians interested in highlighting tensions within the Hindu world.[38] What must have particularly irked him was the Adi Hindu Mahasabha's open defiance of the sanatan Hindu dharma model of social evolution—it claimed 'achhuts (untouchables) were the original inhabitants of India', 'rejected Hindu social reforms' and 'demanded separate electorates for dalits'.[39] Jinnah, Poddar argued, preyed on such divisions; Jogendra Nath Mandal, a Dalit leader from Bengal, had joined the Muslim League (he later became the first law and labour minister of Pakistan). Such instances of the 'lure of money and power' were creating bitterness and divisions among the Hindus.

Before Malaviya's death, Bihar had seen unprecedented violence against Muslims. In the first riot in Muzaffarpur, fourteen Muslims were killed and there were reports that 'roving Hindu mobs have sought to exterminate the Muslim population'.[40] The *Malaviya Ank* justified the violence as an act of reprisal for what Hindus had undergone in Bengal.[41] Though admitting that the Hindus of Bihar had 'gone mad', Poddar discovered virtues in the violence perpetrated by them. 'In Bihar there were no instances of rape, forcible marriage, kidnapping of women and conversion. What took place were murders, loot and arson. It was nothing compared to the atrocities in East Bengal, yet it was a sign of moral decay.' Poddar descended into his signature ambivalence, lamenting the Hindu behaviour at one moment, justifying it at another. He evaluated the reaction of politicians that he claimed differed in the two cases—Governor Burrows and the Muslim League government having meticulously planned the violence in Bengal, while in Bihar the government swung into action immediately to stop the killing and national leaders like Jawaharlal Nehru, Rajendra Prasad, Jayaprakash Narayan and Muslim League leaders visited the sites of violence. 'Nehru and Rajendra Prasad told the Hindus they would have to attack them first before killing the Muslims. These great leaders cannot be expected to say the same thing to Mian Jinnah. But they should have issued similar warnings in East Bengal.'

To quell the violence in Bihar, Poddar alleged, the government had deployed British and Muslim army personnel who indulged in brutal repression. He cited Hindu Mahasabha leader Jagat Narayan Lal (who incidentally joined the Congress and became a minister in the first Bihar government after Independence) as reported in the newspaper *Sanmarg*, started by Karpatri Maharaj. Lal described the firing in Nausa (now part of Vaishali district) in which allegedly old men, women and even bedridden people were shot. Lal equated the incident to the Jallianwala Bagh massacre of 1919 in Amritsar.

Poddar criticized Gandhi for his decision to visit Noakhali 'to wipe the Hindu tears', saying that the same Muslim League leaders who had hatched the conspiracy against the Hindus would accompany him. Saying that the company one keeps colours one's views, Poddar alleged this was the case with Gandhi: 'He is not opposing Suhrawardy's government openly. Instead, he is supporting the proposal for a peace committee that would include Suhrawardy. He (Gandhi) might even promise to get some prominent Hindus in the committee. But would that help Hindus forget the trauma of violence? As for the threat of the army, what will government do if 30 crore Hindus decide to face the army's bullets?'

Syama Prasad Mookerjee also criticized Gandhi in the *Malaviya Ank*, saying his idea of fasting could further complicate the situation instead of offering any solution. He said Jinnah should learn a lesson from Bihar: 'He should know wrong actions by Muslims in one part of the country could lead to retaliation in another part. If he understands this he will be able to free himself from British imperialism and work for cordial relations between the two communities.'[42]

For Poddar, the larger threat was of pan-Islamism; the demand for Pakistan, he believed, was part of an international movement. He referred to a proposal by Jinnah to hold a meeting in India of representatives from Muslim countries like Iran, Iraq, Saudi Arabia, Syria and Lebanon. 'Jinnah says (India's) Muslims have a lot in common with these countries and they would discuss issues of mutual interest like culture and ideology.'[43] Poddar also cited works of Chaudhary Rahmat Ali, one of the earliest proponents of Pakistan, to illustrate the futility of efforts to create brotherhood between the two communities, contradicting his token call for Hindu–Muslim amity in the same issue.

One of the most burning issues was that of missing Hindu women. *Malaviya Ank* claimed that 10,000 abducted Hindu women of Bengal had been saved while 20,000 were still in Muslim homes. The task of locating these women, Poddar said, was difficult as most of them were clad in burqas; however, educated women in Bengal were working to find them and Syama Prasad Mookerjee was hopeful of success in this endeavour. Women were advised to seek the help of government officials, 'otherwise it would be difficult to achieve any success in areas that have already become Pakistan'.[44] If given police security, *Malaviya Ank* said, female swayamsevaks (RSS volunteers) could locate Hindu women among those wearing burqas.

The issue also carried letters from two Hindu women, called Hindu Deviyan (Hindu Goddesses) by *Kalyan* for having suffered and come out of the harrowing time in Noakhali.[45] A self-righteous and tokenistic editorial comment prefixed to the letters told readers not to get provoked to take revenge, but instead to work towards Hindu–Muslim amity so that the two communities could coexist in peace.

The first letter by Amar Behen (immortal sister) reminded women that they had the responsibility to make men brave and prescribed a sixfold path to serve Hindu samaj (society). First, they must convince the men in their family that Hindu women were in danger. Men should help with 'tan' (body, but in this context strength) and 'dhan' (wealth), otherwise women would be robbed of their 'dhan', i.e., virtue. Women were told to encourage men not to fear riots but be prepared to face them bravely. Besides, a woman should be able to protect her own satitva (virtue). If that was not possible, a woman should not succumb to a mlechchha (non-Aryan/barbarian/Muslim man)—'In such a situation it is better to take one's own life or ask men in the family to do it.' Women were advised not to wear make-up or venture out unaccompanied by a male member of the family. Finally, while accepting gifts from near and dear ones, women should ask for cash instead of valuables, as cash would help in building a corpus for social welfare in times of distress.

The second letter, '*Banga Kanya Ki Marmasparshi* Appeal' (A Touching Appeal from a Bengali Girl) was a first-person account of a woman from Noakhali who had been raped. 'My virtue has been destroyed by wicked men who could not be controlled. I wanted them to take my life but they took my dharma (religion, but in this context, purpose in life), my izzat (honour), my entire being. My husband and father were killed right in front of me; my children were not spared either. I was raped in front of them, my father, father-in-law and sons.'

Making a fervent appeal to saints like Shankaracharya, she lamented their absence in her hour of distress and asked what had happened to their sense of dharma (duty). Next she berated men of all castes, asking how their blood did not boil on hearing of their sister's travails. She also called on the Sikhs (known for their bravery yet having failed her), Madan Mohan Malaviya (who, she thought, presumably died on hearing about her state), and then the students of his Banaras Hindu University who did nothing to help a woman like her. She reserved the worst for Gandhi, accusing him of having a heart harder than a flint. 'I have faced this in your lifetime. You have seen the condition of Bengal. Are you not ashamed of imparting the lesson of peace at a wrong time? Are you not afraid of God to talk of peace and aligning with ruthless people who did the worst things to helpless women? Is it not a cruel ridicule?' Nehru, Patel, Subhash Chandra Bose, Aurobindo Ghose, followers of Rama and Hanuman were not spared either for their inertia. The beleaguered woman branded Hindu men 'impotent' and appealed to Hindu women to come together and forget their dependence on men.

This letter of appeal is a vivid example of collaboration between the Hindu Mahasabha, Gita Press and some other publishing houses that espoused the cause of Hindu nationalism. The United Provinces government was immediately alerted to this appeal in the *Malaviya Ank*, and the Criminal Investigation Department discovered the same account in a leaflet 'published and printed at Allahabad by the mantri (secretary), Hindu Mahasabha, Prayag' that was distributed on 13 December 1946. The CID's weekly report on political activities said the leaflet 'appeals to Hindus and especially to Hindu women to counter the Muslim tyranny with the sword'.[46]

F.R. Stockwell of the CID, Special Branch, sent a copy of the special issue of *Kalyan* to Rajeshwar Dayal, home secretary of the United Provinces, and recommended that it be proscribed. He specifically told Dayal, '*Kalyan* has a very wide circulation in India and the effect of the article mentioned may be extremely bad.'[47]

Within a day of receiving Stockwell's letter, Rajeshwar Dayal issued an order. While agreeing that the effect of the 'appeal must no doubt have been unfortunate', he said it would be 'profitless to take any action in respect of the October number which is already in circulation', and it would 'suffice if the DM (district magistrate, Gorakhpur) were to warn the editor against the future publication of incitory matter such as the appeal'.[48] Dayal himself wrote to the district magistrate on this matter.[49]

In the period between Dayal's order and its execution, the CID, Special Branch reported that 'copies of a highly provocative leaflet entitled *Banga Kanya Ki Marmasparshi Appeal* printed at Kailash Press, Allahabad' were in circulation. The leaflet consisted of extracts from the *Kalyan* letter. The CID said that after a search of Kailash Press 4,000 copies of the leaflet had been taken into police possession. It was discovered that Vishwanath, a local Hindu Mahasabha leader, was responsible for its publication and that similar leaflets had also been printed in the Central Press, Allahabad.[50]

Stockwell wrote again to Dayal suggesting that the particular issue of *Kalyan* 'be now proscribed and that the printer and publisher be either prosecuted, or called upon to deposit security as a guarantee that they will not publish any further such communally objectionable article'. Stockwell was of the opinion that the ban would 'have a good effect in preventing further publications of this type, as printers and publishers would know that they cannot turn out with impunity communally objectionable matter'.[51]

Even as the United Provinces' home department was deliberating, Dayal received a letter from his counterpart G.C. Drewe of the Bombay government saying that the 'Appeal' had been published in the 13 December 1946 issue of the *Mahratta* of Poona. Drewe informed Dayal that the Bombay government proposed to take action against the *Mahratta* under the Indian Press (Emergency Powers) Act, 1931, and wanted to know whether the UP government had taken, or was considering, any action against *Kalyan*.[52]

However, Dayal made it clear that 'as the editor of that paper (*Kalyan*) has already been warned, I do not think further action against him, such as prosecution, is necessary'.[53] Just a few days later, thousands of pamphlets from Allahabad consisting of the same article were confiscated,[54] but Dayal's order remained unchanged.

The *Kalyan* article continued to nag the United Provinces government as news of its publication in a booklet form appeared from Gwalior barely four months before Independence.[55]

Returning to politics, *Malaviya Ank* presented a picture of Noakhali where all the levers of power and economy were under Muslim control. Calling the situation there the precursor to the formation of Pakistan, *Malaviya Ank* cited news reports of converted Hindus dressed like Muslims submitting applications to courts that they had decided to leave the 'darkness of Hinduism' of their own will and had embraced the pious light of Islam to remove their blindness. 'New methods are being adopted and Muslim League is out to prove that all conversions have taken place through free will.' Various religious leaders put forward their views on reconversion (shuddhi) of Hindus who had become

Muslims, urging that they should be welcomed back to the fold after performing the elaborate rituals deemed necessary to purify them.[56]

Even an administrative decision could not be seen outside the context of the communal divide. Poddar was angered by the proposed legislation by the Bombay government to ban untouchability and attempts to bring in a Hindu marriage bill and divorce bill. He castigated Ashfaq Ali, railway minister in the interim government, saying his decision to end the system of separate provision of tea, water and food for Hindu and Muslim passengers was an attack on the sanctity of Hindu religion.[57]

A Clarion Call for Hindus

Poddar elaborated on his twelve-point solution for Hindu unity and protection in the *Malaviya Ank*.[58] His first suggestion was to create an all-India organization that would protect the interests of Hindus of all castes and sects. Next, emphasizing the role the media could play in the dissemination of the values of sanatan Hindu dharma, Poddar suggested publication of a slew of newspapers in different languages from different parts of the country. While he praised the work done by the English daily *Amrita Bazar Patrika* of Calcutta to highlight the oppression of Hindus in Bengal, and lauded Hindi dailies like *Bharat*, *Aaj*, *Sansar* and *Pratap*, he said the only newspaper working towards propagation of the Hindu faith was *Sanmarg* of Banaras. Poddar's vision was to have a *Sanmarg*-like newspaper from each major city, published in English, Hindi and regional languages. Here Poddar raised the spectre of the Muslim League, saying there was a rumour that the leading party of Muslims was planning to bring out nine newspapers from Bombay.

Wealthy Hindus were asked to spend liberally for the cause of Hindus and in defence of Hinduism, its honour and growth. Poddar envisioned the setting up of a nationwide Rakshak Dal, a kind of Hindu militia, of five million youth. In this context Poddar praised the work of the RSS and encouraged Hindu youth to participate in its programmes. Sanghchalaks (local RSS organizers) were told to emphasize the humane aspects of the Hindu religion, its philosophy and the need to protect its supremacy.

In his convoluted fashion, Poddar told readers to replace the word

'Muslims' with 'Hindus' in a speech by Jinnah delivered in Delhi that read: 'We do not want to fight. We want to live peacefully. But to save ourselves from any attack we should conserve our energy so that the other side should realize doing anything against Muslims would cause more harm to them and would be suicidal.'

Hindu women were asked to be alert, not to venture out unnecessarily, to carry a knife and not to let children out alone. People were generally advised not to go for late-night movie shows and fairs. Hindu industrialists and landlords were told to be magnanimous with their staff and treat them as part of their families so that in times of crisis they would not turn into adversaries. They were also told to employ only Hindus as guards and drivers at home as well as in factories and offices. Temples, ashrams and monasteries should be fortified, Poddar advised.

In the charged communal environment of 1946, *Kalyan*'s December issue that had carried the article '*Hindu Kya Karen*' and the *Malaviya Ank* (also published in December) had both raised considerable controversy and drawn the attention of the establishment. In February 1947, after much hesitation, the Governments of Bihar and the United Provinces decided to ban the two issues.[59] By then lakhs of copies of these issues had already been circulated, and '*Hindu Kya Karen*' had been re-published separately by Gita Press and by many well-heeled readers who spent their own money on its printing and free dissemination.

The ban under section 153-A of the Indian Penal Code—for spreading communal disaffection—came as a surprise to Poddar. In the March 1947 issue of *Kalyan*, he castigated the Congress governments of the two states for missing the bigger picture. He claimed that both issues were aimed at communal amity and reproduced extracts from them to make his point. He also mocked the government for its delayed decision: 'I do not know if *Kalyan*'s influence will wane or be enhanced.'[60] Further, he queried why Muslim League publications, 'brought out only to spread communal disharmony', had been left untouched. 'Is it because they are Muslims and government has to take every step cautiously? The fact is, action against *Kalyan* is also a ploy to please the Muslims.' He pointed out that while *Kalyan*'s anti-government stand during World War II had not resulted in any action by the colonial government, now, on the eve of freedom, a government of Indians had banned two issues.

Poddar saw the ban as an act of God that Gita Press did not regret or wish to complain about. He went ahead with the annual number of 1947—a mammoth 725-page issue on the *Markandeya* and *Brahma Puranas*. Unlike the annual issues of previous years, devoted entirely to their subjects, in 1947 space was lent to themes related to nationhood and to reports on Hindu–Muslim violence.

What better way to open the debate than with an extract of the speech by RSS chief M.S. Golwalkar, '*Sachcha Rashtravad*', that presented his interpretation of Indian nationhood and how external influences caused the nation to lose the plot.[61] Golwalkar stated that the RSS wanted to unite the Hindus; and once united, to make them powerful; and when they were powerful, to work for their prosperity. Innocuous, some would say. But Golwalkar's idea of history and prescription for Hindu supremacy was chilling in its conviction.

Golwalkar believed the biggest problem in India was the creation of nationalism. Although the intention was to create one rashtra (nation), the model was borrowed from outside. The second mistake in the formulation of nationalism, Golwalkar said, was the acceptance of the theory of Aryan invasion and that India was a continent comprising many nations. This belief, he argued, led to another blunder: 'We accepted India has many nations and like the Americans agreed to have a federation. This gave rise to a mutilated version of sub-nationalism in India' that 'lacks true Bharatiyata (Indianness)'. In his opinion, the nationalism built against colonial rule in India would not last forever: 'The central pivot of Indian life cannot be outside India. Extraterritorial inspiration and extraterritorial idealism is the biggest example of extraterritorial loyalty. And it is the biggest act against the nation.'

Kalyan's tryst with Noakhali continued unabated in January 1947. The issue carried eight instances of how divine intervention had saved Hindus in Bengal from attacks by Muslims.[62]And if God came to the rescue of Hindus, *Kalyan* cited many instances of Hindus coming to the defence of Muslims in and around Meerut. In a rare case, it reported that two Muslims, Kale Khan and Mohammad Omar, saved a Hindu woman from losing her property to rioters.[63]

Then there was an exhaustive report on the current situation in the country and what Hindus should do.[64] The message was not to depend on the Central government as it had ceased to exist insofar as security of citizens in Muslim League–ruled states was concerned. The report encouraged Hindus to defend themselves. It cited Patel's speech at the Meerut session of Congress in which he had warned Muslim League leaders that 'sword would be answered with sword' and that 'Pakistan cannot be achieved through loot, murder, arson, religious conversion and rape.'

Comparing the relative state of Muslim and Hindu refugee camps, *Kalyan*'s contention was that camps in Bihar for Muslims had better conditions since most of them were run by Muslim League volunteers. Citing Sucheta Kripalani, the report painted a sorry state of Hindu refugee camps in East Bengal with poor hygienic conditions and inadequate food.

The article also expressed concern that the Muslims in Bihar were getting more gun licences than the Hindus: 'A statement by the Bihar government shows 52 per cent gun licences are with Hindus constituting 89 per cent, whereas 11 per cent Muslims have 48 per cent gun licences.'

Kalyan gave instances of Muslim propaganda—the claim that the Muslims had suffered more in Bihar than the Hindus in Bengal, and the distribution of a pamphlet at the meeting of the United Nations General Assembly alleging that the Indian delegation did not have a single Muslim while, as Vijaya Lakshmi Pandit pointed out, the delegation had two Muslims, Mahommedali Currim Chagla and Nawab Ali Yawar Jung.

Throughout the article, Jinnah was portrayed as the new-age Aurangzeb, a comparison that had been made in his praise for the first time by Mohammad Ismail, a Muslim League leader from Madras. 'It is good that Jinnah has been exposed by his own party leader. He has removed the cloak of tolerance and secularism Jinnah was wearing. The Muslim League should remember that Jinnah will meet the same fate as Aurangzeb.' Jinnah's Direct Action led to the spread of violence across north India, and *Kalyan* stated that this had to be countered: 'The time has come for every Hindu man and woman to become a soldier in self-defence. They should launch a movement demanding reservation in government jobs in proportion to their percentage in the population. Just like Muslims rally around at the call of *Allah-O-Akbar*, Hindus should learn to come together on hearing the blowing of conch shells and the slogans of *Har Har Mahadev* and *Bajrang Bali Ki Jai*.'

Posturing and strident opposition apart, the reality of Pakistan was something the Hindu nationalists and Gita Press had come to terms with by the first quarter of 1947, and *Kalyan* presented their vision of soon-to-be-born independent India based on the paradigm of Hindi-Hindu-Hindustan.

The most vivid articulation of this dream was through a poem—'*Hindutva Viheen Swarajya Se Kya Hoga?*'(What Good Is Independence Without Hindutva?)—in the February 1947 issue of *Kalyan*.[65] The author, one is led to believe, was a person who had been to prison six times for participating in the Congress-led national movement.

Provocative, passionate and filled with patriotic fervour of the Hindutva variety, the poem had all the markings of a high school magazine effort while touching upon key aspects of the Hindu nationalism discourse:

Yadi ham mein hindutva na hota, kyon swaraj-hit ladte?
Ho jate sab yavan-christian, kyon jhagron mein aate?
Kyon datkar qurbani karte, kyon jailon mein sadte?
Kyon goli seenon par sahte, kyon phansi par chadhte?
Aaj kisi ko khush karne-hit dharma diye kya hoga?
Kya hoga aise swarajya se, jo hindutva na hoga?

If we had no Hindutva in us, why would we fight for Swaraj?
We would have become foreigners or Christians then, why would we fight?
Why did we sacrifice so boldly, why did we rot in jail?
Why did we take bullets on our chests, why did we go to the gallows?
What will we get today by sacrificing our religion to please someone?
What will we get from Swaraj without Hindutva?

In another verse the Hindi-Hindu mission was blended with the fear of Hindustani or Urdu taking over the language of Hindus. Killing of Hindi was seen as another way of killing Hindus.

Hindi-Hindu dharma Hind ka, pyari Hindi bhasha!
Hindi-bhojan basan, pran main behti Hindi shwasa!!
Aaj chal raha hai Hindi par, Hindustani phansa!
Har prakar Hindu hatya ho, dekhe Hind tamasha!!

Hindi-Hindu is the religion of Hind, Beautiful is the Hindi language!
Hindi is our food and cloth, Hindi flows in our breath!!
Today Hindi is facing the trap of Hindustani!
Hindus are killed in every manner, while Hind is a witness to the show!!

And then there was the clarion call to Hindus to arise:

Aaj chahen to Pakistani ada sudur baha dein!
Aaj chahen to hum avani se atyachar mita dein!!
Aaj chahen to duniyabhar mein Ramrajya faila dein!
Agar paap par prabal dharma ka ransingha bajwa dein!!

If we wish, today the accomplishment of Pakistan can be drowned!
If we wish, today oppression can be removed from the universe!!
If we wish, today Ram Rajya can be established all over the world!
If only we are able to let dharma dominate over our sins!!

Kalyan continued with selective extracts from newspapers, which became almost a regular column in 1947, showing what it called the tragedy of Hindu jati. The focus remained on Bengal and the 'dangerous policies' of the Muslim League government that was 'openly courting Muslims who were filling most of the administrative posts'.[66]

Poddar termed Gandhi's efforts at a rapprochement between the two communities futile; while he praised Gandhi's principles of ahimsa and tolerance, he argued that they meant nothing to Muslims. Poddar cited the indifference of Bengal Muslims to Gandhi's general call for contributions to help the riot victims, while the Hindus, he said, showered Gandhi with money and valuables. 'Gandhi's influence is on Hindus who by nature are spiritual and respectful towards him. They consider Gandhi a saint and a mahatma. If he says they have committed a sin, Hindus admit it. If he asks Hindus to tolerate, they do that. They should realize what this tolerance will lead to and whether it can save them from the Muslims' well-organized attack. The Hindus will not gain the respect of the Muslims until they are united.'[67]

With each passing month Gita Press became increasingly combative on the Hindu–Muslim front. A month after the ban on two of its issues, *Kalyan* reproduced a full-page call to Hindus to gear up against the Muslim violence that had first appeared in *Prabuddha Bharat*, the journal of the Ramakrishna Mission started by Swami Vivekananda in 1896.The call—'*Hinduon Ka Kartavya*' (Duty of Hindus)—included a direct message to Muslims not to interfere in the affairs of the Hindus: 'Religion is the basis of a Hindu's life. Whoever comes in the way of his freedom to practise or disturbs it is an asura, a demon. Such an act calls for retaliation in some form. Hindus do not force anyone to convert at the point of swords . . . Hindus should fight for their dharma and go down fighting like men of valour. But they should not be the one to initiate the aggression. Violence in self-defence is as fully justified, as aggression is despicable.'[68]

Sometime in April 1947 the government decided to arrest Karpatri Maharaj for his move to initiate dharma yudh (religious war). Born in Pratapgarh, Uttar Pradesh as Har Narayan Ojha, Karpatri was no ordinary god-man. Considered a 'manifestation of Lord Shiva', Karpatri (the one who uses his hand as a vessel for food) also had many Shankaracharyas as his pupils.[69]

Kalyan's May 1947 issue launched a campaign against his arrest.[70] Justifying his call for dharma yudh, the journal said it was a result of the government turning a deaf ear to the various demands of Hindus. 'The government promises religious freedom and justice to all but disregards the demands and views of followers of sanatan dharma who are the largest group in India.' *Kalyan* demanded the early release of Karpatri Maharaj and called on Hindus to strengthen the movement started by him.

In the same issue, Poddar warned that 'Mian Jinnah is not going to remain contented merely with Pakistan . . . the way he is planning he would attack to capture the whole of Hindusthan (literally, abode of the Hindus).'[71] Poddar said that Indian Muslims who chose to stay behind would help Jinnah in the capture-Hindustan campaign. If Poddar were to be believed, one of the key arrangements being made to carry out Jinnah's plan was distribution of arms across a large Muslim network. He said the manufacture of arms by Muslims was under way in Punjab, the United Provinces, Sindh and border areas. Aligarh, he said, had long been an active centre of arms manufacture and distribution. 'It is also being said arms are being offloaded at the ports of Muslim-ruled Kathiawar. Arming of Muslim Guards (associated with Muslim League during the Pakistan movement) is being talked about openly. There are reports of recovery of huge cache of arms from Assam.'

He asked Hindus and Sikhs to remain alert—not to initiate any attack, but to defend themselves valiantly. Poddar's biggest regret was the composition of the two nations: 'Pakistan would forever remain a pure Muslim state but Hindusthan instead of becoming a pure Hindu state would become a khichri (hotchpotch) state.'

In June 1947, *Kalyan* carried another speech Golwalkar delivered at the RSS's annual function in Delhi.[72] Generally making the same point as earlier, Golwalkar, without taking Gandhi's name even once, mocked Hindu–Muslim unity endeavours, calling them an 'effort to assimilate two mutually contradictory cultural streams'. After all, he said, if a brahmin tried to be friends with a demon, the brahmin would always be the loser.

Meanwhile, though Karpatri Maharaj was in jail, the dharma yudh movement was still on in Delhi. A group of sadhus and sanatan dharma organizations like Gita Press sought commitment from the government that it would not bring any legislation that might subvert the age-old shastric order. If the Congress high command refrained from bringing in anti-religious legislations, enacted a law banning cow slaughter and gave an assurance that India would not be partitioned, *Kalyan* assured the government that Karpatri Maharaj could be persuaded to withdraw his dharma yudh.[73]

In July 1947, Poddar was upset that the Muslim League slogan of *Lad Ke Lenge Pakistan, Maar Ke Lenge Pakistan*[74] (We will fight for Pakistan, We will kill for Pakistan) had scored over the Hindu slogan *Jinnah Chahe De De Jaan, Nahi Milega Pakistan* (Jinnah can give his life, He will not get Pakistan). Poddar criticized the Hindu leadership in general and Gandhi in particular for acquiescing in the formation of Pakistan despite their public position against the partition of India. 'It is a riddle to understand Mahatmaji's mutually conflicting views.' He argued that if the political class had been helpless in thwarting the demand for Pakistan, it should have been created two years ago. 'At least the conditions would not have been so extreme and the Muslim League could have been contained.' Poddar denounced the Indian leadership's reluctance to call the new nation Hindusthan, the land of Hindus, and questioned their promise to treat the Muslim minority on a par with the Hindu majority: 'Muslims in India do not deserve good treatment if Hindus in Pakistan are not treated well.'

Poddar then presented a twelve-point template for the Hindu-majority independent India, and appealed to 'Congress, Hindu Mahasabha, Sanatanis, Jains, Sikhs to work together to achieve this'.

a) India should be called Hindusthan or Aryavarta.
b) It should be purely a Hindu nation and entirely organized on the basis of Hindu culture. The national flag should be saffron and Vande Mataram should be the national anthem.
c) As a matter of basic principle, cow slaughter should be banned.
d) The official language should be pure Hindi (not the corrupt Hindustani) and the script Devanagari.
e) Military training should be made compulsory and the Arms Act should be amended.
f) The Indian Army should only consist of Hindus. Therefore, the Army should be divided beforehand.
g) Muslims should not be appointed to any high post.
h) In government jobs Muslims should be appointed based on their percentage in the population. This should be done only if Hindus in Pakistan get government jobs in proportion to their population.
i) Laws should not be made for any religion in the name of social reform.
j) In the border areas of East and West Bengal, East and West Punjab, North-West Frontier Province and Assam and all other borders, the Central government should deploy a strong army so that in future India is not attacked.
k) Pakistan should be treated as a foreign country and passports be made mandatory for travelling there.

l) In India, Muslims and other minorities should be given adequate facilities. Their life and dignity should be protected.

In addition, Poddar spelt out eight principles that every Hindu should follow:

a) Honour India's ancient culture, its glorious history as well as show respect and imbibe the valour and knowledge of great men of the past.
b) Take pride in Hindutva. A Hindu of any varna, jati or faith should know that his primary identity is of a Hindu. Such unity would result in helping each other.
c) Despite social differences, make united efforts to create a great Hindu rashtra.
d) Substitute selfish traits like personal ambition, hankering for power and craving for honour and wealth by service to the nation.
e) Help the weak and poor with dedication, money and might. Never be afraid of oppressors (in the present context this could mean Muslims). They should be exterminated with all possible means. Not doing anything (in retaliation) to their oppression would be a sin just the way it is to oppress the poor.
f) Consider yourself invincible and strong and always work in that direction.
g) Have belief in God's unlimited power and benevolence, and conserve energy to fight internal and external enemies.
h) Consider every work as worship of God.

Surprisingly, political comment was minimal in the August issue of *Kalyan*, except for a negative piece '*Tab Aur Ab*' (Then and Now) that compared the earlier peace, tranquillity, brotherhood, respect for the fourfold varna system, the rule of law and low prices with the current all-round tension among castes and religions, social breakdown and high prices—fruits of the much-awaited swaraj.[75]

In this month of Independence, *Kalyan* also reproduced two instances of 'Pakistan behaviour' that had been carried in *Hindustan*, a Bangla daily from Calcutta, and *Milap* published from Shikarpur, Sindh.[76] The first was a postcard, reportedly written by one Mohammed

Shamsul Hussain to the Hindus of East Bengal. He rejoiced that 'due to the mercy of Allah, Pakistan has already come into being in East Bengal', and advised the Hindus that the only way they could save their lives was through marriage. 'We do not like complications. In plain language, we want to marry your daughters and bring them home.'

The second piece reported a Muslim League speech in Qazi-Arf village in Sindh on 15 July 1947 that threatened Hindus with conversion of their temples into mosques and replacement of brahmin priests with maulvis. The report stated that pleas by Hindus of the village had been disregarded by the Muslims.

In the months following, *Kalyan* carried more accounts on the misdeeds of Pakistan, including Nehru's complaint that the Pakistan government had cut off all communication lines from West Punjab and was not cooperating in the transfer of Hindus and Sikhs stranded there.[77] As refugees from Pakistan started streaming in, *Kalyan* carried an article by Poddar's old acquaintance Prabhudatt Brahmachari who made a fervent appeal for help in setting up relief camps and providing jobs, money, shelter and food.[78] Poddar appended an editorial comment endorsing the appeal. He said Hindus coming from Pakistan should not be considered refugees but 'our own people' who have suffered 'demonic oppression'.

As far as *Kalyan* was concerned, Partition was a misfortune for Hindus.[79] It repeatedly blamed Gandhi and the Congress leadership for this. Regretting the loss of 'everything' Hindus had, *Kalyan* said with the formation of Pakistan yet another Muslim country had been created, whereas there was not a single Hindu country in the world.

Gita Press's advocacy of militant nationalism in the 1940s through the powerful print medium of *Kalyan* was not the reflection of a stand-alone publishing house but the collective voice of Hindu nationalist organizations like the RSS, Hindu Mahasabha and others. In particular, it had originated with the Hindu Mahasabha's thirty-first session in Gorakhpur during 24–25 December 1946. An old Mahasabhaite, Poddar was a delegate at the meeting and entrusted with the task of making arrangements to feed 6,000–7,000 members who had converged from all over the country. The meeting took place in the backdrop of the Calcutta and Noakhali killings and these events dominated the

Mahasabha proceedings. Poddar spoke on both days, calling on Hindus to unite against the Muslim violence in Bengal.[80]

The seeds of what *Kalyan* and Poddar wrote throughout 1947 were sown at this Mahasabha session.[81] L.B. Bhopatkar who presided over the session had given a call to 'Hindus to take up arms in defence of their religion and culture', as 'while it is only human to forget and to forgive, it is divine to resist and to repay'. Poddar was to repeatedly urge such action in the pages of *Kalyan* in 1947, as also the formation of a Hindu National Guard that was advocated at the session along with a call to Hindu women to carry daggers. Even his twelve-point template for Hindustan drew heavily from the Mahasabha session.

The Hindu Code Bill

In 1941, the colonial government had appointed a Hindu Law Committee chaired by Calcutta High Court judge B.N. Rau, which advocated the formation of a Hindu law code. The committee was revived in 1944, when it prepared a draft 'Hindu Code Bill', a piece of social legislation aimed at modernizing the laws of Hindu marriage and inheritance. The intention was to 'extend the rights of Hindu women by enforcing monogamy, recognizing the principle of inheritance through a daughter, and giving a woman complete rather than limited control of her property'.[82] The Hindu Code Bill incensed orthodox Hindu elements who saw the new legislation as an attack on Hindus and an affront to their religion in the name of social reform. As the grand coalition of myriad orthodox elements emerged, Gita Press's *Kalyan* became an important vehicle in the campaign against the bill, not only educating its readers but also exhorting them to protest.

The same *Kalyan* had remained silent about the Sarada Act in 1929 that fixed fourteen as the minimum age of marriage for girls and eighteen for boys. Poddar was opposed to the law but chose to keep his anger out of the pages of *Kalyan*. He wrote to Goyandka: 'I am a big opponent of this law not only because it relates to the age of girls but due to its interference in religious matters. There is a need to get this law revoked so that in future no need is felt to legislate on such matters. To break the law and go to jail is the only way out. I think opposing the legislation from a social and religious perspective would not help. The law has to be opposed politically.'[83] He further stated, '*Kalyan* should not get involved in this. Instead, it should concentrate on propagating humanity, ideal behaviour and devotion to gods. Today, *Kalyan*'s message is spread among thousands of government employees. The moment we turn political they will move away from the journal. It is not about losing subscribers but principles.' But less than two decades later, these principles changed as Hindu nationalism grew more vocal.

An alert *Kalyan* had been keeping an eye on a slew of legislation that was being introduced in the Constituent Assembly that had been elected early in 1946. One early piece of legislation that had caught Jaydayal Goyandka's attention related to the payment of compensation to a wife separated from her husband. Goyandka wrote in *Kalyan* that such 'independence is not promised to women in the Hindu social structure. A woman has to live with her father till marriage, with her husband as a married woman and after his demise she has to live either with her son or some other relative. She cannot be independent at any cost.'[84] Goyandka stressed the supremacy of the shastras that, according to him, already governed each and every aspect of Hindu life, and the inadvisability of tinkering with them. He also expressed his opposition to three more planned pieces of legislation that would legalize inter-caste marriage, marriage within the same gotra (patrilineal kinship group) and divorce. For Goyandka these pieces of legislation would not empower women but would make them morally depraved. Therefore, Hindus should oppose them unitedly. Goyandka stated that Malaviya, the biggest benefactor of Hindus, had been opposed to such social legislation, seeing them as ploys to divert attention from the more serious problems that plagued the country.

The final report of the Hindu Law Committee was submitted to the government on 21 February 1947. Besides Rau, the committee consisted of Dwarka Nath Mitter, a former judge of the Calcutta High Court, R. Gharpure, principal of the Law College in Poona, and Rajratna Vasudev Vinayak Joshi, a lawyer from Baroda. The report was submitted in the face of strong opposition from Mitter, an expert on Hindu law.[85] A bill was introduced in the Central legislature and shelved,[86] only to be taken up again in independent India in April 1948 with B.R. Ambedkar as law minister.

In brief, the Hindu Code Bill 'introduced two types of marriage: the sacramental and civil',[87] and promised a great deal of freedom and flexibility in marriage and divorce, a paradigm shift that immediately invited the ire of Hindu traditionalists. Even those who had the sacramental or traditional marriage could have the marriage registered civilly; this would enable either partner to subsequently seek divorce. The bill also did away with polygamy and caste identity in marriage and the restriction on marriage within the same gotra, and made impotency a ground for divorce.

The Hindu Code Bill 'treated the heirs of intestate succession not as coparcenaries but as individuals entitled to individual property', and gave 'absolute property rights to the heir that would give him power to dispose of his property'. Also, the 'law of inheritance through agnates' was removed and blood relationship was emphasized for deciding inheritance. Thus 'the widow, the daughter and the widow of a predeceased son were brought at par'.

According to Geraldine Forbes, the Rau Committee report 'masterfully blended two views of Hindu society'—it 'nationalized the women's rights movement, claiming that it would be possible to combine the best elements from the ancient Hindu texts with legal principles suitable for contemporary society'.[88]

Kalyan's response was swift and direct. A detailed comment, without the author's name, stated that the proposed legislation was the handiwork of people who knew nothing about the shastras but were so influenced by Western civilization's according of primacy to physical needs that they were out to destroy the Hindu jati.[89] The prime target was Ambedkar. *Kalyan* had been harsh to him in the past for demanding equality for untouchables, and this time too made highly disparaging, casteist remarks about him as the law minister who supported the legislation. Sir Sultan Ahmed, former law minister, who had introduced the bill in the Constituent Assembly in 1944, was not spared either.

Ambedkar bore the brunt of Poddar's hostility throughout his stint as law minister. His resignation was demanded on the slightest pretext. In 1950, newspaper reports of Ambedkar's allegedly negative remarks on Hindu gods Rama and Krishna caused *Kalyan* to launch a fusillade against secularism in general and Ambedkar's anti-Hindu persona in particular: 'Such signs do not augur well for a democracy in its infancy. Till now Hindu public was taking his words seriously but now it is confirmed the Hindu Code Bill introduced by Ambedkar is the most important part of his conspiracy to destroy Hindu dharma. It would be a matter of great humiliation, shame for the Hindus and a blot on Hindu dharma if a man like him remains their law minister. Through peaceful but effective means we should force the government to remove him and withdraw the Hindu Code Bill.'[90]

Kalyan called on India's 'religiously inclined' president (Dr Rajendra Prasad), 'international statesman' prime minister (Jawaharlal Nehru), 'elderly experienced' home minister (Sardar Patel) and top Congress functionaries to sack Ambedkar and withdraw the Hindu Code Bill in order to exhibit their sense of justice, secular credentials and belief in democratic principles.

The magazine claimed that the bill was being forced through parliament despite the clear lack of support the committee had found when it travelled across the country eliciting people's opinion. The journal relied heavily on Mitter's dissenting note which was, apparently, the result of witnessing 'such strong opposition to the reforms suggested'.[91] Mitter had maintained an exhaustive record of the deliberations of the Hindu Law Committee, and the views of the opponents and supporters of various provisions of the Hindu Code Bill. He had come to the conclusion 'that the majority of the Hindus incline to the view that the codification of Hindu Law is neither possible nor desirable'. He said 'most of the Hindu rules are now well settled and well understood, and a code is not, therefore, called for at all'.[92]

For Gita Press, Mitter's chronicle of public hearings on the Hindu Code Bill that included opposition by orthodox groups like Bharat Dharma Mahamandal, Hindu Mahasabha, Akhil Bharatiya Dharma Sangh, Akhil Bharatiya Varnashram Swaraj Sangh and Jain associations was a godsend. *Kalyan* used these views to make the point that the votaries of the Hindu Code Bill were in a hopeless minority. The journal also emphasized opposition to the bill by leading conservative politicians like Malaviya and Kailash Nath Katju and women novelists like Anurupa Devi of Bengal. 'Are they all bereft of wisdom? Are only a handful of reformists wise?'[93]

In response to the progressive argument that legislating the Hindu Code would bring caste and gender equality in society, the same article asked if equality had brought happiness in the Western domestic world: 'Abundance of unmarried women, innumerable abortions, rising divorce rate, women working in hotels and shops in complete disregard to their honour and purity are telling us loudly that Western civilization is a curse on women. The system created by the sages and saints for Indian women at home and in society was endowed with their knowledge.'

Gita Press realized that its arguments against the Hindu Code Bill would have even greater resonance in the orthodox world if they were articulated through the Hindu–Muslim prism, citing the legislation as an instance of Muslim assault in their domestic domain. Thus, the provision in the bill giving a daughter inheritance rights to her father's property was seen as a straight lift from Muslim law: 'Since the bill is the brainwave of Sir Sultan Ahmed it is natural such a provision has been made.' *Kalyan* painted a dreadful picture of the repercussions of daughters getting inheritance rights: 'The battle between bhai-bhai (brothers) would now become a battle between bhai-behen (brother and sister). Daughters would get rights from their fathers but would have to give away similar rights to their nanads (husband's sister). So there would be no benefit, but the peace and tranquillity of our homes would be gone. Daughters live with their husbands, so how would it benefit the family if they get a share of their father's wealth?'

Further, the fear was raised that giving girls of sixteen and above the freedom to marry anyone of their choice might lead to their tying the knot with Muslim boys. 'In one corner of the house Bhagwan would be worshipped and in the other end there would be recitation of Quran and beef would be cooked. Which Hindu is going to tolerate such a law?' A similar fear was expressed for lifting the ban on marriage within gotras and allowing divorce. *Kalyan* said that Hindu marriage was a spiritual bond between two individuals, and cited one A. Mark Mathews as having said, 'Divorce is a blot on American society', to drive home the point that India was merely adopting this social disease. While requesting readers to write protest letters to Prime Minister Jawaharlal Nehru, *Kalyan* made it clear only pandits and scholars of shastras had the right to interpret and point out the rights and wrongs in a Hindu marriage.

As a strategy to exercise moral pressure on the government and votaries of the legislation, *Kalyan* reproduced one Phaguram Aggarwal's letter in the Delhi-based *Indian News Chronicle* that quoted disapproval of the Hindu Code Bill expressed by the late Mahatma Gandhi: 'I cannot imagine a situation in which a wife would be doing things separately from her husband. Taking care of children and looking after the house would take away all her energy.'[94]

Swami Karpatri, the old ally of Gita Press, was spewing venom on the Hindu Code Bill. Naturally, their resources were put together and *Kalyan* carried a public notice that first appeared in Karpatri's *Sanmarg*. As the Select Committee was to meet on 20 July 1948 and the Constituent Assembly session was to commence from 4 August, opponents of the Hindu Code Bill—including Jains, Arya Samajists and Sikhs—were urged to be vocal.

'Everyone is caught up in their own troubles. Government will make use of the current situation and pass the bill. Government should follow the principles of democracy. People in the villages are not even aware (of the Hindu Code Bill). We request Nehru to carefully read the note of dissent by Mitter. We also request everyone opposed to the bill to send letters and telegrams before 4 August to the government. If this is not done, later we will be told there was not enough opposition to the bill.'[95]

The next month, *Kalyan* made another fervent appeal to the government not to go ahead with the bill. Apart from reiterating earlier arguments, the journal requested the government to consider the views of Malaviya, 'the uncrowned king of Hindu India', as well as those of four judges of Calcutta High Court who had said: 'Most of the rules of Hindu law are now well settled and well understood, and a code is not, therefore, called for at all. We are not aware that the whole of the personal law of any community in any country has been, or is sought to be, embodied in a code, and it is our conviction that all communities in India, like the Muslims for instance, will stoutly resist any attempt to foist a code of personal law upon them. We see no reason why the Hindus should be treated differently.'[96]

The Hindu Code Bill could not be taken up during the August 1948 session of the Constituent Assembly, but *Kalyan* kept up its campaign. In an editorial comment, Poddar advised readers not to think the bill had been shelved: 'President Rajendra Prasad had advised shelving of the bill on legal grounds but it has not been accepted. Only the debate on the bill has been put on hold till the next session. As before, the general public and organizations should continue to hold protest meetings and send letters and telegrams.'[97]It was true that 'Prasad had strongly opposed the Hindu Code Bill right from the beginning. He felt the bill would destroy our strong family links and our cultural tradition would go haywire.'[98]

Having got to know about government's plan to take over the management of temples, in the same editorial comment *Kalyan* justified the huge tracts of land given to temples so that they could generate revenues to sustain themselves economically. 'To protect these temples, their founders, feelings of devotees and of Hindu culture it is important to save these zamindaris that had continued even during the Muslim and British rule.'[99] Lamenting the situation of being hounded under independent India's 'own' rule, Gita Press said such a takeover of temple zamindari would be a sin and a matter of great shame. The proposal of government providing a fixed monthly contribution to temples for running their affairs was of little use as the value of money was bound to come down in the future, making any contribution ineffective. However, it agreed to government intervention to protect the rights of farmers working on land owned by temples.

By 1949 *Kalyan* had sharpened its attack on the Hindu Code Bill. Its criticism that had so far comprised religious and communal rhetoric was now at least attempting to sound meaningful. In a full-length critique, the journal challenged the proposed legislation on three grounds.[100] One, the Constituent Assembly had no right to legislate on religious matters, as neither the voter nor the voted were required to have any knowledge of religion, and if there was no knowledge of religion how could they decide on a religious issue? Two, the same Constituent Assembly had principally agreed not to interfere in matters of religion, and this was such a matter as, for Hindus, marriage was the holiest ritual. Three, in a secular country, making laws relating to one religion was outright objectionable. The last charge—interfering with the religious code of the majority community while letting off minorities, especially Muslims—was levelled against what was seen as Nehru's preferential treatment of minorities, especially Muslims.

Kalyan even attacked the very basis of the Constituent Assembly, saying it did not truly represent the people as it had been constituted by the provincial assemblies that were elected by a minuscule thirty-five million of the total population of 400 million. 'And if Muslim votes are taken out of this . . . the voter percentage goes down even further.'[101]

As for the specific clauses of the bill, the same article painted a gruesome picture of their impact. Allowing marriages within the gotras meant that distant cousins and even uncle and niece could marry each other. Inter-caste marriages would become legal and marriage between Hindus of any caste and other religions would be valid. *Kalyan* presented a scenario in which a capricious son of a brahmin, kshatriya or vaishya could bring home any girl, either a lower caste, or a Christian or Muslim, and even consume meat, causing immense pain to family members who followed the tenets of varna system. If a Christian or Muslim declared himself a Hindu and married a Hindu girl, their son could inherit the mother's wealth and then revert to the original faith of his father. A bigger loss expected was the gradual redundancy of shastric marriage rituals as court marriages would become more common and acceptable. Divorce, as *Kalyan* understood it, could take place simply if one of the partners levelled allegations against the other. This would destroy the great tradition of women being pativrata (worshipping their husbands). The loss to a woman (especially to her character) was stressed, as the husband 'in order to escape paying of maintenance could cook up stories to prove her to be immoral'. Adoption was another issue raised—*Kalyan* maintained it was a religious process that had to follow an elaborate ritual, but the provisions for adoption in the bill allowed a man without a child to adopt a non-Hindu child.

The Hindu Code Bill was also perceived as a threat to the joint family system. *Kalyan* argued: 'It is due to this system that, despite suffering thousands of years of oppressive foreign rule, Hindu families could retain their fortune.' For *Kalyan*, giving an individual the right to his/her share of property could create a situation in which one member of a family could decide to sell off his share without consulting other members. The inheritance clause in the new law threatened the time-tested system of succession on the basis of seniority among male descendents.

The protest against the Hindu Code Bill intensified as *Kalyan* took upon itself the task of involving its readers. Claiming that even within the Congress there were differing opinions, readers were asked to send protest letters to Prime Minister Nehru and Lok Sabha Speaker G.V. Mavalankar.[102] Appeals by Karpatri Maharaj and Algu Rai Shastri, a Congress member of the legislative assembly who worked in various districts in the United Provinces and made his name working for untouchables,[103] were also published in *Kalyan*. While Karpatri said the bill was neither 'tarksammat' (based on logic), nor 'shastrasammat' (based on shastras) or 'loksammat' (based on public opinion), Shastri strangely forgot his work among untouchables and asked the government to leave such matters to religious gurus and not fall into the myth of social reform: 'It is as if you send someone to your house to make arrangements to feed your guests and he sells off your property.'[104]

A novel literary tool employed by *Kalyan* during the Hindu Code Bill controversy was an account of a dream a swami had from 'midnight to dawn' on 15 June 1949. Possibly the longest anyone could have had, the dream was set in a courtroom and included Ambedkar as a lawyer. The swami reproduced every dialogue he claimed to have heard.[105]

The case was of a brahmin woman who had been lured into marriage by her doctor who claimed to be a brahmin from Madras but turned out to be a chamar (untouchable caste of leather workers). The man who had testified to the doctor's caste was also found to be of low caste. While married, the brahmin lady alleged, she had received a share in her father's property; this was sold and the money pocketed by her husband. In the dream, Ambedkar was counsel for the husband and argued his client had done nothing wrong under the Hindu Code Bill. However, the judge termed the law illegal and ruled in favour of the brahmin woman. When Ambedkar protested and even threatened the judge with dismissal, the judge replied that he would request 'mother nature' to throw out 'black English rulers' just the way 'real English rulers' had been made to leave, and then 'pure democratic government would be established'.

In 1950–51, when the Hindu Code Bill finally came up for discussion in parliament, it was stalled through a series of motions. Prabhu Dayal

Himmatsingka, Poddar's friend of youth and an accomplice in the Rodda Arms Robbery case, had become an eminent lawyer and was a member of the Constituent Assembly. Along with Biswanath Das, he moved a motion seeking wider discussion on the bill. A series of motions were moved by others, some demanding the bill be sent to another Select Committee and others demanding the law be 'universally applicable to all religions',[106] Eventually the bill was put in cold storage for a few years, and a disappointed Ambedkar resigned.

While reformist and conservative politicians were engaged in intense battle in the legislature, Poddar and *Kalyan* reworked their opposition to the Hindu Code Bill. Instead of harping on the threat to Hindu existence, Poddar said there were more urgent tasks at hand for the government of the new nation than passing the Hindu Code Bill.

He reminded the government of various problems afflicting the nation: 'Somewhere there is drought, somewhere there is flood. There is an outcry for food. On the other hand Pakistan is giving a call for jihad and Mian Liaquat is raring to fight. In such a situation our policy should be to forge unity and affection so that everyone supports the government in one voice and strengthens it. But unfortunately, at such a juncture our government is bringing the Hindu Code Bill.'[107]

Poddar realized the bill could be used as a potential poll issue during the first general election of 1951–52; however, his appeal to voters in *Kalyan* could not prevent the landslide victory of the Congress party. A confident newly elected government under Nehru reworked the Hindu Code Bill, dismembering it into four separate bills—the Hindu Marriage Bill, the Hindu Succession Bill, the Hindu Minority and Guardianship Bill, and the Hindu Adoptions and Maintenance Bill. In a span of three years between 1954 and 1956, the four bills were passed by huge majorities.[108]

Still, Poddar did not give up. In 1954, when the people's opinion was sought on the Hindu Succession Bill, he reiterated his stated opposition and requested his readers—'Hindu janta (populace), educated, learned, Hindu institutions, religious gurus, business organizations'—to write to the law minister protesting against the bill.[109] But it was a lost battle, and Gita Press would never forgive the Congress, especially Nehru, for what it saw as an assault on the majority community.

Questions of Caste and Conversion

Much of Gita Press's critique of the Hindu Code Bill stemmed from its opposition to lower castes gaining liberty of access to upper-caste homes through marital alliances that had the sanction of law. This would undermine the fourfold varna system that was the very basis of sanatan Hindu dharma. Right from its inception Gita Press had not wavered from its stance that the caste stratification not only had shastric sanction but also at a social level was responsible for peace and mutual respect among the four castes. The varna system was built into Gita Press by its managing trust, Gobind Bhawan Karyalaya, where membership was open to 'any Sanatan Dharmi Hindu by caste brahmin, kshatriya and vaishya'[110] and not to the fourth class—shudras—or to the 'untouchables' (Harijans) and tribals (adivasis) who were not among the 'twice-born'.

The first test for Gita Press was the Poona Pact of 1932 negotiated between Gandhi and Ambedkar at Yerwada jail and signed by representatives of depressed classes and upper-caste Hindus, which promised increased representation to depressed classes. Poddar opposed it vociferously and engaged with Gandhi in a long argument in a series of letters, each refusing to budge from his position and trying to convince the other. Gandhi's endorsement of inter-dining and temple entry for Harijans was something Gita Press could never come to terms with. Poddar pointed to Gandhi's ambivalence on the caste question, quoting his old writings that justified varnashram dharma, but Gandhi did not budge.

In 1946, a Harijan called Prabhakar presided over a marriage as a priest. Gandhi blessed the married couple, and Kaka Kalelkar and Vinoba Bhave translated the Vedic mantras for the wedding into Hindi. A *Kalyan* reader brought news of this marriage to Poddar's notice and asked his views, since he was a known follower of Gandhi. Poddar replied: 'I consider him a saint and have always respected his truthfulness. I loved him and continue to do so. But as far as I know he is not a saint in the Indian tradition. More than the Indian saints, gods and their incarnations, Gandhi is influenced by Western saints and social reformers. Therefore, at times he does things that are strongly against Indian culture.'[111] Poddar stated that 'hating Harijans is a sin' and 'there is no difference between a brahmin and a Harijan'. He argued the atman (soul) is the same, be it of a well-educated brahmin, a chandal (worker at the cremation ground), a cow, an elephant or a dog. Therefore, the learned man looks at them all with the same eyes. 'But this does not mean his behaviour towards all of them would be the same.' He argued that a Harijan did not have the right to do what was designated for others, but 'is best suited to do what his body is intended for. In this regard what Mahatma Gandhi has done is neither in tune with Hindu culture nor sanatan dharma. This is his free will and an assault on Hindu culture and varna dharma. The assault is serious since Gandhi is considered a saint and innumerable people believe in him and there is no dearth of people who would blindly follow him. Detractors of Hindu religion feel strengthened when they find Gandhi's action in endorsing their belief. The biggest problem is Gandhi considers himself a sanatani Hindu and despite believing in marriage rituals, participates in and encourages such un-shastric acts.'

On Gandhi's decision to attend only those weddings where at least one of the partners was a Harijan, Poddar fumed: 'If this is true it is really dangerous. Now anyone wanting the Mahatma to bless their child would have to marry their son/daughter to a Harijan. What does one say about Mahatmaji?'

The issue of temple entry for untouchables was seen by Gita Press on one level as an attempt by Muslim League politicians to lure untouchables towards their party and eventually towards Islam. Jinnah's appointment of Jogendranath Mandal to the Viceroy's Council was shown as a case in point. Two, it was seen as the classic British ploy of divide and rule—with new categories of interest groups such as workers, untouchables, mill owners, peasants and zamindars being created. Taking a leaf from history to make a larger point, howsoever flawed, Gita Press said Hindus and Muslims had fought the war of 1857 together without making demands on each other. 'By giving a call for Hindu–Muslim unity we actually turned them into two distinct communities. Now by seeking to integrate Harijans we are distancing ourselves from them. Hindu–Muslim unity gave birth to Jinnah and the call for the emancipation of untouchables has given rise to Ambedkar.'[112]

In its wisdom, Gita Press ascribed the demand for temple entry to the mixing of religion with politics, for which Gandhi was held fully responsible, and saw it as a pressure tactic by the lower castes for greater representation. Gita Press claimed that Ambedkar himself was opposed to the Temple Entry Bill of 1933–34: a complete and deliberate misinterpretation of Ambedkar's opposition. For Ambedkar the far more important issues for untouchables were 'higher education, higher employment and economic advancement' rather than temple entry that could only 'destroy the basis of the claim of the untouchable for political rights by destroying the barrier between them and the Hindus'.[113]

Deliberately ignoring the multilayered complexities of the temple entry debate, an article by Madangopal Singhal used the opposition to the bill by various provincial governments and organizations of untouchables to construe that the Hindu world was indeed united against the legislation.[114]

Singhal raised the aspect of purity. Untouchables, he said, had the right to worship nature gods, the sun, the moon, the fire, the earth, the Ganga, the banyan tree, etc. The other forms of gods, i.e., the 'cultural statues' brought to life through the chanting of Vedic hymns, could be worshipped 'only by a dwija (twice-born)', and this was 'the basis on which the dharmashastras bar the entry of untouchables into temples'. It was argued that social reform was possible only through transformation of the heart and not through legislation. The untouchables were told that exclusive temples could be built for them, but they should pay attention to education, health and employment. Ostensibly repeating Ambedkar's priority concerns for the untouchables was not as innocent as Gita Press would have us believe, but reflected deep-seated prejudices. 'Scientific' reasons were advanced to justify the practice of untouchability: 'Through their sharp eyes the Maharishis had come to the conclusion that doing the job of a bhangi (a low caste associated with cleaning) for generations leaves germs in their body and therefore there is need to persist with the system of untouchability.'

In the *Hindu Sanskriti Ank, Kalyan*'s annual number of 1950, criticism of the demand for temple entry became more blatant and provocative, even resorting to the use of highly pejorative terms for untouchables. An article by the Varnashram Swarajya Sangh stated:

'Those who did noble deeds are born as brahmins or kshatriyas and those who indulged in bad deeds are born as chandals . . . A human being who commits sin has an impure body. He carries the impurity to his next birth. Therefore, such men are banned from entering temples . . . Untouchables should acknowledge that the ban on temple entry for them is the result of their past misdeeds. Regretting those misdeeds would purify them more than entry into temples.'[115]

Claiming that the untouchability rules were not discriminatory, the Varnashram Swarajya Sangh cited the case of women being considered 'impure': 'In the *Manusmriti* where bathing is recommended after coming in touch with a chandala it is also stated that one should do the same thing in case of physical contact with a menstruating or lactating woman, even if she is one's mother, sister or wife.' In patronizing tones, untouchables were told that if the upper castes had truly ill-treated them they would have been in a similar state to the natives of the USA and the Aborigines of Australia—millions of them would not be alive.

The new republic was nothing like Poddar's dream of a Hindu rashtra. Not only did secularism become the sine qua non of India's constitution, something Poddar would always regret, but so many leaders at the helm of affairs were imbued with the reformist zeal that the voice of orthodoxy became weak. Bihar took the first step on 27 September 1953 when Chief Minister Sri Krishna Sinha along with Congress leaders Mahesh Prasad Singh and Vinodanand Jha led a group of 800 Harijans through the main gate of Baidyanath temple in Deoghar (now in Jharkhand).[116] For Poddar this was an outrageous act that needed to be condemned in the strongest possible language.

Baidyanath Dham, one of the twelve most venerated seats of Shiva in the country,[117] was not new to such controversy. In 1934, Gandhi had come here at the invitation of the Harijan Sevak Sangh and met with near-assault from orthodox groups, who violently opposed the idea of opening the temple gates and letting untouchables worship the Shivalinga. Before leaving Deoghar, Gandhi told thousands of his followers that he would enter the temple only if Harijans could accompany him.

The behaviour of the sanatanis towards Gandhi had created considerable public opinion against them, expressed in a resolution passed in a public meeting at Munger on 3 May 1934. It was decided to hold a disputation between representative scholars on what the Hindu shastras actually said in this context. Lakshman Shastri Joshi, who had conducted the wedding of the daughter of C. Rajagopalachari to Devdas Gandhi, was called on behalf of the Harijans while Pandit Akhilananda appeared for the sanatanis. It is believed that Joshi 'proved beyond doubt that the Vedic view did not stand in the way of Harijans' entry into the temple of Baidyanath Dham'. Though Akhilananda protested, the debate had its impact and 'sanatanis gave up the practice of organizing public lectures in the premises of Deoghar temple against the cause of Harijans'.

Sri Krishna Sinha's entry with Harijans into Baidyanath Dham was the final act in the long struggle. Poddar reacted sharply in a twelve-page pamphlet—*Balpurvak Dev Mandir Pravesh Aur Bhakti* (Forceful Entry into Temples and Devotion). He claimed that after the Bihar incident he had been inundated with letters from a shocked public who wanted to know his views.

While granting that Harijans had the right to devotion, Poddar contended that bhakti did not require access to temples. Temples, he said, were not public places, as each had different gods with specific rules for their worship. Images of gods might be made of stone, metal or wood but they were worshipped on the basis of the shastras. 'The same shastra that infused life into a god's statue has also made rules about who can worship. If we do not agree there is life in the image of the god inside a temple then there is no point making demands to worship such a god. One might as well worship the image and statue of the god sold in the market or kept in the museum. Why demand entry into temples?'[118] Poddar, like others in the sanatan fold, dismissed the changed discourse in the newly independent nation that emphasized equality of all citizens. While it was possible for the government with its majority to make laws of its choice and open temples to all, or even take over temples and change the rules of worship, 'such changes brought through law cannot change what is there in the shastras. God ceases to exist in an image or statue inside a temple that does not follow shastras . . . Forceful entry is rape, violence and misuse of power. What kind of a democracy or Swaraj is it that allows an individual, a political party or ruling establishment to interfere and forcibly enter a place of worship of one particular faith?' Reacting to reports of Vinoba Bhave having supported government takeover of temples, Poddar wondered how he, a supporter of Gandhi, could support rape. Warning of possible violence, Poddar in the same breath criticized those sanatanis who had attacked Vinoba Bhave and a woman accompanying him.

Poddar's pamphlet included a letter Gandhi had written to him on 5 November 1932 criticizing those who 'taunt and slander santanists, commit himsa (violence) and undoubtedly injure the cause of the removal of untouchability . . . Sanatanists who see untouchability as a part of religion should not be subjected to attacks of any kind. They have as much right to stand firm on their belief as we have to stand on ours.'[119]

In October 1967, *Kalyan* carried an extract from a religious discourse delivered by Shankaracharya Niranjan Dev Tirth in Delhi.[120] The speech was highly contemptuous of changes in urban lifestyles and consumption patterns, from the manner in which men urinated in public to the use of 'biscuits consisting eggs, toothbrushes made of pig hair and impure tooth powder'. Far more serious was Tirth's argument in defence of the caste system as the ultimate marker of social identity. He said 'caste' was not unique among the Hindus but existed in both animate and inanimate worlds—stones, metals, birds, animals, plants and flowers. He derided those who were striving for a casteless society. Tirth saw such an act as a mahapap (grave sin). He contended that being born in a certain caste was an act of fate that could not be changed through knowledge and imbibing of a pure lifestyle. At most he was willing to grant that good deeds in the present life could be rewarded in the next life, whereby even a shudra could be reborn as a brahmin. He said the converse was also true—a non-believer brahmin was likely to be a shudra in his next life.

On 6 December 1968, the Lok Sabha debated Tirth's article in *Kalyan*. Union home minister Yashwantrao Chavan, replying to a question by George Fernandes, stated: 'Government strongly disapprove of the views of Shankaracharya and consider that such articles are harmful to national unity'. However, he made it clear that the 'article was not actionable under the law'.[121] *Kalyan*'s issue of December 1968 was in press when the matter came up in parliament, but it lost no time in putting up a defence on the inside back cover, arguing that Tirth's article did not demean other religions.[122] There is no missing Poddar's style in the unsigned piece: 'The article should be read properly. We think those who raised the issue in parliament and Mr Chavan did not make the effort to read and understand the article properly. Despite being a scholar and an intelligent man who holds such a responsible position, Chavan's words against the Shankaracharya do not behove him. A man in high position of a secular country has no reason or the right to make such a comment against Hindu sanatan dharma and its religious leaders.' *Kalyan* also reproduced the solidarity telegram the Shankaracharya of Dwarka had sent to the president seeking withdrawal of Chavan's statement. He termed Chavan's statement 'highly objectionable' that 'denounces intentionally the dignity of Hindu religious heads and interferes with Hinduism and their religious practices when the so-called secular government does not utter a word about the activities of other minority communities'.

On the question of the status of tribals, Gita Press reflected the relative silence of Hindu nationalists. Unlike the marginalized castes that had began asserting themselves from the 1920s onwards, the voice of the vast spectrum of tribal India was not substantially raised in mainstream politics or among the assertive conservative Hindu groups.

However, the formation of the Bharatiya Jana Sangh in October 1951,[123] the first attempt by the RSS to depute its cadres for political work, saw a surfeit of new issues brought into the public and electoral arena. Though, as Christophe Jaffrelot points out, 'the presence of Hindu traditionalists within the Congress served to deprive the Jana Sangh of many of its strongest arguments on which its appeal was based, such as the promotion of Hindi, the protection of the cow and the fight against Christian missions',[124] the Jana Sangh had begun asserting itself separately. In August 1953, the party's All India General Council in Allahabad expressed 'concern over the recent spurt in the activities of American, British and other foreign missionaries who are exploiting illiteracy and poverty of the backward sections of our people for converting them to Christianity'.[125] The creation of 'denationalized elements in an already weak society', they said, was giving rise to demands for 'independent states of Naga and Jharkhand regions' and such demands were 'proofs of their anti-national and disruptive influence'.

In January 1954, the Jana Sangh demanded the government 'keep a watchful eye on the anti-national activities of foreign missionaries' and ensure that 'foreign money does not influence these missions'.[126] The party's 'Anti-Foreign Missionary Week' protest resulted in the Madhya Pradesh government setting up a commission to inquire into the activities of Christian missionaries under Justice Dr Bhawani Shankar Niyogi, former chief justice of the Calcutta High Court.[127]

For Gita Press, politically inclined and active since the 1940s, the subject of foreign missionaries working in tribal areas became an immediate cause for concern and counteraction. But the first task was to establish that the tribals were an integral, though independent, part of the Hindu fold. *Kalyan* was pressed into the job of historicizing the Hindu origin of vanvasis (literally, forest dwellers), and simultaneously various affiliates of the Gita Press descended into the tribal regions with the mission of reconversion. The Vanvasi Kalyan Ashram, set up as an arm of the RSS in 1952 to work among the adivasis (literally, original dwellers), was already active in the tribal regions of Madhya Pradesh and what is now Chhattisgarh.

Writing in *Kalyan*, politician-sadhu Prabhudatt Brahmachari said the largely accepted theory of the Aryan invasion having pushed tribes to the interior forested areas was a Western one and reflected their ignorance and irreligious bent.[128] He said India had two kinds of adivasis: the Kols, Bhils, Oraons, Gonds, Baiga, Matiya and others were listed as forest tribes, and Nishad, Mallah, Kevat, Kahar and Mahar as riverside tribes. The latter, *Kalyan* would have us believe, also lived by occasionally robbing city dwellers.

Brahmachari's version of the origin of tribal people was equally offensive. Ven, the ruler of the forests, oppressed the ascetics living there and had to be killed. But his death had caused anarchy, and so the rishis had to revive the corpse. This led to the birth of a 'black man, short in height, flat nose and red eyes'. Thus was born the first 'Hindu tribal' who was told never to leave the forest. Brahmachari claimed that during his fourteen-year forest exile Rama was instrumental in forging cordial relations between forest and non-forest dwellers and transforming the religious habits of various tribes. 'They had their own gods and goddesses and worshipped the forest, mountain, trees, cow, ghosts. But interaction with followers of varnashram dharma made them followers of Rama.'

Blaming the British for attempting to convert the whole country to Christianity, something that even Muslim rulers had not attempted, Brahmachari chronicled the rise in the number of Christians in the tribal belt across Madhya Pradesh, parts of Uttar Pradesh, Gujarat, Maharashtra and Bihar. Repeating the Jana Sangh's fears, Brahmachari said the report of the Niyogi Commission was 'hair-raising' and a proof of how missionaries were exploiting innocent tribals by converting them to Christianity in exchange for food, education and medicine.

In fact, as Baxter states, the Niyogi report continued to 'form the basis of the anti-missionary stance of all communal Hindu political parties, of such Hindu groups as the Arya Samaj and the sanatan dharma, and of many conservative Hindus in other political parties'.[129] The Niyogi Commission stated that it had found an 'appreciable increase of American personnel since independence'; that conversion was being brought about through undue influence; there were instances of political activities by the Church; and that missionary work was 'part of the uniform world policy to revive Christendom for re-establishing the western supremacy'. In Baxter's view, the Commission had 'made up its mind in advance as to what it would find', and found exactly that.

Brahmachari demanded quick action on the recommendations of the Niyogi Commission, especially sending home those missionaries who were 'primarily engaged' in evangelism; banning all kinds of inducements including school and medical facilities; the formation of a United Christian Church in India not dependent on foreign funds; and an amendment in the Constitution of India giving only Indian citizens the right to propagate religion.[130]

Gita Press had hoped that Madhya Pradesh chief minister Ravi Shankar Shukla would take action, but his untimely death led the press to take up cudgels on behalf of orthodox Hindus to work in tribal regions and check conversions to Christianity. Brahmachari highlighted the work done by Kalyan Ashram, run by Gita Press, especially its efforts to convince those who had already converted to return to their original faith. Gita Press provided 100 copies of the Ramayana with commentary to be distributed among adivasis.

Brahmachari, who travelled more than 1,000 kilometres within tribal India, reported how thousands of adivasis thronged to his discourses.[131] According to him, '. . . vanvasi bandhu (forest-dwelling brothers) might have become Christian due to their greed but they have the same love for their country'. He was confident that dedicated work among them would lead to their returning to Hinduism in droves. He gave instances of adivasis having taken to the Ramayana in a big way—at one place he found night-long recitations of the text taking place along with the construction of a temple, meeting hall and a room for religious discourse.

Ramayana mandalis were formed in tribal regions. Bhimsen, an RSS swayamsevak working in Jashpur, wrote that the inspiration for mandalis came from Golwalkar, who attended a meeting of these mandalis held in 1963 by Kalyan Ashram. But the initiative had major backing from Gita Press that ensured free supplies of Ramayana and other religious texts to these groups.

Special Issue on Hindu Culture

The publication of good-quality religious texts at low prices was set out as the primary task of Gita Press, but it was not enough. It was backed by an extraordinary zeal to provide for the masses, especially women and children, lessons on sanatan Hindu dharma—bhakti, rituals, morality, conduct in public as well as private, and necessary self-defence and retaliation against threats from the Muslims on the one hand and from the secular government on the other. Gita Press articulated these lessons in *Kalyan* and other publications from time to time but a comprehensive ready reckoner on Hinduism was missing. This was published in 1950 in the *Hindu Sanskriti Ank* of *Kalyan,* an 800-page issue on Hindu culture, leaving no aspect out of its purview. Still in print, the *Hindu Sanskriti Ank* has gone through seven print runs and sold 147,200 copies so far.

The striking feature of the *Hindu Sanskriti Ank,* henceforth *HSA,* was its sweep in terms of contributors as well as themes. From the

Shankaracharyas, right-wing political leaders of the Hindu Mahasabha like sadhu-politician Mahant Digvijaynath and Chandkaran Sharda, RSS chief M.S. Golwalkar and politician-sadhus like Swami Karpatri Maharaj, to Gandhians like Vinoba Bhave and Hindi writers like Ayodhya Singh Upadhyay 'Harioudh' and Sumitranandan Pant, the pages of *HSA* had an eclectic mix of voices. However, all the writings, even if notionally different, had the twin purpose of establishing the supremacy of sanatan Hindu dharma and shedding light on its glorious history. This was sought to be achieved through emphasis on the comprehensive nature of Hindu culture with its long tradition of education, philosophy, medicine, architecture, science, music, language and literature, besides its numerous religious texts and ritual practices. Many of these articles had political and communal overtones.

Settling the foremost question of Hindu identity, Swami Brahmananda Saraswati stated that anyone who believed in religious texts like the Vedas and followed the principles of varnashram dharma would be considered a Hindu.[132] The fourfold varna system and the four stages of Hindu life—brahmacharya (student life), garhasthya (householding), vanaprastha (retirement to forest) and sanyasa (renunciation)—were the foundation on which Hindu identity was constructed. The Swami, unfazed by the establishment of the new secular republic, called on the rulers of independent India to follow Hindu culture in their administration of the country since Hindustan was the nation of Hindus. Non-Hindu citizens were welcome as long as they chose to 'live like guests'. The government was warned not to interfere in religious and social matters, to desist from making laws that would blur caste lines and allow untouchables to enter temples. 'Attempts to forge equality are destined to fail. In the past Buddhist rulers like Ashoka and Kanishka tried to force equality but it had an adverse impact on the society.' However, a law banning slaughter of cows was demanded immediately.

Rabble-rouser Swami Karpatri was impatient with the new narrative of composite 'Hindustani' culture that talked of peaceful coexistence of Hindus and Muslims.[133] For Karpatri this was a khichri culture. 'Whenever any aspect of Indian culture came under foreign influence it became inactive. This can be seen in the case of Indian philosophy, art and literature . . . I can understand Hindu castes, culture, religion, Vedas, temples and Rama-Krishna; I can also understand Quran, Masjid, Islam, Arabic-Urdu . . . it is impossible to believe in such an artificial culture and its artificial basis.'

Sri Bharat Dharma Mahamandal, the all-India representative association of orthodox Hindus,[134] expanded on the definition of Hindu by specifying elaborate rules and rituals a Hindu ought to follow. It also listed sixteen basic principles of Hindu religion, calling them sixteen art forms.[135]

Mahant Digvijaynath, head of the Nathpanthis headquartered in Gorakhpur and a prominent leader of the Hindu Mahasabha, negated the view of Hindutva as communalism. 'This has become a popular slogan of our times. But I can say with total force there can be no slogan more incoherent and misleading than this. Hindutva and communalism are as far apart as heaven and earth.'[136] Citing the Hindu Mahasabha's definition of a Hindu—one who lives in the region from the Sindhu river to Kanyakumari—Digvijaynath said there could not be a more non-communal definition. In the next breath the militant Hindu in him emerged: 'A Hindu is one who considers India his pitribhumi (fatherland) and punyabhumi (holy land). Anyone who considers this land his pitribhumi and punyabhumi will never become a traitor.' Digvijaynath explained punyabhumi as a place where an individual went on pilgrimage and where holy men of his faith were born. Discarding any semblance of tolerance he had displayed so far, Digvijaynath contended that the heart of an Indian citizen should always be filled with a prayer to be born here again and again, and not with a prayer for a call to Medina. 'A British or a Muslim might consider Bharatbhumi as his pitribhumi but he would not be called Hindu until he considers Indian places of pilgrimage as his own. He would have to forget the memory of Mecca or Palestine and become pure Indian.' Digvijaynath asked readers to imagine a war between India and Mecca, when Muslims who did not consider India their punyabhumi would side with Mecca. In his vision of Hindutva, the implied meaning was clear: 'The minorities must accept the leadership and protection of the majority.'

There was also an attempt to expand the Hindu base by bringing under its umbrella religions like Buddhism and Jainism, despite the fact that the two religions openly opposed sanatan Hindu dharma, its caste system and elaborate rituals. It was often argued that Buddhism and Jainism were 'Hindu' because they 'originated in India out of debates and critiques that are internal to Hinduism'.[137] Digvijaynath designated various sects holding opposing views as Hindu: the Veda-baiter Charvak was Hindu as was Vyasa, the supreme believer in Vedas; Shaktas who believed in violence were Hindus and so were the Buddhists and Jains who followed the ideology of non-violence.[138] In the ultimate analysis, Hinduism for Digvijaynath was like an ocean in which many rivers merged. 'Hinduism is the name of a big nation and not some communal ideology. Hinduism is an ideal Indian national socialism. Hinduism is not communalism but nationalism of a kind that has no parallel in the world. Bharat will cease to exist if Hindutva is threatened.'

Kunwar Chandkaran Sharda, another prominent Hindu Mahasabha leader, filled the gap that Digvijaynath had left in his narrative of Hinduism-communalism. Sharda focused on the definition of Hindu culture, a culture in which 'all citizens believe in God, treat each other as brothers, practise non-discrimination and where Ram rajya, i.e., a state of peace, love, simplicity and understanding, exists'.[139] But that definition was not good enough until it was counterposed with Muslim culture. A comparison had to be drawn between Rama's sacrifice of power and his younger brother Bharata's reluctance to rule in his place, and the Muslim emperor Aurangzeb who killed his brothers and imprisoned his father for the throne. 'We do not want a culture whose fundamental principle is to kill people of other faiths, destroy their places of worship, burn their holy texts and keep men and women as captives.'

Sharda glorified the Hindu tradition of sacrifice demonstrated by '14,000 Rajasthani women who leapt into fire in Chittor fort to save their honour from infidels', by Guru Gobind Singh's sacrifice of his children, and the hard times faced by Shivaji, Rana Pratap, Durga Das Rathore and others in defence of Hindu culture. In his endeavour to establish the supremacy of Hindu culture, Sharda argued that the Muslims, despite conquering major parts of Asia, Africa and southern Europe, could not truly conquer India. Mughal power reached its zenith under Akbar because he decided to rule according to Hindu principles and in cooperation with Hindu rulers. In Sharda's tale, the decline of the Mughal Empire set in when the successors of Akbar adopted a hostile attitude towards their erstwhile Hindu allies. Sharda's account highlighted the triumph of Hindu culture and civilization despite going through '1,100 years of lawlessness, aggression, massacres and loot'.

In contrast to these flawed narratives, Golwalkar wrote a cogently argued and complex article on what constitutes Hindu sanskriti (Hindu culture).[140] He emphasized the impossibility of fulfilling all human needs, and the importance of transforming oneself from 'I' to 'We' so that societal needs replaced individual ambitions. Golwalkar pointed out the limitations of state power and how uncontrolled power instead of providing the joy of independence could result in slavery and sorrow. 'In Hindu culture there is a concept of selfless great men who were above power. Such individuals had the freedom to point out injustice and the courage to bring about change.'

Expounding on the dialectics of power, Golwalkar argued that Hindu culture made a distinction between political power and creation of wealth. 'Wealth is power, so is control of state. The two can be intoxicating and give rise to injustice. One can imagine what control of state power and means of production can do. But if control of the two gets into one hand, society will suffer. It would be natural that such a society would refuse to suffer in silence and would revolt. In Hindu culture, society is constituted after considering factors that would give birth to mutual cooperation, mutual dependence and fraternity.'

An attempt was also made to explain the Hindu concept of independence not merely as freedom from foreign rule, but also in terms of independence of mind, body and spirit. Contributing his bit to the history project of Hindu nationalists, Justice Jivji traced Hinduism to Mohenjo-Daro and Harappa.[141] Questioning the new wave of modernity brought by science, he said discarding one's own culture to accept the Western-influenced Hindu Code Bill and depending on the West for technology and food grains was not the Hindu idea of independence. 'Independence is constituted by individual freedom and national freedom. Hindu culture retained its freedom even when it was colonized.' This freedom faced its first threat when Lord Macaulay brought English education to India; modern education, Jivji maintained, spawned a new culture of consumption, giving rise to massive imports of tea, cigar, biscuits, condensed milk and a whole host of products at a crippling cost. For Jivji, independence essentially meant protection of Hindu culture. Muslim culture, he argued, did not have much to offer to the world. Jivji feared that the British would rejoice in the destruction of Hindu culture that was taking place after Independence.

In a similar vein, noted Hindi writer Kishori Das Vajpayee wrote on Hindu culture and nationalism being one. Though his formulation was less strident than Digvijaynath's, Vajpayee agreed that Hindu culture meant Indian culture and subsumed other religious groups. He argued that secularism should not mean the country became neutral to culture.[142]

Jugal Kishore Birla, the eldest of the Birla brothers, wrote about the threat to Hindu culture in independent India. Presenting a grand sweep of his version of history, Birla concluded that Europe, Iran, Afghanistan and Baluchistan were all part of the Aryan culture but people considered themselves different since they practised different religions. 'Culture can survive only if religion is defended. Only then the nation will prosper.'[143] What was worrying Birla was the resistance to sanatan Hindu dharma by organizations demanding equality. He criticized reformist women who attended public meetings, calling them kulta (promiscuous) and patit (fallen), saying they had harmed the great tradition of Sita, Savitri and Padmini. Co-education and lack of moral education to children, he wrote, had resulted in students suffering from physical and mental illnesses. 'The campaign for social equality is giving rise to differences. The demand for equality has reached a stage where the categorization of male and female is also being questioned. If the situation does not improve Indian society and culture is on the verge of total destruction.'

One of the conservatives within the Congress, Sampurnanand was education minister of the United Provinces when he wrote for *HSA*.[144] Limited by the fact that he was a full-time politician and could not afford to strike a strident Hindu nationalist note, Sampurnanand moderated his views to the extent of saying Indian culture was a composite one. But at the same time, he said, 'The threads of this tapestry have come from various places but the design is of Hindu culture.' He glorified Hindu tolerance, unlike other religions that, he said, believed in the destruction of religious places. 'The tolerance shown by Hindus towards other religions is unprecedented.'

Governor General C. Rajagopalachari also termed Hindu culture as Indian culture and Indian culture as the culture of the world.[145] An old contributor to *Kalyan*, Rajagopalachari was steeped in the Hindu tradition but kept away from Hindu–Muslim conflict. Instead, he stressed the importance of spiritual knowledge, religious teachers and the need to surrender to God without whom there would be no end to sorrow and failure, no peace of mind. 'Rich or poor, scholar or a fool, for everyone, whatever he might be doing professionally, Hindu culture is the only reality.'

Gandhian Vinoba Bhave limited himself to an encapsulated definition of a Hindu—one who believed in the varna system, in the four ashrams of life, and in cow worship; one who treated Shruti (the received Vedic texts) as his mother, respected all religions, did not disrespect idols, believed in rebirth and abhorred violence.[146]

The National Language

As editor of a high-selling Hindi journal, Poddar was a keen proponent of the Hindi language. In 1941, the Sasta Sahitya Mandal (founded in 1925 for the spread of cheap Hindi literature with the blessings of Gandhi and a host of top Congress leaders) in an attempt to expand the reach of its publications asked Poddar to share the subscriber list of *Kalyan*. The Mandal planned to hold a book fair that would move from city to city, in which Gita Press publications would also be sold. In the margin of the communication from Sasta Sahitya Mandal, Poddar's old friend Haribhau Upadhyay, later a prominent Congress leader in Rajasthan, had written a note of assurance that the subscriber data would not be misused. The Mandal intented to make similar requests to other Hindi journals. Poddar, ever the Hindi enthusiast, obliged.[147]

In Poddar's vision of independent India, Hindi was to play a central role as the lingua franca of the new nation, its unifying force. Always closely associated with the Hindi Sahitya Sammelan, leading Hindi writers and various strands of language discourse, Poddar and *Kalyan* never wavered from their support of Hindi as the language of the Hindus and a key component of identity politics.

Replying to a reader who had expressed concern at the dominance of Urdu/Hindustani, an angry Poddar said he was not against Persian or Urdu or in favour of banning them, but the introduction of Persian words in Hindi to make it Hindustani and forcing people to read both Nagari and Persian scripts were oppressive acts that 'would not lead to equality in society but breed language communalism. One can already see it happening.' Poddar said Muslims would not study Hindi, while Hindus would forget Hindi and this would have an adverse impact on culture: 'What to do? These are the days of adverse happenings. Proponents of Hindi should resist imposition of Hindustani and start an agitation. The effort is to turn Hindi into Urdu, Urdu into Persian so that Hindi is killed forever. This should not be allowed to happen.'[148]

The Hindi–Urdu battle was to get intense and even intemperate in the pages of *Kalyan*. A month after Poddar stirred the Hindustani/Urdu language pot, his journal carried a lengthy two-part article '*Hindustani Ka Rahasya*' (The Mystery of Hindustani).[149] The first instalment did not reveal the author's name, using the byline '*Ek Hindi Ke Mukh Se*' (From the Mouth of a Hindi-speaker). The second part identified the writer in insignificant type as Ravi Shankar Shukla, a Congress stalwart from the Central Provinces. A Hindu traditionalist and part of Malaviya's Independent Congress Party, Shukla had been introduced to the Congress by B.S. Moonje of the Hindu Mahasabha.[150] Moonje, a close aide of Tilak, had spent a number of years in the Congress before gravitating towards militant Hindu nationalist groups.

Shukla was a champion of Sanskrit but did not bring that up here. He was outraged by the nationalist Muslims of the Andhra region in Madras state petitioning Maulana Azad to change their medium of instruction from Telugu to Urdu. This move, Shukla said, only proved that Kangresi Musalman (Muslims sympathetic to the Congress), not more than the proportion of salt in cooked lentils (meaning an insignificant number), were with other Muslims on the issue of language. For Shukla the demand by Andhra Muslims would mean the communal division of social, cultural and political life in the Andhra region, mistrust, and spending of taxpayers' money on the opening of Urdu schools and colleges.

Shukla felt there was complete confusion on the language front, and part of his ire was directed against Gandhi. On the one hand there was a demand for reorganization of Indian states on the basis of language, and on the other Gandhi was campaigning for Hindustani instead of Hindi as well as compulsory teaching of Urdu and Devanagari scripts.

Shukla bitterly criticized Gandhi's Hindustani formula as 'nothing more than an appeasement policy'. He said if Congress governments implemented it, Muslims would learn only Urdu language and literature and use Urdu for all official purposes. Shukla painted a grim scenario in which Urdu would become the dominant language since it was part of Hindustani, and this would lead to the death of regional languages in the long run. Muslims, Shukla said, cared only for Urdu and not the regional languages. Shukla said the need was for Urdu to change its course and for votaries of the language to adopt Hindi rather than force Hindiwalas to take to Hindustani.

Pakistan had become a reality by the time the second instalment of Shukla's article appeared in *Kalyan*, and his attack on the Congress intensified on multiple fronts. Citing noted linguist Suniti Kumar Chatterjee's *Indo-Aryan and Hindi*, Shukla repeated the claim of Hindi nationalists that Hindi existed prior to Hindustani. He asked: 'Would people be taught both the scripts (i.e., Urdu and Devanagari)? If not, which country's state language would Hindustani become, which country's radio would use it and which country's university would make it the medium of instruction? I think it is meant only for the Hindus of Hindustan. Hindus beware.'

Shukla, also a member of the Constituent Assembly, appealed to the Congress to do whatever it wanted with Hindustani but spare Hindi. He said Hindi should have total suzerainty in the United Provinces and Bihar, and all administrative work be carried out in Hindi. At the level of the Central government, Shukla suggested Hindustani be used on a trial basis in the defence and home departments. Shukla was in favour of making Urdu an optional language but only if Pakistan extended the same favour to Hindi. Further, 'Hindusthan should become a Hindu rashtra and its state religion should be Hinduism. Hindus or non-Muslims should hold the top posts. Any person who does not believe . . . in Hindu culture should not be made a part of the government of Hindusthan. Muslims, as demanded by the premier of Central Provinces, should not be given the rights of citizenship. Muslims asserted their separate identity and got Pakistan.'

Shukla blamed Nehru, 'a man who as Maulana Azad says even dreams in English', for preferring 'India' to 'Hindusthan'. 'English might be his own language but not of 99.9 per cent of Indians.' He argued that the Persian 'stan' be replaced with 'sthan' so that the nation became Hindusthan instead of Hindustan.

Shukla's vituperative text was not considered convincing enough by another Hindi language fanatic Raghuvira, then a Congressman, who joined the 'save Hindi' chorus, deploying different language to make the same argument. He described those at the helm of Indian affairs as leaders who 'had surrendered their mind and heart to Muslims and Britishers with little love for Hindu culture and religion'.[151] Lamenting the failure of India's leaders to understand the simple concept of a Hindu nation for the Hindu majority, he set forth on a long explanation about the wider acceptability of Devanagari as the script for many regional languages like Marathi, Nepali and Gujarati.

Raghuvira appealed to readers to write to members of the provincial assemblies expressing support for Sanskritized Hindi as India's sole language and Devanagari as the only script. As if this was not enough, Poddar's short editorial comment[152] forewarned of 'disastrous times ahead from which it would be difficult to come out' if Hindustani replaced Hindi and Persian script was used instead of Devanagari. He again requested readers to write directly to Rajendra Prasad, Abul Kalam Azad and members of the provincial assemblies.

As the votaries of Hindi were confronted with the task of developing a standardized lexicon and grammar for it, one that could straddle multiple uses, Ghanshyam Singh Gupt, Speaker of the Central Provinces and Berar assembly, sounded a cautionary note. He explained the difference between the simple vocabulary of conversation and the specialized vocabulary needed for administration and education in various subjects, describing the problems he had faced when trying to use Hindi words for legislative purposes.[153] He cited many examples of legislative terms to explain the complexity of the task. He did not share the view of language fanatics who insisted on introducing Sanskritized terms in place of common Hindi words. Though Gupt was confident Sanskrit had the potential to provide new words, he advocated that proper rules of inclusion in Hindi be followed.

The language kettle remained cold for many years after the constitution adopted Hindi as the national language with the express provision that English would cease to be the official language after 1965. But as the deadline for abolition of English approached, widespread language riots were reported from southern India, especially Madras state.[154] Hindi, spoken only by 35 per cent people in north India, was seen as an imposition by south Indian states that also feared the decline of their regional languages. Even though the Official Languages Act was passed in 1963 as a way out of the impasse and to ensure that 'English would coexist alongside Hindi for the foreseeable future', anti-Hindi riots were reported even in 1965.

In Gita Press's scheme of things Hindi was the language of the Hindus. After an elaborate account of the efforts of Muslim and British rulers to use their languages—Persian, Urdu and English—to colonize the minds, bodies and souls of their subjects, *Kalyan* argued that Hindi and Sanskrit epitomized Hindu religion, culture and ancient thought. Without referring to the conflict between the languages of north and south India, *Kalyan* stressed the unity of religious and language identity: 'Studying Sanskrit and Hindi is integral to our religion. What kind of a Hindu is the one who does not know them? Hindi creates emotional unity in the country and binds it together.'[155]

Articles promoting Hindi and Sanskrit have continued to grace the pages of *Kalyan* over the decades, as regular re-statements of Gita Press's mission as the custodian of Hindi, Hindu and Hindusthan—part of its role as foot-soldier of the Sangh Parivar.

९: Religion as Politics, Politics of Religion

Through the power of print, Gita Press sought to influence the policies and politics of free India, supporting various movements, ideologies and organizations that promoted Hindu identity and culture, and opposing those seen as a threat to sanatan dharma. The role of Gita Press was not limited to that of a cog in the wheel; the purpose was much more subtle. Gita Press had the sanction of Indian nationalism and had a deep reach through *Kalyan* to middle-class homes. Where else would you get articles by Mahatma Gandhi, S. Radhakrishnan, Rajendra Prasad, C. Rajagopalachari and Govind Ballabh Pant as well as M.S. Golwalkar, Karpatri Maharaj and Prabhudatt Brahmachari, all in one special issue?[1]

Hindu nationalists used *Kalyan*'s novelty and reach among the Hindu reading public to the full, with Gita Press and Poddar as willing partners. Disillusioned with what he called the anti-Hindu policies of the first Congress government, the clear option for Poddar was to openly support, and even get actively involved in, the politics and struggles of Hindu nationalist groups and later political parties like the Jana Sangh. *Kalyan* was used not only to disseminate their world view but also become a propaganda vehicle in 'using ethno-religious appeals to build up agitational movements'.[2] This was on full display during the cow-protection movement.

Cow Protection: The Early Years

A sacred symbol of militant Hindu identity and nationality, representing mother (gau mata), the cow was central to the Gita Press project.[3] Divisive politics and widespread violence had accompanied the issue of cow protection since the late nineteenth century when Arya Samaj founder Swami Dayanand Saraswati established the first cattle sanctuary in 1879 and the first gaurakshini sabha at Agra in 1881.

By the time Gita Press entered the discourse on cow protection in the first quarter of the twentieth century, the broad contours of the debate were already well drawn. The cow had emerged as the 'rallying symbol for the mobilization of the Hindu community'.[4] While the movement for cow protection had created a common enemy in the Muslims who practised cow slaughter, the colonial government was not spared either for interfering with the Hindu belief system and its ritualistic universe.

Peter van der Veer asks the question: Why would people want to die and kill for the protection of cow?[5] He looks at the centrality of the cow at four levels. One, in brahminical rituals the cow is akin to mother, a 'symbol of the earth, the nourisher, goddess who fulfills every wish (*kamadhenu*), symbol of wealth and good fortune (*lakshmi*)' who is integral to rituals related to 'death, pollution and sin, and devotional worship of gods and goddesses'. Two, sacredness is also attached to cow products like milk, dung and urine. Consumption of milk, butter and ghee (clarified butter) is believed to make a person satvik (pure) and a mixture of five cow products—milk, curd, butter, urine and dung—is used to prepare the panchgavya that is used to purify a polluted person (it was offered as a solution for Hindu women who had lost their modesty during the communal riots at the time of Partition). Three, the symbol of cow as the wish-fulfilling mother of Krishna is celebrated in the bhakti cult. Finally, gaumata was symbolic of both family and community. Protecting the cow meant reiterating the patriarchal authority like the kingdom of Rama (Ramrajya), the ideal Hindu state.

Politically, cow protection assumed national importance during the Khilafat movement of 1919 in support of the khalifa (caliph) of Turkey. At the behest of Gandhi, Congress supported the Khilafat cause as a 'nationalist programme of non-cooperation'.[6] This support was used by votaries of cow protection as a bargaining point to persuade Muslims not to slaughter cows. Gandhi, though a staunch defender of the cow, was opposed to the idea of mixing support to the Khilafat cause with the demand for a total ban on cow slaughter. He was hopeful that even without the quid pro quo Muslims would make the gesture of banning cow slaughter. The Muslim League did pass a resolution to 'curtail slaughter' in its annual conference in December 1919–January 1920.

However, the Congress itself dithered on passing a resolution against cow slaughter despite attempts by cow-protection societies in various provinces. Later in 1927, the Congress call for Hindus and Muslims to work together, and to put aside their differences over cow slaughter and music processions before mosques, only added to the party's long history of taking ambiguous positions on contentious religious issues.

Gita Press's engagement with the cow was at three levels: ritualistic, devotional and economic. Though *Kalyan* had been writing about the importance of the cow in Hindu life, and threats to it, for a long time, an annual number on the cow was planned only in 1945. Poddar's letter to prospective contributors said that the *Gau Ank* would discuss religious, social, economic as well as scientific measures to protect cows. Disregarding a bevy of works by scholars and Indologists like Rajendra Lal Mitra, L.L. Sundara Ram, P.V. Kane, H.D. Sankalia and Laxman Shastri Joshi, that quoted passages from the dharmashastras to prove that the practice of cow sacrifice and beef-eating prevailed in ancient India,[7] Poddar lamented that it was 'indeed deplorable that (the cow) should have been reduced to such a woeful predicament' in the land of 'Bharat Varsa, the scene of many endearing pastimes of the divine Sri Krsna'.[8]

The 663-page *Gau Ank* has a diverse range of contributors of varied ideological affiliations—from ultra-conservatives like the Shankaracharyas, Swami Karpatri and Prabhudatt Brahmachari to Hindu nationalist politicians and Congress conservatives like Madan Mohan Malaviya, Syama Prasad Mookerjee, Govind Ballabh Pant, Rajendra Prasad, K.N. Katju, Sir Purshottamdas Thakurdas and Jankidevi Bajaj, wife of Jamnalal Bajaj. Gandhi sent a brief message to *Kalyan* for the *Gau Ank*, merely stating that India's prosperity was linked to the well-being of the cow and its progeny,[9] but a long article was compiled from his previous speeches and articles on the cow. Senior Congress leader Pattabhi Sitaramayya in his short statement said that Hindustan was nurtured by three matas (mothers): gau mata, bhu mata (mother earth) and Ganga mata. Maulana Kabil, president of Hindu–Muslim Gauraksha Sabha, and Gandhians Vinoba Bhave and Kaka Kalelkar also wrote, keeping the focus away from the communal angle. Poet Maithilisharan Gupt, a keen votary of Hindu nationalism, wrote a poem '*Gau Geet*' comparing the cow to the mother as a selfless giver who sustained life and agriculture, even her dung and urine being a source of salvation.[10] The cow's sacredness was also celebrated by another leading Hindi poet, Ayodhya Singh Upadhyay 'Harioudh'.

Gau Ank extended the 'cow as mother' metaphor to another plane, claiming it was natural to see women as cows and cows as women.[11] In ancient times, it said, wars were fought for women and cows. Also, women nurtured cows, source of a family's prosperity. *Kalyan* said the cow embodied non-violence, compassion and tolerance—attributes of an ideal Hindu woman. 'The ideal Hindu woman sees success of her womanhood in being a wife and a mother. To achieve them she sacrifices her personal happiness. She is happy if others around her are happy. In the animal world, the cow displays similar characteristics.'

The Shankaracharyas of Dwarka, Jyotishpeeth and Kanchi dwelt on the religious, scientific and economic bases for protecting cows, with the last even suggesting that the cow and its products could save the world from the post-war economic crisis. He also talked of the medicinal powers of milk and its potential to cure various epidemics that had broken out after World War II.[12]

But the task of establishing the relationship between Hindutva and the cow was left to Prabhudatt Brahmachari, who wrote: '. . . anyone who considers cow a mother is a Hindu. It is the most beautiful definition of a Hindu. One swayamsevak said it is an incomplete definition. I told him if we say those who believe in the Vedas are Hindus it would not be appropriate since many among Hindus like the Jains and the Sikhs do not consider the Vedas as theirs.'[13]

Brahmachari's larger argument was that, even in the age of all-round moral decay, a Hindu nation like Nepal had imposed a total ban on cow slaughter. Brahmachari recounted tales from the Vedas, Puranas and Mahabharata to illustrate that all was well in society when primacy was given to cows. There was no crime more despicable than killing a cow and no charity greater than feeding cows. In the 'classical past' people would do anything, even lay down their lives, to defend cows. Brahmachari lamented the present state of affairs when even Hindus had become direct murderers of cows, especially aged animals who were sold to slaughterhouses. Referring to the time of the 1857 rebellion, he wrote, 'In Meerut such a big revolt took place to protest against taking the cartridge in the mouth. But today I have proof that barristers and lawyers are even eating beef.'

Brahmachari prescribed a tenfold path for Hindus and Hindutva to survive. He asked Hindus to keep cows at home even if this meant they had to have fewer motor vehicles. Those consuming beef should be shunned—others should not marry into or dine with these families. Cows should not be sold to slaughterhouses at any cost; they should be treated as family members; grass should be grown at home for cows; cow milk and ghee should be consumed; people should vote only for those who promised to ban killing of cows; artificial methods to enhance milk production should be shunned; to improve the ox breed they must be fed milk, should not be made to work beyond capacity, and old oxen should not be sent to the slaughterhouse. Instead, ox and cow protection societies should be established.

In their editorial comment, Poddar and co-editor Chimmanlal Gosvami prepared an even more exhaustive list of dos and don'ts. Among the many suggestions, stress was put on influencing Muslim opinion.[14] To do this, they said, Urdu translations of articles in favour of cow protection by Muslims could be published in 'Muslim newspapers'—a perpetuation of the stereotype of Urdu as the language of all Muslims.

Poddar and Gosvami proposed a fresh approach to heighten respect for cows, saying measures should be taken to raise the price of cows. 'As a result cows would not only be precious from the point of religion but would also tempt people to make a profit.' This was an interesting mix of religion and commerce by the editors of a publishing house entirely patronized by Marwaris. Rich Marwaris had bankrolled gaurakshini sabhas from the late nineteenth century, but for the cow-protection movement to be successful the bait of profit was needed—a business model for bhakti.

This was also in tune with the overall attempt to cast cow-protection arguments within 'secular terms', and (like the rest of *Gau Ank*) reflected three highlights of the reworked debate, as pointed out by Therese O'Toole.[15] One, the cow had high economic utility, and there was a direct relationship between the quality of cattle and general prosperity in the country. Two, national pride was associated with economic prosperity that was in turn wrought by the cow economy. Three, the cow issue had the potential to 'cement harmonious relationship between Hindus and Muslims'. At the same time, emphasis on an economy based on cow protection could be 'a way to pursue an economic boycott of Muslims and make the Hindu economically more prosperous'.[16]

So strong was the stress on the economic factor that *Gau Ank*'s extract from Swami Dayanand's *Gaukarunanidhi*, the pamphlet written in 1881 highlighting the state of cows, was entirely confined to the argument that prosperity would be guaranteed if cow and ox were not slaughtered. Dayanand had come up with startling figures. According to him, if on an average a cow conceived thirteen times, one cow alone could provide milk to 25,740 human beings. Each time a cow conceived, he calculated, 1,980 human beings consumed her milk. Similarly, he had calculated how a pair of oxen contributed to the production of 200 tonnes of foodgrain in their lifetime. On the other hand, he claimed, the beef of a slaughtered cow could provide only a single meal for eighty human beings.[17]

The special issue also had a large number of experts on cattle, dairy scientists and veterinarians providing the scientific rationale for protecting cows. Sir Datar Singh, advisor, cattle utilization to the colonial government, had spent his lifetime working for cow protection (his granddaughter is BJP leader and animal rights activist Maneka Gandhi). His argument, entirely economic in nature, was in favour of creating more cowsheds and shelters. Reeling out a series of data on cows, Singh, a close friend of Poddar, said India had 2.1 million of the world's 6.1 million milch cattle but the per capita consumption of milk was abysmally low at 7 ounces compared to 56 ounces in New Zealand and 45 ounces in Australia. Singh admitted that cow varieties in India were inferior to those in developed countries, and recommended getting superior varieties of bulls for breeding. But Singh believed cows could not be protected till there was a paradigm shift in the government's attitude. He asked provincial governments to appoint officers who would take interest in the development of cowsheds and shelters. One, he demanded these be shifted out from cities so that cows would get good pastureland. Two, no distinction should be made between old and young cows in terms of the food they were provided. Three, better medical facilities should be provided for the animal.[18]

Sociologist-ecologist and a scholar of many parts, Radha Kamal Mukerjee talked of the inevitable threat to livestock if immediate steps were not taken to create pastureland for them, while existing forests should be conserved and new ones created.[19] Mukerjee said the increasing fragmentation of landholdings had brought an end to the system of leaving farms fallow for one season so that animals could graze there. He also regretted the introduction of new crops like cotton, sugar cane and jute, which though beneficial to farmers, were harmful for cattle as they were grown at the cost of crops like lentils and legumes that also provided fodder. Mukerjee gave a province-wise break-up of the skewed ratio of jungle to cultivable land.

Madan Mohan Malaviya, a reluctant writer as Poddar used to complain, wrote a long article that relied heavily on the reports of various committees and commissions set up by the colonial government.[20] His blueprint for protecting cows was also entirely economic in nature. He recommended popularization of mixed farming in which the cow played an important role, and incentives to farmers to keep more than one cow and ox. In densely populated cities Malaviya wanted government to encourage people to establish cooperative dairies and designate areas on city outskirts for this purpose. Each district, he said, should have committees to look after fodder and grazing areas for cattle. A movement should be launched in the country with a slogan 'Produce More, Have More'.

Astute businessman and conservative politician Purshottamdas Thakurdas regretted that excessive communal conflict was coming in the way of an amicable solution to cow slaughter. He asked atheists and non-Hindus to at least protect the cow for her economic worth, if not for religious and ritualistic reasons.[21]

Rajendra Prasad called for a more scientific approach towards the breeding of cows, provision of extra pasturelands, improvement in agriculture techniques, and most importantly not allowing obscurantism to come in the way of extracting the most from body parts—skin, flesh, bones—of dead cows.[22]

For Gita Press an important aspect of secularizing the cow debate was to establish that eating beef did not have the sanction of Islam.

Dharam Lal Singh claimed that *Sur-e-Baqr*, the second chapter of the Quran contained rich details about cow worship in Saudi Arabia, Turkey and other Muslim states.[23] In wide-ranging extracts from different Islamic texts, Singh argued that Prophet Muhammad was kind-hearted and did not hurt any creature; in fact, there were various instances in his life when he saved animals from harm. Singh cited *Sur-e-Haj* that stated, 'Allah does not want animal blood and flesh in sacrifice; He wants your piety.' Turning to the long period of Muslim rulers in India, Singh maintained they had respected the sensibilities of Hindus and discouraged cow slaughter. He reproduced a decree of 5 June 1593 from Akbar's reign that barred residents of Mathura and adjoining areas from hunting peacocks and disturbing cows in pastureland.

Separately, the *Gau Ank* carried a small piece from Major Charles Stuart's translation of the reminiscences of Zohar, a servant of Humayun.[24] Zohar wrote how once, during his journey to Iran, Humayun did not get anything to eat. During the night halt, Humayun discovered his stepbrother Kamran and his mother camping nearby and sent his staff to fetch some food from them. The food consisted of vegetables and meat. Humayun had doubts about the meat, and when he found out it was beef, said, 'Oh Kamran, is this the way to fill your stomach? You feed the same meat to your holy mother. Now you are incapable of getting four goats for your mother.' Zohar said Humayun did not touch the food and retired after having a glass of sherbet.

Maulana Kabil Saheb made a case for cow protection, stressing that the entire issue must be looked at from a non-religious perspective—from the point of livelihood, economic prosperity, politics and national progress, as the cow formed the backbone of agriculture.[25] He pointed out that the country could progress if Hindus and Muslims were united. The Maulana said Muslim rulers of India had understood this need for unity and taken steps to save cows. 'There is no other subject more important than cow protection to bring Hindus and Muslims on the same platform.' He specifically told Muslims that the Quran did not mention eating of beef, and said that Sufis did not touch beef. To the Hindus, the Maulana's appeal was to respect Muslims who were part of the cow-protection movement and not taunt them on religious grounds.

A Law to Ban Cow Slaughter

Come 1947 and Gita Press's conciliatory tone was fast evaporating. Poddar was all set to become a crucial player in the united Hindu campaign against cow slaughter. Even as *Kalyan* was mostly devoted to opposing Partition, the cow was not forgotten.

In July 1947, *Kalyan* appealed to its readers to send telegrams to Rajendra Prasad, president of the Constituent Assembly, demanding that the first law of the Indian Union should be that 'in no circumstance would a single cow be slaughtered'.[26] Readers were reminded that 'cow protection alone could save life and religion since the cow is the life of the Indian nation'. Newspapers were asked to be part of the cow-protection movement.

Popularizing ghee as a cooking medium that promised to make a person satvik (pure) was central to the cow protection debate. The first threat it faced was from the large-scale production of hydrogenated vegetable oil or vanaspati that was cheaper; provincial governments were giving incentives to entrepreneurs for setting up vanaspati units. *Kalyan* called vanaspati a 'sweet poison scientifically proven to be a source of indigestion, constipation, impotence and several ailments'.[27] Reporting that Gandhi, who was 'till recently opposed to vanaspati', had asked for suspension of the agitation against the new cooking medium, *Kalyan* said, 'if it is true one does not know the mystery behind it'.

However, Gandhi was consistently critical of vanaspati. As late as April 1946, he agreed with Sir Datar Singh, who was also an active member of the Goseva Sangh, on the superiority of ghee. Gandhi summarized Singh's article for wider dissemination. Vanaspati, he said, is a 'poor substitute for *ghee*' but 'due to the great margin of profit in this industry [its production] has developed from 26 thousand tons per annum in 1937 to 105 thousand tons in 1943'.[28] Such rapid growth of the vanaspati industry, Gandhi feared, 'will not only adversely affect the welfare of the cultivators, but will have a deleterious effect on the cattle industry upon which the prosperity of the whole nation directly depends'. Gandhi suggested that if manufacture of vanaspati could not be banned, at least it should be strictly controlled by immediately bringing it under a licence regime.

By 1950, *Kalyan* would become the vehicle for the anti-vanaspati lobby to campaign in favour of a bill brought by Thakurdas Bhargava, a Congress leader, seeking a ban on the vegetable oil business.[29] The spirited campaign had more than a fair sprinkling of experts and scientists taking sides. After scientist Shanti Swarup Bhatnagar endorsed it, it became tough for the anti-vanaspati lobby to denounce a cooking medium they had alleged was made from animal fat. Equally tough to deal with were allegations that those who opposed vegetable oil were anti-poor and pro-rich. In his editorial comment appended to an article, Poddar said the vegetable oil lobby had earmarked Rs 700,000 for the campaign to fool the people, and alleged that vanaspati consumers were being asked to sign in favour of vegetable oil, extolling its nutritional value.

On 10 August 1947, five days before Independence, Gita Press and other Hindu conservative bodies were busy organizing an anti-cow-slaughter day throughout the country.[30] Baba Raghav Das claimed that 400,000 letters had been sent to the chairperson of the legislative council, demanding a comprehensive law totally banning cow slaughter. He also boasted of the inclusive nature of the movement—sarvajatiya (all castes), sarvaprantiya (all provinces)—and exhorted readers not to give up till the demand was met. Raghav Das said pressure should be put on local bodies—assembly, council, district board, municipal board, cantonment board, etc.—as well as legislative bodies to make cow slaughter illegal. Three politicians, Rajendra Prasad, Jawaharlal Nehru and Sardar Patel, were to be sent letters and telegrams. Hindus were asked to canvas for support especially from Sikhs, Muslims, Parsis and Christians.

In the early months of freedom, cow protection made slow and steady progress, widening the circle of supporters by reaching out to Congress leaders and industrialists. The idea was to influence the Constituent Assembly that had recently started working on the Constitution of India. The initiative was taken by Poddar's close friend of many decades, Ram Krishna Dalmia, 'an orthodox Hindu industrialist of great wealth',[31] who set up the Gaubadh Nivarani Sabha. However, the campaign for a law banning cow slaughter had not evoked all-round support from the Hindu members of provincial legislative assemblies and legislative councils. In the opinion of Gita Press, the main cause of their reluctance was Gandhi's opposition to a ban through a law. The rift between Gita Press and Gandhi was fast widening; *Kalyan* said many of the political leaders who opposed the ban were Gandhi bhakts, and they followed a general policy not to oppose him, besides lacking the courage to do so.[32]

After a mammoth meeting on cow protection organized by Ram Krishna Dalmia, a delegation consisting of Jayantilal Mankar of the Bombay Humanitarian League, Baba Raghav Das, Hanuman Prasad Poddar, Lala Hardev Sahay, Jaidayal Dalmia and Ram Narsingh met Dr Rajendra Prasad with the demand to make the ban on cow slaughter a fundamental right just as Sikhs had been given the fundamental right to carry the kirpan. A committee was formed to look into the matter but ultimately the demand was rejected.[33]

Nevertheless, Gita Press persisted. Various proposals that could be made a part of the final draft of the constitution were collated to present a united Hindu view on the issue of cow protection. An interesting mix of personalities like Congressmen Seth Govind Das, Thakurdas Bhargava, Sardar Jaydev Singh, Shibban Lal Saksena, R.V. Dhulekar and Nihal Singh Takshak gave written submissions to *Kalyan*.

During the Constituent Assembly debates, Thakurdas Bhargava proposed that the ban on cow slaughter be made a part of the Directive Principles of State Policy. Though his argument that the ban was needed as the cow was central to 'agriculture economics'[34] did not convince many members of the Constituent Assembly, who felt religion was the real reason behind the demand, ultimately Bhargava's amendment to the draft constitution was accepted and prohibition of cow slaughter was included in the Directive Principles. Article 48 of the Constitution reads thus: 'The State shall endeavour to organise agriculture and animal husbandry on modern and scientific lines and shall, in particular, take steps for preserving and improving the breeds, and prohibiting the slaughter, of cows and calves and other milch and draught cattle.' However, this merely meant that cow protection became a guiding principle of public policy; it could not be enforced in a court of law.

Gita Press stepped up the pressure on the government, especially against the model bill on cow slaughter that was sent to the states. A specific provision in the model bill that used the terms 'useful' and 'not useful' when referring to cows attracted the wrath of Gita Press and the All India Gosevak Samaj.[35] The bill allowed slaughter of cows above the age of fourteen and those that could not conceive. Endorsing an editorial in the orthodox *Sanmarg*, *Kalyan* asked, if this was the treatment to be meted out to old cows, would the same be done to old people who had ceased to be useful? Another objectionable provision in the model bill allowed cow slaughter for religious, medicinal and research purposes. A statement from Hardev Sahay, secretary, All India Gosevak Samaj, dismissed the arguments for such provision and called on the government to learn from Muslim rulers who had completely banned cow slaughter—even Aurangzeb had banned the killing of cows.

Gita Press realized the battle needed to now involve readers in protests. When news came of the setting up of a brand new slaughterhouse in Bombay, Poddar immediately requested readers to join the protest.[36] He reminded them of how, during the British rule, a proposal to build slaughterhouses in Punjab and Sindh had to be shelved because of protests led by Madan Mohan Malaviya.

Keeping a keen watch on government action on the cow front, Poddar had news for his readers in December 1949. After the devaluation of the Indian rupee, a committee had been set up to suggest measures to increase exports. The committee, on finding a gradual decline in leather extraction business, had recommended that the ban on cow slaughter imposed by a few provincial governments should be lifted. Poddar said the leather extraction business was at the core of cow slaughter; in 1940 alone, 52,700,000 cows had been slaughtered. He reminded politicians in power about their promise of a complete ban on cow killings in free India, and made an impassioned plea to readers: 'If Hindus are left with any sense of national interest and religiosity, they should protest this unethical move. I also request eminent journalists to protest against the proposal to set up a new slaughterhouse and lift the ban imposed by many provincial governments.'[37]

For the cow-protection movement, the years from the 1950s to mid-1960s were quiet ones but no less intense as the battle was fought in legislatures and the Supreme Court. It appeared that the cow protectionists had the upper hand. Much to the discomfiture of Nehru, who 'was prepared to stake his prime ministership on this issue',[38] the Congress-ruled state governments of Uttar Pradesh, Bihar, Rajasthan and Madhya Pradesh banned cow slaughter. In 1954, while the Central government's Expert Committee on the Prevention of Slaughter of Cattle in India concluded that 'a total ban on slaughter of all cattle would not be in the best interests of the country', the Supreme Court upheld the constitutionality of the ban on slaughter of cows by the four state governments.[39] However, the apex court allowed slaughter of bulls, bullocks and buffaloes as well as sheep and goats.

While efforts, mainly through private members' bills, to bring a Central legislation did not meet with success, the orthodox elements within the Congress always sided with the Hindu nationalists when it came to the cow. When voting took place on Seth Govind Das's private member's bill—the Indian Cattle Preservation Bill—in 1955, despite the party whip, two Congress leaders (Purushottam Das Tandon and Thakur Das Bhargava) voted in favour of the bill.[40] In proposing the bill Seth Govind Das had not only defied Nehru but was colluding with RSS chief M.S. Golwalkar.

By the mid-1960s the venerable gau mata had been turned into an aggressive rallying point for Hindu nationalists. The death of Lala Hardev Sahay, possibly the most dominant voice in the cow-protection movement, on 30 September 1962, was a turning point.

From 1946 till his death, Sahay had been involved in the establishment of various cow-protection organizations, like the gaurakshini sabha, Bharat Gosevak Samaj, Gau Hatya Nirodh Samiti and Bharat Gau Raksha Sangh.[41] The relationship that he had with Jayantibhai Naradlal Mankar of the Bombay Humanitarian League resulted in the birth of the Bharat Gosevak Samaj in 1948. Seth Govind Das of Congress was made its president, while Sahay and Mankar became secretaries of the new body. It was an indication of the ideological fluidity of the times that the head office of the Samaj was at the residence of Seth Govind Das in Delhi.

After Sahay's death, his friends decided to revive the Bharat Gosevak Samaj since it was the first formal organization he had been associated with. His friends like M.S. Golwalkar of the RSS and Lala Hansraj

Gupta, Arya Samajist industrialist who became the RSS sanghchalak of Delhi in 1947, were party to this decision.[42] Thakurdas Bhargava, old and ailing, was co-opted in the revival exercise. Bhargava suggested that *Godhan*, a journal edited by Sahay, also be revived. However, Bhargava did not live to see the revival as he died in December 1962.

The meeting to reorganize the Bharat Gosevak Samaj took place on 28 February 1963 at the residence of Hansraj Gupta. The meeting approved the revival plan, Seth Govind Das became the chairperson and selected a ten-member central committee. Hanuman Prasad Poddar was one of the four vice-presidents of the Bharat Gosevak Samaj, and another ten-member executive committee was set up that included his close friend Jaidayal Dalmia.[43]

In August 1964 the Samaj held a meeting at Vrindavan and 'demanded that the government should take upon itself the task of banning cow slaughter'[44] and 'pass a legislation to ban cow slaughter completely by Gopashtami (a date falling in October or November) in 1965'.[45] The entire galaxy of Hindu nationalist leaders attended the conference: Golwalkar gave the inaugural speech and Deendayal Upadhyaya addressed the gathering, while Prabhudatt Brahmachari declared that, if the government failed to fulfil its commitment, a nationwide agitation should begin.

By 1966 there was no sign of the government acceding to the demand for a complete ban on cow slaughter. Though contemporary accounts of the cow-protection movement do not refer to any big protest before November 1966, the June issue of *Kalyan* carried an appeal made by Poddar to the government to release around twenty sadhus who had undertaken a fast unto death in a Delhi jail, demanding a complete ban of cow slaughter.[46] Poddar accused the government of subverting the principles of democracy. 'Government succumbs only if violent means are adopted for unfair demands. But if courteous appeal is made no value is attached to it. Undesirable noise reaches government but a demand that is nationalistic, inspired by national interest and in accordance with the Indian culture is being disregarded by the government.'

Poddar further blamed the Central government for dragging its feet on banning cow slaughter, first asking the states to enact laws and then not cooperating in their implementation.

The movement was fast gaining momentum. Though Golwalkar was an active supporter of the cow-protection movement, Poddar formally requested him to join the collective effort: 'This struggle would get some life only if you actively join it.'[47] Poddar also informed Golwalkar that Karpatri Maharaj and Prabhudatt Brahmachari had agreed to work together. RSS support was not limited to Golwalkar, or in providing funds and foot soldiers; its senior functionaries were involved in the day-to-day operations of the movement. Rajendra Singh, 'Rajju Bhaiya', who became the head (sarsanghchalak) of the RSS in 1994, was managing the funds of Gorakhsha Maha Abhiyan Samiti, Uttar Pradesh. He reported directly to Poddar who was the president of the state unit apart from being national treasurer of Sarvadaliya Goraksha Maha Abhiyan Samiti.[48]

On 25 September 1966, various cow-protection groups united to form the Sarvadaliya Goraksha Maha Abhiyan Samiti (SGMS) and mount the most formidable challenge to the Congress government of Indira Gandhi. Barring the left parties and socialists, the new organization represented an ultimate coming together of members of the Congress, Jana Sangh, RSS, Arya Samaj, Hindu Mahasabha, and an assorted group of sadhus and religious leaders of different faiths.

Poddar was part of the supreme council of the SGMS that included Golwalkar, Prabhudatt Brahmachari, Swami Karpatri Maharaj, Jagadguru Shankaracharya of Puri, Jain spiritual leader Muni Sushil Kumar and Swami Guru Charan Das of the Bharat Sadhu Samaj. The executive committee comprised Mahant Digvijaynath (Hindu Mahasabha), Seth Govind Das (Congress), Ramgopal Shalwale (Arya Samaj), Hansraj Gupta (RSS), V.P. Joshi (Delhi RSS and Jana Sangh), Nand Lal Shastri (MP and former member of Ram Rajya Parishad), and Ram Singh (Hindu Mahasabha, Delhi).[49]

As treasurer of SGMS, Poddar did not confine himself to the movement but used *Kalyan* to carry the propaganda of cow protection far and wide. The role played by Gita Press and Poddar in the cow-protection movement has been largely ignored in serious accounts.

Four months before the November 1966 demonstration outside parliament, Prabhudatt Brahmachari wrote a scathing article in *Kalyan*, calling on Hindus to be prepared to give up their lives to protect the cow.[50] Brahmachari claimed that cow protection had been at the centre of the national movement. He cited Motilal Nehru as having said he did not eat beef but could eat the flesh of those who consumed beef. During the non-cooperation movement, Brahmachari said, a patriot was one who wore and spun khadi, propagated Hindi and worshipped cows. Therefore, it had come as a rude shock when the Congress government dragged its feet on banning cow slaughter after Independence.

Brahmachari spelt out various initiatives taken by Golwalkar, Karpatri Maharaj, Sahay and Poddar to put pressure on the government to ban cow slaughter. There is an interesting aside to Nehru's meeting with the delegation (including Poddar at an earlier date) that called on him with a petition demanding the ban. Nehru is believed to have told the delegation that he would consider the demand and then asked, 'Why do you people run a campaign that I eat beef?' The delegation, consisting of the leading lights of the cow-protection movement, denied being behind the canard but told Nehru the best way to silence the critics would be to ban cow slaughter completely.

Though the SGMS was yet to be formally announced, the same July issue of *Kalyan* carried an appeal in its name asking people to undertake fasts and conduct pujas and reading of religious texts to exert moral pressure on the government to impose an early ban on cow slaughter.[51] The decision of Brahmachari and others to undertake a fast unto death from 20 November 1966 was announced. Poddar, on his part, made a personal appeal for people to boycott all those who contributed to the killing of cows. In August, *Kalyan* asked its readers to fight unitedly for a ban on cow slaughter under the aegis of SGMS, and in September, Brahmachari issued another appeal to readers asking them to join the November agitation in large numbers to combat the government's 'devil-may-care attitude'.[52]

Brahmachari also began a campaign from 22 September 1966 to galvanize support for the cow cause, while Poddar wrote an account of the spread of the cow-protection movement among people and organizations of all religions and castes throughout the country.[53]

Poddar reported that Jamat-e-Imano-Hind, a Lucknow-based Muslim organization, had moved a resolution stating it would be better to give up cow slaughter before government banned it completely. In Banaras, a foreign-educated, high government official who had become a mauni (one who has taken a vow of silence) sadhu was reported to have given up water for seventeen days. In Delhi, a parliamentary cow forum had been set up consisting of Seth Govind Das, Kamal Nayan Bajaj, M.S. Aney, Atal Bihari Vajpayee, Hari Vishnu Kamath, Dagabhai Patel and Prakash Veer Shastri. The mandate of the forum was to raise public opinion against cow slaughter. The movement, Poddar claimed, had even spread to Nepal where thousands were willing to give up their lives. *Kalyan* appealed to the general public to not only protest but also not to vote for any candidate who supported the killing of cows.[54]

It seems that in September 1966, Prime Minister Indira Gandhi had a meeting with Acharya Sushil Kumar in which she gave some assurances; *Kalyan* reported that what the PM had told the Acharya sounded 'reassuring' and based on that Mauni Baba of Banaras had given up his fast.[55] However, Pandit Ramchandra Vir who was on fast in Delhi was arrested and jailed. The journal reiterated that the ban on cow slaughter could not be left to states. 'If need be the Constitution should be amended. It has already been amended twenty-one times. Our movement should be peaceful but aggressive and nationwide.'

As pressure on the government was building up, Shankaracharya Niranjan Dev Tirth of Puri delivered an inciting speech in Meerut. This was reproduced in *Kalyan*: 'One (Potti) Ramulu could get Andhra state by giving up his life. One Sant Fateh Singh could get Punjab merely by threatening to give up his life. I will see how cow slaughter does not get banned if one gau bhakt agrees to die for the cause. We do not need one lakh youth. Police and army will shoot them and yet the tyrannical Congress government would not budge. In the entire country we need five to six men who are willing to give up their lives to end killing of cows.'[56]

Niranjan Dev Tirth offered himself as the first Shankaracharya to be willing to lay down his life for the cow cause. The Shankaracharya reminded the crowd of Meerut's glorious past and how the first spark of the revolt of 1857 was lit there by soldiers who refused to use the cartridges that had been greased with cow and pig fat. He also reminded the government that the assurance of a total ban on cow slaughter had been given by the former prime minister Lal Bahadur Shastri before his sudden death in Tashkent.

In the same November issue, Poddar provided an update on the movement.[57] He said the movement had reached a decisive phase and there was a need to make it a success. An appeal was issued to everyone to contribute with whatever funds they could. Those who were able were urged to participate in the mammoth rally in Delhi, while others should intensify the struggle in their areas. Poddar thanked the Shankaracharyas, Golwalkar, Muni Sushil Kumar and Prabhudatt Brahmachari for their contributions. He did not specify the work being done by the RSS but called it 'great'. Similarly, 'leaders of the Hindu Mahasabha are believed to have put their heart and soul into save-the-cow campaign'.

Poddar had separately thanked Golwalkar for the support the swayamsevaks were lending to the movement. What emerges is that special training was being given to them to work for cow protection. 'RSS swayamsevaks are ideal, skilled, dutiful and true people. The training at Shri Brahmachari's place was really useful. The entire credit goes to the swayamsevaks. They have been preparing for weeks,' Poddar informed Golwalkar.[58] He gave instances of huge public gatherings at Deoria and a few other places for which he gave the swayamsevaks full credit.

As it had done before, *Kalyan* included Muslim endorsement of the movement. An article by one Atiqur Rehman Kidwai, first published in *Gandiv*, a prominent Hindi journal, was extracted in *Kalyan*.[59] Kidwai argued that the cow-protection movement of the Hindus was not directed against Muslims, and blamed the government for dithering on the issue. The main purpose, he said, was to merely get the slaughterhouses closed. He appealed to Muslims to appreciate the precarious situation and not do anything to aggravate it.

The months of planning to put up a united face and speak in a single Hindu voice went completely awry on 7 November. Delhi had never witnessed such a surge of people, estimated between 125,000 and 700,000, who had begun congregating days before the event.[60] The mega event was to terminate in front of parliament with a galaxy of cow-protection movement leaders, otherwise belonging to ideologically diverse groups, set to address the crowd. Golwalkar, Karpatri Maharaj and Prabhudatt Brahmachari, Congress's Seth Govind Das, Jana Sangh's Atal Bihari Vajpayee and Gita Press's Poddar were on the stage.

For some time, speeches were made as planned, even as inside parliament Swami Rameshwaranand, the Jana Sangh MP from Karnal who had been suspended for ten days in September, was disrupting Lok Sabha proceedings. He was finally suspended for the rest of the session. Outside, protest speeches went on smoothly till the just-suspended Rameshwaranand took the stage and made a provocative appeal to the lakhs of protesters to stop anyone from entering or leaving Parliament House. This was taken as an open call for a physical assault on parliament. Even as Vajpayee and Brahmachari tried to calm the crowd, masses of people surged towards Parliament House, and stone throwing and fighting began, followed by a lathi charge by the police. A few kilometres away, part of the crowd had laid siege to Congress president K. Kamaraj's residence and injured his staff. At the end of the day, the movement for non-violence against the cow had led to widespread violence in the heart of New Delhi with eight dead and several more injured.

The first fallout of the unanticipated violence was the dismissal of Home Minister Gulzarilal Nanda by Indira Gandhi. The Jana Sangh, that had made the ban on cow slaughter part of its 1952, 1957 and 1962 election manifestos,[61] made desperate attempts to distance itself from the likes of Rameshwaranand and others. However, top Jana Sangh leaders could not escape arrest. Nanda, already a keen votary of cow protection, became a part of the movement by 1968,[62] addressing meetings with Niranjan Dev Tirth.

Undeterred, Brahmachari and Niranjan Dev Tirth decided to continue with their fast as planned earlier, from 20 November. The Jana Sangh, RSS and the Gita Press were soon back. In the case of the Jana Sangh, cow protection again became a part of the 1967 election manifesto,[63] complete with the promise of pasturelands, dairies and improvement of goshalas (cow shelters).

But Poddar was rattled by the violence and unsure of its consequences for him personally and for the cow-protection movement in general. In a long and tedious explanation, Poddar claimed, 'Though according to

Hindu religion I do not consider Hindu politics separate from religion, I have no links with any political party.'[64] He said it was god's wish that made him a part of the cow-protection movement. Admitting that critics would not be wrong in mocking the protestors for demanding protection of cows but allowing human beings to be killed, Poddar said it would be almost a sin to blame the organizers for the violence of 7 November. Men were killed; those who rejoiced in the misery of others set a few buildings and old vehicles on fire. Poddar requested leaders of the movement not to lose heart but maintain peace and calm. At the same time, he urged the government to fast-track the legislation banning cow slaughter.

Elsewhere in the same issue of *Kalyan*, Poddar dismissed allegations that the violence of 7 November was part of a conspiracy: 'What can we tell them? If it was a well-planned conspiracy to loot and kill why would 1,000,000 people come without arms? Why would they bring 50,000 women with them, some of them with infants, while a few others needed walking sticks? The idea was to hold a peaceful, disciplined rally.'[65]

Poddar regretted the loss to life and property and demanded a judicial inquiry. More painful for him was the arrest of Prabhudatt Brahmachari and Shankaracharya Niranjan Dev Tirth. He said no government had ever thus humiliated a Shankaracharya. Poddar referred to Jayaprakash Narayan's speech in Simla blaming the government for the violence, as an example of public sympathy for the cow-protection movement.

In a long letter to Indira Gandhi, in which he addressed her as sister, Poddar mentioned his past as revolutionary during the colonial period.[66] He reeled out names of nationalist leaders—Bal Gangadhar Tilak, Lala Lajpat Rai, Deshbandhu Chittaranjan Das and Madan Mohan Malaviya—with whom he claimed close association. For Mahatma Gandhi, Poddar said, he had been like family. Poddar attempted to show he was equidistant from all political parties and nursed no political motive.

Poddar admitted that cow protection was close to his heart, but for spiritual reasons. Coming to the violent incident, Poddar said he was hurt by the government's response. He gave his version of the incident and denied the organizers had any hand in it. Poddar maintained that lakhs of people consisting of the elderly and young, men and women and even infants had come together out of reverence for the cow and not to indulge in wanton violence. He requested Indira Gandhi to view the facts of the case: 'I still remember how non-violent satyagrahis were attacked by the British police. Is it justified to repeat such a thing on our own people under our own rule? I request you to think about it with a sympathetic heart. You are the nation's sister.' His belief in cow protection was still firm, though, and he asked her to give it priority.

The January 1967 issue of *Kalyan* challenged the repeated argument of Indira Gandhi and her home minister Y.B. Chavan that cow protection was a state subject; that many states had already passed laws banning cow slaughter and the states that had not would be pressured by the Centre to pass the law. Poddar said the laws prevailing in the states were based on the Supreme Court order that allowed slaughter of aged oxen.[67] He contended these were inadequate since in the name of old oxen, not only young oxen, but even cows were being killed every day. Poddar's demand was for a complete and comprehensive ban on the killing of any member of the gau-vansh (cow family that included cows, bulls, oxen, calves of all ages) and severe punishment to offenders. He said the law in Uttar Pradesh was so flawed that a cow killer could be out of jail after paying a small fine.

Poddar suggested the most amicable solution to the cow question would be a Central law. He said under Articles 249 and 250 of the Constitution of India, the Centre had the right to make laws on state subjects in the national interest. Another suggestion was that the president promulgate an ordinance banning cow slaughter. The 1967 elections were barely two months away, so Poddar argued that this would be better than mere assurances from ministers.

The 1967 elections were turning out to be the most crucial since Independence, posing a serious challenge to the Congress hegemony from socialists and Hindu nationalists. While Poddar issued an unsigned appeal stating that the SGMS had nothing to do with the elections, and that he personally had no link with any political party, he could not resist taking a dig at the Congress and warning it of the consequences of turning a blind eye to the demand for a ban on the killing of cows: 'In the present context those who have committed the sin of forcing revered acharyas and sadhus to die of hunger and put thousands of men and women into jail in biting cold should expect votes only from those who are Hindus only in name, have abandoned the belief of their ancestors and are engaged in acquiring wealth and power, and from those who are too innocent or too scared.'[68]

By 30 and 31 January 1967, both Niranjan Dev Tirth and Prabhudatt Brahmachari had given up their fast on the government's promise of setting up a new twelve-member committee with the mandate to propose an amendment of the Constitution if protection of the cow required it.[69] The committee had Golwalkar, Rama Prasad Mookerjee (former chief justice of Calcutta High Court and brother of Jana Sangh leader Syama Prasad Mookerjee) and Niranjan Dev Tirth as members. However, Golwalkar said he could not attend for three months and Tirth resigned on the ground that government was not serious about implementing the ban. A certain level of fatigue had set in. Karpatri Maharaj who had taken over as head of the SGMS, was in favour of forming a united front with the Jana Sangh, Hindu Mahasabha and his own Ram Rajya Parishad that would go to people with the sole promise of banning cow slaughter. But the Jana Sangh did not show any interest in the proposal—though it retained the plank of cow protection for the elections.

After the February 1967 elections saw Indira Gandhi return to power, *Kalyan* carried a piece by Brijlal Biyani, a Congress leader. Biyani's concern was the parallel discourse against the cow-protection movement that argued: one, the cow-protection movement was religious in nature; two, such a movement had not existed under colonial rule; three, the movement had been timed to coincide with the general election; four, cow protection had become a political subject; and five, undertaking a fast as a strategy was not productive.[70] Biyani countered each criticism, contending that: one, if a secular state interfered with religion and faith, there was bound to be a movement against it; two, gaurakshini sabhas had been formed throughout the country during the British period and there was no reason why a movement should not take place now even if it had not before; three, it was natural to initiate a movement when the possibility of its success was the highest; four, every political party had its core ideological principles and there was nothing wrong if a party that believed in cow protection joined the movement; and finally the fast was an accepted form of protest as demonstrated by Gandhi against the British and more recently by Potti Sriramulu's fast to death for the creation of the state of Andhra Pradesh.

Biyani took exception to Congress leader S.K. Patil's remark that if the Shankaracharya of Puri had died in the course of the fast it would have been a blot on the Hindu religion. On the contrary, Biyani countered, had the Shankaracharya died it would have been a blot on the present government.

Poddar in his short comment on Biyani's article merely said that only the future would tell who would win the battle.[71] Frustrated with the long-drawn struggle, a despondent Poddar said it was unlikely that Biyani's hope of triumph would materialize. However, he asked those demanding a comprehensive legal ban on cow slaughter to remain faithful to God and not allow dilution of their enthusiasm. A wide network of businessmen, mostly Marwari, was working closely to provide food and shelter to agitationists who were coming out of jail or were part of the camp that had been set up in the Arya Samaj temple in Delhi.

As the fortunes of the cow-protection movement dwindled, there came news of an alleged attack on sadhus in Delhi's Tihar Jail by some dreaded criminals in the presence of prison officials. The attack on the evening of 29 June 1967, Poddar reported in *Kalyan*, was carried out when Karpatri Maharaj was delivering a lecture to fellow agitationists in the jail.[72] Poddar said the criminals who attacked the sadhus with rods, lathis and stones had broken the locks of the barracks. After visiting the injured sadhus in the Tihar Jail hospital, Poddar said some of them had been impaired for life. Karpatri Maharaj was severely injured in one eye. Poddar claimed to have enough evidence—photographs and testimonies—of government involvement. But this evidence was withheld from the public as the government had immediately set up a commission of inquiry under S.S. Dulat, retired judge of the Punjab and Haryana High Court.

Poddar said the reason for the attack was unknown, but it was likely that the jail officials wanted to scare the sadhus so that the movement was called off. He described another disturbing incident that had taken place on 5 July 1967, as 105 sadhus stepped out of Tihar after their release. A criminal had approached them at the prison gate and warned them that they would be killed if they continued to participate in the cow-protection movement.

The year 1967 saw an unprecedented drought in Bihar, followed by devastating floods the following year. Under the aegis of SGMS, Poddar collected Rs 5,000 and then another Rs 20,000, which was donated to the Bihar unit of the Central Cattle Relief Committee. The money was used to organize cattle fodder for 2,624 families spread over 147 relief centres.[73]

The SGMS had collected a considerable fund in the name of cow protection, the bulk of which came from anonymous patrons of the cow in Delhi and Calcutta.[74] Hitsharan Sharma, a trusted employee of Jaidayal Dalmia, was managing the funds of SGMS in Delhi. He regularly reported, often in a resentful tone, about expenditure on various heads, some avoidable—for instance, the telephone bills of Niranjan Dev Tirth and Karpatri Maharaj and the expenses of naga sadhus stationed on the banks of Yamuna, who had declared they would not give up the satyagraha till the ban on cow slaughter was announced. The SGMS was also paying the medical and legal expenses of those injured in Tihar Jail in June 1967.[75] The court case was mishandled, with the lawyer duping the SGMS. Further, there was distrust and disharmony among senior leaders.

By the last quarter of 1967, Poddar began distancing himself from the SGMS, partly due to indifferent health but mainly owing to his growing disenchantment with the movement. Yet, *Kalyan* continued as a faithful chronicler of the cow agitation in the street and in parliament. Occasionally the journal would have an article on a Muslim putting his life at stake to protect a cow, as a result of which gaumata would bless him with darshan.[76] There were always reiterations of the social, religious and economic benefits of protecting cows.[77]

On 21 December 1967, two Lok Sabha MPs—Atal Bihari Vajpayee, who was the Jana Sangh leader in parliament and Om Prakash Tyagi, initially an Arya Samajist from Uttar Pradesh and the party's chief whip—asked if cow and pig fat were being used to manufacture soap, and whether the government was aware that a majority of Indians had a problem with touching animal fat. In his reply, K. Raghuramaiah, minister of state for petroleum, chemicals and social welfare, admitted the use of animal fat in soap manufacturing. He said fat constituted 11 per cent of the ingredients of soap; however, he said edible fat imported from the US was not mixed in soaps and also refused to confirm if pig fat was used. The minister claimed consumers had made no complaints.

The Vajpayee–Tyagi question in parliament and the response was reproduced in *Kalyan* with Poddar's comment: 'Government is not afraid to hurt the religious sensibilities of the Hindus. But it is scared of the Muslims. Therefore, a clear reply was not given about the use of pig fat in soaps. This can be found out directly from the importers of fat from the United States. The soap packet should specify what fat it consists of.'[78]

What Poddar considered a crisis and an affront to Hindu sensibilities provided a big business opportunity for the manufacture of soap without animal fat. Poddar had asked readers to send him names of manufacturers of soap that did not contain any fat. By June 1968, *Kalyan* had a list of sixty-eight such manufacturers,[79] the first on the list being Gobind Bhawan Karyalaya, the parent organization of Gita Press, always in search of business that could fetch it a small profit to subsidize its publications. The list was dominated by Indian companies like Rohtas Industries (by the late 1960s under the control of Ram Krishna Dalmia's son-in-law Shanti Prasad Jain), Bengal Chemicals, Modi Soap Works, DCM Chemical Works, Ganesh Flour Mills, Marwari Soap Works, Kutch Oil & Allied Industries, Tata Oil Mill and a host of others. Even the large multinational Hindustan Lever claimed it had switched over to making fatless soaps, both for washing clothes and bathing.

In 1968, *Kalyan* admitted that there were differences of opinion among the leaders of the cow-protection movement.[80] An unsigned article that bore the definite stamp of Poddar stated that vying for top posts within the SGMS had led to rivalry and opposing views being articulated. The biggest mistake made by the SGMS, the article said, was joining the government's Goraksha Samiti and suspending the cow-protection movement. *Kalyan* pointed out that despite the movement's suspension, government had not fulfilled its promise of withdrawing the cases against those who had been booked for allegedly inciting violence on 7 November 1966.

More disturbing were the deliberations of the Goraksha Samiti that, *Kalyan* feared, had been set up as an attempt to blunt the cow-protection movement. The Samiti had started examining cow experts who were against any ban on killing, and voted for a decision to discuss the pros and cons of a 'complete ban', 'partial ban' and 'no ban' on cow slaughter. This was opposed in *Kalyan*, along with the suggestion by certain economists that if cows could not be slaughtered in India they could be exported so that India could earn some foreign exchange. Saying 'this is a demonic articulation of madness for money', the *Kalyan* article advocated a revival of the cow-protection movement: 'The last agitation shook the government's throne. But this time . . . if people work with enthusiasm and better management the situation can be even better. The movement should be such that the government is forced to succumb. There is need for a serious discussion and not some hurried decision. All mutual differences should be buried and the movement should keep a distance from politics. Members of legislative assemblies and parliament should be convinced in favour of the law.'

The same issue of *Kalyan* criticized the book brought out by the Central government's Publications Division titled *Gandhiji Aur Goraksha* (Gandhi and Cow Protection). The Hindi publication, to be distributed free, was seen as a clever ploy by the government to muddle the debate on cow slaughter and to try and prove that Gandhi was not completely in favour of a ban on cow slaughter. In a three-part article in *Kalyan*, Jaidayal Dalmia cited two lines from the monograph, originally written by Gandhi in *Harijan*, 1938: 'After all, butchers also have to do their business' and 'We should make it economically unnecessary and impossible to sell cows to butchers.' Dalmia said it was impossible to understand the correct meaning of these lines unless one knew the context in which Mahatma Gandhi wrote them. 'It is possible when the Mahatma wrote these lines there had been a Hindu–Muslim riot and some butchers may have got beaten up by Hindus.'[81]

Dalmia collected copious excerpts from Gandhi's writings to prove that he was not ambivalent towards cow slaughter. To show that the cruelty involved in the slaughter of cows and other animals was not mere rhetoric, Dalmia cited various government reports that contained graphic details of the process of animal slaughter.

While keeping Gandhi beyond criticism, Dalmia squarely blamed Nehru for the continuance of cow slaughter in the country. He referred to Nehru's speech during the debate in parliament in 1955 when he had said cows could not be given more importance than the economy of a country, or more importance than human beings. During the debate on the Indian Cow Protection Bill in 1955, Nehru had said, 'I am willing to resign from the post of Prime Minister but I will not give in . . . My advice to people who do not understand economics and agriculture is not to take a step which will ruin our cattle wealth . . .'[82]

In the final instalment of his article, Dalmia demanded that, if the government was not keen to bring a law banning cow slaughter, it should at least accept the demands made by Gandhi in an article in *Young India* way back in 1923, and which still held true even after Independence: government should pay the highest price and buy every cow sold in the open market; should run dairies in big cities so that milk would be sold at a reasonable rate; should make full efforts to use the hide and bones of dead cows; should open a leather factory under its protection; should open model animal farms so that people could be trained to rear cattle; and should make available pasturelands and open a separate department for cattle welfare.

In many ways Dalmia was now steering the cow-protection movement. In a bid to resolve the confusion created by diverse opinion about cow slaughter and consumption of beef in the Vedas, he wrote to Krishna Chandra, who worked at Gita Press, to suggest to Poddar that a book be compiled in English and Hindi, to prove that neither beef eating nor cow slaughter were practised in the times of the Vedas and the Upanishads.[83]

Dalmia cited a portion from A.B. Shah's *Cow Slaughter: Horns of a Dilemma* that claimed 'slaughter of cows on ceremonial occasions was considered auspicious in ancient India'. Shah had said 'bride and bridegroom were made to sit on the raw skin of a red bull before the altar', and that such a skin was also used during the coronation of kings. According to Shah, the practice was still prevalent in Nepal, the only Hindu kingdom in the world. He said at the time of the coronation of

King Mahendra, *The Times of India* reported that 'the sacred skin of an ox on which the throne of King Mahendra was mounted for the dazzling coronation ceremonies was personally flown to Kathmandu by Pakistan's foreign minister Hamidul Haq Choudhury'.

Poddar's response to Dalmia's suggestion is not known, but for Dalmia the resolution of this question had become a personal mission. Dalmia decided to put together an edited volume himself—*Prachin Bharat Mein Gomans: Ek Samiksha* (Beef in Ancient India: An Analysis)—with the avowed aim of disproving that the cow was ever slaughtered or its meat consumed in ancient India. Even though the Dalmia group was past its peak, Jaidayal Dalmia had enough resources to get 10,000 copies printed of which 5,000 were to be distributed free.[84] Dalmia sent the first draft of the chapters to Poddar's associate Harikrishna Dujari in Gorakhpur, with a request that Dujari seek Poddar's approval the moment his health improved.[85]

Prachin Bharat Mein Gomans: Ek Samiksha was published under the Gita Press imprint and became an instant hit with cow protectionists. From rave reviews of the book in the RSS weekly *Panchjanya* as well as ultra-conservative publications from Banaras and many small towns of UP, to letters of commendation from Golwalkar, Seth Govind Das, spiritual leaders and even judges of the Allahabad High Court, Dalmia's efforts drew considerable praise.

A long spell of ill health had kept Poddar away from the success of Dalmia's book. By the end of 1969, Poddar requested Dalmia to inform Niranjan Dev Tirth that he must get a new treasurer for the SGMS.[86] He made it clear that contributions to SGMS did not get income tax exemption and there was no likelihood of it; in the same breath, he revealed the method SGMS adopted to avoid income tax. Poddar said SGMS used the receipts of Bharat Gosevak Samaj, a tax-exempt organization. He asked Dalmia to talk to them again and organize more receipts.

Two years later, Poddar was no more. As a tribute to his contribution to the cow-protection movement, the Bharat Gosevak Samaj brought out a special issue of its journal *Godhan* in his memory.

Vishwa Hindu Parishad

On 29 and 30 August 1964 a meeting of leading members of Hindu right-wing organizations was held in Bombay at the Sandipani Ashram of Swami Chinmayananda, founder of the Chinmaya Mission and a known Gita expert. The meeting was called by RSS leader Golwalkar to address the all-round feelings of 'insecurity, irreligiosity and oppression' among Hindus and to 'unite the Hindus in India with the crores of their co-religionists living abroad'.[87] Though only sixty of the 150 invited individuals attended,[88] the meeting with one voice created the Vishwa Hindu Parishad, a council to represent the interests of the Hindus of the world. With time the VHP became the special-purpose vehicle of the RSS and a 'consistory for Hinduism' that would 'engage in ethno-religious mobilizing campaigns'.[89]

The VHP was the Hindu right's first major joint venture that drew strength and sustenance from individuals (including powerful sadhus, politicians, businessmen and former royalty) and a host of organizations led by the RSS. Two of its important functions were to propagate the Hindu religion among Indian expatriates and initiate a countermovement of reconversion to deal with Christian 'proselytization particularly among India's tribal people'.

Though invited, Poddar could not attend the Sandipani Ashram congregation, but he had the stature to be made a founding trustee of the VHP[90] along with other big names—among them, Jayachamaraja Wodeyar (the former ruler of Mysore and a keen proponent of the theory of Hinduism-in-danger), Sadguru Jagjit Singh (spiritual head of the Namdhari Sikhs), Sikh leader Master Tara Singh, Swami Chinmayananda, Sir C.P. Ramaswamy Aiyar (former diwan of Travancore state who had been an associate of Annie Besant in the Home League movement, a Congress leader, vice chancellor of Banaras Hindu University and chairman of the committee on the reform of Hindu temples),[91] Rama Prasad Mookerjee, Bharatiya Vidya Bhavan's K.M. Munshi, M.S. Golwalkar and Keshavram Kashiram Shastri (a Gujarati and Sanskrit writer and teacher). Shivram Shankar Apte, who had been a junior lawyer and associate of K.M. Munshi in his days of legal practice and later a journalist and RSS pracharak (worker), became the first general secretary of the VHP.

For Poddar, the birth of the VHP was a moment of celebration. He had long advocated a strong Hindu organization and the VHP fitted the bill. An additional gratification was the involvement of his dear friend Jaidayal Dalmia's son Vishnu Hari Dalmia.

He was also excited about the new organization holding a first-of-its-kind mega meeting of Hindus from all over the world for three days, 22–24 January 1966, during the Kumbh Mela at Prayag (Allahabad). Poddar asked Hindu representatives from all over the world to participate in the Vishwa Hindu Sammelan for better understanding, love and cooperation among themselves and the future formation of VHP branches all over the world. Reviving memories of the assembly at Kanauj held by Harshavardhana in the seventh century CE to honour the Buddhist pilgrim Xuan Zang, 20,000 to 30,000 Hindus attended the VHP meeting in 1966.[92] Representatives of more than 2,500 Hindu groups were present, including the Shankaracharya of Dwarka. Three state governors attended—Biswanath Prasad Das of Uttar Pradesh, K.N. Katju of West Bengal and Ananthasayanam Ayyangar of Bihar. Tulsi Giri, former prime minister of Nepal, represented the king of Nepal and read out his message. Rama Prasad Mookerjee presided over the meeting. Again, Poddar could not attend the Vishwa Hindu Sammelan owing to sudden illness. Regretting his absence, Sriman Narayan, India's ambassador in Nepal, sent him a copy of the message from King Mahendra Vir Vikram Shah Deo of Nepal.

The VHP often drew on the networking skills of Poddar, and Apte would remind him to contribute to its journal *Hindu Vishva*. Apte said Poddar through his 'effective and powerful articles could appeal to religious gurus and sadhus in pilgrimage places to take responsibility of the society at this crucial juncture', and sought his continued cooperation, giving him the total freedom to 'write on anything you consider to be right'.[93]

Ram Janmabhoomi Movement

The seeds of what was to be a long-drawn battle were sown in the temple town of Ayodhya in the 1940s. Hindus contended that, at the site of the birth of Lord Rama, there had been a temple that Mughal emperor Babur had demolished in 1528 to construct the Babri Masjid. Not backed by archaeological evidence, the Hindu claim was disputed by the Muslims who continued to offer namaz in the Babri Masjid. A series of events in 1948–49 were to have repercussions in Ayodhya and ultimately in Indian politics over four decades later.

Baba Raghav Das, Poddar's long-time friend, had won the June 1948 by-election from the Faizabad assembly constituency on a Congress ticket. His opponent, Congress Socialist Party's Acharya Narendra Dev, a native of Faizabad and well steeped in Hindu religious thought as well as Marxian ideology, had lost by a slender margin of 1,312 votes (Das: 5,392; Narendra Dev: 4,080). The Baba's victory was a shot in the arm for 'Hindu communalists, whether inside the Congress or outside it'.[94] The Muslims of Ayodhya had overwhelmingly voted for Narendra Dev, the reason being Chief Minister Govind Ballabh Pant's public display of affection towards conservative Hindu groups and the communal campaign run by Baba Raghav Das. Even before the by-election, Muslims had been threatened by local sadhus and Hindu Mahasabha not to offer namaz in the Babri Masjid. Pant, engaged in a battle of supremacy within the UP Congress, was not only involved in the communal campaign in favour of Baba Raghav Das but was dismissive of Muslim fears. The Baba's victory offered an opportunity for further action.

On the night of 22–23 December 1949, an idol of Lord Rama appeared in the Babri Masjid, an event that was immediately portrayed as divine intervention and unambiguous proof that Rama had indeed been born there. The first information report (FIR) filed at the Ayodhya police station named Abhiram Das, Ram Sakal Das, Sudarshan Das and fifty to sixty unnamed persons for rioting, trespassing and desecrating a religious place.[95] As it turned out, the police investigation hardly helped in sifting truth from myth. A conniving district and state administration (Pant was still chief minister) muddied the waters further by creating the fear of a Hindu backlash if the idol was removed. As a result, Hindus got the right to worship where the idol had allegedly manifested itself, and the mother of all legal disputes was born. Subsequently it has been proved beyond doubt that the act of the emergence of the idol was the handiwork of Abhiram Das of Nirvani

Akhara and his associates, as part of a larger conspiracy of Hindu communalists.[96]

Noted Hindi journalist and an RSS insider Ram Bahadur Rai recently provided a new and shocking revelation about the sudden appearance of the idol in Ayodhya. Rai wrote that he had been told by RSS leader Nanaji Deshmukh that the idol had been introduced into the Ayodhya complex after holy immersion in the Sarayu river under the leadership of Poddar.[97] When Rai expressed a wish to record this fact, Deshmukh did not agree, though he maintained it was the truth. Deshmukh's claim has not found any mention in scores of published works on Ayodhya, but points at a web of conspiracy whose threads are yet to be untangled.

Poddar, who throughout the 1940s had been involved in Hindu nationalist propaganda, received the news of the appearance of the idol of Lord Rama with great joy. Irrespective of his involvement or otherwise, the news must have meant a lot to him as he was already working on a plan to restore places related to Hindu deities—Ayodhya (Rama), Mathura (Krishna) and Salasar (Hanuman).

Within days of the appearance of the idol, fondly called Ramlalla by the devout and the Sangh Parivar, Poddar reached Ayodhya for confabulations about the future course of action.[98] For a man whose own life was full of claims of direct communion with the gods, the emergence of the idol of Rama was not to be questioned at all. Instead, he was interested in planning the future of the idol that needed a magnificent abode in the shape of an imposing temple.

When he heard government might remove the idol, Poddar wrote to prominent people: 'Ayodhya has the ancient site of Ram Janmabhoomi. Muslims came and built a masjid there. It is said that an idol of Rama has appeared there. Akhand recitation of Ramayana and kirtans is taking place there. I have heard government wants to remove the idol and efforts are being made in that direction. The birthplace of Lord Rama is related to the Hindus of India. If the idol is removed, it would become impossible to wrest control of places of worship that were occupied by Muslims.'[99]

During his stay in Ayodhya, Poddar found that the local Hindu groups did not have the financial means to bear the cost of performing daily puja at the disputed site. Another big burden was going to be the cost of fighting the legal battle that promised to be protracted and messy. Poddar made a promise of Rs 1,500 each month for akhand kirtan (uninterrupted religious recitation) and daily worship of the idol, and additionally, promised to take care of the legal costs and other major or minor expenditure that might have to be incurred from time to time.[100]

As the court case dragged on and the Hindu–Muslim communal fault lines further deepened in Ayodhya, Poddar got involved in the task of finding a permanent solution to the dispute. However, his solution was majoritarian in nature—he wanted to convince the leading Muslims of Ayodhya and outside that the existence of a mosque inside a temple was unnatural and un-Islamic. A few liberal Muslims were sent to Ayodhya with the message of Poddar's solution that basically meant Muslims relinquishing their right over the Babri Masjid. Poddar claimed some of these liberal Muslims were even willing to go on a fast in Delhi against the Muslim agitation for restoring the site to them. He did not live to see the tragic outcome of the dispute.

Krishna Janmabhoomi Movement

The battle to restore the Shri Krishna Janmabhoomi temple in Mathura was less acrimonious but more interesting as it brought Gita Press and the Congress on a common platform. After the initial efforts of Madan Mohan Malaviya, with support from Jugal Kishore Birla, the two main dramatis personae were Hanuman Prasad Poddar and Seth Govind Das who was a member of the Congress Working Committee, the party's highest decision-making body.

Poddar's tryst with Krishna Janmabhoomi began simply as a pilgrim in the early 1950s. He was soon turned into the main driving force behind the restoration plan. Addressing a meeting held in his honour during one of his trips to Mathura, Poddar rued the irony that while Mathura received thousands of pilgrims every year, the Krishna Janmabhoomi was in a state of total neglect. He asked who would not be troubled with the state of this site of Lord Krishna's birth, and announced that he would personally give Rs 10,000 towards its restoration.[101] It was first decided to have a massive yagna or ritual fire offering at Shri Krishna Janmabhoomi.

Aware that such a project at Mathura would involve huge costs, Poddar collaborated with Seth Govind Das, a fellow Marwari, writer and a conservative Congress politician. Das and Poddar had similar views on many issues, and agreed on the need to restore Lord Krishna's birthplace to its pristine glory. Being a Congressman, Das also knew that if he was to be involved with the Shri Krishna Janmabhoomi movement, it had to be conducted within the parameters of his party's ideology of secularism.

By July 1955, Das had a plan that he felt Nehru's government would agree to be involved with. Das wrote to Poddar: 'In this letter I am sending you the complete plan of Sri Krishna Dham in Hindi and English. In English, the plan is called Govardhan. This has been done because we are a secular state and in case we want any help from the government then the name should be secular. It took a lot of discussion and hard work to finalize the plan.'[102]

Das requested Poddar to read the plan carefully as it was an 'unparalleled' attempt. He said if 'Bharat has to remain Bharat', it was 'the duty of devotees of Indian culture to give shape to this plan'. Das said that he himself would be writing to the Central and state governments, and had already consulted President Rajendra Prasad who had willingly agreed to provide all help. Das felt that government help would come if Rs 500,000 to 1,000,000 could be collected, some land bought near the site of Govardhan/Krishna Janmabhoomi and the foundation of a new building laid by the president. He asked Poddar to do whatever was possible in the matter. Das suggested to Poddar, '*Kalyan* has 1.25 lakh subscribers. If you appeal, at least a lakh of subscribers can easily contribute between five to ten rupees and the sum would be easily organized.' Das also asked Poddar and Jaydayal Goyandka to reach out to their wide circle of devout-minded contacts—mainly Vaishnavites in Bombay and Ahmedabad—for resources. The money collected by them could be retained by Gita Press till the trust deed for Govardhan was ready.

By 1958, Keshavdev Mandir had come up as the first building in the complex. Poddar's speech at the inauguration of the mandir shows his important position in the nationwide movement to liberate Hindu places of worship from alleged past desecrations by Muslim rulers. Thanking Madan Mohan Malaviya and Jugal Kishore Birla for initiating the Krishna Janmabhoomi movement, Poddar said: 'Forcible occupation of a place of religious worship or laying right on the birthplace of a great man is a sin. While such forcible right exists it reminds people of that sin and causes enmity. Removal of that blot from here has brightened the face of the nation. Till recently we were under foreign rule and now we have swarajya. Now no such blots should exist. Sommath Temple has been rebuilt due to the efforts of Sardar Patel. Similarly, the holy temple in Kashi, Ayodhya, temple at Sidhpur and various other religious places should be liberated.'[103]

For Poddar, a nation retained its splendour and pride if people of different religious faiths—Hindus, Muslims and Sikhs—worshipped their gods in their respective religious places. Liberation after so many years had restored some glory to the nation, Poddar said. But he expressed his disgust with Christian missionaries for luring poor Indians to convert. The speech also included a long story about the life of Krishna and his popularity among Muslim poets like Ras Khan, Hazrat Nafis Khalili, Hindu poet-writers like Bihari and Bharatendu Harishchandra, saint-poets like Jaidev and Chaitanya Mahaprabhu, politicians like Tilak, Gandhi and Aurobindo.

Seth Govind Das too was taking no rest. Even during his tour of Uttar Pradesh as a Congress Working Committee member, Das asked Poddar to organize a meeting of prominent religious-minded individuals on Sri Krishna Dham and Braj. Das said the meeting should be held at Poddar's house in Gorakhpur and organized in consultation with the city Congress office so that it would not be disturbed.[104]

Over the next few years, slowly and steadily more structures came up in the Shri Krishna complex. In 1962 the foundation of the Shri Krishna Chabutra (platform) was laid, and construction was completed in 1965. Speaking at the inauguration of the final structure, Poddar said that in the more than 350 years since Aurangzeb had demolished the temple in Mathura, the inauguration of the new complex and recitation of the Gita there were the most significant events in the life of the holy city.[105] Jhavarmal Sharma, former editor of *Calcutta Samachar* and Poddar's friend from his Calcutta days, was present at the inauguration. Sharma penned a poem on Poddar, singing his praises for his efforts in securing the Krishna Janmabhoomi.

Religion in Electoral Politics

Much as Poddar claimed to keep a safe distance from politics, he acknowledged the power politics had over religion as well as religion's role in stirring up politics. In India's first general election of 1951–52, a reader of *Kalyan* asked Poddar whom to vote for. In an attempt to maintain his public persona of aloofness and disdain for politics, Poddar quoted Shaw Desmond's *World Birth*: 'Like horse-racing, there is something in politics which degrades. It turns good men into bad men and bad into worse.'[106] Poddar stated that the ablest candidate should win, irrespective of the party, and told the reader not to nurse any feeling of ill will or preconceived notion about a candidate or party, whether Congress or Hindu Mahasabha. He pointed out that in pre-Independence elections, 'The feeling was to vote for even a dog of the Congress but not for a god outside the Congress.' Now, he said, 'we should not say we will support even a dog opposed to the Congress and not gods inside the Congress'. A voter should make his choice impartially, on the basis of his conscience and a sense of justice.

In an article on voters' responsibilities in the Indian republic, Poddar claimed that as a spiritual person he was least equipped to offer advice on political matter.[107] Yet, he could not resist the temptation to dispense political wisdom, having been so involved in the protests against the Hindu Code Bill. He was opposed to the idea of India as a secular republic as he felt this undermined the superiority of the Hindu majority. He was also against the electoral process and its emphasis on numbers at the cost of intelligence, knowledge, experience, wisdom, character and other positive qualities in an individual: 'In this system only people above a certain age can vote and everything depends on such votes. One extra vote could make an unintelligent and unworthy candidate defeat an experienced, intelligent and righteous opponent.'

Poddar also resented the dominance of money, particularly of the illegal variety, in the elections. A rough estimate by Poddar put the use of black money at one billion rupees. He said leaders of big political parties had been collecting election funds for a long time by resorting to various methods: deceit, force, allurement and forgery. 'In many states people are facing a huge crisis of food and clothes, and here crores of rupees are being spent on petrol, paper, printing and campaigning.' Poddar was also critical of the false claims made by the candidates and their tendency to show opponents in poor light. 'This system is such that even intelligent people lose their minds and attack their opponents as a matter of routine.'

Poddar, who had faced arrest for his alleged role in the conspiracy to assassinate Mahatma Gandhi, felt that Nehru was wrong in making it an election issue. Without mentioning the Hindu Mahasabha and the RSS, Poddar wrote: 'In order to prove the supremacy of his own organization and run down others the Congress president and our prime minister, our country's priceless treasure, someone who has given his entire life in the service of the nation, is calling other organizations killers of Mahatma Gandhi. He is talking of exercising his powers as prime minister and threatening to crush so-and-so organizations. Newspaper readers can read the last few speeches of respected Nehru to understand the problems of this system.'

Finally, Poddar settled for the safe option. Instead of asking readers of *Kalyan* to support any specific political party he exhorted them to vote for those candidates who met four conditions. The ideal candidate was the one who 'opposed the anti-religious Hindu Code Bill or any legislation that encroached on any religion'; one who was genuinely interested in working for a Central legislation to ban cow slaughter; one who promised to make efforts to provide food, clothing, education and medical facilities at affordable rates; and finally, one who did not seek pecuniary benefits for himself or for his party. It was not difficult to see that only members of the Hindu Mahasabha and the newly formed Bharatiya Jana Sangh would pass the Poddar test.

In another article in the same issue of *Kalyan*, Poddar added two more conditions: a candidate should uphold the ancient Indian culture and system of education; and he should publicly state that Partition had been a mistake and promise to work for the reunification of India.[108]

In this article, Poddar made more categorical statements against

Nehru and the Congress, and asked votaries of the anti-cow-slaughter law, opponents of the Hindu Code Bill and supporters of akhand Bharat (undivided India) to vote for the candidates of Swami Karpatri Maharaj's Ram Rajya Parishad. Further, 'In constituencies where there is no Ram Rajya Parishad candidate, the vote should be in favour of either Hindu Mahasabha or Jana Sangh candidates . . . But it should be remembered opposition to the Congress is based on principles not individuals or the institution itself.'

Poddar's support to the Ram Rajya Parishad was not confined to the pages of *Kalyan*. He and Goyandka actively campaigned for the party. In Calcutta, the duo had attended public meetings in support of the Parishad. Poddar was particularly strident in his speeches: 'It is a sin like cow slaughter to put the Congress and the supporters of Mr Nehru into power again by supporting them in the coming general elections . . . It is very regrettable that today the followers of Mahatma Gandhi, who revered the cow even more than Swaraj, are encouraging cow slaughter.'[109]

In his *Kalyan* article, Poddar also discussed the scene in Allahabad where a battle royale was being waged between Jawaharlal Nehru and Prabhudatt Brahmachari. The latter had agreed to join the fray at the behest of Golwalkar and Rajendra Singh of the RSS.[110] Brahmachari was not the sole sadhu to join the electoral fray in defence of cow protection and against the Hindu Code Bill. Madhav Acharya stood as an independent candidate from Karnal against Subhadra Joshi of the Congress.

Prabhudatt Brahmachari was contesting the elections, Poddar explained, on the issue of Hindu Code Bill, and therefore all those opposed to the bill should support him. Poddar also made it clear that Brahmachari would quit the fray if Nehru promised to withdraw the Hindu Code Bill. Poddar did not spare Ambedkar either, asking voters to wholeheartedly oppose the Dalit leader who was contesting as a candidate of his Scheduled Castes Federation (later the Republican Party) from one of the two constituencies of Bombay City North (it was a double-member constituency with one seat in the reserved category), and actively campaigning in favour of the Hindu Code Bill.[111]

After indulging wholesale in politics and canvassing in favour of the

Ram Rajya Parishad, Hindu Mahasabha and Jana Sangh, Poddar took care to reiterate that he was not against specific individuals and political parties. However, the results were disappointing for him, as the Congress swept the polls. Though for Poddar it would have come as some relief that Ambedkar lost to Congress's Narayan Sadoba Kajrolkar, by just 15,000 votes. Overall, the Ram Rajya Parishad, Hindu Mahasabha and Jana Sangh won three seats each.

By the time of the 1967 general election, the Congress hegemony was under threat. The grand old party posted one of its worst performances, winning only 283 seats out of the 516 it contested. In the state elections, three big states of the Hindi heartland, Uttar Pradesh, Bihar and Madhya Pradesh, saw the formation of Samyukta Vidhayak Dal governments—an unlikely coalition of the Jana Sangh, Samyukta Socialist Party, communists and Congress rebels—signalling that Congress was no longer invincible.

Reviewing the elections, Poddar again lamented the dominance of money power in the electoral process, something he alleged had been introduced by the Congress.[112] This trend was viewed by Poddar as a serious challenge to the very basis of democracy, as the funding of politicians by businessmen was nothing but an investment for future return. Poddar also cited widespread violence like stone pelting and arson at polling stations during the election, including attacks on Indira Gandhi during her campaign in Bhubaneswar in 1967 and on Madhu Limaye, as being indicative of a new India that had derailed from the path of non-violence and forgotten Gandhi's ahimsa.

Though happy about the diminishing stature of the Congress, Poddar alleged that the 1967 parliamentary elections had not been free and fair.[113] In an indirect reference to the formation of SVD governments in Bihar, UP and MP made possible through defections and dissensions, Poddar highlighted the new subculture of money power being used to lure MLAs to defect. He doubted that governments with such dubious foundations would have the ability to do any public good. Invoking Mahatma Gandhi, Poddar said it would have been beneficial if mutually opposed governments or parties had placed Gandhi's ideals as their goal instead of putting all their energies, resources and thought into pulling down each other. 'Post-Independence there has been a rise in corruption, immorality, mutual antagonism, violence and counter-violence.'

The 1967 general election was the last on which Poddar commented at length, though there was no participation this time unlike in 1951–52, when Gita Press and all the Hindu nationalist groups had participated in an enthusiastic campaign in favour of their agenda to protect cows, junk the Hindu Code Bill and undo Partition. By the 1971 general election, the involvement of an ailing Poddar was limited to issuing an appeal on behalf of media baron Ramnath Goenka who was contesting on a Jana Sangh ticket from Vidisha in Madhya Pradesh. As we have seen, Goenka won.

Twin Enemies: Communism and Secularism

The steady spread of communist ideology in the first half of the twentieth century was considered by Gita Press a serious challenge not only to the idea of a hegemonic Hindu–Hindi rule but to private enterprise and profit-making—of great significance to its Marwari patrons. Therefore, one finds *Kalyan* devoting a disproportionately large amount of space to debunking communism and its ideal of a society devoid of religion, based on equality.

The Communist Party of India, established in Tashkent (then in the USSR, now the capital of Uzbekistan) on 17 October 1920, was in its formative years when Gita Press was established. Organized labour and peasant movements were then sporadic in nature, confined mainly to the new centres of industrial production like Bombay, Madras and Calcutta. Gita Press's initial fear of the communist ideology was similar to that of the colonial government. In both cases it was 'grossly exaggerated'[114] and emanated from the worldwide impact of the Bolshevik Revolution of 1917. The Soviet Union became a hated and feared alien force, and the overactive home department of British India saw anyone who resisted the Empire—from tall nationalist leaders like Gandhi and C.R. Das to obscure leaders of the peasant movement in the United Provinces and Mewar—as a Bolshevik. And for a religious publishing house like Gita Press, any ideology that advocated a religion-free society was a serious threat.

In 1928, news of intense anti-religious propaganda in the USSR and Germany caused great apprehension among the orthodox Hindu set. *Kalyan* was among the early publications to warn its readers of the disastrous consequences of communism in a country like India where religion 'is a way of life and the centre of existence'.[115] Sadanand, the writer of the *Kalyan* article, said any attempt to exterminate religion from the life of a nation would mean extermination of the concepts of community and fraternity, the two key ingredients of nationalism. He said mutual jealousy, pride, obstinacy, blind faith and selfishness among followers of different religions had already created enough division within Indian society.

At the end of 1928, when news of a mammoth anti-God meeting in Moscow attended by 700 delegates came in, *Kalyan* got worked up again. Though the resolutions passed at the meeting were not known, the unsigned article said the theme of the meeting—anti-God—was self-explanatory: 'There cannot be a worse movement than this. Any one who is sympathetic to it is committing a great mistake. Whatever the outward manifestation of religion, and even if it needs to be reformed, attacking the supreme power of God is nothing but a reflection of the overall decline of the human race. Equality and world peace, the two main goals of the meeting, cannot be achieved through this conclave. In fact, it would be like chasing a mirage that would end only in chaos, pain and restlessness.'[116]

The biggest cause for worry for Gita Press was the birth of such 'polluted thought' in India, where people had unflinching faith in God. Expressing regret that educated and cultured people wrote articles and organized lectures questioning the existence of God, the *Kalyan* article urged people to 'refrain from either speaking against God or listening to any criticism'.

Gita Press realized the need to provide an alternative to the new ideology, something that would not threaten the tenets of sanatan Hindu dharma yet celebrate the concept of equality. This alternative was discovered in the Bhagavadgita—an Indian version of communism, divinely ordained.

A ready reckoner of the similarities and differences between the Indian and Russian versions of communism was prepared.[117] While

Indian communism was based on the principle of equality as defined by the Supreme Being, the Russian version had economic equality at its core. To follow Indian communism, one had merely to purify the mind, while only fear of the authorities forced Russians to become communists.

The comparison took an even more bizarre turn when it came to listing the forces behind the ancient godly Indian communism and the modern godless Russian communism. On the Indian side it was a crowded list including Arjun, Yudhishthir, Vidhur, Vyas, Narada, Tulsidas, Chaitanya Mahaprabhu, Mirabai, Guru Nanak, Sant Tukaram, Ramdas, Raidas, Sant Gyaneshwar, Tiruvalluvar, Narsi Mehta and others. How and why these mythological and real characters—epic heroes, poets, seers and religious gurus—were chosen as the founding fathers of Indian communism is not known, but the list was certainly weightier compared to the three masterminds of Russian communism: Lenin, Trotsky and later Stalin.

Bhakti was cited as a necessary condition to internalize Indian communism, unlike the Russian one that opposed religion and God yet encouraged building of statues of Karl Marx and Lenin. When talking of the relative impact of the two communisms, the Indian version was seen to make a man compassionate towards all living beings, while Russian communism was limited to creating equality among human beings—only the hard-working ones. Besides, the stress on family life and respect for parents was integral to Indian communism unlike in Russia where, *Kalyan* said, thousands of children were orphans and clueless about their parents.

Two similarities were noted between Indian and Russian communisms. The first would delight even the most serious of political theorists: it said that Lord Krishna, the originator of Indian communism, dallied with gopis—hard-working milkmaids—just as the fathers of Russian communism were involved with humble peasants and workers. The second similarity was more to the point: that both versions were aimed at the betterment of the poor and the downtrodden.

By the time *Kalyan*'s *Ishwar Ank* was planned in 1932, communism had made further inroads into Europe, while the Communist Party of India had begun taking firm root. Laxman Narayan Garde, Poddar's associate in *Kalyan* and a scholar of some repute, was given the task of putting the modern theory of atheism into perspective.[118] Through a detailed analysis of historical materialism, Garde argued that atheism was necessary in the context in which communism was born. However, he stated, one of the principles of material philosophy is that change is inevitable. Going by this principle, the state of communists as non-believers would change, and the needs of society would change as well, putting an end to atheism.

Kalyan kept up the attack on communism at regular intervals. The spread of communist ideology even among a section of the Congress was seen as contributing to the political flux of the 1940s as well creating the bogey of inequality in Muslim minds.[119] Besides, communism's stress on gender equality and the individual spirit threatened the shastric concept of the Indian woman's sphere being limited to the four walls of her father's, husband's or son's home.

A two-part article by Charu Chandra Mitra argued that the basic mantra of communism—from each according to his ability, to each according to his need—was already practised in India through the joint family system.[120] While the USSR was divided into communes, in India every joint family was a commune. However, in the Indian system, he said, the freedom of an individual was not diminished, unlike in the Soviet system.

Pitching the Gita as a counter to communism became a favoured practice among Hindu nationalists. Kailash Nath Katju wrote for the *Hindu Sanskriti Ank* lamenting the mental slavery of Indians to modern concepts, in the process discarding ancient Indian traditions.[121] For Katju it was nothing but ignorance to think that the concept of equality was a modern one; such a concept had been delineated in the Gita and seriously followed by our forefathers. Katju argued: 'These days there is a view that the nation can make maximum progress if there is an end to profiteering/profit from business and social prestige based on economic worth. It is also believed if there is no right to property and profit from property, a classless society would be formed without any rich or poor. This is considered a new ideology. But it is already a part of our ancient pedagogy. Our system teaches sacrifice, not of karma, but of fruits of karma.'

Katju contended that the Gita taught that renunciation would not bear any fruit. Instead, he argued, it stressed activity to maintain the dignity of life. 'Such a confluence of the spiritual and the physical cannot be found in any religious or secular literature.' In the overall analysis, Katju argued, minus the component of class struggle and enmity, communism was another name for the Gita.

Dismissing communism's ideal of a classless society, an article by Nardev Shastri defended the varna system of Hindus in which the four castes carried out their pre-ordained duties. He believed the slogan 'workers of the world unite' from the *Communist Manifesto*, the 1848 text by Karl Marx and Friedrich Engels, was at the cost of the other classes. On the other hand, the Indian social structure had a deep-seated relationship with spiritualism that had helped it to survive through the long history of slavery, colonial rule and injustices. 'Now that the British rule is over, if India acts independently and preserves its culture it will once again show the way to the world.'[122]

Occasionally, *Kalyan* would reassure its readers not to be afraid of the new ideology. Karl Marx, it said, was a sagacious mind who propounded communism on observing the inequality in the world. Principally, *Kalyan* argued, communism wanted to establish what should ideally exist in any society, so there was nothing to be afraid of: 'India of sanatan dharma has no reason to worry if it imbibes communist values because the ideal that communism wants to establish already exists in our religious and saintly traditions in a purer form.'[123]

Gita Press's approach to communism was thus based on moral superiority, claiming that a more refined manifesto of an equal society existed in the Gita. However, it was not prepared for the new direction the government was about to take, when, at its 1955 session in Avadi (near Madras), the Congress 'resolved to establish a socialistic pattern of society'.[124] The Avadi session's most notable feature was not the 'speed with which the government acted' but the 'change in the atmosphere'. The presence of Vinoba Bhave in Avadi—he had not attended Congress sessions for a long time—provided the moral endorsement of the party's plan of implementing the tenets of socialism and its 'progressive shift to Left'.[125]

The government's subsequent stress on the public sector and nationalization of industry raised the hackles of Gita Press, a product of Marwari philanthropy. This move towards state control of resources and business was an attack by an adversarial Congress government on the concept of profit that had been advanced as moral justification in the pages of *Kalyan*. Nardev Shastri questioned the Congress version of socialism.[126] He expressed concern that through nationalization the state would become even more powerful: 'Government already has the resources of power. Would it not go berserk if economic resources come under its control?' Shastri's prescription was simple: 'In India only the socialism of Vedic times, as recommended by saints and sages, can be popularized.'

In its overenthusiasm to showcase the failure of the socialist economy, *Kalyan* published an anonymous article that had first been written in Marathi.[127] The article said the communist idea of distributing wealth equally among citizens would leave everyone a pauper, as proved by the fact that the per capita national income and wages of workers were among the lowest in the Soviet Union compared to other countries. The article claimed that the controlled economy of the Soviet Union was another form of monopoly capitalism, since the ruling class controlled the land and other modes of production. Further, communism fed war and therefore encouraged the defence industry—while the United States spent 6 per cent of its production on defence, Soviet Union spent 18 per cent. It was also shown that compared to Soviet Union, the US spent Rs 19 more per capita on education, Rs 140 more on social security and insurance and Rs 370 more on social welfare. 'Thus it is proved that, despite having an opposite goal, a controlled economy like Russia has created an economic structure that can put capitalism to shame.' A comparative analysis of the prices of essential items between Washington and Moscow again proved that the Soviet capital was a more expensive place to live in. The article, unlike others, advocated communism as an alternative, but with a different economic model to the one the Soviet Union had adopted.

In 1959, when Kalyan brought out its annual *Manavta Ank*, it actually carried an article in favour of communism. C. Nesterenko, a Russian writer on philosophy, outlined the moral principles of communism, arguing that in a socialist society there was a perfect blending of public good and private interest.[128] For a citizen of the

Soviet Union, the country's success was considered personal success. He said every citizen got the collective help and support of the society. For Nesterenko, the best example of communist morality was the way individuals came together and turned 355,000 hectares of fallow land cultivable and helped in establishing over 10,000 public enterprises. His myth of morality in the Soviet Union would get exposed in subsequent years, based as it was on a fragile foundation of fear. But in *Kalyan* he did not miss an opportunity to declare the supremacy of communism and its endeavour to create a society based on collective good.

Nesterenko's paean to communism was an aberration for Gita Press. In the late 1960s, as the government came down heavily on the cow-protection movement, Gita Press saw the state action as a reflection of its leftist leanings.[129] Leftist ideology, *Kalyan* said, considered madira (alcohol), maans (meat), machhli (fish), mudra (money) and maithun (sex) as liberating agents, and the Congress, though attacking the communists, had itself turned leftist. 'What communists desire to do is being done by the government. Today if communism is on the rise in this country, the policies of the government are to be blamed . . . Communism has no measure of equality, no definition of equality and morality.'

The 1960s were a period of intense churning in leftist ideology, leading to a split in the Communist Party of India and the formation of the Communist Party of India (Marxist) (CPI-M) in 1964. Widespread violence by leftist groups, which started in West Bengal on the issue of food shortage, soon encompassed many issues—culminating in May 1967 in the Naxalbari incident. The unrest spread to Andhra Pradesh, Kerala and elsewhere.

In Bengal, the left violence of the 1960s was largely directed against Marwari traders and industrialists. Industrial disputes and labour problems became the order of the day as the left gained a stronghold in the state. 'Between March and August 1967, 915 gheraos had been recorded, and by October, the Puja season, there was a sharp rise in the number of bonus disputes.' However, '. . . despite various concessions to industrialists by the state government, they seemed chary of committing themselves to a course of investment and expansion, no doubt on the lookout for better terms and a more sympathetic government'.[130]

As the Calcutta Marwari world closed ranks, their first port of call was Poddar in Gorakhpur. Marwaris, even if aware of the various nuances of leftist ideology, did not make a distinction between these. Various methods were discussed and devised to counter the anti-business rhetoric and campaign of the communists in general and Naxals in particular. Purshottam Dass Halwasiya, an activist of the Calcutta Marwari world, was at the helm of building this counter narrative.

Writing to Poddar, Halwasiya suggested the large-scale publication of cheap literature putting forth views on economic and social issues that would show the error of communist ideology. 'This is one way to deal with the ideological struggle with the communists. They have done the maximum in popularizing communist literature. Therefore, we should distribute our literature at the lowest price.'[131] Explaining his plan to Poddar, Halwasiya said he had decided to enlist the help of 'various disciplined departments of the RSS who could face up to the communist and anarchist elements'. He had not limited himself to RSS outfits like the Bharatiya Mazdoor Sangh, Akhil Bharatiya Vidyarthi Parishad and Swastik Prakashan, but had also reached out to the Bharatiya Jana Sangh and organizations like the Calcuta Citizens' Forum, Secondary Teachers' Association and Syama Prasad Mookerjee Study Circle. He told Poddar that if necessary a new organization—Rashtriya Suraksha Samiti—would be formed. Halwasiya estimated 'an expenditure of Rs 3–4 lakh' on the entire exercise but expected that in the 'prevailing circumstances in Calcutta organizing funds would not be a problem'.

Soon the Bharatiya Sanskritik Suraksha Parishad (BSSP) was established with the basic goal of resisting violent and anarchist tendencies through cultural means. The BSSP's tenfold supplementary mission was to encourage nationalist elements and ordinary citizens of states where law and order was in disarray due to anti-national violence; cooperate with nationalist organizations without getting involved in party politics; and popularize the tenets of cultural purity, sacrifice and public service.[132]

The BSSP included Poddar's *Kalyan* article on the West Bengal situation in its propaganda literature. In this piece, Poddar regretted the rapid decline in the country's divine tradition.[133] The widespread and dreadful violence in West Bengal, from Calcutta to Siliguri, Poddar said, was a reminder of how our thinking on nationalism had become so narrow and limited that on the basis of language and boundary, people of other states were being attacked. He presented a grim view of society under Naxal siege in West Bengal, and the divisive tendencies in Assam and Maharashtra: 'The entire society has gone haywire. Looting and arson are on the rise. There is no one to protect, to listen. Women are being humiliated. Buses, trains and shops are being burnt. A crowd can hold anyone to ransom. Schools are being attacked, students and teachers are getting killed. Since there is no one to stop this, it has resulted in closure of factories and rise in economic difficulties. It is difficult to procure items of daily need. In the name of welfare of the poor, the life of the poor is being made more difficult . . . many peace-loving people are thinking of migrating to other places. In Assam, there is general resentment against people of other states. In Maharashtra, the Shiv Sena is doing the same.'

It is interesting to note Poddar's inclusion of the right-wing Shiv Sena in his criticism.

One can safely assume that of the many new ideologies of the twentieth century, communism was considered by Gita Press the most threatening to the Hindu way of life. This assumption stems from the continued publication of Swami Karpatri Maharaj's *Marxvad Aur Ram Rajya* by Gita Press. Since the first edition in 1957, the total sales of the book have amounted to just 23,500 copies, an abysmally low figure for a publishing house that has sold millions of copies of the Ramayana, Mahabharata and Gita. However, seven editions have been printed, the last one in 2009, indicating that communism, though no longer the alternative it had sought to become, still rankles with the Hindu right.

Karpatri began writing the book in 1953 in jail after he was arrested for involvement in the Jammu and Kashmir Andolan (J&K Agitation) a joint initiative of Ram Rajya Parishad, Hindu Mahasabha and Jana Sangh. The book began as an article in Sanskrit, based on whatever Marxist literature was available in the jail. Before he could finish the article, Karpatri was released. On two subsequent incarcerations in a

Banaras jail for participating in the movement to liberate the Kashi Vishwanath temple, Karpatri had better access to books on Marxism, and enlarged the scope of his commentary that soon took the form of a book. He continued to write sporadically after his release, and by 1956, the handwritten manuscript, though highly unorganized, landed in Gita Press. Janaki Nath Sharma, who was on the editorial staff of *Kalyan* and had also spent time in jail with Karpatri, was entrusted with the task of editing the text and proofreading the manuscript.[134]

Ultimately *Marxvad Aur Ram Rajya* turned out to be a treatise of 800-plus pages. Juxtaposed with each Marxian theory and principle was Karpatri's alternative of Ram rajya. Karpatri chose a simplistic mode of writing. First he would cite heavily from Marx and then demolish his arguments through wisdom from Hindu religious texts. Of course, he never deviated from the assertion of not only the pre-existence of principles of equality in Hindu dharma, but also its moral and ethical superiority over communism.

Karpartri mocked Marx's theory of class struggle and triumph of the oppressed. He was dismissive of the Marxian tenet of state ownership of land, industry and other assets and argued that it was against dharma and individual liberty and growth.[135] Under the theocratic Ram rajya, Karpatri argued, an individual used his strength and ability to earn for his family, and secured his present and afterlife through acts of sacrifice, penance and charity. He was also not convinced with Marx's description of the plight of the working class. Karpatri's view was that the working class was not so oppressed and definitely not naive; in times of emergency, a motor mechanic or a rickshaw puller extracted undue payment from hapless customers. Karpatri also disputed the virtue of equal distribution of wealth, justified profit-making and questioned Marx's prediction of class struggle.

Among several examples of Karpatri's regressive views, the most offensive were his statements on women. The new concept of women workers and the liberty it provided them, a product of the industrial revolution, common to both capitalist and communist ideologies, was considered a threat to the Hindu social order where a woman was limited to the domestic sphere as daughter, wife or mother. Karpatri said Lenin had challenged the concept of pativrata nari (devoted wife);

in Marxism, since everything was state-owned there was no need for a woman to be in a relationship with one man.[136] As there were no laws of inheritance and private ownership of property, Karpatri said, a woman became like a bucket of water that could quench the thirst of many men. He went even further to state that, in order to facilitate multiple relationships, the Soviet Union had legitimized abortion. Karpatri said he could already see the impact of such international social trends on India, where the government was planning to introduce a divorce law to give women more independence. Scornful of both capitalist and communist societies for making women part of the workforce, Karpatri painted in contrast the 'utopian' Ram rajya under which there was no breach of gender turf—men working outside and women ruling the domestic world. In the world that the Ram Rajya Parishad promised, girls would be married off in their childhood so that they could rule the household and become queens of their domestic world.

Parallel to Gita Press's antagonism to communist principles was its attack on the secular ideals of the new Indian republic. Secularism was always an anathema to the conservative Indian political class that had strongly rooted for India to be declared a Hindu nation. In the eyes of Gita Press, the government's actions—opening the gates of temples to untouchables, introduction of the Hindu Code Bill and ambivalence on cow slaughter—were all manifestations of the evils of secularism.

By the 1960s it had become apparent to the likes of Poddar that India was not the nation they had envisioned it to be. As violence raged across India on a range of emotive issues like language in the south, religion in UP and ethnicity in Assam, Poddar saw this as symptomatic of a loss of values of sanatan Hindu dharma in the country and over-reliance on secularism.[137] In the name of secularism, Poddar said, the country was 'engaged in the vile work of making man a beast, devil or demon'.[138] He sounded the death knell for India in the absence of sanatan dharma: '... sanatan dharma is declining ... This is a very dangerous thing for the future of the world. It is a supremely essential and immediately inevitable duty to understand this sanatan dharma, to arrange for the instruction of sanatan dharma in the syllabus of all the educational institutions ...'

Poddar blamed the liberal attitude of Indian leaders and a foreign conspiracy for the rise of secularism, which he said created such a feeling of helplessness among the majority Hindus that they feared any expression of religious feelings would be termed communal.[139]

Secularism was branded a 'curse' in an article in *Kalyan* in 1968.[140] It was blamed not only for obliterating India's Hindu past but also for the creation of two distinguishable categories—Indians and Hindus. Gita Press attacked the separation of nation and religion. The dream of an exclusive Hindu nation had been shattered by the new inclusive India that had too many competing interests based on affiliations to caste, sect or ideology; this was seen as an assault on Hindu unity. Secularism led to appeasement of minorities while the 'responsibility of being peaceful was entirely on the Hindus'.

The author of the article Rajendra Prasad Jain gave a call for a dharmayudh (religious war) against secularism, which, he said, was the cause of religious, social and moral bankruptcy in the country. Citing a reported statement of former chief justice of India K. Subba Rao, he said that the word 'secularism does not occur anywhere in the Constitution'.[141] In 1966, Jain had come up with the thesis that, given the experience of the first two decades of Independence, it was imperative that the country be declared a Hindu rashtra (nation).[142] Two years later, he asked, 'If secularism is an ideal, countries dominated by Muslims, communists and Christians should also follow it. Why should only Hindu-majority Bharat be made a sacrificial lamb?'[143]

As had been the case with the Hindu Mahasabha in the 1940s, there was a total unity of purpose between Gita Press and the Jana Sangh in the 1960s. Right from its inception, the Jana Sangh had been opposed to the espousal of secularism by the Congress. During the first general election in 1951–52, opposition to secularism made it to the Jana Sangh's manifesto. In a language remarkably similar to Gita Press's critique of secularism, the party promised dharma rajya that was not to be theocracy but merely rule of law, saying: 'Secularism, as currently interpreted in this country, however, is only a euphemism for the policy of Muslim appeasement. The so-called secular composite nationalism is neither nationalism nor secularism but only a compromise with communalism of those who demand a price even for their lip loyalty to this country.'[144]

Bharatiya sanskriti (Indian culture) and maryada (dignity) were to be the basis of Jana Sangh's dharma rajya. Indian culture was the assimilation of contributions of 'different peoples, creeds and cultures' to the main current in such a way as to make it 'one and indivisible . . . Any talk of composite culture, therefore, is unrealistic, illogical and dangerous for it tends to weaken national unity and encourage fissiparous tendencies.' For the Jana Sangh, Bharat itself was an 'ancient nation' whose 'recently obtained freedom only marks the beginning of a new chapter in her long and chequered history, and not the birth of a new nation'.

Gita Press's grouse was that secularism had worked against Hinduism, allowing other religions to spread at its expense. Hindus were faulted for being too soft, compassionate and law-abiding. Facts and figures, often unsubstantiated, like the Christian population having gone up to ten million, the existence of 7,000 missionaries in the country and the alleged conversion of 30,000 Hindus to Christianity every month, were dished out regularly to prove that secularism had worked against the Hindus while other religions had prospered.[145]

Making a fine distinction between Hinduism and other religions like Christianity and Islam, *Kalyan* said, while others resorted to the sword to convert, Hinduism followed the path of non-violence. An appeal was made to Hindus not to sit idle as their religion was going through its darkest hour. *Kalyan* advised that the only way to deal with secularism was through Hindu unity, religious education of youth and large-scale mobilization—not only of the various Hindu sects but also religions that had emerged from Hinduism, such as Buddhism and Jainism. 'Today our religion is in danger. Cows are being slaughtered. The honour and chastity of our mothers and daughters are under threat. Hindus wake up! Hindus unite!'

Gita Press and its various publications continue to attack the Indian state for its secular nature. The writings of ultra-conservatives like Swami Karpatri are reprinted in *Kalyan* to reiterate that secularism leads to the erosion of religious values in society.[146]

Times of Crises

The Chinese aggression of 1962, the first major failure of Nehru's foreign policy, posed a challenge to Poddar and the entire Hindu right. They needed to live up to their claim of putting the nation before everything. Poddar termed the Chinese aggression an act of treachery that needed immediate and comprehensive retribution: 'China should be taught such a lesson for this vile act that in future they have no courage or are left in no position for such misadventures.'[147] He praised the Indian government and public for making the right efforts to punish the Chinese aggressors. He was particularly pleased with the manner in which an 'unfortunate incident had resulted in creating a fortunate result—unity among men and women across religions and belief systems'. An appeal was made to readers of *Kalyan* to contribute whatever they could to the nation, reminding them that it was the duty of every Indian to fight the aggressor.

Even here, Poddar gave the strategic affair a spiritual and religious twist. India, he said, should also resort to 'spiritual means' to destroy China for casting an evil eye on the holy Himalayas. Such an effort, he said, would also liberate Tibet from the anti-God and anti-religion China.

Considering Nepal's geographical proximity to China, Poddar hoped the Hindu kingdom would come to India's rescue. In what would today be considered an attitude of aggressive domination by the citizens of the larger neighbour, Poddar coolly claimed: 'India and Nepal are entirely one, India is Nepal and Nepal is India . . . Nepal is a matter of pride for India and Hindus because it is the only sanatan dharma Hindu rashtra (nation) . . . India and Nepal have one religion, one shastra and one God . . . It should be expected that in a moment of crisis when sanatan Hindu dharma is under attack from anti-religion, anti-God China, Nepal would lend adequate support.'

Days before this article appeared, Poddar had already written to King Mahendra of Nepal, saying that, though he had nothing to do with politics, he was making a religious appeal. He requested King Mahendra not to cooperate with anti-God China in its unjust and barbaric attack on India.[148]

Three years later, at the time of the India–Pakistan war of 1965, Poddar again justified Indian military action, saying Pakistan had become a nagging wound: 'Just as one gets rid of a wound surgically, India is doing the same to Pakistan. This is out of beneficence, not animosity. This is not enmity. Though it has taken a serious form, all believers in truth and justice should support India . . . Pakistanis should be punished and at no cost should an unjust demon be supported.'[149]

A month later, Poddar produced a comprehensive analysis of the wars with Pakistan and China, blaming the two nations for provoking India. He regretted the very existence of Pakistan as 'the biggest mistake . . . had India remained undivided there would not have been any attack nor would China have threatened India or US and Britain could have indulged in diplomatic manoeuvres'.[150]

Reiterating what had been the demand of the RSS, Hindu Mahasabha and Gita Press itself, Poddar said the best solution to deal with Pakistan would be its reintegration with India—this was the only way out for citizens of both nations. Poddar's recipe to deal with China was no less straightforward: he suggested China be thrown out of Buddhist Tibet, as this would be 'beneficial to India and the world'.

The two successive wars, especially the one with Pakistan, emboldened Poddar to raise the Hindu–Muslim identity question again. He reiterated the demand Gita Press and the Hindu Mahasabha had made on the eve of Independence, that the task of securing the nation should be left to Hindus. 'The burden of India's security indeed lies with the Hindus and only a Hindu can carry out this task properly. This principle should be fully internalized. Hindus should be trusted, given more opportunity and allowed to run India's defence establishment. This is the only way we can be safe.'

Poddar said that, after the two wars, it could no longer be hidden that 'in many provinces, most towns and villages, there are enough traitors, people who are sympathetic to Pakistan and China'. Without naming Muslims, Poddar contended there were people who had ties with Pakistan and China, those who helped Pakistan illegally and considered it to be their country. He warned against such people and demanded exemplary punishment for them.

However, months before the 1971 war with Pakistan that led to the birth of Bangladesh, when a severe flood engulfed East Pakistan Poddar wrote to Prime Minister Indira Gandhi conveying Gita Press's 'heartfelt sympathy' and enclosing a cheque of Rs 5,000 as contribution to the relief fund. He requested Gandhi to ensure that the money was 'transmitted to the Pakistan government or towards any relief fund started by you or your government . . .'[151]

Given Poddar's acrimony towards Pakistan, it is possible that this help was his way of lending support to East Pakistan where the Awami League was fighting a lone battle against the Pakistan People's Party. The likely prospect of Pakistan disintegrating must have been something for him to be happy about. In fact, Poddar's charity intervention for the natural calamity was among the few of his last public acts before his death in March 1971.

६ : The Moral Universe of Gita Press

In the winter of 1939 Hanuman Prasad Poddar was camping in Ram Krishna Dalmia's cement factory at Dalmia Dadri in present-day Haryana. It was a period of deep despondency and one of the several points in his life when he would threaten to leave Gita Press. At such times, Poddar would move out of Gorakhpur, often to Ratangarh and sometimes, as in this case, to his dear friend Dalmia's factory.

Poddar's voluminous correspondence would be redirected to him wherever he went, and much of his time would be spent replying to letters, mostly queries from readers of *Kalyan*. Many were personal in nature, seeking Poddar's spiritual guidance.

One of the letters Poddar received at Dalmia Dadri was from Bajrang Lal, a senior functionary of Gita Press. Lal, as Poddar's reply reveals, asked Poddar whether over-dependence on God was a good thing. Poddar replied that in one's devotion to God even in the face of adversity one should be like a 'pativrata nari (loyal wife) who does not desert her husband even if he troubles her a lot, humiliates her in public' and 'does not cheat on him even if seduced with money'.[1]

Such a reply to an innocuous spiritual query, using a shockingly regressive image of an ideal Hindu wife, was neither inadvertent nor innocent. The 'devoted and self-sacrificing'[2] female was at the centre of the moral universe that Gita Press inhabited both as practitioner and as propagator of sanatan Hindu dharma. The central role assigned to a woman by the patriarchal system was one that confined her to the inner recesses of the household and burdened her with responsibility for the family's moral compass.

Gita Press's advocacy of patriarchal control over women's public and private spheres was not as out of tune with the times as one might expect. The reformist zeal that had marked the second half of the nineteenth century had not progressed, as it logically should have, to second-generation social reform at the beginning of the twentieth century. Just the reverse had happened, and by the time Gita Press came into existence, the situation was ripe to further the conservative agenda, at the centre of which stood the hapless Hindu nari (woman).

What went wrong? Historian Ghulam Murshid has attributed the slowdown in social reform to the rise of nationalism that 'glorified India's past and tended to defend everything traditional', but Partha Chatterjee contests Murshid's claim as based on 'rather simple and linear assumptions'.[3] Chatterjee is more in agreement with Sumit Sarkar who highlighted the 'limitations of the nineteenth-century renaissance' in which 'instead of any autonomous feminist pressure to improve their lot', the 'initiative came essentially from men'.[4]

Further, Sarkar argues, the campaign for social change could not metamorphose into a full-blown movement because the efforts made in the ninteenth century had a 'strong personal dimension'. Reforms in Hindu society were focused on 'upper-caste social evils like sati, the widow-remarriage taboo or *kulin* polygamy', leaving intact the 'emphasis on puritanical norms and restraints' that had a 'strong patriarchal aspect'.

Extending Sarkar's argument, Partha Chatterjee contends that 'the material/spiritual distinction was condensed into an analogous, but ideologically far more powerful dichotomy: that between the outer and the inner'.[5] The outside world with its unpredictable nature and infirmities was the 'domain of the male' and the inner world, the home, had to 'remain unaffected by the profane activities of the material world' and therefore was the domain of the woman. The construct of the outer/inner world also emanated from the nationalist contention that while the European power with its might and 'superior material culture' ruled India, it 'had failed to colonize the inner, essential, identity of the East which lay in its distinctive, and superior, spiritual culture'. Chatterjee concludes that by fusing the 'home/world dichotomy' with 'gender roles', nationalists dealt with the women's question: 'It was not a dismissal of modernity; the attempt was rather to make modernity consistent with the nationalist project.'

Writing at length on the concept of ghar/bahar (home/outside world), Poddar argued the two were not exclusive: 'Man and woman together form a ghar, the home, the family. A man goes outside for his ghar and woman remains inside for the same ghar. If need be, for social and religious reasons and within certain limits, a woman can step outside the ghar with her husband and sons. Similarly, a man comes to the ghar not to rule and demonstrate his achievements of bahar, but to live. The system of ghar-bahar is to secure the family and make it prosperous.'[6]

Preserving the Purity of Women

As early as 1926, the year of *Kalyan*'s birth, among the dozen-odd books brought out by Gita Press was a forty-six-page monograph *Stri Dharma Prashnottari* (Questions and Answers on Women's Dharma), a sort of compendium of a woman's duties, by Hanuman Prasad Poddar. Its popularity can be discerned from the simple fact that it is still in print, over a million copies having been sold over the decades. It is currently priced at Rs 5.

Stri Dharma Prashnottari was just the beginning—over its years of existence, Gita Press has published innumerable tracts on women, their education, their duties as housewives, their sexuality and hygiene and in general their role in society. Prominent among these are *Nari Dharma* and *Striyon Ke Liye Kartavya Shiksha* by Jaydayal Goyandka, *Bhakt Nari, Nari Shiksha* and *Dampatya Jivan Ka Adarsh* by Poddar, *Grihasta Mein Kaise Rahen* and *Prashnottar Manimala* by Swami Ramsukhdas.[7] In 1948, *Kalyan* published its *Nari Ank*. Besides this, articles on subjects relating to women regularly appeared in the monthly issues of *Kalyan* and in the special issues on *Manavta* (Humanity, 1959), *Sadachar* (Ideal Behaviour, 1978), *Shiksha* (Education, 1988) and *Charitra Nirman* (Character Building, 1983).

Stri Dharma Prashnottari provided the model for the Gita Press's oeuvre on women. Written in the style of a conversation between two women, the monograph stands out for its misogynist intent. The choice of the women's names is interesting: the one seeking knowledge is Sarala, the simpleton (saral meaning simple or uncomplicated), and the one educating her about women's duties is Savitri, the devoted wife of ancient Indian mythology, the ideal Hindu woman. Each answer Savitri gives to Sarala's questions is an instruction, a lesson that liberally cites the shastras.

In all Gita Press publications on women, the language used is reformist in tone and prescriptive in nature. Poddar and others made it clear that a woman's non-adherence to the set rules could affect the broader Hindu society. The onus was on the woman to be the flag bearer of morality, purity and chastity. Only then could an ideal family—and by extension an ideal nation—be formed.

One factor that possibly played an important role in Gita Press's overemphasis on women and their purity may be the Marwari community's trajectory of migration from the small towns and nondescript villages of Rajasthan to the then colonial capital Calcutta or other big cities. It was common practice among first-generation migrants to leave the elders, womenfolk and children in Rajasthan, where a well-lubricated network of relatives provided support for each other. However, this practice came with a huge social cost. In November 1929, the hugely popular Hindi journal *Chand* published a special issue on the Marwaris that, as we saw in an earlier chapter, shook the Marwari world. The articles primarily focused on the uncontrolled sexuality of lonely and unfulfilled Marwari women, citing at length the pulp literature coming out of Jaipur—works like *Khayal Chhote Kanth Ko* (Thinking of a Younger Husband), *Kaki Jetuth Ka Khayal* (Thinking about Aunt and Nephew), both published by Kanhaiyalal Bookseller of Jaipur's Tripolia Bazar, and *Do Gori Ka Balma* (A Lover of Two Women) by Ishwarlal Bookseller. These were all written in Marwari and claimed to be based on real incidents that highlighted the promiscuity of Marwari women and related tales of sexual escapades and incestuous relationships within households.

Eight years after the controversial *Marwari Ank*, *Chand* carried an article by Sukhda Devi, the late wife of Chandkaran Sharda, Poddar's friend and a respected figure among Marwaris, also a leading light of the Arya Samaj movement. While Sharda wrote on the virtues of Hindu dharma for *Kalyan*, Sukhda Devi's article in *Chand* exposed the pitiable condition of Marwari women.[8] In many ways, it was a first-person account of life in the inner chambers of a prosperous Marwari mansion. Wealth, she said, had not brought happiness. She condemned the duplicity of the community that did not think twice when contributing Rs 50,000 to Gandhi for the popularization of Hindi, but had shown no such enthusiasm in opening schools for Marwari girls. Without education, the world of a Marwari woman had shrunk to narrow interests in dress and jewellery, gossip and the desire to marry off sons the moment they reached the age of sixteen.

Sukhda Devi exposed the ills in the Marwari domestic world, from marriages of young girls with older men, to domestic violence. She said there was not a single Marwari household where the men had not married twice or thrice. On the other hand, Marwari widows, often young, were not allowed to remarry, as a result of which, Sukhda Devi said, 'widows have become immoral'.

She appealed to Marwari women to make efforts to open schools that would teach girls home science, economics, cooking, medical care and midwifery along with providing a general education. 'We should take steps forward along with the world. Marwari girls should not be any less than girls of other communities.' She concluded with the remark, 'God helps those who help themselves', after urging women to protest against oppressive social practices.

The theme of loneliness and the confinement of Marwari women to the domestic sphere continues to inspire literary works in present times, as seen in the 2001 Hindi novel *Peeli Aandhi* (Yellow Storm) by Prabha Khaitan, a member of the community. Her book is a portrayal of three generations of Marwari women spread across 100–150 years, their struggles and successes in carving an identity for themselves in the wider progressive social context of Bengal.[9]

Poddar and Goyandka, who were to become the conscience-keepers of the community, had themselves lived the double life of migrant bachelors in Calcutta and married men in Rajasthan. In their view, women were a source of social malaise, and they needed to aspire to the ideals of purity represented by their ancient predecessors like Savitri and Shakuntala. This purity was a comprehensive concept that had to manifest itself in every aspect of a woman's being: education, marriage, domestic affairs, sex life and health. The promiscuity of men was neither part of the debate nor considered a problem. It was only women who were expected to remain chaste under all circumstances, to bear the unfaithful behaviour of their husbands and resist being seduced by other men.

Women's Education

In *Stri Dharma Prashnottari*,[10] as the dialogue between the two women proceeds, Sarala asks if education for women is a bad thing; could it result in her becoming a widow as was widely believed? Savitri rubbishes this: 'If that is the case then in jatis (communities) among whom education is common all women would have become widows.' Sarala then asks if education makes a woman immoral, and Savitri emphatically denies this too. Education, she says, fuels dharma in a woman, makes her more able in her domestic work. This kind of education comes from religious texts that not only enhance knowledge and give one strength to deal with any crisis, but also helps one avoid bad habits and imbibe good traits. 'Immorality and decadence set in not due to education but a host of other factors like lack of education, living in the company of promiscuous women, roaming from household to household, indulging in immoral talk and quarrelling with husbands.'

Now Sarala pointedly asks what kind of education should be imparted to women; should it be of the kind prevalent in schools? Savitri replies that education for girls should on the one hand help them to understand the teachings of the Ramayana, Gita, *Manusmriti*, Mahabharata and other religious texts, and on the other enhance their domestic skills—cooking, sewing and needlework, taking care of the male child and following the orders of her husband. She disapproves of the education currently being imparted in girls' schools: 'English and English (Western) culture has entered these schools, destroying the Hindu ideals. Fashion is on the rise and so is the love for sensuous pleasure. Women despise and have lost interest in housework. A better part of their time is spent beautifying themselves. The importance of religion is on the wane. Such an education is definitely not needed for Hindu women.'

Savitri strongly advocates educational reform so that the Hindu girl can become an ideal Hindu woman with qualities like love for religion and ethics; devotion to her husband and her elders; compassion for the poor and selflessness in service to mankind; interest in household work; control of expenses; and hatred for sensual pleasure.

With school education denied to a girl, Sarala wants to know if she should forever remain under the command of her parents. Savitri says this is not only necessary but also dharma for girls: 'According to our shastras, in all situations the stri-jati (women) should not become independent . . . At a young age, the girl should be under the command of her father, in her youth under the control of her husband and after the death of her husband under the care of her sons.'

Poddar did not remain content with the Sarala–Savitri debate in his attempt to counter the spread of the 'wrong' type of education in the country. He employed every possible incident that could further his argument against Western education for women. Even a remote incident of marriage between a brahmin girl and a Muslim boy in Poona was used to illustrate the pitfalls of modern education for women. He also extracted other writers' articles to make his point. One such piece, by Parshuram Mehrotra in *Madhuri,* a literary journal for women, was written in the form of a letter from a sister to her elder brother. The anguished sister, though supportive of women's education, pointed out three problems: lack of good schools for girls, a curriculum that was too Western in content and the lack of good women teachers. Such education, she said, would wreak havoc in society in general and within the family in particular.[11]

Stri Dharma Prashnottari had gone into multiple reprints by the time Goyandka's *Nari Dharma* came out in 1938. Delving into similar territories of women's public and private existence, *Nari Dharma* established Poddar as the milder of the two and even progressive, if such a term could be used in the context of Gita Press. Highly opinionated, judgemental and unambiguously biased, Goyandka did not mince words—his language was direct, sometimes even crude.

Writing to Poddar in highly contemptuous terms about women's freedom in Europe, Goyandka had expressed fear about what such freedom could do in India 'where women are so murkh (foolish) that they cannot even count till 100'.[12] At the very start of his book he stated that 'educated women get nasht-brasht (destroyed)'.[13] He believed there was a lack of teachers with good character, which led to illicit relationships in educational institutions becoming the norm, though these rarely came out in the open. He stated that such relationships had become common even in temples, places of pilgrimage and religious congregations, and the solution lay in men and women having minimal contact with each other.

Dismissing the solution of having women teachers, Goyandka said it was a difficult task to find those of good character—'As a result hardly any of the hundreds of girls' schools in the country are run as per the ideals of sanatan Hindu dharma.' Goyandka denied there was any evidence in the shastric texts of schools, gurukuls or universities for women or the practice of co-education in ancient times. The education of females traditionally took place in the home, he said.

To educate and build the character, strength and mental purity of girls and women, Goyandka laid stress on hard physical labour. Even harsh words and rebukes by elders were to be considered by a woman as a form of education.[14]

Unlike Goyandka, Poddar was not impervious to the sweeping changes taking place throughout the country. He was aware that, despite the best efforts of Gita Press and other revivalist organizations to push for home-based shastric education for women, the colonial machinery and changing Indian mindset could not be countered. It remained for him to critique the colonial education that sought to destroy the gendered basis of the ghar/bahar (home/world) concept.

In 1936, in an elaborate essay—'*Vartaman Shiksha*'—Poddar regretted the new wave of modernity that aimed to put men and women on an equal educational footing, so much so that even women were becoming 'teachers, clerks, lawyers, barristers, writers, politicians and members of municipalities and councils'.[15] Such ideas of progress, Poddar said, were turning women anti-God and anti-religion. Though, due to their inherent qualities of gentleness, kindness, devotion and shyness, women had not yet begun defying the tenets of religion like men, Poddar felt that the seeds of such defiance had been sown. The first manifestation of this decline, he said, was that women were becoming less patient.

Modern education, as Poddar saw it, was creating a parallel universe, an immoral one, in which women were writing letters to men who were not related to them, were joking, playing chess and dancing with these men. The most important aspect, Poddar wrote, was the loss of virtue. Never short of instances to prove his argument, he cited a letter in a reformist newspaper of Lahore in which a reader opposed to co-education had written about a report by a lady health officer of a school which indicated that 90 per cent of girls above twelve had become pregnant at some point. Poddar wrote that it was possible this figure was a printing error, but the situation was alarming enough even if 10 per cent of girls were getting pregnant. He said Lahore-like incidents were on the rise because in the co-education system there was a high probability of schoolgirls 'losing their character'.

The concept of co-education, Poddar argued, interfered with the basic purpose of education, which is to highlight and draw out the inherent strength of an individual. Since in his view shakti (power) was not evenly distributed between boys and girls, it was wrong to give them similar education in the same schools. Besides, he argued, co-education could bring about great mutual attraction between a boy and a girl, because of the difference in the physical constitution of the two sexes: 'It is impossible to resist temptation if one stays in close proximity.'

An article on the modern woman in *Kalyan*'s *Nari Ank* (1948) praised the Sanskrit scholar and vice chancellor of Allahabad University Ganganath Jha for his opposition to co-education at the university. Jha also did not allow a dance performance by the daughter of a faculty member and refused to budge despite a campaign against him by the local daily *Leader*. The *Kalyan* article also claimed that Madan Mohan Malaviya regretted the opening of a girl's wing in Banaras Hindu University.[16]

Extending the ghar/bahar dichotomy, the article designated offices, bazaars, congregations, courts and councils as places for men, and the home for women. The writer asked women why they should waste their time and energy in offices instead of savouring the pleasure of motherhood and the independence of their home. In his view, the purpose of education for women should be to further develop their inherent qualities so that they became good mothers. Like Goyandka, he dismissed the argument that co-education had existed in the gurukuls of ancient India. Poddar too wrote there was no evidence to prove such a claim. Only the daughters of gurus studied with boys, but the relationship between them was of brother and sister. Also, strict surveillance was maintained.

By the time of the *Nari Ank*, Gita Press's narrative was changing, not so much in its obscurantist tone but in its resistance to the spread of women's education, as it believed all its fears about Western education for women had come true. Poddar's '*Vartaman Shiksha*' was partially reproduced in *Nari Ank* with some new footnotes and an attempt to articulate more practical reasons against giving institutional education to girls.[17] In a way, the 882-page special issue, Gita Press's ultimate compendium on women, was an attempt to present a comprehensive sanatani view on questions relating to women. According to the current editor of *Kalyan*, Radheshyam Khemka, the articles in *Nari Ank* compare modern and ancient women.[18]

An article by Kishori Das Vajpayee, a votary of sanatan dharma, writer, poet, teacher, journalist and activist, stated that girls were mentally sharper than boys but softer both physically and mentally. 'Therefore, a woman who masters a dry and mentally sapping subject like mathematics becomes physically weak and loses shine. Such women present a pathetic picture in domestic affairs. They are always unwell and depressed. Even their relatives are not happy. The purpose of education is happiness.'[19]

This was certainly a novel argument against the education of women. Further, Vajpayee raised a practical fear against women pursuing degrees like BA and MA, saying that it was nearly impossible to find suitable grooms for such girls, who 'willingly or unwillingly remain unmarried throughout their life and become lonely and helpless'. He advocated that girls should instead acquire qualifications like Vidya Vinodini, Vidushi, etc., that were on offer from institutions popularly called vidyapiths. These institutions imparted education based on the Indian knowledge system, on religion, ancient science, history, culture and a huge dose of morality. Vidyapiths were the sanatanis' counter to Western-type schools and colleges. Women were meant to be the harbingers of knowledge and purity within the family, and vidyapith education was argued to be complete, one that posed no threat to the family or to the woman herself, yet was sufficient to enable her to successfully carry out her household work and educate her children.

Gita Press also resorted to what had been done in Bengal during the mid-nineteenth century—parodying educated women and ridiculing their efforts to be on an equal footing with men.[20] Who better than an educated woman to take the lead in doing this? Shakuntala Gupta, herself a graduate in Hindi, mocked Western-educated women for adding to the list of unemployed, a category that had so far been exclusively composed of men.[21] In a more serious vein, she wrote of the threat these educated women posed to the existing social and moral order. Gupta listed a host of immoral practices among educated women—frequenting clubs and cinema halls, playing cards, drinking alcohol, smoking, eating meat and spending time with men at unearthly hours. Her remedy was complete revision of the curriculum for women, with emphasis on Indian languages, domestic science and parenting.

But again, a note of ambivalence crept in. *Nari Ank* carried a laudatory article on Anandibai Joshi, India's first Western-educated woman doctor and a cousin of Pandita Ramabai, 'a reputed champion of Indian women's education'.[22] Joshi, praised by Gita Press for leading the life of a devout Hindu wife as a student in Pennsylvania, USA, had been at the receiving end of conservatives in India—she and her friend, the Marathi novelist Kashibai Kanitkar, had been stoned for wearing shoes and walking out with umbrellas, two symbols of male authority.[23] But this fact was not mentioned in the Gita Press narrative.[24] The article also deliberately papered over the reasons that forced Joshi to go abroad for medical education.

The *Kalyan* article on Joshi was a mere translation of parts of her biography by Caroline Healey Dall,[25] with significant omissions. It spoke of how she carried her saris, glass bangles, sindoor and photographs of gods and goddesses to the USA, thus preserving her Hindu identity as a woman and a wife in a foreign land. *Kalyan* chose to ignore portions of Dall's book where Joshi criticized Hindu priests as 'prejudiced and corrupt'—'I dislike them as a class.' The article thus presented a one-dimensional image of Joshi as a woman wedded to her cultural ethos, when she was also a freethinker with an eclectic taste in books, authors and ideas.

Kalyan's *Nari Ank* did not confine itself to Indian women like Joshi, but also gave space to Western female icons who had chosen to spend their life in the service of mankind. So we find profiles of Florence Nightingale, Joan of Arc, Elizabeth Fry and Helen Keller. Notably, Poddar had earlier written a booklet on European women to propagate the values of the Victorian age among Indian women.[26]

Marriage and Domesticity

In 1929, writing to an unidentified woman who was in a bad marriage and who seemed to have bared her pain and sought his advice, Poddar displayed the conflict between his sanatani Hindu core and pretentious reformist face.[27] Possibly the woman had experienced physical torture at the hands of her husband, which made Poddar hesitate to give the usual advice that she should display the classic tolerance of Bharatiya matri jati (Indian mothers). Addressing the woman as behen (sister), Poddar took an unprecedented stand, saying that he would not find it wrong if she walked out of the marriage and left her husband's home.

But then his sanatani self got the better of him, and Poddar cited the glorious tradition of sati dharma (sati in this context exemplifying wifely devotion) among Indian women as the reason for his hesitation in advising her to leave her husband. As if to console her, Poddar predicted doom for the husband, but this was a ploy to reignite the sati in her. 'God only knows the evil plight that awaits such a man. I am hesitant to spell it out as the Indian sati does not want to hear anything untoward about her husband, even if he is the meanest and the worst human being.'

After creating considerable confusion about what he stood for, Poddar dished out the standard sanatani fare and told the woman to have faith in God and to pray, not for his end but the end of his base thinking. Though Poddar had earlier supported the idea of the woman leaving her matrimonial home, he now painted a picture of a highly immoral outside world, one she should not step into. So, in the end, he left the woman to languish in her abusive marriage.

Poddar's position was hardly surprising. For him, Hindu marriage was a religious rite, a spiritual quest that did not require registration or a contract of the type prevalent in marriages of other religions, as there was no question of it breaking. The relationship between husband and wife did not end with death, as marriage was between two bodies and one soul: 'This oneness is what makes the Hindu marriage special.'[28] This construct of the sanctity and eternity of marriage was the driving force behind Gita Press's opposition to widow remarriage.

It was not mutual love between a man and a woman that formed the basis of a marriage, Poddar believed. Instead, marriage was a means to moderate sensual desire and pleasure and to exercise self-control, so that a man could move towards renunciation. He advised boys and girls to marry according to the wishes of their family elders, to consider marriage a religious ritual, not to marry outside caste and religion, not to go in for registered marriages and to spend less on the ceremony. He also wrote against newlyweds going on a honeymoon.[29]

In Poddar's view, the appropriate age of marriage for girls was just before they reached puberty. In *Stri Dharma Prashnottari*, Savitri prescribes marriage for girls at the age of twelve, unless a suitable groom is not found, in which case parents may wait a year or two. She does state that marrying a girl before she turns twelve could adversely affect her health and even result in early death; further, a woman should have some right in the selection of her life partner. 'Savitri, Rukmini and Damayanti (considered ideal Hindu women of ancient times) chose their husbands. Had they been girls, this could not have happened.'[30] This contrasts with Goyandka's view that women should have no say in their choice of partner, but should accept the decision of their father or brother, and live with their husband loyally for the rest of their life.

Yet, Poddar vociferously opposed the Child Marriage Restraint Act of 1929 (popularly known as the Sarda Act) that fixed the age of marriage for girls at fourteen and for boys at eighteen. He argued that the proposed law would 'take away a major right of the Hindus and would cause a big blow to believers in the dharmashastras'. Besides, he questioned the wisdom of allowing a government that had done so much harm to the nation to attempt to carry out social and religious reform.[31]

Presenting his skewed understanding of female sexuality, Poddar wrote that, during her menstrual period, a woman had an uncontrollable urge for sex, and 'to channelize this vasana (sexual urge) there is the system of marrying girls by the time they attain puberty. In her husband's shelter, a woman's sexual desire does not reach others and she is saved from getting polluted. If she is not married, her sexual desire degenerates into debauchery, just the way it is happening in Europe.'[32]

The core job of a woman was to serve the world. How? Poddar used two terms—utpadan (literally translated it would mean manufacturing or production) and nirman (literally construction or creation). Thus a woman's job was to procreate and nurture 'quality men'.[33]

In *Stri Dharma Prashnottari*, Savitri's very first statement is: 'The most important dharma for a woman is loyalty to her husband . . . Her entire purpose should be to make her husband happy.'[34] Saying that for a woman her husband is the God, Savitri cites passages from Manu to emphasize that, even if a husband is without any character, lacks skill or is libidinous, it is the duty of his wife to worship him, as pure devotion to the husband is the sure-shot and only ticket to swargalok (heaven).

Poddar believed that loyalty to her husband endowed a woman with such unprecedented power that even the gods would be afraid of her. And, a man who raped a woman devoted to her husband was sure to die, as pativrata (devotion to husband) was a fire that could engulf a rapist as if he were a mere straw.[35]

Poddar's Sarala is not as naive as one might believe, as she asks whether husbands do not have any dharma (duty). Citing instances of wife abuse, Sarala innocently asks if the shastras sanction such acts. Savitri at first makes the right noises, and quotes Manu to say that God resides where women are respected. She even states that men who do not treat their wives properly, or do not give them enough food, are neglecting their dharma. But then she chides Sarala for deviating from the subject of their conversation which is 'stri dharma': 'Men have a different dharma. To argue that since men do not follow their own dharma, women should also give theirs up, is neither justified nor a valid argument. For us (women) it is important to follow our own dharma. Whatever be the husband's behaviour towards us, it is not the job of a pious and devout wife to assess him. I am of the firm belief that if a wife is devoted to her husband, her purity of heart can bring him back to the right path.'[36]

The image of the Muslim male as the lustful 'other'[37] and the threat he posed to the Hindu woman does not fail to come up either. Sarala asks if it is advisable for women to visit pirs and paigambars (holy men in Islam). Savitri's reply is clear: 'To believe in Muslim pirs and paigambars is a sin and sacrilege. Despite so many Hindu gods and goddesses, if someone worships Muslim pirs, believes in them, becomes a part of their tazia processions, offers money and flowers on their graves, this would be an act against the Hindu religion.'[38]

Poddar condemned any kind of interaction between Hindu women and Muslim men. Even the innocent bangles made of lac, popular among Hindu women in many provinces, were turned into a Muslim symbol as they were primarily made by Muslim artisans. Hindu nationalist organizations, including Gita Press, called on Hindu women not only to avoid lac bangles, but also not to 'board ekkas (horse carts) driven by Muslims, not to keep Muslim servants, not to invite Muslim prostitutes or singers on joyous occasions, not to buy any household items from Muslim, etc.'.[39] Though ostensibly this was to avoid contact with the 'lustful Muslim other male', there was also probably the motive of cutting off economic patronage to Muslims.

Poddar also gave his argument against lac bangles a 'purity' twist, arguing lac was an animal product and therefore the food cooked by women wearing lac bangles became impure. Further, he said, 'The money paid for bangles goes to Muslims and is occasionally used against our religion. Also, one has to touch Muslim men. Therefore, women should wear swadeshi glass bangles.'[40] The word swadeshi to signify Hindu was used deliberately to label the Muslim 'other' as an alien who would sully the purity of the Hindu woman.

Hindu women were advised not to go alone on pilgrimage; and if they did go, it should be only with their husband's permission. In *Stri Dharma Prashnottari* Savitri explains: 'Through darshan of God and priests' advice, temples were once a source of fulfilment for devotees. But this is no longer so. Pilgrim centres have turned into dens of vice populated by thieves, crooks, immoral and greedy people, and hardly a saint or a mahatma can be found there.'[41] Rather than wasting time on excursions to temples and pilgrimage centres, Savitri reiterates that for a woman there is no God greater than her husband whose feet she should touch and wash every day—the water that washes her husband's feet is as pure as any holy water.

With so much stress on the primacy of the domestic world for women, Sarala asks about their domestic duties. Savitri's list has elements of 'Victorian fetishes of discipline, routine and order'.[42]

Keep the house clean, put things in order.
Spend less than the income; keep a tab on the expenditure.

Have knowledge about how to protect health.
Take care of the children; pass on to them your character and knowledge.
Do all the household work with your own hands.
Know the family's relatives and friends and behave with them as required.
Never feel lazy.
Have knowledge about religion and show enthusiasm in religious activities.
Be munificent.
Serve your husband, suppressing carnal desire in a sweet voice and with love; keep your husband satisfied.
Be content with whatever is given.
Do not encourage buying of luxurious items.
Speak sweetly.
Remain alert and retain purity.
Be affectionate to all relatives and friends of your husband; all your actions should enhance your husband's name, fame, wealth and happiness.[43]

Basing his arguments to a large extent on the *Manusmriti*, Goyandka more or less regurgitated what Poddar had already laid out as a woman's duty in her in-laws' home, but pushed the bar even higher. Goyandka's advice was to avoid six things Manu had prohibited for women: tobacco, hemp leaves (bhang), leaving a place without her husband, roaming around freely, staying with others and sleeping at odd hours. Also, women should not sing obscene songs in groups during the Holi festival or in the presence of men, but it was all right to sing songs celebrating various manifestations of God. Similarly, they were asked to shun obscene literature and read only texts like the Ramayana and Mahabharata.

A married woman was warned not to undertake a fast without her husband's permission as this could have an adverse impact on his life. She was barred from giving charity or going on pilgrimage without her husband's consent: 'Husband is the pilgrim centre, husband is the fast, husband is God and husband is the respected guru.'[44]

Gita Press's criticism of obscene songs had a lot to do with the publishing house's Marwari origin. The practice of Marwari women singing bawdy songs 'at marriages and other festive occasions' had attracted widespread criticism, including in *Chand*'s infamous *Marwari Ank*. Even before the advent of Gita Press, various efforts had been made to end this practice.[45] As we saw, in the very first year of *Kalyan* there was disproportionate emphasis on how the festival of Holi should be observed without resorting to obscenity of any kind.

In Goyandka's view, women became shameless and useless if they did not do the housework themselves.

A woman without culinary skills was warned of humiliation, while one who cooked well earned the respect and love of the family—especially the husband. Four necessary qualities every woman was expected to have before entering the kitchen were good health and no communicable disease, a fair knowledge of cooking simple food, a pure mind and a feeling of love towards everyone who would eat the food. Women of rich households were told not to outsource the job of cooking. Food should be cooked keeping the weather in mind, and a woman should not raise contentious domestic issues while cooking.[46]

Poddar's Savitri also warns a woman to keep away from all kinds of women who would be a bad influence: prostitutes; immoral women; those who criticize their husbands; those with adversarial relationships with their husbands; those who are cunning; those who gamble and steal; those who believe in shamans; those who are always quarrelling; those without shame; those who are arrogant; those who speak bitterly and those who get sexually aroused.[47]

In addition to her earlier list, Savitri enumerates sixty-four more duties of a woman that range from behaviour towards in-laws and relatives to her role in shaping the character of her children.[48] She is expected to teach her daughter to serve her in-laws, especially her husband, and not criticize them before anyone: '. . . do not listen to your daughter's diatribe against her in-laws. Instead, convince her that her welfare lies in the service of in-laws. In case her grievance is genuine, try to resolve it amicably so that the relationship between the two families is not affected.'

The mother also has a major role in educating the male child, the balak. 'With your efforts, the male child can inculcate good habits and become a scholar that would help him serve the nation.' Interestingly, Savitri tells Sarala that in case a son is not born or he dies in childbirth it should be considered divine providence; a woman can seek treatment from a vaidya (traditional healer) but should not take the step of adopting a male child. Savitri assures Sarala that salvation is possible even without giving birth to a male child.

Nari Ank celebrated ideal mothers and the mothers of 'strong heroic sons' throughout world history—from Mary the mother of Jesus, to the mothers of Napoleon, George Washington, Lenin, Mussolini, Hitler, Chiang Kai-shek, and closer home Syama Prasad Mookerjee and Jawaharlal Nehru.

While both Poddar and Goyandka laid great stress on the wife's duty to obey her husband, at one point Goyandka did caution the wife not to follow the orders of her husband in case of an act that would lead him to narak (hell). An order inspired by anger, sexual urge, greed or desire was to be disregarded, as also an order to serve poison to someone, to misbehave with anyone, to commit feticide or cow slaughter.[49]

Kalyan's Nari Ank listed women who had followed the nari dharma throughout their life and reaped the benefits. Ideal wives such as Ramabai Ranade, Kundan Devi Malaviya, Kasturba Gandhi, Maharani Lakshmi Ammani of the Mysore royal family and Sarada Devi, wife of Ramakrishna Paramahamsa were showcased by *Kalyan* as those who had followed the path of religion and devotion to their husbands and never wavered from the path of God.[50]

Nari Ank told the story of Arya Samaj leader Swami Shraddhanand as an example of how a wife's devotion to a wayward husband helped in transforming him. Son of a kotwal (police officer), Munshiram, as Shraddhanand was known before he took sanyas, was addicted to alcohol, gambling and non-vegetarian food, and despite occasional remorse could not bring his life back on track, even after marriage to Shiv Devi. One night he returned home completely drunk and dishevelled after visiting a prostitute. Shiv Devi nursed him like a mother, waiting for him to get back to his senses and eat, before she herself ate anything. When Munshiram apologized and confessed his misdemeanours, Shiv Devi replied that as a wife it was her duty to serve him without fail. The incident changed Munshiram, and he became Swami Shraddhanand.[51]

Even eighty years after *Stri Dharma Prashnottari*, Gita Press, unmindful of the grand social and educational changes that had swept the nation, was still doling out recipes for good behaviour that women should follow to keep their husbands under their control.[52] On offer this time was an extract from the Mahabharata, a conversation between Satyabhama and Draupadi. Visiting the Pandavas during their exile in the forest, Satyabhama was surprised to find the five brothers under the complete control of Draupadi. Draupadi explained that a wife could win over her husband and keep him under control by being dutiful to him and his family, forgetting herself. She reeled out the specific duties she performed for her five husbands, mother-in-law and others in the family, with total devotion and suppressing her own desires and needs.

Unlike the duties of women that have remained cast in stone for Gita Press, some changes have been incorporated in a mother's duties towards her children. While the emphasis on inculcating values of Indian culture, tolerance, contentment, speaking in swadeshi language (i.e., Hindi) has remained unchanged, an interesting addition is the duty of a mother to regulate what her children watch on television. In the view of Gita Press, TV is a medium that causes tension and promotes materialistic culture, so mothers are first advised to control their own habit of watching TV and only let children view programmes that would help in building their character.[53]

Women's Emancipation as a Cause of Moral Decay

Ramnath 'Suman', a leading Hindi writer and a friend of both Poddar and Goyandka, was worried about the fast depleting numbers of India's grihalakshmis (Lakshmis of the household).[54] The author of numerous books on women and domesticity,[55] Suman strongly disputed that education had brought freedom to women. Despite their membership of clubs and societies, and big lectures on citizen's rights and freedom, he said, educated women had become 'more than before instruments of enjoyment for men'.[56] Suman said the 'pilgrim centres of modern civilization' in which women played a central role, like clubs, cinemas, colleges, beauty parlours, exhibitions like craft fairs, flower shows, baby shows and parties, were proof that they were being objectified. In these 'pilgrim centres', well-dressed women were either gazing at men or being gazed upon by them. Suman reduced craft exhibitions to nothing more than a cheap—the entry fee being three annas—opportunity for men to prey on women, even if from a distance. He pointed out that these places were not frequented by women with inner beauty and strength of character.

The premium on physical beauty and fashion in cinema and other facets of the public sphere had a spiralling impact on society, Suman said, that resulted in men seeking only beautiful and fashionable women in marriage, pointing to matrimonial ads in papers as evidence. 'Civilized and independent modern women have created a thirst for beauty among men. Today it is easier for an ill-behaved but beautiful girl to get married than one who is healthy, hard-working and talented but not so beautiful.' He further lamented that self-assertive educated women led to disintegration of homes: 'Grihalakshmis are disappearing and so are grihas (homes).'

Of the various modern 'pilgrim centres' listed by Suman, Poddar detested cinema the most. His quarrel was with the intrinsic nature of movies. Even if the script was good and the film had educative value, there was still the emphasis on physical beauty and the possibility of men and women coming closer. He said as long as men played the roles of women it was fine, but when women started acting problems began. 'Howsoever good the character of a man may be, the constant company of a woman causes lust. Men and women are constructed differently and there is always a desire for physical union, especially when young.'[57] He said modern cinema presented pitfalls at every step: obscene songs, sexual jokes, semi-naked dancing, stories replete with immorality, and the suggestive looks and gestures of actresses. Poddar was worried that cinema had moved away from its early missionary zeal and become a moneymaking enterprise in which businessmen were investing crores of rupees. Even educated women, he said, were getting attracted to act in movies with men and willing to sacrifice their family's honour and prestige.

For Poddar the seeds of decay had been sown in Europe, where, 'A woman can joke and play with anyone, drink with other men, go out with them while her father and husband are not supposed to say anything. This is the sign of civilization. O Indian devis who once considered sati supreme, you have lost sight of your pious goal by gravitating towards the well of doom.'[58]

Using the oft-repeated cliche of female physical weakness that necessitated protection by father, brother, husband or son, Poddar argued that even in Western countries, where women were more independent, they could not venture out like men. This was because women had maternal instincts and had to bear children. Poddar consoled woman for her weakness, saying, 'in her physical dependence she is free in spirit because of her intrinsic qualities of forbearance, selflessness, tolerance and ascetic fervour. Men may work all their life to acquire these qualities but they rarely succeed.'[59]

Kalyan's Nari Ank extracted short pieces from the writings of diverse people, from noted progressive Hindi writer Premchand who admonished his Indian 'sisters for borrowing from Western ideals and reducing themselves to instruments of pleasure'[60] to Adolf Hitler appealing to German women not to get involved with the outside world but confine themselves to becoming good housewives and mothers.[61] An extract from Colonel James Tod and William Crooke's *Annals and Antiquities of Rajasthan* praised the domestic happiness and independence of Rajput women who stayed within the home by choice.[62]

Poddar cited a Labour MP's speech in the British parliament in which he reportedly said 40 per cent of girls under twenty got pregnant before marriage, and among married women the first child was illegitimate in 25 per cent of the cases. If Poddar was to be believed, the Labour MP had said British society had never before witnessed such moral decay.[63] Taking Britain to be representative of the entire Western world, Poddar said that Western family life had been destroyed: 'Women there are no longer the queens of homes. A beautiful and ideal domestic life is beyond their imagination . . . Lure of individual liberty and free love has made them run from one man to the other. They have to sell their love at various places, knock on the doors of several employers for jobs and return home disappointed after finding "No Vacancy" notices. What kind of a freedom and happiness is this? Unfortunately, Indian women are also moving towards this . . .'

As before, Poddar ascribed the blame to the education system that made women literate but failed to provide complete education or elevate their mind. Real education, he argued, prepared a person to carry out his/her duties as sanctioned by dharma. In the present context, Poddar was referring to nari dharma: 'In Europe, women's education has failed. Had they received education naturally suited to their gender it would have done them a world of good. Unnatural education to women has caused immense damage to them.'

Citing rather strange findings from an unknown source, Poddar said 70 per cent of women in America had been found incapable of performing domestic chores and 60 per cent were single and past the age of marriage (not mentioning what that age was). In the absence of marriage, Poddar said, women acted as they felt, led unprincipled lives and indulged in debauchery. 'The population of unmarried women is on the rise. They do not have the pleasure of home. In Europe, at least 50 per cent of educated women remain spinsters. Is this all-round development?'

Another matter for concern, Poddar claimed, was the blurring of gender differences—with women taking to physical exercise in a big way, making them more masculine at the cost of their feminine and maternal selves. On the other hand, he noticed, there was a growing tendency among men to beautify themselves like women. Women—whose bodies and minds needed to be disciplined through an exhaustive set of rules 'to ensure the birthing and nurturing of strong heroic sons for the Hindu community-nation'[64]—were not expected to shy away from their duty by assuming masculine traits. However, Poddar as well as the RSS supported the idea of women not being pacifists in the public sphere.[65] Poddar said that a woman should become Durga to punish anyone who caused harm to her husband or son; the fierce Hindu goddesses Kali and Durga are worshipped as the Mother.[66]

For Gita Press, nothing was more serious or posed a greater threat to the religious sanctity of Hindu marriage than divorce. While the dharmashastras 'liberally permitted the husband to remarry during the lifetime of the first wife', they denied the 'remedy of divorce' to the wife, 'even when completely forsaken by the husband'.[67] Livia Holden makes a compelling argument when she says: 'It seems, in other words, that the indissolubility of marriage is not particularly mobilized to prevent the celebration of subsequent marriages altogether, but rather to prevent the conceptualization of the Hindu divorce on the woman's initiative.'[68]

Gita Press was barely four when the All India Women's Conference (AIWC) was born in Poona in 1927. In the coming years AIWC became the most effective flag bearer of rights for women. In the mid-1930s, AIWC petitioned the government to set up an 'all-India commission to consider the legal disabilities of women'.[69] Put together in a pamphlet—*Legal Disabilities of Indian Women: A Plea for a Commission of Enquiry*—written by Renuka Ray, legal secretary of AIWC, the thrust was on comprehensive legal reforms for women, especially personal and domestic laws. Following this, several new laws were passed, including the Hindu Woman's Right to Divorce Act and the Muslim Women's Right to Divorce Act.

The wave of reforms, even if half-hearted and seldom implemented, was enough to disturb Gita Press. *Kalyan* carried a piece by Ruprani 'Syama', a graduate, who ridiculed the view of divorce as a marker of civilized society.[70] Syama wrote that talking of divorce in India, the land of sati and jauhar, was an insult to its women. Marriage in India was not a contract but a blending of two bodies and souls in which the woman completely merged herself with her husband, became part of him without caring for her own identity. Calling a woman who divorced her husband the daughter of either a demon or an animal, Syama said that, in a Hindu marriage, the woman was not only an object to satisfy her husband's sexual needs but was meant to serve him selflessly, as had been the case since the dawn of civilization. The abala (weak) woman underwent pain, humiliation, oppression, but the joy of becoming a mother was the ultimate reward that outweighed all the suffering. Of course, Syama only talked of giving birth to a balak (male child) when describing the heavenly experience of being called maa (mother). She stressed throughout that the position of a woman in society was of a volunteer (swayamsevika) who did selfless service, not for recognition or money.

Syama contrasted the pious woman with one who sought divorce on the grounds that her husband abused or beat her, or had gone astray. In Europe and America, she said, newspapers were full of reports of divorce because marriage in that part of the world was a contract. 'As long as I get food, clothes and freedom, I belong to you. The day freedom is curtailed there would be no relationship between us. Such self-obsessed, uninhibited women are a blot on the nation and society. They become rolling stones and either commit suicide or regret their acts for the rest of their lives.' Divorce, she wrote, was an immoral act resorted to by women who wanted to move from one man to another. This entailed loss of character or satitva, a heavy price for a little freedom, which exposed the woman to sexual predators and often forced her to seek customers in the marketplace.

She also chided men for seeking divorce on the grounds that their wives were quarrelsome, insensitive or made life hell for them. Her advice that men should become like Lord Rama if they wanted their wives to act like Sita. Syama advised them to treat their wives with sensitivity and win them over to the right track. But this advice to men was brief; it was woman who was the villain in a divorce.

Divorce came in for more criticism by Poddar in the late 1940s when the Nehru government was pursuing the Hindu Code Bill. Unlike the colonial period, when resistance to government's social legislation could be couched in the garb of nationalism, the government of free India had to be opposed differently. Therefore, Poddar's anti-divorce argument that had so far heavily relied on religious texts to show it as an alien practice unknown to the Hindu world was expanded now to include Western views on the evils of divorce. He cited the Pope's concern about rising divorce rates in Europe. One M. McIntosh, a lady, was quoted as saying that the life of a man and a woman depended on two things, marriage and home, but the evil of divorce was destroying both of them. Another individual, a Doctor Denevel, stated that marriage meant responsibility and keeping a little window of divorce open could lead to regular attempts to escape from this responsibility.[71]

Poddar admitted that women, whether wives or widowed sisters, were at the receiving end of male oppression. But he was quick to argue that such cases were rare and the state should not bring in new legislation just because a few individuals/families had lost track of the adarsh (ideal), of respecting and caring for women.

In any case, using a veiled threat, Poddar argued that the divorce law if enacted would be more harmful to women than men. More men would resort to divorce, as moral decline was far greater among men than among women. He called on women to oppose the proposed legislation, regretting that educated Indian women were mistakenly welcoming it as a sign of progress.

Widowhood

In the December 1949 issue of *Kalyan*, Poddar's column '*Kaam Ke Patra*' featured a letter from a widow belonging to an affluent family.[72] All of twenty and mother of a child, her family wanted her to get married again, which she was resisting. She sought Poddar's help, asking him what the shastras said about widow remarriage.

In his reply, Poddar lauded her 'high thoughts', saying that her resistance showed she was born in the tradition of Sita and Savitri, and encouraging her not to succumb to family pressure. Her present state of widowhood, he said, was the result of actions or sins of the previous life and the only way to emerge out of that condition could be through good deeds and worshipping God.

Poddar accused those who were in favour of getting her remarried of indulging in a grave sin to fulfil their own selfish motives. Remarriage was akin to throwing her in hell, he said, citing *Manusmriti*. Poddar described the future of the widow's son in case she got married again: 'When he is grown up, his mother's misdeed would deprive him of all respect.' Poddar's reply was a reinforcement of the larger argument that a Hindu marriage did not end with the death of the husband and the woman had to remain a pativrata nari even after becoming a widow.

Much of Poddar's advice to the young widow in 1949 is contained in his earlier *Stri Dharma Prashnottari*. There, Savitri sings the praises of widows whose supreme sacrifice brings laurels to the Hindu religion. She asks, if they cannot be revered who else should be? She ascribes cases of failure to follow vidhva dharma (duties of widows) to the lack of religious education, ill treatment of widows and in general lustful tendencies among men. Savitri recommends that girls be married to boys not younger than eighteen and men not older than thirty-five, which will bring down the number of widows substantially. And then she spells out the twelve rules that comprise vidhva dharma:[73]

1. A woman should become sati after her husband's death. This is considered illegal today, but dying on her husband's pyre is not the sole way of becoming sati. A widow should consider God as her husband and immerse herself in worship, suppressing her inner desire. This is how one becomes sati.
2. A widow should detach herself from worldly pleasures and study texts like the Gita and Ramayana that inculcate the virtues of gyan (knowledge), vairagya (renunciation) and bhakti (devotion).
3. A widow should not participate in festivities. She should avoid listening to conversations of young girls and married women, discard jewels, stop braiding her hair, eating paan (betel leaf) or using any aromatic product. (As an afterthought, or probably to keep up the pretence of being a reformist, *Stri Dharma Prashnottari* explains why widows should shun festivities—it is not, as popularly believed, that the shadow of a widow is inauspicious, but that a woman has uncontrollable sexual urges that need to be kept in check. 'They are advised not to attend festivities so that the pomp and glitter do not cause deterioration of mind.')
4. To the maximum possible extent, a widow should sleep on the floor, avoid a soft bed, eat food that does not provoke desire and wear hand-spun thick clothes and not colourful garments.
5. Widows should resist eight kinds of sexual union (maithuna). These are: seeing a man; touching a man or woman; enjoying the company of another in a lonely place; talking to others; reading or talking about a man or woman; playing together; thinking about a man or woman; and actual sexual intercourse.
6. A widow should undertake fasts without water or food.
7. A widow must not sit idle, but immerse herself in household work.
8. A widow should attend religious and moral lectures, and completely give up bad company.
9. A widow must remain within the control of rakshaks (protectors) like her mother-in-law, father-in-law, jeth (husband's elder brother), devar (husband's younger brother), father, mother or brother. She should not do anything without the permission of the rakshak.
10. A widow is advised not to talk too much or express anger; to stay happy by remaining helpless; to believe in religion and never let the heart be led astray.

11. A widow must not sit in the company of young women, but always be with elderly women who strictly follow dharma. As regards immoral women, widows should not even glimpse them.
12. If a widow has money, it should be spent on the impoverished, orphans and other widows. If a widow does not have enough money, she should earn to survive and never ask anyone for monetary help.

Goyandka further advised widows to eat a simple vegetarian meal once a day and shun items like ghee, milk, sugar and spices since these enhanced the sexual urge. His argument against widow remarriage was entirely based on Manu's prescription. He argued that a woman could be given away (kanyadan) in marriage only once and she had the right to have her father bear the expense of only one marriage.[74] It is interesting to note how, while citing the dharmashastras, Goyandka did not forget to highlight the subtext against widow remarriage—namely the cost her family would have to incur again, and its consequences for the male inheritance. This position was articulated sharply during the agitation against Nehru's Hindu Code Bill in the early 1950s.

As years passed, more restrictions were added, prohibiting widows from watching movies and dramas, reading 'obscene' literature and looking at 'dirty' pictures.[75] Some earlier prohibitions became more pronounced, like the one on seclusion. Widows were asked either to sleep alone or with other women or children. Since widows were considered more vulnerable than girls or married women, they had to maintain a safe distance from men other than those in the immediate family. Those to be particularly abhorred were mendicants and sadhus, though Poddar did not forget to mention 'alcoholic Muslims who frequent prostitutes'.[76]

In *Stri Dharma Prashnottari*, Poddar was relatively mute on the practice of sati, though he referred to the law banning it. However, in the 1948 *Nari Ank* he celebrated the magic of sati.[77] Poddar's narrative rested on his genuine 'scientific' belief that fire could emanate from a distraught widow's shoulder and heart. Poddar explained that fire existed everywhere including the human body, and could be produced on being rubbed, as in the case of stone or wood. He also gave the instance of high body fever that often resulted in death. Referring to a Parsi journal, Poddar said he had read about ductless glands in the body that played a crucial role in contributing to the physical features and character of a human being. He argued that, just as these glands had an impact on human character, the character also influenced these glands. Drawing from this 'science', Poddar said it was difficult to imagine the impact on the glands of a true sati whose body, mind and heart were pure, who had survived only on the love of her husband, who had not given the same place to any other man, who had led a selfless life and who was incapable of suffering the loss. 'In such a condition of grief for her husband, if some special internal action results in fire, it can hardly be a matter of surprise.'

Taking his scientific argument further, Poddar zeroed in on the thyroid gland whose task he said was to invigorate love and physical desire in human beings. He quoted from the work of one Dr Louis Berman who had said that 'since the presence of thyroxin (secreted by the thyroid) in tissues determines the rate at which they burn themselves, it is obvious that, if there were no mechanism for retarding its action, the tissues would set fire to themselves'. Based on this, Poddar said, if the condition of a woman grieving for her husband reached the extraordinary stage of affecting her thyroid gland, it was possible her body could catch fire. Thus, 'becoming sati is a completely natural phenomenon and not possible through outside influence'.

Mindful of the fact that many women did not commit sati for a variety of reasons, Poddar praised them too, in fact more than those who immolated themselves. He said it was not easy for a woman to observe brahmacharya (celibacy), take care of children selflessly and make her husband in the 'other world' happy.

Celebrating the system of sati and those who had actually committed it, the *Nari Ank* profiled Ramrakhi, wife of Bal Mukund who with three others had thrown a bomb at the viceroy, Lord Hardinge, on 23 December 1912 at Chandni Chowk. All of them were later hanged. *Nari Ank* claimed that Bal Mukund who had been married just a year before the bomb incident had not yet consummated the marriage. It said that when Ramrakhi got to know about the hardship that Bal Mukund was undergoing in jail, she also created jail-like conditions for herself at home. She went on a fast the day Bal Mukund was hanged, and died as a result eighteen days later.[78] *Nari Ank* profiled more than a hundred such satis from myth, folklore and history, including Sati Parvati, Savitri, Anasuya, Sanyogita, Padmini and Lakshmi Bai.

Female Hygine, Health and Sexuality

Gita Press's overemphasis on women's hygiene emanated from the premium the Hindu social system laid on 'purity'. A woman was considered intrinsically 'impure', the ostensible reason being her monthly menstrual cycle. But the subtext was deeper—to stress that women were not equal to men physically and thus counter the growing forces of gender equality. In a tone that smacked of patriarchy, women were told that since they personified the nation as mothers and the producers of great sons, they had to take care of their hygiene and health.

Women's hygiene and health were strangely limited to gynaecological issues, and Gita Press thus not only accentuated the gender distinction but also managed to underscore woman's vulnerability. This was used as a pretext to control her sexuality that, as we have seen, was already declared to be a patriarchal business since women were believed to be incapable of putting a lid on their sexual urges. Goyandka's advice to women to avoid 'father, brother and son' in a lonely place 'since the 'strength of senses can attract even the most intelligent of men'[79] loudly proclaimed where Gita Press stood on women.

As Tanika Sarkar argues, subjecting the 'Hindu woman to community discipline' was an attempt by Hindu revivalists to preserve the 'ritual sphere as the source of authentic meaning and value, the site of difference and uniqueness'. The Hindu woman's body, her sexuality 'became a deeply politicized matter—it alone could signify past freedom and future autonomy'.[80] This was reflected in the patriarchal cultural and social practices that Gita Press advocated.

Goyandka in his *Nari Dharma* claimed that women suffered from special defects of body and character and therefore were unfit to live a life of freedom. These 'defects' were a deadly mix of impurity, anger, obstinacy, lack of intelligence, cunningness, defiance, frivolousness, restlessness, harshness, shallowness and false daredevilry. It seems that

Goyandka would go to any lengths to deprive women of their liberty, even invoking the damage such freedom could cause to the 'nation, jati (other women) and society'.[81]

In the appendix of Poddar's *Stri Dharma Prashnottari,* Sarala asks Savitri for tips about protecting one's health as well as rearing children. Savitri says sharir-raksha (protecting the body) is part of a woman's dharma as she bears sons who may one day be great men. She says most of a woman's ailments emanate from complications related to menstruation that normally starts at the age of twelve or thirteen—once again raising the question of age of consent.

Gita Press waged battle on the right age of marriage for girls till the late 1940s. An article by one Charu Chandra Mitra in *Kalyan* cited passages from accounts as diverse as Havelock Ellis's *Psychology of Sex* and Anton Vitalivich Nemilov's *Biological Tragedy of Women* to debunk the Western practice of not marrying girls before the age of sixteen, twenty or twenty-five and to 'educate the theoretician social reformers'.[82] Mitra extracted a passage from Ellis that is self-explanatory: 'The first ovulation signifies sexual maturity and is the last link in the chain of important processes which began in her infancy. The sexual apparatus is now ready for service for the benefit of the race.'[83]

By reducing a woman's childbearing capacity to a mechanized process carried out by her 'sexual apparatus' from the age of puberty to serve the race, Gita Press was papering over the menarche versus menstruation debate. Mitra's long essay, serialized over the next two issues of *Kalyan,* ignored the fact that, during the period of menarche, it could be dangerous for a girl to give birth. Instead, he justified the 'use' of the 'organ of maternity' (matritva ka ang) from the time a girl began menstruating to serve the Aryan race.

Mitra, an attorney-at-law, had a Western education, but supported conservative practices such as the segregation of women during the menstrual cycle. He quoted Nemilov who argued, 'man, under the domination of the hormones, becomes energetic to the point of audacity, whereas woman, eroticized by the hormones, becomes feeble and passive to a degree of self-abnegation', and 'sexual desire weighs down upon woman whose activity normally does not go beyond coquetry'.[84] Thus, for a man, fulfilling his sexual desire was seen almost as a right, while a woman exercising her sexuality was overstepping the patriarchal line. This acceptance of the 'difference between the bodies and sexual urges of women and men accentuated the power of the husband over the wife, whereby the man could escape with many wrongs but the woman could not'.[85]

Writers like Mitra and publications like *Kalyan* ignored the changing complexion of gender equations. With his carefully chosen citations from Western works, Mitra was only stressing the centrality of the shastras and *Manusmriti* in governing woman's sexuality.

Returning to Savitri's prescription for women's health, there are six primary rules a woman needs to follow during her menstrual cycle: 'Never sleep with your husband; do not do physical labour; do not sleep on the floor in cold places; do not bathe; do not catch a cold; and avoid lifting heavy objects, climbing stairs or getting on and off vehicles.[86]

According to Savitri, physical union during the menstrual period can give rise to 'illness', pain, physical weakness, hysteria and an irregular menstrual cycle that will cause a lot of problems during childbirth. Sexual union during the menstrual cycle is also considered bad for men, resulting in the weakening of eyes, intelligence and strength, and faster ageing.

Catching a cold during the period, says Savitri, will lead to its sudden arrest and that can become a source of many ailments. Therefore, she claims, the visionary chroniclers of the shastras had argued in favour of isolating a menstruating woman: 'Such a provision helped the woman in carrying out her dharma (duty) and protecting her health.'

Sarala then asks about precautions to be taken during pregnancy. Again, a woman must abstain from sex during this period—Savitri says even in normal circumstances the husband and wife should not share a bed, and this should be even more strictly adhered to during pregnancy. The rest of the rules are more in the nature of common sense—a pregnant woman should not lift heavy things, she should not consume tea, coffee or bhang, or any medicine without consulting a vaidya, she should wear light and clean clothes and avoid fighting, shouting or crying. An expecting mother is advised to frequently eat small quantities of nutritional food, drink clean water, maintain cleanliness in the house and bathe at least once every day. For positive energy she should keep photographs of sadhus or brave men before her, avoid anger, greed and arrogance, not listen to immoral stories but instead select sections of scriptures like the Shantiparva of the Mahabharata, the third and the eleventh chapters of the Bhagavadgita, the *Ramcharitmanas* of Tulsidas and important stories from other religious texts.

Savitri assures Sarala that if the rules of pregnancy are followed, a woman can have a child like Prahlad, Dhruv, Narada, Harishchandra, Buddha, Sita or Savitri—this would be beneficial to herself and to the world.[87]

The birth of a male child was not about chromosomes, but the responsibility of the mother. 'An intelligent, talented, brave and religious male child' could be produced only if she followed some additional rules of piety and self-control.[88] These included not piercing the nose or any part of the body; not touching impure things; not conversing with cunning people; not stepping out of the house without tying the hair, covering the body and keeping words under check; not eating food served by a shudra; not sleeping with her head towards the north or west; not sleeping in the evening; and not sleeping next to anyone else. In the morning, a pregnant woman was expected to wear washed clothes and worship the cow, brahmin, Narayan and Lakshmi. The husband was to be venerated separately with sandal paste, garland and food items.

The regimen for a woman desiring a male child kept getting longer and more complex, curious and comical. Citing Charaka, Poddar said that a woman who wished for a healthy and famous son should have a darshan of a white bull every morning after her bath,[89] as the Hindu shastras clearly spelt out that whoever a pregnant woman saw in the morning impacted her mind and a similar child was born. He claimed that a white pregnant woman, whose room had a picture of an African, gave birth to a son who also looked like an African, and in another case, a brahmin woman who had seen a Pathan man in the morning became mother of a son who in life became a 'characterless Pathan'. In order to dissuade women from having sex during pregnancy, Poddar created the disturbing possibility of this leading to a fetus without limbs.

At the time of childbirth, there were more rules to be followed. Apart from emphasizing the cleanliness of the place where the child was to be delivered, Savitri stressed the importance of the personal hygiene of the dai (traditional midwife). Further, it said that since most dais were either Muslim or belonged to the lower chamar caste—two communities outside the realm of twice-born (brahmin, kshatriya and vaishya) and hence despised by caste Hindus—their cleanliness was a major issue; besides, Gita Press was caught in a dilemma of sorts between the traditional system of dais helping in childbirth at home, and the new system of hospitals and nursing homes with doctors and nurses trained in advanced Western methods of child delivery, that was slowly making inroads in cities and small towns.

Significantly, Savitri makes it clear that no distinction be made in rearing a male and a female child. The importance of mother's milk and its nutritional and medicinal values is stressed, and those 'fashionable educated women' who do not breastfeed their children for fear of losing their youth are criticized. Like a doctor, Savitri prescribes feeding at fixed intervals and provides a clear chart of the time and quantity of milk that a child should be fed. She warns against overfeeding or underfeeding a child, and says a mother should avoid feeding when angry, excited or sorrowful.

This positive discourse on mother's milk turns regressive and patriarchal once again when it comes to a new mother's sexual relationship with her husband. Savitri states that early resumption of the sexual relationship has an adverse impact on mother's milk and by extension on the child's health. More to the point, she warns, 'Repeated pregnancy permanently destroys her health.'[90]

Regarding the health of mother and child, Savitri tells Sarala that older women in the family have more knowledge and wisdom than doctors or vaidyas. Further, good health is considered a by-product of a healthy and clean mind that, again, is possible only if one follows a strict regimen of self-control, piety and devotion to God.

Even in the 1940s, by which time modern medicine had taken deep root in India, *Nari Ank* listed four reasons why women fell ill, one of which was their indulging in too much fashion—wearing high-heeled shoes, applying cream, powder and lipstick.[91] However, more plausible reasons were also given—lack of exercise, irregular food habits, leading an extravagant life. Women were told to maintain a healthy lifestyle and work hard; only then was it possible that 'no man would cast an evil eye on them'. Grinding corn in a hand mill was showcased as the epitome of hard work that could prevent ill health. Most of the health issues mentioned in *Nari Ank* related to the menstrual cycle (irregular, excessive bleeding), childbirth and stomach ailments. Women were advised to resort to home remedies, and only consult a vaidya if these did not work, never a modern medical practitioner.

Goyandka specifically warned women to avoid foreign medicines as he claimed they consisted of a mix of garlic, onion, alcohol, meat, animal fat, blood and eggs—all of which 'destroys religion and health'.[92] Western medicine was included in the long list of prohibited foods for women, like biscuits, ice, soda water, lemonade and foreign-made syrups. Also to be avoided were foods that were sour and tasty, including betel leaf and betel nut.

Further, only children of those mothers who were careless and themselves led an undisciplined and thoughtless lives fell sick. *Nari Ank* offered indigenous remedies for twenty-one common ailments among children, ranging from the common cold to stomach ache, with express advice to mothers not to give any other medicines—or administer only small amounts if need be.[93] Even today, Gita Press continues to dole out home remedies for children's ailments, though its resistance to doctors has ebbed somewhat.[94]

However, when it comes to AIDS, Gita Press invokes morality and blames the prevalence of the disease in India to the erosion of 'self-control and traditional values' under the influence of Western culture. *Kalyan* traces the cause of AIDS to 'illegitimate, immoderate sexual relationships', and recommends the study of religious texts, the Ramayana and the Gita, as the best way to curb such desires.[95]

Gita Press's patriarchal stranglehold over a woman's sexuality was not limited to her biological self but also extended to deciding what she should wear.[96] Prescribing a certain style of dress was not just about protecting women's modesty, but was directed against women who were challenging traditional notions of appropriate attire. Gita Press highlighted the 'magical or transformative use' of clothes 'in which the moral and physical being of the wearer/recipient was perceived to be actually changed by the innate qualities of the cloth or the spirit and substance (holy, strengthening, or polluting) it conveyed'.[97]

Ramcharan Mahendra, a writer from the Gita Press stable who penned many monographs, made a distinction between Hindu and Muslim dress.[98] Mahendra's thesis was that dress had a relationship with culture and religion. While this itself was nothing new, Mahendra highlighted the relative superiority of Hindu dress—sari, dhoti and kurta— 'worn by the likes of Lal Bahadur Shastri, Indira Gandhi and Vijaya Lakshmi Pandit even abroad'. Hindu dress was considered the best for its cleanliness, beauty and dignity.

On the other hand, he demonized the culture of the Christians and Muslims: 'Angrezi (Christian) and Islamic religion and culture are based on the concept of pleasure. Obscenity, frivolousness and nudity are prevalent in them. They only stress external beauty. By consuming alcohol and meat, they have forgotten human values and indulge only in pleasure for the senses.' He asked people to wear Angrezi or Muslim dress and experience its influence on their thinking and attitude: 'Just like the military dress gives rise to the feeling of violence, animal instincts, terror, pride and desire to oppress others, the dress of Muslims gives birth to sensual desires, selfishness, exhibitionism and frivolousness.'

Such a moral twist to dressing, howsoever powerful, could not have made much difference had it not been married to the economic factor of threat to Indian textiles from cheap British imports. As Emma Tarlo explains, the nationalist movement wove together 'political, economic, aesthetic and moral arguments under the leadership of Gandhi who tried to encourage all Indians to revert to Indian dress'.[99]

The Gita Press template on women's dress, as on every other issue, was provided by its forty-six-page all-time best-seller *Stri Dharma Prashnottari* and reinforced in *Nari Ank*. Arguments based on morality, religion, politics and economics were blended to dissuade women from wearing Western clothes or using too much jewellery. Any woman breaching this code was considered as challenging the very notion of simplicity, the hallmark of a devout Hindu wife. Such an attitude was termed a 'love for luxury' and included in the inexhaustible list of 'corrupting characteristics of women' (nari ke dushan).[100]

In the Sarala–Savitri dialogue, Savitri says a woman should dress up only for her husband's happiness and not to show-off in public. A woman who moves around shabbily at home but dresses up before venturing out, commits a huge mistake, she says. One, there is a fear of getting robbed. Two, 'jewellery and clothes become a reason for women to start fighting within the family that often creates division among brothers and even father and sons. Such developments sound the death knell of the family.'[101]

When Sarala inquires whether it is wrong if a woman who dresses up at home makes demands on her husband for clothes and jewels, Savitri replies that too much interest in make-up, clothes and jewellery takes a woman on the path of luxury and she starts shunning household work. 'Making constant demands on the husband reduces love between the two. A woman should be attached to her husband. It is also the duty of the husband to provide clothes and jewels to his wife from time to time. If he is stingy, it is his fault, but it is the husband's task, so only he should think about it. A woman's happiness lies in what makes her husband happy. If the husband does not have the economic wherewithal to get new clothes and jewels and his wife harasses him every day, it has an adverse impact on him.'

In tune with the nationalist narrative, Savitri also advises women to discard foreign-made silk clothes. Besides arguing that the use of foreign cloth causes a big loss to the nation's economy, she introduces the old concept of pure versus impure, ethical versus unethical. Foreign or mill-made cloth, Savitri says, consists of animal fat: 'Lakhs of tons of animal fat is used to make such cloth. Similarly, silk is made after killing innumerable worms. Therefore as far as possible you should wear hand-spun (khadi) clothes. They do not consist of fat but help poor brothers and sisters to remain employed . . . animals would not be killed, purity would be retained, lajja (shame or sanctity) would not be lost and dharma would be saved.'[102]

In this demonizing of foreign cloth, 'arguments far removed from Gandhi's' were often made—for example one of Gandhi's associates telling people in Gujarat that cow fat was mixed in the manufacture of foreign cloth, or a leaflet stating that a thousand pounds of coloured Manchester cloth consisted of 300 pounds of cow and pig blood.[103]

On his part, Poddar argued that khadi should be worn both for the sake of Swaraj and of religion: 'I consider khadi to be of help in artha (economy), dharma (religion), kama (sexuality) and moksha (freedom from rebirth).'[104] Even after the attainment of Swaraj, he appealed to people to adopt khadi, as the 'moment it is worn a person forgets all his desires and loses many defects of character'.[105]

Birth Control and Abortion

Even though, by the mid-1930s, Poddar's relationship with Gandhi had started wearing thin on many counts, certain ideas and principles the Mahatma held helped the Gita Press counter threats to its views on women's sexuality. One such threat was the use of contraceptives by women as a means of 'birth control'—a term coined by Margaret Sanger, the American feminist and propagator of the slogan 'every child should be a wanted child'. The use of contraceptives by women was still in its infancy worldwide and was being resisted by conservative elements, and Sanger was tirelessly lobbying for a woman's right to choose when to have a child.

At the end of 1935, Gandhi in a long interview to Sanger had argued that the remedy did not lie in contraception or any other artificial birth-control measure but in women saying 'no to their husbands when they approach them carnally'.[106] Confident that husbands, not all of whom were 'brutes', would understand this resistance from their wives, a method he claimed to have taught to many women, Gandhi upheld another principle—that physical union should take place only to produce children. Otherwise, he told Sanger: 'When both want to satisfy animal passion without having to suffer the consequences of their act it is not love, it is lust . . . When a husband says, "Let us not have children, but let us have relations", what is that but animal passion?'

Sanger's counter that Gandhi's method of self-restraint could result in 'irritations, disputes and thwarted longings' did not convince him. When she gave 'hard cases' of people who had experienced nervous breakdowns as a result of sexual restraint, he responded that these must be 'based on examination of imbeciles'. Gandhi reiterated his sex-only-for-procreation position in *Harijan* in March 1936, while also expressing admiration for Sanger's 'zeal'.[107]

For Poddar, the Gandhi–Sanger debate was a godsend. In his April 1936 article '*Vartaman Shiksha*', Poddar acknowledged that in India having too many children was a cause of misery for parents, but called it divine providence. 'Birth is pre-ordained . . . If someone does not believe in this, then self-restraint is the only solution.'[108] Echoing Gandhi, Poddar said he did not want to be disrespectful to Sanger as her intentions were right, but contraception in the Indian context was both harmful and sinful. He argued the sole purpose of birth-control measures was to satisfy sexual passion, and that could encourage adultery.

Without mentioning the source (a common habit with him), Poddar referred to an article by Gandhi that warned of negative consequences of artificial birth control, many of which were still not apparent. One consequence was the wave of sexual liberty among school- and college-going females, as restricting the use of contraceptives to married women was impossible. Besides, with the availability of contraceptives, marriage had lost its sanctity and become merely a means to satisfy the sexual urge.

Even as late as 1969, *Kalyan* used a relevant portion from Gandhi's *Navjivan* article of 1925 to make its point against contraception. Gandhi had appealed to doctors, saying that that they would do a great service to mankind if they stopped prescribing artificial methods of birth control. 'Encouraging artificial methods is like encouraging evil. It makes men and women frivolous. Artificial methods would result in impotence and decline in sperm count. This remedy would prove to be worse than the disease.'[109]

Gandhi's stance on birth control through abstention was integral to his view of marriage as an institution that, as he told C.F. Andrews, 'is a status lower than that of celibacy'.[110] Writing to Andrews way back in 1920, Gandhi had said, 'Take it from me that there is no happiness in marriage.'[111] Sex between husband and wife was abhorrent for him: 'I cannot imagine a thing as ugly as the intercourse of man and woman. That it leads to the birth of children is due to God's inscrutable way'[112] and '. . . the occasion of marriage should remind us of self-restraint. If desires cannot be conquered, they should be harnessed.'[113]

Vinoba Bhave, one of Gandhi's closest disciples, lent his support to Gita Press's campaign against family planning that for him represented the defeat of 'spiritual and moral values'.[114] Disputing the theory of population becoming a burden, Bhave warned that birth control would negatively impact not only the birth of children but also intelligence: 'The creative energy we call sperm has given birth to the great poet Valmiki and fearless Hanuman. People are now misusing that creative energy. Husband and wife are making such an arrangement (using birth control) so that they can have sex but not produce children. If they continue like this, the nation will lose power.' Bhave's one-point solution was to return to a life divided into four ashrams—brahmacharya, garhasthya, vanaprastha and sanyas—in which the garhasthya (householder) phase was to last from the age of twenty-five to forty-five, the right age for having children.

Charu Chandra Mitra's 1948 serialized article '*Nari*' included a scathing attack on the practice of birth control and its impact on women's freedom. For him, the freedom that birth control promised was harmful to women and the nation, and would have a direct and adverse impact on marriage since the age-old concept of marriage as 'the sole way to contain the sexual urge' would no longer hold. Marriage and domesticity—the pleasure of bearing and rearing children—would be the biggest casualty of this freedom, he contended. Men and women who practised birth control, he predicted, would lead a lonely old age.[115]

Gita Press's opposition to artificial birth-control measures continued into the late 1960s. *Kalyan* now turned to K.C. Mishra, a medical practitioner who articulated a medico-religious argument. With over three decades of practice, as he claimed, Mishra regretted the adoption of Western methods, 'that was akin to people in the plains wearing winter clothing required in Kashmir'.[116] Mishra said birth-control measures being used in the cold countries of Europe could not be used in a warm country like India. Listing their side effects, Mishra said that even Dr Robert B.M.C. Clure, who had worked on family planning in China for twenty-four years, in the Arab world for four years and in India for twelve years, had found problems with contraceptives. Clure had said that 'until public health education made sterilization acceptable, there would be no good contraceptive available in rural areas', and that 'unnatural methods all have serious side effects on the nervous system besides leading to digestive trouble, etc.'. Mishra's invocation to Indian youth was not to go in for sterilization as it would in the long term weaken the nation. 'If youth lose their power to produce, the nation would face a shortage of soldiers.'

The subtext of Gita Press's sustained, often shrill, campaign with religious and moral overtones was not so much resistance to modern methods of birth control as it was another reflection of an Islamophobic mindset.[117] Population was an important ingredient in the communal competition, the bogey of the Muslim population rising at an unimaginably greater pace than that of the Hindus being one of the many used by Hindu nationalist groups.[118]

Right from its inception, through the intense communal polarization during the 1940s and 1960s, Gita Press made repeated use of common Hindu nationalist phrases such as 'Muslim violence against Hindus', 'Muslim rape of Hindu women', 'Muslim pillaging of Hindu property', 'Muslim virility' and 'increasing Muslim population' to drive home the story of victimhood of the Hindus at the hands of invader Muslims.

Already, Gita Press had carried Hitler's appeal to German women to confine themselves to the roles of wives and mothers. Drawing from Hitler's Germany was not an innocuous act, but Gita Press's affirmation of its regard for the fascist ruler. In fact, when it comes to the 'women question', there is a great deal of similarity between Nazi Germany, Gita Press and other Hindu nationalist organizations like the RSS, Hindu Mahasabha and others; in particular, the 'hysterical protective anxiety about numbers' vis-à-vis the Muslims shown by Gita Press and the entire Hindu right owes a lot to Hitler.[119]

Much of Gita Press's concern about the declining Hindu population emanated from successive census reports that created the fear of Muslims racing past the Hindus, at least in the politically and socially volatile United Provinces. The census report in 1911 gave official credence to the Hindu nationalist narrative by making statements like 'Musalmans are more fertile than Hindus',[120] and in 1921, 'prohibition of remarriage of widows does not affect Muhammadans' and 'both relatively and absolutely Hindus have lost'.[121] Further, between 1911 and 1921, 'Hindus decreased by 347 persons per 1,000'. Such reports only fuelled fears based on the belief that 'the social and political influence of a population is in direct proportion to its size'.[122]

The hysteria of 'saffron demography', a term coined by Particia and

Roger Jeffery, was echoed by Poddar himself in reply to a *Kalyan* reader who wanted his views on family planning. Poddar severely criticized the government for its family planning programme. Repeating the moral and physical problems caused by the government initiative, he said the biggest threat was to 'the future of the Hindu jati'.[123]

Poddar was angry that the government's family planning was gaining ground only among Hindus, while Muslims had termed it 'anti-religious' and kept away from it. Muslims, he said, were allowed to keep more than one wife and, therefore, their population was rising at a greater pace while that of the Hindus was declining and was likely to dip further: 'If the situation continues like this, the number of Muslims would be the same as the Hindus or may even surpass them. The adverse impact of such a scenario can be gauged from the formation of one Pakistan. Even the Christian population is rising. Every law-abiding citizen should pay heed to this, especially the Hindus.'

Poddar batted for self-restraint as the best form of birth control. It seems the reader had expressed concern about the shortage of food due to rising population; Poddar dismissed such a fear and told him to leave the task of feeding everyone to God.

A Discursive Space for Women

Late nineteenth-century United Provinces saw the birth of Hindi journals for women. The earliest was the short-lived *Bal Bodhini*, probably the first in the country, started by the maverick Bharatendu Harishchandra of Banaras in 1874. But its attempt to raise 'consciousness about emerging democratic ideas and nationalism'[124] came to a premature end with the demise of the owner at a young age.

Gita Press was still far from being born when two women from the Nehru clan of Allahabad, Rameshwari Nehru and Roop Kumari Nehru, came out with the radical *Stri Darpan* in 1909. Unmatched in its 'gravity and depth',[125] there was a great deal of synergy between *Stri Darpan*'s advocacy of women's rights and the equal importance it laid on their traditional duties or dharma. What marked out *Stri Darpan* was its clarity of purpose and firm belief that the fate of women lay in their own hands 'because husbands, brothers and fathers cannot promote the welfare of the country while treating women like animals'.[126] The journal had a mix of male and female contributors who wrote on a range of issues: domestic, national and international. From the purdah system, health and hygiene, to international events, women's education and women's movements in other states of India, and news of the national movement, *Stri Darpan* had an enviable range of coverage.

The same year saw the birth of another journal, again in Allahabad, a few kilometres away from *Stri Darpan*. The wife–husband team of Gopaldevi and Sudarsanacharya brought out *Grihalaksmi* (literally, Goddess Lakshmi of the home). The journal began with an impressive circulation of 4,000 and, as the name suggests, represented all that *Stri Darpan* vocally opposed. *Grihalaksmi*'s conservatism and 'practical, lower middle class orientation' was a counter to the elitist *Stri Darpan*, as it talked of 'moral education for girls and stressed their role as wives and mothers' and how it was important for them to learn to sacrifice their aspirations and desires at the altar of family.[127]

Critical of men who, instead of treating their wives as companions in dharma (sahadharminis), looked on them as lovers (pranayini), *Grihalaksmi* saw companionship in marriage as not only a marker of equality but something that had the sanction of the scriptures. The disparate worlds of *Grihalaksmi* and *Stri Darpan* often clashed as each published rebuttal and rejoinders to the other's views.[128]

Chand, the most iconic of Hindi women's journals, was also born in Allahabad. In 1922, more than a decade after *Stri Darpan* and *Grihalaksmi*, the discursive sphere of the United Provinces had undergone a great transformation. As Francesca Orsini points out, a 'kind of rapprochement was taking place between women's journals and general magazines', as a result of which issues related to women were finding a place in 'mainstream journals'.[129] While this change was about the recognition of women as a new class of readers, it also reinforced through dedicated columns that they were a separate category. *Chand*, as Orsini argues, demolished the trend of women's journals carrying articles that were 'stri-upyogi' (useful for women). Instead, she says, *Chand* brought women and issues related to them to the centre of the nationalist movement.

Chand, which means the moon, was started by Ramrakh Singh

Sahgal, who was originally from Lahore. Ramkrishna Mukund Laghate was the co-editor and Ramrakh's daughter, Vidyavati Sahgal, the office manager. Eclectic and diverse in its contents, *Chand* became the front-line journal of its time, with a circulation that at its peak reached 15,000. The idea of special issues—*Achhut Ank, Kayastha Ank, Marwari Ank, Vidushi Ank*—was another dimension of *Chand*'s innovative editorial policy. Within a few years, the journal was recommended for school and public libraries in many states.

Chand's biggest achievement was the manner in which it supported and strongly advocated women's access to the public sphere through the concept of seva dharma (the duty to serve). This 'redefined' and 'legitimized' a woman who was active in the public sphere, 'bestowing moral capital' on her. The journal caught the imagination of women, educated and uneducated alike, by urging them to join its mission if they wanted to 'save the millions of women drowning in an ocean of ignorance', 'if the heart-rending cries of thirty-five million Indian widows affect you somehow' and if they wished 'to destroy the evil custom of child-marriage and dowry'.

With the change in editorship of *Chand* (Sahgal had to resign in the face of strong state action and precarious financial position), the radical spirit and mission of the journal lost its direction. Under Mahadevi Varma, who had written some of her earliest pieces for *Chand* and had done the unthinkable in those days by opting out of her marriage, the journal became a women's magazine. It also became more middle class in its orientation by 'accepting class and caste distinctions and gender limitations'.

These and other women's journals became educated and uneducated women's windows to the world.[130] They not only 'redefined gender roles within the domestic sphere, they also tackled women's new role as members of a nation-to-be' and 'responsible female citizens'.[131] Despite the fact that it was men who financed most of these journals, they contested and produced a counter to what 'male reformers had long deemed appropriate for women'.[132]

The celebration of colonial education for women by these journals was a major challenge to Gita Press's mission of creating a world where women were confined to the inner spaces, holding the reins of domesticity and morality, while men were the masters outside.

For Gita Press, religious, social and cultural matters concerning women were important—these were addressed through *Kalyan*, a journal edited by men. A majority of the articles too were written by men, and reminded women about their duties towards family and nation, which could be accomplished only through strict adherence to scriptures and codes. The fact that *Kalyan* could be read by both men and women in the family made its journey into Hindu households easier. *Kalyan* carried the promise of bhakti (worship), gyan (knowledge) and vairagya (renunciation) to all its readers, irrespective of gender.

What also worked to *Kalyan*'s advantage was Gita Press's attempt to remain apolitical, at least in its first decade. There would be an occasional article critical of the government or the Congress, but the journal ensured it did not run foul of the colonial government as its contemporaries *Chand* and *Hindu Panch* had. It was only in the 1940s that *Kalyan*'s open advocacy of violence was noticed and acted upon by the government. The initial period of non-confrontation, coupled with the wide Marwari network eager to distribute *Kalyan* across India, gave the journal an advantage that none of the women's journals had. In a few years' time, *Kalyan* had built an enviable and unheard-of circulation running into a few lakhs.

Gita Press was wise enough not to let men do all the talking. *Kalyan* opened its pages to women writers, even those who had been to Western-style schools and universities. But these women were role models, adarsh nari (ideal women) who were so well grounded in the Hindu ethos that the 'polluting' influence of colonial education could not permeate their souls. These were women who, despite modern education, argued in favour of women confining themselves to the private sphere. Their writings in *Kalyan* did not 'reflect women's real worlds and their real experiences'.[133]

As *Kalyan* did not welcome voices of dissent, the two leading women writers in Hindi of that period—Subhadra Kumari Chauhan and Mahadevi Varma—do not find place in the journal, either as role models or as contributors. Chauhan, a few years senior to Varma at Crosthwaite Girls School, Allahabad, was her close friend. A woman of the public sphere, Chauhan did not let her conservative background act as a barrier to her being a satyagrahi during the nationalist movement and a writer demanding equality for women.[134]

Varma was a rebel in both private and public spheres. Married at the insistence of her grandfather at the age of nine, she refused to join her husband after completing her graduation. The years at her parents' home were spent in getting educated and dabbling in literary pursuits. Varma made her mark as a poet and writer in *Chand*, and went on to become one of the big four of the chhayavad movement in Hindi poetry. Breaking away from marriage and remaining single for life made Varma a pariah for Gita Press. Her lifelong work for women's education through the Prayag Mahila Vidyapith, where she introduced innovations like 'private study followed by formal certification',[135] challenged the core of the moral order that Gita Press was seeking to establish.

Of the hundreds of women who contributed to *Kalyan*—within the limitations imposed by Gita Press—just three stand out for their achievements outside the home. However, in writing for *Kalyan*, they too confined themselves to subjects and views that did not challenge the journal's prescribed patriarchal norms for women.

R.S. Subbalakshmi, or Sister Subbalakshmi as she was called, came from an educated family of Madras. Born in 1886 to an engineer father and a housewife mother, she was married at eleven, after little over four years of schooling. Early widowhood brought her back to her parents in Tanjore district. Father Subramania Iyer, instead of following the prescribed rules for widows, chose to educate his daughter. In order to escape the violent reaction his decision created in Tanjore, a seat of brahmin conservatism, the family moved to Madras city. After a mix of home and convent school education, Subbalakshmi did her matriculation and joined Presidency College, drawing the further wrath of conservatives. She was 'threatened with excommunication, harassed in the streets and ostracized in the classroom'.[136]

After her graduation, Subbalakshmi opened a school for widows at her parents' home. With the support of Miss Christina Lynch, inspectress of female education in Coimbatore, Subbalakshmi shifted the school to Triplicane in Madras, where it was run from a former ice house, drawing scorn from the conservative locals. Later, she became the principal of Lady Willingdon Training College and Practice School that trained women as elementary, high school and secondary school teachers, maintaining a balance between teaching in English and moral and religious training. She then opened Sarada Vidyalaya, a boarding school for adult widows. However, this school was run in an orthodox fashion, a contrast with her own life as a widow.

Decorated with the Padma Shri in 1958, Subbalakshmi wrote for *Kalyan* in the 1930s. But we do not find a single article by her related to the pioneering work she did in women's (particularly widows') education. The four articles she penned for *Kalyan* were on the topics of oneness of God, Shiva, Krishna and spiritual power. This choice of subjects by Gita Press was clearly deliberate, ignoring her identity as an educationist.

Vijaya Lakshmi Pandit was all that Gita Press would not want to see in a Hindu woman. A sister of Jawaharlal Nehru, educated at home by English tutors and then abroad, Vijaya Lakshmi entered public life in the 1930s. In 1937, she was elected to the provincial assembly of the United Provinces and became a minister. She had married Ranjit Sitaram Pandit, a barrister and nationalist, of her own volition and was Western in her outlook. A successful diplomat, Vijaya Lakshmi served as India's ambassador to various nations. The high watermark of her career was her election as the first woman president of the UN General Assembly in 1953.

Poddar would have never considered Vijaya Lakshmi Pandit as a contributor. But in the mid-1960s, her article '*Aaj Ka Bharat*' (Today's India) in *Navbharat Times,* a Hindi daily, came to his notice. *Kalyan* reproduced it in full with an editorial comment lauding her for the definition of modernity she had provided.[137] Poddar appealed to readers to learn from her article not to confuse everything contemporary with modernity.

Pandit wrote of her varied experiences abroad and how she had not succumbed to the Western lifestyle. In 1954, when she had delivered a lecture to a group of women in Japan, one young woman had asked her: 'You are wearing the traditional Indian dress. How can you be modern?'

When a question arose as to how to greet Queen Elizabeth of England and other members of the royal family, Pandit said that while many 'modern' Indian women resorted to Western methods she stuck to the Hindu system of namaskar and found that many in the gathering followed suit. Further, when the wife of a diplomat got an audience with the Pope and the question of how she should greet him arose, the Vatican authorities told her to do a namaskar.

Wherever Pandit lived, the food in her house, she said, was served even to foreign guests in the Indian thali. Also, she preferred to eat with her hands rather than use fork and knife. She spoke of the mad rush in India to become modern, often reflected in dress, especially of women, and expressed concern that this could lead to the demise of the sari and salwar-kameez.

Pandit was particularly irked that Indians, instead of understanding what had made the Britishers successful in India, merely imitated their manners. The worst reflection of this mindset, she said, could be seen in the way many Indians were discarding their mother tongue in favour of English. She recalled that, despite the importance given to English language and literature in her home, the children were always encouraged to speak with each other and family members in Hindi or Urdu. Pandit wrote: 'In order to imitate Western manners and customs symbolically, we have abandoned solid values of sanatan . . . What we have embraced in their place does look like part of the new world but I am confident it is not suitable for us.'

Far removed from the world of Subbalakshmi and Pandit was Raihana Tyabji, whose Radha–Krishna relationship with Poddar has been dealt with earlier. Her life deserves a full book, but here I confine myself to her writings in *Kalyan*. She was, of course, best known as author of *The Heart of a Gopi* published in 1936, an eternal classic that was translated into many European languages and widely quoted in varied fora, from 'academic studies of Hinduism and websites on spirituality to a blog on God and even the official George Harrison messageboard'.[138]

Of the nine pieces she wrote for *Kalyan*, at least four were directly about Krishna, written in a highly evocative, conversational style. In contrast to Raihana's numerous letters to Poddar, that often talked of her innermost feelings, her articles drew a 'metaphorical veil' over her personal experiences, yet are 'valid accounts' of these.

Coming from a family where women had been at the forefront of breaking the barriers of patriarchy, Raihana not only participated in the national struggle but supported the Sarda Act of 1929. This reformist streak in Raihana as well as her single status are possible reasons why Poddar did not commission her to write on women's issues either in *Nari Ank* or any other issue of *Kalyan.*

The restriction of its discursive sphere to women writers of a certain kind—firm followers and practitioners of the male-created code—kept *Kalyan* in the good books of its readers, many of whom looked to it for moral and spiritual succour as long as Poddar was alive. It was this conservatism that would attract women readers of *Kalyan*, struggling to come to terms with the changes in society, to share their angst with Poddar either through private correspondence or through the pages of *Kalyan.* Poddar took their faith in him very seriously.

Take the case of Anasuya Devi who wrote to Poddar of her terrible experience. She told him that in certain cities innocent and unsuspecting women were being picked up and taken to army camps by female agents. Once in the camp, she wrote, the women were made to sleep with jawans—each woman was expected to have sex with twenty-four jawans for fifteen minutes each. According to Anasuya, the women were paid Rs 10 per jawan, and in the morning they would be sent back. The women agents who procured these helpless women were paid Rs 100. Anasuya wrote that she could not believe that the Indian government would stoop to this level of moral decay, and was also at a loss to comprehend how soldiers, entrusted with the task of defending the nation, could indulge in such an activity. She said at this rate India would become Pakistan, and requested Poddar to intervene.[139]

Anasuya's threat to commit suicide may have propelled Poddar to write to the then defence minister Swaran Singh: 'Her tearful appeal to me to save her sisters from this fearful and hateful situation has led me to approach a man of high character and strict discipline like you for doing the needful in the matter which demands immediate and strong attention.'[140]

Poddar reminded the defence minister of the 'proud reputation of the Indian army, which never indulged in the molestation of women even of conquered territories'. He demanded an inquiry into Anasuya's allegations and, if found true, an immediate end to the practice with 'iron hands'. Swaran Singh's reply, if any, is not among the Poddar Papers, but what is established is the public perception of Gita Press as defender of the virtue of Hindu women.

Education of the Male child

The moral universe of Gita Press had women at its core, while men and children, the male child to be specific, inhabited the concentric sphere around. Women with their knowledge of the religious texts were supposed to foster the right atmosphere in the home and keep their men from getting carried away by Western influences so that they remained loyal to Hindu values and morals. An abiding concern of Gita Press was that colonial education had led Hindu men to forget their religion and that the strength of the community was weakening as a result.

Gita Press considered the entire nation as a classroom, and its journal *Kalyan* and hundreds of other publications as the means of pedagogy.[141] The exercise of training and educating the Hindu male child was undertaken in parallel to the colonial education that he was getting in school, that allowed for 'no possibility of the inclusion of the indigenous knowledge and cultural forms.'[142]

Even more fearsome for Gita Press than colonial education, was the influence that social reformers—imbued with Western ideals—wielded over the masses. While the reformist agenda was to 'use the liberal philosophy of the West' in their nationalist project, the revivalist aim was to use India's ancient history, its heritage, its religious texts and heroes to 'culturally train the masses in their own tradition' to take on the colonial rulers.[143]

While Gita Press took upon itself the task of educating the masses, its primary focus was the Hindu male child. This education was to begin even before the child went to school, his first step into the outer world. If women were contributors to the nation's 'present', children—specifically male children—were crucial to its 'future'. Maybe it was concern for the future of the newly born India that was behind the decision to bring out a special issue of *Kalyan* on the male child (*Balak Ank*) within three years of India becoming a republic, while *Nari Ank* had come out a year after Independence.

By 1953, the year of *Balak Ank*, there was a growing realization among Hindu nationalists that Nehruvian India and its new temples—dams and heavy industry—did not correspond to their vision of a Hindu nation. *Kalyan*'s special issue had a bit of everything to make the male child an ideal Hindu citizen: lessons in morality, politics, religion; emphasis on physical education, religious texts, family values; examples from the lives of leaders like Tilak, Gandhi, Malaviya, Sri Aurobindo, Chittaranjan Das, Subhas Chandra Bose, Napoleon, George Washington, Henry David Thoreau, Bharatendu Harishchandra, Birbal, Ishwar Chandra Vidyasagar and many more.

Hindu Mahasabha leader N.C. Chatterjee wrote about the uncertain and gloomy future of the Hindus, and by implication of India, if the policy of secularism was followed.[144] Chatterjee's article was a rabble-rousing appeal to youth to embrace Hindutva. He said Hindutva had not rejected the importance of secularism and worldly things, but if the nation had to make the right kind of progress the necessary energy would come only from the Hindu dharma.

Chatterjee's anger was directed at the helplessness of the Nehru government to get Hindus in Pakistani jails released. He said when he raised the matter in the Lok Sabha, the minister in charge of minority affairs only said that he had written to the Pakistan government. 'At this Gwalior MP Narayan Bhaskar Khare protested, but all that Nehru and his cabinet colleagues could do was to look the other way,' Chatterjee wrote. He asked the 'coward rulers who hide behind the notion of secularism' to protect the interests of the Hindu minorities in Kashmir and East Pakistan.

Chatterjee said India's future did not lie in communism, Marxism or Gandhism but only in following the principles of selfless service enshrined in the Gita. He appealed to Hindus not to step back as the bugle call for change had been made and the time had come to fight the unholy forces.

RSS leader Madhav Sadashiv Golwalkar in a highly complex article explained what it takes to be free from the cycle of rebirth. Asking parents to take up the job of bringing up a child seriously, Golwalkar said an education system that gave importance only to information and learning by rote could not inculcate moral values in a child. Educational institutions, he said, saw themselves as nothing more than factories producing useless servants without any moral values.[145]

Arguing that creation of a morally superior male child depended on a host of factors ranging from values inherited from parents to the social context he inhabits, Golwalkar gave an instance of how inherited values could be subsumed or corrupted by social influences. Golwalkar said, while attending the funeral procession of Sardar Patel, he found that even as leaders like Jawaharlal Nehru and others looked sombre and walked slowly, a section of the crowd was shouting as if in celebration. On inquiry, he was told that the appearance of a film actor in funeral procession had caused excitement among the people, causing them to forget the solemnity of the occasion. Education, Golwalkar said, should strive to build respect for truly great men.

In a short message, N.B. Khare said, as future citizens, male children were the real asset of the nation. Children should be made aware of the consequences of indiscipline and impoliteness that were themselves a result of spouting the slogan of secularism all the time, the existence of cinema halls and lack of religious education in schools.[146]

Regardless of what Chatterjee, Golwalkar and Khare expected from Hindu youth, the task of cultivating Hindu morality among them had many impediments. Gita Press considered the impact of obscene literature, journals and cinema to be the most damaging of these.

Through three separate articles, the *Balak Ank* mapped the moral danger posed by the printed word and moving pictures. Stories, novels and drama, it was said, were full of obscenities and it appeared that highlighting lust and immorality in literature had become an art form. The article severely criticized the dictum of 'art for art's sake' and argued that such art spelt doom for society.[147] Obscene literature worked differently for a young male child and an adult; at a young age the tendency was to learn and imitate: 'Therefore, if obscenity is dished out to them they will learn it immediately and get habituated to it.' The perils of such imitation were already evident in the manner in which loyalty to husband (pativrata) was termed as slavery and in the rude behaviour of boys and girls towards their teachers. The article asked how it was possible to maintain high moral standards if obscene literature continued to corrupt young minds.

More than literature, cheap and easily accessible newspapers and journals had become potent vehicles of obscenity, arousing sexual tendencies among young male children. The *Kalyan* article accused them of regularly publishing semi-naked photographs of women along with obscene poems and stories, and questioned their motive in pushing the nation and society into the well of darkness.[148] It said once a boy got used to such writings he wanted to read them repeatedly and even secretly. 'He imbibes bad habits like being disrespectful to elders and teachers, and teases women. Repeated reading of obscene journals arouses him, forcing him to masturbate and that leaves him with sperm-related problems.' Besides, such moral decay caused boys to become irreverent towards India's ancient heritage, history, its customs, saints and heroes. The article made a plea for parental control over the reading material that was accessible to their male children.

Gita Press's critique of literature and journals paled before what it had to say about cinema and film journals, considered the worst vehicle of moral decay among youth. *Balak Ank* claimed there was near unanimity among scholars and learned politicians like C. Rajagopalachari, K.M. Munshi and others that cinema was polluting the minds and bodies of the younger generation.[149]

Cinema was accused of spawning a craze for fashion among boys and girls, from *Awaara* and *Barsaat* bush-shirts to saris named after successful female actors like Madhubala, Nargis and Suraiya. There were other ways in which cinema was influencing the new generation, the article said. As models for consumer products, actors were omnipresent in everyday life, staring out from soap wrappers, hair oil bottles and even medicines. Their influence had extended to college elections where the support of some actor was needed to ensure victory.

Gita Press, that had worked consciously to popularize Hindu iconography, could not fathom the way film actors had eclipsed gods and sages as icons among the youth. Requesting the government to exercise control on cinema, Gita Press also demanded a ban on film magazines as they made children aspire to a life of glamour and luxury. *Balak Ank* pointed to the growing trend among boys and girls to run away from home to try their luck in Bombay films. Thereafter, lack of work often forced the girls to become prostitutes, while the boys returned home after spending all their money. Readers were requested to discontinue subscriptions to film magazines to exert pressure on their publishers to dilute the content that had destroyed etiquette, modesty and morality among people.

Another article recommended that rather than entertainment, films should become a tool of education for children, as the combination of visuals and sound could help them grasp complex issues easily: 'Educating the male child can be a comprehensive experiment. It can emphasize many subjects like literature, religion, geography, history, science and commerce . . . Indian economy is not so robust as to allow making of big-budget educational films. Therefore, we need small-budget documentaries that can be taken to the remotest of villages.'[150]

In his editorial comment, Poddar agreed it would be impossible to ban cinema completely. However, he suggested widespread reforms to make cinema socially relevant: 'First and foremost, female actors should be thrown out completely. They are the root cause of all evil. Second, films should not consist of anything that perverts the mind. There will be hungama (noisy protest) at first, but then people will get used to the changes. In any case, entertainment value will still be there in films sans the immoral stuff. The Censor Board can also usher in some changes.'[151]

Whenever possible, Poddar and people close to him kept a keen eye on movies and their contents. In 1957, Vishnu Hari Dalmia, the eldest child of Jaidayal Dalmia, wrote to then information and broadcasting minister, complaining against film producers who 'frequently distort mythological stories, on which many of their productions are based', as a result of which 'instead of educating the masses in the virtues which our mythology is intended to convey and which draw their inspiration from our ancient literature and culture, they tend to give rise in the minds of the common man disrespect for our religion and our gods'.[152] These were Vishnu Hari's pre-VHP days, but his communal tone and tenor were very much in place. He told the I&B minister that it was 'tragic that our Hindu society should tolerate a violation of such fundamentals by film producers'. He reminded the minister that 'in no other community would this be allowed' and gave instances (without getting into specifics) of Muslims and Christians taking exception to movies that had incorrectly shown aspects of their religions. He called for 'early and suitable provisions in the regulations governing the functioning of the Film Censor Board' for attention to be paid to mythological films.

Within a few months, Dalmia had a specific complaint about a film's distortion of Hindu mythology. The movie was *Rama–Hanuman Yudh* that showed Rama and Hanuman battling each other, whereas in the Ramayana, Hanuman is an acolyte of Rama. When an outraged Dalmia complained to the Censor Board, the Board replied that reference to such a battle existed in *Sudarshan Samhita*. Dalmia then referred the matter to Chimmanlal Gosvami.[153] Within three days, Dalmia was informed by another source that Valmiki's *Uttar Ramayana* indeed talked of such a battle; still, he wanted to be sure and asked Gosvami to check further.[154]

In the mid-1960s it was Poddar's turn to be aggrieved with what he saw on Doordarshan, the state-owned television network. He was upset that immediately after the telecast of the film *Bal Ramayana*, a foreign film called *Bull Fighting* had been shown. In this film a bull was violently incapacitated by a sword and other weapons before being tied to a horse carriage, dragged and killed. The movie, Poddar told I&B minister Satyanarayan Sinha, showed the flesh of the bull being cut and eaten. Claiming that *Bull Fighting* had caused grievous injury to Hindu sensibilities, Poddar requested Sinha to ensure such movies were never telecast in the land of 'Rama, Krishna and Mahatma Gandhi'.[155]

To the triad of literature, journals and cinema, Gita Press added beauty products and the obsession to look beautiful as another factor destroying Indian youth, male and female alike. An article in *Balak Ank* exhibited a deep-seated bias against refugees from Punjab, especially girls and women, who were mocked for paying more attention to their outer beauty and less to the soul.[156] To make the point, a story was narrated, full of gaping holes, when a few girls living in post-Partition refugee camps were said to have complained to a government official about beauty products being in short supply. The article continued, 'Even today there are enough instances of such addiction (to products like powder, perfume, cream and lipstick) especially among families that have been uprooted from Punjab. Economically their life is very tough. They regularly face shortage of food and clothes, but still spend a major chunk of their income on beauty products.'

The use of beauty products, the article continued, was not only a drain on a family's finances but also destroyed character and health. However, at the base of this criticism was insecurity about women crossing the threshold of patriarchal control, which led to an argument of the type common among male and female guardians of morality even today: 'These women decorate themselves like butterflies and roam in the market without covering their head and with naked arms and half-naked body. Then they complain of men leering and teasing them. What else can be the motive behind becoming an object of exhibition?'

Repeating the old argument that women should dress up only for their husbands, the same article made another offensive statement: 'I remember that in our childhood there was a notion that a woman who wears make-up and gaudy saris and shamelessly mixes with men has to be a prostitute. But the manner in which girls of respectable families come out in public today—even prostitutes did not behave like that 25–30 years ago.'

Balak Ank maintained that it was the lack of good children's literature in the country that had resulted in the growth and popularity of obscene literature and film journals. Banarsi Das Chaturvedi, a leading figure of the Hindi world and its internecine politics, asked why a country like India, where 9,000 children were born every day, could not find ten to twenty writers who could study the children's literature of the world and present the best of this to Indian children.[157] Though an upholder of Indian cultural values, Chaturvedi was not averse to borrowing good children's literature from all over the world. He also criticized the government for not setting up any commission to study the needs of primary education in the country. Quoting English writer and poet G.K. Chesterton, Chaturvedi said that one of the key requirements of children's literature was that the stories should lend themselves to illustration. He suggested that stories around Hindu pilgrimage centres could easily be converted into illustrated stories for children.

Aggrieved with pedagogy in general and the quality of textbooks in particular, Gita Press attempted to push *Balak Ank* as some sort of extra reading for school children. Madhya Pradesh under Ravi Shankar Shukla, a known Congress conservative, was among the first to sanction the purchase of copies of *Balak Ank* as prizes for competitions and in school libraries in the state.[158]

Poddar claimed some following in Patiala and East Punjab States Union (PEPSU) that existed between 1948 and 1956. Here too, the government approved purchase of *Balak Ank* for school libraries.[159] The governments of Saurashtra and Vindhya Pradesh—both created in 1948—followed suit.[160]

In the mid-1930s, when Gita Press had started the Gita Society, Poddar had pushed for inclusion of the Gita in school curricula and also proposed publishing school textbooks. This evoked immediate response. From faraway Kunjah (in Gujrat district of present-day Pakistan's Punjab province), the headmaster of Shri Krishna High and Middle School for Boys and Girls wrote to Poddar asking for a list of titles that he could order. He had met Poddar a year earlier in Rishikesh where the proposal had been discussed. The headmaster asked for Poddar's help in 'making a suitable selection of books for the boys and girls of high, middle and primary schools in the Punjab, where the standard in Hindi is the lowest'.[161] From Assam, the president of Assam Sanskrit Board wrote to inform Poddar that the Gita or at least some chapters of it were already being taught at various levels.[162]

Soon there were others knocking on the doors of Gita Press seeking its expertise on textbooks for children. Set up in 1929, the Birla Education Trust (BET), based in Pilani, was run by Lt Commander (retired) Sukhdeo Pandey under the direct supervision of G.D. Birla and ran a clutch of schools in Rajasthan. In 1957, Pandey wrote to Poddar praising Gita Press for its religious and moral texts for children. Pandey said that religious and moral education was non-existent in Hindu households, and even though rituals were performed at home, very few understood their true meaning. Visiting temples, he said, had been reduced to offering flowers without knowing the purpose behind the ritual. He told Poddar: 'I think it is important that religious and moral education be imparted in schools. But there is a shortage of such books which can be read and understood by children.'[163]

Pandey said he had expressed similar concern to teachers of BET-run schools and they had prepared manuscripts of textbooks on religion and morals up to class X. Pandey inquired if Poddar would be interested in publishing these books, complete with illustrations, and if it would be possible to pay the authors.

Poddar, who was at the time in his native Ratangarh, agreed in principle and told Pandey that he would put the proposal before Gita

Press's publications committee. He made it clear that, since Gita Press books were priced very low, royalties could not be promised to the authors, but instead they could be given one-time payment.[164] Pandey agreed with the proposal of one-time payment and sent Poddar the manuscripts of textbooks for classes III to X.[165] By February 1958, Poddar had seen most of the manuscripts and told Pandey he was hopeful that the Gita Press publications committee would give them the go-ahead.[166]

The same month, the publications committee scrutinized the manuscripts and gave in-principle approval. Poddar put forward a few conditions to Pandey: Gita Press should have the freedom to change the language and make additions to the manuscript in case any special instance or incident was missing; Pandey should seek the approval of the authors in case changes were carried out; and three, Gita Press should have the freedom to publish more editions of the books.[167] Pandey agreed to all the conditions,[168] but the books were only published at the end of 1959. Gita Press continues to publish textbooks on religion and morals for school children.

Gita Press's pocket-sized Ramayana as well as the separate publication of each of its chapters became popular educational tools. In 1970, in celebration of Tulsi Jayanti, the Allahabad district education authority decided to distribute the pocket-sized Sundarkand of the Ramayana to 3.5 lakh school children throughout the district. Then district education inspector Kedar Nath Singh wrote requesting Poddar to fulfil the order at the earliest.[169]

If the *Balak Ank* presented Gita Press's vision for the nation's future, *Kalyan*'s *Shiksha Ank*, published thirty-five years later, was a compendium of accounts of successive governments' failure to blend moral teaching with Western pedagogy—especially the failure to dismantle the structure of education created through Macaulay's minutes of 1835.[170]

Shiksha Ank looked at an entire gamut of issues from ancient to the contemporary times. The idea was to establish the superiority of an ancient education system while presenting a severe critique of modern state policy. It was argued that the word shiksha emanates from the Vedic concept 'to give', unlike the English word 'education' which means rule-based learning for a specific purpose.[171] Macaulay's dispatch of 1835 was dismissed as a product of ignorance, as it was unaware of the Indian discourse on education, be it the dialogue between Nachiketa (son of sage Gautama) and Yamraj, or what the *Chhandogya Upanishad* says about the relationship between the teacher and the taught.

The purpose of education—to create an ideal Hindu male child—was clearly delineated through a poem by Ramchandra Shastri Vidyalankar.[172] The gist of the poem was that to serve one's parents, teachers and nation was the primary dharma of any child. A child must not be cunning or foxlike; should have faith in religion, God and truth; and must respect time and fellow citizens. He should be hard-working, courageous and fearless, charming, knowledgeable, skilled, cultured and should learn art, science, philosophy and policy, to grasp the essence of knowledge. He was advised to shun fashion, music and dance and not be a spendthrift; and further stay away from playing taash (cards), chaupar (a board game) and shatranj (chess). Educated children were asked to teach others, help the downtrodden and learn new ways to serve society. The cow should be protected, as should the interests of the twice-born castes and the nation.

The special number on education highlighted the note of dissent that Hindu nationalist leader Mahant Digvijaynath had raised in opposition to the National Education Policy of 1968. An important leader of the Hindu Mahasabha, he was an independent member of parliament from Gorakhpur and had objected to the broad outlines of the policy in 1967. He said the basic problem with the policy was that its core was still based on Macaulay's minutes on education of 2 February 1835.[173] Macaulay's aim had been to create a class of interpreters between the British imperialist rulers and the ruled. This class, Macaulay had said, should be Indian in flesh and blood but British in its interests, thinking, morality and intelligence.

Digvijaynath had lamented that Macaulay's mindset still continued to dominate policy formulation more than a century later. He was particularly upset that instead of creating a national identity, the new policy stressed India's diversity—this was nothing more than a clear rejection of the majoritarian politics of the Hindu nationalists. 'There is no big country in the world without minority groups. But a country's identity is not altered by minorities. Therefore, it is not true that India is a country of many religions and languages,' Digvijaynath said.

Opposed to the idea of giving English the status of associate national language, Nath had wanted pride of place for Sanskrit and a massive programme for translation of school and college textbooks into Indian languages. The final policy did talk of promotion of Sanskrit, but did not match the aspirations of the sadhu-politician from Uttar Pradesh.

Shiksha Ank carried in full Prime Minister Rajiv Gandhi's speech on the New Education Policy of 1986 to the National Development Council, along with an article criticizing it.[174] Dubbing the New Education Policy the 10+2+3 scheme, the writer Vedram Sharma maintained that it was an old and incomplete scheme, first proposed by Calcutta University in 1919. He argued that the system of uniform school education for ten years did not make any distinction between urban and rural contexts, and between boys and girls. The common syllabus, he said, failed on the touchstone of the 'unity in diversity' principle, as it disregarded distinctions of gender and culture and ignored the relationship between education and culture.

Making a plea for a different education system for rural students, Sharma said the essence of the nation resided in its villages and historically it had been proven that if urban India, while sustaining itself on the people and culture of rural India, did not give them anything in return, the country suffered. Therefore, he favoured a parallel education system specific to the needs and aspirations of people living in villages. It had to be a three-layered scheme with basic primary schools, rural middle schools and rural universities.

Sharma's arguments would have found enough backers among liberal educationists, but it began to falter as his intentions became apparent. His problem with a gender-neutral education system was based on the belief that girls needed a different syllabus that would prepare them for a life that was clearly different from boys. He even cited the Radhakrishnan Commission report of 1950 that while advocating equality in education for both sexes, also insisted on 'practical laboratory experience for them [girls] in the care of a home and family'.

The special issues of *Kalyan* on education and the male child were supplemented by scores of monographs on how to build moral character through a disciplined life, devotion to God and obedience to elders. Narrating heroic tales of mythic and historical personalities, Gita Press emphasized that an ideal 'Hindu nation' could be built only through the adoption of their values. While investment for the future was made in the Hindu male child, the adult male was also expected to follow the codes to maintain his hold over the community and to ensure that the movement for revivalism did not falter.

As usual Poddar made no bones about his contempt for the colonial education system, stating in a 1928 tract: 'An education that enhances the number of clerks, an education that makes you dependent on others, an education that looks down upon farming, shopkeeping, manual labour and considers them to be the work of the uneducated, an education that only teaches how to use the pen and makes a person arrogant and lazy can never be a source of happiness.'[175]

In his famous 1936 essay '*Vartaman Shiksha*', portions of which were carried in *Nari Ank* and after his death in *Shiksha Ank*, Poddar dwelt on the ideal education for the Hindu male child. According to him, Indian education would be successful as long as it was based on the Aryan system of the four stages (ashrams) of life. Education should result in physical, mental, material and moral growth in this world and salvation after death. 'Good education is one that liberates us from darkness,' he said, quoting an unnamed sage.[176]

The essay expands on the social ills caused by colonial education which, Poddar warned, was turning a whole generation of college-going youth into atheists and agnostics. He said questions and comments like 'God is an imagination of mankind', 'To talk of God is a waste of time', 'Who has seen God?' or 'Religion is a farce' had become common among youth. This lack of faith in God, he said, would encourage youth to act out of free will and result in erratic behaviour.

Poddar also blamed colonial education for making youth impatient, impolite and insensitive to social/religious norms as well as to family values. In his inimitable style, full of illustrations from his experience, the *Kalyan* editor gave various instances of rude and abusive behaviour by young men in the presence of women and the elderly. He claimed that the intermingling of youth from different caste, class and religious backgrounds had created a new lifestyle of eating and drinking from the same plate and even sharing the same morsel of food. He specially referred to the popularity of soda water and likened the manner in which a single bottle was shared among friends to a mother's breast being shared by all the children. Poddar could not hide his specific apprehension of Muslims sharing food and drinks with their Hindu friends.

Poddar criticized the lifestyle in student hostels. While their parents struggled to send them money, students spent lavishly. As Poddar described it, they often had multiple pairs of shoes, wasted time singing and dancing, went out with girls and maintained intimate relationships with them, gambled, drank tea before taking a bath, wore perfume, watched movies and read obscene novels. He classified these habits as the biggest contributors to the erosion of patience, politeness and sensitivity among the youth.

The absence of chastity among students was blamed on inadequate textbooks, fashion, reading of gandey (dirty) plays and novels, popularization of obscene literature, luxurious and decadent lifestyles, co-education, spending time with inexperienced young teachers, schools and hostels modelled on Western lines and the practice of writing obscene letters to each other. Poddar claimed, without substantiation, that sexually transmitted diseases were prevalent among nearly 50 per cent of students.

Poddar lamented that students had become disrespectful to their parents and teachers: 'The Aryan system of touching the feet of elders is no longer there. Instead, educated youth consider it below their dignity to even acknowledge their parents. There is very little respect for the mother and father. To disregard and treat them as inferior is considered a sign of progress.'

Poddar discredited Western education by questioning the end product itself—namely the quality of students who had completed university education. His contention was that such education had imbued students with a false sense of superiority to the extent that they considered doing any manual or household work below their dignity. Poddar doubted if the job market would be able to accommodate the thousands of university graduates each year, and raised the spectre of large-scale unemployment among educated youth.

Poddar offered a way out, advocating the production of indigenous textbooks as a counter to the Western-oriented books used in schools. Strategically, this was a clever move, but it derived from the very system he reviled, 'built on bureaucratic control through textbooks and centralized examinations', and suffered from the same problem of bias as the textbooks of the colonial education system did. Like the colonial educationists, Poddar also aimed at a makeover of people's minds. What followed was a plethora of cheap texts by Gita Press, full of moral, social and religious lessons. Most of them proved successful and have gone through several reprints.

An article in *Balak Ank* had also raised serious questions about the authenticity of a centralized examination system, and cited rising unemployment among graduates and diploma holders as proof of its failure.[177] Again it harked back to the traditional gurukul (residential school, usually in the teacher's home) system of education where teaching was considered a form of devotion to Saraswati, the goddess of learning, and a student was evaluated continuously.

Lamenting the abandonment of the ancient system, the article demanded higher salaries for teachers and a greater consciousness in society towards education. Tests/examinations should be held without prior notice, and due importance be given to evaluation of debates and discussions in the class so that students could be judged on the basis of their arguments, ability to think on their own and presence of mind. As for the written examination, Gita Press was in favour of objective-type questions with overwhelming emphasis on general knowledge.

As for the textbooks and monographs published by Gita Press, Poddar had clear opinions on what they should contain. The ideal textbook, he stated, should contain truthful depictions of India's ancient Aryan culture and examples from the lives of great men of the era that could be used for value education.[178] Poddar wanted textbooks to carry extracts from Hindu religious texts, especially the Gita. He argued for religious education to be taught as an independent subject, but not confined to religious texts. The idea was to 'cultivate Hindu morality' through this subject, and the textbook was expected to contain a grand sweep of issues, ranging from the inculcation of belief in gods, devotion to parents, and values of truth, love, celibacy and fearlessness. The textbook, he said, should also help children not to nurse ill will towards others; to treat women as their mothers or sisters; not to criticize others; not to look down upon religious leaders of other faiths; not to resort to illegitimate methods at the workplace; and to value physical strength and earning through hard work. Poddar wanted schools to teach crafts to students so that after passing out they would not consider it beneath their dignity to take up jobs that entailed working with their hands. Strangely, Poddar also made a plea that textbooks should be shorn of material that encouraged communal tension—a principle that he himself would disregard by the 1940s in the pages of *Kalyan*.

The task of evolving a pedagogy for the Hindu male child was a gargantuan job. Unlike the education of the girl child, confined to the teaching of religious texts at home, a boy's education had to be all-encompassing. After all, a Hindu male child had to become a model citizen equally versed in the ways of the outside world as in the cultural, social and moral foundation of the inner one.

Way back in 1935, Poddar had written to one 'Chaturvediji Maharaj', who seems to have been Banarsi Das Chaturvedi, the leading light of the Hindi movement, about Gita Press's plans to bring out a five-volume graded Hindi Reader.[179] Poddar said the press management had long been asking him to write the volumes, but he had been too busy to do so. He was hopeful that Chaturvedi would undertake the task and that the Hindi Reader would be accepted in private schools and schools run by Indian states. (He was not hopeful of getting them introduced in schools run by the colonial government, as he feared tough competition from other publishers who, he said, indulged in corrupt means.)

Poddar wanted the Hindi Reader to talk of dharma (religion), ishwarbhakti (devotion to God) and sadachar (good behaviour). He told Chaturvedi that the text should be such that boys did not easily become anti-religion, anti-God or anti-parent. 'Instead of *ga* of the Hindi alphabet denoting gadha (donkey) and *kha* denoting khargosh (rabbit), children should memorize *ga* for Ganesh. The reader should be respectful to the Hindu way of life and illustrations should convey that children after getting up in the morning pray to God, touch the feet of parents, etc.'

Though Chaturvedi agreed to write the book, Poddar offered to write a few chapters and wanted his name to appear as a co-author after Chaturvedi's, as including his name would help sales in the schools of Rajputana, Punjab and Sindh: 'I have been asked by people there to write a book and I have made the promise.' Alternatively, there should be no author mentioned.

Coming to the price of the Hindi Reader, Poddar requested Chaturvedi to be considerate since the book was meant for free dissemination. Poddar said a one-time payment for the author would be possible, and in case the education department accepted the book, the one-time sum could be enhanced.

The Hindi Reader in five volumes titled *Hindi Bal Pothi* was published without the name of Chaturvedi or Poddar. The first year of publication is not mentioned in any of the volumes. However, according to the 2011 edition of Volume I, 32.1 million copies had so far been printed, including the 50,000 copies printed that year. More than twenty million copies each of the other volumes have been printed.[180]

Among the surfeit of Gita Press literature for the male child, much of it repetitive, *Balak Ke Acharan* (Behaviour of a Male Child, hereafter referred to as *BKA*) has become a classic of sorts.[181] The thirty-two-page booklet priced at Rs 4 had gone through thirty-seven reprints till 2010 and sold more than 700,000 copies. With its emphasis on character building, it includes lessons for young children on saving the nation, dharma (both religion and duty) and jati (both religion and caste), and doles out sermons on the primacy of money, physical strength and intelligence, and ways to improve memory power—all in the form of rhymed verse.

BKA presents Poddar's attempt to promote a sense of national pride and honour in the child. But this project, as its contents strongly suggest, is exclusive in nature. As Veronique Benei puts it: 'This entails building an exclusively Hindu raj whence the members of the Muslim as well as other non-Hindu—as well as "improperly Hindu"—communities would be excluded.'[182] In fact, *BKA* and most other Gita Press monographs contributed to what Benei calls the 'daily production of banal nationalism, the experience of nationalism being so integral to people's lives that it goes unnoticed most of the time'.

'Desh Ki Laaj' (Nation's Honour), the very first poem in *BKA* tells the male child that the nation he was born in is where Rama and Krishna were born as incarnation of gods, where sages like Valmiki and Vyasa composed the Ramayana and Mahabharata.[183] The poem spans the millennia, presenting a mix of mythological and historical righteous Hindus such as Yudhishthira and Harishchandra, Maharana Pratap and Shivaji. The inclusion of Guru Gobind Singh but omission of Guru Nanak seems to be deliberate, emanating from the Gita Press practice of treating the Sikh religion as an offshoot of Hindu dharma and highlighting India's heroic masculine past. Among the nationalists, Tilak, the karamveer (one who performs his duty nobly) and Malaviya, the nishthavan (devout) get precedence over Gandhi, the apostle of non-violence.

The Hindu women considered worth showcasing in *BKA* are Savitri and Anasuya, the two ideal Hindu wives considered the pillars of female morality. Tulsidas and bhakti poet Surdas barely make it to the list, and the poem completely ignores the Buddhist/Jain heritage, not to speak of the centuries of Muslim influence.

Securing the nation's honour hinges on two things: following the path of dharma and retaining the purity of jati. *BKA* makes it clear that only those who follow the well-ordained path of religion can gain immortality and respect. Dharma, *BKA* tells the male child, is not only about religion per se, but high moral behaviour and living a righteous life. Dharma, therefore, is the secret of happiness, peace, fame and beneficence: 'Only where dharma exists, compassion resides; where dharma dominates, truth also rules; if there is dharma, there is forgiveness; where there is dharma there is renunciation and dharma brings the ultimate joy.'[184]

While exhorting the balak to protect the Hindu jati, Poddar stresses that the rules of jati should not be subverted, condemned or broken at any cost. The sanctity of jati should be preserved through leading a disciplined and controlled life, not belittling others or spreading hatred against them.[185]

The rest of *BKA* is about honing various aspects of the male child's character, teaching him not to borrow without permission, to admit mistakes and seek forgiveness, to renounce worldly pleasures including of the senses, to imbibe celibacy, to lead a simple life by learning to forgive and to help the needy.

As a Marwari enterprise, Gita Press never lost sight of the concept of profit as a tool to make people turn to God, religion, scriptures and leading a pure life. The bania model of bhakti created by Gita Press promised quick and sure-shot returns if a person maintained devotion, simplicity and humility. *BKA*, through an instructive poem, made an early attempt to acquaint the male child with various manifestations of wealth; why only a few are born with it and the manner in which it should be handled for it to remain with a person forever. '*Dhan Ka Upyog*' (Right Use of Wealth) was addressed to children born in wealthy families. They were told the wealth they possessed was the result of their good deeds in previous lives. But it should not be wasted in building a kothi (palatial house), buying a car, keeping a retinue of domestic help, leading a luxurious life and lording over others. '*Dhan Ka Upyog*' advised children not to get so overwhelmed with wealth as to discard simplicity, self-control and good behaviour. It argued that wealth would be short-lived if a person became lazy, arrogant and miserly.

In a certain sense, *BKA* spelt out the contours of education that Gita Press wanted the male child to get. But it was not a textbook and at best could only become a supplementary reader. Hooked to the idea of textbooks, Gita Press came up with the five-volume *Bal Pothi* (Book for Children) a set of textbooks full of moral lessons. A statement at the beginning of the Volume II of the *Hindi Bal Pothi* tells us that these texts were prepared in collaboration with experts in modern education, and an appeal was made to the education departments of the provinces to adopt the books as school textbooks.[186] Till 2011, this volume has sold 1,943,000 copies and gone into sixty-three reprints.

The five volumes of *Bal Pothi* constitute a primer aimed at the male child, again doling out moral lessons on ideal behaviour at school and home, and with elders, teachers and guests. Interspersed with character-building stories and tales are lessons on how a motor car works and how vapour forms while cooking. Though there is an acknowledgement of India being home to many religions, the entire gamut of lessons on history and morality is drawn from the Hindu past.

From 1988 to 2012, the Gita Press discourse on education did not undergo any change despite changes in the education system and the promulgation of the Right to Education Act in 2010. In October 2012, *Kalyana-Kalpataru* brought out a special *Shiksha Number* that aimed to 'bring out some of the forgotten areas of human development which might be helpful in reducing the prevailing darkness in educational field'.[187] The darkness that *Kalyana-Kalpataru* talked of was (as before) brought by 'modern education'. 'Our English education has destroyed everything and left nothing in its place. Our boys have lost their politeness and humility. To talk nicely has become degrading. To be reverential to one's elders is degrading. Irreverence has become the sign of liberty. Violence has become so rampant that classmates go to the extent of murdering another class fellow . . .' For *Kalyana-Kalpataru* the solution lay in the 'educational methodology used in ancient India for developing a young *brahmachari* to tackle the dimensions of life which is yet to unfold before him'.

The *Shiksha Number* also carried extracts from Poddar's much-published essay '*Vartaman Shiksha*' of 1936. In 2012, the primary aim of educating girls remained unchanged: 'developing their qualities of chastity and motherliness, and their capacity as an ideal mistress of the home'.[188]

Kalyana-Kalpataru editor Keshoram Aggarwal echoed Poddar's world view when he talked of turning to the 'saints and seers who are the architects of this great land for light and guidance for reorienting the present education in India'.[189]

In order to put into practice its vision of education, Gita Press runs a Vedic School in Churu, Rajasthan. The school is based on the gurukul system of learning and only admits children belonging to brahmin, kshatriya and vaishya castes.[190] An all-male school, it teaches the Vedas, Sanskrit, Hindi, English and modern secular subjects. Students are charged a modest fee.[191]

Through its publications, Gita Press pointed out flaws in the colonial education system in the hope that independent India would adhere to the Hindu nationalist template of politics, society and education. With the adoption of a secular Constitution, their dream of a Hindu India did not materialize, and Gita Press continued with its bitter criticism of government policies that in its view turned a blind eye to the aspirations of the majority and imposed education systems that have turned generations of male and female children into non-believers who have no value for Hindu identity. The relentless attempts by Gita Press to popularize the ancient system of education evidently failed to have the desired effect, though its monographs for children and the *Balak Ank* itself went through numerous editions and became best-sellers. Though some Gita Press writers (including Poddar) did raise some valid points—like rise in materialism and Western influence in day-to-day life—on certain issues, these were obscured by the mass of regressive and illogical arguments that dominated their publications. Still, Gita Press has not given up hope. Its numerous moral tracts continue to attract readers in schools and homes, and its journals and books carry its ideology across India and overseas, propagating the dream of a time when Hindu and India will become synonymous.

Epilogue

Though Gita Press and *Kalyan* now lack the towering presence of Poddar, attempts are still made to influence readers of the journal at the time of elections. What has also not changed is the oblique nature of appeal that does not overtly favour any particular party yet gets its message across to nearly 200,000 subscribers and their families.

In April 2014 as the process of the sixteenth Lok Sabha elections got under way, *Kalyan* editor Radheshyam Khemka wrote a piece titled '*Vote Kisko Dein*' (Whom to Vote For).[1] Khemka began with the statement, laced with excerpts from religious texts, that an unjust ruler can squander away the empire inherited from his forefathers in the same way as wind blows away clouds. So, Khemka said, every alert citizen should vote for a leader who was immersed in the service of religion and had the potential to cleanse the system of corruption. He asked readers to extract the following promises from their chosen leaders: to pass a Central law banning cow slaughter; to make cheap food, clothing, education and medical care easily available, and to put an end to the rising demonic spirit as well as growing insecurity in society. He also wanted *Kalyan* readers to seek assurance from leaders that they would not indulge in financial corruption for personal benefit or to help their party.

Without the heft Poddar brought to the publishing house with his networking skills, *Kalyan* no longer attracts the bouquet of contributors who brought the journal substance, subscriptions and success. Though the format has changed, the journal still relies on the writings of Poddar and Goyandka, recycling their old published articles. But *Kalyan* seems to have lost its position as spokesperson of the conservative section of the Hindus. The regular features that made it the foremost voice on religious issues as reflected in society and politics have been replaced by an occasional outburst. What has not changed, however, is Gita Press's missionary zeal, its supremacist belief in sanatan Hindu dharma and steadfast resolve to achieve that goal. The template remains unchanged; so does the highly complex Sanskritized Hindi of *Kalyan* and its other publications, though Khemka says an attempt is being made to make the language less daunting.

Khemka personifies the continuing orthodox tradition of Gita Press. He has been associated with the press from his childhood, first as a reader and later as a key member of the staff. His father Sita Ram Khemka was an important leader in the cow-protection movement after Independence who worked closely with Poddar, Swami Karpatri Maharaj and M.S. Golwalkar. Despite the odds, Khemka is convinced that the route to the country's salvation and arrest of its continuing moral decay lie in the tenets of sanatan Hindu dharma—something his organization has propagated for over eight decades.[2]

The continuity is remarkable in two other respects. As in the Poddar era, Gita Press through *Kalyan* regularly comments on important contemporary political events and forcefully intervenes on issues of religious conflict. Gita Press has also retained an undiluted stance on the sanctity of the cow, the place of women being in the home, and the fear of Muslims one day outnumbering Hindus in India. Its moral universe has remained impervious to the larger changes in Hindu society.

It is interesting to consider two issues that *Kalyan* took up in the years following Poddar, both related to Lord Rama. First, the matter of Ram Janmabhoomi, which had remained unresolved for years after Poddar was no more. In 1989–90, VHP laid the foundations of a Rama temple on a property adjacent to the site under dispute. On 6 December 1992, VHP and its allies, including BJP, organized a huge rally of kar sevaks (volunteers) at the site, with disastrous consequences. The mob of kar sevaks swarmed into the disputed site and demolished the Babri Masjid within the space of few hours, all under the watchful eyes of BJP stalwarts L.K. Advani, Murli Manohar Joshi and Uma Bharati and a galaxy of top functionaries of the RSS, VHP and Bajrang

Dal. What followed was a chain of incidents of rioting and communal violence on an alarming scale.

Kalyan took a bizarre position on the event. Poddar had been dead for more than two decades now, but the culture of ambiguity that he had fostered was on full display. (An interesting aside is the then prime minister P.V. Narsimha Rao's decision to issue a postal stamp in memory of Poddar earlier in 1992.) Two months after the demolition, editor Radheshyam Khemka began by calling the events in Ayodhya a 'mistake' and played down the spiral of communal violence throughout the country: 'I see no relevance of the political frenzy that is being created after the events in Ayodhya and subsequent violence. As long as the Hindus and the Muslims have to stay together, they will have to respect each other. There is no option but to bring the situation to normal.'[3]

After a long appeal for peace that was general in nature, Khemka came to the demolition. 'The fact is a temple cannot be demolished to build a mosque and a mosque cannot be demolished to erect a temple. Both are against Indian culture. Ram Janmabhoomi is not a mandir–masjid issue. A temple can be built anywhere but a janmabhoomi cannot be changed and much less the birthplace of the avatar of Vishnu. This janmabhoomi is a magnificent memorial for crores of citizen and is among the holiest of places.'

Next, Khemka played the oft-repeated Hindus-as-victim card. He said temples in Kashmir, some of them ancient, had been demolished in the last few years, and after the demolition of Babri Masjid, Hindu temples had met the same fate in Pakistan, Bangladesh and Britain. 'But unlike the sensitivity being shown for the demolition of this structure in Ayodhya built by Babur, no sensitivity was shown for the destruction of these temples. According to some people, the structure in Ayodhya was not a mosque since no prayer had taken place there for 400 years. It also did not have minarets and a well for ablutions before prayers. It was just a structure that for the past fifty years was being used as a temple.'

Khemka reserved his best for the end, concluding that what had been demolished in Ayodhya was not a mosque but a temple: 'Till this clarity dawns on the political class, India will be a lost nation. Hindus and Muslims have to live together in India. The country belongs to both of them. If one of the two says India is not their homeland and they will not respect it, that community needs help.'

Months before the demolition, *Kalyan* had put out what it claimed was evidence from the shastras and Puranas about the birthplace of Lord Rama being the spot where the Babri Masjid stood.[4] Khemka's discussion of the problem took note of the communal tension that was building up due to the continuous agitation of the BJP, led by L.K. Advani, the RSS, VHP and numerous Hindu right-wing organizations. *Kalyan* was not in favour of abandoning or brushing under the carpet an issue as important as Lord Rama's birthplace in the name of secularism. The journal said it would be ironic if a place of worship where no namaz had been offered for half a century but from where only the Ramdhun (recitation of the name of Rama) reverberated were to be called a mosque. 'No honest Muslim would favour ruffling Hindu sentiments and aggravating the problem further. He would choose to settle the dispute.' Politicians were told that a solution could be easy if they saw the problem from a larger perspective and not for their narrow political ends.

When a Delhi-based newspaper raised the question of the purity–impurity of the site, saying, 'If the spot inside the Babri Masjid where the idol of Ramlalla is kept is the exact spot where he was born, then it cannot be a place of worship because in any childbirth, blood is spilt, which renders the place unfit for worship,' *Kalyan* reacted sharply, stating that the human mind was limited and such limitations often resulted in illogical behaviour.[5] Khemka liberally quoted from the Gita, Ramayana and other religious texts to argue that the birth of a god—whether Rama or Krishna—did not involve the usual labour pains or spilling of blood.

Even earlier, in 1990, as the Ram Janmabhoomi movement was gathering steam, *Kalyan* had lauded the efforts of India's first home minister Sardar Vallabhbhai Patel who had begun the project of protecting Indian culture by announcing the reconstruction of the Somnath Temple in Dwarka, Gujarat.[6] After Patel's death, Khemka said, Indian politicians had not paid attention to such matters as they were too busy looking after their political interests. Khemka's refrain was that Ram Janmabhoomi should not be viewed as a political issue but purely as a spiritual matter and one of national pride. Repeating the argument that a site of birth could not be shifted, Khemka said that Hindus and Muslims could live as brothers only if there was mutual regard and willingness to sacrifice. He suggested that the Babri Masjid be respectfully shifted from its present site and rebuilt elsewhere. This would facilitate the revival of Ram Janmabhoomi as a place of worship of Lord Rama.

In 2007 *Kalyan* took up cudgels against the United Progressive Alliance (UPA) government's Sethusamudram project. Officially called the Sethusamudram Shipping Channel Project, it proposed the 'dredging of a ship channel across the Palk Straits between India and Sri Lanka'.[7] This would allow ships sailing between the east and west coasts of India, providing a shorter passage through India's territorial waters, instead of having to circumnavigate Sri Lanka, saving up to 424 nautical miles (780 km) or thirty hours in sailing time. Though the seeds of this project had been sown during the BJP-led National Democratic Alliance (NDA) government's rule between 1999 and 2004, when the Sethusamudram project was revived by the UPA in 2007, the conservative Hindu set—BJP, RSS, VHP, Bajrang Dal and a whole host of militant Hindu organizations—sensed an opportunity to turn it into an emotive issue.

Completely disregarding archaeological or scientific evidence, the conservatives claimed the Sethusamudram project would result in the destruction of the Ram Setu—the bridge that, according to the Ramayana, Rama built at Rameshwaram with the help of Sugriva's large army of monkeys, including Hanuman, to reach Sri Lanka and rescue Sita from Ravana.

Kalyan led the Hindu protest, claiming that though the mythic Ram Setu had not been sighted for thousands of years, in 1860 a British sailor had experienced a huge obstruction submerged between Sri Lanka and Rameshwaram.[8] Radheshyam Khemka wrote that many committees had been formed over the past 145 years to remove the obstruction since it was making sea travel difficult. To give a scientific edge to his arguments, Khemka said an image collected by a NASA satellite had revealed that a bridge 48 km long and nearly 2 km wide was submerged between Sri Lanka and Rameshwaram. The water level above the bridge varied from 1 to 10 metres. Khemka quoted the NASA report as stating that the bridge was 1,750,000 years old, which according to the Hindu belief system corresponded to Treta Yuga, the 'second of the four yugas (Krita, Treta, Dvapara and Kali) lasting for 12.96 lakh years'.

Responding to an affidavit by the Archaeological Survey of India, which said that Rama and Ramayana had no historical basis, Khemka resorted to a Poddar-like response. He criticized the ASI for being a useless institution on which thousands of crores were spent. The ASI's job was to protect ancient heritage, but it was doing the opposite. The government's Sethusamudram Shipping Channel Project at a cost of Rs 25,000 crore would destroy India's oldest bridge.

Khemka wrote: 'Work has started. Foreign-made dredgers have been pressed into action and attempt is being made to demolish the bridge. It is claimed this project will reduce sea travel between India and Sri Lanka by 400 nautical miles and reduce the journey time by sixteen hours. But according to experts the new route can be made without removing the Ram Setu.' Khemka suggested that removing sand dunes between Rameshwaram and Mandapam village near Dhanuskodi could create a sea route that would not only save journey time but would also help in preserving a timeless piece of heritage like the Ram Setu.

Khemka then pressed the religious panic button. He described the unprecedented havoc that would take place if the Ram Setu was destroyed: 'It is a big crime for which all of us would be held guilty. To protest against the government's short-sightedness and indifference and to protect the sanatan Hindu values, many religious leaders have launched an agitation and warned of dire consequences. If any untoward incident takes place the government will be held accountable.'

The ASI's affidavit was too hard to digest for the BJP and others of their ilk who attacked it vigorously. Under pressure, the UPA capitulated, the affidavit was withdrawn and the project was put on hold.

Kalyan's response to situations has always been selective; at times, significant events have been ignored. The imposition of Emergency by the Indira Gandhi government in June 1975 went largely unnoticed in

Kalyan, barring an oblique reference in an article (six months after its lifting) stressing the role of religion in society. It is possible that fear of the censor had put *Kalyan* on the defensive to the extent that the article talked in general terms about 'disturbances in society and selfish motives that lead to unjust fights',[9] and traced them to the decline of religious values.

In the 1980s, when Punjab was in the midst of militancy, *Kalyan* could not keep itself aloof. Giving a brief overview of the glorious history of the Sikhs, Khemka regretted the entry of a 'few elements who are spreading disaffection in the name of religion and distracting ordinary Sikhs from the path of peace'.[10] Despite clear resistance by Sikhs against any attempt to define their religion as an extension of Hinduism, Khemka did not hesitate to invoke the unity of the two religions. He said the Golden Temple at Amritsar and the Kashi Vishwanath Temple at Banaras exemplified that unity, since Maharaja Ranjit Singh had donated gold for both places of worship.

As sporadic violence continued in Punjab, *Kalyan* regretted the killing of innocent men, women and children travelling in buses, and appealed to the Sikh community to unite for the safety and security of the nation and to exterminate militancy from the 'pious land of Punjab'. Sikhs were asked not to provide shelter and cover to militants or to help misguided youth.[11]

In the late 1980s, as India plummeted to new depths of political uncertainty and corrupt practices, such as the Bofors gun purchase, *Kalyan*, slowly coming out of Poddar's shadow, took a moral position reminiscent of the journal's early years. The consistent decline of India's standing in the comity of nations despite its spiritual superiority was deemed unacceptable. Resorting to a sensational style of presentation, incongruous for a religious journal, *Kalyan* said that principles had lost value in society and gave an elaborate account of aspects where such degradation was most visible. This included the new trend of violence inside parliament, assemblies and secretariats; the lure of money and threat of muscle power being used to encourage political defections; military consolidation by enemy nations across the border; growth of discontentment among the general public; and rise in illegal labour practices. *Kalyan* asked readers to keep away from such negative activities and work towards nation building.[12]

Pakistan, the proverbial bugbear of the Hindu right, became the target of intense attack by Gita Press at the time of the Kargil war in 1999. In his editorial, Khemka justified the Indian action against the aggressor Pakistan. Adopting Poddar's tone and tenor during the Indo-Pak war of 1965, Khemka said resistance and retaliation alone would not be enough. He pitched for the extermination of Pakistan's devilish tendencies as it would be beneficial to mankind. Only bilateral relationships based on true intent, action and commitment were successful, he argued. Khemka stressed on the wide gap between Pakistan's promise of peace and the intrusion by the Pakistan army across the Line of Control. He saw it as nothing less than a grand conspiracy that needed swift retaliation. As if on cue, Khemka revived Poddar's wound analogy about Pakistan, and said this time the poisonous wound consisted of intruders who needed to be operated upon.[13]

About Godhra and the subsequent Gujarat violence of 2002 against the Muslims, *Kalyan*'s annual number *Nitisar Ank* (Issue on Principles, January–February 2002) was silent. Instead, Khemka wrote against what he called the new trend of dissociating religion from politics. He argued that, without religion, a society and its politics would become uncontrollable and this could even result in the withering away of the state's power.[14]

Gita Press's focus on protection of cows and consistent demands for ban on their slaughter has continued through the decades. In 1995, fifty years after the *Gau Ank* and twenty-four years after the death of Poddar, Gita Press published its *Gau Seva Ank*. This was a reiteration of the *Gau Ank* insofar as the social, religious and economic benefits from cows were concerned. Consisting mainly of extracts of old articles by leading cow campaigners, many of them dead by then, the novelty of the *Gau Seva Ank* was its review of the cow-protection movement of the late 1960s. Prabhudatt Brahmachari's article explained how joining the government-sponsored Goraksha Samiti had sounded the death knell of the cow-protection movement, and regretted that, despite so many years of self-rule, cows were still under threat in India.[15] He listed out and dismissed the various arguments advanced by opponents of the ban on cow slaughter. What outraged him the most was the argument that, in order to respect the sensitivity of Muslims, a minority community, the ban on cow slaughter should not be insisted upon.

Radhakrishna Bajaj, sarvodaya leader and an important member of the Goseva Sangh,[16] chronicled the cow-protection movement after the failure of the 1960s movement.[17] In 1975, at a meeting of the Goseva Sammelan (Cow Service Conference), Vinoba Bhave had declared that if cow slaughter was not banned by his next birthday (11 September 1976), he would sit on a fast unto death. News of Bhave's threat was not cleared by the censorship in operation under the Emergency regime. Pamphlets and journals were confiscated and the CID issued a nationwide circular to stop solidarity marches and fasts.

Bajaj wrote that, even after the change of regime in 1977, the Janata government did not bring a central law to ban cow slaughter. He said, parallel to Bhave's movement, a nationwide protest colloquially coined Roko Bhai Roko (Stop Brother Stop) was initiated at major centres of cow slaughter like Kosi Kalan in western Uttar Pradesh and Deonar in Maharashtra. The idea was to physically stop the transfer of cattle to slaughterhouses. According to Bajaj, sporadic protests, often localized, continued through the 1980s. In 1987, a mammoth Goseva Sammelan was held in Delhi's Rajghat attended by 1,000 representatives from all over the country with the demand to ban cow slaughter through a Central law. As a result, Bajaj said, the Madhya Pradesh, Rajasthan, Himachal Pradesh and Uttar Pradesh assemblies passed laws banning cow slaughter. However, UP's law did not get the president's assent. For Bajaj, the best performing state was Gujarat, which not only passed the legislation but also implemented the law in letter and spirit. He was upset with the pace of implementation in Maharashtra, where the massive slaughterhouse in Deonar continued to function despite a protest at its gate for twelve years. Elsewhere in Maharashtra, Bajaj said, killing of cows continued unabated.

The lack of a Central law banning cow slaughter remained a sore point with *Kalyan*, which continued to be reflected in regular writings on the subject. In a 2012 issue, the subject of treatment of cows in the Quran was revived. The example of Saudi Arabia, with its ultra-modern dairies, was showcased as an example of Muslim love for cows.[18] Al Shafi, a dairy farm in a place called Al Khiraj in Saudi Arabia, was said to house 36,000 cows in an air-conditioned environment attended by a 1,400-strong staff. *Kalyan* also claimed that in the Al Shafi farm there were 5,000 Indian cows whose milk, around 400 litres daily, was consumed by the royal family at Riyadh. The article went on to stress that the cow could be a means to unite the Indian Hindus and Muslims, like Ganga and Yamuna.

In early 2015, as BJP-ruled Maharashtra and Haryana completely banned cow slaughter, *Kalyan* celebrated the news with aplomb. Editor Khemka thanked the two state governments, especially Maharashtra that had passed the legislation nineteen years ago but was waiting for presidential assent. He lamented that many states, like Meghalaya, Arunachal Pradesh, Manipur, Sikkim and Kerala, still allowed cow slaughter. Khemka said the present government at the Centre has the ability to pass a Central legislation and hoped God will give it the strength to do so.[19]

Since Gita Press's moral universe is unchanged, almost cast in stone, its fear of modern education for women has also not subsided. Radheshyam Khemka parroted Poddar when he said, 'Though modern education among women has become common, they get so consumed with their passion for education that their ambition touches the sky.' Further, 'Women do whatever they feel like to fulfil their aspirations but it often results in tension, worry and disturbance and ultimately suicide.' Khemka blamed women's lack of religious education for their current state.[20]

Similarly, the anti-sati law coupled with intensification of the women's movement in the new century has not resulted in a review of Gita Press's stance on sati. Sitting in his well-appointed drawing room in Banaras, Khemka in 2011 expounded on the merits of sati and how in ancient times even women who lost their husbands at a young age immolated themselves willingly. 'This is not possible in this day and age. Therefore, a widow should lead a sage-like life as spelt out in the shastras. Widow marriage is not sanctioned in the shastras. The reason is that a woman becomes a widow due to sins in her previous life. Sin is the cause behind sorrow, hardship and adversity. Bearing it happily is the only way in which a person can overcome the sins of the previous life. If, against the diktats of the shastras, a woman gets remarried what happens is that even before her cycle of sin is completed, a new sin is added which she has to pay for in the future.'[21]

In 2013, after the popular god-man Asaram Bapu and his son Narayan Sai were arrested on charges of rape and molestation, *Kalyan* warned its readers, especially women, to beware of such god-men. 'Allegations of sexual exploitation have been levelled against a man who had a special standing in the spiritual world and one who had lakhs of devotees. While the truth will come out from courts, such incidents bring bad name to sadhus. Naturally, it shakes the faith of people in them.'[22]

Khemka severely criticized men who impersonate sadhus and sexually exploit innocent girls and women. He dismissed as 'baseless' Asaram Bapu's reported claim that allegations of sexual impropriety had also been levelled against Swami Ram Tirth, Swami Ramsukh Das and Swami Vivekananda. Khemka stated that Swami Ramsukh Das, who was closely associated with Gita Press, never met a woman alone, and if by mistake any woman touched his feet he would go on a fast that day.

The static moral world of Gita Press wakes up every time any arm of the state makes a progressive intervention. The changes wrought by an evolving jurisprudence is hard for it to accept. In early 2013, the Supreme Court ruled that live-in relationships would not be considered illegitimate. Earlier, the Madras High Court had ruled that a man and a woman in a physical relationship without marriage would have the status of a married couple and a child born out of such a union would be their legal heir. These two decisions shook the very foundations of the edifice of Hindu marriage that Gita Press had propagated for ninety years.

Khemka could not accept the Supreme Court's argument that, under Article 21 of the Constitution, a citizen is free to lead a life of his choice. In a restrained but angry editorial, he wrote that the apex court in one stroke had not only destroyed the sanctity of fire and God being witness to a marriage but even bypassed the formality of civil marriage (notwithstanding Khemka's antipathy to the latter). Aware that the Supreme Court could not be attacked like other institutions, Khemka merely called the orders 'desh ka durbhagya' (nation's misfortune) and lamented that the 'liberty and sexual freedom prohibited to youth by Indian culture as well as other religions are gaining legitimacy instead of being labelled waywardness'.[23]

Khemka employed the old Hindu nationalist arguments of 'nation in danger', saying that even the British government had maintained an arm's-length distance from the religious sphere. These arguments had been used at the time of the Hindu Code Bill and cow-protection movement with mixed success, and Khemka resorted to them: 'After Independence, there is a tendency to make laws that are against the shastras. We can already see a rise in cases of divorce, female infanticide and widow remarriage. Earlier, perpetrators of infanticide were punished, now, under the family planning rules they have been designated as vaidyas.' Khemka warned the courts and 'responsible judges' to be careful and avoid passing orders against the shastras and dharmashastras—only then would the nation's future be bright.

However, *Kalyan* has not so far reacted to the Supreme Court's order of 2013 decriminalizing same-sex relationships.

Under Khemka, *Kalyan*'s Islamophobic drive continues too, holding the government's family-planning programme responsible for the falling Hindu and rising Muslim population. Like Poddar, Khemka laments the government's failure (that he believes is deliberate) to bring Muslims under the family-planning umbrella; this is followed by what Patricia and Roger Jeffrey call 'scare-mongering'[24] of the worst kind: 'Recently newspapers carried a report on Islamic population in the world. It shows out of India's 102.86 crore population, 22.64 crore are Muslims, which roughly means 22 per cent of the total. Additionally there are 2 per cent Christians and other communities. In 1991, the Hindus were 85 per cent of population; that has come down to 76 per cent in 2002.'[25]

Khemka adds that the country is on the verge of a major crisis as the Muslim population is rising by a crore every year. He fears family planning will have disastrous consequences for Hindu culture and pride, and blames politicians for their vote-bank politics and for working against Indian culture by appeasing Muslims. He also ascribes the failure of the cow-protection movement to vote-bank politics.

A related issue that is cause for concern is abortion. Poddar had passed away the year parliament passed the Medical Termination of Pregnancy Act, 1971, which made abortion partially legal. A pregnancy could be terminated if it endangered the physical and mental life of a woman; if there was danger of a woman giving birth to a physically challenged child; if an unmarried under-eighteen girl got pregnant; if a mentally ill woman got pregnant; or if a woman got pregnant due to failure of contraceptives.

Gita Press published the views of the noted Gandhian Siddharaj Dhadda, minister of commerce and industry in the first Rajasthan government after Independence, who later quit the Congress. He attacked the government for making abortion 'simple' and the law 'lax': 'A woman would express the desire to abort and a doctor would agree. The new law paves the way for both. For a doctor, abortion has become a means to make money. It is beneficial for him to meet demands for abortion. The law gives all the power and responsibility to the doctor. The law stresses "good faith" but it would be impossible to prove if a doctor works in that spirit or not . . . The new law has several loopholes and so many exceptions that a doctor need not fear.'[26]

Dhadda said the real intention behind the new legislation was not to secure the physical and mental security of a woman but to 'arrest the growth of population'. He supported the idea of resorting to artificial birth-control measures, but to justify 'infanticide is a dangerous idea and needs a serious rethinking'. He asked the votaries of abortion how many women died in the process of getting their child aborted. Using the Gandhian idiom of non-violence, he made a fervent plea that the 'sanctity of life should not be sacrificed at the altar of trivial selfish goals'.

Gita Press continues its serious engagement against abortion even today. The book *Garbhpat: Uchit Ya Anuchit, Faisla Aapka* (Abortion: Right or Wrong, You Decide) first published in the 1990s by Jain Book Agency, a noted publisher of government Acts, statutes, the Constitution of India and other legal documents, was brought under the aegis of the Gita Press in 2011 and reworked. Penned by Gopinath Aggarwal, author of a series of similar moral texts, the work has gone into thirty-eight editions and sold more than 300,000 copies in its earlier and current versions.

Quoting varied sources in support, from Mahatma Gandhi's 'God alone can take life because he alone gives it' to the Supreme Court's 'the foetus is regarded as a human life from the moment of fertilization', the monograph through illustrations (of poor quality) explains the stages of gradual growth of the fetus inside the mother's womb.[27] The narrative is laced with tales from the epics, the most common being the story of Abhimanyu learning the art of breaking the circular formation (chakravyuh) of the enemy's army in his mother's womb. Such tales are mixed with medical expert opinions and descriptions of the 'violence' involved in various methods of abortion.

A contribution by Shailendra Kumar Jain explains the dangers to the mother while aborting the child. These range from haemorrhage to infection, damage to the cervix, perforation of the uterus and perforation of the bowel; the long-term implications are even more serious—impaired childbearing ability, giving birth to stillborn or handicapped children, suffering miscarriages, premature births, low birthweight of child and ectopic pregnancies. Jain refers to Japan's Nagode Survey of 1968, according to which more than 30 per cent of women who had undergone abortions were found to be suffering from mental problems. Citing a report in the *Hindustan Times*, Jain says that, of the fifty million abortions worldwide, nearly half were illegal and resulted in the death of 200,000 women. Jain also estimates that between six and eight million women become ill for lifetime as a result of undergoing abortion.[28]

The book blames the rise in abortion on sex-determination tests being conducted by birth clinics. Aggarwal says prenatal testing began with the intention of detecting chronic illness in the fetus or other abnormal characteristics—it can comprehend seventy-two kinds of chronic and hereditary diseases in a yet-to-be born child and thus helps in their prenatal treatment. But it soon degenerated into sex detection that led to many a girl child being aborted. Aggarwal writes that not only have sex-detection clinics become common throughout the country, but authoritative figures suggest that they are sites of female feticide, 97 per cent of aborted fetuses being female.

The book states that despite specific laws by many states to ban prenatal diagnostic techniques, the scourge has not been arrested as people are getting the sex of their to-be-born child determined in one way or another. Through interviews with doctors, Aggarwal shows how such tests are also not risk-free as there is danger of damage to the fetus and placenta; besides, they do not always give accurate results.

Aggarwal makes a moral pitch for gender equality and tells mothers that a girl child is as much a part of them as a son. Spinning out a long list of great women, including Sita, Rani Lakshmi Bai, Mother Teresa and others, Aggarwal reminds everyone of the saying 'there is a woman behind every successful man'. He says it is illogical to believe that a male child would take care of his parents in their old age, whereas a girl child would only be a cause for major expenditure on her marriage and dowry. Aggarwal cites cases he knows of where the daughters have taken better care of their old parents than the sons. It is worth noting that the argument of giving equal status to sons and daughters and arguing that a daughter will look after her parents in their old age would not have gone down well with Poddar. He would have considered it as contradicting the tenets of the shastras, and hence blasphemy.

The continuity that characterizes Gita Press's ideology also extends to its business model. The economics of the organization has not changed much. At present, Gita Press runs primarily on Gobind Bhawan's cloth business, the income from subscriptions to *Kalyan* and *Kalyana-Kalpataru* and from the sale of books, and contributions from patrons and trustees. The newsprint business closed a long time ago. The subscription-based circulation of *Kalyan* is over 200,000 while that of *Kalyana-Kalpataru* is over 100,000. In addition, a few thousand copies of these journals are sold at counters in different parts of the country. Facing the fast-changing world in which religion and spiritualism have fallen to the diktats of the market and packaging, Gita Press has refused to change its rules, especially the promise made to Gandhi that it would not accept advertisements. However, Khemka acknowledges: 'We are not able to get new customers. With limited resources I do not know for how long we will survive.'[29]

Khemka's despondency stems from the battle Gita Press is fighting in a liberal economy, taking small steps to keep pace with new trends in business. In 2012, Gobind Bhawan Karyalaya tested its economic worth through ICRA, a top credit-rating agency. ICRA gave a BB rating to the 'Rs 8.5 crore of fund-based limits of Gobind Bhawan Karyalaya', stating that the 'outlook on the long-term rating is stable'.[30] The rating factored in the 'modest scale of operations of Gobind Bhawan Karyalaya, subdued profitability on account of non-profit making aim of the society and high working capital intensity due to high inventory days'. The practice of utilizing most of the cash towards capital expenditure has resulted in limited cash balances. In 2013, Gobind Bhawan Karyalaya made a profit of Rs 0.5 million on its operating income of Rs 859.8 million, a slight improvement from the profit of Rs 0.4 million on an operating income of Rs 792.9 million in 2012.

ICRA's contention that Gobind Bhawan Karyalaya has a stable future may be of some solace to Khemka. Stability stems from its 'strong presence for almost nine decades with established brand in religious books like Shrimad Bhagwadgita, Ramayana, etc., strong distribution network throughout India and market position supported by limited publications by peers in similar price bands'. Although books are sold at negative margins, there is a steady flow of income from other businesses—selling food, cloth and Ayurvedic medicines—which augurs well for the world of Gita Press.

As Gita Press stands within striking distance of a century, the only organization that may be said to parallel its success is the Bible Society. No other publishing house in India has marketed religion so successfully. And despite claiming to maintain a safe distance from politics, Gita Press has regularly taken political stands. Not only has it played a pivotal role in 'popular efforts to proclaim Hindu solidarity (sangathan), pious self-identity and normative cultural values',[31] as a player in the theatre of Hindu nationalism it has also stood side by side with the majoritarian narrative of the RSS, Hindu Mahasabha, Jana Sangh and BJP at every critical juncture since 1923. And in times of intense communal division, *Kalyan* has exchanged the sobriety of a religious journal for the language of hate and religious identity. The fact that its publications reach even secular Hindu homes adds to the might and mystique of Gita Press. And as Indian politics becomes more polarized with a definite right turn, organizations like Gita Press may get their second wind. If Goyandka and Poddar are watching as their publishing house persists in pursuing its larger goal of protecting and propagating sanatan Hindu dharma, they must indeed be a proud pair.

Notes

Introduction

1. Information on Goyandka and the foundation of Gita Press from Bhagwati Prasad Singh, *Kalyan Path: Nirmata Aur Rahi*, Radha Madhav Seva Sansthan, Gorakhpur, 1980, pp. 287–89.
2. Details of Bajaj's speech from B.R. Nanda, *In Gandhi's Footsteps: The Life and Times of Jamnalal Bajaj*, Oxford University Press, Delhi, 2011, pp. 145–47.
3. C.A. Bayly, *Empire and Information: Intelligence Gathering and Social Communication in India, 1780–1870*, Cambridge University Press, New Delhi, 1996, pp. 1–9.
4. Sumit Sarkar, *Modern India, 1885–1947*, Macmillan, New Delhi, 1983, p. 235.
5. Vasudha Dalmia, *The Nationalization of Hindu Traditions: Bharatendu Harishchandra and Nineteenth Century Banaras*, Oxford University Press, Delhi, 1997, p. 197; Shamsur Rehman Faruqi, 'A Long History of Urdu Literary Culture, Part I,' in Sheldon Pollock (ed.), *Literary Cultures in History: Reconstructions from South Asia*, University of California Press, Berkeley, 2003, p. 815.
6. Harish Trivedi, 'The Progress of Hindi, Part 2,' in Pollock (ed.), 2003, pp. 965–66.
7. Christopher R. King, *One Language, Two Scripts: The Hindi Movement in Nineteenth Century North India*, Oxford University Press, New Delhi, 1994, p. 15.
8. '*Nij Bhasha Unnati Ahe, Sab Unnati Ko Mool; Bin Nij Bhasha Gyan Ke Mitat Na Hiye Lo Sool*,' couplet from Bharatendu Harishchandra, '*Hindi Ki Unnati Par Vyakhyan*', 1877, published in *Bharatendu Samagra*, Hindi Pracharak Publication, Banaras, 2009.

9. Alok Rai, *Hindi Nationalism*, Orient Longman, New Delhi, 2001, pp. 17–49.
10. Avinash Kumar, 'Making of the Hindi Literary Field: Journals, Institutions, Personalities (1900–1940)', Ph.D. thesis, Jawaharlal Nehru University, Delhi, 2001.
11. Obituary of M.P. Dwivedi by Babu Shyamsundar Das, *Saraswati*, February 1939.
12. See Ramvilas Sharma, *Mahavir Prasad Dwivedi Aur Hindi Navjagran*, Rajkamal Prakashan, Delhi, 1977, pp.183–84.
13. Kumar, 2001.
14. Trivedi, 2003, p. 961.
15. Abhik Samanta, 'The Gita Press, Gorakhpur: A Discursive Study', M.Phil. dissertation, Delhi University, 2007.
16. Ganesh Damodar Savarkar, '*Sanatan Dharma Hi Ekmatr Dharma Hai*' (Sanatan Dharma Is the Sole Religion), *Hindu Panch*, 29 November 1928.
17. '*Panch Karyalaya Mein Adarsh Veer*' (The Ideal Hero in Panch Office), *Hindu Panch*, 4 October 1928.
18. Bal Mukund Gupt, '*Marwari Mahashayon Ke Naam*' (To Great Marwaris), *Bharatmitra*, 27 February 1904, reproduced in K.C. Yadav (ed.), *Chhithe Aur Khat*, Haryana Academy of History and Culture, 2012, pp. 35–39.
19. The following arguments are based on Philip Lutgendorf, *Life of a Text: Performing the Ramcaritmanas of Tulsidas*, University of California Press, Berkeley, 1991, p. 423.
20. Thomas A. Timberg, *The Marwaris: From Traders to Industrialists*, Vikas, New Delhi, 1978, p. 60.
21. Lutgendorf, 1991, p. 423.
22. Christophe Jaffrelot, *India's Silent Revolution*, Permanent Black, Ranikhet, 2003, pp. 189–99.
23. Chandraraj Bhandari 'Visharad', Bhramarlal Soni and Krishnalal Gupt, *Aggarwal Jati Ka Itihas*, Aggarwal History Office, Indore, 1937, pp. 106–18.
24. See for example Bhalchand Modi, *Desh Ke Itihas Mein Marwari Jati Ka Sthan*, published by Raghunath Prasad Singhania, Calcutta, 1939; Rishi Jaimini Kaushik Barua, *Main Apne Marwari Samaj Ko Pyar Karta Hoon*, Jaimini Prakashan, Calcutta, 1967.

25. Satyakam Vidyalankar, '*Path Pravartak*' (Guide), *Navneet Hindi Digest*, November 1971, pp. 93–96.
26. Krishna Bihari Mishra, *Hindi Patrakarita: Rajasthani Aayojan Ki Kriti Bhumika*, Akhil Bhartiya Marwari Yuva Sangh, Delhi, 1999, pp. 21–22.
27. Ibid., pp. 17–18.
28. Ibid., p. 27.
29. Paul Arney, 'The "Mouth" of Sanatana Dharma: The Role of Gita Press in Spreading the Word', paper presented at the American Academy of Religion Annual Meeting, Washington DC, November 20–23, 1993.
30. Shivpujan Sahay, Editorial Comment in *Marwari Sudhar*, Vol. 7, cited in Mishra, 1999, p. 61.
31. Sarkar, 1983, p. 157.
32. Peter Robb, 'The Challenge of Gau Mata: British Policy and Religious Change in India, 1880–1916', *Modern Asian Studies*, Vol. 20, No. 2, 1986, pp. 285–319.
33. Gyanendra Pandey, *The Ascendancy of the Congress in Uttar Pradesh*, Anthem Press, London, 2002, p. 97.
34. Sandria B. Freitag, *Collective Action and Community: Public Arenas and the Emergence of Communalism in North India*, Oxford University Press, Delhi, 1990, pp. 208–09.
35. Ibid., p. 225.
36. M.K. Gandhi in *Young India*, 9 April 1931, reproduced in *Collected Works of Mahatma Gandhi*, Vol. 51, pp. 361.
37. Hanuman Prasad Poddar, *Kalyan*, Vol. 6, No. 5, 1931, title page.
38. Freitag, 1990, p. 235.
39. I owe this argument to educationist Krishna Kumar.
40. Review of *Sanatan Dharma Pataka* in *Madhuri*, 1 January 1925, p. 843.
41. Dalmia, 1997, p. 7.
42. Monika Hortsmann, 'Towards A Universal Dharma: *Kalyan* and The Tracts of the Gita Press', in Vasudha Dalmia and Heinrich von Stietencron (eds), *Representing Hinduism*, Sage, New Delhi, 1995, p. 303.
43. Benedict Anderson, *Imagined Communities: Reflections on the Origin and Spread of Nationalism*, Verso, London, 2003, pp. 38–39.

44. Paul Arney, 'Gita Press and the Magazine *Kalyan*: The Hindu Imperative of Dharma-pracar', paper presented at the 24th Annual Conference on South Asia, University of Wisconsin, Madison, October 1995.
45. Jaydayal Goyandka, *'Dharma Aur Uska Prachar'* (Religion and Its Propagation), *Kalyan*, Vol. 2, No. 3, 1927, p. 186. Cited in Arney, 1995.
46. Arney, 1995.
47. William A. Graham, *Beyond The Written Word: Oral Aspects of Scripture in the History of Religion*, Cambridge University Press, London, 1987, p. 77.
48. Singh, 1980, p. 318.
49. Kathryn Hansen, *Stages of Life: Indian Theatre Autobiographies*, Permanent Black, Ranikhet, 2011, p. 103.
50. Lutgendorf, 1991, pp. 66–67.
51. Ibid.
52. In the 1931 census, UP had 2,309,000 literates (20.91 lakh male, 2.18 lakh female) that went up to 4,728,000 in the 1941 census (40.97 lakh male, 6.30 lakh female); the literacy rate was higher than in Central Provinces and Bihar.
53. Cited in Ulrike Stark, *An Empire of Books: The Naval Kishore Press and the Diffusion of the Printed Word in Colonial India*, Permanent Black, Ranikhet, 2007, p. 35.
54. Stark, 2007, pp. 43–44, 51–52.
55. Samanta, 2007.
56. Goyandka's diatribe in *Kalyan* is quoted in Monika Freier, 'Cultivating Emotions: The Gita Press and Its Agenda of Social and Spiritual Reform,' *South Asian History and Culture*, Vol. 3, No. 3, July 2012, pp. 397–418.
57. Ibid.
58. *Hindu Code: Hindu Sanskriti Ke Vinash Ka Ayojan* (Hindu Code: A Plan for the Destruction of Hindu Culture), *Kalyan*, June 1948, pp. 1110–13.
59. Varnashram Swarajya Sangh: *Antyajan Ke Liye Mandir Pravesh Ka Nishedh Kyon* (Why Temple Entry Be Banned for Lower Castes), *Hindu Sanskriti Ank, Kalyan*, January 1950, pp. 214–17.
60. Arney, 1993.

61. Ibid.
62. '*Gita Press Ke Karyon Ka Sankshipt Vivaran*' (A Short Description of the Activities of Gita Press), *Kalyan*, June 1955, pp. 1118–20.
63. http://gitapress.org/Pub.htm. Accessed on 5 February 2014.
64. Arney, 1993 and 1995.
65. Chandrima Chakraborty, *Masculinity, Asceticism, Hinduism: Past and Present Imaginings of India*, Permanent Black, Ranikhet, 2011, p. 5.
66. I owe this line of inquiry to a suggestion from historian Ulrike Stark.
67. Charu Gupta, 'Articulating Hindu Masculinity and Femininity: "Shuddhi" and "Sangathan" Movements in United Provinces in the 1920s', *Economic and Political Weekly*, Vol. 33, No. 13, 26 March–3 April 1998, pp. 727–35.

1. A Twentieth-century Hindu Missionary and His Mentor

1. Monika Hortsmann, 'Towards a Universal Dharma: *Kalyan* and the Tracts of the Gita Press', in Vasudha Dalmia and Heinrich von Stietencron (eds), *Representing Hinduism: The Construction of Religious Tradition and National Identity*, Sage, New Delhi, 1995, pp. 294–305.
2. As described by Rishi Jaimini Kaushik Barua, *Main Apne Marwari Samaj Ko Pyar Karta Hoon*, Jaimini Prakashan, Calcutta, 1967, Vol. 7, p. 1296.
3. Hanuman Prasad Poddar's interview to Gambhirchand Dujari for a biography that got published partially as *Shri Bhaiji: Ek Alaukik Vibhuti, Rasa-Siddha Sant Bhaiji Shri Hanuman Prasad Poddar Aur Sant Pravar Sethji Shri Jaydayalji Goyandka Ka Jivan Darshan*, Gita Vatika Prakashan, Gorakhpur, 2000. The manuscript is in the collection of Harikrishna Dujari. Also see, Bhagwati Prasad Singh, *Kalyan Path: Nirmata Aur Rahi*, Radha Madhav Seva Sansthan, Gorakhpur, 1980. These are the sources for the details of Hanuman Prasad Poddar's life provided in this section.
4. Bhalchand Modi, *Desh Ke Itihas Mein Marwari Jati Ka Sthan*, published by Raghunath Prasad Singhania, Calcutta, 1939, pp. 739–40.
5. See Jayeeta Sharma, *Empire's Garden: Assam and The Making of India*, Permanent Black, Ranikhet, 2011.

6. Abhik Samanta, 'The Gita Press Gorakhpur: A Discursive Study', MPhil dissertation, Delhi University, 2007.
7. Suhas Chakravarty, *Raj Syndrome*, Penguin, New Delhi, 1995.
8. Sumit Sarkar, *Modern India: 1885–1947*, Macmillan, New Delhi, 1983, p. 75.
9. Karmendu Shishir, *Navjagrankalin Patrakarita Aur Matwala*, Anamika Prakashan, Delhi, 2012, p. 330.
10. Francesca Orsini, *The Hindi Public Sphere 1920–1940: Language and Literature in the Age of Nationalism*, Oxford University Press, New Delhi, 2002, p. 442.
11. '*Samayik Vichar Pravah*' (Contemporary Thought), *Saraswati*, November 1931, p. 563.
12. Sumit Sarkar, *The Swadeshi Movement in Bengal*, Permanent Black, Ranikhet, 2010, p. 221.
13. Singh, 1980, pp. 84–85.
14. Madan Mohan Malaviya to Poddar, 25 May 1935. Poddar Papers.
15. Sarkar, 2010, p. 226.
16. Singh, 1980, pp. 90–91.
17. *Calcutta Samachar*, 22 July 1916. NMML, Microfilm Section.
18. *Calcutta Samachar*, 24 July 1916. NMML, Microfilm Section.
19. Native Newspapers Report, Bengal, 1916. NMML.
20. Medha M. Kudaisya, *The Life and Times of G.D. Birla*, Oxford University Press, New Delhi, 2003, p. 37.
21. Report of the Sedition Committee, 1918, p. 66. Poddar Papers.
22. Barua quoted in Kudaisya, 2003, p. 36.
23. Kudaisya, ibid., p. 35.
24. Sarkar, 2010, p. 83.
25. Poddar's interview to Akhil Bharatvarshiya Marwari Sammelan, 1955. Poddar Papers.
26. B.V. Paradkar, '*Sati Bhagwati*', *Kalyan*, November 1938.
27. Summation of narrative about the conspiracy culled from Poddar Papers, Prabhu Dayal Himmatsingka's account of the incident in the commemorative volume on Poddar (1971), extracts from James Campbell Ker, *Political Trouble in India, 1907–1917*, Oriental Publishers, Delhi, 1917, and Barua as cited in Kudaisya, 2003.
28. Native Newspapers Report, Bengal, 1916, citing a report in *Dainik Basumati* of 18 July. NMML.

29. Ashutosh Lahiry's interview to Raghunath Prasad Singhania for a book on the role of Marwaris in the freedom struggle. Poddar Papers.
30. D.P. Mandelia, *G.D. Birla: A Superb Master Sculptor,* cited in Kudaisya, 2003.
31. Political Department Records (Special Intelligence Branch), Government of Bengal. Poddar Papers.
32. Ibid.
33. Report on the meeting of the Marwari Association, *The Statesman,* Tuesday, 8 August 1916. NMML, Microfilm Section.
34. *The Oxford Encyclopaedia of the Music of India,* Sangit Mahabharati and Oxford University Press, Mumbai and New Delhi, 2011, Vol. III, p. 788.
35. B.K. Birla to Poddar, 6 October 1955. Poddar Papers.
36. Questionnaire by G.S. Ghurye and R.V. Athaide. Poddar Papers.
37. Dhananjay Keer, *Lokmanya Tilak: Father of the Indian Freedom Struggle,* S.V. Kangutkar, Bombay, 1959, pp. 428–29.
38. Gandhi to Poddar, 16 May 1935. Poddar Papers.
39. Rajmohan Gandhi, *The Good Boatman: A Portrait of Gandhi,* Viking, 1995, p. 362.
40. Rajmohan Gandhi, *Mohandas: A True Story of a Man, His People and an Empire,* Penguin-Viking, New Delhi, 2006, p. 366.
41. Telegram from Gandhi to Poddar, 16 June 1932. Poddar Papers.
42. Rajmohan Gandhi, 2006, p. 310.
43. Request dated 18 June 1932. Poddar Papers.
44. Press communique sent by Poddar. Poddar Papers.
45. Gandhi's letter dated 21 July 1932 from Yerwada jail, *Collected Works of Mahatma Gandhi,* Vol. 56, p. 226.
46. Gandhi to Poddar, 2 August 1932. Poddar Papers.
47. Narandas Gandhi to Poddar, 3 August 1932, from Satyagraha Ashram Udyoga Mandir, Sabarmati. Poddar Papers.
48. Rajmohan Gandhi, 2006, p. 370.
49. Ibid., p. 373.
50. Poddar to Gandhi, Kartik Shukla 1, Samvat 1989 (1932). Poddar Papers.
51. *Navjivan,* 9 October 1921.
52. *Navjivan,* 12 December 1920.
53. *Navjivan,* 17 April 1921.

54. In the Ramayana, Sabari was a tribal woman devotee of Rama and fed him fruits, tasting them first to check that they were good. While Lakshman chided Rama for eating the 'impure' fruits, Rama blessed Sabari for her act of devotion.
55. Gandhi's letter to Poddar, 5 November 1932. *Collected Works of Mahatma Gandhi,* Vol. 57, pp. 339–40.
56. Poddar to Anand Puri, 8 July 1956. Poddar Papers.
57. Poddar to Prabhashankar Gupt, Kartik Shukla, 1988 (1931). Poddar Papers.
58. Poddar to Gandhi, date not clear, 1937. Poddar Papers.
59. Gandhi to Poddar, 18 February 1937. *Collected Works of Mahatma Gandhi,* Vol. 70, p. 420.
60. Jamnalal Bajaj to Poddar, 4 October 1940. Jamnalal Bajaj Papers, NMML.
61. Poddar to Jamnalal Bajaj, undated. Jamnalal Bajaj Papers, NMML.
62. Hindu Mahasabha Papers, NMML.
63. Kudaisya, 2003, p. 270.
64. Manuscript of Poddar's biography, most likely compiled by Shyamsundar Dujari. Poddar Papers.
65. Weekly Report on Political Activities, for the week ending 15 July 1949, No. 28. CID Archives, Lucknow.
66. Weekly Report on Political Activities, for the week ending 2 September 1949, No. 35. CID Archives, Lucknow.
67. Poddar's statement to the press, 24 March 1928. Poddar Papers.
68. Text of Poddar's speech at the Tenth Marwari Aggarwal Mahasabha Meeting, Bombay, published by the Reception Committee and printed by Gita Press, 1928. Poddar Papers.
69. Hari Shankar Dwivedi and Vishnu Hari Dalmia (eds), *Sant Shri Jaidayal Dalmia Smriti Granth* (Jaidayal Dalmia Commemorative Volume), published by Harishankar Dwivedi, New Delhi, n.d., p. 13.
70. Ibid., pp. 126–29.
71. Ibid., pp. 156–57.
72. Ibid., pp. 152–53, quoting letters from Poddar to Jaidayal Dalmia, Sravana Shukla 14, 1989 (1932), and 1 October 1933.
73. Poddar to Ram Krishna Dalmia, Ashwin Shukla 1988 (1931), reproduced in *Saras Patra* compiled by Shyamsundar Dujari, Gita Vatika Prakashan, Gorakhpur, 2005, pp. 59–60.

74. Dwivedi and Dalmia, n.d., p.16.
75. Ibid., pp. 14–15.
76. Dwijendra Tripathi, *The Oxford History of Indian Business*, Oxford University Press, New Delhi, 2004, p. 195.
77. Poddar to Bajaj, 26 November 1939. Jamnalal Bajaj Papers, NMML.
78. Poddar to Bajaj, 15 December 1939. Jamnalal Bajaj Papers, NMML.
79. Tripathi, 2004, p. 195.
80. Neelima Dalmia Adhar, *Father Dearest: The Life and Times of R.K. Dalmia*, Roli Books, New Delhi, 2003.
81. Ram Krishna Dalmia to Poddar, 11 November 1969. Poddar Papers.
82. R.K. Dalmia to Poddar, 27 April 1970. Poddar Papers.
83. Jaidayal Dalmia to Poddar, 2 August 1970. Poddar Papers.
84. The nine companies being inquired into were Dalmia Jain Airways Ltd, Dalmia Jain Aviation Ltd (later known as Asia Udyog Ltd), Lahore Electric Supply Company Ltd (later known as South Asia Industries Ltd), Shapurji Broacha Mills Ltd, Madhowji Dharamsi Manufacturing Company Ltd, Allenberry & Co. Ltd, Bharat Union Agencies Ltd, Dalmia Cement and Paper Marketing Co. Ltd (later known as Delhi Glass Works Ltd) and Vastra Vyavasaya Ltd. Dalmia Dadri Cement Ltd was later added to the list.
85. Report of the Commission of Inquiry (Inquiry on the Administration of Dalmia–Jain Companies), Department of Commerce & Industry, 1963, p. 1.
86. Nasir Tyabji, 'Of Traders, Usurers and British Capital: Managing Agencies and the Dalmia Jain Case', in S.R. Hashim, K.S. Chalapati Rao, K.V.K. Ranganathan and M.R. Murthy (eds), *Indian Industrial Development and Globalisation: Essays in Honour of Prof. S.K. Goyal*, Academic Foundation, New Delhi, 2008, pp. 109–30.
87. Report of the Commission of Inquiry, 1963, p.71.
88. Ibid., p. 73.
89. Ibid., p. 72.
90. Ibid., p. 75.
91. Ibid., p. 83.
92. Ken Auletta, 'Citizens Jain: Why India's Newspaper Industry is Thriving', *The New Yorker*, 8 October 2012, pp. 52–61.
93. Poddar to Lal Bahadur Shastri, 16 March 1965, *Saras Patra*, 2005, pp. 140–41.

94. Seth Govind Das to Poddar, 14 December 1935. Poddar Papers.
95. Vimla Thakkar's letters to Hanuman Prasad Poddar, 11 January 1959 and 17 January 1959. Poddar Papers.
96. http://natnagarsitamau.com/english/history_sitamau.html. Accessed on 5 November 2013.
97. Godbole to Poddar, 1 January 1935. Poddar Papers.
98. Godbole to Poddar, dt3 November 1935. Poddar Papers.
99. Godbole to Poddar, 18 August 1936. Poddar Papers.
100. Swami Sahajanand Saraswati, *Mera Jivan Sangharsh,* edited by Avadhesh Pradhan, Granth Shilpi, New Delhi, 2000, p. 248.
101. Radheshyam Banka, *Parikar Malika,* Vol. II, Hanuman Prasad Smarak Samiti, Gita Vatika, Gorakhpur, 2013, pp. 20–21. Banka does not give details of Golwalkar's article but cites it verbatim.
102. Copy of Poddar's letter to Govind Ballabh Pant, undated (1950s). Poddar Papers.
103. Poddar's letter to Sampurnanand, 1959. Poddar Papers.
104. Paul R. Brass, *An Indian Political Life: Charan Singh and Congress Politics, 1937–1961,* Sage Publications, New Delhi, 2011, pp. 254–68.
105. Sampurnanand's letter to Poddar, 28 August 1967. Poddar Papers.
106. Poddar to Ramnath Goenka, 6 July 1969, *Saras Patra,* 2005, pp. 65–66.
107. Poddar's appeal to vote for Goenka in the 1971 election, undated. Poddar Papers.
108. Poddar's letter to an unnamed person, undated. Poddar Papers.
109. Singh, 1980, p. 477.
110. Lee Siegel, *Sacred and Profane Dimensions of Love in Indian Traditions as Exemplified in the Gitagovinda of Jayadeva,* Oxford University Press, New Delhi, 1990, p. 3.
111. Irene Wolfington to Poddar, 21 December 1965. Poddar Papers.
112. G.D. Birla to Poddar, 1 August 1941. Poddar Papers.
113. G.D. Birla to Poddar, 9 August 1941. Poddar Papers.
114. Poddar to Gulzarilal Nanda, 9 March 1965. Poddar Papers.
115. Undated letter from Irene to Swami Chakradhar. Poddar Papers.
116. Poddar's undated letter (probably of June 1965) to Irene. Poddar Papers.
117. Irene's undated letter, presumably her reply to Poddar. Poddar Papers.

118. Siobhan Lambert-Hurley, *The Heart of a Gopi: Raihana Tyabji's Bhakti Devotionalism as Self-Representation*, Loughborough University, Leicestershire, 2013, pp. 1–19.
119. Ibid.
120. Gandhi to Raihana, 3 June 1927, *Collected Works of Mahatma Gandhi*, Vol. 38, p. 491.
121. Gandhi to Raihana, 4 January 1931, 25 January 1931 and 10 October 1932, *Collected Works of Mahatma Gandhi*, Vol. 50, p. 462; Vol. 51, p. 64; Vol. 57, p. 207.
122. Gandhi to Raihana, 3 June 1927. *Collected Works of Mahatma Gandhi*, Vol. 38, pp. 491–92.
123. Lambert-Hurley, 2013, also Ved Mehta, *Mahatma Gandhi and His Apostles*, Penguin Books, Harmondsworth, Middlesex, 1976, p. 211 cited in Lambert-Hurley.
124. Ibid.
125. Ibid.
126. Ibid.
127. Poddar to Raihana Tyabji, 18 November 1939. Poddar Papers.
128. Raihana Tyabji to Poddar, 21 November 1939. Poddar Papers.
129. Poddar to Raihana Tyabji, 28 November 1939. Poddar Papers.
130. Raihana Tyabji to Poddar, 7 December 1939. Poddar Papers.
131. Poddar to Raihana Tyabji, 16 December 1939. Poddar Papers.
132. Lambert-Hurley, 2013.
133. http://www.swarthmore.edu/library/friends/ead/5267nile.xml. Accessed 29 May 2014.
134. *The Times of India*, 19 May 1975.
135. Jaydayal Goyandka to GD Birla, undated. Poddar Papers.
136. Samanta, 2007.
137. A ritual among Hindus in which balls of meal, flour or rice, are offered to the spirits of ancestors during a particular fortnight in a year. Carrying out this ritual in Gaya is considered most auspicious.
138. The accounts of Poddar's visions are taken from Dujari, 2000, and from the complete manuscript of Poddar's life by Dujari that is part of the Poddar Papers.
139. Dujari, 2000, pp. 85–87.
140. Poddar to Ramjivan, 29 June 1964. Poddar Papers.
141. Singh, 1980, pp. 85–86.

142. Poddar to Goyandka, Asadha Krishna 4, Samvat 1991 (1934), *Saras Patra*, 2005, pp. 10–11.
143. Goyandka to Poddar, Asadha Shukla 6, Samvat 1991 (1934), *Saras Patra*, 2005, pp. 11–15.
144. Poddar to Madan Lal, date not clear. Poddar Papers.
145. Poddar to Pitambar Prasad Aggarwal, 15 November 1939. Poddar Papers.
146. Singh, 1980, pp. 178–79.
147. Poddar to an unnamed acquaintance, 19 July 1964. Poddar Papers.
148. Poddar to Yogi Shiv Narayan, 14 December 1967. Poddar Papers.
149. Poddar to Chimmanlal Gosvami, 28 March 1939, *Saras Patra*, 2005, pp. 107–09.
150. Shankarrao Deo's letter to Poddar inviting him to the All India Cultural Conference, 3 March 1951. Poddar Papers.
151. Rules and Regulations of Bharatiya Chaturdham Veda Bhawan Nyasa, 24 March 1965. Poddar Papers.
152. Ibid.
153. Hanuman Prasad Poddar, *Desh Mein Aasuri Sampada Ka Vistar Aur Hamara Kartavya*. Undated. Poddar Papers.
154. Brochure, '*Hanuman Prasad Abhinandan Granth*', 1958. The list of contributors included Vice-president S. Radhakrishnan and chief minister of Madras C. Rajgopalachari; Poddar's old friends and associates Govind Ballabh Pant, Purushottam Das Tandon, K.M. Munshi, Sampurnanand and Kamlapati Tripathi; scholars and writers like Vasudev Sharan Aggarwal, Suniti Kumar Chatterji, Makhanlal Chaturvedi, Rahul Sankrityayan, Nand Dulare Vajpayee, Sumitranandan Pant, Seth Govind Das, Maithilisharan Gupt, Banarsidas Chaturvedi, Omkarnath Thakur and others; comrades-in-arms like Swami Karpatri Maharaj and Prabhudatt Brahmachari; industrialist friends like Ghanshyam Das Birla and intimate associates like Shanti Prasad Jain, Jaydayal Goyandka, Jaidayal Dalmia and Chimmanlal Gosvami. Poddar Papers.
155. Poddar to Nageshwar Dixit, 13 December 1953. Poddar Papers.
156. Varma to Poddar, 21 December 1953. Poddar Papers.
157. Poddar to Varma, 27 December 1953. Poddar Papers.
158. S.N. Mangal to Jaidayal Dalmia, 7 October 1967. Poddar Papers.
159. Mangal to Jaidayal Dalmia, 28 March 1968. Poddar Papers.

160. Mangal to Jaidayal Dalmia, 10 April 1968. Poddar Papers.
161. Copy of the Appeal Issued by Shanti Prasad Jain, Ramnath Goenka and Omkarmal Saraf, April 1968. Poddar Papers.
162. Mangal to Jaidayal Dalmia, 20 April 1968. Poddar Papers.
163. Jaidayal Dalmia to Mangal, 22 April 1968. Poddar Papers.
164. Mangal to Jaidayal Dalmia, 6 May 1968. Poddar Papers.
165. Jaidayal Dalmia to Mangal, 9 May 1968. Poddar Papers.
166. Prabhupada to Poddar, 21 July 1970. www.prabhupadabooks.com. Accessed on 1 October 2013.
167. '*Ajar Amar Gun Nidhi Sut Hohu, Karahu Bahut Raghunayak Chhohu*', couplet 16, Sundar Kand, Ramayana. Telegram from Teji Bachchan to Poddar, 27 September 1970. Poddar Papers.
168. Prabhudatt Brahmachari's undated letter to Poddar and the latter's reply, 9 Kartik Krishna, Samvat 2027 (1970). Poddar Papers.
169. Prabhupada to Achyutananda and Jaya Govinda, 13 October 1968. www.prabhupadabooks.com. Accessed on 1 October 2013.
170. Prabhupada to Poddar, 4 March 1970. www.prabhupadabooks.com. Accessed on 1 October 2013.
171. Hanuman Prasad Poddar, '*Meri Esthiti Ka Spastikaran*' (Explanation of My Position), 1969. Poddar Papers.
172. Ishwari Prasad Goenka to Parmeshwar Prasad Fogla, 13 May 1971. Poddar Papers.
173. Ishwari Prasad Goenka to Shyamsundar Dujari, 31 May 1971. Poddar Papers.
174. Chimmanlal Gosvami's statement, 15 April 1972. Poddar Papers.
175. Radheshyam Banka to Seth Govind Das, 4 August 1972. Seth Govind Das Papers, NMML.
176. See Dujari, 2000.
177. See detailed description of Goyandka's role as arbiter in the division of business and assets of the family of Mohanlal Goyanka, a leading coal miner of Raniganj, in Rishi Jaimini Kaushik Barua, 1967, p. 1296.
178. Dujari, 2000, pp. 528–29.
179. Christophe Jaffrelot, *Religion, Caste and Politics in India,* Primus Books, New Delhi, 2010, p. 174.
180. Poddar to Gambhirchand Dujari, 5, Chaitra Shukla, 1936. Poddar Papers.

181. Poddar to Lal Bahadur Shastri, 15 March 1965, *Saras Patra*, 2005, pp. 140–41.
182. *Kalyan*, May 1965, pp. 1 and 1020.

2. The World of Gita Press

1. Krishan Bihari Mishra, *Hind Patrakarita: Rajasthani Ayojan Ki Kriti Bhumika*, Akhil Bharatiya Marwari Yuva Manch, Delhi, 1999.
2. *Kalyan*, Inaugural Issue, August 1926, pp. 2–3. All translations are by this writer.
3. Ibid., pp. 30–33.
4. *Kalyan*, Vol. 1, No. 2, September 1926, p. 49.
5. Bhupendranath Sanyal (1877–1962), considered a doyen of Kriya Yoga, is said to have been a child prodigy with mythic tales about his spiritual prowess. Born in Nadia (West Bengal), Sanyal set up yogic ashrams all over the country.
6. Bhagwati Prasad Singh, *Manishi Ki Lokyatra: Gopinath Kaviraj Ka Jivan Darshan*, Vishwavidyalaya Prakashan, Banaras, 2010, pp. 188–89.
7. Partha Chatterjeee, 'History and the Nationalisation of Hinduism', in Vasudha Dalmia and Heinrich von Stietencron (eds), *The Oxford India Hinduism Reader*, Oxford University Press, New Delhi, 2009, pp. 231–61.
8. Bhupendranath Sanyal, '*Hamara Param Lakshya*' (Our Supreme Goal), *Kalyan*, Vol . 1, No. 5, 1926, pp. 130–36.
9. Chatterjeee, 2009.
10. '*Kya Bhagwan Ke Pratyaksh Darshan Ho Sakte Hain*' (Can there be direct vision of god?), *Kalyan*, Vol. 1, No. 6, pp. 184–86.
11. '*Shri Bhagwan Naam: Param Awashyak Soochna*' (Name of Shri Bhagwan: Most Urgent Notice), *Kalyan*, Vol. 1, No. 7, 1926, pp. 114–15.
12. P.S. Chauhan, 'Hindi Novel Before Premchand', shodhganga.inflibnet.ac.in/bitstream/10603/ . . . /06_chapter%202.pdf, 2012. Accessed on 1 September 2012.
13. '*Pandit Lajjaramji Mehta Ka Patra*' (Letter from Pt Lajjaram Mehta), *Kalyan*, Vol. 1, No. 7, 1926, pp. 222–23.
14. '*Holi Par Hamara Kartavya*' (Our Duty during Holi), *Kalyan*, Vol. 1, No. 8, 1926, p. 249. Prahlad is a character from the Puranas known

for his deep devotion to God. He could not be dissuaded from his path despite attempts by his demon father Hiranyakashipu.

15. Rajnish Kumar Chaturvedi, '*Patrakarita Ke Kshetra Mein Kalyan Dharmik Patrika Ka Yogdan*' (Contribution of religious journal *Kalyan* to the field of journalism), unpublished Ph.D. dissertation, Mahamana Madan Mohan Malaviya Hindi Patrakarita Sansthan, Mahatma Gandhi Kashi Vidyapith, Banaras, 2006, p. 367.
16. *Hindu Panch*, Vol. 2, No. 10, 8 September 1927, p. 36.
17. '*Awashyak Suchnayen*' (Important Notices), *Kalyan*, Vol. 2, No. 2, 1927, last page.
18. Shahid Amin, 'Gandhi as Mahatma: Gorakhpur District, Eastern UP, 1921–2', in Ranajit Guha (ed.), *Subaltern Studies*, Vol. III, Oxford University Press, New Delhi, 1984, p. 7.
19. Information in this paragraph is from Arjun Tiwari, '*Poorvi Uttar Pradesh Mein Hindi Patrakarita Ka Udbhav Aur Vikas*', Ph.D. thesis, Gorakhpur University, 1978, cited in Amin, 1984.
20. William R. Pinch, *Peasants and Monks in British India*, University of California Press, 1996, p. 121. http://ark.cdlib.org/ark:/13030/ft22900465. Accessed on 1 September 2012. GOI, Home Department, Public Proceedings, December 1893, No. 212. Cited in Pinch, 1996.
21. Cited in Pinch, 1996, p. 43.
22. Information in this paragraph is from Bhagwati Prasad Singh, *Kalyan Path: Nirmata Aur Rahi*, Radha Madhav Seva Sansthan, Gorakhpur, 1980, pp. 289–90.
23. Jaydayal Goyandka's letter to Nandlal Joshi, date unclear, 1927. Poddar Papers.
24. Information in this and the following paragraph from Singh, 1980, pp. 259–61.
25. Karmendu Shishir (ed.), *Shivpujan Sahay Samagra*, Vol. 8, Anamika Publishers, New Delhi, 2011, pp. 430–31.
26. Singh, 1980, p. 260.
27. Yagik to Poddar, 30 December 1936, 26 January and 25 February 1937. Poddar Papers.
28. Yagik to Poddar, 15 March 1937. Poddar Papers.
29. Yagik to Poddar, 25 March 1937. Podhdar Papers.
30. Pinch has explained in detail the debate within the Ramanandi sect on caste rules of commensality.

31. Cited in Pinch, 1996, p. 66.
32. Francesca Orsini, *The Hindi Public Sphere: Language and Literature in the Age of Nationalism, 1920-1940,* Oxford University Press, New Delhi, 2002, pp. 451–52.
33. Viyogi Hari to Poddar, 20 October 1970. Poddar Papers.
34. Interview transcript of Hanuman Prasad Poddar. Poddar Papers.
35. '*Bhul Sudhar*' (Correction), *Kalyan,* June 1936.
36. Letter of complaint by trustee B.J. Oza to Hanuman Prasad Poddar, 7 October 1940. Poddar Papers.
37. *Kalyan,* December 1960.
38. Ibid.
39. '*Sarvagya, Gobind Bhawan*' (Omniscient, Gobind Bhawan), *Hindu Panch,* Vol. 2, No. 41, 31 May 1928, pp. 17–18.
40. Pannalal Sharma, '*Kalkatte Ka Samajik Jivan*' (Social Life of Calcutta), *Chand* (*Marwari Ank*), November 1929, pp. 152-65, 221-23.
41. *Hindu Panch,* Vol. 2, N. 41, 31 May 1928, pp. 17–18.
42. Goyandka's statement. Poddar Papers.
43. *Hindu Panch,* Vol. 2, N. 41, 31 May 1928, pp. 17–18.
44. Ibid.
45. G.D. Birla (ed.), *Bapu: A Unique Association,* Vol. I, Bharatiya Vidya Bhavan, Bombay, 1977, pp. 95–96.
46. *Kalyan,* Vol. 2, No. 11, 1927, pp. 508–09.
47. Mahatma Gandhi, '*Bhakti Ke Naam Par Bhog*' (Sex in the Name of Devotion) *Hindu Panch,* Vol. 2, No. 40, 24 May 1928, p. 39 (reproduced from *Navjivan*).
48. Satyadev Vidyalankar, '*Gobind Bhawan Aur Sthaniya Samachar Patra*' (Gobind Bhawan and local newspapers), *Hindu Panch,* Vol. 2, No. 42, 7 June 1928, pp. 39–42.
49. Transcript of interview with Hanuman Prasad Poddar for his biography. Poddar Papers.
50. Government Gazette of the United Provinces, Allahabad, Saturday, 1 March, 1939, No. XI, Vol. LXI, p. 235. Commissioner's Record Room, Gorakhpur.
51. Poddar to Gambhirchand Dujari, Ashadha Krishna, Samvat 1985 (1928). Poddar Papers.
52. Poddar to Gambhirchand Dujari, Vaisakha Shukla, Samvat 1985 (1928). Poddar Papers.

53. '*Sampadakiya Tippniyan*' (Editorial Comments), *Kalyan*, Vol. 2, No. 2, 1927, pp. 190–91.
54. Monika Freier, 'Cultivating Emotions: The Gita Press and Its Agenda of Social and Spiritual Reform', *South Asian History and Culture*, Vol. 3, No. 3, 2012, pp. 397–413.
55. Hanuman Prasad Poddar, *Samaj Sudhar*, Gita Press, Gorakhpur, 1928, pp. 34–36.
56. Philip Lutgendorf, *Hanuman's Tale: The Message of a Divine Monkey*, Oxford University Press, New Delhi, 2007, p. 294.
57. Harold A. Gould, *Grass Roots Politics in India: A Century of Political Evolution in Faizabad District*, Oxford & IBH, New Delhi, 1994, p. 180.
58. Orsini, 2002, pp. 398–99.
59. All Gita test details from *Kalyan*, Vol. 2, Nos. 6 and 8, 1927.
60. Ritu Sinha, 'Educating the Hindu Child Citizen: Pedagogy of the Gita Press', paper presented at a workshop on education, Jammu University, November 2012.
61. *Kalyan*, Vol. 2, No. 8, 1927.
62. '*Shri Gita Pariksha*' (Gita Examination), *Kalyan*, August 1939, p. 1072.
63. Poddar's invitation letter for Gita Society, 2 April 1935. Poddar Papers.
64. Akshaya Mukul, 'History Joshi Wants to Censor,' *Times of India*, 24 February 2002, http://articles.timesofindia.indiatimes.com/2002-02-24/india/27124654_1_hindu-mahasabha-savarkar-muslims. Accessed on 5 September 2012.
65. Partha Chatterjee, *A Princely Impostor? The Kumar of Bhawal and the Secret History of Indian Nationalism*, Permanent Black, Ranikhet, 2002, p. 342.
66. *Marwari Stores Ltd*, vs *Gouri Shankar Goenka*, AIR 1936 Cal 327, 165 Ind Cas 408.
67. The list also had names like I.J.S. Taraporewala of Bombay's Muncherjee Framji Cama Athornan Institute who was a leading writer on Zoroastrianism; Sophia Wadia of the United Lodge of Theosophists, Bombay; Mohammad Hafiz Syed of Allahabad University, who was a regular contributor to *Kalyan* and a friend of Poddar's and Jwala Prasad Kanodia. List based on Gita Society pamphlet. Poddar Papers.

68. Ernest P. Hortwitz to Poddar, 5 May 1935. Poddar Papers.
69. Davar to Manager, Gita Press, 2 December 1934. Poddar Papers.
70. Purshottamdas Thakurdas's secretary to Gita Press, 29 November 1934. Poddar Papers.
71. Ganganath Jha to Hanuman Prasad Poddar, 27 November 1934. Poddar Papers.
72. Rev. Edwin Greaves to Poddar, 23 April 1935. Poddar Papers.
73. Ragbans Kishore Balbir to Poddar, 14 September 1935. Poddar Papers.
74. *London Gazette*, Vol. I, printed and published by His Majesty's Stationery Office, London, 1947, p. 22. http://www.london.gazette.co.uk/issues/37842/pages/124/page.pdf. Accessed on 5 September 2012.
75. Hanuman Prasad Poddar, *'Shri Bhagwan Naam Jap Ke Liye Sadar Prarthana'* (Request to recite God's Name), 1948. Poddar Papers.
76. Pamphlet on membership of Shri Gita-Ramayana Prachar Sangh. Poddar Papers.
77. Quotes in this paragraph are from Philip Lutgendorf, *The Life of a Text: Performing the Ramcaritmanas of Tulsidas*, University of California Press, Berkeley, 1991, p. 62.
78. In 1954, Devdas Gandhi as editor of *The Hindustan Times* helped bring out a full-verse translation in English of the Ramcharitmanas by Rev. A.G. Atkins, an American priest. In his introduction Atkins wrote that he had followed the edition of Ramcharitmanas of Chaturvedi Dwarikaprasad Sharma in close consultation with the editions of Dr Mataprasad Gupta of Gita Press and Dr Shyam Sundar Das. I owe this information to Ramachandra Guha and Gopalkrishna Gandhi.
79. S.S. Suryanarayana Sastri to Poddar, 5 August 1938. Poddar Papers.
80. Gopi Kisan Bhartia to Poddar, 12 October 1939. Poddar Papers.
81. Letter from president, Mandir Committee, 4 Training Battalion, 1, EME Centre, 26 August 1966. Poddar Papers.
82. Gita Piramal, *Business Legends*, Viking (Penguin), New Delhi, 1998, pp. 24–25.
83. S.N. Mangal to Poddar, 2 February 1967. Poddar Papers.
84. Harold A. Gould, *Sikhs, Swamis, Students, and Spies: The Indian Lobby in the United States, 1900-1946*, Sage Publications, New Delhi, 2006, p. 70.

85. Vinesh Y. Hookoomsing, 'Chhota Bharat, Mauritius: The Myth and The Reality', in Bhikhu Parekh, Gurharpal Singh and Steven Vertovec (eds), *Culture and Economy in the Indian Diaspora*, Routledge, London, 2003, pp. 13–32.
86. Tarachand Roy to Poddar, 30 October 1935. Poddar Papers.
87. G.A. Bernard to Poddar, 2 September 1935. Poddar Papers.
88. www.shantisadan.org. Accessed on 10 September 2012.
89. Uttama Devi to Poddar, 15 March 1945. Poddar Papers.
90. Uttama Devi to Poddar, 24 February 1945. Poddar Papers.
91. Louise Wilding to editor, *Kalyana-Kalpataru*, 11 January 1943. Poddar Papers.
92. Louise Wilding to editor, *Kalayana-Kalpataru*, 22 February 1943. Poddar Papers.
93. P. Adaros to editor, *Kalyana-Kalpataru*, 21 December 1944. Poddar Papers.
94. http://henrythomashamblin.wwwhubs.com/. Accessed on 10 September 2012.
95. Hamblin to Poddar, 20 September 1944. Poddar Papers.
96. Hamblin to Poddar, 23 February 1945. Poddar Papers.
97. Herbert to Poddar, 10 February 1945. Poddar Papers.
98. W.D. Padfield to editor, *Kalyana-Kalpataru*, 26 June 1958. Poddar Papers.
99. Krishna Dutt Bharadwaj to Poddar, 29 October 1958. Poddar Papers.
100. Curator, Sri Chitra Central Hindu Religious Library, Trivandrum, to manager, *Kalyana-Kalpataru*, 18 December 1945. Poddar Papers.
101. Bhandarkar Institute's Mahabharata project began in 1919. Various editions came out before a Critical edition running into nineteen volumes was produced in 1966. The institute is still working on the project. It plans to bring out a translation of the critical edition and interpretive epilogue, and digitize the text. Source: http://www.bori.ac.in/mahabharata_project.html. Accessed on 5 June 2014.
102. Poddar, '*Sampadak Ka Nivedan Aur Kshama Prarthana*' (Editor's Submission and Prayer for Forgiveness), *Mahabharata*, Vol. 3, No. 12, 1958, pp. 247–48.
103. Eric Hobsbawm, 'Introduction: Inventing Traditions', in Eric Hobsbawm and Terence Ranger (eds), *The Invention of Tradition*, Cambridge University Press, Cambridge, UK, 1983, pp. 1, 4.

104. Dieter Conrad, 'The Personal Law Question and Hindu Nationalism', in Vasudha Dalmia and Heinrich von Stietencron (eds), *The Oxford India Hinduism Reader*, Oxford University Press, New Delhi, 2007, p. 192.
105. Singh, 1980, pp. 262–63.
106. Poddar's invitation letter dated 10 June 1949 for contribution to *Hindu Sanskriti Ank*. Purshottamdas Thakurdas Papers, NMML, File No. 661.
107. Poddar's letter in Hindi inviting articles for *Ishwar Ank* of 1932. Poddar Papers.
108. Copy of Poddar's invitation letter for *Gau Ank* of 1945. Poddar Papers.
109. Editor, *Kalyan*, to officiating director of statistics, Department of Commercial Intelligence and Statistics, India, 16 September 1945; Editor, *Kalyan*, to director of farms, general headquarters, Simla, 24 August 1945. Poddar Papers.
110. Editor, *Kalyan*, to Sir Datar Singh, 15 September 1945. Poddar Papers.
111. For example, editor, *Kalyan* to K.C. Sen, director of dairy research in Bangalore, 15 September 1945; editor, *Kalyan*, to B.N. Mankar of the Bombay Humanitarian League, 25 August 1945. Poddar Papers.
112. Editor, *Kalyan*, to secretary, Imperial Council of Agricultural Research, 25 August 1945. Poddar Papers.
113. Editor, *Kalyan*, to the manager, Prabhat Film Company, 5 July 1945. Poddar Papers.
114. Niranjanananda Swamy to Poddar, 10 July 1945. Poddar Papers.
115. Gandhi to Poddar, 8 April 1932, *Collected Works of Mahatma Gandhi*, Vol. 55, p. 213.
116. Gandhi to Poddar, 23 May 1932, *Collected Works of Mahatma Gandhi*, Vol 55, p. 415.
117. Gandhi to Poddar, 21 June 1932. *Collected Works of Mahatma Gandhi*, Vol. 56, p. 35.
118. C.F. Andrews to Poddar, undated (in the file related to 1935). Poddar Papers.
119. '*Kalyan Ka Manas Ank*', *Arya Mahila*, September 1938. Poddar Papers.
120. Review of *Manas Ank* by *Bharata Dharma*, clippings in Poddar Papers.

121. Review of *Yoga Ank* by *Bombay Chronicle*, clippings in Poddar Papers.
122. Review of *Yoga Ank* by *Cherag*, clippings in Poddar Papers.
123. Poddar to Ambika Prasad Vajpayee, Magh Krishna 4, Samvat 1991 (1934), *Saras Patra* compiled by Shyamsundar Dujari, Gita Vatika Prakashan, Gorakhpur, 2005, pp. 111–12.
124. Partha Mitter, 'Mechanical Reproduction and the World of the Colonial Artist', in Sumathi Ramaswamy (ed.), *Beyond Appearances*, Sage, New Delhi, 2003, p. 15.
125. Partha Mitter, *Art and Nationalism in Colonial India, 1850-1922*, Cambridge University Press, New Delhi, 1994, p. 122.
126. Mitter, 2003, p. 25.
127. Christopher Pinney, *Photos of the Gods: The Printed Image and Political Struggle in India*, Reaktion Books, London, 2004, p. 72.
128. Kajri Jain, 'The Efficacious Image: Pictures and Power in Indian Mass Culture', in Richard H. Davis (ed.), *Picturing the Nation: Iconographies of Modern India*, Orient Longman, New Delhi, 2007, p. 156.
129. Kajri Jain, 'More Than Meets the Eye: The Circulation of Images and the Embodiment of Value', in Ramaswamy (ed.), 2003, p. 41.
130. Jain, 'The Efficacious Image', 2007, pp. 158–59.
131. Ibid., p. 160.
132. Kajri Jain, *Gods in the Bazaar: The Economies of Indian Calendar Art*, Duke University Press, Durham, 2007, p. 148.
133. Singh, 1980, p. 283; James G. Lochtefeld, *The Illustrated Encyclopedia of Hinduism*, Vol. I, Rosen Publishing Group Inc., New York, 2002, p. 152.
134. Singh, 1980, p. 283; Lochtefeld, 2002, Vol. II, p. 582.
135. Singh, 1980, p. 283.
136. Walter Benjamin, *Illuminations: Essays and Reflections*, translated by Harry Zohn, edited by Hannah Arendt, Schocken Books, New York, 2007, p. 224.
137. *Kalyan, Bhakta Ank*, Vol. 3, No. 1, 1928, plate between pp. 30 and 31.
138. Typewritten copy of Gandhi's letter to Poddar, 16 May 1935. Poddar Papers. The letter is not in the *Collected Works of Mahatma Gandhi*.
139. Ramcharan Mahendra, '*Devi Devtaon Ke Chitron Ke Darshan Se Tamogun Aur Mansik Rog Dur Ho Jate Hain*' (Viewing Pictures of

Gods and Goddesses Takes Away Dark Thoughts and Mental Illness), *Kalyan*, May 1960, pp. 951–54.

140. Ramcharan Mahendra, '*Hindu Devtaon Mein Vibhinn Rangon Ka Chhipa Hua Gupt Aphipraya*' (The Secret Meaning of Colours Hidden in Hindu Deities), *Kalyan*, April 1967, pp. 849–54.
141. Shivram Krishna Godbole to Poddar, 3 November 1935. Poddar Papers.
142. Singh, 1980, pp. 375–76.
143. Goyandka to Poddar, Magha Shukla, Samvat 2011 (1954). Poddar Papers.
144. R.R. Diwakar to Poddar. 28 July 1952. Poddar Papers.
145. Singh, 1980, pp. 282–84.
146. Ibid.
147. Jain, 'The Efficacious Image', p. 161; *Gods in the Bazar*, p. 86.
148. Pinney, 2004, p. 82; Jain, 'More Than Meets the Eye', 2003, p. 54.
149. R.K. Vashistha, *Art and Artists of Rajasthan*, Abhinav Publications, New Delhi, 1995, p. 87.
150. Pinney, 2004, p. 89.
151. Prem Narendra Ghasiram Sharma to Poddar, 6 December 1931. Poddar Papers.
152. Prem Narendra Ghasiram Sharma to Poddar, 9 March 1932. Poddar Papers.
153. Prem Narendra Ghasiram Sharma to Poddar, 14 June 1932. Poddar Papers.
154. Satyendranath Banerjee to manager, Gita Press, 18 March 1932. Poddar Papers.
155. Testimonial for Banerjee: by Nandalal Bose, 21 July 1923; by C.F. Andrews, 18 July 1923. Poddar Papers.
156. Banerjee to *Kalyan* editor, 29 March 1932. Poddar Papers.
157. Mitter, 1994, p. 297.
158. Dhanpat Rai (Premchand) to Poddar, date not clear but postmark on the postcard shows 1932. Poddar Papers.
159. Mohd. Hakim Khan to Poddar, 16 March 1932. Poddar Papers.
160. Mohd. Hakim Khan to Poddar, date not clear but he mentions having received Poddar's letter of 14 June 1932. Poddar Papers.
161. Mohd. Hakim Khan to Poddar, 1 July 1932. Poddar Papers.
162. Yashodhara Dalmia, *Amrita Sher-Gil: A Life*, Penguin-Viking, New Delhi, 2006, p. 62.

163. Tapati Guha-Thakurta, *The Making of A New Art: Artists, Aesthetics and Nationalism in Bengal, C. 1850-1920*, Cambridge University Press, Cambridge, UK, 1992, p. 323.
164. Vivan Sundaram, *Amrita Sher-Gil: A Self-Portrait in Letters & Writings*, Vol. I, Tulika Books, New Delhi, 2010, p. 332.
165. Sarada Ukil to Poddar, 17 December 1935. Poddar Papers.
166. Sarada Ukil to Poddar, 20 February 1936. Poddar Papers.
167. Sarada Ukil to Poddar, 18 May 1939. Poddar Papers.
168. Poddar to Sarada Ukil, 27 June 1939. Poddar Papers.
169. Sarada Ukil to Poddar, 14 July 1939. Poddar Papers.
170. Sarada Ukil to Poddar, 19 July 1939. Poddar Papers.
171. Poddar to Sarada Ukil, 26 March 1940. Poddar Papers.
172. Sarada Ukil to Poddar, 3 April 1940. Poddar Papers.
173. Poddar to Sarada Ukil, 6 April 1940. Poddar Papers.
174. Sarada Ukil to Poddar, 24 April 1940. Poddar Papers.
175. Sarada Ukil to Poddar, 1 June 1940 and 3 June 1940. Poddar Papers.
176. Sarada Ukil to Poddar, 10 June 1940. Poddar Papers.
177. Partha Mitter, *The Triumph of Modernism: India's Artists and the Avant-Garde 1922—1947*, Reaktion Books, London, 2007, p. 16.
178. Guha-Thakurta, 1992, p. 217.
179. See ibid., and Mitter, 1994, for detailed debates on art and aesthetics.
180. O.C. Gangoly to Poddar, 10 January 1937. Poddar Papers.
181. Poddar to Gangoly, 7 February 1950. Poddar Papers.
182. Poddar's letter to chief secretary, Tranvancore state, 9 November 1949. Poddar Papers.
183. Dyaneshwar Nadkarni, *Husain: Riding the Lightning*, Popular Prakashan, Bombay, 1996, pp. 31–33.
184. Deolalikar's telegrams to Poddar, 13 August 1930 and 16 August 1930. Poddar Papers.
185. Poddar to Deolalikar, 1930 (exact date not clear). Poddar Papers.
186. Deolalikar to Poddar, 12 October 1931. Poddar Papers.
187. Deolalikar to Poddar, 29 November 1931. Poddar Papers.
188. Deolalikar to Poddar, 30 March 1932. Poddar Papers.
189. Mitter, 1994, pp. 331–32.
190. Gulammohammed Sheikh, 'The Backdrop', in Sheikh (ed.), *Contemporary Art in Baroda*, Tulika, New Delhi, 1997, pp. 42–43.
191. Kanu Desai to Poddar, 5 November 1938. Poddar Papers.

192. Kanu Desai to Poddar, 16 May 1939. Poddar Papers.
193. Savitri Khanolkar to Poddar, 31 October 1939. Poddar Papers
194. Savitri Khanolkar to Poddar, 17 February 1940. Poddar Papers.
195. Hanuman Prasad Poddar and Chimmanlal Gosvami, '*Kshama Prarthana*' (Prayer for Forgiveness), *Upasana Ank, Kalyan,* January 1968, pp. 699–700.
196. Gita Dwar and Leela Chitra Mandir inauguration pamphlet, 29 April 1955. Poddar Papers.
197. Ibid.
198. Dr Rajendra Prasad's speech at the inauguration of Gita Dwar and Leela Chitra Mandir of Gita Press on 29 April 1955, Gorakhpur, published in *Kalyan,* June 1955, pp. 1113–15.
199. Hanuman Prasad Poddar, '*Lalaji Ka Parlokvas*' (Demise of Lalaji), *Kalyan,* March 1928, p. 566.
200. Hanuman Prasad Poddar, '*Pt Motilalji Ka Dehavasan*' (Death of Pt Motilal), *Kalyan,* April 1931, p. 1152.
201. Hanuman Prasad Poddar, 'Emperor George V', *Kalyan,* April 1936, p. 1359.
202. Hanuman Prasad Poddar, '*Vinashi Jagat*' (Destructive World), *Kalyan,* December 1936, p. 984.
203. Shivnath Dubey, '*Paramadarniya Dr Hedgewar*' (Revered Dr Hedgewar), *Kalyan, Hindu Sanskriti Ank,* January 1950, last page.
204. Hanuman Prasad Poddar, '*Nehruji Ke Prati Shraddhanjali*' (Tribute to Nehru), *Kalyan,* June 1964, page not numbered.
205. Hanuman Prasad Poddar, '*Shri Lal Bahadur Shastri*', *Kalyan,* January 1966, page not numbered.
206. Information and quotes in this and subsequent paragraphs are from Bhimsen, '*Shri Guruji: Ek Adhyatmik Vibhuti*' (Guruji: A Spiritual Icon), *Kalyan,* July 1973, pp. 852–58.
207. '*Shrimati Indira Gandhiji Ke Prati Shraddhanjali*' (A Tribute to Mrs Indira Gandhi), *Kalyan,* November 1984, p. 901.
208. Klaus K. Klostermaier, *A Survery of Hinduism,* State University of New York Press, New York, 2007, p. 109.
209. Radheshyam Khemka, '*Himsa Ka Nanga Tandav*' (Naked Dance of Violence), *Kalyan,* May 1991, p. 568.
210. Poddar to Gambhirchand Dujari, Sravana Shukla 5, Samvat 1983 (1926). Poddar Papers.

211. Poddar to Jwala Prasad Kanodia, Kartik Krishna 8, Samvat 1989 (1932), *Saras Patra*, 2005, pp. 112–13.
212. Singh, 1980, p. 157.
213. Gyanendra Pandey, *The Ascendancy of the Congress in Uttar Pradesh*, Anthem Press, London, 2002, p. 40.
214. Singh, 1980, pp. 158–59.
215. Ibid.
216. Notification of Industries Department, 3 April 1939, No. 1127/ XVIII–625-D, Commissioner's Record Room, Gorakhpur.
217. CID, United Provinces, Weekly Reports on Political Activities, weeks ending 5 March, 2 April and 30 April 1948. CID Archives, Lucknow.
218. '*Dushkal Ke Sambandh Mein*' (About Unfortunate Times), *Saraswati*, September 1943, p. 464.
219. J.E. Pedley's testimonial, 25 March 1940. Poddar Papers.
220. H.S. Ross's testimonial, 11 July 1942. Poddar Papers.
221. H.S. Ross to chief price controller, Bihar government, 8 July 1942. Poddar Papers.
222. Memorandum by Gita Press; Note by B.L. Chandgothia, 14 May 1953; Chandgothia to Seth Govind Das, 16 July 1953. Seth Govind Das Papers, NMML.
223. B.L. Chandgothia to the labour commissioner, Uttar Pradesh, 16 July 1956. Poddar Papers.
224. Copy of legal opinion sought by Jaidayal Dalmia. Poddar Papers.
225. Jaidayal Dalmia to Krishna Chandra, Gita Press, 30 March 1968. Poddar Papers.
226. Poddar to Ishwari Prasad Goenka, 11 February 1967, *Saras Patra*, 2005, pp. 113–16.
227. Letters from Gobind Bhawan to Poddar, 5 and 12 December 1969. Poddar Papers.
228. Communication from the Office of Labour Commissioner, West Bengal, to Gobind Bhavan Karyalaya, 1 July 1970. Poddar Papers.
229. Annual statement of accounts, 1968–69. Poddar Papers.
230. Minutes of the meeting of the trustees of Gobind Bhawan Karyalaya, 7 March 1970. Poddar Papers.
231. Singh, 1980, pp. 162–63.
232. This and further quotes are from Poddar's letter to Pandit Hari Prasad, 24 February 1966. Poddar Papers.

233. Jaidayal Dalmia to *TOI* and *The Indian Express*, 10 March 1968. Poddar Papers.
234. Copy of estimate sent by *TOI* to Dalmia, 18 March 1968. Poddar Papers.
235. Ramnath Goenka to Dalmia, 27 March 1968. Poddar Papers.
236. G.P. Birla to Poddar, 19 March 1970. Poddar Papers.
237. S.S. Goenka to Poddar, 9 April 1970. Poddar Papers.
238. Poddar to G.P. Birla, 27 July 1970; Gobind Bhawan functionary to Poddar, 18 July 1970. Poddar Papers.
239. Jaidayal Dalmia to Harikrishna Dujari, 17 April 1970. Poddar Papers.
240. Poddar to Bihari Lal, 15 June 1970. Poddar Papers.
241. Poddar to Ishwari Prasad Goenka, 27 July 1970, *Saras Patra*, 2005, pp. 116–17.
242. Poddar to Bihari Lal, 15 May 1970; Jaidayal Dalmia to Krishna Chandra, undated (contents reveal it was around the same time). Poddar Papers.
243. Draft of Gita Press's application to assistant controller, Exchange Control Department, Reserve Bank of India, Kanpur, undated. Poddar Papers. However, the idea for application was mooted by Jaidayal Dalmia on 15 September 1970. Also part of Poddar Papers.
244. Draft of Gita Press's application to RBI, undated. Poddar Papers.

3. Contributors: Local, National, Transnational

1. Bhagwati Prasad Singh, *Kalyan Path: Nirmata Aur Rahi*, Radha Madhav Seva Sansthan, Gorakhpur, 1980, p. 269.
2. Poddar Papers.
3. Klaus K. Klostermaier, *A Concise Encyclopedia of Hinduism*, Oneworld Publications, London, 1998, pp. 176–77.
4. A.L. Basham, *The Wonder That Was India*, Rupa Paperback, New Delhi, 1981, p. 113.
5. Klostermaier, 1998, p. 174.
6. Basham, 1981, p. 113.
7. Ritu Sinha, 'Educating the Hindu Child Citizen: Pedagogy of the Gita Press', paper presented at a workshop on Education, Jammu University, November 2012.
8. Poddar Papers.
9. Singh, 1980, p. 268.

10. See Paul Brunton, *A Search in Secret India*, Samuel Weiser Inc., Maine (USA), 1934.
11. C.D. Deshmukh to Poddar, 31 May 1941. Poddar Papers.
12. Madhav Ashish to Poddar, undated but talks of *Manavta Ank* of 1959. Poddar Papers.
13. Letter from Bharat Dharma Mahamandal to Poddar, 22 October 1934. Poddar Papers.
14. Shyam Swarup Sharma to Ghanshyam Das Jalan, publisher, Gita Press, 2 November 1968. Poddar Papers.
15. Poddar to Vishwanath Malhotra, 22 November 1968. Poddar Papers.
16. *Kalyan*, December 1968, pp. 1374–75.
17. Prabhupada to Satsvarupa, 31 December 1968. www.prabhupada books.com. Accessed on 1 October 2013.
18. Prabhupada to Satsvarupa, 23 January 1968. www.prabhupada books.com. Accessed on 1 October 2013
19. Prabhupada to Brahmananda, 5 February 1969. www.prabhupada books.com. Accessed on 1 October 2013.
20. Prabhupada to Radhe Shyam Banka, 13 March 1970; Prabhupada to disciple Gargamuni, 16 February 1971. www.prabhupada books.com. Accessed on 1 October 2013.
21. Prabhupada to Poddar, 4 and 5 February 1970. www.prabhupada books.com. Accessed on 1 October 2013.
22. Prabhupada to Poddar, 4 March 1970. www.prabhupadabooks.com. Accessed on 1 October 2013.
23. Prabhupada to Poddar, 23 May 1970. www.prabhupadabooks.com. Accessed on 1 October 2013.
24. Prabhupada to N.C. Chatterjee, 9 July 1970. www.prabhupada books.com. Accessed on 1 October 2013.
25. Singh, 1980, p. 117. Also part of Poddar Papers.
26. Ibid., pp. 134–35.
27. '*Shri Krishna Aur Mahatmaji Ka Anashakti Yoga*' (Krishna and Mahatma's *Anashakti Yoga*), *Saraswati*, November 1931, pp. 569–70.
28. Pyarelal's letter to Hanuman Prasad Poddar, 8 January 1945. Poddar Papers.
29. G.D. Birla to Poddar, 31 May 1958. Poddar Papers.
30. Poddar to Jugal Kishore Birla, 9 Shravan Krishna, Samvat 2006 (1949). Poddar Papers.

31. Interview of Hanuman Prasad Poddar. Poddar Papers.
32. Singh, 1980, p. 117. Also part of Poddar Papers.
33. Claim made in the advertisement of *Bharata Dharma* in *Theosophist Magazine*, October–December 1927.
34. Prefatory note for the book on the Bible by Verrier Elwin sent by C. Rajagopalachari to Poddar. Poddar Papers.
35. C. Rajagopalachari to Poddar, 14 August 1935. Poddar Papers.
36. C. Rajagopalachari to Poddar, 28 June 1952. Poddar Papers.
37. Radhakrishnan to Chimmanlal Gosvami, 17 June 1958. Poddar Papers.
38. K.M. Munshi to Hanuman Prasad Poddar, 17 April 1959. Poddar Papers.
39. Munshi to Poddar, 10 July 1957. Poddar Papers.
40. Poddar to Sampurnanand, 13 Shravan Shukla, Samvat 2006 (1949). Poddar Papers.
41. Poddar to Sampurnanand, Bhadra Amavasya, Samvat 2006 (1949). Poddar Papers.
42. Sampurnanand to Poddar, Bhadra Shukla, Samvat 1994 (1937). Poddar Papers.
43. Sampurnanand to Poddar, 22 October 1937. Poddar Papers.
44. Poddar to Sampurnanand, 21 October 1957. Poddar Papers.
45. Copy of Poddar's editorial comment. Poddar Papers.
46. Katju to Poddar, 4 August 1949. Poddar Papers.
47. Katju to Poddar, 6 October 1952. Poddar Papers.
48. Purshottamdas Thakurdas Papers, NMML, F No. 107(I)/1931 and File No. 81/III-IV/1929.
49. Thakurdas to Poddar, 4 May 1942. Poddar Papers.
50. Thakurdas's letter through secretary, 7 August 1945. Poddar Papers.
51. Thakurdas to Poddar, 27 December 1948. Thakurdas Papers, NMML, File No. F 358.
52. Bhalchand Modi, *Desh Ke Itihas Mein Marwari Jati Ka Sthan*, published by Raghunath Prasad Singhania, Calcutta, 1939, p. 504; Philip Lutgendorf, *The Life of a Text: Performing the Ramcaritmanas of Tulsidas*, University of California Press, Berkeley, 1991. http://ark.cdlib.org/ark:/13030/ft796nb4pk/. Accessed on 14 February 2012.
53. Das to Poddar, 2 December 1959. Poddar Papers.

54. B.L. Chandgothia, general manager, Gita Press to Seth Govind Das, 16 July 1953. Govind Das Papers, NMML.
55. Poddar to Jawaharlal Nehru, 10 June 1949; Prime Minister's Secretariat to *Kalyan* editor, June 1949. Poddar Papers.
56. Pant's letter to Poddar, 19 January 1959. Poddar Papers.
57. Copy of Poddar's letter to G.B. Pant, undated. Poddar Papers. Also cited in Singh, 1980, pp. 479–80.
58. Valmiki Chaudhury to Poddar, 7 July 1952. Poddar Papers.
59. Oral History Transcript of interview with Gyanwati Darbar, private secretary to Rajendra Prasad, by Dr Hari Dev Sharma, 14 March 1969. NMML.
60. Gyanwati Darbar to editor, *Mahabharata,* 27 July 1956. Poddar Papers.
61. Librarian, Delhi University to editor, *Kalyan,* 17 October 1956. Poddar Papers.
62. N. Krishnaswamy to Poddar, 19 January 1949. Poddar Papers.
63. Sri Prakash to Poddar, 12 May 1957; Shriman Narayan to Poddar, 7 June 1958. Poddar Papers.
64. Srikrishna Saral, *Indian Revolutionaries: A Comprehensive Study, 1757–1961,* Vol. 2, Ocean Books, New Delhi, 1999.
65. Cited in Charu Gupta, *Sexuality, Obscenity and Community,* Permanent Black, Ranikhet, 2001, p. 230.
66. Chandkaran Sharda, *'Hindu Sanskriti Kya Hai'* (What is Hindu Culture?), *Kalyan, Hindu Sanskriti Ank,* January 1950, pp. 201–03.
67. Golwalkar to Poddar, 25 December 1949, *Sri Guruji Samagra,* Vol. 7 (Correspondence), Suruchi Prakashan, Delhi, pp. 192–93.
68. Golwalkar to Poddar, 5 July 1955, ibid., pp. 310–11.
69. Thate to Poddar, February 1956, Poddar Papers.
70. Golwalkar to Poddar, 25 February 1956, *Sri Guruji Samagra,* Vol. 7, pp. 211–12.
71. Craig Baxter, *Jana Sangh: A Biography of an Indian Political Party,* Oxford University Press, New Delhi, 1971, pp. 62–63.
72. Mookerji to Poddar, 25 June 1952. Poddar Papers.
73. N.C. Chatterjee to Poddar, 29 June 1952. Poddar Papers.
74. Christophe Jaffrelot, *The Hindu Nationalist Movement in India,* Viking, New Delhi, 1996, p. 94 (fn).
75. N.B. Khare, Oral History Transcript, NMML, Accession No. 301.

76. Jaffrelot, 1996, p. 94.
77. Raghuvira to Poddar, 1 May 1958. Poddar Papers.
78. Raghuvira to Poddar, 8 January 1958. Poddar Papers.
79. Jaffrelot, 1996, p. 103.
80. http://www.swamisridindayaluji.in/karpatri.php. Accessed on 5 September 2012.
81. H.L. Erdman, *The Swatantra Party and Indian Conservatism*, Cambridge University Press, Cambridge, UK, 2008, p. 52.
82. B.D. Graham, *Hindu Nationalism and Indian Politics: The Origin and Development of the Bharatiya Jana Sangh*, Cambridge University Press, New York, 2008, p. 95.
83. Ibid., p. 149.
84. Jaffrelot, 1996, p. 199.
85. Ibid.
86. Kaka Kalelkar's letter and Poddar's reply, *Kalyan*, January 1969, p. 691.
87. *Kaka Kalelkar Granthavali*, Vol. 11, Gandhi Hindustani Sahitya Sabha, New Delhi, 2002, pp. 258–59.
88. Sumit Sarkar, *Swadeshi Movement in Bengal*, Permanent Black, Ranikhet, 2010, p. 143.
89. Ibid., p. 423.
90. Read Sabyasachi Bhattacharya's introduction in Radha Kumud Mookerji, *The Fundamental Unity of India*, Bharatiya Vidya Bhavan, Chronicle Books, New Delhi, 2008.
91. Ram Lal Wadhwa, *Hindu Mahasabha (1928–1947)*, Radha Publications, New Delhi, 1999, p. 179.
92. Mookerji to Poddar, 14 October 1949. Poddar Papers.
93. Mookerji to Poddar, 3 July 1954. Poddar Papers.
94. Ram Moorti Loomba in G.R. Madan (ed.), *Radha Kamal Mukerjee: An Eminent Scholar, Saint and Social Worker*, Radha Publications, New Delhi, 2008, p. 3.
95. Ramachandra Guha, 'The Ones Who Stayed Behind', *Economic & Political Weekly*, 22 March 2003.
96. Loomba in Madan (ed.), 2008, p. 3.
97. Radha Kamal Mukerjee to Poddar, 15 December (year not mentioned). Poddar Papers.
98. S.N. Sen to Poddar, 4 November 1938. Poddar Papers.

99. Sekhar Bandyopadhyay, *Caste, Culture & Hegemony: Social Dominance in Colonial Bengal,* Sage Publications, New Delhi, 2004.
100. Sen to Poddar, 18 July 1945. Poddar Papers.
101. Amartya Sen, Foreword to Kshitimohan Sen, *Hinduism,* Penguin India, New Delhi, 2005.
102. Ibid.
103. Anil K. Chanda, Tagore's secretary, to Poddar, 29 October 1936. Poddar Papers.
104. Altekar to Poddar, 8 February 1934. Poddar Papers.
105. Poddar to Suniti Kumar Chatterjee, 1 August 1949. Poddar Papers.
106. Ganganath Jha to Poddar, 1 October 1938. Poddar Papers.
107. See Hugh Tinker, *The Ordeal of Love: C.F. Andrews and India,* Oxford University Press, New Delhi, 1979.
108. Copy of letter from Andrews to Poddar, 18 July 1923. Poddar Papers.
109. Arundale to Poddar, 29 November 1935. Poddar Papers.
110. Gandhi's Foreword to Sophia Wadia, *Brotherhood of Religions,* International Book House, Bombay, 1939.
111. Wadia to Baba Raghav Das, 30 November 1934. Poddar Papers.
112. http://roerich.org/nr.html?mid=bio_rus. Accessed on 5 October 2012.
113. Roerich's secretary to Poddar, 29 March 1932. Poddar Papers.
114. Roerich to Poddar, 11 March 1932. Poddar Papers.
115. For biographical sketch see Sunil Raman, *C.Y. Chintamani: The Liberal Editor Politician,* Rupa Charitavali Series, New Delhi, 2002; Gyanesh Kudaisya, *Region, Nation, 'Heartland': Uttar Pradesh in India's Body Politic,* Sage, New Delhi, 2006.
116. Nico Slate, *Colored Cosmopolitanism,* Harvard University Press, Cambridge, Mass., 2012, p. 75.
117. Tikekar to Poddar, 16 February 1935. Poddar Papers.
118. Tikekar to Poddar, 21 March 1935. Poddar Papers.
119. Tikekar to Poddar, 8 April 1935. Poddar Papers.
120. Singh, 1980, pp. 144–45.
121. Harish Trivedi, 'Progress of Hindi, Part 2', in Sheldon Pollock (ed.), *Literary Cultures in History: Reconstruction from South Asia,* University of California Press, Berkeley, 2003, p. 976.
122. Allison Busch, 'An Early Moment in the Development of Hindi Literary Theory by Mishrabandhu', in Shobna Nijhawan (ed.),

Nationalism in the Vernacular, Permanent Black, Ranikhet, 2010, p. 343.

123. *Mishrabandhuvinod,* Vol. 1, 4th edition, Ganga Pustakmala Karyalaya, Lucknow, 1934, p. 77.
124. Preface to the second edition of *Mishrabandhuvinod* reproduced in the fourth edition of 1934.
125. *Mishrabandhuvinod,* Vol. IV, 1934, p. 393.
126. See Francesca Orsini, *The Hindi Public Sphere, 1920-40: Language and Literature in the Age of Nationalism,* 2002, Oxford University Press, New Delhi, pp. 401–02.
127. Ayodhya Singh Upadhyay 'Harioudh', *Hindi Bhasha Aur Uske Sahitya Ka Vikas,* Patna University, 1934, printed by Babu Manik Lal, United Press Limited, Bhagalpur, pp. 544–45, 703, 719.
128. Singh, 1980, p. 273.
129. Gambhirchand Dujari, *Shri Bhaiji: Ek Alaukik Vibhuti,* Gita Vatika Prakashan, Gorakhpur, 2000, pp. 307–08.
130. Ruth Vanita, *Love's Rite: Same Sex Marriage in India and the West,* Palgrave, New York, 2005, p. 162.
131. Karmendu Shishir (ed.), *Navjagrankalin Patrakarita Aur Matwala,* Vol. I, Anamika Prakashan, New Delhi, 2012, p. 38.
132. Chaturvedi to Ugra, undated, marked personal in Narayan Dutt (ed.), *Banarsidas Chaturvedi Ke Chuninda Patra,* Vol. I, IGNCA and Rajkamal Prakashan, New Delhi, 2006, p. 237.
133. Another undated letter to Ugra, ibid.
134. Copy of Poddar's letter to Chaturvedi, 1931. Poddar Papers.
135. Chaturvedi to Poddar, 11 August 1941. Poddar Papers.
136. Chaturvedi to Poddar, May 1958. Poddar Papers.
137. Shamshur Rahman Faruqi, 'A Long History of Urdu Literary Culture, Part I,' in Pollock (ed.), 2003, p. 819.
138. Dujari, 2000, p. 307.
139. Trivedi, 2003, p. 990
140. This and the following quotes are from Karine Schomer, *Mahadevi Varma and the Chhayavad Age of Modern Hindi Poetry,* Oxford University Press, New Delhi, 1998, pp. 26, 95–96, 101.
141. Trivedi, 2003, p. 995.
142. Ibid., p. 994.
143. This and the following information is from Shishir (ed.), 2012, pp. 24, 31, 39; and Schomer, 1998, p. 103.

144. Dujari, 2000, p. 307.
145. Poddar to Pant, date not clear. Poddar Papers.
146. Schomer, 1998, p. 21.
147. Ibid., pp. 95–96.
148. Trivedi, 2003, p. 988.
149. Sudhir Chandra, *Hindu, Hindutva, Hindustan*, Rajkamal Prakashan, New Delhi, 2005, pp. 134–35.
150. Shishir (ed.), 2012, Vol. II, p. 116.
151. Poddar to Gupt, 1949. Poddar Papers.
152. Gupt to Poddar, 1945. Poddar Papers.
153. Orsini, 2002, pp. 424–25.
154. Phrase attributed to Nirala in Shishir, 2012, Vol. 1, p. 32.
155. Ibid., p. 31.
156. Poddar to Sahay, 23 May 1932. Shivpujan Sahay Papers, NMML.
157. Poddar to Sahay, 6 September 1931. Shivpujan Sahay Papers, NMML.
158. Poddar to Pravasi Lal Varma, date not clear. Shivpujan Sahay Papers, NMML.
159. Lutgendorf, 1991, pp. 59–60.
160. Orsini, 2002, pp. 415–16.
161. Singh, 1980, pp. 35, 37, 50, 275.
162. Mangal Murthy (ed.), *Shivpujan Sahay Sahitya Samagra*, Vol. II, Anamika Prakashan, New Delhi, 2012, pp. 397–98.
163. See Singh, 1980, pp. 471–74.
164. Garde to Poddar, 12 July 1957. Poddar Papers.
165. Garde to Gosvami, 2 December 1957. Poddar Papers.
166. Harivansh Rai Bachchan, '*Geet*', *Kalyan*, June 1960, p. 1008.
167. Harivansh Rai Bachchan, *In the Afternoon of Time: An Autobiography*, edited and translated from Hindi by Rupert Snell, Viking, New Delhi, 1998, pp. 402–03.
168 . Radheshyam Banka, *Parikar Malika*, Vol. IV, Hanuman Prasad Poddar Smarak Samiti, Gorakhpur, 2013, pp. 274–75.
169. Biographical details from Shishir (ed.), 2012, Vol. I, pp. 329, 331; Orsini, 2002, pp. 400–01.
170. Tripathi to Poddar, 7 July 1952. Poddar Papers.
171. Orsini, 2002, pp. 404–05.
172. Jainendra Kumar to Poddar, 6 December 1958. Poddar Papers.

173. Biographical details of writers from Shishir (ed.), 2012, Vol. I; Orsini, 2002, pp. 384–452; Murthy (ed.), 2012, p. 398.
174. Syed to Poddar, 11 November 1934. Poddar Papers.
175. Syed to Poddar, 27 November 1936. Poddar Papers.
176. Syed to Poddar, 15 December 1936. Poddar Papers.
177. Syed to Poddar, 25 November 1938. Poddar Papers.
178. Syed to Poddar, 11 January 1943. Poddar Papers.
179. Syed to Poddar, 12 June 1944. Poddar Papers.
180. Singh, 1980, p. 273.
181. Syed to Chimmanlal Gosvami, 17 June 1958. Poddar Papers.
182. Kasim Ali to Poddar, 10 October 1952. Poddar Papers.
183. Kasim Ali to Poddar, 11 November 1952. Poddar Papers.
184. Hussain to Poddar, 19 February 1932. Poddar Papers.
185. Firoze C. Davar, *Parsis and Racial Suicide*, Dinar Printing, Bombay, year unknown, pp. 8, 5.
186. Davar to Poddar, 11 December 1935. Poddar Papers.
187. Davar to Poddar, 28 November 1936. Poddar Papers.
188. Davar to Poddar, 18 June 1958. Poddar Papers.
189. Biographical details from http://archives.gcah.org/publicdata/gcah2723.htm. Accessed on 5 November 2012.
190. Biographical details from http://christianlarson.wwwhubs.com/ Accessed on 5 November 2012.
191. Edwin Greaves, *Hindi Grammar*, Indian Press, Allahabad, 1921, pp. III, 6.
192. Greaves to Poddar, February 1935. Poddar Papers.
193. Johan Van Manen's prefatory note in Schrader's *Introduction to the Pancaratra and Ahirbudhaya Samhita*, Adyar Library, Madras, 1916.
194. Schrader to Poddar, 14 March 1935. Poddar Papers.
195. Schrader to Chimmanlal Gosvami, 6 September 1937.
196. John George Woodroffe, *Is India Civilised?: Essays on Indian Culture*, Ganesh & Co. Publishers, 1919, Madras, pp. 1, XII, XVI.
197. Constance A. Jones and James D. Ryan, *Encyclopedia of Hinduism*, Facts on File (an imprint of Infobase Publishing), New York, 2007, p. 502.
198. Poddar to Woodroffe, 13 January 1934. Poddar Papers.
199. Ridgway F. Shinn, *Arthur Berriedale Keith (1879-1944): The Chief Ornament of Scottish Learning*, Aberdeen University Press, Aberdeen, Scotland, UK, 1990.

200. Keith to editor, *Kalyana-Kalpataru*, 31 October 1936. Poddar Papers.
201. Strauss to editor, *Kalyana-Kalpataru*, 6 November 1936. Poddar Papers.
202. Schrader to editor, *Kalyana-Kalpataru*, 8 January 1937. Poddar Papers.
203. Whitwell to editor, *Kalyana-Kalpataru*, 20 August 1958. Poddar Papers.
204. Fabio Scialpi's commemorative speech at the seminar on G. Tucci held at the Italian Embassy Cultural Centre, New Delhi, on 19 October 2004, citing R. Gnoli, 'L'India nell'opera di Giuseppe Tucci,' in Giuseppe Tucci, *Nel Cenenario Della Nascita, a Curadi Melasecchi*, Rome, June 1994.
205. *Modern Review*, January 1926, pp. 130–31.
206. Gargano to Gosvami, 12 August 1958. Poddar Papers.
207. Lessing to editor, *Kalyan*, 27 June 1958. Poddar Papers.
208. Shiv Sharan to Poddar, 8 September 1949. Poddar Papers.
209. Sasaki to editor, *Kalyan*, 1 July 1958. Poddar Papers.
210. K. De Vreese to Chimmanlal Gosvami, 12 July 1958. Poddar Papers.
211. Letter to Poddar (sender's name undeciphered), 3 September 1941. Poddar Papers.
212. Letters to Poddar (sender's name undeciphered), 11 and 14 March 1945. Poddar Papers.
213. V.N. Sharma to Poddar, 25 April 1958; Homer L. Bradshaw to Gita Press, 12 January 1958. Poddar Papers.
214. Turbiani to Poddar, 24 August 1949. Poddar Papers.
215. Turbiani to Poddar, 13 November 1957. Poddar Papers.
216. Turbiani to Poddar, 9 January 1958. Poddar Papers.
217. Turbiani to Poddar, 31 March 1958. Poddar Papers.
218. Turbiani to Poddar, 30 June 1958 and 30 November 1958. Poddar Papers.
219. Turbiani to Poddar, 2 February 1959. Poddar Papers.
220. Turbiani to Poddar, January 1961. Poddar Papers.
221. R.S. McGregor (ed.), *Devotional Literature in South Asia: Current Research (1985-1988)*, Cambridge University Press, Cambridge, UK, 1992, pp. 49–55.
222. Miltner to Poddar, 16 March and 8 June 1961. Poddar Papers.
223. A series of letters by Karl G. Gesh to Poddar between 1956 and 1960. Poddar Papers.

224. Raymond F. Piper to director, Gita Press, 20 August 1960. Poddar Papers.
225. B.K. Goyal to Poddar, 5 January 1970. Poddar Papers.
226. Manager, Gita Press, to B.K. Goyal, 15 January 1970. Poddar Papers.
227. G.P. Mishra to Poddar, 13 January 1961. Poddar Papers.
228. R.K. Srivastava to Poddar, 27 January 1961. Poddar Papers.
229. Ramesh Kumar Prasad to Poddar, 20 May 1960. Poddar Papers.
230. Letter from Swami Swayamprabhananda to editor, *Kalyan*, 28 June 1956. Poddar Papers.

4. *Foot Soldier of the Sangh Parivar*

1. Romila Thapar, 'Imagined Religious Communities' and 'Syndicated Hinduism', in *Cultural Pasts: Essays in Early Indian History*, Oxford University Press, New Delhi, 2000, pp. 966, 972, 1046–47.
2. Sumit Sarkar, 'Indian Nationalism and the Politics of Hindutva,' in David Ludden (ed.), *Making India Hindu*, Oxford University Press, New Delhi, 1996, p. 273.
3. V.D. Savarkar, *Hindutva: Who is a Hindu?*, Central Hindu Yuvak Sabha, New Delhi, 1938, p. 5.
4. Antony Copley, *Hinduism in Public and Private: Reform, Hindutva, Gender and Sampraday*, Oxford University Press, New Delhi, 2003, pp. 6–7, 9.
5. K.B. Hedgewar, 'Hindusthan Belongs to Hindus Only', reproduced in K.M. Talreja (ed.), *Awake and Arise*, September–October, 1974. (Hedgewar died in June 1940.)
6. Christophe Jaffrelot, *Religion, Caste and Politics in India*, Primus Books, New Delhi, 2010, p. 31.
7. *The Communal Problem, Report of the Kanpur Riots Enquiry Committee*, National Book Trust, 2007, pp. 150–51.
8. '*Sampadakiya Tippniyan*' (Editorial Comments), *Kalyan*, Vol. 1, No. 1, 1926, pp. 33–34.
9. '*Jaydayal Goyandka Ke Patra*' (Letters of Jayadayal Goyandka), *Kalyan*, Vol. 2, No. 11, 1927, p. 489.
10. Hanuman Prasad Poddar, '*Mahamana Malaviyaji Aur Bhagwan Naam Mahima*' (Revered Malaviyaji And Benefits of God's Name), *Kalyan*, *Bhagwan Naam Mahima Aur Prarthana Ank*, January 1965, pp. 160–65.

11. '*Purane Sansmaran*' (Reminiscences), *Kalyan, Bhagwan Naam Mahima Aur Prarthana Ank,* January 1965, pp. 158–60.
12. '*Safalta Prapti, Durghatna Se Raksha Aadi*' (Secured Success, Escaped Accidents, etc.), *Kalyan, Bhagwan Naam Mahima Aur Prarthana Ank,* January 1965, p. 616.
13. *Kalyan,* November 1951, p. 1459.
14. 'Communal Clash in Gorakhpur: Twenty-Seven Injured', *Times of India,* Bombay, 23 December 1939.
15. Poddar to Chimmanlal Gosvami, 14 Margashirsh Shukla, Samvat, 1996 (1939). Poddar Papers.
16. Poddar to Chimmanlal Gosvami, 26 December 1939. Poddar Papers.
17. Poddar to Chimmanlal Gosvami, 29 December 1939. Poddar Papers.
18. Poddar to Shukla, undated but contents suggest it was written between 1 and 3 January 1940. Poddar Papers.
19. Ibid.
20. Poddar to Bajrang Lal, 3 January 1940. Poddar Papers.
21. Poddar to Chimmanlal Gosvami, 4 January 1940. Poddar Papers.
22. Ramnaresh Tripathi, '*Ur-Prerak*' (Catalyst), *Kalyan,* December 1939, pp. 1361–63.
23. Hanuman Prasad Poddar, '*Vishwa Hindu Parishad*', *Kalyan,* December 1965, p. 4.
24. SGPC to Gita Press, 14 March 1934. Poddar Papers.
25. Office of the Chief Khalsa Diwan to Gita Press, 14 March 1954. Poddar Papers.
26. SGPC to Gita Press, 3 April 1934. Poddar Papers.
27. Stanley Wolpert, *Shameful Flight: The Last Years of The British Empire in India,* Oxford University Press, New York, 2006, p. 120.
28. Sumit Sarkar, *Modern India, 1885–1947,* Macmillan, New Delhi, 1983, pp. 432–33.
29. Short Report of Hindu Mahasabha Relief Activities During Calcutta Killings and Noakhali Carnage, published by Bengal Provincial Hindu Mahasabha, 162, Bowbazar Street, Calcutta, 1946, p. 6.
30. Hanuman Prasad Poddar, '*Vartaman Vikat Paristhiti Aur Hamara Kartavya*' (Present Troubled Times and Our Duty), *Kalyan,* November 1946, pp. 1312–18.
31. Hanuman Prasad Poddar, '*Vartaman Paristhiti Ke Sambandh Mein Vichar*' (Thoughts about the Present Situation), *Kalyan,* December 1946, pp. 1377–79.

32. *'Chhapne Ka Sabko Adhikar Hai'* (All Have the Right to Publish), *Kalyan, Malaviya Ank,* 1946, p. 1441.
33. *'Yah Ank Kyon Aur Kis Liye'* (Why This Issue of *Kalyan*?), *Kalyan, Malaviya Ank,* 1946, p. 1440.
34. 'Pujyapad Mahamana Sri Malaviyaji Maharaj' (Devoted Malaviya the Great), *Kalyan, Malaviya Ank,* 1946, p. 1387.
35. *'Mahamana Malaviyaji Ka Antim Pura Vaktavya'* (Malaviya's Last Full Statement), *Kalyan, Malaviya Ank,* 1946, pp. 1389–91.
36. H.L. Erdman, *The Swatantra Party and Indian Conservatism,* Cambridge University Press, New York, 1967, p. 52.
37. Swami Karpatri Maharaj, *'Utho-Jago'* (Arise, Awake), *Kalyan, Malaviya Ank,* 1946, p. 1393.
38. Hanuman Prasad Poddar, *'Hinduon Ki Kamjori Ka Karan Aur Uske Mitane Ka Upay'* (Causes of Hindu Weakness and Ways to Remove Them), *Kalyan, Malaviya Ank,* 1946, pp. 1400–03.
39. Ramnarayan S. Rawat, *Reconsidering Untouchability: Chamars and Dalit History in North India,* Permanent Black, Ranikhet, 2012, p. 148.
40. Bihar governor Dow to Wavell, 9 November 1946, 'Transfers of Power, IX, The Fixing of a Time Limit', pp. 38–39, cited in Wolpert, 2006, p. 125.
41. Hanuman Prasad Poddar, *'Manavta Ka Patan: Bengal Aur Bihar'* (Decline of Humanity: Bengal and Bihar), *Kalyan, Malaviya Ank,* 1946, pp. 1409–18.
42. *'Dr Syama Prasad Mookerjee Ka Vaktavya'* (Statement of Dr Syama Prasad Mookerjee), *Kalyan, Malaviya Ank,* 1946, p. 1404.
43. *'Khatre Ki Ghanti'* (Danger Bell), *Kalyan, Malaviya Ank,* 1946, p. 1418.
44. *'Bengal Ki Apharan Ki Hui Mahilayen'* (Abducted Women of Bengal), *Kalyan, Malaviya Ank,* 1946, p. 1420.
45. *'Hindu Deviyon Ke Patra'* (Letters of Hindu Goddesses), *Kalyan, Malaviya Ank,* 1946, pp. 1424–27.
46. Weekly Report on Political Activities, No. 49, for the Week Ending 29 December 1946. CID Archives, Lucknow.
47. F.R. Stockwell to Rajeshwar Dayal, 20 December 1946. Home Department (Police), File No. 1116/1947, UP State Archives, Lucknow.

48. Order of Rajeshwar Dayal, 21 December 1946. Home Department (Police), File No. 1116/1947, UP State Archives, Lucknow.
49. Rajeshwar Dayal to District Magistrate, Gorakhpur, 2 January 1947. Home Department (Police), File No. 1116/1947, UP State Archives, Lucknow.
50. Home Department (Police), File No. 1116/1947, UP State Archives, Lucknow.
51. F.R. Stockwell to Rajeshwar Dayal, 11 January 1947. Home Department (Police), File No. 1116/1947, UP State Archives, Lucknow.
52. G.C. Drewe to the secretary to the Government of the United Provinces, Home Department, 4 January 1947. Home Department (Police), File No. 1116/1947, UP State Archives, Lucknow.
53. Rajeshwar Dayal's order dated 15 January 1947. Home Department (Police), File No. 1116/1947, UP State Archives, Lucknow.
54. T.B. Crossley to Rajeshwar Dayal, home secretary, United Provinces, 24 January 1947. Home Department (Police), File No. 1116/1947, UP State Archives, Lucknow.
55. N.C. Misra of Criminal Investigation Department, Lucknow, to Rajeshwar Dayal, home secretary, United Provinces, 1 May 1947. Home Department (Police), File No. 1116/1947. UP State Archives, Lucknow.
56. '*Dharmantarit Bhai-Behnon Ki Shuddhi*' (Purification of Converted Brothers and Sisters), *Kalyan, Malaviya Ank*, 1946, pp. 1430–32.
57. '*Hindu Dharma Par Kanooni Prahar*' (Legal Trouble for Hindu Religion), *Kalyan, Malaviya Ank*, 1946, pp. 1432–33.
58. '*Sangathan Aur Sangrakshan Ke Dwadash Sadhan*' (Twelve Paths to Achieve Unity and Protection), *Kalyan, Malaviya Ank*, 1946, pp. 1435–36.
59. Report of the Administration of the United Provinces, 1947, Allahabad, Superintendent, Printing and Stationery, United Provinces. Printed by P.N. Bhargava, Bhargava Bhushan Press, Banaras.
60. Hanuman Prasad Poddar, '*Kalyan Par* Congress *Sarkaron Ki Kripa*' (Benevolence of Congress Governments on *Kalyan*), *Kalyan*, March 1947, pp. 851–53.
61. M.S. Golwalkar, '*Sachcha Rashtravad*' (True Nationalism), *Kalyan*, January 1947, pp. 656–66.

62. *'Bhagwan Ko Arthbhav Se Pukarte Hi Raksha Ho Gayi'* (How Calling God with Sincerity Helped), *Kalyan,* January 1947, pp. 666–68.
63. *'Manavta Ke Adarsh'* (Ideals of Humanity), *Kalyan,* January 1947, pp. 675–80.
64. *'Desh Ki Vartaman Paristhiti Aur Hinduon Ka Kartavya'* (Current Situation in the Country and Duty of Hindus), *Kalyan,* January 1947, pp. 686–96.
65. *Kalyan,* February 1947, pp. 785–86.
66. *'Hindu Jati Par Vipatti'* (Misfortune of Hindus), *Kalyan,* February 1947, p. 787.
67. Hanuman Prasad Poddar, *'Bhagwatprityarth Dweshrahit Kartavyapalan'* (Carrying Out Duty Towards God Without Any Rancour), *Kalyan,* March 1947, pp. 839–49.
68. *'Hinduon Ka Kartavya'* (Duty of Hindus). From *Prabuddha Bharat,* reproduced in *Kalyan,* April 1947, p. 718.
69. Chitra Sinha, *Debating Patriarchy: The Hindu Code Bill Controversy in India (1941–1956),* OUP and New India Foundation, New Delhi, 2012, p. 185.
70. *'Hindu Dharma Aur Sanskriti Par Prahar'* (An Assault on Hindu Religion and Culture), *Kalyan,* May 1947, p. 969.
71. Hanuman Prasad Poddar, *'Bhayanak Khatra Aur Turant Kartavya Palan Ki Avashyakta'* (Terrible Danger and Immediate Duties to Be Carried Out), *Kalyan,* May 1947, pp. 970–81.
72. M.S. Golwalkar, *'Hamari Sanskriti Ki Akhand Dhara'* (The Continuous Stream of Our Culture), *Kalyan,* June 1947, pp. 1035–41.
73. *'Dharma Yudh Ke Liye Aavahan'* (Call for Religious War), *Kalyan,* June 1947, pp. 1042–43.
74. Hanuman Prasad Poddar, *'Bharat Vibhajan Ke Baad Kya Hoga'* (What Will Happen after India's Partition), *Kalyan,* July 1947, pp. 1099–1106.
75. Hanuman Sharma, *'Tab Aur Aab'* (Then and Now), *Kalyan,* August 1947, pp. 1165–70.
76. *'Pakistani Vartav Ke Namune'* (Specimen of Pakistani Behaviour), *Kalyan,* August 1947, inside back cover.
77. *'Punjab Ke Atyachar Aur Hamari Sarkar, Pradhan Mantri Ka Vaktavya'* (Oppression in Punjab and Our Government: PM's Statement), *Kalyan,* September 1947, pp. 1232–33.

78. Prabhudatt Brahmachari, '*Sarnarthiyon Ki Seva Sarvasreshtha Dharma Hai* (Helping Refugees is Supreme Dharma), *Kalyan*, October 1947, pp. 1289–91.
79. R. Shukla, '*Hinduon Ka Durbhagya*' (Misfortune of Hindus), *Kalyan*, November 1947, pp. 1361–62.
80. Gambhirchand Dujari, *Shri Bhaiji: Ek Alaukik Vibhuti*, Gita Vatika Prakashan, Gorakhpur, 2000, pp. 230–31.
81. The information in this paragraph is from Ram Lal Wadhwa, *Hindu Mahasabha, 1928–1947*, Radha Publications, New Delhi, 1999, pp. 208–09.
82. B.D. Graham, *Hindu Nationalism and Indian Politics: The Origins and Development of the Bharatiya Jana Sangh*, Cambridge University Press, New York, 1990, p. 19.
83. Poddar to Goyandka, 8 Kartik Krishna, Samvat 1986 (1929). Poddar Papers.
84. Jaydayal Goyandka, '*Hindu Vivah Ki Pavitrata Evam Tatsambandhi Kanoon*' (Sanctity of Hindu Marriage and Laws Related to Them), *Kalyan*, August 1946, pp. 1124–27.
85. Sinha, 2012, pp. 51, 63.
86. Donald Eugene Smith, *India as a Secular State*, Princeton University Press, New Jersey, 1963, p. 279.
87. Information in this and the next paragraph from Sinha, 2012, pp. 64–65.
88. Geraldine Forbes, *Women in Modern India*, Cambridge University Press, New Delhi, 1996, pp. 118–19.
89. '*Hindu Code: Hindu Sanskriti Ke Vinash Ka Ayojan*' (Hindu Code: A Plan for the Destruction of Hindu Culture), *Kalyan*, June 1948, pp. 1110–13.
90. '*Hindu Dharma Aur Hinduon Ke Aradhya Dev Bhagwan Sri Ram Aur Sri Krishna Par Aakshep*' (Sri Rama and Sri Krishna: Attack on Hindu Dharma's Presiding Deities), *Kalyan*, May 1950, p. 1158.
91. Sinha, 2012, p. 88.
92. Ibid., p. 93.
93. '*Hindu Code: Hindu Sanskriti Ke Vinash Ka Ayojan*, (Hindu Code: Plan to Destroy Hindu Culture)', *Kalyan*, June 1948.
94. '*Hindu Code Ke Sambandh Mein Mahatmaji Ka Mat*' (Mahatma's Views on Hindu Code Bill), *Kalyan*, June 1948, pp. 1113–14.

95. '*Hindu Code: Virodh Mein Sabha Kijiye, Tar Patra Bhejiye*' (Hindu Code: Hold Meetings to Oppose, Send Letters and Telegrams), *Kalyan*, July 1948, inside back cover, reproduced from *Sanmarg*.
96. Bhagwan Das Halna, '*Hindu Code Bill Ka Virodh*' (Opposition to the Hindu Code Bill), *Kalyan*, August 1948, pp. 1242–45.
97. '*Hindu Code Bill Aur Mandiron Ki Zamindari*' (Hindu Code Bill and Control of Temples), *Kalyan*, October 1948, pp. 1375–76.
98. Oral History Transcript, Gyanwati Darbar, NMML, Acc. No. 547.
99. '*Hindu Code Bill Aur Mandiron Ki Zamindari*' (Hindu Code Bill and Control of Temples), *Kalyan*, October 1948, pp. 1375–76.
100. '*Sanskriti Aur Dharma Ka Ghatak Hindu Code Bill*' (Hindu Code Bill: A Danger to Culture and Religion), *Kalyan*, March 1949, pp. 900–04.
101. Ibid.
102. 'Hindu Code Bill', *Kalyan*, April 1949, inside back cover.
103. Gyanendra Pandey, *The Ascendancy of the Congress in Uttar Pradesh: Class, Community and Nation in Northern India, 1920–1940*, Anthem Press, London, 2002, p. 41.
104. '*Hindu Code Bill Par Sammatiyan*' (Views on Hindu Code Bill), *Kalyan*, July 1949, inside back page.
105. Swami Parasnath Saraswati, 'Hindu Code Bill', *Kalyan*, August 1949, pp. 1200–03.
106. Sinha, 2012, pp. 72–73.
107. Hanuman Prasad Poddar, 'Hindu Code Bill', *Kalyan*, September 1951, p. 4.
108. Smith, 1963, p. 281.
109. '*Naye Roop Mein Hindu Code Bill*' (Hindu Code Bill In a New Form), *Kalyan*, July 1954, p. 1182.
110. Rules and Regulations of the Gobind Bhawan Karyalaya. Poddar Papers.
111. *Kalyan*, February 1946, pp. 933, 935.
112. Madangopal Singhal, '*Harijan Mandir Pravesh*' (Harijan Temple Entry), *Kalyan*, January 1947, pp. 715–22.
113. Nicholas B. Dirks, *Castes of Mind: Colonialism and the Making of Modern India*, Permanent Black, Ranikhet, 2002, p. 269.
114. '*Harijan Mandir Pravesh*', *Kalyan*, January 1947.
115. Varnashram Swarajya Sangh, '*Antyajon Ke Liye Mandir Pravesh Ka*

Nishedh Kyon' (Why Temple Entry Should Be Banned for Lower Castes), *Kalyan, Hindu Sanskriti Ank,* January 1950, pp. 214–17.

116. *Bihar, 1912–2012,* Bihar State Archives, 2012, p. 60.
117. The discussion in this and the next paragraph is based on Hetukar Jha, 'Promises and Lapses: Understanding the Experience of Scheduled Castes in Bihar in Historical Perspective', *Journal of Indian School of Political Economy,* Vol. XII, July–December 2000, pp. 431–32.
118. Hanuman Prasad Poddar, *Balpurvak Dev Mandir Pravesh Aur Bhakti* (Forceful Entry into Temples and Devotion), Gita Press, Gorakhpur, 1953.
119. *Collected Works of Mahatma Gandhi,* Vol. 57, pp. 339–40.
120. *Param Pujyapad Shri Jagatguru Shankaracharya Shri Swami Niranjan Dev Tirth Maharaj Ke Mahatvapurna Sadupadesh* (Important Discourse of Niranjan Dev Tirth Delivered in Delhi), *Kalyan,* October 1967, pp 1219–26.
121. Lok Sabha Debates, Sixth Session, Vol. 22, Nos. 10–20, 2–6 December 1968, Lok Sabha Secretariat, pp. 14–18.
122. '*Sanatan Dharma Par Anuchit Aakshep*' (Inappropriate Comments on Sanatan Dharma), *Kalyan,* December 1968, inside back cover.
123. See Graham, 1990; Craig Baxter, *The Jana Sangh: A Biography of an Indian Political Party,* OUP, New Delhi, 1971 and Christophe Jaffrelot, *The Hindu Nationalist Movement in India,* Viking, New Delhi, 1996.
124. Jaffrelot, 1996, p. 164.
125. Bharatiya Jana Sangh (1952–1980), Party Document, Internal Affairs, Vol. 4, p. 112. BJP, 2005.
126. Ibid., pp. 101–02.
127. Jaffrelot, 1996, p. 164.
128. Prabhudatt Brahmachari, '*Vanvasi Bandhuon Ke Beech Mein*' (In the Midst of Forest Dwellers), *Kalyan,* May 1963, pp. 917–25.
129. Baxter, 1971, p. 133.
130. Ibid., pp. 143–45.
131. '*Vanvasi Bandhuon Ke Beech Mein*' (In the Midst of Adivasi Brothers), *Kalyan,* May 1963.
132. Swami Brahmananda Saraswati, '*Hindu Sanskriti*' (Hindu Culture), *HSA, Kalyan,* January 1950, pp. 23–32.
133. Swami Karpatri Maharaj, '*Sanskriti Vimarsh*' (Discourse on Culture), *HSA,* pp. 35–39.

134. Sri Bharat Dharma Mahamandal, *The World's Eternal Religion*, Naval Kishore Press, Lucknow, 1920, p. III.
135. Sri Bharat Dharma Mahamandal, '*Hindu Sanskriti*,' *HSA*, pp. 41–50.
136. Mahant Digvijaynath, '*Kya Hindutva Sampradayikta Hai*' (Is Hindutva Communal?), *HSA*, pp. 61–62.
137. Partha Chatterjee, 'History and the Nationalisation of Hinduism', in Vasudha Dalmia and Heinrich von Stietencron (eds), *The Oxford India Hinduism Reader*, Oxford University Press, New Delhi, 2007, p. 258.
138. Mahant Digvijaynath, '*Kya Hindutva Sampradayikta Hai*', *HSA*.
139. Kunwar Chandkaran Sharda, '*Hindu Sanskriti Kya Hai*' (What is Hindu Culture?), *HSA*, pp. 201–03.
140. Madhavrao Sadashiv Golwalkar, '*Hindu Sanskriti*', *HSA*, pp. 57–61.
141. Justice Jivji, '*Hindu Sanskriti Aur Swadhinta*' (Hindu Culture and Freedom), *HSA*, pp. 136–44.
142. Kishori Das Vajpayee, '*Hindu Sanskriti Aur Rashtriyata*' (Hindu Culture and Nationalism), *HSA*, pp. 152–53.
143. Jugal Kishore Birla, '*Arya Hindu Dharma*' (The Aryan Hindu Religion), *HSA*, p. 200.
144. Sampurnanand, '*Hindu Sanskriti*', *HSA*, pp. 69–73.
145. C. Rajagopalachari, '*Hindu Sanskriti Hi Vishwa Sanskriti Hai*' (Hindu Culture Is World Culture) *HSA*, p. 63.
146. Vinoba Bhave, '*Hindu Kaun*' (Who is a Hindu?), *HSA*, p. 63.
147. Jitmal Lunia to Poddar, 8 March 1941. Poddar Papers.
148. Hanuman Prasad Poddar, '*Hindi Aur Hindustani, Kaam Ke Patra*' (Hindi and Hindustani: Meaningful Letters), *Kalyan*, June 1947, pp. 1030–31.
149. Ravi Shankar Shukla, '*Hindustani Ka Rahasya*' (Mystery of Hindustani), in two parts, *Kalyan*, July and August 1947, pp. 1090–97, 1156–61.
150. Jaffrelot, 1996, p. 162.
151. Raghuvira, '*Hindi Bhasha Ki Raksha Karo, Yahi Samay Hai*' (Defend Hindi Language: This is the Occasion), *Kalyan*, September 1947, pp. 1229–31.
152. Editorial comment at the end of Raghuvira's article. *Kalyan*, September 1947, p. 1231.
153. Ghanshyam Singh Gupt, '*Swatantra Bharat Ki Bhasha*' (Independent India's Language), *Kalyan*, March 1948, pp. 890–92.

154. Robert D. King, 'Language Politics and Conflicts in South Asia', in Braj B. Kachru, Yamuna Kachru and S.N. Sridhar (eds), *Language in South Asia*, Cambridge University Press, New York, 2008, pp. 316–19.
155. Ramcharan Mahendra, '*Hindu Veshbhusha Aur Hindi Bhasha Ko Apnane Mein Garv Ka Anubhav Karen*' (Feel Proud to Adopt Hindu Attire and Hindi Language), *Kalyan*, November 1966, pp. 1312–16.

5. Religion as Politics, Politics of Religion

1. I owe this argument to Jyotirmaya Sharma of University of Hyderabad.
2. Christophe Jaffrelot, *The Hindu Nationalist Movement in India*, Viking, New Delhi, 1996, p. 112.
3. Charu Gupta, 'The Icon of Mother in Late Colonial North India: Bharat Mata, Matri Bhasha and Gau Mata', *Economic & Political Weekly*, Vol. 36, No. 45, 10–16 November 2001, pp. 4291–99; Peter van der Veer, *Religious Nationalism: Hindus and Muslims in India*, University of California Press, Berkeley, 1994, p. 86.
4. Ibid.
5. Ibid., pp. 86–88.
6. Therese O'Toole, 'Secularizing the Cow: The Relationship between Religious Reform and Hindu Nationalism', in Antony Copley (ed.), *Hinduism in Public and Private*, Oxford University Press, New Delhi, 2003, pp. 95–98.
7. D.N. Jha, *The Myth of the Holy Cow*, Verso, London, 2004.
8. Poddar's letter to prospective contributors to *Gau Ank*, *Kalyan*'s annual issue of 1945. Poddar Papers.
9. Mahatma Gandhi, '*Bharat Ki Sukh Samridhi*' (India's Prosperity), *Kalyan*, *Gau Ank*, October 1945, p. 17.
10. Maithilisharan Gupt, '*Gau Geet*' (Poem on the Cow), *Gau Ank*, p. 5.
11. Shanti Kumar Nanuram Vyas, '*Gau Aur Nari*' (Cow and Woman), *Gau Ank*, pp. 280–84.
12. Shankaracharya of Kanchi, '*Gau Raksha Hi Prapanch Raksha Hai*' (Cow Protection is the Protection of the World), *Gau Ank*, p. 4.
13. Prabhudatt Brahmachari, '*Gaumata Aur Hindutva*' (Mother Cow and Hindutva), *Gau Ank*, pp. 14–16.
14. Hanuman Prasad Poddar and Chimmanlal Gosvami, '*Kshama Prarthana*' (Prayer for Forgiveness), *Gau Ank*, pp. 662–63.

15. O'Toole, 2003 p. 102.
16. Gupta, 2001, pp. 4291–99.
17. Swami Dayanand Saraswati, '*Gau Se Anant Labh*' (Countless Benefits from Cow), *Gau Ank*, p. 248.
18. Sir Datar Singh, '*Bharatvarsha Mein Gaushalaon Aur Pinjrapolon Ka Sudhar*' (Improvement in India's Cowsheds and Shelters), *Gau Ank*, pp. 20–23.
19. Radha Kamal Mukerjee, '*Jangalon Aur Gocharbhumiyon Ka Prabandh*' (Management of Jungles and Pastureland), *Gau Ank*, pp. 315–16.
20. Madan Mohan Malaviya, '*Gorakhsha Ke Sadhan*' (Ways of Cow Protection), *Gau Ank*, pp. 100–06.
21. Sir Purshottamdas Thakurdas, '*Vartaman Bharat Mein Gau Ki Dasha*' (State of Cow in Present-day India), *Gau Ank*, pp. 25–26.
22. Dr Rajendra Prasad, '*Gau Palan Sanatan Dharma Hai*' (Rearing Cows is Sanatan Dharma), *Gau Ank*, p. 24.
23. Dharam Lal Singh, '*Musalman Aur Gau Raksha*' (Muslims and Cow Protection), *Gau Ank*, pp. 219–29.
24. '*Humayun Ki Gau Mans Se Ghrina*' (Humayun's Hatred for Beef), *Gau Ank*, p. 215.
25. Maulana Kabil Saheb, '*Gau Raksha Kyon Avashyak Hai*' (Why Is Cow Protection Necessary?), *Gau Ank*, pp. 626–27.
26. '*Bharat Mein Gau Badh Sarvatha Bandh Ho*' (Cow Slaughter Should Be Completely Banned in India), *Kalyan*, July 1947, back page.
27. Srinivas Poddar, *Gau Ko Bachaiye* (Save the Cows), *Kalyan*, August 1947, pp. 1138–40.
28. *Collected Works of Mahatma Gandhi*, Vol. 90, pp. 203–05.
29. Kishorelal Mashruwala, '*Vanaspati Pratibandhak Kanoon*' (Law to Ban Vegetable Oil), *Kalyan*, July 1950, pp. 1287–88.
30. Baba Raghav Das, '*Gau Hatya Bandh Honi Hi Chahiye*' (Cow Slaughter Must Stop), *Kalyan*, September 1947, p. 1224.
31. Donald Eugene Smith, *India As A Secular State*, Princeton University Press, Princeton, New Jersey, 1963, p. 484.
32. '*Gaubadh Nishedh Shighra Ho*' (Cow Slaughter Should Be Banned Immediately), *Kalyan*, October 1947, pp. 1298–1301.
33. Smith, 1963, pp. 484–85.
34. Ibid.
35. '*Gau Badh Sarvatha Bandh Ho*' (Cow Slaughter Should Be Completely Banned), *Kalyan*, August 1949, pp. 1217–18.

36. Hanuman Prasad Poddar, '*Gau Badh Ko Protsahan*' (Encouragement to Cow Slaughter), *Kalyan*, November 1949, inside back cover.
37. Hanuman Prasad Poddar, '*Gau Badh Ko Doosra Ek Aur Protsahan*' (Another Encouragement to Cow Slaughter), *Kalyan*, December 1949, inside back cover.
38. Smith, 1963, p. 486.
39. Ibid.
40. Ibid.
41. Bharat Gosevak Samaj: Report on the Last Six Month's Work. Poddar Papers.
42. Jaffrelot, 1996, p. 73.
43. Bharat Gosevak Samaj: Report on the Last Six Month's Work. Poddar Papers.
44. Jaffrelot, 1996, p. 205.
45. B.D. Graham, *Hindu Nationalism and Indian Politics*, Cambridge University Press, New York, 1980, pp. 148–49.
46. Hanuman Prasad Poddar, '*Gohatya Nivaran Tatha Delhi Jail Mein Anshan Karnewale Sadhuon Ko Turant Chhorne Ki Appeal*' (An Appeal to Immediately Release Sadhus on Fast in a Delhi Jail), *Kalyan*, June 1966, inside back cover.
47. Bhagwati Prasad Singh, *Kalyan Path: Nirmata Aur Rahi*, Radha Madhav Seva Sansthan, Gorakhpur, 1980, pp. 341–42.
48. Rajendra Singh, 'Rajju Bhaiya', to Poddar, 9 May 1967. Poddar Papers.
49. Craig Baxter, *Biography of a Political Party: Jana Sangh*, Oxford University Press, Bombay, 1971, p. 259.
50. Prabhudatt Brahmachari, '*Gau Ki Raksha Balidan Ke Bina Nahin*' (Cow Protection Is Not Possible Without Sacrifice), *Kalyan*, July 1966, pp. 1045–54.
51. '*Gauhatya Bandh Karane Ke Liye Bhagwad Aaradhana*' (Worshipping Gods to Put an End to the Slaughter of Cows), *Kalyan*, July 1966, inside back cover.
52. Prabhudatt Brahmachari, '*Goseva Aur Gohatya Nishedh Ke Nimitt Amaran Anshan*' (Fast Unto Death in the Service of the Cow and Prohibition of Cow Slaughter, *Kalyan*, September 1966, pp. 1185–91.
53. Hanuman Prasad Poddar, '*Goraksha Maha Abhiyan*' (Massive

Campaign for Cow Protection), *Kalyan*, September 1966, pp. 1210–12.

54. '*Goraksha Maha Abhiyan Sambandhi Kuch Suchnayen*' (Some Information Regarding Gorakhsa Maha Abhiyan), *Kalyan*, September 1966, inside back over.
55. '*Goraksha Maha Abhiyan*,' *Kalyan*, October 1966, inside back over.
56. Swami Niranjan Dev Tirth, '*Gau Hatya Ko Poorna Roop Se Bandh Karane Ke Liye Balidan*' (Sacrifice for Total Ban on Cow Slaughter), *Kalyan*, November 1966, pp. 1279–83.
57. Hanuman Prasad Poddar, '*Govansh Ki Hatya Shighra Se Shighra Bandh Ho*' (Killing of Cattle Should Stop at the Earliest), *Kalyan*, November 1966, p. 1331.
58. Poddar to Golwalkar, 20 October 1966, in *Saras Patra*, compiled by Shyamsundar Dujari, Gita Vatika Prakashan, Gorakhpur, 2005, pp. 136–37.
59. Atiqur Rehman Kidwai, '*Gohatya Samasya: Sarkar Aur Musalman*' (Problem of Cow Slaughter: Government and Muslims), *Kalyan*, November 1966, pp. 1335–36.
60. The information in this paragraph is sourced from Jaffrelot, 1996, pp. 206–07 and Baxter, 1971, p. 260.
61. Bharatiya Jana Sangh (1952–1980), Party Document, Policies and Manifestoes, Vol. I, pp. 212–13, 266, 288. BJP, 2005.
62. '*Gorakshharth Nanda Bhi Jagadguru Ke Saath Satyagraha Karenge*' (For Cow Protection Nanda Will Join Satyagraha with Jagadguru), *Veer Arjun*, 30 May 1968. Poddar Papers.
63. Bharatiya Jana Sangh (1952–1980), Party Document, Policies and Manifestoes, Vol. I, p. 291. BJP 2005.
64. Hanuman Prasad Poddar, '*Main Bhagvat Ichcha Se Hi Goraksha Maha Abhiyan Samiti Mein Sammilit Hua*' (By God's Grace I Became Part of Goraksha Maha Abhiyan Samiti) *Kalyan*, December 1966, p. 1392.
65. Hanuman Prasad Poddar, '*Bharat Sarkar Ki Maans Utpadan Ki Panchvarshiya Yojana*' (Indian Government's Five-Year Plan for Meat Production), *Kalyan*, November 1966, p. 1394.
66. Hanuman Prasad Poddar to Indira Gandhi, Kartik Shukla 11, Samvat 2023 (1966), in *Saras Patra*, 1999, pp. 137–40.
67. Hanuman Prasad Poddar, '*Gohatya Nirodh Ka Prayas*' (Efforts to Ban Cow Slaughter), *Kalyan*, January 1967, pp. 699–703.

68. '*Sarvadaliya Gorakhsha Maha Abhiyan Samiti Ka Chunav Se Sambandh Nahin*' (SGMS Has Nothing to Do with the Elections), *Kalyan*, February 1967, p. 765.
69. Information in this paragraph is from Jaffrelot, 1996, p. 211; Baxter, 1971, pp. 260–61.
70. Brijlal Biyani, '*Gohatya Nirodh*' (Cow Slaughter Ban), *Kalyan*, March 1967, pp. 813–17.
71. Hanuman Prasad Poddar, comments on Biyani's article, *Kalyan*, March 1967, p. 817 (concluding paragraph).
72. Hanuman Prasad Poddar, '*Delhi Tihar Jail Mẹin Gorakhsha Ke Satyagrahi Sadhuon par Amanushik Prahar*' (Inhuman Attack in Delhi's Tihar Jail on the Cow Protectionist Sadhus), *Kalyan*, August 1967, p. 1146–47.
73. Dharmlal Singh to Poddar, 14 July 1967 and 30 May 1968. Poddar Papers.
74. Statement of Accounts of Sarvadaliya Gorakhsa Maha Abhiyan Samiti from the beginning to 31 August 1967. Poddar Papers.
75. Hitsharan Sharma to Poddar, 19 August 1967. Poddar Papers.
76. '*Padho, Samjho Aur Karo*' (Read, Understand and Do), *Kalyan*, August 1967, p. 1149.
77. Swami Keshavpuri Vedantacharya, '*Goraksha Kyon Aur Kaise Karen*' (Cow Protection: Why and How To Do It), *Kalyan*, September 1967 pp. 1197–1200.
78. '*Sabun Mein Gai Ki Charbi: Sarkarki Svikarokti*' (Cow Fat in Soap: Government's Admission), *Kalyan*, February 1968, inside back cover.
79. '*Charbirahit Sabun Bananewalon Ke Naam Pate*' (Name and Address of Manufacturers of Fatless Soaps), *Kalyan*, June 1968, pp. 1009–12.
80. '*Goraksha Andolan*' (Cow-Protection Agitation), *Kalyan*, August 1968, pp. 1227–29.
81. Jaidayal Dalmia, '*Gandhiji Aur Goraksha*' (Gandhi and Cow Protection), *Kalyan*, August 1968, pp. 1130–34. The second and third instalments of this article were published in *Kalyan*, September 1968, pp. 1190–95, and October 1968, pp. 1242–45.
82. *Lok Sabha Debates*, Part II, Vol. III, Ninth Session (2–21 April 1955), Lok Sabha Secretariat.
83. Jaidayal Dalmia to Krishna Chandra, 16 May 1968. Poddar Papers.
84. Jaidayal Dalmia to Harikrishna Dujari, 7 October 1969. Poddar Papers.

85. Jaidayal Dalmia to Harikrishna Dujari, 26 December 1969. Poddar Papers.
86. Poddar to Dalmia, 15 October 1969. Poddar Papers.
87. Raghunandan Prasad Sharma (ed.), *Satat Sadhana Yatra Ke Tees Barsh (1964–1994)*, VHP Publications, New Delhi, 1995, pp. 4–5.
88. Manjari Katju, *Visva Hindu Parishad and Indian Politics*, Orient Blackswan, New Delhi, 2010, p. 5.
89. Jaffrelot, 1996, pp. 193, 196.
90. Sharma (ed.), 1995, p. 7.
91. Katju, 2010, p. 23.
92. Sharma (ed.), 1995, p.6.
93. Apte to Poddar, 23 July 1970. Poddar Papers.
94. Krishna Jha and Dhirendra K. Jha, *Ayodhya The Dark Night: The Secret History of Rama's Appearance in Babri Masjid*, Harper Collins, New Delhi, 2012, p. 44.
95. Ibid., Prologue, p. 1.
96. Ibid.
97. Ram Bahadur Rai, *'Babri Masjid: Dhwansh Ki Rajniti'* (Babri Masjid: Politics of Demolition), *Yathawat*, 1–15 December 2013, pp. 6–11.
98. Singh, 1980, pp. 326–27.
99. Extract of Poddar's letter cited by Gopal Singh Visharad in Radheshyam Banka (ed.), *Sant Hriday Poddarji*, Hanuman Prasad Poddar Smarak Samiti, Gorakhpur, 1991, pp. 86–88.
100. Singh, 1980, pp. 326–27.
101. Singh, 1980, pp. 328–29.
102. Seth Govind Das to Hanuman Prasad Poddar, 5 July 1955. Seth Govind Das Papers, NMML.
103. Hanuman Prasad Poddar's Speech at the Inauguration of Shri Krishna Temple at Mathura, 6 September 1958, pamphlet published by Gita Press.
104. Seth Govind Das to Poddar, 18 November 1958. Poddar Papers.
105. Singh, 1980, p. 329.
106. Hanuman Prasad Poddar, *Kalyan*, July 1951, p. 1199.
107. Hanuman Prasad Poddar, *'Vartaman Gantantra Tatha Matdataon Ka Kartavya'* (Present Republic and Responsibility of Voters), *Kalyan*, December 1951, p. 1516.
108. Hanuman Prasad Poddar, *'Vote Kiskon Dein'* (Whom Should You Vote For?), *Kalyan*, December 1951, p. 1519.

109. 'Ushering in Ram Rajya in India: Call at Bengal Parishad', *The Times of India*, 6 April 1951, p. 5.
110. Jaffrelot, 1996, p. 199.
111. Poddar, '*Vote Kiskon Dein*,' December 1951.
112. Hanuman Prasad Poddar, '*Jantantra Ya Asur Tantra*' (Democracy or Demonocracy), *Kalyan*, March 1967, pp. 818–20.
113. Hanuman Prasad Poddar, '*Jantantra Ki Raksha Kaise Ho*' (How to Save Democracy), *Kalyan*, June 1967, p. 1011.
114. Sumit Sarkar, *Modern India*, Macmillan, New Delhi, 1983, p. 177.
115. Sadanand, '*Rajniti Se Dharma Ka Sambandh Vichchhed*' (Desegregating Religion from Politics), *Kalyan*, Vol. 3, No. 7, 1928, pp. 652–53.
116. '*Ishwar Virodhi Sammelan*' (Anti-God Congregation), *Kalyan*, Vol. 3, No. 12, 1928, pp. 1048–49.
117. Rajendra, '*Sri Gita Ka Samatva Aur Aaj Ka Samvyavad*' (Equality in Gita and Today's Communism), *Kalyan*, Vol. 4, No. 1, 1929, pp. 349–50.
118. Laxman Narayan Garde, '*Adhunik Anishwarvad*' (Modern Atheism), *Kalyan*, August 1932, pp. 212–19.
119. Hanuman Prasad Poddar and Chimmanlal Gosvami, '*Kshama Prarthana*' (Prayer for Forgiveness), *Kalyan*, January 1947, pp. 722–25.
120. Charu Chandra Mitra, '*Nari*' (Woman), *Kalyan*, (two instalments) May and June 1948, pp. 1049–54 and 1115–18.
121. Kailash Nath Katju, '*Srimad Bhagavadgita Aur Communistvad*' (Gita and Communism), *Kalyan*, *Hindu Sanskriti Ank*, January 1950, pp. 64–67.
122. Acharya Nardev Shastri Vedtirth, '*Hindu Sanskriti Aur Paschatyavad*' (Hindu Culture and Western Ideology), *Kalyan*, *Hindu Sanskriti Ank*, January 1950, pp. 171–74.
123. Ram Vallabh Chaturvedi, '*Communism Se Hum Kyon Daren?*' (Why Should We Be Afraid of Communism?), *Kalyan*, March 1950, pp. 1023–25.
124. 'The Great Endeavour,' *Economic Weekly*, 14 May 1955. p. 561.
125. 'Further Left,' *Economic Weekly*, 13 June 1955, p. 698.
126. Nardev Shastri, '*Yeh Kaisa Samajwad Hai*' (What Kind of Socialism Is This?), *Kalyan*, May 1955, pp. 1017–19.
127. '*Rus Ki Anarthpurn Arth Vyavastha*' (Russia's Meaningless Economy), *Kalyan*, May 1955, pp. 1050–56.

128. C. Nesterenko, '*Samyavadi Naitikta Ka Audarya*' (Communism's Liberal Morality), *Kalyan*, January 1959, pp. 571–72.
129. Indralal Shastri Jain, '*Ashanti Aur Himsatmak Pravrittiyon Ka Utardayitva Prashasan Niti Par*' (Administration Responsible for Disturbance and Violent Tendencies), *Kalyan*, February 1967, pp. 750–51.
130. Rabindra Ray, *The Naxalites and Their Ideology*, Oxford University Press, New Delhi, 1988, pp. 88–89.
131. Purshottam Dass Halwasiya to Poddar, 4 September 1967. Poddar Papers.
132. From a pamphlet of Bharatiya Sanskritik Suraksha Parishad. Poddar Papers.
133. Hanuman Prasad Poddar, '*Desh Mein Aasuri Sampada Ka Vistar Aur Hamara Kartavya*' (Growth of Evil Forces in the Country and Our Duty), *Kalyan*, September 1967, pp. 1196–97.
134. Ganga Shankar Mishra, '*Prastavana*' (Foreword) to Swami Karpatri Maharaj, *Marxvad Aur Ram Rajya*, Gita Press, Gorakhpur, 2009, pp. 3–5.
135. Swami Karpatri Maharaj, 2009, pp. 256, 262–63, 306–07, 313–14.
136. Ibid., pp. 574, 576, 577.
137. Hanuman Prasad Poddar, '*Sanatan Dharma Ke Harash Honewale Deshvyapi Anarth*' (Nationwide Crisis Due to Erosion of Sanatan Dharma), *Kalyan*, March 1968, pp. 817–19.
138. Hanuman Prasad Poddar, 'Necessity of the Knowledge, Grasping and Spreading of the Sanatan (Universal) Dharma', undated typed article. Poddar Papers.
139. '*Kaam Ke Patra*' (Important Letters, a column through which Poddar replied to readers' queries), *Kalyan*, August 1968, pp. 1137–39.
140. Rajendra Prasad Jain, '*Dharmnirpekshata Ka Abhishaap*' (Curse of Secularism), *Kalyan*, November 1968, pp. 1300–02.
141. Through the forty-second constitutional amendment in 1976 the words secular and socialist were included in the Preamble to the Constitution of India.
142. Rajendra Prasad Jain, '*Dharmnirpeksh*' (Secularism), *Kalyan*, October 1966, pp. 1255–57.
143. Jain, '*Dharmanirpekshata Ka Abhishaap,*' November 1968.
144. Bharatiya Jana Sangh, (1952–1980), Party Document, Vol. I, Policies and Manifestoes, BJP, 2005, pp. 284–85.

145. Sundarlal Vohra, '*Hindu Dharma Ki Agni Pariksha*' (Hindu Dharma's Trial by Fire), *Kalyan*, June 1966, pp. 1003–06.
146. Late Swami Karpatri Maharaj, '*Dharma Aur Rajniti*' (Religion and Politics), *Kalyan*, January 2002, pp. 106–11.
147. Hanuman Prasad Poddar, '*Chin Par Purna Vijay Prapt Karne Ke Liye Adhyatmik Sadhan Bhi Kiye Jayen*' (Spiritual Efforts Should Also Be Made to Attain Absolute Victory over China), *Kalyan*, December 1962, p. 1347.
148. Poddar to King Mahendra, 19 November 1962. Poddar Papers.
149. Hanuman Prasad Poddar, '*Pakistan Yudh Aur Hamara Kartavya*' (Pakistan War and Our Duty), *Kalyan*, October 1965, p. 3.
150. Hanuman Prasad Poddar, '*Pakistan-Chin Sangharsh Mein Hamara Kartavya Tatha Vijay Aur Vishwa Shanti Ke Sadhan*' (Our Duty in the Conflict with Pakistan and China and Ways to Become Victorious and Achieve World Peace), *Kalyan*, November 1965, pp. 1317–19.
151. Poddar to Indira Gandhi, 23 November 1970. Poddar Papers.

6. The Moral Universe of Gita Press

1. Poddar to Bajrang Lal, 16 November 1939. Poddar Papers.
2. Geraldine Forbes, *Women in Modern India*, Cambridge University Press, New Delhi, 1996, p. 1.
3. Ghulam Murshid, *Reluctant Debutante: Response of Bengali Women to Modernisation, 1849–1905*, Rajshahi University Press, 1983, cited in Partha Chatterjee, 'The Nationalist Resolution of the Women's Question', in Kumkum Sangari and Sudesh Vaid (eds), *Recasting Women: Essays in Colonial History*, Zubaan, New Delhi, 2010, p. 234.
4. Sumit Sarkar, 'The Women's Question in Nineteenth Century Bengal', in *A Critique of Colonial India*, Papyrus, Calcutta, 2000, p. 89.
5. Partha Chatterjee, 'Colonialism, Nationalism, and Colonised Women: The Contest in India', *American Ethnologist*, Vol. 16, No. 4, November 1989, pp. 622–33.
6. Hanuman Prasad Poddar, '*Vartaman Shiksha*' (Present-day Education), *Kalyan*, April 1936, p. 1297.
7. *Nari Dharma* (Women's Duty) was first published in 1938; till 2000 it was priced at Rs 3, had sold 1,395,000 copies and gone into seventy-four editions.

Striyon Ke Liye Kartavya Shiksha (Education in Duties for Women) was first published in 1954; till 2000, 1,025,000 copies were sold in forty-five editions; it is priced at Rs 5.

Bhakt Nari (Devout Women) priced at Rs 4 was first published in 1931 and till 2002 had gone into thirty-nine editions and sold 462,000 copies. *Nari Shiksha* (Women's Education), first published in 1952, till 2010 has gone into fifty-seven editions and sold 1,027,000 copies; priced at Rs 8 it is expensive by Gita Press standards.

Dampatya Jivan Ka Adarsh (Ideals of Marital Life) is a late compilation of Poddar's articles. First published in 1991; till 2002 it had seventeen editions with 181,000 copies sold, priced at Rs 7.

Grihasta Mein Kaise Rahen (How to Live in the Household) first published in 1990, had thirty-seven editions till 2004 with 930,000 copies sold; priced at Rs 6.

Prashnouttar Manimala (A Garland of Questions) was first published in 2001 and in the first year itself went through five editions; by 2002 it had six editions with 10,000 copies sold, priced at Rs 7.

8. Sukhda Devi, '*Marwari Samaj Mein Striyon Ki Hin Dasha*' (Deplorable State of Women in the Marwari Community), *Chand*, July 1937, pp. 278–79.
9. Prabha Khaitan, *Peeli Aandhi*, Rajkamal Paperbacks, Delhi, 2001.
10. Hanuman Prasad Poddar, *Stri Dharma Prashnottari*, Gita Press, Gorakhpur, 1926, pp. 12–15.
11. Hanuman Prasad Poddar, *Samaj Sudhar*, Gita Press, Gorakhpur, 1928, pp. 21, 23.
12. Jaydayal Goyandka to Hanuman Prasad Poddar, 1925 (date and month not clear). Poddar Papers.
13. Jaydayal Goyandka, *Nari Dharma*, Gita Press, Gorakhpur, 1938, pp. 2–3.
14. Ibid., p. 25.
15. Hanuman Prasad Poddar, '*Vartaman Shiksha*,' *Kalyan*, April 1936, p. 1293.
16. Dwarika Prasad Chaturvedi, '*Adhunik Nari*' (Modern Women), *Kalyan, Nari Ank*, January 1948, pp. 155–56.
17. Hanuman Prasad Poddar, '*Shiksha Aur Sah-Shiksha*' (Women's Education And Co-education), *Kalyan, Nari Ank*, January 1948, pp. 230–32.

18. Interview with Radheshyam Khemka, editor, *Kalyan*, February 2011 in Banaras.
19. Kishori Das Vajpayee, '*Ladkiyon Ki Shiksha*' (Girls' Education), *Kalyan, Nari Ank*, 1948, p. 227.
20. Chatterjee, 'Colonialism, Nationalism, and Colonised Women,' 1989.
21. Shakuntala Gupta, '*Vartaman Shiksha Mein Parivartan Ki Avashyakta*' (Need to Change Modern Education), *Kalyan, Nari Ank*, January 1948, pp. 232–34.
22. Meera Kosambi, Introduction in *Pandita Ramabai's American Encounter: The People of the United States* (1889), Indiana University Press, Bloomington, USA, 2003, p. 3.
23. Meera Kosambi cited in Radha Kumar, *The History of Doing*, Zubaan, New Delhi, 1993, p. 32.
24. Sudarshan Singh, 'Dr Anandibai Joshi', *Kalyan, Nari Ank*, January 1948, pp. 816–18.
25. Caroline Healey Dall, *The Life of Dr Anandibai Joshee*, Roberts Brothers, Boston, 1888, p. 50.
26. Hanuman Prasad Poddar, *Europe Ki Bhakt Striyan*, (Women Devotees of Europe) Gita Press, Gorakhpur, 1934.
27. Poddar to an unidentified woman, 1929 (date and month not clear). Poddar Papers.
28. Hanuman Prasad Poddar, '*Hindu Vivah Ki Visheshta*' (The Speciality of Hindu Marriage), in *Nari Shiksha*, Gita Press, Gorakhpur, 1952, p. 100.
29. Hanuman Prasad Poddar, *Dampatya Jivan Ka Adarsh* (Ideals of Married Life), 38th ed., Gita Press, Gorakhpur, 2013, p. 14.
30. Poddar, *Stri Dharma Prashnottari*, 1926, p. 16.
31. Poddar, *Samaj Sudhar*, 1928, p. 15.
32. Hanuman Prasad Poddar, '*Vivah Ka Mahan Uddeshya Aur Vivah Kaal*' (Great Purpose Behind Marriage and Married Life), in *Nari Shiksha*, 1952, pp. 27–28.
33. Poddar, *Nari Shiksha*, 1952, p. 21.
34. Poddar, *Stri Dharma Prashnottari*, 1926, p. 1.
35. Hanuman Prasad Poddar, *Dampatya Jivan Ka Adarsh* (Ideals of Married Life), 38th ed., Gita Press, Gorakhpur, 2013, pp. 82–83.
36. Poddar, *Stri Dharma Prashnottari*, 1926, p. 4.
37. Charu Gupta, 'Articulating Hindu Masculinity and Femininity:

"Shuddhi" and "Sangathan" Movements in United Provinces in the 1920s', *Economic and Political Weekly*, Vol. 33, No. 13. 26 March–3 April 1998, pp. 727–35.

38. Poddar, *Stri Dharma Prashnottari*, 1926, p. 11.
39. Gupta, 1998, pp. 730–31.
40. Poddar, *Samaj Sudhar*, 1928, p. 26.
41. Poddar, *Stri Dharma Prashnottari*, 1926, p. 16.
42. Dipesh Chakrabarty, 'The Difference-Deferral of a Colonial Modernity: Public Debates on Domesticity in British Bengal', in David Arnold and David Hardiman (eds), *Subaltern Studies*, Vol. VIII, Oxford University Press, New Delhi, 1996, p. 55.
43. Poddar, *Stri Dharma Prashnottari*, 1926, pp. 23–34.
44. Goyandka, *Nari Dharma*, 1938, pp. 13–14, 26–27.
45. Charu Gupta, *Sexuality, Obscenity, Community*, Permanent Black, Ranikhet, 2001, pp. 90–108.
46. '*Nari Aur Bhojan Nirman Kala*' (Women and the Art of Cooking), *Kalyan, Nari Ank*, January 1948, pp. 346–49.
47. Poddar, *Stri Dharma Prashnottari*, 1926, p. 35.
48. Ibid., pp. 27–28.
49. Goyandka, *Nari Dharma*, 1938, p. 33.
50. *Kalyan, Nari Ank*, January 1948, pp. 819–20, 821–23, 831–35, 836–38.
51. '*Pativrata Kya Kar Sakti Hai*' (What a Loyal Wife Can Do?), *Kalyan, Nari Ank*, January 1948, pp. 333–34.
52. '*Kaise Acharan Se Nari Pati Ko Vash Mein Kar Sakti Hai*' (With What Kind of Behaviour Can a Woman Keep Her Husband under Control?), *Kalyan, Sanskar Ank*, January 2006, pp. 194–95.
53. Ramnivas Lakhotia, '*Bachchon Ke Prati Maa Ka Uttardaitwa*' (Mother's Duties Towards Children), *Sanskar Ank*, January 2006, pp. 258–60.
54. Chakrabarty, 1996, p. 60.
55. *Nari: Grihalakshmi Aur Kalyani* (1946), *Anand Niketan, Ghar Ki Rani, Bhai Ke Patra, Kanya and Nari Jivan, Kuch Samasyayen*. All published by Sadhana Sadan, Prayag (Allahabad).
56. Ramnath 'Suman', '*Bharatiya Grihon Se Lupt Hoti Hui Grihalakshmiyan*' (Lakshmis Vanishing from Indian Homes), *Kalyan, Nari Ank*, January 1948, pp. 133–36.
57. Poddar, *Vartaman Shiksha*, (monograph) 1936, pp. 30–32.

58. Poddar, '*Vartaman Shiksha*', *Kalyan*, April 1936, p. 1294.
59. Poddar, *Nari Shiksha*, 1952, pp. 21–22.
60. Premchand, '*Nari Ka Vastavik Swarup*' (Woman's Real Self), *Kalyan, Nari Ank*, January 1948, p. 351.
61. Adolf Hitler, '*Striyon Ka Kartavya*' (Women's Duty), *Kalyan, Nari Ank*, January 1948, p. 724.
62. Colonel James Tod, '*Aitihasik Tathya*' (Historical Facts), *Kalyan, Nari Ank*, January 1948, p. 200.
63. Poddar, *Nari Shiksha*, 1952, pp. 21–22.
64. Chandrima Chakraborty, *Masculinity, Asceticism, Hinduism*, Permanent Black, Ranikhet, 2011, p. 193.
65. Amrita Basu, 'Feminism Inverted', in Tanika Sarkar and Urvashi Butalia (eds), *Women And the Hindu Right*, Kali For Women, New Delhi, 1995, p. 159.
66. Poddar, *Nari Shiksha*, 1952, pp. 24–25.
67. A.S. Altekar, *The Position of Women in Hindu Civilization*, Motilal Banarsidass, Delhi, 1938, p. 83.
68. Livia Holden, *Hindu Divorce: A Legal Anthropology*, Ashgate, England, 2008, pp. 15–16.
69. Forbes, 1996, pp. 112–13.
70. Ruprani 'Shyama', '*Talaq Sabhyata Ka Chinh Hai?*' (Is Divorce a Symbol of Civilization?), *Kalyan*, March 1936, pp. 1280–83.
71. Hanuman Prasad Poddar, '*Vivah-Vichched*' (Dissolution of Marriage), *Kalyan, Nari Ank*, January 1948, pp. 192–95.
72. Hanuman Prasad Poddar, '*Kaam Ke Patra*' (Useful Letters), *Kalyan*, December 1949, pp. 1467–75.
73. Poddar, *Stri Dharma Prashnottari*, 1926, pp. 20–23.
74. Goyandka, *Nari Dharma*, 1938, p. 36.
75. '*Vidhva Jivan Ko Pavitra Rakhne Ka Sadhan*' (Means to Keep a Widow's Life Pure), *Kalyan, Nari Ank*, January 1948, pp. 241–43.
76. Poddar, *Samaj Sudhar*, 1928, p. 6.
77. Hanuman Prasad Poddar, '*Sahmaran Ya Sati Chamatkar*' (Dying Together or Sati Magic), *Kalyan, Nari Ank*, January 1948, pp. 257–59.
78. Acharya Chandrasekhar Shastri, '*Bharatiya Atankvad Mein Ek Sati Mahila*' (A Sati Woman in the Indian Revolutionary Movement), *Kalyan, Nari Ank*, January 1948, pp. 867–68.

79. Goyandka, *Nari Dharma*, 1938, p. 14.
80. Tanika Sarkar, *Hindu Wife, Hindu Nation*, Permanent Black, Ranikhet, 2001, p. 228.
81. Goyandka, *Nari Dharma*, 1938, p. 2.
82. Charu Chandra Mitra, '*Nari: Paschatya Aur Hindu Samaj Mein*' (Women: In Western and Hindu Society), *Kalyan*, May 1948, pp. 1049–54.
83. Havelock Ellis, *Psychology of Sex*, Vol. VI, p. 524 as cited in Mitra.
84. Anton Vitalivich Nemilov, *Biological Tragedy of Women*, Chapter VII, pp. 128–33, as cited in Mitra, *Kalyan*, May 1948.
85. Gupta, 2001, p. 126.
86. Poddar, *Stri Dharma Prashnottari*, 1926, p. 37.
87. Ibid., pp. 40–41.
88. '*Sarvashreshth Santan Prapti Ke Liye Niyam*' (Rules for Getting the Best Child), *Kalyan, Nari Ank*, January 1948, p. 294.
89. Hanuman Prasad Poddar, '*Garbhadhan Ke Shreshth Niyam*' (Best Rules for Pregnancy), in *Nari Shiksha*, 1952, pp. 33–38.
90. Poddar, *Stri Dharma Prashnottari*, 1926, p. 41.
91. Gangadhar Trivedi, '*Striyon Ke Rog Aur Unki Gharelu Chikitsa*' (Ailments among Women and Their Home Remedies), *Kalyan, Nari Ank*, January 1948, pp. 300–03.
92. Goyandka, *Nari Dharma*, 1938, p. 24.
93. '*Shishu Rog Aur Unki Gharelu Chikitsa*' (Ailments among Children and Their Home Remedies), *Kalyan, Nari Ank*, January 1948, pp. 304–12.
94. Vaidya Badrudin Ranpuri, '*Bal Rogon Ki Kuchh Adbhut Davaiyan*' (Some Magical Medicines for Ailments among Children), *Kalyan*, June 2001, pp. 730–31.
95. Siddhgopal, '*AIDS Evam Adhyatm*' (AIDS and Spiritualism), *Kalyan*, November 2005, p. 961.
96. Emma Tarlo, *Clothing Matters: Dress and Identity in India*, Penguin-Viking, New Delhi, 1996, p. 1.
97. C.A. Bayly, 'The Origins of Swadeshi (home industry): Cloth and Indian Society, 1700–1930', in Arjun Appadurai (ed.), *The Social Life of Things: Commodities in Cultural Perspective*, Cambridge University Press, USA, pp. 286–87.
98. Ramcharan Mahendra, '*Hindu Bheshbhusha Aur Hindi Bhasha Ko*

Apnane Main Garv Ka Anubhav Karen' (Take Pride in Adopting Hindu Dress and the Hindi Language), *Kalyan*, November 1966, pp. 1312–13.

99. Tarlo, 1996, p. 11.
100. Hanuman Prasad Poddar, '*Nari Ke Dooshan*' (Faults of Women), *Kalyan, Nari Ank*, January 1948, pp. 324–28.
101. Poddar, *Stri Dharma Prashnottari*, 1926, pp. 17–18.
102. Ibid., p. 35.
103. Tarlo, 1996, p. 95.
104. Poddar, *Samaj Sudhar*, 1928, pp. 30–31.
105. Hanuman Prasad Poddar, *Purna Samarpan*, Gita Press, Gorakhpur, 1953, pp. 250–64.
106. M.K. Gandhi interview to Margaret Sanger, 3–4 December 1935, *Collected Works of Mahatma Gandhi*, Vol. 68, pp. 190–91.
107. Mahatma Gandhi, 'Birth-Control', *Harijan*, 14 March 1936. *Collected Works of Mahatma Gandhi*, Vol. 68, pp. 296–98.
108. Poddar, '*Vartaman Shiksha*', *Kalyan*, April 1936, pp. 1289–1300; and an expanded version published as a separate monograph in 1936 by Gita Press, Gorakhpur, pp. 21–22.
109. Mahatma Gandhi, '*Santati Ya Parivar Niyojan Par Mahatma Gandhi Ke Vichar*' (Mahatma Gandhi's Thoughts on Raising a Family vs Family Planning), *Navjivan*, 12 March 1925, as quoted in *Kalyan*, August 1969, p. 1107.
110. *Collected Works of Mahatma Gandhi*, Vol. 17, p. 54, cited in J.T.F. Jordens, *Gandhi's Religion: A Homespun Shawl*, Oxford University Press, New Delhi, 2012, p. 209.
111. Ibid., Vol. 23, Publications Division, p. 102, cited in Jordens, 2012.
112. Ibid., Vol. 29, p. 415.
113. Ibid., Vol. 30, p. 235–36.
114. Vinoba Bhave, '*Parivar Niyojan Aur Bharatiya Sanskriti*' (Family Planning and Indian Culture), *Kalyan*, June 1997, pp. 516–17 (original year of publication not known).
115. Mitra, '*Nari: Paschatya Aur Hindu Samaj Mein*', *Kalyan*, August 1948, pp. 1235–41.
116. Dr K.C. Mishra, '*Parivar Niyojan Par Ek Adhyatmik Drishtikon*' (A Spiritual View on Family Planning), *Kalyan*, December 1967, pp. 1389–91.

117. Patricia Jeffery and Roger Jeffery, *Confronting Saffron Demography*, Three Essays Collective, New Delhi, 2006, p. 1.
118. Chandrima Chakraborty, *Masculinity, Asceticism, Hinduism*, Permanent Black, Ranikhet, 2011, p. 181.
119. Charu Gupta, 'Politics of Gender: Women in Nazi Germany', *Economic and Political Weekly*, Vol. 26, No. 17, 27 April 1991, pp. WS40–WS48.
120. Census of India, 1911, Vol. XV, Part I, Allahabad, 1912, pp. 109–10, cited in Gupta, *Sexuality, Obscenity, Community*, 2001, pp. 307–08.
121. Census of India, 1921, UP, p. 53 cited in Gupta, 2001, p. 308.
122. Jeffery and Jeffery, 2006, p. 2.
123. Hanuman Prasad Poddar, '*Parivar Niyojan Hanikarak Hai*' (Family Planning is Harmful), in '*Kaam Ke Patra*', *Kalyan*, August 1968, pp. 1140–41.
124. Vir Bharat Talwar, 'Feminist Consciousness in Women's Journals in Hindi, 1910–20', in Kumkum Sangari and Sudesh Vaid (eds), 2010, p. 205.
125. Ibid., p. 207.
126. Francesca Orsini, *The Hindi Public Sphere, 1920–1940: Language and Literature in the Age of Nationalism*, Oxford University Press, Delhi, 2002, pp. 264–65.
127. Ibid., p. 262.
128. Talwar, 2010, p. 208.
129. The details about *Chand* provided here are sourced from Orsini, 2002, pp. 266–74.
130. Ibid., pp. 245, 260, 269.
131. Shobna Nijhawan, *Women and Girls in the Hindi Public Sphere*, Oxford University Press, New Delhi, 2012, pp. 13, 18.
132. Ibid., p. 4.
133. Susie Tharu and K. Lalita (eds), *Women Writing in India*, Vol. I, Oxford University Press, New Delhi, 1993, p. 14.
134. Ibid., pp. 419–20.
135. Ibid., p. 459.
136. Information on Subbalakshmi sourced from Forbes, 1996, pp. 57–60.
137. Vijaya Lakshmi Pandit, '*Adhunikta: Saar Aur Asaar*' (Modernity: Its

Essence and Non-Essence) *Kalyan*, December 1965, pp. 1367–70 (first published in *Navbharat Times*, Bombay, 23 April 1965).

138. This and following quotes are from Siobhan Lambert-Hurley, 'Heart of a Gopi: Raihana Tyabji's Bhakti Devotionalism as Self-Representation,' Loughborough University, 2011 (published in *Modern Asian Studies*, Vol. 48, No. 3, May 2014, pp. 569–95).
139. Anasuya Devi to Poddar, address and date not given but probably January–February 1970. Poddar Papers.
140. Poddar to Swaran Singh, 20 February 1970. Poddar Papers.
141. Ritu Sinha, 'Hindi and Hindu Nationalism: A Sociological Study of Contemporary Trends in Hindi Literary Sphere', doctoral thesis in submission, JNU, Delhi.
142. Krishna Kumar, *Political Agenda of Education*, Sage, Delhi, 2005, p. 16.
143. Sinha, 'Hindi and Hindu Nationalism'.
144. N.C. Chatterjee, '*Hindu Jati Aur Bharat Ka Bhavishya*' (The Future of the Hindus and India), *Kalyan, Balak Ank*, January 1953, pp. 37–38.
145. Madhav Sadashiv Golwalkar, '*Abhyudaya Aur Nihshreyas Tatha Unki Prapti Ke Upaye*' (How to Achieve Progress and Freedom from Rebirth), *Kalyan, Balak Ank*, January 1953, pp. 285–90.
146. N.B. Khare, '*Dharmik Siddhanton Ko Jagane Ki Avashyakta*' (Need to Invoke Tenets of Religion), *Kalyan, Balak Ank*, January 1953, p. 36.
147. '*Gande Sahitya Se Balakon Ke Jivan Par Kuprabhav*' (Adverse Impact of Obscene Literature on Children), *Kalyan, Balak Ank*, January 1953, pp. 331–33.
148. '*Vartaman Kuchh Patra-Patrikaon Ki Anaitik Pravritti Aur Balakon Ko Usse Bachane Ki Avashyakta*' (Immoral Tendencies of a Few Current Journals and the Need to Protect Boys from Them), *Kalyan, Balak Ank*, January 1953, pp. 333–36.
149. '*Cinema Sahitya Evam Cinema Abhinetriyon Ke Chitron Ke Prachar Se Balakon Ka Patan*' (Moral Decline among Male Children Due to Cinema Literature and Photographs of Film Actresses), *Kalyan, Balak Ank*, January 1953, pp. 337–39.
150. Gurty Subramaniam, '*Chalchitra Ke Sadupayog Se Bal Shiksha*' (Educating the Male Child through Beneficial Use of Cinema), *Kalyan, Balak Ank*, January 1953, pp. 339–41.

151. Hanuman Prasad Poddar, *Kalyan, Balak Ank*, January 1953, p. 341.
152. Vishnu Hari Dalmia to I&B minister, 10 June 1957. Poddar Papers.
153. V.H. Dalmia to Chimmanlal Gosvami, 15 October 1957. Poddar Papers.
154. V.H. Dalmia to Chimmanlal Gosvami, 18 October 1957. Poddar Papers.
155. Poddar to Satyanarayan Sinha, date not clear. Poddar Papers.
156. '*Bilasita Ki Samagriyon Ke Prachar Se Yuvak Yuvtiyon Ke Dhan, Swasthya Tatha Charitra Ka Nash*' (Destruction of Money, Health and Character Due to Popularization of Cosmetic Products), *Kalyan, Balak Ank*, January 1953, pp. 344–46.
157. Banarsi Das Chaturvedi, '*Bharatiya Bal Sahitya*' (Children's Literature in India), *Kalyan, Balak Ank*, January 1953, pp. 388–92.
158. Office of the Director of Public Instruction, Madhya Pradesh, circular dated 26 March 1953. Poddar Papers.
159. Directorate of Education, PEPSU, Nabha, circular dated 29 July 1953. Poddar Papers.
160. Circular of Education Directorate, Government of Saurashtra, 27 January 1953, and order of Education Section of Development and Social Services Department, Government of Vindhya Pradesh, 9 March 1953. Poddar Papers.
161. Headmaster of Shri Krishna School to Poddar, 13 February 1935. Poddar Papers.
162. President, Assam Sanskrit Board to Poddar, 29 October 1935. Poddar Papers.
163. Sukhdeo Pandey to Poddar, 30 December 1957. Poddar Papers.
164. Poddar to Pandey, 20 January 1958. Poddar Papers.
165. Pandey to Poddar, 24 January 1958. Poddar Papers.
166. Poddar to Pandey, 7 February 1958. Poddar Papers.
167. Poddar to Pandey, 20 February 1958. Poddar Papers.
168. Pandey to Poddar, 21 February 1958. Poddar Papers.
169. Kedar Nath Singh to Poddar, 25 July 1970. Poddar Papers.
170. Mahant Digvijaynath, '*Rashtriya Shiksha Niti*' (National Educational Policy), *Kalyan, Shiksha Ank*, January 1988, pp. 97–98.
171. Paripurnanand Varma, '*Bharat Mein Prachin Shiksha Tatha Adhunik Shiksha*' (Ancient and Modern Education in India), *Kalyan, Shiksha Ank*, January 1988, pp. 225–30.

172. Ramchandra Shastri Vidyalankar, '*Balakon Ko Shiksha*' (Education of Boys), *Kalyan, Shiksha Ank*, January 1988, p. 401.
173. Digvijaynath, '*Rashtriya Shiksha Niti*', *Shiksha Ank*, January 1988.
174. Rajiv Gandhi, '*Rashtriya Shiksha Niti*' (National Education Policy) and Vedram Sharma, '*10+2+3 Shiksha Pranali: Purani Aur Apoorn Yojna*' (10+2+3 Education System: Old and Incomplete System), *Kalyan, Shiksha Ank*, January 1988, pp. 347–53 and 375–78.
175. Poddar, *Samaj Sudhar*, 1928, p. 5.
176. Poddar, '*Vartaman Shiksha*,' *Kalyan*, April 1936, pp. 1290–92, 1295, May, 1433–34.
177. Jaswantrai Jaishankar Hathi, '*Parikshak Aur Pariksha*' (Examiner and Examination), *Kalyan, Balak Ank*, January 1953, pp. 792–93.
178. Poddar, '*Vartaman Shiksha*,' *Kalyan*, May 1936, p. 1434.
179. Poddar to Chaturvediji Maharaj, 28 September 1935. Poddar Papers.
180. *Hindi Bal Pothi, Shishu Path*, Vol. 1; *Hindi Bal Pothi*, Vol. 4, Gita Press, Gorakhpur, 2011.
181. Hanuman Prasad Poddar, *Balak ke Acharan*, Gita Press, Gorakhpur, 2010.
182. Veronique Benei, *Schooling India: Hindus, Muslims and the Forging of Citizens*, Permanent Black, Ranikhet, 2009, pp. 1–2.
183. Poddar, '*Desh Ki Laaj*' (Nation's Honour), in *BKA*, 2010, pp. 5–8.
184. Poddar, '*Dharma Ka Palan*' (Following Dharma), in *BKA*, pp. 9–10.
185. Poddar, '*Jati Ki Maryada*' (Sanctity of Religion/Caste), in *BKA*, pp. 11–12.
186. *Hindi Bal Pothi, Shishu Path*, Vol. II, Gita Press, Gorakhpur, 2011, Introduction.
187. Editorial, *Kalyana-Kalpataru*, October 2012, p. 10.
188. Hanuman Prasad Poddar, 'The Present Day Education', *Kalyana-Kalpataru, Shiksha Number*, October 2012, pp. 51–58.
189. Editorial, *Kalyana-Kalpataru, Shiksha Number*, October 2012, pp. 9–12.
190. Rules and Regulations of Shri Rishikul Brahmacharya Ashram, Churu, *Kalyan*, June 1969, back cover.
191. http://gitapress.org/Vedic_school.htm. Accessed on 27 November 2013.

Epilogue

1. Radheshyam Khemka, '*Vote Kisko Dein*', *Kalyan*, April 2014, p. 29.
2. Interview with Radheshyam Khemka, editor, *Kalyan*, in Banaras, February 2011.
3. Radheshyam Khemka, '*Ayodhya Ki Ghatna: Samasya Aur Samadhan*' (Incident in Ayodhya: Problem and Solution), *Kalyan*, February 1993, pp. 447–48.
4. Editor, '*Shri Ram Janmabhoomi Ka Vivad*' (The Controversy of Shri Ram Janmabhoomi), *Kalyan*, July 1992, pp. 647–48.
5. Editorial comment, '*Ayodhya Mein Bhagwan Shri Ram Ka Prakatya Hua Tha*' (Lord Rama Appeared in Ayodhya), *Kalyan*, September 1992, p. 768.
6. Radheshyam Khemka, '*Shri Ram Janmabhoomi*', *Kalyan*, June 1990, pp. 602–04.
7. http://sethusamudram.gov.in/What/What.htm. Accessed on 5 January 2013.
8. Radheshyam Khemka, '*Setubandh Rameshwaram Ki Raksha Karen*' (Protect Setu at Rameshwaram), *Kalyan*, March 2007, pp. 595–96.
9. Ramchandra Mahendra, '*Samaj Ke Liye Dharma Ka Mahatvapurna Yogdan*' (Important Role of Religion in Society), *Kalyan*, September 1977, pp. 346–47.
10. Radheshyam Khemka, '*Sikh Dharma Bharatiya Darshan Evam Hindu Sanskriti Ka Abhinn Ang*' (Sikh Religion Is an Integral Part of Indian Philosophy and Hindu Culture), *Kalyan*, June 1984, pp. 658–60.
11. '*Aatankvad Aur Nar Hatya*' (Militancy and Human Killing), *Kalyan*, July 1987, p. 880.
12. *Kalyan*, July 1988, p. 3.
13. Radheshyam Khemka, '*Desh Ki Simaon Ko Surakshit Rakhna Hamara Kartavya*' (It is Our Duty to Protect the Country's Boundaries), *Kalyan*, March 1999, p. 4.
14. Radheshyam Khemka, '*Dharma, Rajya Aur Niti*' (Religion, State and Principles), *Kalyan*, *Nitisar Ank*, January–February 2002, pp. 542–46.
15. Prabhudatt Brahmachari, '*Swarajya Evam Go Raksha*' (Self-rule and Cow Protection), *Kalyan*, *Gau Seva Ank*, January 1995, pp. 78–82.
16. M.V. Kamath, *Gandhi's Coolie: Life and Times of Ramakrishna Bajaj*, Allied Publishers, New Delhi, 1988. p. 253.

17. Radhakrishna Bajaj, '*Goraksha Evam Gosamvardhan*' (Cow Protection and Cows' Development), *Gau Seva Ank*, January 1995, pp. 341–46.
18. Muzaffar Hussain, '*Gai Aur Quran*' (Cow and the Quran), *Kalyan*, March 2012, pp. 514–16.
19. Radheshyam Khemka, '*Purn Go Hatyabandi Ki Disha Mein Maharashtra Ka Ek Kadam*' (A Step by Maharashtra Towards Total Ban on Cow Slaughter), *Kalyan*, April 2015, p. 50.
20. Interview with Khemka, February 2011.
21. Interview with Khemka, February 2011.
22. Radheshyam Khemka, '*Savdhan Rehne Ki Avashyakta*' (Need to Be Alert), *Kalyan*, November 2013, pp. 49–50.
23. Radheshyam Khemka, '*Desh Ka Durbhagya*' (Nation's Misfortune), *Kalyan*, September 2013, p. 50
24. Patricia Jeffery and Roger Jeffery, *Confronting Saffron Demography*, Three Essays Collective, New Delhi, 2006, p. 2.
25. Radheshyam Khemka, '*Bharatiya Sanskriti Aur Parivar Niyojan*' (Indian Culture and Family Planning), *Kalyan*, August 2002, pp. 743–44.
26. Siddharaj Dhadda, '*Ek Drishtikon: Garbhpat Kanoon Ya Hatya Ko Manyata*' (A Viewpoint: Abortion Law or Licence to Kill), *Kalyan*, July 1971, pp. 1063–65.
27. Gopinath Aggarwal, *Garbhpat: Uchit Ya Anuchit, Faisla Aapka*, Gita Press, Gorakhpur, 2011, p. 3.
28. Shailendra Kumar Jain in Aggarwal 2011, pp. 13–15.
29. Interview with Khemka, February 2011.
30. ICRA rating, August 2013.
31. *Merriam-Webster's Encyclopedia of World Religions*, Massachusetts, 1999, pp. 379–80.

Bibliography

Primary Sources

All India Hindu Mahasabha Papers, List No. 8, Nehru Memorial Museum and Library, New Delhi (NMML).

Amiya K. Samanta (ed.), *Terrorism in Bengal: A Collection of Documents*, Vols I—VI, Government of West Bengal, Calcutta, 1995.

Ashutosh Lahiry Papers, List No. 64, NMML.

Bengal Native Newspapers Report, NMML, National Archives of India.

Bharatiya Jana Sangh: Party Documents, Vols. I—V, BJP, 2005.

Census of India, 1911, 1921, United Provinces.

CID Archives, Lucknow.

Commissioner's Record Room, Gorakhpur.

Dr Sampurnanand, Oral History Transcript, Acc. 265, NMML.

G.D. Birla Papers, List No. 41, NMML.

Gyanwati Darbar, private secretary to Rajendra Prasad, Oral History Transcript, NMML.

Hanuman Prasad Poddar Papers. In the collection of Harikrishna Dujari, Gorakhpur.

Hari Shankar Dwivedi and Vishnu Hari Dalmia (eds), *Sant Shri Jaidayal Dalmia Smriti Granth* (Jaidayal Dalmia Commemorative Volume), published by Hari Shankar Dwivedi, New Delhi.

The Hindu Library, Chennai.

Jamnalal Bajaj Papers, List No. 124, NMML.

Lok Sabha Debates, Part II, Vol. III, Ninth Session (2–21 April, 1955), Lok Sabha Secretariat.

Lok Sabha Debates, Sixth Session, Vol. 22, Nos. 10–20, 2–6 December, 1968, Lok Sabha Secretariat.

Madan Mohan Malaviya Papers, Microfilm section, NMML.

Marwari Library, New Delhi.

Marwari Stores Ltd. vs *Gouri Shankar Goenka*. AIR 1936 Cal 327, 165 Ind Cas 408.

N.B. Khare, Oral History Transcript, Acc. 310, NMML.

Nagari Pracharini Sabha Library, Banaras.

O.P. Ralhan, Hindu Mahasabha Documents, Vols I & II, Anmol Publications, New Delhi, 1997.

Pamphlet of Bharatiya Sanskritik Suraksha Parishad

Prabhu Dayal Himmatsingka, Oral History Transcript, Acc. 785, NMML.

Purshottamdas Thakurdas Papers, List No. 11, NMML.

Raghunandan Prasad Sharma (ed.), *Satat Sadhana Yatra Ke Tees Barsh (1964–1994)*, VHP Publications, New Delhi, 1995.

Report of the Administration of the United Provinces, 1947, Allahabad, Superintendent, Printing and Stationery, United Provinces. Printed by P.N. Bhargava, Bhargava Bhushan Press, Banaras.

Report of the Commission of Inquiry (Inquiry on the Administration of Dalmia–Jain Companies), Department of Commerce and Industry, 1963.

Seth Govind Das, Oral History Transcript, Acc. No. 155, NMML.

Seth Govind Das Papers, List No. 107, NMML.

Shivpujan Sahay Papers, List No. 473, NMML.

Short Report of Hindu Mahasabha Relief Activities during Calcutta Killings and Noakhali Carnage, published by Bengal Provincial Hindu Mahasabha, 162, Bowbazar Street, Calcutta, 1946.

Sitaram Sekhsaria, Oral History Transcript, Acc. 701, NMML.

Theosophical Society Library, Banaras and Adayar, Chennai.

UP State Archives, Lucknow.

Visva Hindu Parishad Ki Bayalish Varshiya Vikas Yatra (1964-2006), VHP Publication, New Delhi, 2007.

Viyogi Hari, Oral History Transcript, Acc. 659, NMML.

Dictionaries

Kalika Prasad, Rajballabh Sahay and Mukundi Lal Srivastava (eds), *Brihat Hindi Kosh*, Gyanmandal Limited, Banaras, 2011.

R.S. McGregor, Oxford Hindi–English Dictionary, Oxford University Press, New Delhi, 2011.

Ramchandra Varma (ed.), *Sanskshipt Hindi Shabd-Sagar*, Nagari Pracharini Sabha, Banaras, 1987.

The Student's Practical Dictionary, Ram Narain Lal Publisher and Bookseller, Allahabad, 1936.

e-Sources

http://natnagarsitamau.com/english/history_sitamau.html

http://www.swarthmore.edu/library/friends/ead/5267nile.xml

www.prabhupadabooks.com

http://ark.cdlib.org/ark:/13030/ft22900465

http://articles.timesofindia.indiatimes.com/2002-02-24/india/27124654_1_hindu-mahasabha-savarkar-muslims

http://www.london.gazette.co.uk/issues/37842/pages/124/page.pdf

www.shantisadan.org

http://www.bori.ac.in/mahabharata_project.html

http://henrythomashamblin.wwwhubs.com/

http://www.swamisridindayaluji.in/karpatri.php

http://archives.gcah.org/publicdata/gcah2723.htm

http://christianlarson.wwwhubs.com/

http://gitapress.org/Vedic_school.htm

http://sethusamudram.gov.in/What/What.htm.

Journals, Newspapers

Arya Mahila

Bharata Dharma

Bombay Chronicle

Calcutta Samachar

Chand

Cheerag

Economic & Political Weekly

Economic Weekly

Hindu Panch

Journal of Arts and Ideas

Madhuri

Modern Review

Navbharat Times

Navjivan

Navneet Hindi Digest

Saraswati

Stri Dharma Shikshak

The Statesman

The Times of India

Veer Arjun

Yathawat

Unpublished Theses and Dissertations

Abhik Samanta, 'The Gita Press, Gorakhpur: A Discursive Study', M.Phil. dissertation, Delhi University, 2007.

Avinash Kumar, 'Making of the Hindi Literary Field: Journals, Institutions, Personalities (1900–1940)', Ph.D. thesis, Jawaharlal Nehru University, Delhi, 2001.

Rajnish Kumar Chaturvedi, *'Patrakarita Ke Kshetra Mein Kalyan Dharmik Patrika Ka Yogdan'*, Ph.D. thesis, Mahamana Madan Mohan Malaviya Hindi Patrakarita Sansthan, Mahatma Gandhi Kashi Vidyapith, Banaras, 2006.

Ritu Sinha, 'Hindi and Hindu Nationalism: A Sociological Study of Contemporary Trends in Hindi Literary Sphere', Ph.D. thesis, JNU, Delhi, 2015.

Sarah K. Broome, *Stri-Dharma: Voice of the Indian Women's Rights Movement* 1928-1936, History Thesis, Paper 57, Georgia State University, 2012.

Secondary Sources

A.L. Basham, *The Wonder That Was India*, Rupa Paperback, New Delhi, 1981.

A.S. Altekar, *The Position of Women in Hindu Civilization*, Motilal Banarsidass, Delhi, 1938.

Abhijit Gupta and Swapan Kumar Chakravorty, *Print Areas: Book History in India*, Permanent Black, New Delhi, 2004.

— *Movable Type: Book History in India*, Permanent Black, Ranikhet, 2008

Alan Ross, *The Emissary: G.D. Birla, Gandhi and Independence*, Collins Harvill, London, 1986.

Alok Rai, *Hindi Nationalism*, Orient Longman, New Delhi, 2001.

Amrit Rai, *A House Divided: The Origin and Development of Hindi/Hindavi*, Oxford University Press, New Delhi, 1984.

Andrew J. Nicholson, *Unifying Hinduism: Philosophy and Identity in Indian Intellectual History*, Permanent Black, Ranikhet, 2011.

Anna S. King and John Brockington (eds), *The Intimate Other: Love Divine in Indic Religions*, Orient Longman, New Delhi, 2005.

Anton Vitalivich Nemilov, *Biological Tragedy of Woman*, (translated by Stephanie Ofental), Covici Friede Inc, New York, 1932.

Antony Copley, *Hinduism in Public and Private: Reform, Hindutva, Gender and Sampraday*, Oxford University Press, New Delhi, 2003.

Arjun Appadurai (ed.), *The Social Life of Things: Commodities in Cultural Perspective*, Cambridge University Press, USA, 1988.

Asoka Mehta and Achyut Patwardhan, *Communal Tangle in India*, Kitabistan, Allahabad, 1942.

Axel Michaels, *Hinduism: Past and Present*, Orient Longman, New Delhi, 2006.

B.D. Graham, *Hindu Nationalism and Indian Politics: The Origin and Development of the Bharatiya Jana Sangh*, Cambridge University Press, New York, 2008.

B.R. Nanda, *In Gandhi's Footsteps: The Life and Times of Jamnalal Bajaj*, Oxford University Press, Delhi, 2011.

Barbara Daly Metcalf, *Perfecting Women: Maulana Ashraf Ali Thanawi's Bihishti Zewar*, Oxford University Press, New Delhi, 2002.

Benedict Anderson, *Imagined Communities: Reflections on the Origin and Spread of Nationalism*, Verso, London, 2003.

Bernard Cohn, *The Bernard Cohn Omnibus*, Oxford University Press, New Delhi, 2008.

Bhikhu Parekh, Gurharpal Singh and Steven Vertovec (eds), *Culture and Economy in the Indian Diaspora*, Routledge, London, 2003.

Braj B. Kachru, Yamuna Kachru and S.N. Sridhar (eds), *Language in South Asia*, Cambridge University Press, New York, 2008.

Brajlal Verma, *Hanuman Prasad Poddar*, Publications Division, New Delhi, 1987.

C.A. Bayly, *Empire and Information: Intelligence Gathering and Social Communication in India, 1780–1870*, Cambridge University Press, New Delhi, 1996.

Carey A. Watt and Michael Mann (eds), *Civilizing Missions in Colonial India and Postcolonial South Asia: From Improvement to Development*, Anthem Press India, New Delhi, 2012.

Carol A. Breckenridge and Peter van der Veer, *Orientalism and the Postcolonial Predicament: Perspectives on South Asia*, University of Pennsylvania Press, Philadelphia, 1993.

Caroline Healey Dall, *The Life of Dr Anandibai Joshee*, Roberts Brothers, Boston, 1888.

Chandrima Chakraborty, *Masculinity, Asceticism, Hinduism: Past and Present Imaginings of India*, Permanent Black, Ranikhet, 2011.

Charu Gupta, *Sexuality, Obscenity, Community*, Permanent Black, Ranikhet, 2001.

Chitra Sinha, *Debating Patriarchy: The Hindu Code Bill Controversy in India (1941–1956)*, OUP and New India Foundation, New Delhi, 2012.

Christophe Jaffrelot, *India's Silent Revolution*, Permanent Black, Ranikhet, 2003.

— *Religion, Caste & Politics in India*, Primus Books, New Delhi, 2010.

— *Hindu Nationalism*, Permanent Black, Ranikhet, 2009.

— *The Hindu Nationalist Movement in India*, Penguin-Viking, New Delhi, 1996.

Christophe Jaffrelot (ed.), *The Sangh Parivar: A Reader*, Oxford University Press, New Delhi, 2005.

Christopher Pinney, *Photos of the Gods: The Printed Image and Political Struggle in India*, Reaktion Books, London, 2004.

Christopher R. King, *One Language, Two Scripts: The Hindi Movement in Nineteenth Century North India*, Oxford University Press, New Delhi, 1994.

Collected Works of Mahatma Gandhi, Publications Division, New Delhi 1958–94.

Constance A. Jones and James D. Ryan, *Encyclopedia of Hinduism*, Facts on File (an imprint of Infobase Publishing), New York, 2007.

Craig Baxter, *Jana Sangh: A Biography of an Indian Political Party*, Oxford University Press, New Delhi, 1971.

D.A. Low, *Congress and the Raj: Facets of the Indian Struggle 1917—47*, Oxford University Press, New Delhi, 2004.

D.N. Jha, *The Myth of the Holy Cow*, Verso, London, 2004.

David Arnold and David Hardiman (eds), *Subaltern Studies*, Vol. VIII, Oxford University Press, New Delhi, 1993.

David Ludden (ed.), *Making India Hindu*, Oxford University Press, New Delhi, 1996.

David N. Lorenzen, *Who Invented Hinduism? Essays on Religion in History*, Yoda Press, New Delhi, 2009.

Dhananjay Keer, *Lokmanya Tilak: Father of the Indian Freedom Struggle*, S.V. Kangutkar, Bombay, 1959.

Dharampal, *Collected Writings*, Vol. I—V, Society for Integrated Development of Himalayas, Mussoorie, 2007.

Dharampal and T.M. Mukundan, *The British Origin of Cow-Slaughter in India,* Society for Integrated Development of Himalayas, Mussoorie, 2002.

Dhirendra K. Jha and Krishna Jha, *Ayodhya: The Dark Night: The Secret History of Rama's Appearance in Babri Masjid,* HarperCollins, New Delhi, 2012.

Donald Eugene Smith, *India as a Secular State,* Princeton University Press, New Jersey, 1963.

Dwijendra Tripathi, *The Oxford History of Indian Business,* Oxford University Press, New Delhi, 2004.

Emma Tarlo, *Clothing Matters: Dress and Identity in India,* Penguin-Viking, New Delhi, 1996.

Eric Hobsbawm and Terence Ranger (eds), *The Invention of Tradition,* Cambridge University Press, Cambridge, UK, 1983.

Francesca Orsini, *The Hindi Public Sphere 1920—1940: Language and Literature in the Age of Nationalism,* Oxford University Press, New Delhi, 2002.

— *Print and Pleasure: Popular Literature and Entertaining Fictions in Colonial North India,* Permanent Black, Ranikhet, 2009.

Francesca Orsini (ed.), *Before the Divide: Hindi and Urdu Literary Culture,* Orient Blackswan, New Delhi, 2010.

G.D. Birla (ed.), *Bapu: A Unique Association,* Vol. I, Bharatiya Vidya Bhavan, Bombay, 1977.

G.R. Madan, *Radha Kamal Mukerjee: An Eminent Scholar, Saint and Social Worker,* Radha Publications, New Delhi, 2008.

Gail Minault, *Gender, Language and Learning: Essays in Indo-Muslim Cultural History,* Permanent Black, Ranikhet, 2009.

Geoffrey A. Oddie, *Imagined Hinduism: British Protestant Missionary Constructions of Hinduism, 1793–1900,* Sage, New Delhi, 2006.

Geraldine Forbes, *Women in Modern India,* Cambridge University Press, New Delhi, 1996.

Ghulam Murshid, *Reluctant Debutante: Response of Bengali Women to Modernisation, 1849–1905,* Rajshahi University Press, 1983.

Gita Piramal, *Business Legends,* Penguin-Viking, New Delhi, 1998.

Gulammohammed Sheikh (ed.), *Contemporary Art in Baroda*, Tulika, New Delhi, 1997.

Gyanendra Pandey, *The Ascendancy of the Congress in Uttar Pradesh*, Anthem Press, London, 2002.

— *The Construction of Communalism in Colonial North India*, Oxford University Press, New Delhi, 2008.

Gyanesh Kudaisya, *Region, Nation, 'Heartland': Uttar Pradesh in India's Body Politic*, Sage, New Delhi, 2006.

H.L. Erdman, *The Swatantra Party and Indian Conservatism*, Cambridge University Press, Cambridge, 2008.

Harivansh Rai Bachchan, *In the Afternoon of Time: An Autobiography*, edited and translated from Hindi by Rupert Snell, Viking, 1998.

Havelock Ellis, *Studies in The Psychology of Sex*, Random House, USA, 1937.

Hans Harder (ed.), *Literature & Nationalist Ideology*, Social Science Press, New Delhi, 2011.

Harold A. Gould, *Grass Roots Politics in India: A Century of Political Evolution in Faizabad District*, Oxford & IBH, New Delhi, 1994.

— *Sikhs, Swamis, Students, and Spies: The Indian Lobby in the United States, 1900-1946*, Sage Publications, New Delhi, 2006.

Hugh Tinker, *The Ordeal of Love: C.F. Andrews and India*, Oxford University Press, New Delhi, 1979.

J.E. Llewellyn, *The Arya Samaj As a Fundamentalist Movement: A Study in Comparative Fundamentalism*, Manohar, New Delhi, 1993.

J.N. Farquhar, *Modern Religious Movements in India*, Low Price Publications, New Delhi, 1999.

J.T.F. Jordens, *Gandhi's Religion: A Homespun Shawl*, Oxford University Press, New Delhi, 2012.

James G. Lochtefeld, *The Illustrated Encyclopedia of Hinduism*, Vol. I—II, Rosen Publishing Group Inc., New York, 2002.

James Campbell Ker, *Political Trouble in India, 1907—1917*, Oriental Publishers, Delhi, 1917.

Jayeeta Sharma, *Empire's Garden: Assam and The Making of India*, Permanent Black, Ranikhet, 2011.

John George Woodroffe, *Is India Civilized? Essays on Indian Culture*, Ganesh & Co. Publishers, 1919, Madras.

K.L. Gauba, *The Assassination of Mahatma Gandhi*, Jaico Publishing House, Bombay, 1969.

K.M. Sen, *Hinduism*, Penguin, New Delhi, 2005.

K.M. Talreja (ed.), *Awake & Arise*, September–October, 1974.

Kajri Jain, *Gods in the Bazaar: The Economies of Indian Calendar Art*, Duke University Press, Durham, 2007.

Karine Schomer, *Mahadevi Varma and the Chhayavad Age of Modern Hindi Poetry*, Oxford University Press, New Delhi, 1998.

Kathryn Hansen, *Stages of Life: Indian Theatre Autobiographies*, Permanent Black, Ranikhet, 2011.

Kenneth W. Jones, *Arya Dharm: Hindu Consciousness in 19th Century Punjab*, Manohar, New Delhi, 2006.

— *Religious Controversy in British India: Dialogues in South Asian Languages*, State University of New York Press, New York, 1992.

Klaus K. Klostermaier, *A Survery of Hinduism*, State University of New York Press, New York, 2007.

Krishna Kumar, *Political Agenda of Education*, Sage, Delhi, 2005.

Kumkum Sangari, *Politics of the Possible: Gender, History, Narrative, Colonial English*, Tulika, New Delhi, 1999.

Kumkum Sangari and Sudesh Vaid (eds), *Recasting Women: Essays in Colonial History*, Zubaan, New Delhi, 2010.

Leah Renold, *A Hindu Education: Early Years of the Banaras Hindu University*, Oxford University Press, New Delhi, 2005.

Lee Siegel, *Sacred and Profane Dimensions of Love in Indian Traditions as Exemplified in the Gita Govinda of Jayadeva*, Oxford University Press, New Delhi, 1990.

Lionel Carter (ed.), *United Provinces' Politics, Congress in Mid-Term: Governors' Fortnightly Reports and Other Key Documents, 1938*, Manohar, New Delhi, 2009.

Livia Holden, *Hindu Divorce: A Legal Anthropology*, Ashgate, England, 2008.

Manjari Katju, *Vishva Hindu Parishad and Indian Politics,* Orient Blackswan, New Delhi, 2010.

Medha M. Kudaisya, *The Life and Times of G.D. Birla,* Oxford University Press, New Delhi, 2003.

Neelima Dalmia Adhar, *Father Dearest: The Life and Times of R.K. Dalmia,* Roli Books, New Delhi, 2003.

Nicholas B. Dirks, *Castes of Mind: Colonialism and the Making of Modern India,* Permanent Black, Ranikhet, 2002.

Nico Slate, *Colored Cosmopolitanism,* Harvard University Press, Cambridge, Mass., 2012.

Nita Kumar, *Lessons from Schools: The History of Education in Banaras,* Sage, New Delhi, 2000.

— *The Politics of Gender, Community, and Modernity: Essays on Education in India,* Oxford University Press, New Delhi, 2011.

Pandita Ramabai, *Pandita Ramabai's American Encounter: The People of the United States* (1889), Indiana University Press, 2003.

Partha Chatterjee, *A Princely Impostor? The Kumar of Bhawal and the Secret History of Indian Nationalism,* Permanent Black, Ranikhet, 2002.

Partha Mitter, *Art and Nationalism in Colonial India, 1850-1922,* Cambridge University Press, New Delhi, 1994.

— *The Triumph of Modernism: India's Artists and the Avant-Garde 1922—1947,* Reaktion Books, London, 2007.

Patricia Jeffery and Roger Jeffery, *Confronting Saffron Demography,* Three Essays Collective, New Delhi, 2006.

Paul Brunton, *A Search in Secret India,* Samuel Weiser Inc., Maine, USA, 1934.

Paul R. Brass, *An Indian Political Life: Charan Singh and Congress Politics, 1937–1961,* Sage Publications, New Delhi, 2011.

— *Language, Religion and Politics in North India,* Authors Guild Backinprint.com Edition, New England, USA, 2005.

— *The Production of Hindu-Muslim Violence in Contemporary India,* Oxford University Press, New Delhi, 2003.

Peter van der Veer, *Religious Nationalism: Hindus and Muslims in India,* University of California Press, Berkeley, 1994.

— *Gods on Earth: Religious Experience and Identity in Ayodhya*, Oxford University Press, New Delhi, 1997.

Philip Lutgendorf, *Hanuman's Tale: The Message of a Divine Monkey*, Oxford University Press, New Delhi, 2007.

— *Life of a Text: Performing the Ramcaritmanas of Tulsidas*, University of California Press, Berkeley, 1991.

Prabhu Bapu, *Hindu Mahasabha in Colonial North India, 1915-1930*, Routledge, London (UK), 2013.

R.K. Vashistha, *Art and Artists of Rajasthan*, Abhinav Publications, New Delhi, 1995.

R.S. McGregor (ed.), *Devotional Literature in South Asia: Current Research (1985-1988)*, Cambridge University Press, Cambridge, UK, 1992.

Rabindra Ray, *The Naxalites and Their Ideology*, Oxford University Press, New Delhi, 1988.

Radha Kumar, *The History of Doing*, Zubaan, New Delhi, 1993.

Radha Kumud Mookerji, *The Fundamental Unity of India*,

Bharatiya Vidya Bhavan, Chronicle Books, New Delhi, 2008.

Rajmohan Gandhi, *Mohandas: A True Story of a Man, His People and an Empire*, Penguin-Viking, New Delhi, 2006.

— *The Good Boatman: A Portrait of Gandhi*, Viking, 1995.

Ram Lal Wadhwa, *Hindu Mahasabha (1928-1947)*, Radha Publications, New Delhi, 1999.

Ramnarayan S. Rawat, *Reconsidering Untouchability: Chamars and Dalit History in North India*, Permanent Black, Ranikhet, 2012.

Ranajit Guha (ed.), *Subaltern Studies*, Vol. III, Oxford University Press, New Delhi, 1984.

Romila Thapar, *Cultural Pasts: Essays in Early Indian History*, Oxford University Press, New Delhi, 2000.

S.R. Hashim, K.S. Chalapati Rao, K.V.K. Ranganathan and M.R. Murthy (eds.), *Indian Industrial Development and Globalisation: Essays in Honour of Prof. S.K. Goyal*, Academic Foundation, New Delhi, 2008.

Sandria B. Freitag, *Collective Action and Community: Public Arenas and the*

Emergence of Communalism in North India, Oxford University Press, New Delhi, 1990.

Sekhar Bandyopadhyay, *Caste, Culture and Hegemony: Social Dominance in Colonial Bengal*, Sage Publications, New Delhi, 2004.

Sheldon Pollock (ed.), *Literary Cultures in History: Reconstructions from South Asia*, University of California Press, Berkeley, 2003.

Shobna Nijhawan (ed.), *Nationalism in the Vernacular*, Permanent Black, Ranikhet, 2010.

— *Women and Girls in the Hindi Public Sphere*, Oxford University Press, New Delhi, 2012.

Shraddhananda Sanyasi, *Hindu Sangathan: Saviour of the Dying Race*, Publisher Unknown, 1926.

Sri Bharat Dharma Mahamandal, *The World's Eternal Religion*, Naval Kishore Press, Lucknow, 1920.

Srikrishna Saral, *Indian Revolutionaries: A Comprehensive Study, 1757-1961*, Vol. 2, Ocean Books, New Delhi, 1999.

Stanley Wolpert, *Shameful Flight: The Last Years of The British Empire in India*, Oxford University Press, New York, 2006.

Stuart Blackburn and Vasudha Dalmia (eds), *India's Literary History: Essays on the Nineteenth Century*, Permanent Black, Ranikhet, 2010.

Stuart Blackburn, *Print, Folklore and Nationalism in Colonial South India*, Permanent Black, Ranikhet, 2006.

Suhas Chakravarty, *Raj Syndrome*, Penguin, New Delhi, 1995.

Sumathi Ramaswamy (ed.), *Beyond Appearances*, Sage, New Delhi, 2003.

Sumit Sarkar, *A Critique of Colonial India*, Papyrus, Calcutta, 2000.

— *Modern India, 1885–1947*, Macmillan, New Delhi, 1983.

— *The Swadeshi Movement in Bengal*, Permanent Black, Ranikhet, 2010.

Sumit Sarkar and Tanika Sarkar, *Women and Social Reform in Modern India*, Vols. I—II, Permanent Black, Ranikhet, 2007.

Sunil Raman, *C.Y. Chintamani: The Liberal Editor Politician*, Rupa Charitavali Series, New Delhi, 2002.

Susan Bayly, *Caste, Society and Politics in India: From the Eighteenth Century to the Modern Age*, Cambridge University Press, New Delhi, 2005.

Susie Tharu and K. Lalita (eds), *Women Writing in India*, Vol. I, Oxford University Press, New Delhi, 1993.

Tanika Sarkar and Urvashi Butalia (eds), *Women And the Hindu Right*, Kali For Women, New Delhi, 1995.

Tanika Sarkar, *Hindu Wife, Hindu Nation*, Permanent Black, Ranikhet, 2001.

Tapati Guha-Thakurta, *The Making of A New Art: Artists, Aesthetics and Nationalism in Bengal, C. 1850-1920*, Cambridge University Press, Cambridge, UK, 1992.

The Communal Problem, Report of the Kanpur Riots Enquiry Committee, National Book Trust, 2007.

The Oxford Encyclopaedia of the Music of India, Sangit Mahabharati and Oxford University Press, Mumbai and New Delhi, 2011.

Thomas A. Timberg, *The Marwaris: From Traders to Industrialists*, Vikas, New Delhi, 1978.

Thomas Blom Hansen, *The Saffron Wave: Democracy and Hindu Nationalism in Modern India*, Oxford University Press, New Delhi, 1999.

Thomas R. Metcalf, *Ideologies of the Raj*, Cambridge University Press, New Delhi, 1995.

Ulrike Stark, *An Empire of Books: The Naval Kishore Press and the Diffusion of the Printed Word in Colonial India*, Permanent Black, Ranikhet, 2007.

V.D. Savarkar, *Hindutva: Who is a Hindu?*, Central Hindu Yuvak Sabha, New Delhi, 1938.

Vasudha Dalmia, *The Nationalization of Hindu Traditions: Bharatendu Harishchandra and Nineteenth Century Banaras*, Oxford University Press, Delhi, 1997.

Vasudha Dalmia and Heinrich von Stietencron (eds), *Representing Hinduism: The Construction of Religious Tradition and National Identity*, Sage, New Delhi, 1995.

— *The Oxford India Hinduism Reader*, Oxford University Press, New Delhi, 2009.

Vasudha Dalmia and Rashmi Sadana (eds), *The Cambridge Companion To Modern Indian Culture*, Cambridge University Press, New Delhi, 2012.

Ved Mehta, *Mahatma Gandhi and His Apostles*, Penguin Books, Harmondsworth, Middlesex, UK, 1976.

Veronique Benei, *Schooling India: Hindus, Muslims and the Forging of Citizens*, Permanent Black, Ranikhet, 2009.

Vivan Sundaram, *Amrita Sher-Gil: A Self-Portrait in Letters & Writings*, Vol. I, Tulika Books, New Delhi, 2010.

Walter Benjamin, *Illuminations: Essays and Reflections*, translated by Harry Zohn, edited by Hannah Arendt, Schocken Books, New York, 2007.

William A. Graham, *Beyond the Written Word: Oral Aspects of Scripture in the History of Religion*, Cambridge University Press, London, 1987.

William Gould, *Hindu Nationalism and the Language of Politics in Late Colonial India*, Cambridge University Press, New Delhi, 2005.

— *Religion and Conflict in Modern South Asia*, Cambridge University Press, New Delhi, 2012.

William R. Pinch, *Peasants and Monks in British India*, University of California Press, Berkeley, 1996.

Yashodhara Dalmia, *Amrita Sher-Gil: A Life*, Penguin-Viking, 2006.

Hindi

Ayodhya Singh Upadhyay 'Harioudh', *Hindi Bhasha Aur Uske Sahitya Ka Bikas*, Patna University, 1934, printed by Babu Manik Lal, United Press Limited, Bhagalpur.

Bhagwati Prasad Singh, *Kalyan Path: Nirmata Aur Rahi*, Radha Madhav Seva Sansthan, Gorakhpur, 1980.

— *Manishi Ki Lokyatra: Gopinath Kaviraj Ka Jivan Darshan*, Vishwavidyalaya Prakashan, Banaras, 2010.

Bhalchand Modi, *Desh Ke Itihas Mein Marwari Jati Ka Sthan*, published by Raghunath Prasad Singhania, Calcutta, 1939.

Bharatendu Harishchandra, *Bharatendu Samagra*, Hindi Pracharak Publication, Banaras, 2009.

Chandraraj Bhandari 'Visharad', Bhramarlal Soni and Krishnalal Gupt, *Aggarwal Jati Ka Itihas*, Aggarwal History Office, Indore, 1937.

Dhirendranath Singh, *Adhunik Hindi Ke Vikas Mein Khadagvilas Press Ki Bhumika*, Bihar Rashtrabhasha Parishad, Patna, 1986.

Gambhirchand Dujari, *Shri Bhaiji: Ek Alaukik Vibhuti, Rasa-Siddha Sant Bhaiji Shri Hanuman Prasad Poddar Aur Sant Pravar Sethji Shri Jaydayalji Goyandka Ka Jivan Darshan*, Gita Vatika Prakashan, Gorakhpur, 2000.

Ganeshbihari, Shyambihari, Sukhdevbihari Mishra, *Mishrabandhuvinod*, Ganga Pustakmala Karyalaya, 4th ed., Lucknow, 1934.

Gopinath Kaviraj, Chimmanlal Gosvami, Bhagwati Prasad Singh (eds), *Bhaiji: Pawan Smaran*, Radha-Madhav Seva Sansthan, Gorakhpur, 1972.

Hanuman Prasad Poddar, *Samaj Sudhar*, Gita Press, Gorakhpur, 1928.

K.C. Yadav (ed.), *Chitthe Aur Khat*, Haryana Academy of History and Culture, 2012.

Kaka Kalelkar, *Kaka Kalelkar Granthavali*, Vol. I– XI, Gandhi Hindustani Sahitya Sabha, New Delhi, 2002.

Karmendu Shishir (ed.), *Shivpujan Sahay Samagra* , Vol. 8, Anamika Publishers, New Delhi, 2011.

Karmendu Shishir, *Navjagrankalin Patrakarita Aur Matwala*, Anamika Prakashan, Vol. I–III, Delhi, 2012.

Krishna Bihari Mishra, *Hindi Patrakarita: Rajasthani Aayojan Ki Kriti Bhumika*, Akhil Bhartiya Marwari Yuva Sangh, Delhi, 1999.

M.S. Golwalkar, *Sri Guruji Samagra*, Vol. 7 (Correspondence), Suruchi Prakashan, Delhi,

Narayan Dutt (ed.), *Banarsidas Chaturvedi Ke Chuninda Patra*, Vol. I, IGNCA and Rajkamal Prakashan, New Delhi, 2006.

Prabha Khaitan, *Peeli Aandhi*, Rajkamal Paperbacks, Delhi, 2001

Radheshyam Banka (ed.), *Sant Hriday Poddarji*, Hanuman Prasad Poddar Smarak Samiti, Gorakhpur, 1991.

Radheshyam Banka, *Parikar Malika*, Vol. II, Hanuman Prasad Smarak Samiti, Gita Vatika, Gorakhpur, 2013.

Ramvilas Sharma, *Mahavir Prasad Dwivedi Aur Hindi Navjagran*, Rajkamal Prakashan, Delhi, 1977.

Rishi Jaimini Kaushik Barua, *Main Apne Marwari Samaj Ko Pyar Karta Hoon*, Jaimini Prakashan, Calcutta, 1967.

Shyamsundar Dujari, *Saras Patra,* Gita Vatika Prakashan, Gorakhpur, 2005.

Sudhir Chandra, *Hindu, Hindutva, Hindustan,* Rajkamal Prakashan, 2005, New Delhi.

Swami Sahajanand Saraswati, *Mera Jivan Sangharsh,* edited by Avdhesh Pradhan, Granth Shilpi, New Delhi, 2000.

Gita Press Publications

Bhakt Nari

Dampatya Jivan Ka Adarsh

Gribasta Mein Kaise Rahe

Hanuman Prasad Poddar, *Balpurvak Dev Mandir Pravesh Aur Bhakti* (Forceful Entry into Temples and Devotion), Gita Press, Gorakhpur, 1953.

Hanuman Prasad Poddar's Speech at the Inauguration of Shri Krishna Temple at Mathura, 6 September, 1958, pamphlet published by Gita Press.

Hindi Bal Pothi

Kalyan, 1926–2015

Kalyana-Kalpataru, 1934–2015

Nari Dharma

Nari Shiksha

Prashnouttar Manimala

Purna Samarpan

Samaj Sudhar

Stri Dharma Prasnotri

Striyon Ke Liye Kartavya Shiksha

Swami Karpatri Maharaj, *Marxvad Aur Ram Rajya,* Gita Press, Gorakhpur, 2009.

Vartaman Shiksha

Articles

C.A. Bayly, 'Patrons and Politics in Northern India', *Modern Asian Studies,* Vol. 7, No. 3, 1973, pp. 349–88.

Charu Gupta, 'Articulating Hindu Masculinity and Femininity: "Shuddhi" and "Sangathan" Movements in United Provinces in the 1920s', *Economic and Political Weekly,* Vol. 33, No. 13, 26 March–3 April 1998, pp. 727–35.

— 'The Icon of Mother in Late Colonial North India: Bharat Mata, Matri Bhasha and Gau Mata', *Economic & Political Weekly,* Vol. 36, No. 45, 10–16 November, 2001, pp. 4291–99.

— 'Politics of Gender: Women in Nazi Germany,' *Economic and Political Weekly,* Vol. 26, No. 17, 27 April, 1991, pp. WS40–WS48.

— '(Im)possible Love and Sexual Pleasure in Late Colonial North India', *Modern Asian Studies,* Vol. 36, No. 1, February 2002, pp. 195–221.

Hetukar Jha, 'Promises and Lapses: Understanding The Experience of Scheduled Castes in Bihar in Historical Perspective', *Journal of Indian School of Political Economy,* Vol. XII, July–December 2000, pp. 423–44.

Ken Auletta, 'Citizens Jain: Why India's Newspaper Industry is Thriving', *The New Yorker,* 8 October 2012, pp. 52–61.

Krishna Kumar, 'Hindu Revivalism and Education in North-Central India', *Social Scientist,* Vol. 18, No. 10, 1990, pp. 4–26.

Monika Freier, 'Cultivating Emotions: The Gita Press and Its Agenda of Social and Spiritual Reform', *South Asian History and Culture,* Vol. 3, No. 3, July 2012, pp. 397–413.

P.S. Chauhan, 'Hindi Novel Before Premchand', shodhganga.inflibnet.ac.in/bitstream/10603/.../06_chapter%202.pdf, 2012

Partha Chatterjee, 'Colonialism, Nationalism, and Colonised Women: The Contest in India', *American Ethnologist,* Vol. 16, No. 4, November 1989, pp. 622–33.

Paul Arney, 'Gita Press and the Magazine *Kalyan*: The Hindu Imperative of Dharma-pracar', paper presented at the 24th Annual Conference on South Asia, University of Wisconsin, Madison, October 1995.

— 'The "Mouth" of Sanatana Dharma: The Role of Gita Press in Spreading the Word', paper presented at the American Academy of Religion Annual Meeting, Washington DC, 20–23 November, 1993.

Peter Robb, 'The Challenge of Gau Mata: British Policy and Religious Change in India', 1880–1916,' *Modern Asian Studies,* Vol. 20, No. 2, 1986, pp. 285–319.

Ram Bahadur Rai, *'Babri Masjid: Dhwansh Ki Rajniti'*, (Babri Masjid: Politics of Demolition), *Yathawat,* 1–15 December 2013, pp. 6–11.

Ramachandra Guha, 'The Ones Who Stayed Behind', *Economic & Political Weekly,* Vol. 38, No. 12–13, 22 March–4 April 2003, pp. 1121–24.

Richard Gordon, 'The Hindu Mahasabha and the Indian National Congress, 1915 to 1926', *Modern Asian Studies,* Vol. 9, No. 2, 1975, pp. 145–203.

Ritu Sinha, 'Educating the Hindu Child Citizen: Pedagogy of the Gita Press', presented at a workshop on education, Jammu University, November 2012.

Siobhan Lambert-Hurley, 'Heart of a Gopi: Raihana Tyabji's Bhakti Devotionalism as Self-Representation', Loughborough University, 2011, pp. 1–18.

Index

Acknowledgements

This book is the outcome of a long journey enriched by my family, friends, teachers, numerous scholars and colleagues who participated with enthusiasm, some sharing the pain and many others leading me out of the loneliness and void that I frequently experienced. I am a mere chronicler. If the book does not live up to their expectations, the sole blame lies with me.

Once the idea of working on Gita Press was settled, two renowned historians, Shahid Amin and Wendy Doniger, encouraged me to work on the subject. Shahid welcomed the idea with his usual exuberance and Doniger, a doyenne of Hindu studies, gave some vital suggestions that helped me shape my application for the New India Foundation fellowship. She also introduced me to Ulrike Stark, her colleague in the University of Chicago and author of a remarkable book on Naval Kishore Press. Stark asked me to look at the larger colonial politics and how it coincided with the Hindu nationalist project while chronicling the story of Gita Press. In fact, these themes run through the book. A big thank you Ulrike.

The New India Foundation fellowship had eluded me earlier but it taught me the rigour expected of applicants. Thanks to Sunil Khilnani, Krishna Kumar and Tanya Matthan for reading my proposal and making substantive suggestions. I particularly thank Sunil Khilnani for pointing out that the proposal should emphasize the post 1947 history of the Gita Press. Erudite and humble, Tanya read the proposal and made some crucial remarks. Though her own area of interest is far removed from religious politics, Tanya with her eclectic range of reading and knowledge came up with some interesting suggestions. Krishna Kumar, a bilingual education theorist of great repute, reminded me that Hindu nationalism should be seen in the context of competitive communalism. Much of how the Gita Press archives was discovered finds mention in the Introduction. But making sense of it would not have been possible were it not for Charu Gupta, an eminent historian herself. She helped me navigate the maze of archives and constantly encouraged me to complete the work.

A better part of the research was conducted in Gorakhpur, Banaras and Lucknow. I experienced hospitality and made friends during my repeated trips to these towns. In Gorakhpur, Lalmani Tiwari of Gita Press welcomed me with open arms and opened the Press' library. But if there were no Harikrishna Dujari, there would have been no book. He not only gave me full freedom to access the mammoth archives but ensured I was well taken care of in the Gita Vatika guesthouse. Coming from a family that for generations has worked with Gita Press and its founding editor, Hanuman Prasad Poddar, Dujari was my window to a period gone by. Poddar's grandson Rasyendu Fogla and his family were equally hospitable and cooperative during my several visits to the town that has become synonymous with Gita Press. I know the book does not replicate their idea of Gita Press and Poddar. But I am sure they will appreciate that the idea behind the book is not to sing paeans of Gita Press but to place it within the larger canvas of Hindu nationalism in colonial and post-colonial India.

As the ambit of research widened, bureaucrat Vrinda Sarup, who would have made a first-rate historian, helped me get access to the Commissioner's Record Room in Gorakhpur. The then Commissioner, K. Ravindra Babu, and his entire staff need to be thanked for letting me stay in the record room beyond office hours and for plying me with tea and snacks. Ganga Prasad Pandey of Gita Vatika helped with references and material at very short notice. Over my long stays in Gorakhpur the owners of two photocopy shops—Deep Communications and Aman Photocopier—went out of their way to accommodate my almost unrealistic demands and never let me down.

In Banaras, my university friend Ajeet provided me a home away from home. A remarkable man who left a good career to work among sex workers and make a huge difference to their lives, Ajeet, his wife Santwana Manju and little daughter, Barish Brishti, a budding classical singer, gave me company and home food after long days spent in the libraries of the Theosophical Society, Banaras Hindu University and Nagari Pracharini Sabha. In Lucknow, college friend Amrit Abhijat, a bureaucrat, helped me access CID records. The CID Records Office is one of the most efficiently run institutions I have come across. It was on the advice of Malavika Kasturi of the University of Toronto that I went to the office and it was worth the effort. The UP State Archives became my haunt for months. Its staff went out of the way and helped me procure documents at short notice.

In Chandigarh, lawyer Anupam Gupta and his wife Dolly keep an open house and maintain a mammoth library. Thanks to Anupam, I could procure documents and books that would have been impossible to find.

Many Delhi University friends teaching in India and abroad pitched in with research and by reading drafts of various chapters. Thanks to technology, references and material arrived within days and even hours of my demand. It is a long list and I will restrict myself to thank a few of them, the way we have always addressed each other. Thank you A, H, T, N, K and R. Shasank Shekhar Sinha of Routledge India should be singled out for his help in getting me access to academic journals.

Part of the research was conducted in Chennai in the libraries and archives of the Theosophical Society and *The Hindu* newspaper. Thanks to Siddharth Varadarajan, the then editor of *The Hindu,* I was allowed access to the huge archives of the paper. Polite and hospitable, the *Hindu* librarian K. Rajendra Babu presides over the best-maintained archive anywhere in the country that, unlike many other newspapers, has not fallen prey to making money out of its back issues.

In Delhi I made use of, and immensely benefited from, the Nehru Memorial Museum & Library (NMML), National Archives of India (NAI) and Marwari Library in Chandni Chowk. NMML and NAI also boast of some of the finest and most cooperative staff. Historian Mushirul Hasan, the then director-general of NAI, and Jaya Ravindran helped me locate sources and facilitated quick access. Thanks to Hasan's advice I specifically looked at the politics around the cow. Months spent in total silence in NMML's manuscript and microfilm section were the most rewarding. Ever-smiling Deepa Bhatnagar never says no to a researcher and N. Balakrishnan, an NMML veteran, helped me with everything including organizing books through inter-library lending. NMML director Mahesh Rangarajan was a regular source of encouragement while reminding me it is not always a great idea to carry on research indefinitely. Biswamoy Pati read the first chapter and gave some important suggestions on religious concepts.

As the writing progressed so did deviations from the original idea. Novelist and writer Ajaz Ashraf, a dear friend and colleague for many years, was there to pull me out of long blank phases to assure me that deviations can at times result in something more productive. It was he I would look up to for advice, argument and encouragement. Jyotirmaya Sharma of the University of Hyderabad, and author of highly acclaimed books on Hindutva and M.S. Golwalkar, came to my rescue when for days together I could not fine-tune many arguments. Jyotirmaya unravelled the complexity in simple and insightful language. Thank you, Ajaz and Jyotirmaya, for everything. Sociologist Nandini Sundar helped me understand the deeper politics behind Hindu nationalist fascination with adivasis and what it meant for the Gita Press. She has been a big support.

I got in touch with Monika Freier mid-way through my writing. She has worked on Gita Press and immediately shared her article and dissertation. Monika also led me to Paul Arney who is possibly the first scholar to work on Gita Press. She sent me Paul's articles and also secured his permission to use them in my book. Thank you, Monika and Paul.

My former colleague and friend Ronojoy Sen introduced me to Medha M. Kudaisya, his colleague at the National University of Singapore. Medha's magisterial work on G.D. Birla was a big help. She also suggested new sources, especially on the world of Kolkata Marwaris. From the University of Toronto, historian of visual culture and contemporary art Kajri Jain cleared my doubts on artists who worked on Hindu iconography and Gita Press. Friends like Jitendra Kumar and Apoorvanand calmly translated complex Hindi words and sentences over phone or emails. Ravish Tiwari, then with the *Indian Express*, deconstructed small towns of eastern Uttar Pradesh with a quick history. Hridayesh Joshi of *NDTV*, among the finest TV journalists in India, has waited for this book more than anyone else. Long interactions with him have always been enriching. Rakesh Sinha of Delhi University who runs the RSS-funded India Policy Foundation is an old friend who never lets ideological differences come in the way of help. He pitched in with translations of Golwalkar's speeches and references. Ritu Sinha, who is also working on Gita Press, selflessly shared her thoughts, articles and references. In Patna, Srikant helped with dates and references. So did Shamsul Islam. Ram Bahadur Rai's revelation on Babri Masjid point to the multilayered world of the Sangh Parivar.

In Times House, my working abode for fifteen years, a long list of friends and colleagues went out of their way to help. I am thankful to my editors Jaideep Bose, Arindam Sengupta and Diwakar for letting me go on a year's sabbatical. Without the leave, the book would have never seen the light of day. Shankar Raghuraman organized books for me and Rajesh Ramachandran, who had a short stint in Kerala, chipped in with crucial information from Kochi. Mohua Chatterjee and Abheek Barman helped with translations of old-world Bangla. There is another reason why I am indebted to Abheek. During a casual conversation he suggested I look at the report of the Vivian Bose Commission of Inquiry. It literally changed the course of my chapter on Poddar. In my department Rajat Pandit was there to remind me I should not delay the project and colleague Manoj Mitta, a successful author of two remarkable books, had words of constant encouragement.

How does one thank Ramachandra Guha? I will quote what Gandhi wrote to Hanuman Prasad Poddar after son Devdas was released from Gorakhpur jail in 1932. Poddar had taken care of Devdas: '...Why should I feel obliged? The civilized way is to seek such help in silence. Only God can reward for such selfless service, a human being cannot. I think such help should be taken in silence.' Silence will not suffice here since I am no Mahatma. Ram is a liberal in the truest sense. He has been excited about the book right from the beginning and as a managing trustee of New India Foundation runs one of the freest organizations, asks no questions, does not impose his views and is ever ready to help. He was the first one to read the entire manuscript, 60,000 words more than what my readers will go through. His suggestions have become a template for my future books. I have bothered him with minor matters, and possibly more frequently than other Fellows have or would ever do. I will look up to him, always. Thank you, Ram.

Nandan Nilekani, the man behind the NIF, grilled me on the economics of Gita Press. It was not on my agenda but proved crucial to the big picture I was seeking to create.

Thanks also to Gopalkrishna Gandhi for helping me with references, especially the one on the Gita published by the *Hindustan Times* when his father, Devdas Gandhi, was the editor. His kind words and keen interest in the book provided me the much-needed morale boost at the fag end of writing.

Getting an editor who would be scathing yet compassionate made me anxious. My former colleague in *TOI* and dear friend Gopal Tandon agreed to chip in. His comments after reading the first chapter came as a shock but I knew it will come back to me improved. Part of the 1970s set, Gopal, who never got his due, went through each word and every fact, pointed out mistakes, repetitions, verbosity and mercilessly set them right. The process went on for over a year. I also thank his wife Nieru and daughter Saloni for suffering me hours on end in their house, arguing, fighting and devouring good food. It is difficult to meet a man like Gopal.

Then came Rivka Israel, a professional editor with wide experience. She was tasked to cut the flab and put the manuscript in order. I call her the smiling assassin. And what a job she did! Receiving chapters with chunks removed, at times moved to another chapter, was initially painful but once the job was over and I read the full manuscript all I could do was to acknowledge her exceptional editing skills. Due to her long stint with a leading academic publisher, Rivka was well versed with sources and at times even suggested new facts that I accepted with gratitude. If I ever venture to write a book again, Rivka will be my editor.

In HarperCollins I was fortunate to have Ajitha as my editor. Young but cast in the old mould, Ajitha's biggest quality is that she is a great listener. She convinced me to have faith in HarperCollins and has done a great job. Designer Bonita Shimray understood the concept of the book and came up with a cover instantly liked by everyone. Amrita Talwar took up the responsibility of marketing with great enthusiasm. Publisher Karthika took the backseat after passing the baton to Ajitha, appeared occasionally but authoritatively and ensured the deadline is met. Her positive energy and perennial smile makes HarperCollins such a happy place.

Novelist, writer and essayist Pankaj Mishra, who has experienced the influence of Gita Press in his early years, was most welcoming and agreed to not only read the manuscript but also write an advance comment. Thank you, Pankaj, for reposing faith in the book. I am grateful to novelist and essayist Arundhati Roy who too read the manuscript at short notice and agreed to endorse the book.

Delhi's iconic bookshop Bahrisons has been my second home for years, filling me with all I want and with the longest possible credit line. Thanks to Anuj and Rajni for running the best bookshop and having Mithilesh as their Man Friday. I wonder how Mithilesh remembers so many books and knows the mind of so many customers. He got me all I wanted, at times even photocopies of out-of-print editions.

Legendary Prabhu Book Service is located in the most unusual place, Sadar Bazar of Gurgaon. But its fame is international and for decades it has fed researchers with first editions, rare journals and all that makes research such a happy vocation. I still cannot get over how owner Vijay Jain organized copies of *Hindu Panch, Chand, Saraswati, Uma* and many others and got me addicted to first editions. Spending time with him, listening to the tales of authors and politicians, who all drop by, is an education. Thank you Jainsaab.

I am lucky to have a large family and even larger circle of friends who expected the book long ago. As years went by a few of them even stopped enquiring about it but my brothers, sisters-in-law, nephews and nieces did not give up. My father-in-law has waited for it most eagerly. Jyoti, my wife, my best friend, a saathi through the crests and troughs of life, has seen me abandon many projects mid-way. This time she did not let me go astray and took over all the responsibilities to let me chase my dream within a deadline. She has suffered being read out chapters to and being made to read at unearthly hours. Jyoti has been critical and indulgent with her comments on the manuscript in equal measure. Thanks for being there always. The best part of my sabbatical was the time spent with my daughter Jahnavi who would occasionally type for me and sort out research material. All of ten when I started the book, Jahnavi is a teenager now, better informed and more opinionated. Hope she finds the book worth the effort her father made. Thanks also to Krishna and Mary for efficiently running the house and little Riaan for his playful diversions.

The idea for a book on Gita Press came during a discussion with my father way back in 2008, months before he left us without any warning. But his curiosity about the success of Gita Press stayed with me. Much as our ideological worldview differed, I owe it to him for letting me see the world through my own prism and creating an environment where books and ideas mattered the most. It was an atmosphere of free and frank discussion in which all was fair and forgotten the next morning. My disciplinarian mother was happy I was finally doing something substantive. But she followed my father in 2012, two months into my sabbatical, after a night of illness. In fact, the first chapter was completed at my home in Ranchi on the same chair she sat after her walks or when she came down to the ground floor. I miss the two readers who mattered the most. The book is dedicated to them.

About the Author

Akshaya Mukul is a journalist with the *Times of India*. He has contributed to *A Historical Companion to Postcolonial Literatures in English* (2005) edited by Prem Poddar and David Johnson, Edinburgh University Press. He lives in Gurgaon with wife Jyoti, daughter Jahnavi and Dalmatian Bella.